MCAT

CHEMISTRY and ORGANIC CHEMISTRY

Content Review

Printed in the United States of America

Third Printing, 2017

ISBN 978-1-944935-08-5

Next Step Pre-Med, LLC
4256 N Ravenswood Ave
Suite 303
Chicago, IL 60613

www.nextstepmcat.com

ABOUT THE AUTHORS

Bryan Schnedeker is Next Step Test Prep's Vice President for MCAT Tutoring and Content. He manages all of our MCAT and LSAT instructors nationally and counsels hundreds of students when they begin our tutoring process. He has over a decade of MCAT and LSAT teaching and tutoring experience (starting at one of the big prep course companies before joining our team). He has attended medical school and law school himself and has scored a 44 on the old MCAT, a 525 on the new MCAT, and a 180 on the LSAT. Bryan has worked with thousands of MCAT students over the years and specializes in helping students looking to achieve elite scores.

Anthony Lafond is Next Step's MCAT Content Director and an Elite MCAT Tutor. He has been teaching and tutoring MCAT students for nearly 12 years. He earned his MD and PhD degrees from UMDNJ - New Jersey Medical School with a focus on rehabilitative medicine. Dr. Lafond believes that both rehabilitative medicine and MCAT education hinge on the same core principle: crafting an approach that puts the unique needs of the individual foremost.

To find out about MCAT tutoring directly with Anthony or Bryan visit our website:

http://nextsteptestprep.com/mcat

Updates may be found here: http://nextsteptestprep.com/mcat-materials-change-log/

If you have any feedback for us about this book, please contact us at mcat@nextsteptestprep.com

Version: 2017-01-01

FREE ONLINE MCAT DIAGNOSTIC and

FULL-LENGTH EXAM

*Want to see how you would do on the MCAT and understand
where you need to focus your prep?*

TAKE OUR FREE MCAT DIAGNOSTIC EXAM

Timed simulations of all 4 sections of the MCAT

Comprehensive reporting on your performance

Continue your practice with a free Full Length Exam

**These two exams are provided free of charge to students
who purchased our book**

To access your free exam, visit:

http://nextsteptestprep.com/mcat-diagnostic/

TABLE OF CONTENTS

GENERAL CHEMISTRY

ORGANIC CHEMISTRY

CHAPTER 1
Introduction

A. THE NEXT STEP APPROACH TO MCAT CONTENT

The Next Step Chemistry and Organic Chemistry Review is designed to help you understand major concepts in these areas and to use this knowledge to solve problems. Each chapter contains a large number of practice questions to help you review your content in the only format that matters: MCAT-style multiple choice questions.

The MCAT questions are written to test your understanding of basic science concepts and your problem solving abilities; they stress the memorization that is a necessary first step in mastering the MCAT. It is important to note that you cannot prepare for the MCAT the way you have successfully prepared for science exams in school. In your college classes, simple rote memorization is typically all it takes to get a good grade. On the MCAT, memorizing science material is only the first step in a very long journey.

After memorizing the content, you will then need to practice this material on full, timed practice sections and then on full practice tests. This timed work is the only way to simulate the real conditions of test day.

It is critical to note that the time pressure combined with the lengthy and often confusing presentation of facts in the MCAT's passages make for a very demanding exam. It is not enough to learn MCAT content at the level of recognition that is required by most college classes. For the MCAT, you ***must absolutely master the content***. This means that it is not simply enough to recognize a term when you see it. You must know the content so well that you could give a small 10-minute lecture on a given topic, off the top of your head, with no notes whatsoever. This level of mastery requires repetition, practice, and more repetition. That's the main reason we've included hundreds and hundreds of questions through our content review books.

To develop the level of mastery needed, test yourself at the end of each chapter. Flip to the table of contents at the front of the book. Using the table of contents as an outline, can you give a little 5-minute lecture on each bullet point? Test yourself here – make yourself speak out loud to an empty room. If you can, great! It means you've really mastered the content at the level needed. If not, go back and re-read the chapter. Take careful notes.

Finally, one of the best ways to memorize MCAT content is to make study sheets. While flashcards and notes are good and can help, a study sheet is far more effective. A study sheet is a single piece of paper summarizing the important ideas, concepts, relationships, or structures involved in a given MCAT topic. For example, you might make a study sheet of all of the hormones tested on the MCAT – where they are secreted from, where they go, what they do when they get there, what causes them to be released, etc. Then take that study sheet and make a copy, but blank out a dozen pieces of information. Then make a second blank with another dozen pieces of information missing. Then make a final study sheet with almost the whole page blanked out.

Start your practice by filling in the blank spaces on your first copy. Do this over and over, checking the original study sheet until you can get it perfect. Then fill in the spaces on the second blank over and over until you've mastered it. Finally, take the third copy (which is nearly just a blank sheet of paper) and re-create the entire study sheet from memory. That is the level of mastery demanded by the MCAT (and med school!).

B. CHEMISTRY AND ORGANIC CHEMISTRY

Chemistry and organic chemistry are fundamentally the study of change – how molecules change when they interact with each other, and how those interactions then serve as the basis for the reactions that make up living systems. With the recent revision to the MCAT, the exam has an extensive focus on how the various sciences all tie back into living systems, especially those living systems that underpin human physiology.

Chemistry and Organic Chemistry cover an exceptionally broad variety of topics. Organic chem in particular is infamous for being the class where the professor makes you memorize hundreds and hundreds of reactions only to have you promptly forget them all the day after the test. When it comes to mastering these topics, you want to start with a broad-based review of all the topics that the MCAT may ask about. This book has been designed with that goal in mind. To make working with the material more intuitive, we have arranged the chapters as they are usually presented in a typical college textbook. For your reference, here is an outline of all of the chemistry and organic chemistry that will appear on test, organized around the major concepts that the MCAT will focus on:

Chemistry

Biological and Biochemical Foundations of Living Systems

I: Metabolism

    A.   Bioenergetics
        a. ΔG, K_{eq}
        b. Concentration, Le Châtelier's Principle
        c. Exo- and Endo-thermic, Spontaneity
        d. ATP hydrolysis, $\Delta G \ll 0$
        e. Redox: Half-reactions, Soluble Electron Carriers, Flavoproteins

II: Cell Biology

    B.   Plasma Membrane: Osmosis, Osmotic Pressure, Colligative Properties

III: Nervous and Endocrine Systems

    C.   Electrochemistry: Concentration cell, direction of flow, Nernst Equation

IV: Physiology

    D.   Respiratory System: Henry's Law

Chemical and Physical Foundations of Biological Systems

V: Gas Phase

    A.   Absolute Temp, Kelvin Scale, Pressure, Mercury Barometers, 22.4 L/mole @ STP
    B.   Ideal Gas: Ideal Gas Law, Boyle's Law, Charles's Law, Avogadro's Law
    C.   Kinetic Molecular Theory of Gases
    D.   Real Gases: Qualitative, Quantitative, van der Waals's Equation
    E.   Partial Pressure, Mole Fraction, Dalton's Law

VI: Electrochemistry and Circuits

    A.   Electrochemistry
        a. Electrolytic Cell: Electrolysis, Anodes and Cathodes, Electrolytes, Faraday's Law, Electron Flow
        b. Galvanic Cells: Half-reactions, Potential, Electron Flow
        c. Concentration Cell
        d. Batteries: EMG, Voltage, Lead-Storage, Nickel-Cadmium

VII: Atomic Nucleus, Periodic Table, Stoichiometry

    A.   Atomic Nuclei: Atomic Number and Weight, Nucleons, Nuclear Forces, Radioactive Decay, Mass Spectrometer
    B.   Electronic Structure
        a. Hydrogen Atoms, Bohr Model, Effective Nuclear Charge
        b. Quantum Numbers
        c. Ground vs. Excited States
        d. Pauli Exclusion Principle
        e. Paramagnetic and Diamagnetic Elements
        f. Photoelectric Effect
        g. Heisenberg Uncertainty Principle
    C.   The Periodic Table
        a. Alkali Metals, Alkaline Earth Metals, Halogens, Noble Gases, Transition Metals
        b. Representative Elements
        c. Metals and Non-Metals
        d. Oxygen Group
        e. Valence Electrons
        f. Ionization Energy, Electron Affinity, Electronegativity, Atomic and Ionic Radius
    D.   Stoichiometry: Molecular Weight, Molecular and Empirical Formula, Metric Units, Percent Mass, Avogadro's Number, Density, Oxidation, Disproportionation Reactions, Chemical Equations, Yields, Limiting Reagents

VIII: Solutions and Acid/Base

    A.   Acid/Base
        a. Brønsted-Lowry, Auto-ionization of Water, Conjugate Acids and Bases
        b. Strong Acids, Weak Acids
        c. Weak Acids: Dissociation, Salts, Hydrolysis, pH Calculations
        d. K_a, K_b, K_w
        e. Buffers: Concepts, Titration Curves
    B.   Ions and Solutions
        a. Anions, Cations, Familiar Ions, Hydration, Hydronium, Units of Concentration, K_{sp}, Common-Ion Effect, Complex Ions
    C.   Titration: Indicators, Neutralization, Titration Curves, Redox Titration

IX: Covalent Bonds

    A.   Lewis Dot Formulas: Resonance, Formal Charge, Lewis Acids and Bases
    B.   Partial Ionic Bonds: Electronegativity, Dipole Moment
    C.   Sigma and Pi Bonds
        a. Hybrid Orbitals, VSEPR, Resonance

      b. Structural Formulas involving H, C, N, O, F, S, P, Si, Cl
  D. Double and Triple Bonds: Bond Length, Bond Energy, Rigidity
  E. Liquids: Intermolecular Forces, H-bonding, Dipoles, van der Waals, London Dispersion

X: Thermodynamics and Kinetics

  A. Thermochemistry and Thermodynamics
      a. Zeroth, First and Second Laws
      b. PV Diagrams: Work
      c. Entropy: Disorder, Phases
      d. Calorimetry: Heat Capacity, Specific Heat
      e. Conduction, Convection, Radiation
      f. Hess's Law, Enthalpy, Bond Dissociation Energy
      g. Free Energy, Spontaneity
      h. Phase Changes: Phase Diagram, Heat of Fusion and Vaporization
  B. Kinetics and Equilibrium
      a. Rate Law, Rate Constants, Reaction Order, Rate-Determining Step
      b. Temperature and Rate: Activation Energy, Transition State, Reaction Profiles, Arrhenius Equation
      c. Kinetic vs. Thermodynamic Control
      d. Catalysts
      e. Reversible Reactions: Law of Mass Action, K_{eq} and ΔG, Le Châtelier's Principle

Organic Chemistry

Biological and Biochemical Foundations of Living Systems

I: Proteins

  A. Amino Acids: configuration, dipolar ions, acidic/basic, hydrophobic/hydrophilic
  B. Structure
      a. Protein Structure: Primary, Secondary, Tertiary, Quaternary
      b. Protein Stability: Folding, Denaturing, Hydrophobic interactions, Solvation and Entropy
      c. Separation Techniques: Isoelectric Point, Electrophoresis

II: Metabolism

  A. Carbohydrates: Classification, Configuration, Hydrolysis of Glycosides, Monomers and Polymers

III: Cell Biology

  A. Plasma Membrane: Composition: Phospholipids, Steroids, Waxes, Proteins

IV: Nervous and Endocrine Systems

  A. Lipids: Structure, Steroids, Terpenes, Terpenoids

Chemical and Physical Foundations of Biological Systems

V: Light and Sound

    A. Molecular Structure and Absorption Spectra
        a. IR, UV-Vis, Proton NMR

VI: Separation and Purifications

    A. Extraction
    B. Distillation
    C. Chromatography: Column, HPLC, Paper, TLC
    D. Peptides: Electrophoresis, Quantitative Analysis, Size-Exclusion, Ion-Exchange, Affinity
    E. Racemic Mixtures, Separation of Enantiomers

VII: Biological Molecules

    A. Amino Acids and Peptides
        a. Amino Acids: Configuration, Dipolar, Acid/Base, Hydrophobic/Hydrophilic
        b. Peptides: Sulfur Linkage, Polypeptides, 1° - 4° Structure, Isoelectric Point
    B. Lipids: Storage, Triacyl Glycerols, Saponification, Phospholipids, Phosphatids, Sphingolipids, Waxes, Fat-Soluble Vitamins, Steroids, Prostaglandins
    C. Carbohydrates: Classification, Configuration, Cyclic Conformation
        a. Hydrolysis of Glycosides
        b. Keto-Enol Tautomers
    D. Carbonyl Compounds
        a. Nomenclature and Physical Properties of Aldehydes and Ketones
        b. Nucleophilic Addition to Carbonyl Carbon: Acetal, Ketal, Imine, Enamine, Hydrides, Cyanohydrin
        c. Oxidation of Aldehydes
        d. Enolates: Tautomerism, Aldol Condensation, Retro-Aldol, Kinetic and Thermodynamic Enolate
        e. Steric Hindrance of Carbonyl Bond
        f. Acidity of α hydrogens, Carbanions
    E. Alcohols
        a. Nomenclature, Physical Properties
        b. Reactions: Oxidation, S_N1, S_N2, Protection, Mesylates, Tosylates
    F. Carboxylic Acids
        a. Nomenclature, Physical Properties
        b. Reactions: Amides, Lactam, Esters, Lactones, Anhydrides, Reduction, Decarboxylation, Nucleophilic Acyl Substitution
    G. Carboxylic Acid Derivatives
        a. Nomenclature, Physical Properties
        b. Reactions: Nucleophilic Substitution, Transesterification, Amide Hydrolysis
        c. Reactivity, Steric Effects, Electronic Effects, Strain, β lactams
    H. Cyclic Molecules: Phenols, Hydroquinones, Ubiquinones, 2e⁻ Redox Centers, Aromatic Heterocycles

C. THE SCIENTIFIC METHOD

As with all sciences, chemistry research involves methodically searching for information. The procedure associated with this search is called the *scientific method*. It involves

1. asking questions, which are then followed by one or more hypotheses (educated guesses or hunches that answer or explain the question).
2. making predictions from the hypothesis, usually in the form of "if....then" statements (if the influenza virus causes the flu, then those exposed to it will become ill).
3. testing the predictions through experimentation, observation, model building, etc., including appropriate controls with which to compare the results.
4. repeating the investigations and devising new ways to further test the hypothesis (this may include modification of the hypothesis based on the results of the tests).
5. reporting the results and drawing conclusions from them.

A *theory* is similar to a hypothesis in that it is subjected to the scientific method, but a theory usually explains a broad range of related phenomena, not a single one. Theories are well supported hypotheses, shown to be valid under many different circumstances.

In science, there is no real beginning or end. All hypotheses are based on previous work, and all results and conclusions can be expanded in the future. Often experiments raise more questions than they answer.

Understanding this methodical approach to scientific evidence and conclusions is essential for success on the MCAT. Most of the passages you will see in the science sections are ones that describe an experimental procedure and it is critically important that you understand the procedure so that you can answer the questions. You should read the passage carefully, often taking "flowchart" style notes to make sure you've understood the experiment.

D. STABILITY

Chemistry and organic chemistry are fundamentally about reactions. The MCAT isn't concerned with having you memorize hundreds and hundreds of mechanisms. Instead, it wants you to have a firm grasp on the underlying principles. By far the most important of those principles is stability. Molecules want to attain a more stable shape, electronic configuration, or arrangement. As you consider the passages, questions, and answer choices on the exam, find what looks the most reasonable based on stability.

The stability the MCAT will test tends to broadly fall into three categories:

◊   *stable electron configuration*: The most obvious form of stability in chemistry is the complete octet electron configuration. All of the representative elements (Groups IA through VIIA and the Noble Gases) are more stable when they have a complete octet. This explains why we always encounter sodium as Na^+ and never as Na^{2+} or why we see Cl^- but never Cl^{2-}.

◊   *resonance stability*: Molecules in which the electrons are delocalized between several different possible Lewis structures are said to have different resonant forms of the molecule. This resonance creates an unusual stability – the resonant form of the molecule is more stable than any one contributing form that could be drawn with a traditional Lewis diagram. Much of the organic chemistry on the MCAT is driven by molecules that exhibit resonance – carboxylic acids and their derivatives, most especially amides and the peptide bonds they form.

◊   *inductive stability*: when a molecule is attached to a highly electronegative atom or functional group, some of the electron density gets "drawn away" towards that electronegative atom. If an atom has a negative charge on it, you can stabilize that negative charge by putting it near an electronegative group. The negative charge is stabilized through induction. Similarly, if an atom has a positive charge, that positive charge can be stabilized by putting it near a relatively electropositive atom or electron donating functional group.

E. LAB TECHNIQUES

The MCAT, despite including content from a wide variety of science topics, does have one unifying theme: experiment-based passages. While not every passage will feature an experiment, the overwhelming majority will. As such, it is vitally important that you be familiar with common lab techniques. You may want to consider skipping to the end of the book and beginning your studies with the final chapter that explicitly deals with lab techniques. The good news is that, by having taken your pre-requisite courses, you will have carried out many of these procedures yourself. Also, if you have not purchased this book as part of the larger set, you should consider also picking up Next Step's Physics and Math Review book, as it includes a chapter specifically about experimental design and reasoning about data.

F. USING THIS BOOK

Remember: the MCAT stresses your problem solving skills and your knowledge of basic science concepts. Therefore, the work you do in understanding these concepts is a necessary first step, but the first step only. Next Step's Content Review books will help you in this foundational work through a thorough treatment of the major topics included in the MCAT. Study to understand these topics, not just to memorize them.

As a part of the purchase price of this book, you are also entitled to a free copy of Next Step's online MCAT Diagnostic and Science Content Diagnostic exam. See the page at the front of the book with details for how to activate your free online test. If you've purchased this book by itself, we strongly recommend that you consider purchasing the rest of the Next Step Science Content Review package. Success on the MCAT will require a good foundation in Biology, Biochemistry, Chemistry, Organic Chemistry, Psychology, Sociology, and Physics.

It's not enough to simply go through this book as you would one of your textbooks in a class. On the MCAT, you must truly master the content. You have to know it so well that you could write this book yourself. To gain that mastery, you should follow a few simple steps:

1. Don't write in the question portion of the book. You will want to be able to come back and re-do the questions to check your mastery.
2. Begin by taking the Final Exam at the end of the book. This test is a pure content assessment of the relevant content on the MCAT. Taking this test first can help guide you for which chapters merit extra attention.
3. Go through each chapter three times using a "spaced repetition" approach. Spaced repetition has been shown to vastly increase a student's ability to recall information.

    Day 1: Start by skimming the chapter quickly. Get a general sense of the content. Then go back and read the chapter slowly and carefully. Take notes in a separate notebook, make flashcards or study sheets as needed.

    Day 2: Then wait a day.

    Day 3: Come back to the chapter. Re-skim the content and only then do the questions at the end of the chapter. Be sure to analyze all of the questions to make sure you've fully understood them.

    Day 4-5: Then wait two days.

    Day 6: Come back a third and final time. No need to re-skim – simply re-do the questions at the end of the chapter to solidify your understanding.
4. After completing all of the chapters in a section, complete the Section Content Review Problems at the end of the section. These questions are not in the format of the MCAT – they are simply a very large number of short content questions to check that you've understood and memorized the relevant concepts.
5. Come back to the Section Content Review Problems again two days later and re-do them. At this point you should be getting 100% of the questions correct.
6. After working your way through the whole book, come back to the Final Exam and re-take it. As you wrap up your content review work, you should be scoring nearly 100% on this exam.

G. STUDY PLANS

It's absolutely essential that you develop a clear and rigorous study plan and stick to it. Each student's situation is different so you'll need to develop a plan that fits your unique situation.

The best place to start is with Next Step's online Study Plan. We have posted the plan on our MCAT blog on our website. You can find this plan here:

http://nextsteptestprep.com/category/mcat-blog/

H. OTHER RESOURCES

Good MCAT Prep fundamentally requires three things: content review, practice passages, and full test simulation. The book you're holding in your hands can fulfill the first of those goals. To really prepare for the exam, you will also want to pick up materials to provide you with practice and full test simulation

For practice passages, there's no better resource than Next Step's Strategy and Practice books. We have produced one book for each of the four sections on the exam. Each of our Strategy and Practice books includes a concise, focused discussion on strategies for how to deal with the passages, followed by full timed section practice. The timed sections are in the format of the exam, but made slightly harder than the real thing in order to help build up those MCAT muscles.

To get practice simulating the real exam, you'll want to use Next Step's online Full Length exams. These tests are simply the best approximation available of what you'll see on the real test. We're the only MCAT prep company in the world to build our exams from the ground up for the new MCAT. While other big companies are simply re-purposing their old exams into the new MCAT format, we started totally fresh. Our practice tests simulate the content, format, and difficulty level of the real test perfectly.

http://nextsteptestprep.com/mcat-practice-tests/

Finally, the single best resource for MCAT practice is the testmaker: the AAMC. Every student preparing for the MCAT should purchase the official guide, the official AAMC practice test, and any other AAMC practice sets available.

Good luck!

This page intentionally left blank.

GENERAL CHEMISTRY

SECTION 1
Atoms and the Periodic Table

Chemistry is often described as "the study of matter" or "the study of change". Both such descriptions are accurate, and an understanding of the chemistry on the MCAT will require tackling both of these areas at the outset. This first section will start with matter itself through an examination of atoms, the electrons that surround atoms, the molecules formed when atoms are chained together, and then our organization of atoms into the Periodic Table.

We will then move on in the second section to a discussion of the study of change – the chemical reactions that form the foundation not just of the chemistry and organic chemistry tested on the MCAT, but of all living systems.

Though the AAMC will provide you with a periodic table on Test Day, you must still know it like the back of your hand. If you're having to stop in the middle of the test to check basic facts like whether neon is a noble gas or whether carbon has six protons, you'll be losing time – a precious commodity on Test Day. You don't have to memorize the Periodic Table, certainly, but you must be very *very* familiar with it.

CHAPTER 2
Matter

A. INTRODUCTION

A firm grasp of the basic ideas of division of matter is important for the understanding of physical sciences. These basic ideas presented here are not only used in chemistry and physics, but in many diverse fields such as medicine, engineering, astronomy, geology, and so on. In this chapter, we will discuss ideas about atoms and molecules, and related aspects such as moles, Avogadro's number, percentage composition, atomic mass, atomic weight, and subatomic particles.

B. ATOMS

Atoms are the basic units of elements and compounds. In normal chemical reactions, atoms retain their identity. In this section, we will present a quick review of some of the basic terms and concepts such as elements, compounds, and mixtures.

Elements

An element is defined as matter that is made of only one type of atom. Elements are the basic building blocks of more complex matter. Some examples of elements include hydrogen (H), helium (Hc), potassium (K), carbon (C), and mercury (Hg).

Compounds

A compound is matter formed by the combination of two or more elements in fixed ratios. Let's consider an example. Hydrogen peroxide (H_2O_2) is a compound composed of two elements, hydrogen and oxygen, in a fixed ratio.

Mixtures

A combination of different elements, or a combination of elements and compounds, or a combination of different compounds is called a **mixture**. For example, an aqueous solution of potassium hydroxide ($KOH + H_2O$). In this example, the two components are potassium hydroxide and water.

Though these definitions illustrate basic ideas, you need to understand them fully; otherwise it will be almost impossible to decipher higher concepts that are based on these simple ideas. The MCAT tests your understanding of basic concepts by incorporating simple ideas into passages. So in order to succeed on the test, you need to thoroughly understand the basics.

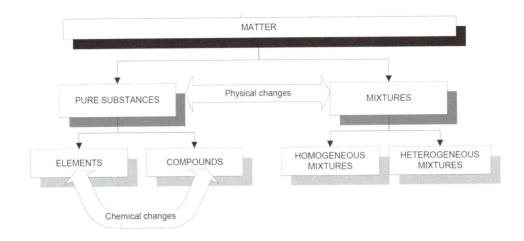

Dalton's Atomic Theory

In 1803, John Dalton proposed the atomic theory of matter. The main postulates of his atomic theory can be summarized as follows:

1. Matter is composed of indivisible particles - atoms.
2. An element is composed of only one kind of atom. These atoms in a particular element have the same properties such as mass, size, or even shape.
3. A compound is composed of two or more elements combined in fixed ratios or proportions.
4. In a chemical reaction, the atoms in the reactants recombine, resulting in products which represent the combination of atoms present in the reactants. In the process, atoms are neither created, nor destroyed. So a chemical reaction is essentially a rearrangement of atoms.

Ramifications of Dalton's Theory

The atomic theory put forward by Dalton is consistent with the law of conservation of mass. As the fourth postulate says, chemical reaction is just a rearrangement of atoms, and thus the total mass remains constant during a chemical reaction.

The postulates also account for the law of definite proportions. Compounds are made of elements in fixed or definite proportions. Since the atoms have fixed mass, compounds should have elements in a fixed ratio with respect to mass. Finally, these postulates predict what is known as the law of multiple proportions. According to this law, if two elements form two or more different compounds, the ratio of the mass of one element of these compounds to a fixed mass of the other element is a simple whole number.

C. THE GENERAL STRUCTURE OF THE ATOM

During the early twentieth century, scientists discovered that atoms can be divided into more basic particles. Their findings made it clear that atoms contain a central portion called the nucleus. The nucleus contains protons and neutrons. Protons are positively charged, and neutrons are neutral. Whirling about the nucleus are particles called electrons which are negatively charged. The electrons are relatively small in mass. Take a look at Table 1-1 for a size comparison.

PARTICLE	ABSOLUTE CHARGE (Coulombs)	RELATIVE CHARGE	MASS (kg)
Neutron	0	0	1.675×10^{-27}
Proton	$+1.6 \times 10^{-19}$	$+1$	1.673×10^{-27}
Electron	-1.6×10^{-19}	-1	9.11×10^{-31}

Table 1-1

D. ELECTRONS AND NUCLEONS

As mentioned above, the late nineteenth century scientists conducted several experiments, and found that atoms are divisible. They conducted experiments with gas discharge tubes.

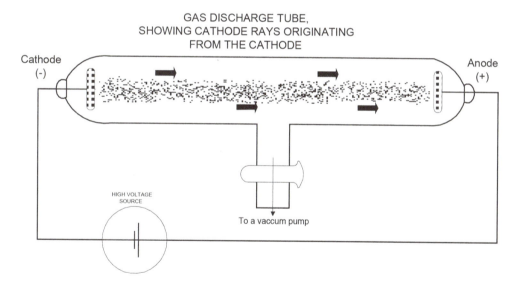

Figure 1-1 Gas discharge tube

A gas discharge tube is shown in Figure 1-1. The gas discharge tube is an evacuated glass tube and has two electrodes, a cathode (negative electrode) and an anode (positive electrode). The electrodes are connected to a high voltage source. Inside the tube, an electric discharge occurs between the electrodes. The discharge or 'rays' originate from the cathode and move toward the anode, and hence are called cathode rays. Using luminescent techniques, the cathode rays are made visible and it was found that these rays are deflected away from negatively charged plates. The scientist J. J. Thompson concluded that the cathode ray consists of negatively charged particles (electrons).

Charge of Electrons

R. A. Millikan conducted the famous oil drop experiments and came to several conclusions: The charge of an electron is -1.602×10^{-19} C. From the charge-to-mass ratio, the mass of an electron was also calculated.

$$\text{charge} / \text{mass} = -1.76 \times 10^{8} \text{ coulombs} / \text{gram}$$

$$\text{mass} = -1.6 \times 10^{-19} / -1.76 \times 10^{8} = 9.11 \times 10^{-23} \text{ g} = 9.11 \times 10^{-31} \text{ kg}$$

Protons

Protons are positively charged nuclear particles. The charge of a proton is (positive electronic charge) $+1.6 \times 10^{-19}$ C. The net positive charge of the nucleus is due to the presence of the protons. A proton is about 1800 times more massive than an electron.

Neutrons

Neutrons have mass comparable to that of protons, but neutrons are devoid of any electric charge. We will talk more about neutrons and their whereabouts when we study radioactivity.

Now a natural question is whether electrons, protons, and neutrons are the most fundamental particles. The answer is no. These fundamental particles can be broken up into smaller particles called quarks. But, we don't have to go that far for the MCAT. Just be aware that such sub-fundamental particles exist, fundamental particles being electrons, protons, and neutrons.

E. MOLECULES AND MOLES

The **atomic number** denotes the number of protons in an atom's nucleus. The **mass number** denotes the total number of protons and neutrons. Protons and neutrons are often called nucleons. By convention, the atomic number is usually written to the left of the elemental notation, and the mass number to the left above the elemental notation as represented by the example below. The element shown is aluminum.

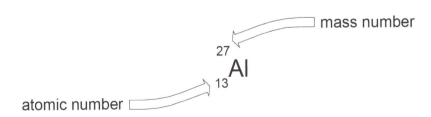

Some atoms have the same atomic number, but different mass numbers. This means different number of neutrons. Such atoms are called **isotopes**.

Atomic Weight

The atomic weight of an element is the average weight of all the isotopic masses of the element, calculated on the basis of their relative abundance in nature. The atomic weights are set on a "carbon-12" scale. This is the standard weight scale that is used worldwide to express atomic weights. Exploring this further, we can say that 12 atomic mass units (amu) make up the mass of one atom of $^{12}_{6}C$ isotope. In other words, one amu is equal to 1/12 the mass of one carbon-12 atom. We can also say that the atomic weight of carbon-12 is 12 amu. Even though it is popular to use the term atomic weight, atomic mass is a more appropriate term since we are really talking about the mass of the atom rather than the weight.

Molecules

A molecule is a set or group of atoms which are chemically bonded. It can be represented by a molecular formula. A molecular formula represents the identity of the different kinds of atoms that are present in a molecule, along with the specific ratio of the atoms that are present in the molecule.

A molecule of H_2O (water) contains two hydrogen atoms bonded to one atom of oxygen.

$$NaOH \quad Sodium\ Hydroxide$$

A molecule of sodium hydroxide contains one sodium atom, one oxygen atom, and one hydrogen atom.

Molecular Weight

Molecular weight represents the sum of the atomic weights of all the atoms in that molecule. Molecular weight is also known as formula weight.

Example 1-1

Calculate the molecular weight of sulfuric acid (H_2SO_4).

2 hydrogens	2 x 1 = 2
1 sulfur	1 x 32 = 32
4 oxygens	4 x 16 = <u>64</u>
	98 g/mole

Example 1- 2

Calculate the molecular weight of carbon dioxide (CO_2).

1 carbon	1 x 12 = 12
2 oxygens	2 x 16 = <u>32</u>
	44 g/mol

Empirical Formula

Empirical formula of a molecule represents the lowest-whole-number (aka the simplest) ratio of the atoms present in the molecule. For example, acetylene has the molecular formula C_2H_2. The empirical formula of acetylene is CH. In essence, empirical formula gives the simplest ratio of atoms in a molecule.

Problem 1-1

Write the empirical formula of the following molecules.

1) H_2O_2
2) C_2H_6
3) H_2O

Answers:

1) HO
2) CH_3
3) H_2O

Notice that sometimes the empirical formula is the same as the molecular formula, as in the case of water (H_2O).

The Mole

The quantity of a given substance that contains as many units or molecules as the number of atoms in 12 grams of carbon-12 is called a **mole**. For example, one mole of glucose contains the same number of glucose molecules as in 12 grams of carbon-12. The mass of one mole of a substance is called its **molar mass**. The number of atoms in 12 grams of carbon-12 is represented by **Avogadro's number (6.022×10^{23})**. So one mole of any substance contains Avogadro's number of units in them.

To understand this concept thoroughly, try different possible scenarios where the Avogadro number can be used. Here are some. One mole of hydrogen atoms contains Avogadro's number of hydrogen atoms. One mole of hydrogen molecules contains Avogadro's number of hydrogen molecules. A mole of water contains 6.022×10^{23} water molecules. These are all different ways of expressing the same concept.

The molar mass of a substance is equal to the molecular weight of that substance. The molecular weight (formula weight) of water is 18 amu. Since this is the molar mass, we can express it as 18 grams/mole.

Example 1-3

Calculate the mass of one molecule of sodium hydroxide (NaOH).

Answer: We know that the formula weight of sodium hydroxide is 40 g/mole.

Sodium	23
Oxygen	16
Hydrogen	1
	40 g/mole

We also know that one mole of NaOH contains Avogadro's number of molecules. So the mass of the NaOH molecule can be found by the following method:

Mass of one molecule of sodium hydroxide

$$= \frac{40g}{6.02 \times 10^{23}} = 6.64 \times 10^{-23} g$$

Example 1-4

Calculate the number of moles in 109.5 grams of hydrogen chloride.

Answer: Just like the last example, we have to find the molar mass of the molecule. The molar mass is 35.5 + 1 = 36.5 g/mole.

$$\text{Number of moles} = 109.5 \text{ g HCl} \times \frac{1 \text{ mol HCl}}{36.5 \text{ g HCl}} = 3 \text{ moles HCl}$$

So, 109.5 grams of HCl correspond to 3 moles of HCl.

You should be able to do these types of conversions back and forth, from grams to moles and moles to grams.

Try the next problem to see whether you have mastered the idea.

Problem 1-2

Calculate the number of grams in 8 moles of sulfur dioxide.

Answer: If your answer is close to 512.8 g, you solved the problem correctly.

F. PERCENT COMPOSITION AND DENSITY

The MCAT often contains percentage composition problems. Percentage composition is the percentage contribution (by weight) of each element to the total mass. Let's explore this idea by looking at some examples.

Example 1-5

Calcium carbonate ($CaCO_3$), commonly known as limestone, is used in the preparation of a variety of compounds. Calculate the percentage composition of each element in calcium carbonate.

Answer:

# of atoms per molecule	molar weight of the atoms	total mass of the element per mol
1 Calcium	1 x 40.1 g	40.1 g
1 Carbon	1 x 12.0 g	12.0 g
3 Oxygen	3 x 16.0 g	48.0 g
		100.1 g

The percentage composition of each element can be found as follows:

$$\% \text{ of calcium} = \frac{40.1}{100.1} \times 100 = 40.1\% \text{ calcium}$$

$$\% \text{ of carbon} = \frac{12}{100.1} \times 100 = 12\% \text{ carbon}$$

$$\% \text{ of oxygen} = \frac{48}{100.1} \times 100 = 47.9\% \text{ oxygen}$$

Predicting Formulas from Percentage Compositions

You should be able to predict the formula of a compound on the basis of data given for percent compositions. Study the next example to understand how it is done.

Example 1-6

A carbon compound contains 27.27% carbon and 72.73% oxygen by mass. Predict the simplest ratio or formula of the compound.

Answer:

The best way to approach this problem is to consider that we have 100 grams of this compound. Logically it should contain 27.27 grams of carbon and 72.73 grams of oxygen. With that in mind, we can calculate the number of moles of each element or atom. After that we can obtain the simple ratio.

Step 1

# of moles of carbon atoms equals 27.27/12 = 2.275 moles of carbon atoms
# of moles of oxygen atoms equals 72.73/16 = 4.546 moles of oxygen atoms

Step 2

Divide every number of moles with the smallest number of moles found for any element. Here the smaller one is 2.2725. So divide the number of moles of carbon atoms and the number of moles of oxygen atoms by 2.2725. That will give you the simplest ratio between them.

$$\text{Carbon: } 2.2725/2.2725 = 1$$
$$\text{Oxygen: } 4.546/2.2725 \approx 2$$

Since the ratio of carbon to oxygen is 1:2, the compound is CO_2.

Example 1-7

Calculate the mass of sulfur in 150 grams of H_2SO_4.

Answer:

The easiest way to calculate this is to find the percentage composition of sulfur. Then, use that percentage to find the mass of sulfur in the given amount of substance.

Step 1

$$\% \text{ of sulfur} = 32.1/98 \times 100, \text{ roughly } 33\%$$

Step 2

The mass of sulfur present in 150 grams of sulfuric acid is

$$150 \times 33\% = 49.5 \text{ g}$$

Density

Density is defined as the mass per unit volume.

$$\text{Density} = \frac{\text{mass}}{\text{volume}}$$

This property can be used to identify a compound or an element, since the density of a pure substance in its solid state is a constant. Since density relates mass and volume, it can be used to find the volume occupied by a given mass, or if the volume is known, we can find the mass.

Density of water is 1.0 g/ml.

Let's explore some calculations involving density. You'll see that these calculations have tremendous laboratory significance.

Example 1-8

The density of carbon tetrachloride is about 1.6 g/ml at 20°C. Calculate the volume occupied by 320 g of CCl_4.

Answer:

$$Density = \frac{mass}{volume}$$

$$Volume = \frac{mass}{density} = \frac{320 \text{ g}}{1.6 \text{g} / \text{ml}} = 200 \text{ ml}$$

So, 320 grams of carbon tetrachloride will occupy a volume of 200 ml.

Example 1-9

A 20 ml sample of mercury has a mass of 271 g. Calculate the density of mercury.

Answer:

$$Density = \frac{mass}{volume} = \frac{271 \text{ g}}{20 \text{ ml}} = 13.55 \text{ g} / \text{ml}$$

This question tests your knowledge of a basic equation. Though the equation is simple, you should be able to manipulate this equation so that you can connect this piece of information with other facts and formulas that are given in your test question or passage.

CHAPTER 2 PROBLEMS

1. A student preparing a solution for an experiment measured the weight of the sample solute to be used. If she is supposed to use 2 moles of calcium hydroxide, she must use:

    A. 57.1 grams.
    B. 74.1 grams.
    C. 114.2 grams.
    D. 148.2 grams.

2. Which of the following best represents the total number of ions present in a sample of NaCl weighing 102 g?

    A. 6.0×10^{23} ions
    B. 10.5×10^{23} ions
    C. 12.0×10^{23} ions
    D. 21×10^{23} ions

3. Experiments conducted with gas discharge tubes during the late 19th century resulted in many important conclusions in atomic chemistry. Among those, one of the most important was the discovery of rays known as cathode rays. Cathode rays when passed near negative plates will most likely:

    A. bend toward the negative plate.
    B. bend away from the negative plate.
    C. will not bend, because they are uncharged.
    D. will not bend, because they are high energy radiations.

4. Which of the following is true regarding a typical atom?

    A. Neutrons and electrons have the same mass.
    B. The mass of neutrons is much less than that of electrons.
    C. Neutrons and protons together make the nucleus electrically neutral.
    D. Protons are more massive than electrons.

5. The empirical formula of butane is:

    A. CH_3
    B. C_2H_5
    C. C_4H_{10}
    D. CH_2

6. The mass of one mole of a substance is numerically equal to:

    A. mass number.
    B. Avogadro number.
    C. molecular weight.
    D. 22.4.

7. If m represents the number of moles of a substance, M represents the molar mass of the substance, and d represents the density of the substance, which of the following expressions equals to the volume of the sample substance?

    A. mM/d
    B. m/dM
    C. d/mM
    D. m/d

8. The mass of oxygen in 96 grams of sulfur dioxide is closest to:

    A. 16 g.
    B. 24 g.
    C. 32 g.
    D. 47 g.

9. Choose the value that most closely corresponds to the percentage composition of chlorine in carbon tetrachloride?

    A. 92%
    B. 90%
    C. 86%
    D. 81%

10. A student researcher analyzing the identity of the by-product of a reaction found that the compound contained 63.6% nitrogen and 36.4% oxygen, by mass. What is the most likely formula of this compound?

    A. NO
    B. NO_2
    C. N_2O
    D. N_2O_3

Questions 11-14 are based on the following passage.

Passage 1

The following reactions were conducted in a lab for studies related to reaction kinetics. Consider the reactions shown:

$$\text{Reaction 1}$$
$$CH_4 + 2O_2 \rightarrow CO_2 + 2H_2O$$

$$2C_2H_6 + 7O_2 \rightarrow 4CO_2 + 6H_2O$$
$$\text{Reaction 2}$$

11. Reaction 2 is best described as which of the following?

    A. A metathesis reaction
    B. A combustion reaction
    C. An endothermic reaction
    D. A decomposition reaction

12. In Reaction 2, if 54 g of water was formed, how much ethane and oxygen must have reacted?

    A. 30 g of ethane and 224 g of oxygen
    B. 60 g of ethane and 224 g of oxygen
    C. 30 g of ethane and 112 g of oxygen
    D. 60 g of ethane and 112 g of oxygen

13. Which of the following is the actual formula of dextrose, if the empirical proportion of carbon, hydrogen, and oxygen is 1:2:1? (Dextrose has a molecular weight of 180 g/mol).

    A. CHO
    B. $C_6H_{12}O_6$
    C. $C_{12}H_6O_3$
    D. CH_2O

14. Which of the following equals the number of hydrogen atoms in 40 grams of methane?

    A. 1.5×10^{24}
    B. 2.4×10^{24}
    C. 6.0×10^{24}
    D. 6.023×10^{23}

CHAPTER 3
Electronic Structure

A. INTRODUCTION

In this chapter, we will discuss the electronic arrangement of atoms. We will also talk about quantum numbers, orbitals, various rules pertaining to electron-filling, and electronic configuration.

B. ATOMIC STRUCTURE

The first ideas about electronic arrangement in atoms were primarily figured out from atomic emission spectra. In various experiments, atoms were made to be thermally or electrically excited, and this resulted in different kinds of bands or lines on photographic plates. Our understanding of atomic structure is based on these types of experiments. All elements have their characteristic line spectra with which they can be analyzed and identified.

Electromagnetic Waves

Before we discuss the atomic structure, we will touch on the topic of electromagnetic radiation to have a better analytical understanding of the key ideas. All electromagnetic radiation travels with a constant speed of 3×10^8 m/s. The electromagnetic spectrum ranges from radio waves to gamma rays.

The Wave Nature

Light has wave nature. It has electric and magnetic fields which are perpendicular to each other, and can travel through space. No medium is required. Because of its wave character, we can define light in terms of frequency and wave length. The distance between two adjacent crests or troughs, or any two adjacent identical points on a wave is called **wavelength** (λ). **Frequency** (f) is the number of wavelengths passing through a point in unit time. Wavelength and frequency are related by the relation given below. Frequency is usually expressed in 1/second (s^{-1}), which is otherwise known as *hertz* (Hz).

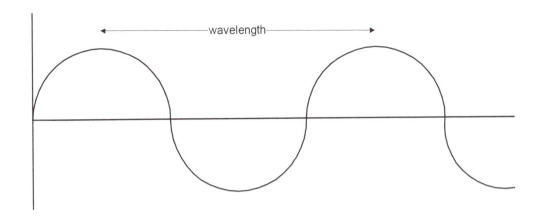

Velocity = frequency x wavelength
c = f λ

The Particle Nature and Quantum Theory

Light has particle nature. These particles or forms (packages) of energy are called quanta. A more modern term for such as particle of light is photon. The energy of a photon can be expressed in terms of the following formula.

Energy = hf,
where h is the Planck's constant, and f is the frequency.
Planck's constant = 6.63×10^{-34} J•s

Wavelength and frequency are related to one another and to the velocity of a wave by the relation given below. For light travelling in a vacuum, its velocity is the constant c. According to **Heisenberg's Uncertainty Principle**, we cannot determine both the momentum and the position of subatomic particles simultaneously. This is because we are using other particles (electromagnetic particles - like photons) of comparable energy to detect these subatomic particles, and by the time these other particles find the subatomic particles (say electrons), they are also disturbing the pathway of these electrons. In essence, the study of something extremely small and fast (about the magnitude of electrons) cannot be done without interference of its natural course or position.

Photoelectric Effect

The Photoelectric Effect can be defined as the ejection of electrons from a metal surface when light rays strike it. The ejected electrons are often called "photoelectrons." The ejection of electrons occurs only if the incident light has a certain minimum or *threshold frequency*. The required threshold frequency is a characteristic specific to each metal. Experimentally, it has been found that the photoelectrons emitted with maximum energy do not have the full energy equivalent supplied by the incident photon. This is because energy is required to break loose the electrons from the surface of the metal. The energy required for this is called "work function," which is characteristic of each metal. The photoelectrons can be accelerated to a positively charged plate, creating a flow of charges along a wire - photocurrent. The current can be measured by an ammeter connected to the wire.

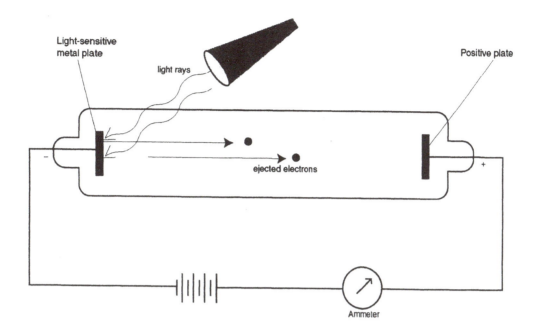

The maximum kinetic energy (K_{max}) of a photoelectron is given by the following equation:

$$K_{max} = 1/2\ m(v_{max})^2 = hf - \phi$$

In this equation, m is the mass of an electron, v_{max} is the maximum velocity of the electrons, h is Planck's constant, f is the frequency of the incident light, and ϕ (pronounced *phi*) is the 'work function' of the metal. The entity hf represents the energy of the incident photon.

Key Observations on Photoelectric Effect

1. The photoelectric effect exemplifies the particle nature of light.
2. Based on conservation of energy, no photoelectron can have energy more than that of an incident photon.
3. The energy of the photoelectrons is always less than that of the incident photons, because some energy (work function) is required to break the electrons loose.
4. The maximum energy of the photoelectrons is independent of the intensity of the incident light.
5. Electrons are not ejected no matter how high the intensity of the incident light is, unless the incident light has the energy corresponding to the threshold frequency characteristic of a particular metal.

Atomic Emission Spectra

When we pass white light through a prism, dispersion of the light occurs resulting in a *continuous spectrum* of wavelengths. Another type of spectrum results when heated gas emits light. This results in a *line spectrum*. Line spectrum contains only certain specific wavelengths of light. The wavelengths in the **visible spectrum** of hydrogen are given by the following formula:

$$\frac{1}{\lambda} = \frac{R}{hc}\left(\frac{1}{4} - \frac{1}{n^2}\right)$$

where λ is the wavelength of the light, R (Rydberg constant) = 2.18 x 10^{-18} J, h (Planck's constant) = 6.63 x 10^{-34} J•s, c (speed of light) = 3.0 x 10^8 m/s, and n is some whole number that is greater than 2 which corresponds to the orbit-number from which the electron is making the transition. For example, if the transition of an electron is from orbit number 4 to 2, the n value is 4.

Bohr's Model of Hydrogen Atom

Niels Bohr's explanation of the hydrogen spectrum was a major breakthrough toward the understanding of atomic structure. The following are the postulates:

1. In each hydrogen atom, the electron revolves around the nucleus in one of the several stable orbits.
2. Each orbit has a definite radius and thus has a definite energy associated with it.
3. An electron in an orbit closest to the nucleus has the lowest energy, and if the electron is in the lowest orbit the atom is said to be in its *ground state*.
4. The electron in an atom may absorb discrete amounts of energy and move to another orbit with higher energy, and this state is called the *excited state*.
5. An electron in an excited atom can go back to a lower energy level and this process will result in the release of excess energy as light.
6. The amount of energy released or absorbed is equal to the difference between the energies of the initial and final orbits.

Based on Bohr's theory, light energy is emitted when an electron in a higher energy level ($E_{initial}$) jumps to a lower energy level (E_{final}). Based on the law of conservation of energy, the sum of energies of the emitted photon (hf) and the electron's final energy (E_{final}) should be equal to the electron's initial energy ($E_{initial}$). This can be represented mathematically as follows:

$$hf + E_{final} = E_{initial}$$

Transitions of the electron in the hydrogen atom result in different spectral lines.

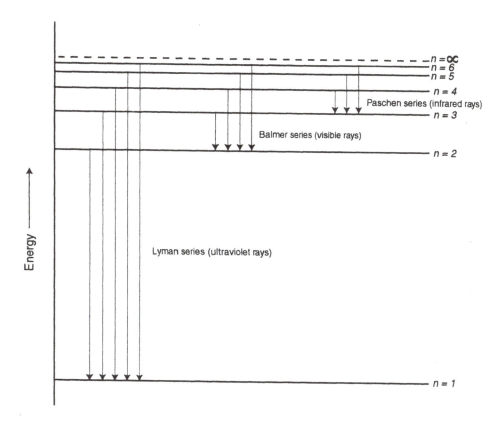

The energy of the emitted photon

$$hf = R\left(\frac{1}{n_{final}^2} - \frac{1}{n_{initial}^2}\right)$$

where n_{final} and $n_{initial}$ are the principal quantum numbers of final and initial energy levels, and R is the Rydberg constant $(2.18 \times 10^{-18}\,\text{J})$. The figure given above shows the transitions that can result in the Lyman (ultraviolet region), Balmer (visible region), and Paschen series (infrared region) for n_{final} values 1, 2, and 3, respectively.

A photon is emitted when an electron in an atom jumps from a higher to a lower energy level.
The energy of the emitted photon is equal to the difference in energy between the two energy levels.

C. QUANTUM NUMBERS

All electrons present in an atom have specific addresses or attributes by which each electron can be referred to. The four quantum numbers are the ones with which we can describe each and every electron that is present in an atom. One of the quantum numbers describes the shape or the most probable area around the nucleus where we can find the particular electrons of interest. This wave function of an electron is called an **orbital**.

Principal quantum number (n). The principal quantum number denotes the energy level of electrons. The larger the principal quantum number is, the larger the energy. The smaller the principal quantum number is, the lower the energy. The shells are often named K, L, M, N, . . ., which correspond to the principal quantum numbers 1, 2, 3, 4, . . ., respectively.

Letter	K	L	M	N . . .
n	1	2	3	4 . . .

Angular momentum quantum number (l). Angular momentum quantum number (azimuthal quantum number) denotes the shape of the orbital. The values range from 0 to n − 1, where n stands for the principal quantum number. If an electron has a principal quantum number of 4, the values of angular momentum quantum numbers are 0, 1, 2, and 3. The angular momentum quantum numbers correspond to different subshells. An angular momentum quantum number 0 corresponds to s subshell, 1 to p subshell, 2 to d subshell, 3 to f subshell, and so on. For instance, $3d$ denotes a subshell with quantum numbers $n = 3$ and $l = 2$

Orbital	s	p	d	f . . .
l	0	1	2	3 . . .

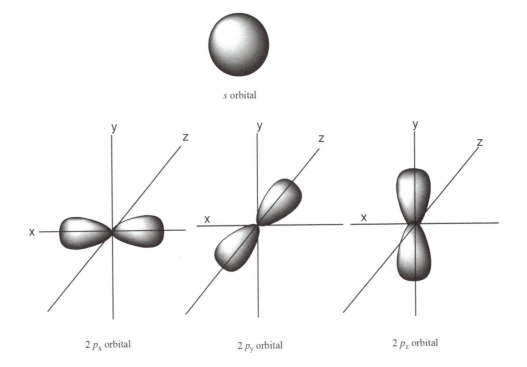

s orbital

2 p_x orbital   2 p_y orbital   2 p_z orbital

Magnetic quantum number (m_l). Magnetic quantum numbers define the different spatial orientations of the orbitals. The values from $-l$ to $+l$. For example, let's say the value of l is 1. So the magnetic quantum numbers will be -1, 0, and $+1$. The l value corresponds to p sublevel and the three magnetic quantum numbers correspond to the three atomic orbitals in the p subshell.

Spin quantum number (m_s). Spin quantum number has to do with the spin orientations of an electron. The two possible spins are denoted by the spin quantum numbers $+1/2$ and $-1/2$.

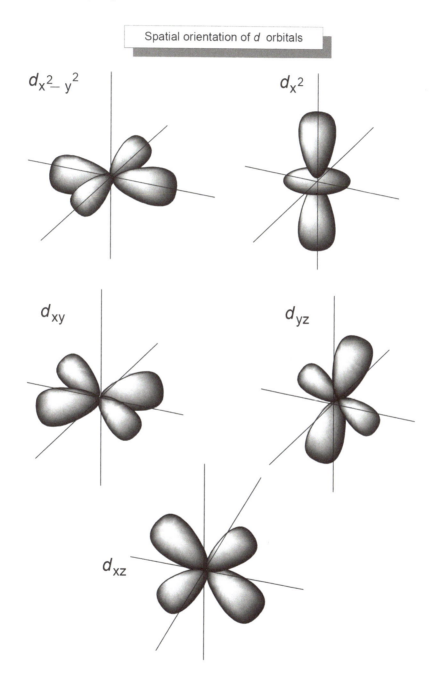

Spatial orientation of d orbitals

$d_{x^2-y^2}$

d_{x^2}

d_{xy}

d_{yz}

d_{xz}

D. ELECTRONIC CONFIGURATION

We talked about quantum numbers and atomic orbitals. In this section, we will focus our attention mainly on writing the electronic configuration of atoms and the rules associated with it. First, let's talk about the ground state electronic configuration. The ground state configuration means the electronic configuration at the lowest energy state.

There are certain rules that should be applied to the filling of orbitals. In order to do that properly, we need to know the Aufbau principle. According to the Aufbau principle, the filling order of electrons obeys a general pattern in which the electrons try to occupy the orbitals in such a way as to minimize the total energy; that is, they occupy the lowest energy orbitals first and then step-by-step go to the next available higher energy levels successively. Of course, there are some exceptions to these generalizations. Filling order can be depicted as follows:

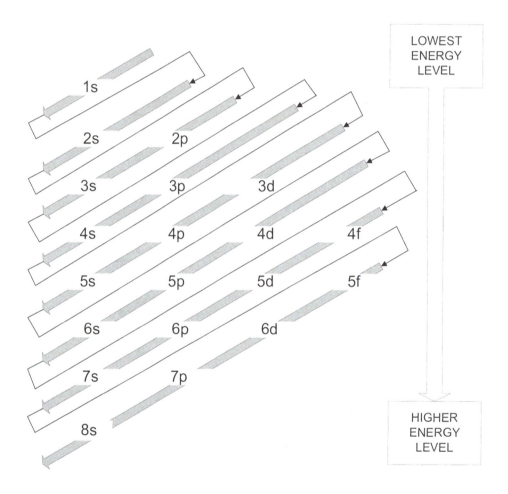

This is an easy way to remember the general order of electron-filling in the subshells. The order of filling is $1s$, $2s$, $2p$, $3s$, $3p$, $4s$, 3d, $4p$, $5s$, . . ., and so on.

An s orbital is spherical in shape. All p orbitals have a dumbbell shape with two lobes aligned along an axis. All d orbitals have slightly complex shapes and are beyond the scope of our discussion. Each orbital can accommodate a maximum of two electrons. Hence, an s subshell, (only one orbital) can accommodate a maximum of two electrons. Similarly, p (three orbitals), d (five orbitals), and f (seven orbitals) subshells can have maximum of six, ten, and fourteen electrons, respectively.

Principal quantum number (n)	Angular momentum quantum number (l)	Magnetic quantum number (m_l)	Subshells	Number of orbitals	Maximum number of electrons
1	0	0	1s	1	2
2	0	0	2s	1	2
2	1	-1,0,+1	2p	3	6
3	0	0	3s	1	2
3	1	-1,0,+1	3p	3	6
3	2	-2,-1,0,+1,+2	3d	5	10
4	0	0	4s	1	2
4	1	-1,0,+1	4p	3	6
4	2	-2,-1,0,+1,+2	4d	5	10
4	3	-3,-2,-1,0,+1,+2,+3	4f	7	14

Table 3-1 Some possible combinations of quantum numbers for atomic orbitals

Example 3-1

Write the electronic configuration of lithium.

Solution: From the periodic table, we can get the atomic number of lithium. The lithium atom has 3 electrons. As we know, the 1s subshell is the first one to be filled. The s orbital can hold a maximum of 2 electrons. We have one electron remaining. It will occupy the 2s subshell which is the next energy level. So the third electron will occupy the 2s subshell. Hence, the configuration of lithium is $1s^2 2s^1$.

Example 3-2

Write the electronic configuration of oxygen in its ground state form.

Solution: The oxygen atom contains 8 electrons. The first 2 electrons will go to the 1s level. The next 2 electrons will occupy the 2s level. We have 4 electrons remaining. What is the next subshell according to the filling order? It is 2p. The p subshell can hold a maximum of 6 electrons in its orbitals. So the remaining 4 electrons will occupy the 2p level. Hence, the configuration of oxygen is $1s^2 2s^2 2p^4$.

Hund's Rule

We have learned the order of filling the subshells. Now let's take a closer look at the filling of electrons in an orbital level. Each orbital can be occupied by a maximum of 2 electrons, and these electrons will have opposite spins as dictated by the spin quantum number. Hund's rule describes the way the electrons fill up the orbitals. According to Hund's rule, each electron starts filling up each orbital of a given subshell. After all the orbitals in a given subshell have been filled singly (half-filled), then the electrons start pairing. Let's look at some examples.

Example 3-3

Write the electronic configuration of sulfur and also show the filling of electrons with orbital notation.

Solution: The sulfur atom has 16 electrons. The electronic configuration is written as $1s^2\, 2s^2\, 2p^6\, 3s^2\, 3p^4$. To see the significance of the Hund's rule, look at the $3p$ subshell. In the $3p$ subshell, we have 3 orbitals.

Note that the electrons first occupy orbitals singly. Altogether there are 4 electrons in the $3p$ subshell. Instead of filling the orbitals in pairs, the first 3 electrons start filling the three orbitals singly, and then the remaining electron occupies the orbital with the other electron as paired electrons. (See the orbital notation of the $3p$ subshell shown above.) If this were not the case, you would have seen two electron-paired orbitals followed by an empty orbital.

Another idea we want to touch on concerns paramagnetic and diamagnetic substances. Substances that have unpaired electrons are called paramagnetic. Substances that have only paired electrons are called diamagnetic. Both paramagnetism and diamagnetism are quantum mechanical effects. Because of the pairing of electrons with oppositely oriented spins in diamagnetic substances, they are weakly repelled by an external magnetic field. In contrast, the unpaired electron or electrons of paramagnetic substances create a net magnetic dipole moment, caused an attractive force oriented in the direction of an external magnetic field.

CHAPTER 3 PROBLEMS

1. Which of the following shows the correct order of filling of subshells?

    A. $3s, 3p, 4s, 3d, 4p$
    B. $3s, 3p, 3d, 4s, 4p$
    C. $3s, 3d, 3p, 4s, 4p$
    D. $3s, 3d, 3p, 4p, 4s$

2. Which of the following represents the outermost shell configuration of an element that is an inert gas under standard conditions?

    A. $4s^2 4p^2$
    B. $4s^2 4p^3$
    C. $4s^1 4p^6$
    D. $4s^2 4p^6$

3. The electronic configuration shown is that of the element:

[Kr] $5s^2 4d^{10} 5p^2$

    A.   Sb.
    B.   Rb.
    C.   In.
    D.   Sn.

4. The maximum number of electrons that can occupy an energy level is calculated using a formula, where n represents the number corresponding to the energy level. The formula is:

    A. n^2
    B. $2n^2$
    C. $2n + 1$
    D. $4n + 2$

5. Consider this statement: no two electrons of an atom can have the same sets of four quantum numbers. This is known as the:

    A.   Heisenberg's uncertainty principle.
    B.   Hund's rule.
    C.   Pauli exclusion principle.
    D.   Aufbau principle.

6. Which of the following is true with respect to the filling of subshells?

    A.   The $4p$ subshell has higher energy than the $5s$ subshell.
    B.   The $3p$ subshell can have a maximum of 3 electrons.
    C.   The $5d$ subshell has higher energy than the $6s$ subshell.
    D.   The $4f$ subshell has higher energy than the $5d$ subshell.

7. Which of the following is NOT isoelectronic with any of the noble gases?

    A. Ca^{2+}
    B. Br^-
    C. S^{2-}
    D. Mg^+

8. Which of the following is NOT a possible set of quantum number values for the nitrogen atom, in the order of principal quantum number, azimuthal quantum number, magnetic quantum number, and spin quantum number?

    A. $1, 0, 0, -1/2$
    B. $2, 1, +1, +1/2$
    C. $2, 0, 0, -1/2$
    D. $2, 1, +2, +1/2$

9. The electronic configuration [Ar] $3d^{10} 4s^2 4p^2$ is that of:

    A.   Ge.
    B.   Zn.
    C.   Se.
    D.   Ar.

10. The electronic configuration of a given element has a $4d$ subshell. This CANNOT be the electronic configuration of:

    A.   Os.
    B.   Cu.
    C.   Ag.
    D.   Ra.

Periodic Table

Group 1	2	3	4	5	6	7	8	9	10	11	12	13	14	15	16	17	18
hydrogen **H** 1 1.0079																	helium **He** 2 4.0026
lithium **Li** 3 6.941	beryllium **Be** 4 9.0122											boron **B** 5 10.811	carbon **C** 6 12.011	nitrogen **N** 7 14.007	oxygen **O** 8 15.999	fluorine **F** 9 18.998	neon **Ne** 10 20.180
sodium **Na** 11 22.990	magnesium **Mg** 12 24.305											aluminium **Al** 13 26.982	silicon **Si** 14 28.086	phosphorus **P** 15 30.974	sulfur **S** 16 32.065	chlorine **Cl** 17 35.453	argon **Ar** 18 39.948
potassium **K** 19 39.098	calcium **Ca** 20 40.078	scandium **Sc** 21 44.956	titanium **Ti** 22 47.867	vanadium **V** 23 50.942	chromium **Cr** 24 51.996	manganese **Mn** 25 54.938	iron **Fe** 26 55.845	cobalt **Co** 27 58.933	nickel **Ni** 28 58.693	copper **Cu** 29 63.546	zinc **Zn** 30 65.39	gallium **Ga** 31 69.723	germanium **Ge** 32 72.61	arsenic **As** 33 74.922	selenium **Se** 34 78.96	bromine **Br** 35 79.904	krypton **Kr** 36 83.80
rubidium **Rb** 37 85.468	strontium **Sr** 38 87.62	yttrium **Y** 39 88.906	zirconium **Zr** 40 91.224	niobium **Nb** 41 92.906	molybdenum **Mo** 42 95.94	technetium **Tc** 43 [98]	ruthenium **Ru** 44 101.07	rhodium **Rh** 45 102.91	palladium **Pd** 46 106.42	silver **Ag** 47 107.87	cadmium **Cd** 48 112.41	indium **In** 49 114.82	tin **Sn** 50 118.71	antimony **Sb** 51 121.76	tellurium **Te** 52 127.60	iodine **I** 53 126.90	xenon **Xe** 54 131.29
caesium **Cs** 55 132.91	barium **Ba** 56 137.33	57-70 *	lutetium **Lu** 71 174.97	hafnium **Hf** 72 178.49	tantalum **Ta** 73 180.95	tungsten **W** 74 183.84	rhenium **Re** 75 186.21	osmium **Os** 76 190.23	iridium **Ir** 77 192.22	platinum **Pt** 78 195.08	gold **Au** 79 196.97	mercury **Hg** 80 200.59	thallium **Tl** 81 204.38	lead **Pb** 82 207.2	bismuth **Bi** 83 208.98	polonium **Po** 84 [209]	astatine **At** 85 [210]	radon **Rn** 86 [222]
francium **Fr** 87 [223]	radium **Ra** 88 [226]	89-102 **	lawrencium **Lr** 103 [262]	rutherfordium **Rf** 104 [261]	dubnium **Db** 105 [262]	seaborgium **Sg** 106 [266]	bohrium **Bh** 107 [264]	hassium **Hs** 108 [269]	meitnerium **Mt** 109 [268]	ununnilium **Uun** 110 [271]	unununium **Uuu** 111 [272]	ununbium **Uub** 112 [277]	ununquadium **Uuq** 114 [289]				

* Lanthanide series

lanthanum **La** 57 138.91	cerium **Ce** 58 140.12	praseodymium **Pr** 59 140.91	neodymium **Nd** 60 144.24	promethium **Pm** 61 [145]	samarium **Sm** 62 150.36	europium **Eu** 63 151.96	gadolinium **Gd** 64 157.25	terbium **Tb** 65 158.93	dysprosium **Dy** 66 162.50	holmium **Ho** 67 164.93	erbium **Er** 68 167.26	thulium **Tm** 69 168.93	ytterbium **Yb** 70 173.04

** Actinide series

actinium **Ac** 89 [227]	thorium **Th** 90 232.04	protactinium **Pa** 91 231.04	uranium **U** 92 238.03	neptunium **Np** 93 [237]	plutonium **Pu** 94 [244]	americium **Am** 95 [243]	curium **Cm** 96 [247]	berkelium **Bk** 97 [247]	californium **Cf** 98 [251]	einsteinium **Es** 99 [252]	fermium **Fm** 100 [257]	mendelevium **Md** 101 [258]	nobelium **No** 102 [259]

A. INTRODUCTION

The periodic table is a systematic representation of elements in a particular order. From the periodic table, we can gather a tremendous amount of information about the characteristics of an element. In this chapter, we will look at the trends and other important aspects of the periodic table.

The properties of elements are periodic functions of their atomic numbers.

B. THE PERIODIC TABLE

The vertical columns of elements represented in the periodic table are called **groups**, and the horizontal rows are called **periods**. There are seven periods in the periodic table. The groups are usually designated by roman numerals followed by the letter A or B as shown in the periodic table.

The groups IA through VIIA are called the main group, or the representative elements. These elements have either *s* or *p* orbital valence electrons. The last group in the periodic table is the noble gas group. The groups ranging from IIIB through IIB are called transition metals, and finally the metals from lanthanum through hafnium and metals from actinium on are called the inner transition metals.

Group IA

The Group IA contains hydrogen, lithium, sodium, potassium, rubidium, cesium, and francium. The Group IA elements are also known as **alkali metals**, with the exception of hydrogen which is not a metal. Alkali metals are very reactive.

All of them react with water to form alkaline solutions.

$$2\,Na\,(s) \;+\; 2\,H_2O \longrightarrow H_2\,(g) \;+\; 2\,NaOH\,(aq)$$

The reactivity of alkali metals to water increases from top to bottom of the periodic table. For example, potassium reacts much more rapidly than lithium. They can also form oxides (For example, lithium can form oxides such as Li_2O.) and a variety of other compounds, since they are highly reactive. Alkali metals are good electrical and thermal conductors. All of them have one valence electron in their outer most shell, which is in the *s* orbital in the ground state. The Group IA elements usually exhibit an oxidation state of $+1$. They have a valence shell configuration of ns^1.

Group IIA

The Group IIA elements are called alkaline earth metals. The alkaline earth metals consist of beryllium, magnesium, calcium, strontium, barium, and radium. Their oxides are basic. They have a valence shell configuration of ns^2, and exhibit an oxidation state of $+2$. These elements are not as reactive as alkali metals.

Metallic character decreases from left to right along a period, and increases from top to bottom of a group.

Group IIIA

The Group IIIA elements consist of boron, aluminum, gallium, indium, and thallium. They have a valence shell configuration of ns^2np^1. They usually have oxidation states of $+1$ and $+3$.

Group IVA

The Group IVA is the carbon family. Carbon is the most versatile element, and thus it has its own separate subject. Yes, you guessed right – organic chemistry. Carbon can exist in many different forms by itself such as graphite and diamond. These forms of carbon are very contrasting in the sense that graphite is relatively soft whereas diamond is very hard. The Group IVA elements have a valence shell configuration of ns^2np^2.

The carbon family consists of carbon, silicon, germanium, tin, and lead. All these form oxides which look like CO_2 (e.g., SiO_2, PbO_2). They also form monoxides. You probably have heard of carbon monoxide, and its harmful effects. CO is a colorless and odorless gas, and it has even higher affinity for hemoglobin than oxygen in the red blood cells.

Group VA

The Group VA is the nitrogen family. The group consists of nitrogen, phosphorus, arsenic, antimony, and bismuth. Nitrogen is a diatomic, colorless, and odorless gas, and is not a very reactive element. The Group VA elements have a valence shell configuration of ns^2np^3.

Group VIA

The Group VIA elements are oxygen, sulfur, selenium, tellurium, and polonium. They have a valence shell configuration of ns^2np^4. Oxygen (O_2) is a diatomic gas, and it also exists in an allotropic form called ozone (O_3). Sulfur forms acidic oxides (e.g., SO_2, SO_3).

Group VIIA

The Group VIIA is more commonly known as the halogen family of elements. They are fluorine, chlorine, bromine, iodine, and astatine. They have an outer configuration of ns^2np^5. Halogens are highly reactive nonmetals, and form diatomic molecules. Halogens form hydrogen halides which are very acidic. These hydrogen halides can dissolve in water to form aqueous acids (e.g., HCl).

Fluorine	-	yellow gas
Chlorine	-	greenish-yellow gas
Bromine	-	reddish brown liquid
Iodine	-	dark colored solid

Group VIIIA

The elements of the Group VIIIA, otherwise known as noble gases are extremely unreactive. They are found as non-combined forms in nature. Because of this, they are called inert gases. They have an outer configuration of ns^2np^6.

C. PERIODIC TRENDS

In this section, we will discuss the periodic properties and trends. It is very important from the MCAT point of view to understand the trends of the periodic table. All of these trends can be memorized, or understood through the atomic property of effective nuclear charge. **Effective nuclear charge** is the net positive charge experienced by valence electrons due to the protons in the nucleus.. It can be approximated by the equation: $Z_{eff} = Z - S$, where Z is the atomic number and S is the number of shielding electrons (aka non-valence electrons).

Atomic Size

As mentioned earlier, the periodic table is very versatile. The periodic table can give you the relative atomic sizes of atoms, and elemental ions. The two trends regarding the atomic radii are given below.

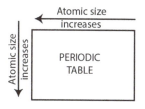

1. From left to right along a period, the atomic radius decreases, as the atomic number increases.
2. Along a group from top to bottom, the atomic radius increases.

One reason for such a trend is attributed to the principal quantum number. As the principal quantum number increases, the size of the orbital increases. Another reason for this trend is attributed to the nuclear shielding by the electron cloud that is between the nucleus and the outermost shells, thereby decreasing the influence of the effective nuclear charge.

Problem 4-1

Arrange the following elements in terms of increasing atomic radius:

Mg, K, Cl, Ba

A) Cl, Mg, K, Cs
B) Cl, K, Mg, Cs
C) Cs, K, Mg, Cl
D) Mg, K, Cl, Ba

Solution: The answer is choice A. Mg and Cl are in the same period (Period 3). But Cl is in Group VIIA and Mg is in Group IIA. So Mg is larger than Cl. The next is K which is in period 4, and thus bigger than both Mg and Cl. Finally, Cs which is in period 6 has the largest atomic radius. So in the increasing order of atomic size is: Cl<Mg<K<Cs.

Ionic Radius

Often you will get questions on arranging ions and atoms according to their sizes. Some of the trends that you should keep in mind regarding ionic radii are listed below:

> 1. *Negatively charged ions have bigger ionic radii than the corresponding neutral atoms.*
> 2. *Positively charged ions have smaller ionic radii than the corresponding neutral atoms.*

Ionization Energy (IE)

Ionization energy is the minimum amount of energy required to remove an electron from an atom. The amount of energy required to remove the first electron is called the first ionization energy (IE_1). The second ionization energy (IE_2) refers to the amount of energy required to remove the second electron. The second ionization energy is always greater than the first ionization energy, since it is more difficult to remove a second electron from an already positive ion, compared to the removal from an electrically neutral atom. The third ionization energy is greater than the second ionization energy, and so on.

First IE < Second IE < Third IE < Fourth IE < Fifth IE < Sixth IE < . . .

The general trend of ionization energy is summarized as follows:

> 1. *Generally, along a period from left to right, the ionization energy increases with increasing atomic number.*
> 2. *The ionization energy decreases from top to bottom along a group as the atomic size increases.*

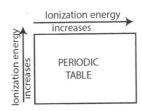

Electron Affinity

Electron affinity is the change in amount (energy either released or absorbed) of energy for the process of adding an electron to an atom (neutral) in its gaseous state, resulting in an ion of -1 charge. The general trend of electron affinity is given below:

The electron affinity increases or in other words, the magnitude (how "big" the negative number is) of the electron affinity increases both left to right along a period and up along a group.

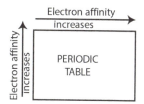

Electronegativity

The relative tendency of an atom to attract the bonding electrons to itself is called **electronegativity**. The popularly used electronegativity scale is based on a system called Pauling's scale, according to which fluorine (the most electronegative element) has an electronegativity value of 4.0. Nonmetals are the most electronegative elements. Electronegativity is an experimentally determined quantity that takes into account the IE and EA for a given species. As a result electronegativity is not subject to the same deviations in its trends like EA and IE are. The general trend of electronegativity is as follows:

1. Generally, electronegativity increases from left to right along a period.
2. Electronegativity decreases down a group from top to bottom.

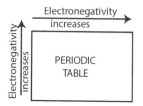

CHAPTER 4 PROBLEMS

1. Sulfur belongs to the classification of elements called the:

    A. inner transition elements.
    B. representative elements.
    C. transition elements.
    D. alkali metals.

2. Which of the following is an alkaline earth metal?

    A. Na
    B. Mn
    C. Sr
    D. Fe

3. Which of the following elements has the lowest electronegativity?

    A. Sr
    B. F
    C. S
    D. Ba

4. Which of the following belongs to the f block in the periodic table?

    A. Sc
    B. U
    C. Si
    D. Pd

5. Which of the following is NOT diatomic?

    A. Oxygen
    B. Nitrogen
    C. Neon
    D. Chlorine

6. Choose the atom that has the biggest atomic radius.

    A. Al
    B. Cl
    C. Ge
    D. Rb

7. Which of the following represents the correct arrangement of atoms according to their atomic radii?

    A. $F < B < Ca < Sr$
    B. $B < F < Sr < Ca$
    C. $Sr < Ca < B < F$
    D. $F < B < Sr < Ca$

8. Choose the true statement regarding the periodic trends.

    A. Along a period from left to right, atomic radius increases.
    B. Along a period from left to right, ionization energy decreases.
    C. Electronegativity of elements increases from right to left along a period.
    D. None of the above

9. Which of the following is the most acidic?

    A. HF
    B. HBr
    C. HCl
    D. HI

10. The outer electronic configuration $ns^2\, np^2$ belongs to which of the following groups?

    A. II A
    B. IV A
    C. IV B
    D. II B

Section 1

CONTENT REVIEW PROBLEMS

1. Which of the following units is most likely used when measuring an atomic radius?

    A. mm
    B. Å
    C. pm
    D. μm

2. What is the charge of 1 electron?

    A. 1.00 C
    B. 1.0087 C
    C. 5.5×10^{-4} C
    D. 1.6×10^{-19} C

3. Which of the following is an uncommon isotope?

    A. ^{12}C
    B. ^{16}O
    C. ^{15}N
    D. ^{32}S

4. What is an amu?

    A. 1/12 of the atomic weight of a ^{12}C atom
    B. The atomic weight of a H atom
    C. The atomic weight of a ^{12}C atom
    D. The weight of one proton or neutron

5. Which of the following is true?

    A. 1 gram = 12 times the weight of one mole of ^{12}C
    B. 1 gram = The weight of one mole of ^{12}C
    C. 1 gram = 6.022×10^{23} amu
    D. 1 gram = 1/12 the weight of one ^{12}C atom

6. What are the rows of the periodic table?

    A. Groups
    B. Orbitals
    C. Periods
    D. Sections

7. What are the columns of the periodic table?

    A. Groups
    B. Orbitals
    C. Periods
    D. Sections

8. Which of the following represents the atomic number?

    A. A
    B. Z
    C. X
    D. n

9. Which of the following represents the mass number?

    A. A
    B. Z
    C. X
    D. n

10. Which group is the most electronegative?

    A. Alkali metals
    B. Alkaline earth metals
    C. Group VIA
    D. Noble Gases

11. Which of the following are located in the nucleus of an atom?

  I. Neutron
  II. Proton
 III. Electron

    A. I only
    B. II only
    C. I and II only
    D. II and III

12. Which of the following are charged particles?

  I. Neutron
  II. Proton
 III. Electron

    A. II only
    B. III only
    C. II and III only
    D. I, II, and III

13. Which of the following is NOT true regarding the structure of an atom?

    A. protons are found adjacent to neutrons
    B. protons and neutrons are of relatively equal mass
    C. electrons and protons have opposite charge
    D. forming an anion changes atomic number

14. Which of the following most exposes a weakness of the Bohr model?

    A. Electrons are best described by probabilities.
    B. Atoms are mostly empty space.
    C. Electrons follow elliptical orbitals rather than spherical.
    D. Neutrons and protons are condensed in the center of the atom.

15. How many protons are in the atom ^{56}Fe?

    A. 23
    B. 26
    C. 30
    D. 56

16. How many neutrons are in the atom ^{56}Fe?

    A. 23
    B. 26
    C. 30
    D. 56

17. How many electrons are in the atom $^{56}Fe^{3+}$?

    A. 23
    B. 26
    C. 29
    D. 56

18. How many protons are in the atom $^{56}Fe^{3+}$?

    A. 23
    B. 26
    C. 30
    D. 56

19. How many nucleons are in the atom $^{56}Fe^{3+}$?

    A. 23
    B. 26
    C. 56
    D. 82

20. Which element has an atomic mass that is closest to its atomic number?

    A. Hydrogen
    B. Helium
    C. Boron
    D. Oxygen

21. How many neutrons are in the nucleus of an average potassium atom?

    A. 19
    B. 20
    C. 21
    D. 39

22. Which of the following atoms would most likely exist in a state with more protons than electrons?

    A. Neon
    B. Nitrogen
    C. Sulfur
    D. Lithium

23. Which of the following atoms is most likely to exist as an anion?

    A. Boron
    B. Aluminum
    C. Nitrogen
    D. Carbon

24. Which of the following has the greatest neutron to proton ratio?

    A. Calcium
    B. Magnesium
    C. Vanadium
    D. Chromium

25. Which of the following is the most important in determining the identity of an element?

    A.   Effective nuclear charge
    B.   Number of electrons
    C.   Number of protons and neutrons
    D.   Number of protons

26. Which of the following correctly orders the mass from greatest to least of the following?
  I. Neutrons
  II. Protons
  III. Electrons
  IV. Alpha particles

    A.   IV, I, II, III
    B.   IV, III, I, II
    C.   I, II, III, IV
    D.   II, I, IV, III

27. Which of the following correctly orders the charge from most positive to least positive of the following?
  I. Neutrons
  II. Protons
  III. Electrons
  IV. Alpha particles

    A.   IV, I, II, III
    B.   IV, II, I, III
    C.   II, IV, III, I
    D.   II, I, III, IV

28. Which of the following is true?

    A.   The number of neutrons in an element is constant.
    B.   The number of electrons in an element is constant.
    C.   The number of nucleons in an element is constant.
    D.   The number of protons in an element is constant.

29. Which of the following is true?

    A.   All nucleons are more massive than electrons
    B.   Protons and electrons are more massive than neutrons
    C.   Electrons are more charged than nucleons
    D.   Protons are more massive than neutrons

30. Which of the following is most likely to contain an equal number of both nucleons?

    A.   Sodium
    B.   Phosphorus
    C.   Chlorine
    D.   Nitrogen

31. Which of the following contains the most atoms?

    A.   100 grams of sodium chloride
    B.   80 grams of calcium chloride
    C.   3 moles of magnesium chloride
    D.   4 moles of sodium chloride

32. Which of the following contains the most molecules?

    A.   30 grams of CO_2
    B.   30 grams of H_2O
    C.   30 grams of NaCl
    D.   30 grams of argon gas

33. Which of the following contains the most atoms?

    A.   1 mole of NaCl
    B.   1 mole of H_2O
    C.   1 mole of CO_2
    D.   1 mole of $AlCl_3$

34. Which of the following weighs the most?

    A.   1 mole NaCl
    B.   2 mole H_2O
    C.   3 mole neon gas
    D.   4 mole helium gas

35. Which of the following weighs the most?

    A.   100 g $CaCO_3$
    B.   1.5 mole $CaCO_3$
    C.   120 g $CaCl_2$
    D.   1 mole $CaCl_2$

36. What volume does 1 mole of water fill?

    A.   18 cm^3
    B.   1 m^3
    C.   18/1000 m^3
    D.   .0018 m^3

37. The density of methanol is .792 g/cm^3. What volume does 2 moles of methanol fill?

    A.   81 cm^3
    B.   1.23 cm^3
    C.   123 cm^3
    D.   8.1 cm^3

38. How many neon molecules are in 5.6 L of neon gas at STP? (the density of neon is .9002 g/L)

    A.   1.5 x 10^{23}
    B.   2.5 x 10^{22}
    C.   5.04 x 10^{23}
    D.   3.03 x 10^{24}

39. Which gas will fill the greatest volume at STP?

    A.   30 g Neon
    B.   30 g Argon
    C.   90 g Krypton
    D.   90 g Xenon

40. Which of the following values is greatest?

    A.   100 moles
    B.   1/Planck's constant
    C.   the number of molecules in 100 g of helium gas
    D.   the number of protons in 200 g of helium gas

41. What is the percent composition of Na^+ in sodium chloride?

    A.   39.5%
    B.   60.5%
    C.   64.7%
    D.   95.3%

42. What is the percent composition of carbon in $C_6H_{12}O_6$?

    A.   20%
    B.   30%
    C.   40%
    D.   60%

43. Given 1 L of both oil and water, which has more mass and why?

    A.   Oil because water has a greater density
    B.   Oil because it has a greater density
    C.   Water because it has a greater density
    D.   Water because oil has a greater density

44. Which of the following has the greatest mass at STP?

    A.   0.5 liter of Ne atoms
    B.   1 liter of water as a gas
    C.   0.5 liter of methanol as a gas
    D.   1 liter of D_2O as a gas

45. Four liquids (A-D) have equal mass and decreasing densities. Which of the following could be the volumes of the liquids?

    A.   Vol A = 1L, Vol B = 2L, Vol C = 3L, Vol D = 4L
    B.   Vol A = 4L, Vol B = 2L, Vol C = 3L, Vol D = 4L
    C.   Vol A = 2L, Vol B = 2L, Vol C = 2L, Vol D = 2L
    D.   Vol A = 4L, Vol B = 3L, Vol C = 2L, Vol D = 1L

46. Which of the following are units of density?

    A. m^3/kg
    B. kg/L
    C. kg/m
    D. kg/m^2

47. Which of the following gives the percent composition of carbon in CO_2?

    A. 12/(12+16*2)
    B. (16*2)/(12)
    C. (16*2)/(12+16*2)
    D. (12+16*2)/(16*2)

48. Suppose air contains 80% N_2 and 20% O_2 by volume, what is the percent composition by mass of O_2 in air?

    A. 20%
    B. 22%
    C. 78%
    D. 80%

49. Suppose air contains 80% N_2 by volume, how much N_2 is in 1 L of air if the density of N_2 is 1.251 g/L?

    A. 1 g
    B. 0.8 g.
    C. 1.25 g.
    D. 6 g.

50. Which of the following is not a quantum number?

    A. l
    B. m
    C. s
    D. n

51. Which of the following does quantum number n represent?

    A. Size of the orbital
    B. Shape of the orbital
    C. Orientation of the orbital
    D. Spin of the electron

52. Which of the following does quantum number l represent?

    A. Size of the orbital
    B. Shape of the orbital
    C. Orientation of the orbital
    D. Spin of the electron

53. Which of the following does quantum number m_s represent?

    A. Size of the orbital
    B. Shape of the orbital
    C. Orientation of the orbital
    D. Spin of the electron

54. Which of the following does quantum number m_l represent?

    A. size of the orbital
    B. shape of the orbital
    C. orientation of the orbital
    D. spin of the electron

55. Which of the following is a possible quantum number set (n, l, m_l, m_s)?

    A. (2,2,1,+1/2)
    B. (2,1,-2,+1/2)
    C. (3,2,-2,+1/2)
    D. (1,0,1,-1/2)

56. Which of the following could be the quantum numbers of the valence electron of Na?

    A. (3,1,0,1/2)
    B. (3,0,0,1/2)
    C. (2,1,1,1/2)
    D. (3,1,1,1/2)

57. Which orbital type corresponds with a quantum number l = 0?

    A. s
    B. p
    C. d
    D. f

58. What is the name of the quantum number n?

    A.   Principal quantum number
    B.   Magnetic quantum number
    C.   Electron spin quantum number
    D.   Azimuthal quantum number

59. What is the name of the quantum number l?

    A.   Principal quantum number
    B.   Magnetic quantum number
    C.   Electron spin quantum number
    D.   Azimuthal quantum number

60. What is the name of the quantum number m_l?

    A.   Principal quantum number
    B.   Magnetic quantum number
    C.   Electron spin quantum number
    D.   Azimuthal quantum number

61. What is the name of the quantum number m_s?

    A.   Principal quantum number
    B.   Magnetic quantum number
    C.   Electron spin quantum number
    D.   Azimuthal quantum number

62. How many orientations are possible for a d orbital?

    A.   1
    B.   3
    C.   5
    D.   7

63. Which of the following gives the number of possible orbitals given a quantum number l?
    A. $2l + 1$
    B. $2l + 3$
    C. $2l + 5$
    D. $2l - 1$

64. Which orbital type corresponds with a quantum number $l = 2$?

    A.   s
    B.   p
    C.   d
    D.   f

65. Which orbital type could NOT have a quantum number $m_l = 1$?

    A.   s
    B.   p
    C.   d
    D.   f

66. Which orbital type could have a quantum number $m_l = -3$?

    A.   s
    B.   p
    C.   d
    D.   f

67. What does Pauli's exclusion principle state?

    A.   Each new electron added as you increase atomic number fills the lowest energy level available.
    B.   Any two electrons in an atom must have different sets of the four quantum numbers.
    C.   Electrons will only exist two in one orbital when all orbitals contain at least one electron.
    D.   No two electrons will ever occupy the same orbital.

68. What is Hund's rule?

    A.   Each new electron added as you increase atomic number fills the lowest energy level available.
    B.   Any two electrons in an atom must have different sets of the four quantum numbers.
    C.   Electrons will only pair up in one orbital when all orbitals contain at least one electron.
    D.   No two electrons will ever occupy the same orbital with the same spin

69. How many orbitals are in the n = 3 shell?

    A. 1
    B. 2
    C. 4
    D. 9

70. How many orbitals are in the n = 4 shell?

    A. 1
    B. 4
    C. 9
    D. 16

71. Which of the following does NOT accurately give the energies in increasing order of electron orbitals?

    A. 2p<3s<3p
    B. 4p<4d<5s
    C. 3p<4s<3d
    D. 5p<6s<4f

72. What is the Aufbau principle?

    A. each new electron added as you increase atomic number fills the lowest energy level available.
    B. any two electrons in an atom must have different sets of the four quantum numbers.
    C. electrons will only exist two in one orbital when all orbitals contain at least one electron.
    D. no two electrons will ever occupy the same orbital with the same spin.

73. Which of the following elements is classified as a metal?

    A. Carbon
    B. Hydrogen
    C. Sodium
    D. Arsenic

74. Which of the following could be the electron filling diagram for the p orbitals of oxygen?

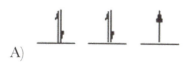

A)

B)

C)

D)

75. Which of the following is the electron configuration of neon?

    A. $1s^2\,2s^2\,2p^6$
    B. $1s^2\,2s^2\,2p^6\,3s^2\,3p^6$
    C. $1s^2\,2p^6$
    D. $1s^2\,2s^2\,2p^6\,3s^2$

76. Which of the following is the electron configuration of chromium 2^+?

    A. $1s^2\,2s^2\,2p^6\,3s^2\,3p^6\,4s^1\,3d^5$
    B. $1s^2\,2s^2\,2p^6\,3s^2\,3p^6\,4s^2\,3d^2$
    C. $1s^2\,2s^2\,2p^6\,3s^2\,3p^6\,4s^2\,3d^4$
    D. $1s^2\,2s^2\,2p^6\,3s^2\,3p^6\,3d^4$

77. Which of the following is the electron configuration of chromium?

    A. $[Ar]\,4s^2\,3d^4$
    B. $[Ar]\,4s^2\,3d^5$
    C. $[Ar]\,4s^1\,3d^5$
    D. $[Ar]\,3d^6$

78. Which of the following is NOT a possible ground state electron configuration?

    A. $1s^2\, 2s^1$
    B. $1s^2\, 2s^2\, 2p^6\, 3s^2\, 3p^6\, 3d^5\, 5s^1$
    C. $1s^2\, 2s^2\, 2p^6\, 3s^2\, 3p^5$
    D. $1s^2\, 2s^2\, 2p^6\, 3s^2\, 3p^6\, 4s^2\, 3d^{10}\, 4p^6$

79. Which of the following elements does not belong to the same group as the other three?

    A.   N
    B.   P
    C.   Se
    D.   As

80. Which of the following groups contains the alkaline earth metals?

    A.   IA
    B.   IIA
    C.   VIIA
    D.   VIIIA

81. Which of the following has the highest charge to mass ratio?

    A.   Proton
    B.   Neutron
    C.   Electron
    D.   Photon

82. What is Avogadro's number?

    A.   The number of hydrogen atoms in 1 gram of H
    B.   1/12 of the number of carbon atoms in 12 grams of 12C
    C.   The number of carbon atoms in 12 grams of 12C
    D.   The number of carbon atoms in 1 gram of 12C

83. Which classification do most of the halogens fall under?

    A.   Metals
    B.   Metalloids
    C.   Nonmetals
    D.   Transition Metals

84. Which group contains the softest metallic solids at room temperature?

    A.   IA
    B.   IIA
    C.   IIIA
    D.   IVA

85. Which of the following is the second most electronegative element?

    A.   Fluorine
    B.   Oxygen
    C.   Chlorine
    D.   Neon

86. Which element's outermost electron experiences the least effective nuclear charge?

    A.   Be
    B.   Li
    C.   C
    D.   N

87. The magnitude of which of the following does NOT generally increase going to the right and up on a periodic table?

    A.   Ionization energy
    B.   Electron Affinity
    C.   Atomic Radius
    D.   Electronegativity

88. Which of the following has the largest atomic radius?

    A.   Cesium
    B.   Fluorine
    C.   Iodine
    D.   Lithium

89. Which of the following has the greatest difference between first and second ionization energy?

    A. Mg
    B. O
    C. F
    D. K

90. Which of the following has the lowest electron affinity?

    A. Na
    B. Rb
    C. F
    D. Ne

91. Which pair of elements has the greatest difference in electronegativity?

    A. Na and Cl
    B. Mg and Cl
    C. C and F
    D. Mg and S

92. Which of the following is an equation used to calculate the number of moles of a substance composed of a single element?

    A. grams/atomic weight
    B. atomic weight/molecular weight
    C. molecular weight/grams
    D. grams/atomic weight*molecular weight

93. Which of the following defines effective nuclear charge?

    A. The amount of shielding done by inner electrons for the outermost electron.
    B. The force felt by the electrons of an atom due to the nucleus.
    C. The force felt by the outermost electron in an atom due to the nucleus.
    D. The total charge of an atom

94. Which of the following are negative values generally?

    A. Electron affinity
    B. Electronegativity
    C. Ionization energy
    D. Atomic radius

95. Which of the following is most likely the electronegativity of F?

    A. 4
    B. 322 kJ/mol
    C. -322 kJ/mol
    D. 0

96. Which of the following gives the definition of ionization energy?

    A. The energy released when an electron is added to an atom
    B. The energy necessary to add an electron to an atom
    C. The energy necessary to remove an electron from an atom
    D. The energy released when an electron is removed from an atom

97. How many hydrogen atoms are in a 100 g sample of water?

    A. $6.7*10^{24}$
    B. $6.022*10^{23}$
    C. $1.11*10^{24}$
    D. $6.022*10^{25}$

98. How much of a 100 g sample of water is hydrogen by weight?

    A. 6 g
    B. 11 g
    C. 22 g
    D. 89 g

99. What is the empirical formula of a molecule that is 37.5 percent carbon, 12.5 percent hydrogen, and 50 percent oxygen by weight?

    A. C_2H_6O
    B. CH_4O
    C. $C_2H_4O_2$
    D. CH_2O

100. Two elements with electronegativities that differ by less than 1, will likely form a(n):

    A. ionic bond because the electronegativities are sufficiently distinct.
    B. ionic bond because the electronegativities are sufficiently close.
    C. covalent bond because the electronegativities are sufficiently distinct.
    D. covalent bond because the electronegativities are sufficiently close.

This page intentionally left blank.

SECTION 2
BONDING AND REACTIONS

When we discuss the idea of chemistry as "the study of change" we primarily mean that it is the study of change in bonds. Chemical reactions are, by and large, nothing more than a change in bonding – either a change in the intramolecular bonds holding a molecule together, or a change in the intermolecular bonds holding a mixture in a certain phase of matter.

In the following chapters we will discuss the types of bonds that can form between atoms and discuss the general classes of chemical reactions that can change those bonds. Even though the chemical reactions that make up living systems are terribly complicated, they still must obey the same basic rules of stoichiometry as any other reaction. A solid grounding in understanding the bonds and reactions that all compounds involve will help you answer a wide variety of chemistry-related MCAT questions.

CHAPTER 5
Chemical Bonding

A. INTRODUCTION

MCAT students are expected to know the electronic structures of atoms and apply this knowledge to the formation of bonds and other related aspects. This chapter is devoted to the review of chemical bonding and related aspects such as ionic character and polarity.

What are Chemical Bonds?

Chemical bonds are strong attractive forces that enable atoms or groups of atoms to hold together. The two major categories of chemical bonds are ionic and covalent bonds. In this chapter, we will discuss ionic bonds, covalent bonds, and other atomic and molecular interactions.

B. IONIC BOND

The major force behind the formation of an **ionic bond** is the electrostatic attractive force that exists between negative and positive ions. It is formed by the transfer of one or more electrons from one atom to another. The atom that donates the electrons becomes positive (cation), and the counterpart atom that receives those electrons becomes negative (anion). The attractive force between two oppositely charged ions or species holds the atoms together in an ionic bond.

In an ionic compound, any ion can attract not only the pairing ion or group, but it can also attract neighboring oppositely charged ions, resulting in strong ionic solids.

Now let us take a look at an example to understand this better. The sodium fluoride (NaF) molecule is a result of ionic bond formation between sodium and fluoride ions. Together with this, you should also try to understand Lewis dot structures. Lewis structure will be discussed in detail later in this chapter.

Lewis Electron-Dot Formulas: *Lewis electron-dot formulas are diagrammatic representations of the atoms involved and their valence electrons. The valence electrons are usually represented as dots around the elemental symbol.*

Formation of the Ionic Bond in NaF

THE ELECTRONIC CONFIGURATION OF SODIUM AND FLUORINE

$$Na \quad - \quad 1s^2 2s^2 2p^6 3s^1$$

$$F \quad - \quad 1s^2 2s^2 2p^5$$

In the formation of the ionic bond, the sodium atom loses the electron from its $3s$ subshell, thereby becoming Na^+.

$$Na \longrightarrow Na^+ + e^-$$

On the other hand, the fluorine atom takes the electron that is being lost from the sodium atom to form a (F^-) fluoride ion.

$$F + e^- \longrightarrow F^-$$

These resulting ions are oppositely charged and therefore have electrostatic attractive forces between them, resulting in the formation of the ionic bond.

$$Na \quad + \quad \cdot \ddot{F} \colon \longrightarrow Na^+ \ [\ F \ ]^-$$

The attractive energy in an ionic bond can be expressed in terms of Coulombic energy, according to Coulomb's law. Imagine this by considering that the ions are spherical and are separated by particular distances. The attractive energy can be expressed as follows:

$$\text{Energy, E} \ = \ \frac{k\,q_1 q_2}{r}$$

Here, k $(= 9 \times 10^9 \ J \cdot m / C^2)$ is a constant, q_1 and q_2 are the charges, and r is the distance between the nuclei of the two ionic entities involved in the bonding.

C. COVALENT BOND

A **covalent bond** is formed as a result of the sharing of a pair of electrons between atoms. Covalent bonds result when the difference in electronegativities between the bonding atoms is very small. Though the intramolecular bonds of covalent compounds are significant, the intermolecular forces are relatively weak. Because of this, covalent compounds have relatively lower boiling and melting points when compared to ionic compounds.

Covalent Bond Formation

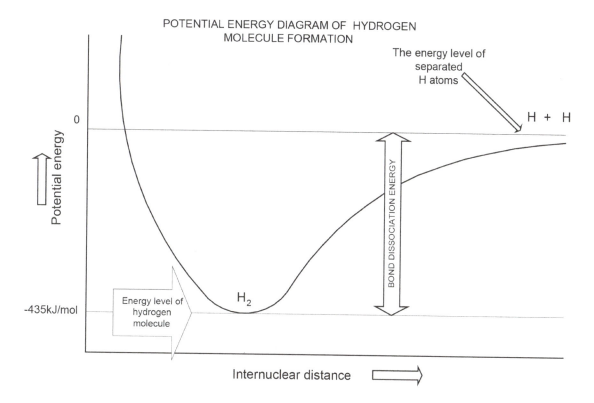

Figure 5-1

In this section, we will look at the covalent bond formation in the hydrogen molecule (H_2). The hydrogen molecule is diatomic. The hydrogen atom has an electronic configuration of $1s^1$. The formation can be expressed in terms of a **Lewis formula** as follows:

$$H\bullet \; + \; \bullet H \longrightarrow H:H \quad \text{or} \quad H–H$$

After the bond is formed, the electrons are shared by both hydrogen atoms, as expected in a covalent bond. This $1s$ overlap makes the configuration of hydrogen atom in the bond the same as that of helium ($1s^2$). Another aspect that you should understand is that the total potential energy (see Figure 5-1) of the hydrogen molecule is lower than that of the hydrogen atoms in their separate forms.

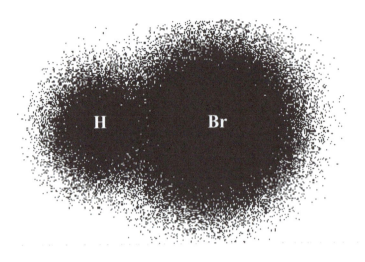

Figure 5-2

The distribution of bonded electrons in the HBr molecule is shown above (Figure 5-2). In this bond formation, hydrogen shares its electron with bromine, whereas bromine gives the one electron that is needed for hydrogen to complete its shell. The bromine atom has 7 electrons in its outermost shell, and it requires 1 more to complete its octet. Octet is the state in which an atom has 8 electrons in its outermost shell. Now, since hydrogen has 2 electrons, and bromine has eight electrons in its valence shell, they are both satisfied in terms of their stability, the stability being facilitated by the formation of the covalent bond.

Coordinate Covalent Bonds

In **coordinate covalent bonds**, the same aspect of the sharing of electrons exists, just as in simple covalent bonds, but the difference is that both shared electrons are supplied by the same atom.

Coordinate covalent bond is formed when the two electrons that are shared in the formation of the bond are donated by one group or atom involved in the bond.

An example of coordinate covalent bond is seen in the formation of ammonium ion (NH_4^+).

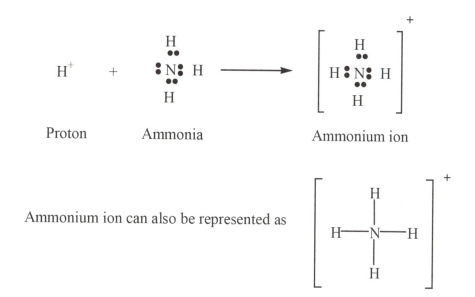

Proton   Ammonia   Ammonium ion

Ammonium ion can also be represented as

Polar and Nonpolar Bonds

When two atoms combine, just like in the formation of a hydrogen molecule, the atoms are one and the same and they have the same electronegativity. But, if the two atoms that are combined via covalent bond are different, then there is unequal sharing of electrons due to the electronegativity difference between those atoms. Such a bond is called a polar covalent bond. The former case (H_2 molecule) is an example of a nonpolar covalent compound. In the HBr molecule, the bonding electrons will be more attracted to the more electronegative of the two atoms, namely bromine. So the bonding electrons are likely to spend more time closer to the more electronegative atom or group. Hence, this bond is polar.

The delta$^+$ (δ^+) indicates the partial positive charge of the hydrogen atom, and delta$^-$ (δ^-) indicates the partial negative charge of the bromine atom. Small and equal charges being separated by a small distance constitute a dipole. The polarity is quantitatively represented in terms of dipole moment, which is the charge times the distance between the charges. Now that you know dipole moment, let's learn how to represent this.

$$\overset{\delta^+}{H}\text{---}\overset{\delta^-}{Br}$$

Here the net dipole moment is as indicated by the arrow.

When there are more than two dipoles, the net effect is the vector sum of all individual dipoles in the molecule. For example, in carbon dioxide (CO_2) the net dipole moment is as shown below.

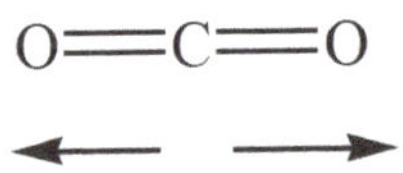

$$O = C = O$$

$$\longleftarrow \qquad \longrightarrow$$

Since the dipoles are equal and opposite, the vectors of the dipoles cancel out.

D. LEWIS DOT STRUCTURES

Lewis Electron-Dot Formulas: *Lewis electron-dot formulas are diagrammatic representations of the atoms involved and their valence electrons. The valence electrons are usually represented as dots around the elemental symbol. It is a two-dimensional way of representing the structural formula, showing the bonding electrons and the lone electrons that are in the valence shells.*

Writing Lewis Formulas

The objective of this section is to become comfortable with writing Lewis structural formulas. We can only predict the Lewis structures of simple molecules. Other complex structures require complicated analysis and predictions based on experimental data.

1. First, determine the main structural makeup of the molecule, such as which atom will be the central atom of the molecule. The central atom of the molecule is usually the atom with the lowest electronegativity.
2. Next, determine the total number of valence (outermost) electrons.
3. Draw the basic skeletal structure of the molecule or ion.
4. Next, determine the distribution of those valence electrons so as to complete the octet of the atoms that are around or bonded to the central atom.
5. The remaining electrons are to be distributed in pairs around the central atom.
6. Sometimes you might find that the central atom is not reaching the octet level even at this point. The most likely reason is that there might be a need of a double bond or a triple bond.

Let's go through an example. Before looking at the solution of the example shown below, determine the Lewis structure on your own.

Example 5-1

Write the Lewis dot formula of carbonate ion

$$(CO_3)^{2-}$$

Solution:

Since carbon is the least electronegative, it is the most likely atom to be in the center. With this information, we can draw the carbonate ion as indicated below.

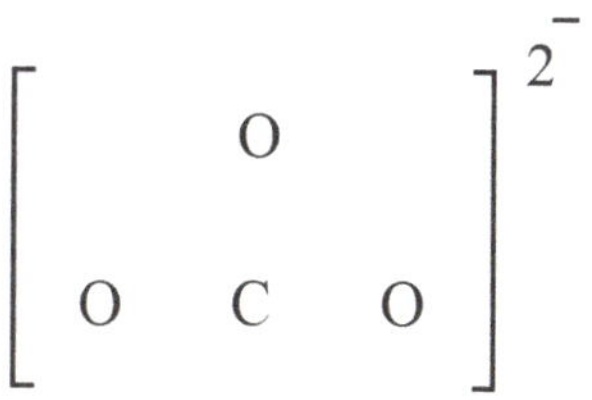

$$\left[\begin{array}{ccc} & O & \\ O & C & O \end{array} \right]^{2-}$$

Next, calculate the number of valence electrons. Carbon has 4 electrons, whereas oxygen has 6 electrons each, and do not forget the net charge of −2, which accounts for two more electrons. This tallies to a total of 24 electrons. We can set up all these valence electrons around individual atoms in the structure drawn so far, as shown below:

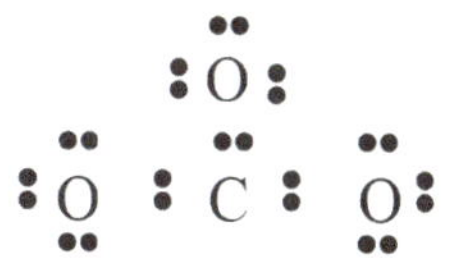

Now that we have set all the valence electrons, we are done, right? No! Watch out for the carbon. The octet of carbon is not satisfied, and thus carbon will not be very stable with this configuration. Since there are no more electrons to spare, we have to move one of the pairs of electrons from an oxygen atom, which results in 1 double bond and 2 single bonds. The completed Lewis structure of the carbonate ion should look as follows:

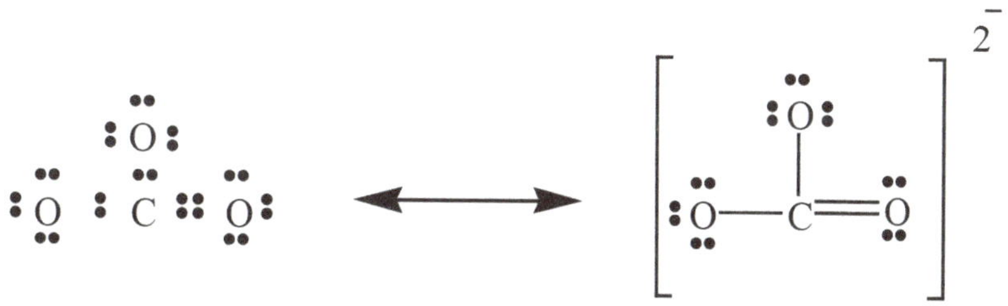

E. RESONANCE

Resonance is an important concept in chemistry. Though we represent definite Lewis structures of molecules, in actuality the electrons are not localized. They are shared and delocalized by atoms in such a way as to be in the most stable electron distribution. This is called **resonance**.

Acetate ion

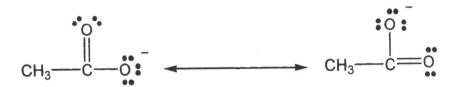

The actual form of these resonance structures is an average of all the possible resonance forms of the group or molecule.

F. FORMAL CHARGE

The concept of **formal charge** is based on the assumption that the electrons involved in the bonds are equally shared between the involved atoms. As you have already seen, this is not exactly the case. But for simplicity and from an analytical point of view, we assume that the electrons are equally distributed.

Formal charge of an atom is the charge of the atom in a formula, under the assumption that the electrons in the bonds are equally distributed between the atoms that contain the bond.

$$\text{Formal charge} = \text{Group number of the atom of interest} - \text{Number of bonds} - \text{Number of unshared electrons}$$

Another way of phrasing this is "Valence number minus sticks minus dots." Since a bond is drawn as a "stick" and the lone pairs are "dots".

There are different ways to find formal charges. One way is mentioned here. You can either choose to do it this way, or whichever way you are comfortable with.

Example 5-2

Find the formal charges of all the atoms in thionyl chloride $(SOCl_2)$.

Solution:

The Lewis structure of thionyl chloride is written below:

$$:\overset{\displaystyle ..}{\underset{\displaystyle }{O}}:$$
$$:\overset{..}{\underset{..}{Cl}}:\overset{..}{\underset{..}{S}}:\overset{..}{\underset{..}{Cl}}:$$

Using the formal charge formula, it is just a matter of plugging in the numbers. Both oxygen and sulfur belong to Group VI. Chlorine belongs to Group VII. Sulfur has 3 bonds and 2 unshared electrons. Oxygen has 1 bond and 6 unshared electrons. Chlorine has 1 bond and 6 unshared electrons.

$$\text{Formal charge} = \text{Group number of the atom of interest} - \text{Number of bonds} - \text{Number of unshared electrons}$$

The formal charge of sulfur = $6 - 3 - 2 = +1$
The formal charge of oxygen = $6 - 1 - 6 = -1$
The formal charge of chlorine = $7 - 1 - 6 = 0$

Notice that the net charge of the molecule is zero, as expected, since it is a molecule and not an ion.

Problem 5-1

Which of the following represents the formal charge of nitrogen in nitric acid (HNO_3)?

    A. 1
    B. +1
    C. 2
    D. +2

Solution:

If you draw the structure, you'll see that nitrogen is the central atom. It has a double bond to one oxygen, a single bond to another oxygen, and a single bond to the OH group. The answer is +1.

G. BOND LENGTH AND BOND ENERGY

Bond length is the distance between the nuclei of the atoms that are bonded together. **Bond energy** is the amount of energy required to pull the atoms involved in the bond away from each other. Bond order is the number of bonds (covalent) that exist between the two bonded atoms. The bond length and bond order are inversely proportional. Hence, as the bond order increases, the bond length decreases and the bond energy increases.

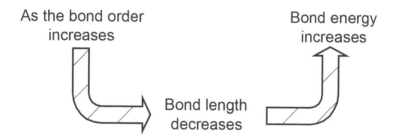

Problem 5-2

Which of the following will have the highest bond energy?

    A.   A carbon-carbon single bond
    B.   A carbon-carbon double bond
    C.   A carbon-carbon triple bond
    D.   A carbon-hydrogen bond

Solution:

The bond order of a triple bond is 3. Carbon-carbon single bond and carbon-hydrogen bond have bond orders of 1. This eliminates choices A and D. The bond order of carbon-carbon double bond is 2. The one with the highest bond order will have the highest bond energy. So the answer is choice C.

H. MOLECULAR GEOMETRY

In this section, we will study the valence shell electron pair repulsion theory and the basis for predicting the shapes of some structures.

Valence Shell Electron Pair Repulsion Theory

Valence shell electron pair repulsion theory (VSEPR) can be used to predict the shapes of molecules. According to this theory, the geometry of a molecule is such that the valence-electron pairs of the central atom are kept farthest apart to minimize the electron repulsions. Again, you have to view molecules in terms of Lewis structure so that the shape of the molecules can be predicted with the VSEPR theory.

Molecular geometry of a molecule is the directional orientation of the bonded pairs around the central atom, excluding the unshared electron pairs.

Let's look at the practical significance of this theory through some examples.

Example 5-3

Predict the molecular geometry of the CO_2 molecule.

Solution:

Carbon, obviously the central atom, has four electrons in its valence shell. In order to complete the octet, carbon requires four more electrons or two pairs of electrons. Oxygen atom has six electrons in its valence shell. In order to complete its octet, each oxygen atom requires two electrons or one pair of electrons. The Lewis structure of CO_2 should look like the figure shown below. Note that the valence electrons of the carbon atom are denoted by asterisks (*) and that of the oxygen are denoted by dots.

$$\overset{\bullet\bullet}{\underset{\bullet\bullet}{:\!O\!:}} \overset{\textstyle *}{\underset{\textstyle *}{}} C \overset{\textstyle *}{\underset{\textstyle *}{}} \overset{\bullet\bullet}{\underset{\bullet\bullet}{:\!O\!:}}$$

The molecule keeps this linear shape, so that the lone-pair electrons are placed far apart as predicted by the VSEPR theory. Also notice that the carbon-oxygen bonds are double bonds. Hence the CO_2 molecule is linear in shape.

Example 5-4

Predict the shape of the BeF_2 molecule.

Solution:

Beryllium has two electrons in its outer most shell. In this case, there is an exception to the octet rule, because in the formation of the molecule, only two pairs (four electrons) are present in the valence shell of beryllium. Each fluorine atom requires one electron to attain the complete octet. Take a look at the structure shown below. Again for clarity, beryllium electrons are denoted by asterisks and fluorine electrons are denoted by dots.

$$:\overset{\bullet\bullet}{\underset{\bullet\bullet}{F}} \ast Be \ast \overset{\bullet\bullet}{\underset{\bullet\bullet}{F}}:$$

$$\Downarrow$$

$$F\text{——}Be\text{——}F$$

$$180^0$$

Example 5-5

Predict the shape of the water (H_2O) molecule.

Solution:

When dealing with bond formation with the possibility of existence of lone pairs, we have to take that into consideration. You will see that in this example. The oxygen atom has six valence electrons, and the hydrogen atom has one valence electron. So in the structural formula, there are two lone pairs in the central oxygen atom. How do you think this will change the shape of the molecule? Well, because of the lone pairs, the molecule will be bent, rather than linear. The structure is shown below.

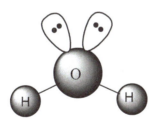

Angular, or bent shape of the water molecule

Problem 5-3

Predict the geometry of the following molecules.

    A. $BeCl_2$
    B. NH_3
    C. $SiCl_4$
    D. BF_3
    E. CH_4

Answers:

    A.   linear

    B.   trigonal pyramidal

    C.   tetrahedral

    D.   trigonal planar

    E.   tetrahedral

SOME COMMON GEOMETRIES AND THEIR CHARACTERISTICS

BONDING ELECTRON PAIRS	LONE PAIRS	GEOMETRY
2	NONE	LINEAR
3	NONE	TRIGONAL PLANAR
2	1	BENT
4	NONE	TETRAHEDRAL
3	1	TRIGONAL PYRAMIDAL
5	NONE	TRIGONAL BIPYRAMIDAL
4	1	SEESAW SHAPED
3	2	T-SHAPED
6	NONE	OCTAHEDRAL

Table 5-1

CHAPTER 5 PROBLEMS

1. Which of the following best represents the Lewis structure of SO_3^{2-}?

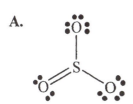
A.

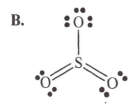
B.

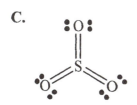
C.

D.

2. Which of the following has a net dipole moment of zero?

    A. H_2O
    B. HCl
    C. CO
    D. CH_4

3. The bond between nitrogen and oxygen in NO_2 is most likely:

    A. an ionic bond.
    B. a covalent bond.
    C. a hydrogen bond.
    D. a dipole-dipole interaction.

4. Ammonia (NH_3) can bond with boron trifluoride (BF_3). For the bond formation, the electrons are most likely supplied by:

    A. nitrogen.
    B. boron.
    C. both boron and nitrogen because the bond formed is covalent.
    D. hydrogen.

5. Which of the following has the highest dipole moment?

    A. HF
    B. CCl_4
    C. HBr
    D. CO_2

6. The molecular geometry of BCl_3 is:

    A. linear.
    B. trigonal planar.
    C. tetrahedral.
    D. trigonal bipyramidal.

7. CCl_4 molecule is:

    A. trigonal planar.
    B. linear.
    C. octahedral.
    D. tetrahedral.

8. Which of the following best describes the geometry of nitrate (NO_3^-)?

    A. Trigonal planar
    B. Trigonal bipyramidal
    C. Tetrahedral
    D. Angular

9. What is the molecular geometry of SF_6?

    A. Hexagonal
    B. Tetrahedral
    C. Octahedral
    D. Trigonal planar

10. CH_4 and SiF_4 are examples of tetrahedral geometry. Which of the following are true regarding these two molecules?

  I. The carbon-hydrogen bonds are dipoles
  II. The silicon-fluorine bonds are dipoles
  III. Methane is nonpolar
  IV. SiF_4 has zero dipole moment

    A. I and II only
    B. II only
    C. II and III only
    D. I, II, III and IV

11. Which of the following types of bonds has the least electronegativity difference between the bonding atoms?

    A. Ionic bond
    B. Polar covalent bond
    C. Nonpolar covalent bond
    D. Cannot be predicted without the actual electronegativity data

12. Which of the following choices represents the vectors of bond dipoles of the indicated (indicated by the arrows) bonds of the compounds A and B, respectively?

Compound A

Compound B

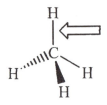

    A.

    B.

    C.

    D.

13. Choose the answer which best denotes the electronic orientation (electronic geometry) of the water molecule.

    A. Angular
    B. Bent
    C. Trigonal planar
    D. Tetrahedral

CHAPTER 6
Chemical Reactions

A. INTRODUCTION

A chemical reaction is a process at the molecular or ionic level by which one or more types of substances are transformed into one or more new types of substances by different modes of combination. In this chapter, we will explore the different types of chemical reactions including oxidation-reduction reactions. We will also learn how to balance equations.

B. CHEMICAL REACTIONS

A chemical reaction can be represented by a chemical equation. In a chemical equation representing an irreversible reaction, the substances that react (reactants) are written on the left side, while the resulting substances (products) are written on the right side of an arrow.

$$2\ H_2 \quad + \quad O_2 \longrightarrow \quad 2\ H_2O$$

In the reaction shown above, two molecules of hydrogen react with one molecule of oxygen, forming two molecules of water. Balancing of equations will be covered a little later in this chapter.

C. REACTION TYPES

There are five types of chemical reactions.

1. Combination reaction
2. Combustion reaction
3. Decomposition reaction
4. Displacement reaction or single-replacement reaction
5. Metathesis reaction or double-replacement reaction

Combination Reaction

A reaction involving the formation of a compound from two or more substances is called a combination reaction.

Some representative combination reactions

$$2Na\ (s)\quad +\quad Cl_2\ (g)\quad \longrightarrow \quad 2\ NaCl\ (s)$$

$$SO_2\ (g)\quad +\quad H_2O\ (l)\quad \longrightarrow \quad H_2SO_3\ (aq)$$

Combustion Reaction

A **combustion reaction** involves the reaction of substances with oxygen, and it is usually accompanied by the release of large amounts of heat. Combustion reactions are thus highly exothermic.

Some representative combustion reactions

$$C\ (s)\quad +\quad O_2\ (g)\quad \longrightarrow \quad C\ O_2\ (g)$$

$$2\ H_2S\ (g)\quad +\quad 3\ O_2\ (g)\quad \longrightarrow \quad 2\ SO_2\ (g)\quad +\quad 2\ H_2O\ (g)$$

Decomposition Reaction

A decomposition reaction is a process in which one compound decomposes or splits to form two or more simpler compounds and/or elements.

A representative decomposition reaction

$$CaCO_3\ (s)\quad \longrightarrow \quad CaO\ (s)\quad +\quad CO_2\ (g)$$

Displacement Reaction (single-replacement reaction)

In a **single-replacement reaction**, an element reacts with a compound, and results in the displacement of an element or group from the compound. An example of a single-replacement reaction is shown.

A single-replacement reaction

$$Zn\ (s) + CuCl_2\ (aq)\ \rightarrow\ ZnCl_2\ (aq) + Cu\ (s)$$

In this reaction, Zn substitutes for Cu.

Metathesis Reaction (double-replacement reaction)

A **metathesis (double-replacement) reaction** involves the exchange of two groups or two ions among the reactants. Remember that in a single-replacement reaction, there is only one group or ion being switched. A metathesis reaction can often result in an insoluble product from soluble reactants, and the insoluble compound formed is called a precipitate.

A metathesis reaction

$$AgNO_3 \ (aq) \ + \ NaCl \ (aq) \ \longrightarrow \ AgCl \ (s) \ + \ NaNO_3 \ (aq)$$

Note that this reaction involves the formation of a precipitate of AgCl.

With respect to the types of reactions, your objective should be to understand the basis behind the categorization.

D. BALANCING REACTIONS

A chemical equation is said to be balanced if all the atoms present in the reactants appear in the same numbers among the products. Here is an example.

Example 6-1

Balance the following equation.

$$Fe \ + \ O_2 \ \longrightarrow \ Fe_2O_3$$

Solution:

Start by balancing the oxygen atoms. There are two oxygen atoms on the reactant side and three oxygen atoms on the product side. To balance this, put 3 as the coefficient of oxygen on the reactant side. When we write '3 O_2,' that means we have 6 oxygen atoms on the reactant side. To make the same number of oxygen atoms on the product side, let's put 2 as the coefficient of Fe_2O_3. Now the oxygen atoms seem to be balanced.

Let's take a look at Fe. Since the coefficient of Fe_2O_3 is 2, we have 4 atoms of Fe on the product side. We can balance this by writing 4 as the coefficient of Fe on the reactant side. So the balanced equation is as follows:

$$4 \, Fe \ + \ 3 \, O_2 \ \longrightarrow \ 2 \ Fe_2O_3$$

Problem 2-1

Balance the following equations:

(a) $Cu + AgNO_3 \longrightarrow Ag + Cu(NO_3)_2$

(b) $Fe_2O_3 + CO \longrightarrow Fe + CO_2$

(c) $H_2SO_4 + NaOH \longrightarrow Na_2SO_4 + H_2O$

(d) $Ba(OH)_2 + HCl \longrightarrow BaCl_2 + H_2O$

Answers:

(a) $Cu + 2\,AgNO_3 \longrightarrow 2\,Ag + Cu(NO_3)_2$

(b) $Fe_2O_3 + 3\,CO \longrightarrow 2\,Fe + 3\,CO_2$

(c) $H_2SO_4 + 2\,NaOH \longrightarrow Na_2SO_4 + 2\,H_2O$

(d) $Ba(OH)_2 + 2\,HCl \longrightarrow BaCl_2 + 2\,H_2O$

E. BALANCING REDOX REACTIONS

Oxidation Number

Electrons are exchanged during oxidation-reduction reactions. The behavior of atoms or ions in terms of the number of electrons transferred is expressed as the oxidation state (oxidation number). We can define oxidation number as the charge of an atom or ion, based on a set of standard rules. If the given species is an ion containing a single atom, then its oxidation state is its charge itself. Let's analyze this by looking at a few examples.

In NaCl, the oxidation state of sodium is $+1$ and the oxidation state of chlorine is -1. Generally, the elements at the top right corner of the periodic table are assigned negative oxidation numbers. Some of the elements on the right side of the periodic table can have positive or negative oxidation numbers depending upon the atom to which the given element is bonded. The elements in the middle and the left portions of the periodic table have almost exclusively positive oxidation numbers.

Table 6-1

General guidelines for assigning oxidation numbers

1. The elemental natural state oxidation number of any atom is zero. e.g., the oxidation number of oxygen atom in O_2 is zero.
2. The sum of the oxidation numbers of the atoms in a compound should be zero.
3. The sum of the oxidation numbers of the atoms in an ionic species (a species with a net charge) should equal the net charge of the ionic species.
4. The oxidation number of a given ion containing a single atom is its charge.

Oxidation numbers of some common elements

1. The common oxidation number of Group IA metals is +1. e.g., lithium, sodium, potassium.
2. The common oxidation number of Group IIA metals is +2. e.g., beryllium, magnesium, calcium.
3. The common oxidation number of Group IIIA is +3. e.g., aluminum, boron.
4. The common oxidation number of Group IVA is +4. +2 is also seen in some compounds such as CO.
5. The common oxidation numbers of Group V A are +5 and –3.
6. The common oxidation number of Group VIA is –2.
7. The common oxidation number of Group VIIA is –1.
8. The common oxidation number of H is +1. In some metal hydrides, hydrogen shows an oxidation number of –1.

The above list of common oxidation numbers is not comprehensive. Nevertheless, it gives you a basic and essential picture about assigning oxidation numbers in common compounds and ionic species. Most elements can have multiple oxidation states, depending on the element or ionic species to which they are bonded. You have to always follow the general guidelines in Table 6-1, and check whether the items listed are satisfied.

Now that we have learned the theory of assigning oxidation numbers, let's do an example to see how it works.

Example 6-2

What is the oxidation number of sulfur in sulfuric acid?

Solution:

Sulfuric acid is H_2SO_4. The oxidation number of hydrogen is +1. But we have two hydrogens which add up to a charge of +2. Since the total charge of this molecule should be zero, we can say that the charge of sulfate ion is –2. We also know that the oxidation number of oxygen is –2. But there are four oxygens in a sulfate ion. So the charge adds to –8. Now let's solve this algebraically.

ON^{Sulfur} - Oxidation number of sulfur
ON^{Oxygen} - Oxidation number of oxygen

$ON^{Sulfur} + 4 \, (ON^{Oxygen}) = -2$
$ON^{Sulfur} + 4 \, (-2) = -2$
$ON^{Sulfur} = +6$

So the oxidation number of sulfur in sulfuric acid is +6.

Problem 6-2

Calculate the oxidation state of the element indicated in each of the following problems.

 A. What is the oxidation state of hydrogen in MgH_2?
 B. What is the oxidation state of chlorine in ClO_3^-?
 C. What is the oxidation state of oxygen in Na_2O_2?
 D. What is the oxidation state of nitrogen in NH_3?
 E. What is the oxidation state of oxygen in O_2?
 F. What is the oxidation state of bromine in $HBrO_2$?
 G. What is the oxidation state of manganese in $KMnO_4$?

Answers:

 A. -1
 B. +5
 C. -1
 D. -3
 E. 0
 F. +3
 G. +7

Redox Reactions

Oxidation-reduction (redox) reactions involve the transfer of electrons from one compound or species to another. In this section, we will discuss oxidation-reduction reactions and learn how to balance them.

Oxidation is the process by which an atom or species loses its electrons. In **reduction**, an atom or species gains electrons. Let's first consider oxidation and reduction separately.

Consider the conversion of iron from its neutral elemental state to its ionic form.

$$Fe \longrightarrow Fe^{2+} + 2e^-$$

Notice that in the process iron lost electrons. The process is oxidation.

Consider another example. An example involving the conversion of bromine to its ionic form.

$$Br_2 + 2e^- \longrightarrow 2Br^-$$

Notice that in the process bromine gained electrons. The process is reduction.

Now let's go one step forward. Consider the next reaction.

$$2 \text{ Fe } + \text{ 3 Br}_2 \longrightarrow 2 \text{ FeBr}_3$$

This reaction is a typical example of an oxidation-reduction reaction. The oxidation number of iron on the reactant side is 0. The oxidation number of bromine on the reactant side is also 0. What are the oxidation numbers of iron and bromine in $FeBr_3$? Well, we know that bromine has an oxidation number of -1. So the oxidation number of iron in $FeBr_3$ is $+3$. Thus iron is oxidized and bromine is reduced. The species that gets oxidized is called the **reducing agent**. The species that gets reduced is called the **oxidizing agent**. In this reaction, iron acts as the reducing agent, and bromine acts as the oxidizing agent.

Oxidation results in an increase in the oxidation number. In the process of oxidation, electrons are lost.
Reduction results in a decrease in the oxidation number. In the process, electrons are gained.

Balancing Redox Reactions

Balancing of an oxidation-reduction reaction is a little more complex than balancing a simple reaction. The main rule that you have to follow when balancing oxidation-reduction reactions is that the absolute value of the increase in oxidation number of all the atoms that are oxidized should equal the absolute value of the decrease in oxidation number of all the atoms that are reduced. Balancing oxidation-reduction reaction is sometimes time-consuming and quite often frustrating. We will look at two methods of balancing oxidation-reduction reactions.

Method A

1. Write the unbalanced equation.
2. Find the oxidation numbers of the atoms that undergo change in oxidation states and write on top of each atom the corresponding oxidation number.
3. By this process, we will be able to see which atoms are getting oxidized and reduced.
4. Compare and indicate the change in oxidation numbers from the reactant side and the product side, and write down the change in the oxidation numbers.
5. Make the necessary changes by writing coefficients that will equalize the changes in the oxidation numbers. In other words, the net decrease in the oxidation numbers should equal the net increase in the oxidation numbers. Add water if necessary.
6. Do a final check on whether all the atoms and charges balance out.

Method B

1. Write the unbalanced equation.
2. Separate the two half-reactions, write them out, and balance any of the atoms. From this point onward, we balance the reactions separately. Do the obvious or the simple balancing by inspection if possible.
3. Balance the oxygen atoms by adding water on the appropriate side of the half-reaction.
4. Balance the hydrogen atoms by adding H^+ on the appropriate side of the half-reaction.
5. Add sufficient number of electrons so that the charges are balanced.
6. Once the half-reactions are balanced, combine the half-reactions and cancel out any common terms that appear on both sides of the equation to get the refined and balanced oxidation-reduction equation.

Example 6-3
Balance the following oxidation-reduction reaction.

$$Zn \; + \; NO_3^- \longrightarrow Zn^{2+} \; + \; N_2O$$

Method A

1. $Zn \; + \; NO_3^- \longrightarrow Zn^{2+} \; + \; N_2O$

2. $\overset{0}{Zn} \; + \; \overset{+5}{NO_3^-} \longrightarrow \overset{+2}{Zn^{2+}} \; + \; \overset{+1}{N_2O}$

3. $\overset{0}{Zn} \; + \; 2\,\overset{+5}{NO_3^-} \longrightarrow \overset{+2}{Zn^{2+}} \; + \; \overset{+1}{N_2O}$

4.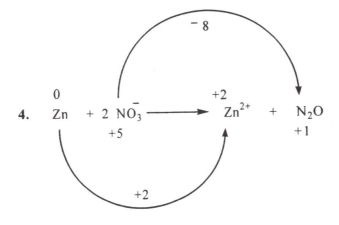

5.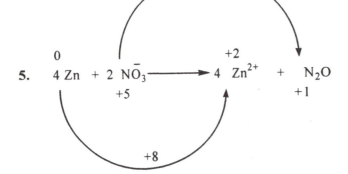

6. $\boxed{10\,H^+ \; + \; 4\,Zn \; + \; 2\,NO_3^- \longrightarrow 4\,Zn^{2+} \; + \; N_2O + 5\,H_2O}$

CHAPTER 6: CHEMICAL REACTIONS

Method B

$$Zn \; + \; NO_3^- \longrightarrow Zn^{2+} \; + \; N_2O$$

Half-reaction I

1. $Zn \rightarrow Zn^{2+}$
2. $Zn \rightarrow Zn^{2+} + 2e^-$

Half-reaction II

1. $NO_3^- \rightarrow N_2O$

2. $2\,NO_3^- \rightarrow N_2O$

3. $2\,NO_3^- \rightarrow N_2O + 5\,H_2O$

4. $10\,H^+ + 2\,NO_3^- \rightarrow N_2O + 5\,H_2O$

5. $8e^- + 10H^+ + 2\,NO_3^- \rightarrow N_2O + 5\,H_2O$

Before we combine the equations, the electrons need to be balanced out. So multiplying the balanced half-reaction # (**I**) by 4, we get

$$4\,Zn \longrightarrow 4\,Zn^{2+} + 8\,e^-$$

Combining the two half reactions

$$4\,Zn \longrightarrow 4\,Zn^{2+} + \cancel{8}e^-$$
$$\cancel{8}e^- + 10\,H^+ + 2\,NO_3^- \longrightarrow N_2O + 5\,H_2O$$
$$\overline{10\,H^+ + 4\,Zn + 2\,NO_3^- \longrightarrow 4\,Zn^{2+} + N_2O + 5\,H_2O}$$

F. STOICHIOMETRY AND LIMITING REAGENTS

In this section, we will look at some chemical equations and find what we can do with the information represented in a chemical equation. The equation shown below represents the reaction of methane and oxygen to form carbon dioxide and water.

$$CH_4 \quad + \quad 2\,O_2 \quad \longrightarrow \quad CO_2 \quad + \quad 2\,H_2O$$

From this balanced equation we can infer many things. Let's consider a few.

1. One molecule of methane reacts with 2 molecules of oxygen to form 1 molecule of carbon dioxide and 2 molecules of water.
2. We can also say that 1 mole of methane reacts with 2 moles of oxygen to form 1 mole of carbon dioxide and 2 moles of water.
3. Since one mole contains Avogadro's number of molecules, we can say that 6.023×10^{23} molecules of methane reacts with 1.2046×10^{24} ($= 2 \times 6.023 \times 10^{23}$) molecules of oxygen to form 6.023×10^{23} molecules of carbon dioxide and 1.2046×10^{24} molecules of water.
4. We can confidently say that 16 g of methane reacts with 64 g of oxygen to form 44 g of carbon dioxide and 36 g of water.

Example 6-4

Calculate the number of moles of water produced when 5.25 moles of methane undergo the reaction depicted below. (Assume there is plenty of oxygen for the reaction)

$$CH_4 \quad + \quad 2\,O_2 \quad \longrightarrow \quad CO_2 \quad + \quad 2\,H_2O$$

Solution:

From the equation, it is clear that for every mole of methane, 2 moles of water are formed. So without any elaborate calculations, you should be able to come up with the correct answer. It is very much like a ratio problem. Since there are 5.25 moles of methane, 10.5 moles of water will be formed.

Number of moles of water formed = 5.25 x 2 = 10.5 moles

Example 6-5

110 g of CO_2 were formed as a result of the reaction shown below. How many grams of oxygen must have reacted to form that much carbon dioxide?

$$CH_4 \quad + \quad 2\,O_2 \quad \longrightarrow \quad CO_2 \quad + \quad 2\,H_2O$$

Solution:

According to the equation, 2 moles of oxygen result in 1 mole of carbon dioxide. For example, if 2 moles of carbon dioxide were formed, 4 moles of oxygen must have reacted. Here, the amount of carbon dioxide formed is given in terms of grams. So the first step is to convert the grams to moles.

$$\text{Moles of carbon dioxide} = \frac{110\ g}{44\ g\ /\ mol} = 2.5\ \text{moles}$$

Hence, <u>5 moles of oxygen</u> must have reacted to form 2.5 moles of carbon dioxide. But the question asks for this quantity in grams. So the final step is to convert moles to grams.

$$\text{The amount of required oxygen} = 5\ \text{moles} \times \frac{32\ g}{1\ mol} = 160\ g$$

Limiting Reagents

So far we have been considering reactions in which all the reactants exist in adequate quantities. In this section, we will consider what happens when the amount of one of the reactants available is less than the amount required to complete the reaction. When such a condition exists, we call that reactant or reagent the limiting reagent.

We will further explore this scenario through the following examples.

Example 6-6

A reaction mixture contains 60.75 g magnesium and 146 g hydrogen chloride. Predict the limiting reagent if the reaction occurs as shown below.

$$Mg\ +\ 2\,HCl\ \longrightarrow\ H_2\ +\ MgCl_2$$

Solution:

First, we have to convert the grams of the substances to moles. Then make the comparison to see which one is the limiting reagent. By now, you should be comfortable with the conversion of moles to grams and vice versa. The number of moles of magnesium present is 2.5 moles. According to the equation, 1 mole of magnesium reacts with 2 moles of hydrogen chloride. For magnesium to completely react, there should be at least 5 moles of hydrogen chloride present. If you calculate the number of moles of hydrogen chloride present, you will get 4 moles. This amount of hydrogen chloride is not enough to completely react with the amount of magnesium present. So the limiting reagent is hydrogen chloride.

G. PERCENT YIELD

If we know the chemical equation and the amounts of reactants, we can calculate the theoretical yield of that reaction. But in reality, the yield depends on many other factors also. Most of the time in synthesis reactions, even in your own lab experiments, you probably noticed that the actual yield is lower than the theoretical yield. The percent yield denotes the amount of actual yield in terms of the theoretical yield. The formula to find the percent yield is given below:

$$\text{Percent yield} = \frac{\text{actual yield of the product}}{\text{theoretical yield of the product}} \times 100\%$$

Example 6-7

$$NaNO_2 \ + \ HCl \ \longrightarrow \ HNO_2 \ + \ NaCl$$

A student conducted the above reaction in a lab as a part of her research assignment. She used 138 g of sodium nitrite, with excess of hydrogen chloride. What is the percent yield of HNO_2, if the actual yield of HNO_2 was 61.1 g?

Solution:

First, you should find the number of moles of $NaNO_2$. Since she used 138 g, the number of moles of $NaNO_2$ is 2 (Mol.wt of $NaNO_2$ is 69 g/mol). Since the ratio of formation of HNO_2 is 1:1 with respect to $NaNO_2$, theoretically 2 moles of HNO_2 should be formed. Two moles of HNO_2 correspond to 94 g. But actually, only 61.1 g of HNO_2 was formed. Now it is just a matter of plug and chug in the percent yield formula.

$$\text{The percentage yield of } HNO_2 = \frac{61.1 \text{ grams}}{94 \text{ grams}} \times 100\% = 65\%$$

In this experiment, the actual yield was not high (i.e., only 65% of the theoretically predicted yield) as expected.

Example 6-8

Match the following reactions with the appropriate type of reaction

1. $2KClO_3 \longrightarrow 2\ KCl\ +\ 3O_2$ **A.** Combination reaction

2. $2K\ +\ Cl_2 \longrightarrow 2KCl$ **B.** Double-replacement reaction

3. $HNO_3\ +\ NaOH \longrightarrow NaNO_3\ +\ H_2O$ **C.** Decomposition reaction

Solution:

$2KClO_3 \longrightarrow 2\ KCl\ +\ 3O_2$ **C.** Decomposition reaction

$2KCl\ +\ Cl_2 \longrightarrow 2KCl$ **A.** Combination reaction

$HNO_3\ +\ NaOH \longrightarrow NaNO_3\ +\ H_2O$ **B.** Double-replacement reaction

CHAPTER 6 PROBLEMS

$$2HI + PbCl_2 \rightarrow PbI_2 + 2HCl$$

1. The reaction shown here can be best classified as a:

    A.   combustion reaction.
    B.   combination reaction.
    C.   single-replacement reaction.
    D.   double-replacement reaction.

2. When combined quantitatively, all of the following reactant combinations give rise to neutralization reactions, EXCEPT:

    A. HNO_2 + NaOH
    B.   KOH + HCl
    C. Al^{3+} + $3OH^-$
    D. H_3PO_4 + NaOH

3. An unbalanced equation is shown. What is the coefficient of aluminum hydroxide in the final balanced equation?

$$H_2SO_4 + Al(OH)_3 \rightarrow H_2O + Al_2(SO_4)_3$$

    A.   1
    B.   2
    C.   3
    D.   7

4. How many grams of sodium chloride are required to synthesize 73 grams of hydrogen chloride, if the reaction involves sodium chloride and sulfuric acid?

$$NaCl + H_2SO_4 \rightarrow Na_2SO_4 + HCl$$

    A.   58.5 grams
    B.   117 grams
    C.   175.5 grams
    D.   234 grams

5. In some reactions, you will often encounter ions in aqueous solutions which are not actually involved in the reaction. Such ions are best termed:

    A.   cations.
    B.   anions.
    C.   salt-bridge ions.
    D.   spectator ions.

6. Some substances can act as a base or an acid. Such substances are called:

    A.   aliphatic substances.
    B.   amphibasic substances.
    C.   lyophilic substances.
    D.   amphoteric substances.

7. Predict the coefficient of iron in the balanced equation for a reaction in which iron reacts with oxygen to form Fe_2O_3.

    A.   1
    B.   2
    C.   3
    D.   4

8. The number of molecules are the same in which of the following pairs?

    A.   32 grams of O_2 and 32 grams of SO_2
    B.   49 grams of NO_2 and 40 grams of NaOH
    C.   20 grams of HF and 36 grams of H_2O
    D.   60 grams of C_2H_6 and 156 grams of C_6H_6

Questions 9-15 are based on the following passage.

Passage 1

Information regarding the amounts of substances that actually react to form the products is of extreme help. Analyzing reactions and having the balanced equations help chemists to determine the correct and optimum proportions of reactants to be used. There are various other factors besides the amount of reactants, which determine the efficiency of reactions.

Experiment 1

$$2\ Al + Fe_2O_3 \rightarrow 2\ Fe + Al_2O_3$$

Student 1 used 40.5 g of aluminum and 80 g of Fe_2O_3 for Reaction I. A second student conducted the same reaction with a different amount for one of the reactants. The second student used 40.5 g of aluminum, and 90 grams of Fe_2O_3. A third student also conducted the same reaction with 54 g of aluminum and the same amount of Fe_2O_3 used by the first student.

Experiment 2

Reaction II involved the production of Al_2O_3 from aluminum hydroxide This was done by heating aluminum hydroxide.

$$2\ Al(OH)_3(s) \rightarrow Al_2O_3(s) + \text{product x}$$

Experiment 3

$$Fe_2O_3(s) + 3\ CO(g) \xrightarrow{\text{heat}} 2\ Fe(s) + 3\ CO_2(g)$$

9. What is the most likely identity of product x?

    A. aluminum
    B. water
    C. hydrogen
    D. oxygen

10. In Experiment 3, which of the following is the limiting reagent?

    A. Fe_2O_3 because there is only 1 mole of it
    B. CO because of its gas phase
    C. Fe because of its insufficiency
    D. Cannot be determined without more data

11. Based on the given information, which of the following are true regarding Experiment 1?
    I. The second student had the highest yield for aluminum oxide.
    II. The third student had a higher yield for aluminum oxide than the first student.
    III. The first and the third students had the same yield for aluminum oxide.

    A. I only
    B. I and II only
    C. I and III only
    D. II and III only

12. Which of the following changes will further increase the overall yield for the reactions conducted in Experiment 1?

    A. Increasing the amount of aluminum used by Student 1
    B. Increasing the amount of aluminum used by Student 2
    C. Increasing the amount of Fe_2O_3 used by Student 2
    D. None of the above

13. Roughly 80 g of Fe_2O_3 was present in Experiment 3, and upon completion of the reaction, it was measured that 22 g of CO_2 was formed. If this is true, how much CO must have reacted before reaching completion of the reaction?

    A. 14 grams
    B. 28 grams
    C. 56 grams
    D. 84 grams

CHAPTER 6: CHEMICAL REACTIONS

14. In the previous question, which of the reactants acts as the limiting reagent?

    A. Fe_2O_3
    B. CO
    C. CO_2
    D.   Cannot be determined

15. If 0.1 mole of CO was reacted with excess of Fe_2O_3, how many molecules of carbon dioxide will be produced?

    A. 6.0×10^{23} molecules
    B. 6.0×10^{22} molecules
    C. 3.0×10^{23} molecules
    D. 18.0×10^{23} molecules

Section 2

CONTENT REVIEW PROBLEMS

1. What is an ionic bond?

   A. A bond between a metal and nonmetal
   B. A bond between two similarly electro-negative elements
   C. A bond in which electrons are shared
   D. A bond between two metallic ions

2. Which of the following pairs of elements will form an ionic bond

   A. S and O
   B. P and C
   C. Na and Mg
   D. Ca and Br

3. Which of the following pairs of elements will NOT form an ionic bond?

   A. K and F
   B. Li and He
   C. Mg and O
   D. Fe and O

4. Which of following pairs of elements will NOT form any bond?

   A. Na and Cl
   B. C and O
   C. Ne and He
   D. Mn and O

5. What is an ion?

   A. A molecule or atom with an electric charge
   B. A molecule or atom involved in an ionic reaction
   C. A molecule or atom with a dipole
   D. A polar molecule or atom

6. Which of the following elements is most likely to exist as a cation?

   A. C
   B. Ga
   C. Be
   D. I

7. Which of the following elements is most likely to exist as an anion?

   A. C
   B. B
   C. Cl
   D. Ca

8. Which of the following compounds contains an ionic bond?

   A. CH_3OH
   B. $KMnO_4$
   C. PO_4^{3-}
   D. SO_2

9. Which of the following compounds does NOT contain an ionic bond?

   A. $CaCl_2$
   B. KF
   C. SO_3^{2-}
   D. NH_4Cl

10. What is an anion?

   A. An atom or molecule with an extra electron
   B. An atom or molecule with a negative electric dipole
   C. An atom or molecule with a loss of electrons
   D. An atom or molecule with a positive electric dipole

11. What is a cation?

   A. An atom or molecule with an extra electron
   B. An atom or molecule with a negative electric dipole
   C. An atom or molecule with a loss of electrons
   D. An atom or molecule with a positive electric dipole

12. How many steps is the reaction to form an ionic bond from two ions?

   A. 1 step
   B. 2 steps
   C. 3 steps
   D. 4 steps

13. What is the order of the slow step in the formation of an ionic bond from two ions?

   A. 1st order
   B. 2nd order
   C. 3rd order
   D. 4th order

14. What is a covalent bond?

   A. A bond between a metal and nonmetal
   B. A bond between a halogen and an alkali metal
   C. A bond in which electrons are shared
   D. A bond between two metallic ions

15. Which of the following pairs will form a covalent bond?

   A. C and O
   B. H and F
   C. Li and Br
   D. NH_4 and MnO_4

16. Which of the following conditions is necessary for the formation of a diatomic ionic bond?

   A. The electronegativities of the two elements be close
   B. The two elements share electrons
   C. The electronegativities of the two elements be sufficiently different.
   D. The two atoms are both nonmetals

17. Which of the following is the least polar covalent bond?

   A. C and H
   B. C and F
   C. C and N
   D. C and O

18. Which of the following is the most polar covalent bond?

   A. C and H
   B. C and F
   C. C and N
   D. C and O

19. Which of the following is the general definition of a polar covalent bond?

   A. A bond with a dipole
   B. A bond between two ions
   C. A bond between a halogen and carbon
   D. A bond with a positive or negative overall charge

20. When is a covalent bond not polar?

   A. When the two elements forming the bond are ions
   B. When the two elements forming the bond are both nonmetals
   C. When the two elements forming the bond are similar.
   D. When the two elements forming the bond have similar electronegativities.

21. How many valence electrons does nitrogen have when in its most stable, unbound form?

    A. 3
    B. 7
    C. 5
    D. 8

22. How many valence electrons does an oxygen atom with a negative charge have?

    A. 6 or 7
    B. 7 or 8
    C. less than 6
    D. 6

23. How many valence electrons does nitrogen contribute to the covalent bonds found in ammonium?

    A. 3
    B. 4
    C. 5
    D. 7

24. What is the formal charge of each of the nitrogens in the following molecule?

$$:N\equiv N:$$

    A. 0
    B. +1
    C. -1
    D. -2

25. Which element in the following molecule has the greatest negative dipole?

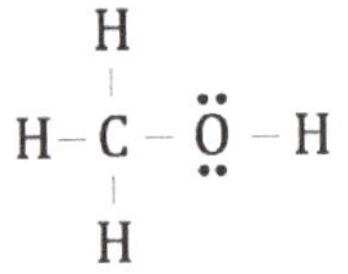

    A. H
    B. C
    C. O
    D. There is no way to tell

26. What is the formal charge of oxygen A?

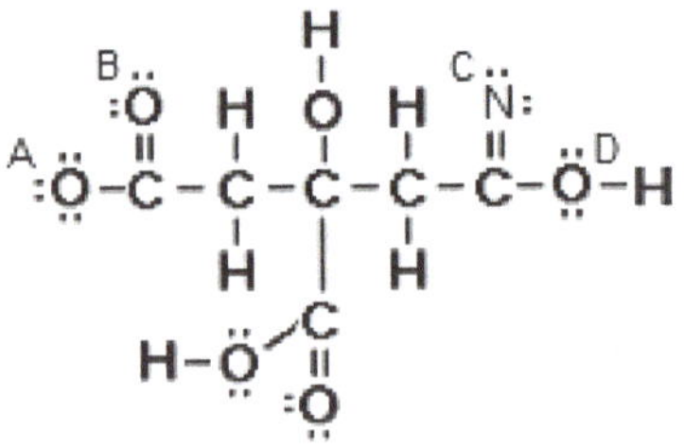

    A. 0
    B. -1
    C. +1
    D. -2

27. What is the formal charge of nitrogen C?

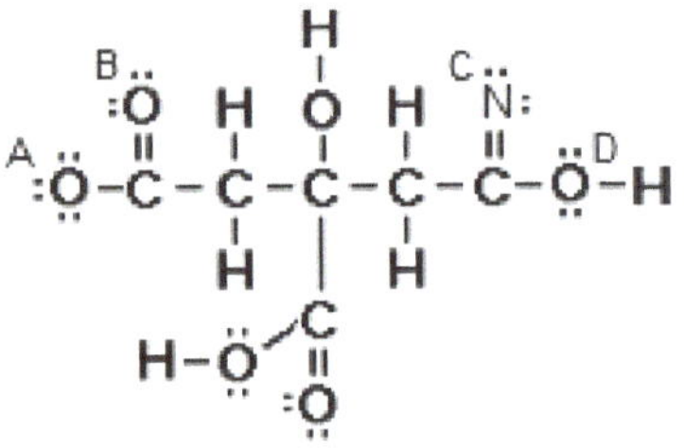

    A. 0
    B. -1
    C. +1
    D. -2

28. How many resonance forms are there of the following molecule?

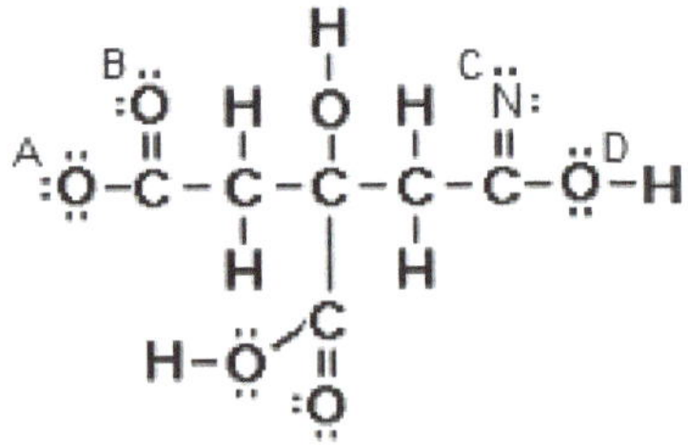

    A. 1
    B. 2
    C. 4
    D. 8

29. Which bond is the longest in the following molecule?

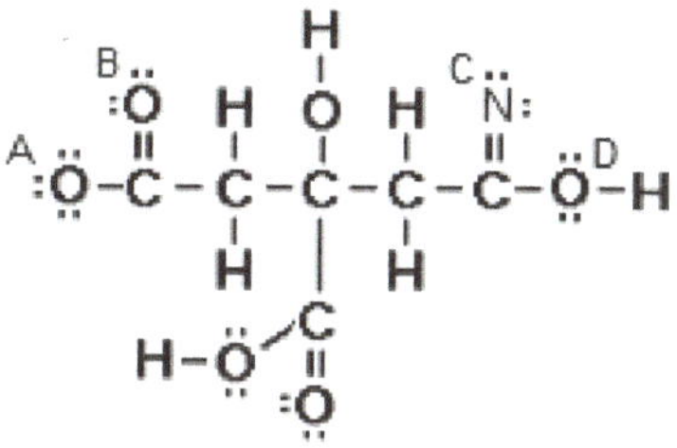

A. The bond involving A
B. The bond involving B
C. The bond involving C
D. The bond involving D

30. What is the overall charge of the following molecule?

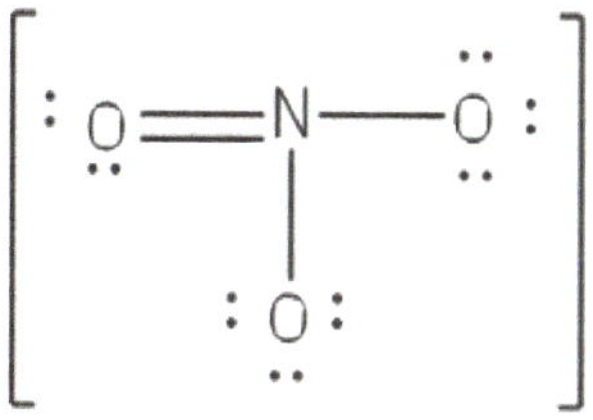

A. 0
B. -1
C. +1
D. -2

31. Which of the following gives the Lewis dot structure of N_2H_4?

A.

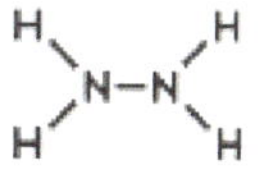

B.

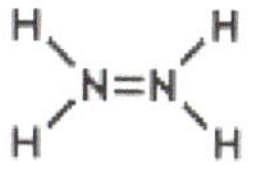

C.

D.

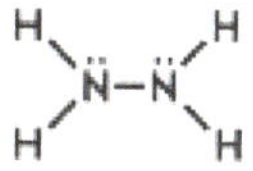

32. What is the formal charge of the phosphorus in the following molecule?

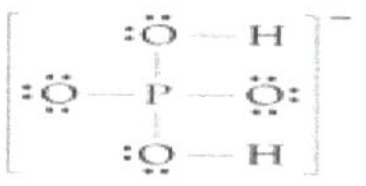

Fe^{3+}

A. 0
B. -1
C. +1
D. -2

33. How many resonance structures exist for the following molecule in which each atom has no more than +1 or -1 formal charge?

$$\left[\begin{array}{c} :\overset{..}{O}: \\ | \\ :\overset{..}{O} - \overset{..}{S} - \overset{..}{O}: \end{array} \right]^{2-}$$

    A. 1
    B. 2
    C. 3
    D. 4

34. What is the bond order character of each bond in the nitrate anion?

    A. 1
    B. 1.33
    C. 1.5
    D. 2

35. On which atom does the negative charge primarily reside in the following molecule?

$$\left[:\overset{..}{\underset{..}{O}} - \overset{..}{\underset{..}{Cl}}: \right]^{-}$$

    A. Cl because it is more electronegative
    B. O because it has 7 valence electrons
    C. Cl because it has 7 valence electrons
    D. O because it is more electronegative

36. Where does the positive charge of the molecule shown primarily reside?

$$\left[\begin{array}{c} H \\ | \\ H - N - H \\ | \\ H \end{array} \right]^{+}$$

    A. The hydrogens because they are less electronegative than N
    B. The nitrogen because it is less electronegative than the hydrogens
    C. The hydrogens because they have positive formal charge
    D. The nitrogen because it has 4 bonds and no lone paired electrons

37. What is the geometry of the following molecule?

    A. Bent
    B. Trigonal planar
    C. Tetrahedral
    D. Trigonal bipyramidal

38. What is bond energy?

    A. The amount of energy input required to break a bond
    B. The amount of energy input required to create a bond
    C. The heat of formation of each part of the bond
    D. The enthalpy of formation of the bond.

39. Which of the following correctly relates bond energy and bond length?

    A.   They are inversely related because the stronger the bond the longer the bond.
    B.   They are directly related because the stronger the bond the longer the bond.
    C.   They are inversely related because the stronger the bond the shorter the bond.
    D.   They are directly related because the stronger the bond the shorter the bond.

40. Which of the following is the shortest bond?

    A.   Single bond between N and H
    B.   Single bond between C and C
    C.   Single bond between O and H
    D.   Single bond between O and C

41. How does bond polarity relate to bond length?

    A.   The relationship changes based on the elements in the bond
    B.   The less polar the bond the stronger
    C.   There is no relationship between bond polarity and bond length
    D.   The more polar the bond the stronger bond

42. Which of the following is the shortest bond?

    A.   C double bonded to C
    B.   C single bonded to C
    C.   C single bonded to O
    D.   C double bonded to O

43. Which of the following is true?

    A.   Breaking bonds requires energy and forming bonds requires energy
    B.   Breaking bonds requires energy and forming bonds releases energy.
    C.   Breaking bonds releases energy and forming bonds releases energy.
    D.   Breaking bonds releases energy and forming bonds requires energy.

44. How many valence electrons form a complete n=2 shell?

    A.   6
    B.   7
    C.   8
    D.   10

45. What is the spatial geometry of the following molecule?

    A.   Trigonal planar
    B.   Trigonal pyramidal
    C.   Tetrahedral
    D.   Trigonal bipyramidal

46. What is the molecular geometry of the following molecule?

    A.   Trigonal planar
    B.   Trigonal pyramidal
    C.   Tetrahedral
    D.   Trigonal bipyramidal

47. What is the coordinate geometry of the S in the following molecule?

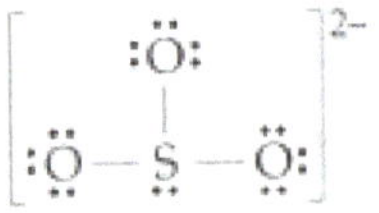

A. Trigonal planar
B. Trigonal pyramidal
C. Tetrahedral
D. Trigonal bipyramidal

48. What is the molecular geometry of the following molecule?

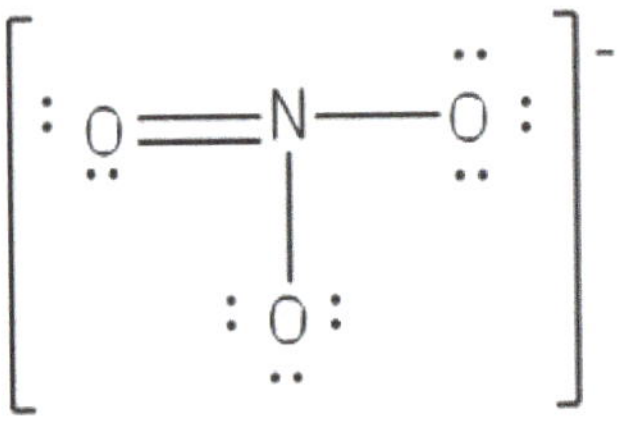

A. Trigonal planar
B. Trigonal pyramidal
C. Tetrahedral
D. Trigonal bipyramidal

49. What is the hybridization of the C in the following molecule?

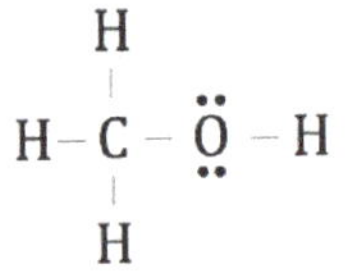

A. sp
B. sp^2
C. sp^3
D. sp^3d

50. What is the hybridization of the carbon attached to A and B?

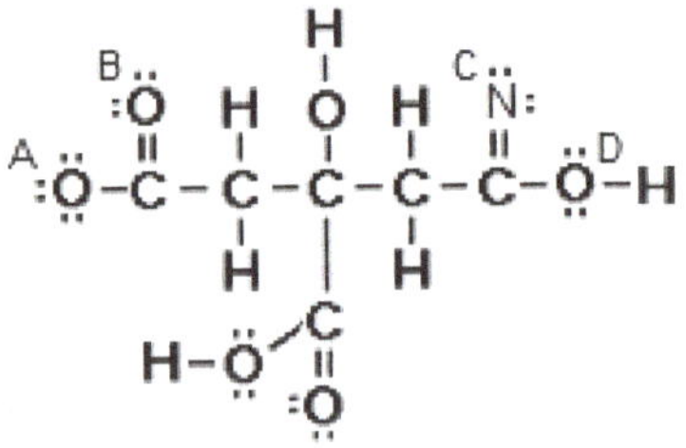

A. sp
B. sp^2
C. sp^3
D. sp^3d

51. What is the molecular geometry of a molecule with a central atom and 4 substituents?

A. Trigonal planar
B. Trigonal pyramidal
C. Tetrahedral
D. Octahedral

52. What is the molecular geometry of a molecule with a central atom and 3 substituents as well as a lone pair of electrons?

A. Trigonal planar
B. Trigonal pyramidal
C. Tetrahedral
D. Octahedral

53. What is the molecular geometry of a molecule with a central atom and 4 substituents as well as two lone pairs of electrons?

A. Trigonal planar
B. Trigonal pyramidal
C. Square planar
D. Octahedral

54. What is the molecular geometry of a molecule with a central atom, 3 substituents, and no lone pairs?

    A.   Trigonal planar
    B.   Trigonal pyramidal
    C.   Tetrahedral
    D.   Trigonal bipyramidal

55. What is the molecular geometry of a molecule with a central atom and 3 substituents as well as two lone pairs of electrons?

    A.   Trigonal planar
    B.   Trigonal pyramidal
    C.   Tetrahedral
    D.   T-shaped

56. What is the molecular geometry of water?

    A.   Bent
    B.   Trigonal planar
    C.   Trigonal pyramidal
    D.   Tetrahedral

57. What is the electronic geometry around the O in water?

    A.   Bent
    B.   Trigonal planar
    C.   Trigonal pyramidal
    D.   Tetrahedral

58. What is the molecular geometry of CO_2?

    A.   Bent
    B.   Trigonal planar
    C.   Trigonal pyramidal
    D.   Linear

59. What is the molecular geometry of XeF_2?

    A.   Bent
    B.   Linear
    C.   Trigonal pyramidal
    D.   Trigonal bipyramidal

60. What is the electronic geometry around Xe in XeF_2?

    A.   Bent
    B.   Straight
    C.   Trigonal pyramidal
    D.   Trigonal bipyramidal

61 Which of the following is not a possible molecular geometry?

    A.   square planar
    B.   square pyramidal
    C.   square bipyramidal
    D.   octahedral planar

62. Which of the following is NOT a type of chemical reaction?

    A.   Single displacement
    B.   Decomposition
    C.   Double displacement
    D.   Triple displacement

The following reaction will be used for 63-65:

$$CH_4 + O_2 \rightarrow CO_2 + H_2O$$

63. Which of the following gives the balanced reaction?

    A. $2CH_4 + 4O_2 \rightarrow 2CO_2 + 4H_2O$
    B. $CH_4 + O_2 \rightarrow CO_2 + 2H_2O$
    C. $CH_4 + 2O_2 \rightarrow CO_2 + 2H_2O$
    D. $2CH_4 + 2O_2 \rightarrow 2CO_2 + 2H_2O$

64. What is the limiting reagent of the reaction if there are 4 moles of CH_4 and 6 moles of O_2 available?

    A. CH_4 because $4 < (6 \times 2)$
    B.   Oxygen because $4 < (6 \times 2)$
    C. CH_4 because $(6/2) < 4$
    D.   Oxygen because $(6/2) < 4$

65. Given the reaction conditions from Q 64, how many grams of CO_2 are produced in a complete reaction?

    A. 44 g
    B. 88 g
    C. 122 g
    D. 132 g

The following reaction will be used for 66-68:

$$C_6H_6 + O_2 \rightarrow CO_2 + H_2O$$

66. Which of the following gives the balanced reaction?

    A. $C_6H_6 + 2O_2 \rightarrow 6CO_2 + H_2O$
    B. $2C_6H_6 + 12O_2 \rightarrow 12CO_2 + 3H_2O$
    C. $2C_6H_6 + 15O_2 \rightarrow 12CO_2 + 6H_2O$
    D. $C_6H_6 + 4O_2 \rightarrow 6CO_2 + 2H_2O$

67. What is the limiting reagent of the reaction if there are 4 moles of C_6H_6 and 35 moles of O_2 available?

    A. C_6H_6 because $(4/2) < (35/15)$
    B. Oxygen because $(4/2) < (35/15)$
    C. C_6H_6 because $(35 \times 15) > (4 \times 2)$
    D. Oxygen because $(35 \times 15) < (4 \times 2)$

68. Given the reaction conditions from Q 67, how many moles of CO_2 are produced in a complete reaction?

    A. 4 moles
    B. 12 moles
    C. 24 moles
    D. 30 moles

69. The following reaction is of which classification?
$A + B \rightarrow C$

    A. Decomposition
    B. Combination
    C. Single Displacement
    D. Double Displacement

70. The following reaction is of which classification?
$A + BC \rightarrow B + AC$

    A. Decomposition
    B. Combination
    C. Single Displacement
    D. Double Displacement

71. The following reaction is of which classification?
$NaCl + AgNO_3 \rightarrow NaNO_3 + AgCl$

    A. Decomposition
    B. Combination
    C. Single Displacement
    D. Double Displacement

72. Balance the following reaction: $CaBr_2 + AgNO_3 \rightarrow AgBr + Ca(NO_3)_2$

    A. $2CaBr_2 + 2AgNO_3 \dashrightarrow 4AgBr + Ca(NO_3)_2$
    B. $CaBr_2 + AgNO_3 \rightarrow 2AgBr + Ca(NO_3)_2$
    C. $CaBr_2 + 2AgNO_3 \rightarrow 2AgBr + Ca(NO_3)_2$
    D. $2CaBr_2 + 2AgNO_3 \dashrightarrow 4AgBr + 2Ca(NO_3)_2$

73. What is the first thing that should be balanced in a combustion reaction?

    A. Carbons
    B. Hydrogens
    C. Oxygens
    D. Electrons

74. Balance the following reaction: $Zn + CuSO_4 \rightarrow ZnSO_4 + Cu$

    A. $2Zn + 2CuSO_4 \rightarrow 2ZnSO_4 + 2Cu$
    B. $Zn + CuSO_4 \rightarrow ZnSO_4 + Cu$
    C. $Zn + 2CuSO_4 \rightarrow ZnSO_4 + 2Cu$
    D. $2Zn + 2CuSO_4 \rightarrow 2ZnSO_4 + Cu$

75. Balance the following reaction: $Au^{3+} + Zn(s) \rightarrow Au(s) + Zn^{2+}$

    A. $2Au^{3+} + Zn(s) \rightarrow 2Au(s) + Zn^{2+}$
    B. $Au^{3+} + 3Zn(s) \rightarrow Au(s) + 3Zn^{2+}$
    C. $3Au^{3+} + 2Zn(s) \rightarrow 3Au(s) + 2Zn^{2+}$
    D. $2Au^{3+} + 3Zn(s) \rightarrow 2Au(s) + 3Zn^{2+}$

76. How many electrons are transferred in the reaction from Q 75?

    A. 2
    B. 4
    C. 5
    D. 6

77. Which reactant from the equation in Q 75 is oxidized?

    A. Au^{3+}
    B. Au
    C. Zn^{2+}
    D. Zn

78. Balance the following reaction: $Al(s) + O_2(g) \rightarrow Al_2O_3(s)$

    A. $Al(s) + O_2(g) \rightarrow Al_2O_3(s)$
    B. $2Al(s) + 2O_2(g) \rightarrow 3Al_2O_3(s)$
    C. $4Al(s) + 3O_2(g) \rightarrow 2Al_2O_3(s)$
    D. $2Al(s) + 3O_2(g) \rightarrow 2Al_2O_3(s)$

79. How many electrons are transferred in the reaction from #78?

    A. 3
    B. 6
    C. 12
    D. 14

80. Which reactant from the equation in Q 78 is the oxidizing agent?

    A. $Al(s)$
    B. $Al_2O_3(s)$
    C. $O_2(g)$
    D. O^{2-}

81. How many moles of C_2H_6 are in 90 grams of C_2H_6?

    A. 2
    B. 3
    C. 3.5
    D. 4

82. How many moles of H_2O will be produced from the perfect combustion of 90 grams of C_2H_6?

    A. 3
    B. 6
    C. 9
    D. 12

83. How many grams of H_2O will be produced from the complete combustion of 90 grams of C_2H_6?

    A. 54 g
    B. 108 g
    C. 162 g
    D. 216 g

84. How many molecules of H_2O will be produced from the complete combustion of 90 grams of C_2H_6?

    A. 1.807×10^{24}
    B. 3.613×10^{24}
    C. 5.420×10^{24}
    D. 7.226×10^{24}

85. How many molecules of H_2O will be produced from the complete combustion of 1.2044×10^{24} molecules of C_2H_6?

    A. 1.807×10^{24}
    B. 3.613×10^{24}
    C. 5.420×10^{24}
    D. 7.226×10^{24}

86. How many grams of CO_2 will be produced from the complete combustion of 90 grams of C_2H_6?

    A. 88 g
    B. 176 g
    C. 264 g
    D. 352 g

87. How many moles of oxygen gas are in 64 grams of oxygen gas?

    A. 1
    B. 2
    C. 3
    D. 4

88. How many grams of H_2O will be produced from the combustion of 90 grams of C_2H_6 if only 64 grams of O_2 are available for the combustion?

    A. 18 g
    B. 31 g
    C. 36 g
    D. 40 g

89. What is the percent yield of the reaction $C_2H_6 + O_2 \rightarrow CO_2 + H_2O$ from # 82-83 if only 121 grams of water are produced?

    A. 50%
    B. 60%
    C. 75%
    D. 80%

90. If only 121 grams of water are produced, how many grams of CO_2 are produced in the reaction described in question #89?

    A. 76 g
    B. 132 g
    C. 198 g
    D. 264 g

91. If only 1.2044×10^{24} molecules of C_2H_6 and 96 grams of O_2 are available, which reactant will be the limiting reagent of the combustion?

    A. Oxygen
    B. C_2H_6
    C. Neither
    D. It's impossible to tell

92. What is the percent yield of a reaction if the theoretical yield is 8 times the actual yield?

    A. 800%
    B. 1/16
    C. 25%
    D. 12.5%

93. What is the actual yield of a reaction whose percent yield is 66% and whose theoretical yield was 120 grams of product?

    A. 80 g
    B. 182 g
    C. 186 g
    D. 120 g

94. What is the theoretical yield of a reaction whose percent yield and actual yield are 20% and 1 gram of product respectively?

    A. .2 g
    B. 2 g
    C. 4 g
    D. 5 g

95. What is the oxidation state of O in CO_2?

    A. -2
    B. -1
    C. 0
    D. +1

96. What is the oxidation state of S in SO_3^{2-}?

    A. -2
    B. 0
    C. +2
    D. +4

97. What is the oxidation state of Mn in MnO_4^-?

    A. +3
    B. +4
    C. +7
    D. +8

98. What is the oxidation state of O in H_2O_2?

    A. -2
    B. -1
    C. 0
    D. +1

99. Which classification applies to the following reaction: $HI + ROH \rightarrow I^- + ROH_2^+$

    A.   Redox
    B.   Double displacement
    C.   Acid-Base
    D.   Combination

100. What is the bond order for each C-O bond in the acetate anion?

    A.   0
    B.   1
    C.   1.5
    D.   2

SECTION 3
PHASES OF MATTER

After dealing with a wide variety of changes to intramolecular bonds in the previous section, we now turn our attention to intermolecular bonds. It is these attractive forces between molecules that determine much of the behavior related to phases and phase changes.

Given the importance of the gas phase on the MCAT – especially in the context of lung physiology – we will start with a thorough discussion of ideal and real gases and the various phenomena related to them. From there we will go on to discuss liquid and solid phases, and what the MCAT will expect you to know about phase transitions.

A. INTRODUCTION

In this chapter, we will review the essential aspects of gases, and the terms that are commonly associated with them. This chapter will also discuss the various laws such as Charles' law, Boyle's law, and ideal gas law. Finally, the kinetic law of gases will be explored.

B. GASES – AN OVERVIEW

Gases are unique when compared to liquids and solids. Gases can be compressed into smaller volumes, and they can be mixed extensively. Compared to their solid and liquid phase, molecules in the gaseous phase have comparatively low densities. Ideally, a gas exerts pressure on all sides of the container it occupies in a uniform manner. These are some of the properties of gases. Let's explore these ideas in detail.

Standard Temperature and Pressure

It is very important to understand the general aspects of gas pressure, its measurements, and calibrations. **Pressure** is force exerted over unit area. The unit of pressure is the pascal (Pa) which is equivalent to $kg/(m•s^2)$. In chemistry, we usually use a mercury-based barometer to measure the pressure. The unit is millimeter of mercury (mmHg). This is the same as the unit torr. Another unit commonly used to denote pressure is atmosphere (atm). You should be able to convert these units back and forth as required.

$$1 \text{ atm} = 760 \text{ mmHg} = 760 \text{ torr}$$
$$1 \text{ atm} = 1.01 \text{ x } 10^5 \text{ Pa}$$

Gases can be compressed or expanded by adjusting the temperature and other conditions that prevail. In order to standardize the quantities of gases measured and conveyed, arbitrary reference conditions called standard temperature and pressure (STP) have been chosen and internationally accepted. The specific values of temperature and pressure at STP are 0°C (273 K) and 1 atm (760 mmHg).

STANDARD TEMPERATURE AND PRESSURE (STP)

Temperature   -   0°C or 273 K

Pressure   -   1 atm or 760 mmHg

You should know what STP is, because in many questions and passages, the actual temperature and pressure situations will not be explicit. Rather, they will say, for example, that the reaction was undertaken at standard temperature and pressure. This means, you have to automatically know that they are talking about the temperatures corresponding to STP reference conditions, which you already know.

Molar Volume

Ideally, one mole of gas at STP occupies a volume of 22.4 L. This is known as **molar volume**. We should bear in mind the fact that this is under standard conditions. Do the example below on your own, before you look at the solution.

Example 7-1

Calculate the number of moles of oxygen at STP present in a volume of 78.75 L.

Solution:

One mole of gas occupies a volume of 22.4 L. To get the number of moles, you have to divide 78.75 L by 22.4 L/mole.

$$\text{Number of moles of oxygen} = 78.75 \text{ L} \times \frac{1 \text{ mol of } O_2}{22.4 \text{ L}} = 3.5 \text{ moles}$$

C. GAS LAWS

Gases behave ideally under reasonably high temperatures and low pressures. The gas laws are helpful in quantitatively relating pressure, volume, temperature, and molar units.

Boyle's Law

According to Boyle's law, the volume of a fixed amount of gas is inversely proportional to the pressure, provided that the temperature is kept constant. A simple and good example with biological significance is the way we take air into our lungs. The way we breathe can be summarized as follows. As the respiratory centers signal, during inspiration the diaphragm contracts resulting in an increase in the thoracic volume, which in turn translates into an increase in the lung volume. This increase in lung volume results in a decrease in pressure. This decrease in pressure inside the lung results in the rushing of air into the lung from the outside – inspiration. The exact opposite conditions result in expiration. The point is that at constant temperature, the volume of a gaseous sample is inversely proportional to its pressure.

$$\text{Volume} \propto \frac{1}{\text{Pressure}}$$

This can be represented mathematically as shown below:

$$\text{BOYLE'S LAW} \qquad V \propto \frac{1}{P} \qquad \text{or} \qquad PV = k \text{ (Constant)}$$

Example 7-2

200 ml of a gas is present in a cylinder at a pressure of 760 torr. If the gas is compressed by using a piston to a pressure of 950 torr, calculate the final volume occupied by the gas. (Assume the temperature to be constant)

Solution:

This problem specifically tests your knowledge of Boyle's law. We know that PV is a constant, provided that the temperature is kept constant. Since the temperature is constant, we can readily apply Boyle's law. We can equate the initial and final stages of the system. P_1 and V_1 represent the initial pressure and volume respectively. P_2 and V_2 represent, the final pressure and volume respectively.

$$P_1 V_1 = P_2 V_2$$

Now it is just a matter of solving for V_2 *(final volume)*.

$$V_2 = V_1 \left(\frac{P_1}{P_2} \right) = 200 \text{ ml} \left(\frac{760 \text{ torr}}{950 \text{ torr}} \right) = 160 \text{ ml}$$

Charles' Law

In 1787, Jacques Charles showed that gas expands to occupy a larger volume as the temperature increases. Volume can be plotted against the temperature at constant pressure, as shown below:

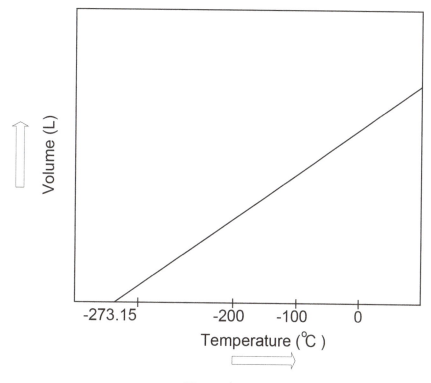

Figure 7-1

When the temperature is increased, the volume increases. Charles found that the volume of a gas is directly proportional to its absolute temperature, provided that the pressure is kept constant. So the volume and temperature have a linear relationship as represented by the graph. Charles's law can be mathematically expressed as follows:

CHARLES' LAW

$$\text{Volume} \quad \propto \quad \text{Temperature}$$

$$V \propto T$$

$$V = kT \qquad \text{or} \qquad \frac{V}{T} = k \text{ (constant)}$$

The volume-temperature graph shows that at zero volume, the corresponding temperature value is $-273.15°C$. This means that at $-273.15°C$, the volume occupied by the gas is zero, also known as 'absolute zero.' This temperature is unique, and scientists so far have not been able to devise a way to lower the temperature to $-273.15°C$.

Combined Gas Law

The gas laws (Charles' and Boyle's law) can be combined to form the combined gas law. The resulting law can be represented mathematically as shown below:

$$\text{COMBINED GAS LAW} \qquad \frac{P_1V_1}{T_1} = \frac{P_2V_2}{T_2} = k \quad \text{(constant)}$$

This relationship can be used to do a variety of calculations involving gases, since it relates pressure, volume, and temperature.

The Ideal Gas Law

This is an extension of the combined gas law. In the combined gas law, we saw the relationship between pressure, volume, and temperature. The ideal gas law can be expressed mathematically as follows:

$$\textit{THE IDEAL GAS LAW} \qquad PV = nRT$$

P - pressure
V - volume
n - number of moles
R - molar gas constant
T - temperature

Here, R (molar gas constant) has values 0.082 L•atm/(K•mol), or 8.31 J/(K•mol), and of course the difference in values is due to the fact that the gas constant is expressed here in two different units.

D. KINETIC THEORY OF GASES

The kinetic theory of gases can be explored in terms of the following assumptions. The theory tries to answer the questions regarding the various properties of gases. It also gives the relationship between the kinetic energy of the molecules and the absolute temperature. The important points in kinetic theory of gases are listed below:

1. A gas consists of small particles (sizes are considered relatively negligible) known as molecules, which are separated widely apart and thus the gas container is mostly empty.
2. The molecules are in a state of continuous random motion, and colliding against each other and also against the sides of the container, and furthermore the collisions are elastic.
3. These collisions result in the pressure of the gas.
4. The molecules are expected to travel in straight lines at different speeds in all directions.
5. The forces (attractive or repulsive) between the molecules are negligible.
6. The average kinetic energy of the molecules is proportional to the temperature.

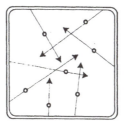

Figure 7-2 *Ideal gas molecules travel randomly in straight lines at different speeds.*

Some Aspects Related to Kinetic Theory

The main aspect of kinetic theory is that the molecules in a gas are in a state of continuous random motion. The speed of molecules depends on the temperature, and can have a range of values. Maxwell's distribution curve is perfect to analyze this fact. In the Maxwell's distribution curve, the relative number of molecules is plotted against the molecular speed on the x-axis. Take a look at the curve in Figure 6-2.

Note that the speed corresponding to the maximum number of molecules is called the **most probable speed**. This is always smaller than the **average speed**, which is in turn smaller than the root-mean-square speed (rms speed).

The formula for root-mean-square speed is given below:

$$\text{Root-mean-square speed} = \sqrt{\frac{3\,RT}{M}}$$

Here, R is the gas constant, T is the absolute temperature, and M is the molar mass of the gas.

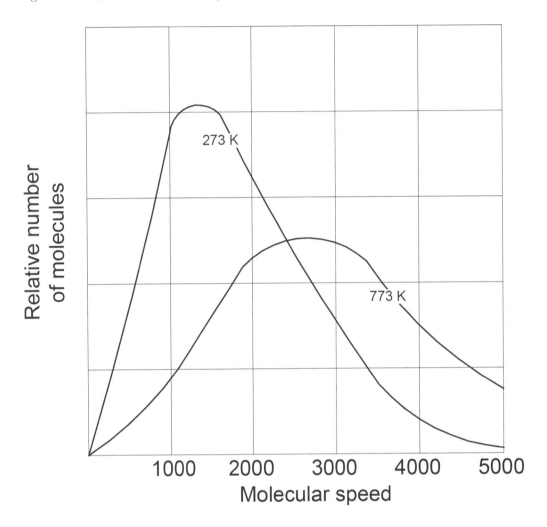

MAXWELL'S DISTRIBUTION CURVE

Figure 7-2

E. PARTIAL PRESSURE

Let's consider a container which has different gases in it. According to Dalton's law of partial pressures, the partial pressures of the gases present in a gaseous mixture can be added to get the net total pressure of the mixture. But, what is partial pressure? Partial pressure is the pressure exerted by a particular gas in a mixture of gases. Now that you know what partial pressure is, take a look at the boxed information which summarizes the whole idea of Dalton's law of partial pressures.

Dalton's Law of Partial Pressures

$$P_{total} = P_A + P_B + P_C + P_D + \ldots \text{ (at constant volume and temperature)}$$
$$P_{total} = \text{Total pressure}$$
$$P_A, P_B, P_C, P_D, \ldots \text{ represent the partial pressures of gases A, B, C, D, and so on.}$$

Another concept you have to understand is mole fraction. The **mole fraction** of a gas is the fraction or ratio of moles of that particular gas against the total number of moles of gases present in the mixture. Mole fraction is defined as follows:

$$\text{Mole fraction} = \frac{\text{Number of moles of gas A}}{\text{Total number of moles of gases in the mixture}} = \frac{n_A}{n_{Total}}$$

Example 7-3

A 1 liter flask contains 0.4 mole of helium and 1.2 moles of hydrogen gas. Find the mole fractions and partial pressures of both gases, if the total pressure of the mixture is 790 mmHg.

Solution:

The total number of moles of gases present in the container is 0.4 + 1.2 = 1.6 moles

The mole fraction of helium = 0.4 / 1.6 = 0.25

The mole fraction of hydrogen = 1.2 / 1.6 = 0.75

Notice that the sum of the mole fractions is always one. If it is not, you probably made an error somewhere in your calculation. Here,

$$0.25 + 0.75 = 1.0$$

Next, we have to find the partial pressures of the gases. We know that sum of the partial pressures of the gases should equal the total pressure of the system. Now that we know the total pressure and the mole fractions, we can calculate the partial pressures of helium and hydrogen.

Partial pressure of gas A = mole fraction of gas A x total pressure

Partial pressure of helium = 0.25 x 790 mmHg = 197.5 mmHg

Partial pressure of hydrogen = 0.75 x 790 mmHg = 592.5 mmHg

F. GRAHAM'S LAW

Diffusion of gases can be described as the process by which a gas spreads to occupy the available and accessible space, thereby creating a uniform pressure throughout the space the gas occupies. A gas having a higher partial pressure will travel or diffuse toward regions of gases having a lower partial pressure, until an equilibrium is reached. To analyze the diffusion of gases, it is much simpler to think in terms of effusion. The difference between diffusion and effusion is that diffusion is the movement of gas through the entire volume of the container, whereas effusion is the movement of gas through a tiny hole of the container.

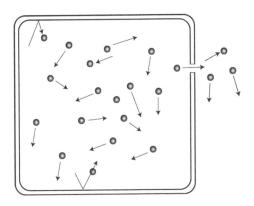

Figure 7-3 The figure depicts the effusion of gas
molecules through a small hole in a container.

According to Graham's law of effusion, the effusion rate of a gas is inversely related to the square root of the molecular weight of the gas. This is true provided that we have the same pressure and temperature conditions. Graham's law can be expressed as shown below:

Graham's law of effusion

$$\text{Effusion rate of gas molecules} \quad \propto \quad \frac{1}{\sqrt{\text{molecular weight}}}$$

Graham's law can be used to approximate the rate of diffusion of one gas in another, or into air, where the rate of diffusion of a gas is inversely proportional to its density. This approximation is valid since under constant conditions of temperature and pressure, the density of diffusing gas particles is proportional to their molecular mass.

Example 7-4

Calculate the ratio of the rates of effusion for the gases oxygen and hydrogen. Assume that the two gases are in the same container having a tiny hole in it.

Solution:

First, we have to consider the fact that according to Graham's law, the rate of effusion is inversely proportional to the square root of the molecular weight of the gas which is effused. This can be represented as follows. Keep in mind that both gases are diatomic.

$$\frac{\text{Rate of effusion of H}_2}{\text{Rate of effusion of O}_2} = \sqrt{\frac{32}{2}} = \frac{4}{1} = 4$$

So the ratio of the rates of effusion of hydrogen and oxygen is 4 : 1.

We should think about the implications of this ratio. This means that the hydrogen molecules will effuse four times faster than the oxygen molecules.

CHAPTER 7 PROBLEMS

1. Consider the reaction between nitric oxide and oxygen to form nitrogen dioxide. If 4 liters of nitrogen dioxide were formed, how many liters of nitric oxide and oxygen must have reacted?

    A. 2 L of NO and 1 L of O_2
    B. 2 L of NO and 2 L of O_2
    C. 4 L of NO and 2 L of O_2
    D. 2 L of NO and 4 L of O_2

2. At a particular temperature and pressure, 1 mole of gas M occupies 45 liters. If the density of gas M at the same temperature and pressure is 1.8 g/L, the molecular weight of gas M is:

    A. 25 g/mole.
    B. 81 g/mole.
    C. 40.5 g/mole.
    D. 4 g/mole.

3. A certain gas behaves ideally at STP. If the density of the gas is 1.4 g/L, what is the most likely identity of this gas? (The gas is diatomic.)

    A. SO_2
    B. N_2
    C. O_2
    D. F_2

4. A hypothetical reaction R occurs only at elevated pressures. It was noted that the optimum pressure required for the reaction was 1330 mmHg. This value is roughly equal to: (1 atm = 101.3 kPa)

    A. 1.3×10^{-2} Pa.
    B. 1.8×10^{5} Pa.
    C. 1.35×10^{8} Pa.
    D. 1.8×10^{2} Pa.

5. $-27^{0}C$ is the same as:

    A. 300 K.
    B. 246 K.
    C. 270 K.
    D. 127 K.

6. The volume occupied by 11.5 g of carbon dioxide at STP is approximately equal to:

    A. 5.9 L.
    B. 22.5 L.
    C. 86 L.
    D. 259 L.

Questions 7-13 are based on the following passage.

Passage 1

The behavior of gases can be predicted to a large extent on the basis of various laws. Gases are expressed mainly in terms of pressure, volume, and temperature. Many gases obey the ideal gas laws and those gases are called ideal gases. If we are not doing precision experiments, we can normally ignore the slight deviations that occur under normal conditions. Nevertheless, we cannot completely ignore the deviation factors.

According to Boyle's law, the pressure is inversely proportional to the volume at a constant temperature. Charles' law states that the volume is directly proportional to the temperature at a constant pressure. Combining these laws and Avogadro's law gives the ideal gas law.

$$PV = nRT$$
(The ideal gas law)

Not all gases behave ideally. There are often deviations from the ideal behavior. At low temperatures, gases often behave differently apart from what is described by the kinetic-molecular theory of gases. Considering these correction factors, the modified gas equation is:

$$\left(P + \frac{n^2a}{V^2}\right)(V - nb) = nRT$$

The correction constants or Van der Waals constants, a and b, of gases are experimentally found. The Van der

Waals constants of some gases are given in Table 1.

Gas	a $(L^2 \cdot atm/mol^2)$	b (L/mol)
Carbon monoxide	1.470	0.039
Hydrogen	0.245	0.026
Chlorine	6.340	0.054
Fluorine	1.170	0.029
Hydrogen sulfide	4.540	0.043
Nitrogen	1.380	0.039
Carbon dioxide	3.660	0.043
Argon	1.360	0.032
Propane	9.390	0.091

Table 1

7. Under which of the following conditions will gases behave most ideally?

    A.   Low temperature and high pressure
    B.   High temperature and low pressure
    C.   Low temperature and low pressure
    D.   Gas behavior does not depend on temperature and pressure if the gas is an ideal gas, and such a gas will behave ideally regardless of the conditions

8. What are the units of universal gas constant R?

    A.   **mol K / L atm**

    B.   **atm / mol K**

    C.   **L atm / mol K**

    D.   **L atm / mol**

9. A group of general chemistry students were assigned to conduct gas experiments. The vessel that contained the gases had a small hole in it. The gases used in the experiments were SO_2 and O_2. What is the ratio of the rate of leakage of SO_2 to O_2 through the hole?

    A.   0.7
    B.   4
    C.   2
    D.   1.4

10. If the van der Waals constants a and b are found to be zero for gas A, what statements are true regarding this gas?
  I.   Gas A does not behave ideally.
  II. Gas A behaves ideally.
  III. Gas A is xenon.

    A.   I only
    B.   II only
    C.   II and III only
    D.   III only

11. What is the most likely van der Waals constant correction factor of bromine?

    A.   0.97 $L^2 \cdot atm/mol^2$
    B.   2.34 $L^2 \cdot atm/mol^2$
    C.   5.32 $L^2 \cdot atm/mol^2$
    D.   9.80 $L^2 \cdot atm/mol^2$

12. Equal volumes of gases will contain the same number of molecules at the same temperature and pressure. This prediction is directly based on:

    A.   Charles' law.
    B.   Boyle's law.
    C.   kinetic-molecular theory.
    D.   Avogadro's law.

13. Based on kinetic-molecular theory, which of the following are true?

I. At a given temperature, all gases have the same average kinetic energy.

II. At a given temperature, different gases have different average velocities.

III. The average kinetic energy is proportional to the absolute temperature.

    A. I only
    B. II only
    C. I and III only
    D. I, II and III

CHAPTER 8

Liquids, Solids, and Phase Changes

A. INTRODUCTION

In this chapter, we will explore the other two important phases of matter tested by the MCAT: liquids and solids. Gases have negligible intermolecular interactions and attractive forces. But this is not the case with either liquids or solids. They both have much stronger intermolecular forces than gases. These forces make substances exist as liquids and solids. As we go along, we will explore the ideas such as hydrogen bonding, London dispersion forces, and dipole interactions.

In addition to just knowing these phases, you will have to know the different theories and their implications, and how to work with some of the formulas involved. We will review the different kinds of molecular interactions that dictate the phase characteristics of molecules. The phase diagram that is discussed in this chapter is also important from the MCAT point of view.

B. THE LIQUID PHASE

Liquids are considered to be relatively incompressible. Unlike gas molecules, liquid molecules are tightly packed. Liquids have a fixed volume, whereas gases do not. Liquids do not have a definite shape. The properties of liquids can be attributed to the presence of various types of intermolecular forces.

C. INTERMOLECULAR FORCES

Intermolecular forces are weak attractive forces that contribute to many of the physical properties exhibited by liquids. From the MCAT point of view, you have to be familiar with the main three types of attractive forces:

1. Hydrogen bonding
2. Dipole-dipole interactions
3. London forces

Hydrogen Bonding

Hydrogen bonding is an intermolecular attractive force that exists between a hydrogen atom covalently bonded to an electronegative atom (fluorine, oxygen, nitrogen), and another electronegative atom in the neighboring molecule. Hydrogen bonding in water is shown below:

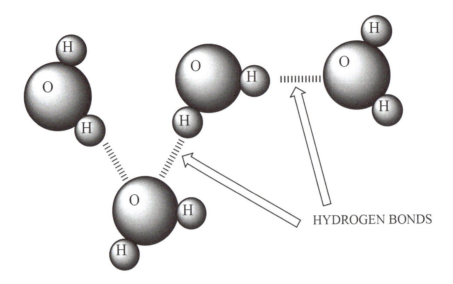

Figure 8-1 Hydrogen bonding in water

As you can see in Figure 7-1, the hydrogen which is covalently bonded to the electronegative atom (in this case it is oxygen), can undergo hydrogen bonding with an electronegative atom (the oxygen of another water molecule) present in the neighboring molecule.

Dipole-Dipole Interactions

Polar molecules have negative and positive polarity. This is because of the difference in electronegativities of the bonded atoms in such molecules. This polarity results in the formation of attractive forces among molecules. Such interactions are called **dipole-dipole interactions**. Consequently, the positive end of one molecule is attracted to the negative end of another. Figure 7-2 illustrates the dipole-dipole interactions between hydrogen chloride molecules.

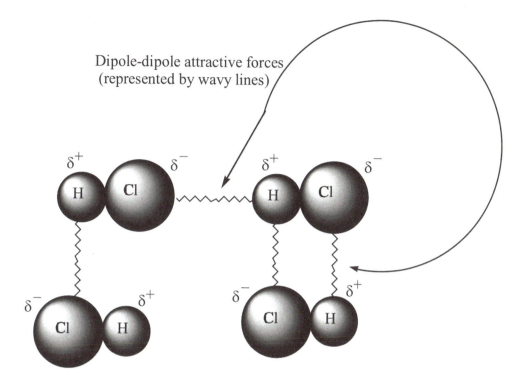

Figure 8-2 Dipole-dipole interaction between HCl molecules

London Forces

London forces are weak attractive forces that exist between instantaneous dipoles. Atoms have a central positively charged nucleus surrounded by electrons. These electrons are constantly moving and the electronic cloud may not always be perfectly distributed. In other words, the electrons at any given moment may be distributed more on one side and less on the other, creating an instantaneous dipole. The side which has more electrons at any moment will have a slight negative charge, whereas the side which is electron deficient will have a slight positive charge. The polarity that results from such charge separations in a molecule can induce polarity in other molecules when they are close enough to the instantaneous dipole molecule. For this reason, London forces are often called instantaneous dipole-induced dipole interactions. London forces are more pronounced in bigger molecules, because they are more polarizable.

It is more likely that a polar molecule will exist as a liquid or solid than a nonpolar molecule. It is because of the intermolecular interactions that are possible among polar molecules.

D. THE SOLID PHASE

A solid has a well-defined shape. Because of the tight packing of the molecules, solids can be considered almost incompressible. There are four types of solids:

1. Ionic solid
2. Metallic solid
3. Molecular solid
4. Network solid

Ionic Solid

An **ionic solid** consists of cations and anions which are held together by the electrostatic attraction between them. These attractive forces are very strong and thus ionic solids have high melting points. Sodium chloride (NaCl), and cesium chloride (CsCl) are examples of ionic solids.

Metallic Solid

A **metallic solid** consists of positive atomic cores surrounded by electrons. Almost all metals are solids at room temperature. The free electrons in metallic solids account for their superior electrical conductivity (e.g., iron, gold, silver).

Molecular Solid

A **molecular solid** consists of atoms or molecules held together by intermolecular attractive forces. In molecular solids, the attractive forces include hydrogen bonds and dipole-dipole forces (e.g., Ice [H_2O (s)]).

Network Solid

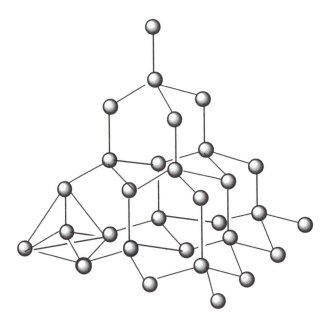

Figure 8-3 Structure of diamond

In a **network solid**, the atoms are held together by large networks of covalent bonds. A perfect example is diamond. Because of such an intricate network (see Figure 7-3) of covalent bonding through the entire crystal, the diamond crystal itself can be considered as one big molecule. Each and every carbon in a diamond is covalently linked to four other carbon atoms. For these reasons, network solids have very high melting points. Other examples of network solids include graphite and asbestos.

E. PHASE CHANGES

Phase transition or change of state refers to the change of a substance's phase from one state to another. In this section, we will talk about the different phase changes, the associated terminology, and the key ideas related to all these.

Types of Phase Transitions

There are different types of phase transitions. From the MCAT point of view, you should have a good grasp of phase transitions. Let's look at the basic terminology.

The conversion of a solid to a liquid is called melting.

The temperature at which a substance changes from solid state to its liquid state is called its melting point.

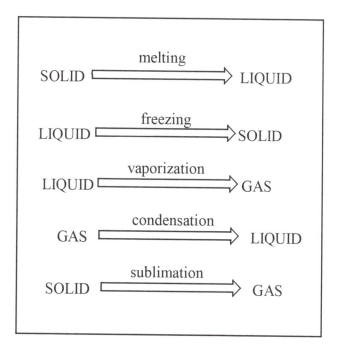

The conversion of a liquid to a solid is called freezing.

The temperature at which a substance changes from liquid state to its solid state is called its freezing point.

The conversion of a liquid to a gas is called vaporization.

The temperature at which a substance changes from liquid state to its gas state is called its boiling point.

The conversion of a gas to a liquid is called condensation.

The direct conversion of a solid to a gas is called sublimation and the reverse is deposition

Heat Transfer

In order to increase the temperature of a substance, we have to supply heat. The heat that should be supplied to increase the temperature varies from one substance to another. So scientists have come up with a way to define this, the specific heat. The **specific heat** ($J/g \cdot C°$) of a substance is the amount of heat that should be added to one gram of that substance to raise its temperature by one degree Celsius. The **Heat capacity** of a given sample substance is the amount of heat that is required to increase the temperature by one degree Celsius. Heat capacity, specific heat, and temperature are related according to the following relations:

$$q = C \, (T_{final} - T_{initial}) = C \, \Delta t,$$

where q is the heat required,
C is the heat capacity, and
Δt is the change in temperature.

$$q = m \, c_{sp} \, \Delta t,$$

where q is the heat required,
m is the mass of the substance in grams,
c_{sp} is the specific heat, and
Δt is the change in temperature.

Let's now talk about the temperature change when heat is added to a substance-the changes in temperature that occur during the change of a substance from its solid state to gaseous state or vice versa. It is easier to understand this from Figure 8-4.

Let's say we are adding heat to a substance which is in its solid state. As the heat increases, the temperature increases until the melting point is attained. Then the temperature will not rise until the substance has melted. Keep in mind that the process of melting requires energy. As more heat is supplied, the temperature again starts increasing until the boiling point has been reached. Then again the temperature will not rise during the process of boiling or vaporization, because the energy that is supplied is used for the process of vaporization. After vaporization is completed, as more heat is supplied, the temperature again starts increasing.

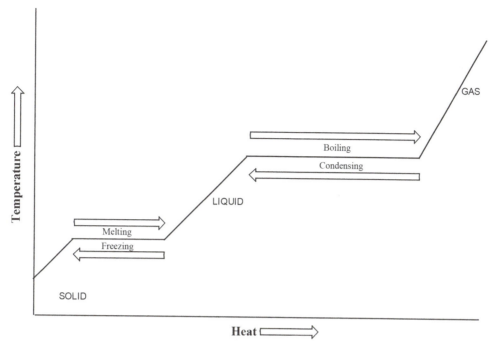

Figure 8-4

Some related terms:

Heat of fusion of a solid substance is the quantity of heat required to melt one gram of that substance at its melting point. The usual unit used is J/g.

Heat of vaporization of a liquid substance is the quantity of heat required to vaporize one gram of that substance at its boiling point. The unit used is J/g.

Heat of condensation of a substance is the quantity of heat that should be removed to condense one gram of that substance at its condensation point. The unit used is J/g.

Heat of crystallization of a substance is the quantity of heat that should be removed to crystallize one gram of that substance at its freezing point. The unit used is J/g.

Phase Diagrams

A **phase diagram** is a graphical representation of phase transitions under different pressures and temperatures. By analyzing the phase diagram of a substance, we can predict the state of that substance at a given temperature and pressure. For the MCAT, you should be familiar with the phase diagram and what exactly it represents, and also be able to predict some of the related trends from a given phase diagram.

In a phase diagram, there are three sections representing the solid, the liquid, and the gas phases. The phase diagram of a substance enables us to determine the phase of that substance at a given temperature and pressure. The phase diagram is actually plotted using experimentally determined values at different temperatures and pressures. Let's take a look at the phase diagram (Figure 8-5) of water.

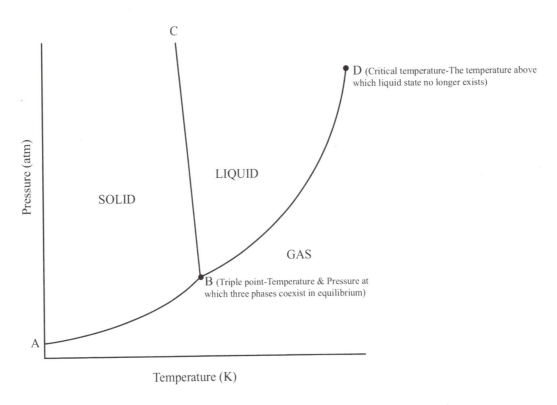

Figure 8-5 Phase diagram of water (diagram not drawn to scale)

As you can see in the phase diagram of water shown above, there are three regions in the graph representing solid, liquid, and gas phases. The segment BC divides the solid and the liquid phases of water. This segment represents the equilibrium region between the solid and the liquid phases. Due to the unique nature of the bent water molecule entering its solid crystal structure, liquid water is denser than ice. While the reasons behind this are outside the scope of the MCAT, you should note that the segment BC for water is slanted toward the left as a result of this behavior. For most phase diagrams (Figure 8-6), the segment BC will be slanted toward the right (positive slope), since the liquid phase is usually *less* dense than the solid phase.

The segment BD divides the liquid and the gas phases in the graph. It also denotes the vapor pressures at different temperatures. The intersecting point of the curves represented by point B is called the **triple point**. This point represents the temperature and pressure at which the three phases of a substance are in equilibrium. How many triple points are likely to exist for a substance? The answer is one. There is only one temperature-pressure combination for a substance at which the three states will be in equilibrium. Figure 8-6 shows a phase diagram representing the majority of other compounds that we see in nature.

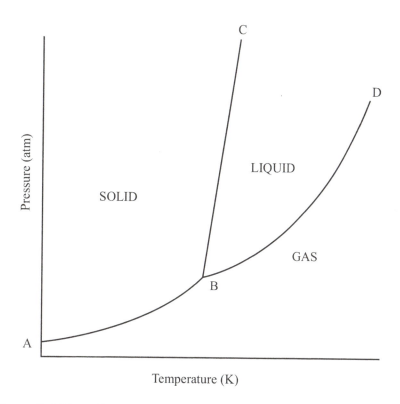

Figure 8-6 Phase diagram of most substances (diagram not drawn to scale)

(Notice the positive slope of segment BC, unlike that of water which has a negative slope)

Substances in their gaseous phase can usually be liquefied by increasing the pressure. But it reaches a point where this conversion is not possible. The temperature above which liquid phase cannot be achieved regardless of the applied pressure is called the **critical temperature**. The vapor pressure at the critical temperature is called the **critical pressure**.

F. COLLIGATIVE PROPERTIES

Colligative properties are properties that depend only on the number (concentration) of solute particles present in a solution. These properties do not depend on the identity of the solute. As an example let's talk about two aqueous solutions; one containing glucose and the other containing urea. As far as the colligative properties are concerned, the two solutions are not different as long as the number of glucose and urea particles are the same. In other words, if the concentration of the given samples of urea and glucose are the same, the colligative properties of both solutions will be the same. The colligative properties that you have to be familiar with for the MCAT are:

1. vapor pressure lowering
2. boiling point elevation
3. freezing point depression
4. osmotic pressure

*A simple **solution** is a mixture of a solute and a solvent.*
SOLUTE + SOLVENT = SOLUTION

Vapor Pressure Lowering

When a solvent contains impurities (solutes), there will be a reduction in its vapor pressure. This means the vapor pressure shown by a solvent when it is pure is lowered by the addition of solutes. The change in vapor pressure is proportional to the quantity of the dissolved solute. Raoult's law explains this relationship.

According to Raoult's law, the mole fraction of the solvent times the vapor pressure of the pure solvent is numerically equal to the vapor pressure of the solution. This is mathematically represented as shown below:

$$P_A = X_A \times P_A$$

Here, P_A is the vapor pressure of the solution (impure solvent),
X_A is the mole fraction of the solvent, and
P_A is the vapor pressure of the pure solvent.

Example 8-1

Calculate the mole fractions of sodium chloride and water in a solution containing 11.7 g of sodium chloride and 9 g of water.

Solution:

In this solution, we have 11.7 grams of NaCl and 9 grams of H_2O. First, you have to find the number of moles of NaCl and H_2O.

$$\text{Number of moles of NaCl} = \frac{11.7 \text{ g}}{58.5 \text{ g / mol}} = 0.2 \text{ mol}$$

$$\text{Number of moles of } H_2O = \frac{9 \text{ g}}{18 \text{ g / mol}} = 0.5 \text{ mol}$$

The total number of moles in the solution = 0.2 + 0.5 = 0.7 mole

$$\text{Mol fraction of sodium chloride} = \frac{0.2 \text{ mol}}{0.7 \text{ mol}} \approx 0.3$$

$$\text{Mol fraction of water} = \frac{0.5 \text{ mol}}{0.7 \text{ mol}} \approx 0.7$$

Boiling Point Elevation

The **boiling point** of a liquid is defined as the temperature at which its vapor pressure equals the prevailing pressure. The prevailing pressure is normally the atmospheric pressure, provided that the container in which the liquid is present is kept open while boiling. When a nonvolatile solute is added to a pure solvent, the boiling point increases.

The increase is proportional to the number of moles of the solute added to the solvent. The relationship is mathematically represented as shown below:

$$\Delta T_b = i K_b C_m$$
Here, ΔT_b is the boiling-point elevation,
i is the ionization factor,
K_b is the boiling-point elevation constant, and
C_m is the molal concentration of the solution.

Example 8-2

Calculate the boiling point of 0.2 m aqueous solution of glucose. (K_b of water is 0.512°C/m.)

Solution:

The formula for finding the boiling-point elevation is:

$$\Delta T_b = i K_b C_m$$

In this problem, we have all the necessary values to find the boiling-point elevation. Here, the ionization factor is 1, since glucose doesn't ionize. Let's substitute the values into the formula.

$$\Delta T_b = K_b C_m = 0.512°C/m \text{ x } 0.2 \text{ } m \approx 0.1°C$$

The boiling point of 0.2 m solution of glucose is 100 + 0.1 = 100.1°C

Freezing Point Depression

The solute concentration affects the freezing point of a solvent. The freezing point of a pure solvent is decreased when solutes are added to it. Just like the boiling-point elevation, freezing-point depression is proportional to the molal concentration. The relationship is shown:

$$\Delta T_f = i K_f C_m$$
Here, ΔT_f is the freezing-point depression,
i is the ionization factor,
K_f is the freezing-point depression constant, and
C_m is the molal concentration of the solution.

Example 8-3

Calculate the freezing point of 2 m aqueous solution of glucose. (K_f of water is 1.86°C/m)

Solution:

The formula for finding the freezing-point depression is:

$$\Delta T_f = i K_f C_m$$

In this problem, we have all the necessary values to find the freezing-point depression. The ionization factor is 1.

$$\Delta T_f = K_f \, C_m = 1.86^\circ C/m \times 2 \, m \approx 3.7^\circ C$$

So the freezing point of $2 \, m$ solution of glucose is $0.0 - 3.7 = -3.7^\circ C$

Osmotic Pressure

Osmotic pressure is also a colligative property. Before we talk about osmotic pressure let's turn our attention to the process of osmosis. Consider two solutions that are made out of the same solvent with different concentrations of solute separated by a semipermeable membrane. The solvent will flow through the semipermeable membrane from the solution of lower concentration to the solution of higher concentration. Thus, **osmosis** is defined as the flow of solvent through a semipermeable membrane resulting in the equilibrium of concentrations on both sides of the semi-permeable membrane.

We will explore the process of osmosis with an experiment. A dilute solution of sodium chloride is taken in a funnel. The mouth of the funnel is covered by a semipermeable membrane. The funnel is then placed upside down into a beaker which is filled with pure distilled water. The setup is done according to the diagram shown (Figure 8-7):

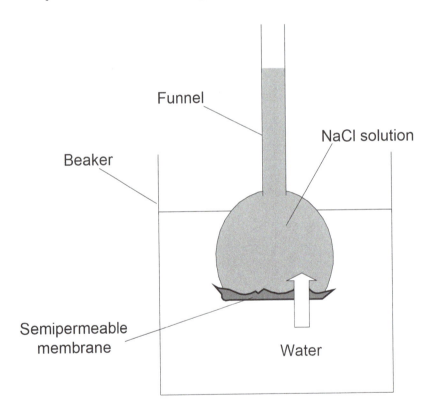

Figure 8-7 Osmosis experiment

The arrow indicates the direction of flow of the solvent (H_2O).

Water will flow into the funnel through the semipermeable membrane, and the liquid level of the funnel will grad-ually increase. The **osmotic pressure** is the pressure required or applied to the solution to stop the flow of the solvent, or in other words, to stop the process of osmosis. The osmotic pressure and concentration are related by the following equation:

Osmotic pressure, $\pi = M R T$

Here, M is the molar concentration of the solute,

R is the gas constant, and

T is the absolute temperature.

CHAPTER 8 PROBLEMS

1. The phase change that involves the conversion of a gas to a solid is called:

    A.   sublimation.
    B.   condensation.
    C.   freezing.
    D.   deposition.

2. Which of the following processes accompanies a release of heat?

    A.   Vaporization
    B.   Condensation
    C.   Sublimation
    D.   Melting

3. Potassium fluoride is:

    A.   a covalent solid.
    B.   a metallic solid.
    C.   a network solid.
    D.   an ionic solid.

4. Which of the following is the strongest type of force that is present in an ionic bonding?

    A.   London forces
    B.   Covalent forces
    C.   Electrostatic forces
    D.   Hydrogen bonding forces

Questions 5-10 are based on the following passage.

Passage 1

A phase diagram illustrates the physical state of a substance with respect to the temperature and the pressure of the surroundings. The points plotted to draw the phase diagram are derived experimentally, and are usually plotted with temperature on the x-axis and pressure on the y-axis. A typical phase diagram is shown in Figure-1.

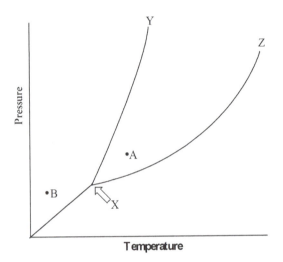

Figure 1

5. Which of the following represents the correct phase diagram of water?

A.

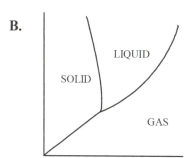

B.

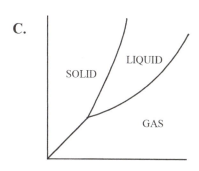

C.

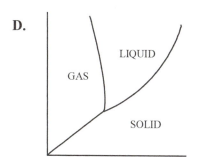

D.

6. The phase diagram given in the passage cannot be that of:

   A. CO_2.
   B. H_2O.
   C. CO.
   D. O_2.

7. From the phase diagram given in the passage, predict the likely phase change if the following changes happen. Consider point A as the current phase of substance M. What is the most likely effect on substance M, if the pressure was decreased without changing the temperature of the system?

   A.   Gas to liquid
   B.   Liquid to gas
   C.   Liquid to solid
   D.   Solid to liquid

8. The point marked 'X' in the phase diagram given in the passage is called:

   A.   the critical point.
   B.   the maximum point.
   C.   the triple point.
   D.   the critical pressure point.

9. The critical temperature of a substance is best defined as:

   A.   the temperature below which a gas cannot be liquefied.
   B.   the temperature above which a liquid cannot be vaporized.
   C.   the temperature above which a substance exists only as a supercritical fluid.
   D.   the temperature which is essential for a substance to obey ideal gas laws.

10. The segment XZ in the phase diagram given in the passage represents the equilibrium between:

   A.   gas and liquid.
   B.   liquid and solid.
   C.   solid and gas.
   D.   gas and plasma.

Section 3

CONTENT REVIEW PROBLEMS

1. Which of the following is Henry's Law?

   A. $P_1V_1 = P_2V_2$
   B. partial pressure $= k_H{}^*c$
   C. $V_1/T_1 = V_2/T_2$
   D. $P_1/T_1 = P_2/T_2$

2. Which of the following is Boyle's Law?

   A. $P_1V_1 = P_2V_2$
   B. partial pressure $= k_H{}^*c$
   C. $V_1/T_1 = V_2/T_2$
   D. $V_1/n_1 = V_2/n_2$

3. Which of the following is Charles' Law?

   A. $P_1V_1 = P_2V_2$
   B. $V_1/n_1 = V_2/n_2$
   C. $V_1/T_1 = V_2/T_2$
   D. $P_1/T_1 = P_2/T_2$

4. Which of the following is the ideal gas law?

   A. $PV = mRT$
   B. $PV/RT = k$
   C. $PT = MnV$
   D. $PV = nRT$

5. Which of the following is Guy-Lussac's Law?

   A. $Rate_1/Rate_2 = \sqrt{(M_{mass2}/M_{mass1})}$
   B. $V_1/n_1 = V_2/n_2$
   C. $V_1/T_1 = V_2/T_2$
   D. $P_1/T_1 = P_2/T_2$

6. Which of the following is Avogadro's Law?

   A. $P_{total} = P_1 + P_2 + ... + P_n$
   B. $V_1/n_1 = V_2/n_2$
   C. $V_1/T_1 = V_2/T_2$
   D. $P_1/T_1 = P_2/T_2$

7. Which of the following is Graham's Law

   A. $P_1V_1 = P_2V_2$
   B. partial pressure $= k_H{}^*c$
   C. $Rate_1/Rate_2 = \sqrt{(M_{mass2}/M_{mass1})}$
   D. $P_1/T_1 = P_2/T_2$

8. Which of the following is Dalton's Law?

   A. $P_{total} = P_1 + P_2 + ... + P_n$
   B. partial pressure $= k_H{}^*c$
   C. $P_1/T_1 = P_2/T_2$
   D. $Rate_1/Rate_2 = \sqrt{(M_{mass2}/M_{mass1})}$

9. If the pressure of a gas is doubled and the temperature is also doubled, with all else held constant, what will be the gas's resulting volume?

   A. It will double
   B. It will be halved
   C. It will quadruple
   D. It will not change

10. If the volume of a gas is doubled and the pressure is halved, with all else held constant, what will be the gas's resulting temperature?

   A. It will double
   B. It will be halved
   C. It will quadruple
   D. It will not change

11. If the volume of a gas is halved and the temperature is doubled, with all else held constant, what will be the gas's resulting pressure?

   A. It will double
   B. It will be halved
   C. It will quadruple
   D. It will not change

12. Given a gas in a closed container, if the container is heated, which value will change?

   A. P
   B. V
   C. n
   D. R

13. Given a gas at constant pressure, if a sealed container is heated, which value will change?

    A. P
    B. V
    C. n
    D. R

14. Given a gas in a balloon at constant temperature, if the balloon is expanded, which value will change?

    A. P
    B. T
    C. n
    D. R

15. What does isobaric mean?

    A. Constant volume
    B. Constant temperature
    C. Constant concentration
    D. Constant pressure

16. Which of the following gives possible units of the gas constant R?

    A. $L\ atm\ K^{-1}\ mol^{-1}$
    B. $J\ K^{-1}\ mol^{-1}$
    C. $L\ J\ K^{-1}\ mol^{-1}$
    D. $atm\ K\ mol^{-1}$

17. Which of the following gives possible units for the gas constant R?

    A. $atm\ J\ K^{-1}\ mol^{-1}$
    B. $J\ L\ K\ mol$
    C. $J\ K\ mol$
    D. $L\ atm\ K^{-1}\ mol^{-1}$

18. What is the value of the gas constant if your pressure is given in atm and volume is given in liters?

    A. .08206
    B. 8.314
    C. 8314
    D. 8.08206

19. What is the value of the gas constant if your pressure is given in atm and volume is given in m³?

    A. .00008206
    B. .08206
    C. 8.314
    D. .008206

20. What is the value of the gas constant if your pressure is given in pascals and volume is given in liters?

    A. .08206
    B. .008206
    C. 8314.7
    D. 8.314

21. What is the value of the gas constant if your pressure is given in pascals and volume is given in m³?

    A. .08314
    B. 8.314
    C. .08206
    D. .8206

22. Which of the following is NOT an assumption or prerequisite of the ideal gas law?

    A. Pressures are low
    B. Temperatures are high
    C. Gases have no mass
    D. Gases have negligible volume

23. Which of the following explains pressure exerted by a gas?

    A. Gas molecules impact with the walls of the container
    B. Gas molecules move randomly around the container
    C. Gas molecules convert kinetic energy into potential energy
    D. Gas molecules collide with each other, creating internal pressure

24. Which of the following will affect the average kinetic energy of gas particles?

    A.   pressure
    B.   temperature of the gas
    C.   volume
    D.   moles of gas

25. Which of the following gives the root mean square velocity of particles in a sample of ideal gas molecules?

    A. $\sqrt{n/3RT}$
    B. $\sqrt{3RT/M}$
    C. $\sqrt{3RT/n}$
    D. $\sqrt{3RT/m}$

26. Which of the following gives the ratio of the rates of effusion for hydrogen gas to that of oxygen gas at the same temperature?

    A.   16:1
    B.   4:1
    C.   1:1
    D.   1:16

27. Which of the following gives the ratio of volumes of equimolar amounts of hydrogen gas and oxygen gas at STP?

    A.   1:16
    B.   1:4
    C.   1:1
    D.   16:1

28. What is the partial pressure of nitrogen in air if air is 80% nitrogen gas?

    A.   608 mmHg
    B.   1.2 atm
    C.   546 mmHg
    D.   .2 atm

The following scenario is for questions 29-31:

64 grams of O_2, 28 grams of N_2, and 1 gram of H_2 are added into one container with a final pressure of 1 atm.

29. What is the approximate partial pressure of the O_2 gas in the container?

    A.   433 torr
    B.   220 torr
    C.   107 torr
    D.   327 torr

30. What is the approximate partial pressure of the N_2 gas in the container?

    A.   433 torr
    B.   220 torr
    C.   107 torr
    D.   540 torr

31. What is the approximate partial pressure of the H_2 gas in the container?

    A.   433 torr
    B.   220 torr
    C.   107 torr
    D.   653 torr

32. How many pascals are 380 mmHg?

    A.   101000
    B.   202000
    C.   55000
    D.   25000

33. Which of the following is equal to 1 atm?

    A.   670 mmHg
    B.   760 torr
    C.   101 Pa
    D.   101,325 kPa

34. Which of the following is true at STP?

    A.   Pressure is 0 atm
    B.   Pressure is 1 atm
    C.   Temperature is 25°C
    D.   Temperature is 298 K

35. Each of the following is true at STP EXCEPT:

    A. Temperature is 273 K.
    B. Pressure is 1 atm.
    C. 44g of $CO_2(g)$ occupies 22.4 L.
    D. 18g of $H_2O(g)$ occupies 11.2 L.

36. The difference between standard conditions and STP is that:

    A. standard conditions means 298K, STP means 273K.
    B. standard conditions require a higher temperature and consequently a higher pressure.
    C. STP is 0 atm, standard conditions is 1 atm.
    D. they are the same temperature and pressure but simply use different units.

37. Which gas will have the highest rate of effusion?

    A. 1 mole of H_2 gas
    B. 0.5 mole of He gas
    C. 0.25 mole of He gas
    D. 2 mole of N_2 gas

38. Which of the following is most useful in separating isotopes by diffusion?

    A. Graham's Law
    B. Boyle's Law
    C. Dalton's Law
    D. Henry's Law

39. Which of the following best describes the liquid phase?

    A. molecules interact but move freely
    B. molecules do not interact with each other but with their container
    C. molecules are in a rigid mosaic structure
    D. molecules are in a fluid crystalline structure

40. Which of the following lists the phases in order from greatest intermolecular attractions to least?

    A. gas, liquid solid
    B. solid, liquid, gas
    C. liquid, gas, solid
    D. liquid, solid, gas

41. Which of the following is most likely a liquid at room temperature?

    A. Ne
    B. Ar
    C. Cl
    D. Br

42. Which of the following is the strongest intermolecular force?

    A. Hydrogen bonding
    B. London dispersion forces
    C. dipole-dipole interactions
    D. induced dipole interactions

43. Which of the following is the weakest intermolecular force?

    A. Hydrogen bonding
    B. London dispersion forces
    C. dipole dipole interactions
    D. ionic bonding

44. Which of the following places the intermolecular forces in order of increasing strength?
    I. Dipole dipole interactions
    II. Hydrogen bonding
    III. London dispersion forces
    IV. Ionic bonding

    A. I, II, III, IV
    B. III, I, II, IV
    C. III, IV, I, II
    D. I, III, IV, II

45. Which of the following elements cannot participate in hydrogen bonding?

    A. O
    B. S
    C. N
    D. F

46. Which of the following will have the highest boiling point?

    A. H_2O
    B. CH_4
    C. CF_4
    D. CH_3OH

47. Which of the following has the weakest intermolecular attractions?

    A. H_2O
    B. CH_4
    C. CF_4
    D. CH_3OH

48. Which of the following orders the following in order of lowest to highest boiling point?

  I. H_2O
  II. CH_4
  III. CF_4
  IV. CH_3OH

    A. I, II, III, IV
    B. III, I, II, IV
    C. II, III, IV, I
    D. III, II, IV, I

49. What is the energy required to transition from the solid phase to the liquid phase?

    A. Heat of evaporation
    B. Heat of fusion
    C. Heat of vaporization
    D. Heat of sublimation

50. What is the energy required to transition from the liquid phase to the gas phase?

    A. Heat of vaporization
    B. Heat of fusion
    C. Heat of evaporation
    D. Heat of sublimation

51. Which of the following bonds has the strongest dipole?

    A. C-F single bond
    B. C-O single bond
    C. C-H single bond
    D. C-N single bond

52. Which of the following molecules is the least polar?

    A. CF_4
    B. CH_3F
    C. CH_2F_2
    D. CHF_3

53. In which phase will H_2O exist at 1 atm and 50 degrees Celsius?

    A. Solid
    B. Liquid
    C. Gas
    D. Not enough information

54. In which phase will H_2O exist at 1 atm and 273 K?

    A. Solid
    B. Liquid
    C. Gas
    D. Not enough information

55. In which phase will H_2O exist at 1 atm 100 degrees Celsius?

    A. Solid
    B. Liquid
    C. Gas
    D. Not enough information

56. Which phase has the least molecular motion?

   A. Solid
   B. Liquid
   C. Gas
   D. Not enough information

57. Which phase conducts sound waves the fastest?

   A. Solid
   B. Liquid
   C. Gas
   D. Not enough information

58. Which phase typically has the least volume per unit mass?

   A. Solid
   B. Liquid
   C. Gas
   D. Not enough information

59. Which of the following will diffuse the fastest?

   A. $^{18}O_2$
   B. O_2
   C. CH_4
   D. Ne

60. According to Charles' law, which of the following values is constant?

   A. PV
   B. P/T
   C. V/T
   D. V/n

61. According to Boyle's Law, which of the following values is constant?

   A. PV
   B. P/T
   C. V/T
   D. V/n

62. According to Avogadro's Law, which of the following values is constant?

   A. PV
   B. P/T
   C. V/T
   D. V/n

The following is a phase diagram of water and will be used for question 63 through 67:

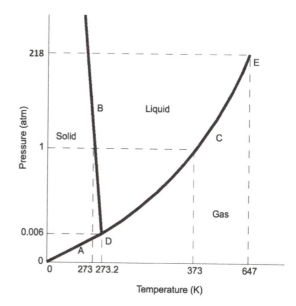

63. Which of the following is the triple point of water?

   A. E
   B. B
   C. C
   D. D

64. Which of the following is the critical point of water?

   A. E
   B. B
   C. C
   D. D

65. At 1 atm and 300 degrees kelvin, if the temperature is raised, which of the following changes will occur?

    A. Liquid to gas
    B. Solid to liquid to gas
    C. Solid to liquid
    D. Solid to gas

66. At 0.01 atm and 273 degrees kelvin, if the pressure is raised, which of the following changes will occur?

    A. Liquid to gas
    B. Solid to liquid to gas
    C. Solid to liquid
    D. Solid to gas

67. At 0.01 atm and 273 K, if the pressure is decreased to 0.002, which of the following occurs?

    A. Liquid to gas
    B. Solid to liquid to gas
    C. Solid to liquid
    D. Solid to gas

68. Which of the following describes a change from solid to liquid?

    A. Freezing
    B. Deposition
    C. Melting
    D. Evaporation

69. Which of the following describes a change from solid to gas?

    A. Sublimation
    B. Condensation
    C. Boiling
    D. Fusion

70. Which of the following describes a change from liquid to gas?

    A. Freezing
    B. Deposition
    C. Melting
    D. Evaporation

71. Which of the following describes a change from gas to liquid?

    A. Fusion
    B. Deposition
    C. Condensation
    D. Sublimation

72. Which of the following describes a change from gas to solid?

    A. Evaporation
    B. Deposition
    C. Condensation
    D. Sublimation

73. Which of the following describes a change from liquid to solid?

    A. Freezing
    B. Deposition
    C. Melting
    D. Fusion

74. Which of the following forms of H_2O is super-cooled?

    A. Ice at 0 kelvin
    B. Water at -5 degrees Celsius
    C. Gas at 373 kelvin
    D. Ice at 298 kelvin

75. What is the effect of solutes in water on boiling point?

    A. It is elevated
    B. It is decreased
    C. There is no effect on boiling point
    D. Not enough information

76. What is the effect of solutes in water on freezing point?

    A. It is elevated
    B. It is decreased
    C. There is no effect on boiling point
    D. Not enough information

77. Which of the following is not a colligative property?

    A. Freezing point depression
    B. Osmotic pressure
    C. Boiling point depression
    D. Vapor pressure lowering

The following information is used for questions 78 – 81:

The K_f of water is 1.86 C/m
The K_b of water is 0.512 C/m
The vapor pressure of water at STP = 23.8 torr
Assume complete solubility for questions 78 - 81.

78. Which of the following solutions has the lowest freezing point?

    A. 1 m NaCl
    B. 0.8 m $CaCl_2$
    C. 0.5 m Na_2SO_4
    D. 1 m KCl

79. What is the boiling point of a 1 m aqueous NaCl solution?

    A. 373.0 K
    B. 373.512 K
    C. 374.24 K
    D. 372.488 K

80. If 2 moles of ions are dissolved in 10 moles of water, what will be the change in vapor pressure of the solution?

    A. 19.8 torr
    B. 28.5 torr
    C. 21.4 torr
    D. 26.2 torr

81. What is the change in freezing point of a 0.5 m $CaCl_2$ solution?

    A. -.26 degrees C
    B. -.93 degrees C
    C. - 2.79 degrees C
    D. -5.58 degrees C

82. Which of the following gives the equation for osmotic pressure of a solution?

    A. $\pi = mRT$
    B. $\pi = MRTi$
    C. $\pi = mRTi$
    D. $\pi = nRTi$

83. Which value of R is used for osmotic pressure calculations?

    A. 0.08206 L atm K^{-1} mol^{-1}
    B. 8.314 J K^{-1} mol^{-1}
    C. 0.08206 L atm K mol^{-1}
    D. 8.314 J K mol^{-1}

84. What are the units of the van't Hoff factor ?

    A. mol
    B. M
    C. L
    D. none

85. Which is the approximate osmotic pressure of 1.5 moles of NaCl in 6 L of water at STP?

    A. 12.23 atm
    B. 7.34 atm
    C. 3.11 atm
    D. 2.5 atm

A CO_2 phase diagram is used for questions 86 – 92:

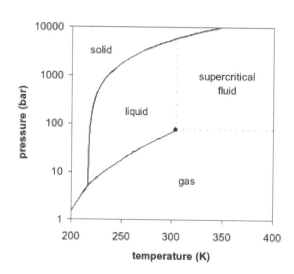

86. What phase is CO_2 at STP?

    A. Solid
    B. Liquid
    C. Gas
    D. Plasma

87. What phase is CO_2 at standard temperature and 100 atm?

    A. Solid
    B. Liquid
    C. Gas
    D. Plasma

88. What is the critical point of CO_2?

    A. 180 K, 1 atm
    B. 273 K, 1 atm
    C. 305 K, 90 bar
    D. 220 K, 8 bar

89. What is the triple point of CO_2?

    A. 180 K, 1 atm
    B. 273 K, 1 atm
    C. 305 K, 90 bar.
    D. 220 K, 8 bar

90. Which of the following phases are possible for CO_2 at -68 degrees Celsius?
  I. Solid
 II. Liquid
III. Gas

    A. I only
    B. I and III only
    C. II and III only
    D. I, II, and III

91. Which of the following phases are possible for CO_2 at Standard pressure?
  I. Solid
 II. Liquid
III. Gas

    A. I only
    B. I and III only
    C. II and III only
    D. I, II, and III

92. At standard pressure, to what temperature must CO_2 be cooled to reach the solid phase?

    A. -50 degrees C
    B. -78.5 degrees C
    C. 200 K
    D. It will never reach the solid phase

93. What is a triple point?

    A. The point at which all matter is in the same phase
    B. The point above which there is no meaningful distinction between phases
    C. The point at which all three phases have the same density
    D. The point at which all three phases can coexist

94. What is the critical point?

    A. The point at which all matter is in the same phase
    B. The point at which the liquid and gas phase have the same density
    C. The point at which gas and liquid phases can coexist
    D. The point at which all three phases can coexist

95. A substance is brought to its critical temperature and then has the pressure increased well past the critical pressure. The substance is now:

    A. a supercritical fluid or a solid.
    B. a gas or a solid.
    C. a supercritical solid.
    D. a solid.

96. Under which of the following conditions would a gas behave least ideally?

    A. $T = 400$ K
    B. $P = 400$ atm
    C. $V = 400$ L
    D. $n = 400$ mol

97. Under which circumstances might the ideal gas law not apply?

    A. $T = 5$ K
    B. $P = 0.5$ atm
    C. $V = 0.5$ L
    D. $n = 0.0001$ mol

98. Which two colligative properties are most interrelated?

    A.   freezing point and boiling point
    B.   vapor pressure and boiling point
    C.   osmotic pressure and vapor pressure
    D.   freezing point and osmotic pressure

99. Given 14 g of N_2 gas in a 2 L container at 25 degrees C, what is the pressure of the container?

    A.   12.2 atm
    B.   6.1 atm
    C.   24.4 atm
    D.   62 atm

100. What is the boiling point of water at 1 atm?

    A.   100 degrees F
    B.   298 degrees K
    C.   373 degrees K
    D.   273 degrees C

SECTION 4
WATER AND ITS SOLUTIONS

Water is arguably the single most important molecule for the MCAT (DNA might come in as a close second). In the previous section we discussed the phases of matter, including the liquid phase. Most of the time when we encounter water on the MCAT it will be as the solvent for some chemical or biological process. As such, we need to fully explore the solutions formed in water.

We'll begin our discussion by talking about the general properties of solutions. What sorts of things can dissolve and why, as well as what happens when you have multiple solutes all trying to dissolve in the same solution at once.

From there, we'll turn our attention to every MCAT student's favorite part of the exam: acid-base chemistry and titrations. While this can be an intimidating topic, it's an important one. Feel free to slow down here and take your time to really understand these concepts. Remember that one of the most important physiological functions the MCAT will ask about is regulating the osmolarity and pH of the body (especially the blood), so a strong foundation in this section is essential to Test Day success.

CHAPTER 9
Chemistry of Solutions

A. INTRODUCTION

When we think of solutions, we normally think of a solution formed by dissolving a solid (e.g., sugar) in a liquid (e.g., water). In reality, any combination of the three states can be considered a solution. In fact, air is a solution which is a mixture of various gases. Carbonated water (soda) is a mixture of a gas (CO_2) dissolved in a liquid (H_2O). Even alloys such as gold-silver alloys are solutions containing two solids. A true solution is a solution which has only one solvent with one or more solutes. In this chapter, we will be limiting our discussion mostly to water-based solutions because of their versatility and importance to life sciences. We will discuss various aspects such as solubility of compounds, and precipitation reactions.

B. SOLUBILITY

Solubility of a substance is defined as the amount of the substance that will dissolve in a particular solvent. Let's consider an example in which sucrose is added to water. When we add sucrose and stir, it dissolves in the water. Let's say we keep on adding more and more sucrose to the solution. Since more and more sucrose is dissolving, the solution is not saturated or it is called an unsaturated solution.

We reach a point where additional sucrose added will not dissolve in that solution. At that point the solution is said to be saturated. We have yet another category in this tradition of categorizing solutions. In some cases, certain solutes become more soluble if the solution is heated. Such solutions are called supersaturated solutions. If we carefully and slowly cool down a supersaturated solution without disturbing its contents, normally we will still have a supersaturated solution. At this stage, even the slightest addition of the solute will result in crystallization.

The Reasons for Solubility

One basic rule that you have to keep in mind is "**like dissolves like**." This means that substances which have similar polarity dissolve one another. We know that water is a polar substance. Since oil is nonpolar, water and oil cannot mix. Solubility helps in maintaining the lowest energy possible when the solute and the solvent are mixed together.

Ionic Solutions

Ionic compounds have peculiar solubility trends. Some are highly soluble, whereas some others have very little solubility. This solubility can be explained in terms of the interactions between the ions and water. Let's take sodium chloride as an example. Sodium chloride has a solubility of 360 g per liter or 36 g per 100 ml at room temperature.

Since water is a polar molecule, when we add sodium chloride to water, the water molecules will orient themselves according to the surrounding ions. Here we have sodium (Na^+) and chloride (Cl^-) ions. So the slightly negative pole (the negative pole is due to the electronegativity of the oxygen atom) of the water molecules will align toward the sodium ions, and the other pole will orient toward the chloride ions. This attraction is otherwise called hydration. Besides hydration, there is another force called lattice energy of the crystal lattice. The higher the lattice energy of an ionic solid is, the lower the solubility of that solid.

C. MEASURES OF SOLUTION CONCENTRATION

Molarity

When we are working with solutions, it is better to have a concentration measure in terms of the volume. **Molarity** is defined as the number of moles of the solute per liter of solution.

$$\text{Molarity} = \frac{\text{moles of solute}}{\text{liter of solution}} = \frac{\text{mol}}{\text{L}}$$

Molality

The **molality** of a solution is defined as the number of moles of the solute per kilogram of solvent.

$$\text{Molality} = \frac{\text{moles of solute}}{\text{kilograms of solvent}}$$

Molarity is usually denoted by the letter M, and molality is denoted by the letter m.

Example 9-1

Calculate the molarity of a solution that contains 18.65 g of KCl in 3 liters of solution.

Solution:

We have 18.65 grams of KCl, and the total volume of the solution is 3 liters. First, find the number of moles of KCl present. The number of moles of KCl is 0.25 mol, which can be calculated from the formula weight and the grams of solute.

$$\text{Molarity} = \frac{\text{moles of solute}}{\text{liters of solution}}$$

$$= \frac{0.25 \text{ mol}}{3 \text{ L}} \approx 0.08 \text{ M}$$

Normality

The normality (N) of a solution is the number of equivalents of solute per liter of solution. The *equivalent* is usually defined in terms of a chemical reaction. For acid-base reactions, an equivalent is the amount of substance that will react or form 1 mole of hydrogen (H^+) or hydroxide (OH^-) ions. For redox (oxidation-reduction) reactions, an equivalent is the amount of substance that will react or form 1 mole of electrons.

$$Normality = \frac{number\ of\ equivalents}{1\ liter\ of\ solution}$$

Normality is a multiple of molarity. The following equation relates normality and molarity.

$$N = n\,M$$

For acids, the number of H^+ available from a formula unit of the acid gives the number of equivalents (n). For example, 1 M H_2SO_4 solution is a 2 N solution, because each molecule of H_2SO_4 can give two H^+. For bases, the number of OH^- available from a formula unit of the base gives the number of equivalents. For example, a 2 M Ca(OH)$_2$ solution is a 4 N solution.

D. K_{sp} AND THE COMMON ION EFFECT

Let's say we are adding silver chloride (AgCl) into a liter of water. We can express the equilibrium as follows:

$$AgCl\,(s) \xrightleftharpoons{H_2O} Ag^+\,(aq) \quad + \quad Cl^-\,(aq)$$

The **solubility product** (K_{sp}) is defined as the equilibrium constant for the solubility equilibrium of ionic compounds. The solubility product of AgCl is expressed as:

$$K_{sp} = \left[Ag^+ \right] \left[Cl^- \right]$$

The solubility product constant is equal to the product of the concentrations of the ions in a saturated solution, each concentration raised to a power equal to its coefficient (number of moles of <u>individual</u> ions formed per mole of the compound) Take a look at the solubility product equation of calcium fluoride (CaF$_2$).

$$CaF_2\,(s) \xrightleftharpoons{H_2O} Ca^{2+}\,(aq) \quad + \quad 2\,F^-\,(aq)$$

$$K_{sp} = \left[Ca^{2+} \right] \left[F^- \right]^2$$

It is imperative that you understand these ideas involving the solubility product constant. Let's look at another example. One mole of aluminum hydroxide [Al(OH)$_3$] gives one mole of aluminum ions and three moles of hydroxide ions in solution.

$$Al(OH)_3 \ (s) \rightleftharpoons Al^{3+}(aq) \ + \ 3 \ OH^-(aq)$$

From the balanced equation, we can see that the coefficient of Al^{3+} is 1 and that of OH^- is 3. So, the solubility constant (K_{sp}) expression for $Al(OH)_3$ is given by:

$$K_{sp} = [Al^{3+}] \ [OH^-]^3$$

The solubility product depends on the temperature, and at a given temperature it is constant for a particular ionic compound. *Molar solubility* is defined as the number of moles of solute dissolved in one liter of its saturated solution. Using the molar solubility of a compound, the solubility product of that compound can be determined or vice versa.

Example 9-2

Calculate the molar solubility of silver chloride (AgCl). The solubility product (K_{sp}) of AgCl is 1.8×10^{-10}.

Solution:

$$AgCl \ (s) \ \xrightarrow{\ H_2O\ } \ Ag^+ \ (aq) \ + \ Cl^- \ (aq)$$

$$K_{sp} = [Ag^+] \ [Cl^-]$$

Let x be the molar solubility of AgCl. So we can write:

$$AgCl \ (s) \ \xrightarrow{\ H_2O\ } \ Ag^+ \ (aq) \ + \ Cl^- \ (aq)$$

	Ag^+	Cl^-
Initial	0	0
Equilibrium	x M	x M

$$K_{sp} = [Ag^+] \ [Cl^-] = (x) \ (x) = (x)^2 = 1.8 \times 10^{-10}$$

So the molar solubility of AgCl, $x = \sqrt{1.8 \times 10^{-10}} = 1.34 \times 10^{-5}$ M

Example 9-3

If 'x' represents the molar solubility of $Al(OH)_3$, find the expression for the solubility product of $Al(OH)_3$ in terms of x. What is the molar solubility of $Al(OH)_3$, if the solubility product constant is 2×10^{-33}?

Solution:

$$Al(OH)_3 \; (s) \rightleftharpoons Al^{3+}(aq) \; + \; 3 \; OH^-(aq)$$

Intial Concentration	0	0
Equilibrium concentration	x	3 x

The solubility product expression is, $K_{sp} = [Al^{3+}] \, [OH^-]^3 = [x] \, [3x]^3 = 27x^4$

$$K_{sp} = 27x^4 = 2 \times 10^{-33}$$

$$x^4 = \frac{2 \times 10^{-33}}{27} = 7.4 \times 10^{-35}$$

The solubility, $x = \sqrt[4]{7.4 \times 10^{-35}} = \sqrt[4]{74 \times 10^{-36}} \approx 2.9 \times 10^{-9} \, mol \, / \, L$

You can approximate numbers to find the correct answer among the choices in the MCAT. In this example, to find the 4th root of 7.4×10^{-35}, first we can rewrite this as 74×10^{-36}. The 4th root of 81 is 3. Since 74 is less than 81, we can approximate the 4th root of 74 as being close to 2.8 or 2.9. Again, the best approximation for the 4th root of 74 is a number below and close to 3. The 4th root of 10^{-36} is 10^{-9}. Such approximation-techniques can save you time during the MCAT.

Ion Product

Ion product is the product of the concentrations of the ions from the compound (solute) in a solution, where each concentration is raised to a power equivalent to that molecule's coefficient in the balanced equation. In other words, the expression for the ion product is the same as that of K_{sp}. In a saturated solution, the ion product is equal to K_{sp}. If the ion product is greater than K_{sp}, the solution is supersaturated and can undergo precipitation. If the ion product is less than K_{sp}, the solution is unsaturated. Thus, by comparing the ion product of a compound against its K_{sp}, we can predict whether or not precipitation is likely to occur.

Ion product $< K_{sp}$	Unsaturated solution	No precipitate is formed
Ion product $= K_{sp}$	Saturated solution	No precipitate is formed
Ion product $> K_{sp}$	Supersaturated solution	Precipitation can occur

Common-Ion Effect

When a salt is added to a solution containing either the same cation or anion, there will be changes in the solubility because of what is commonly known as **common-ion effect**. This is so because the solubility of the salt added is affected by the common ions which are already present in the solution. Consider a solution of sodium fluoride (NaF). We are adding magnesium fluoride (MgF_2) to this solution. Notice the fact that there is a common ion in sodium fluoride and magnesium fluoride, namely fluoride. You will see that the solubility of magnesium fluoride will be less than expected. To be more precise, the solubility of magnesium fluoride will be less than that of its solubility in pure water. The phenomenon can be best explained in terms of Le Châtelier's principle. Consider the dissociation of magnesium and sodium fluorides.

$$MgF_2\ (s) \underset{}{\overset{H_2O}{\rightleftharpoons}} Mg^{2+}\ (aq)\ +\ 2F^-\ (aq) \qquad \text{equation 1}$$

$$NaF\ (s) \underset{}{\overset{H_2O}{\rightleftharpoons}} Na^+\ (aq)\ +\ F^-\ (aq) \qquad \text{equation 2}$$

Magnesium fluoride is not a very soluble salt. It is a mildly soluble salt, whereas sodium fluoride is a highly soluble salt. Because of the higher solubility of sodium fluoride, there will be a lot of fluoride ions in the solution. This increased fluoride ion concentration in the solution will drive the equilibrium of equation 1 to the left. Thus the solubility of magnesium fluoride will be highly diminished because of the fluoride ions already present in the solution.

SOLUBLE IONIC COMPOUNDS
All salts of alkali metals (e.g., sodium, potassium), and ammonium ion are soluble.
All nitrates, acetates, chlorates, and perchlorates are soluble.
All halides (chlorides, bromides, and iodides) are soluble. Exceptions include lead(II), mercury (I), and silver halides.
All sulfates are soluble. Exceptions include calcium, strontium, barium, and lead(II) sulfates.
INSOLUBLE IONIC COMPOUNDS
All carbonates and phosphates are insoluble except those of ammonium ion and alkali metals.
All hydroxides are insoluble except those of calcium, strontium, barium, and alkali metals.
All sulfides are insoluble except those of alkali metals and ammonium ion.

Table 9-1 Some general trends regarding solubilities (in water) of common ionic compounds

E. ELECTROLYTES

Pure distilled water is not a good conductor of electricity. If KCl is added to it, the resulting aqueous KCl solution becomes a good conductor of electricity. Such a substance that dissolves in water to give a solution that can conduct electricity is called an *electrolyte*. The free ions that are present in an electrolytic solution enable the flow of electric current. Most ionic substances are good electrolytes because they dissolve in water ions. A substance that exists almost completely as ions in a solution is called a *strong electrolyte*. Hydrochloric acid is a strong electrolyte because when HCl is dissolved in water, it completely exists as H_3O^+ and Cl^- ions by reacting with water (H_2O).

$$HCl(g) + H_2O(l) \longrightarrow H_3O^+(aq) + Cl^-(aq)$$

Some substances (solutes) form aqueous solutions that weakly conduct electricity. Such substances are called *weak electrolytes*. This weak conduction of electricity is mainly because weak electrolytes only dissociate partially in solution. In other words, only a small fraction of the solute exists as ions, resulting in a solution that conducts electricity very weakly. Acetic acid (CH_3COOH) and ammonia (NH_3) are examples of weak electrolytes.

A substance that can dissolve in water but results in a poorly conducting solution is called *nonelectrolyte*. Glucose ($C_6H_{12}O_6$) is a nonelectrolyte. A nonelectrolyte is not charged in solution because it dissolves as molecules in water rather than ions, and thus cannot conduct electricity.

Acetate: CH_3COO^-	Nitrate: NO_3^-
Ammonium: NH_4^+	Nitrite: NO_2^-
Bicarbonate: HCO_3^-	Oxalate: $C_2O_4^{2-}$
Bisulfate: HSO_4^-	Perchlorate: ClO_4^-
Bisulfite: HSO_3^-	Permanganate: MnO_4^-
Carbonate CO_3^{2-}	Peroxide: O_2^{2-}
Chlorite: ClO_2^-	Phosphate: PO_4^{3-}
Chromate: CrO_4^{2-}	Sulfate: SO_4^{2-}
Cyanide: CN^-	Sulfide: S^{2-}
Dichromate: $Cr_2O_7^{2-}$	Sulfite: SO_3^{2-}
Dihydrogen phosphate: $H_2PO_4^-$	Thiosulfate: $S_2O_3^{2-}$
Hydroxide: OH^-	Superoxide: O_2^-
Hypochlorite: ClO^-	

Table 9-2

CHAPTER 9 PROBLEMS

1. Equivalents of solute per liter of solution is:

    A.   molality.
    B.   molarity.
    C.   normality.
    D.   none of the above.

2. The concentration of a given solution of glucose $(C_6H_{12}O_6)$ is 270 g per liter of solution. What is the molarity of this solution?

    A. $1.5\,M$
    B. $0.67\,M$
    C. $4.86\,M$
    D. $270\,M$

3. You are presented with a $2.5\,M$ solution of hydrochloric acid. If the total volume of the solution is 1.25 L, how many grams of HCl is present in this solution?

    A.   36.5 g
    B.   91.25 g
    C.   111 g
    D.   114 g

4. You are asked to prepare 30 ml of a $2\,M$ solution of HNO_3 from a stock solution of $10\,M$ solution of HNO_3. How much of the stock solution is required to make this 30 ml of $2\,M$ HNO_3 solution?

    A.   3 ml
    B.   6 ml
    C.   10 ml
    D.   30 ml

5. How many grams of NaCl are required to prepare 250 ml of $0.35\,M$ NaCl solution?

    A.   0.0875 g
    B.   20.5 g
    C.   5.1 g
    D.   87.5 g

Questions 6-10 are based on the following passage.

Passage 1

The concentrations of solutions are generally expressed in terms of molarity, molality, normality, and weight percent. The formation of the solutions itself has many ramifications. The solubilities of solutes differ considerably from one other. Some of the factors that can influence the solubility include temperature and pressure. Solubility depends on other factors as well. Given below in Figure 1 is a graph which depicts solubility differences of some solutes.

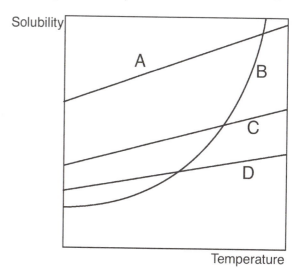

Figure 1

Quite often, the freezing and boiling point changes that are brought about by the dissolved solutes can be predicted reasonably. But this is not always the case.

The predictions and calculations are done for freezing point depression (ΔT_f) based on this formula:

$$\Delta T_f = K_f\, m,$$

where m is the molality and K_f is the freezing point depression constant. $(K_f = 1.86°C/m)$

For boiling point elevation (ΔT_b), the calculations are based on the following formula:

$$\Delta T_b = K_b\, m,$$

where m is the molality and K_b is the boiling point elevation constant. ($K_b = 0.512 \,°C/m$)

6. The graph in the passage shows the solubilities of some compounds (salts). Which of the following is most likely true regarding the Compounds A, B, C and D?

    A.   The solubility process of Compound B is exothermic, and those of Compounds A, C and D are endothermic.
    B.   The solubility process of Compound B is endothermic, and those of Compounds A, C and D are exothermic.
    C.   The solubility processes of Compounds A, B, C and D are exothermic.
    D.   The solubility processes of Compounds A, B, C and D are endothermic.

7. A solution was made by using 315 g of glucose in 750 g of water. What is the boiling point of this solution?

    A. $98.8°$ C
    B. $99.8°$ C
    C. $100.24°$ C
    D. $101.2°$ C

8. Two experiments were conducted for analyzing the solubility properties and their effects on colligative properties. In Experiment I, a 1.0 m solution of KBr was analyzed and in Experiment II, a 2.3 m solution of KBr was analyzed. The experimental values of freezing and boiling points were slightly different from the expected values based on the theoretical calculations discussed in the passage. Which of the following is most likely correct regarding the two experiments?

    A.   The experimental values of the solution in Experiment I were more different from the theoretical calculations than the solution in Experiment II.
    B.   The experimental values of the solution in Experiment II were more different from the theoretical calculations than the solution in Experiment I.
    C.   Both experiments have the same extent of difference from the theoretical predictions.
    D.   The discrepancy noted in the experiments is absolutely a result of instrumental error, because the differences in Experiments I and II cannot change colligative properties.

9. If the amount of glucose used in Question 7 is doubled, while the same 750 g of water was used, what must have happened to the boiling point of the solution?

    A.   It doubled
    B.   It quadrupled.
    C.   It decreased slightly.
    D.   It increased slightly.

10. Which of the following statements is true regarding solutions?

    A.   As the concentration of a solution increases, the vapor pressure increases.
    B.   As the concentration of a solution decreases, the vapor pressure decreases.
    C.   As the concentration of a solution increases, the vapor pressure decreases.
    D.   None of the above

CHAPTER 10

Acid-Base Reactions

A. INTRODUCTION

In this chapter, we will explore different aspects involving acids and bases. We will start with the definitions, followed by ionization reactions, including various key concepts involving strong acids, strong bases, weak acids, weak bases, and buffers. Finally, we will discuss some of the important titration reactions.

B. DEFINITIONS OF ACIDS AND BASES

The Arrhenius Definition

According to Arrhenius, an **acid** is a substance that increases H^+ ions in an aqueous solution. A **base** is a substance that increases OH^- ions in an aqueous solution. The Arrhenius definitions explain the reactions involving acids that contain acidic hydrogens, and bases that contain basic hydroxyl groups (e.g., metal hydroxides). But the definitions are not able to explain the behavior of acids and bases of other types, such as in nonaqueous solutions.

The Bronsted-Lowry Definition

During the early twentieth century, scientists J.N. Bronsted and T.M. Lowry put forth their theories. According to them, an **acid** is a proton donor, and a **base** is a proton acceptor.

Consider the ionization reaction of hydrogen iodide. Since hydrogen iodide is a strong acid, it completely dissociates. In this ionization reaction, note that the water molecule acts as the base.

$$HI\ (aq) \longrightarrow H^+\ (aq)\ +\ I^-\ (aq)$$

$$H^+\ (aq)\ +\ H_2O\ (l) \longrightarrow H_3O^+$$

$$\boxed{HI\ (aq)\ +\ H_2O\ (l) \longrightarrow H_3O^+\ +\ I^-\ (aq)} \quad \text{Overall reaction}$$

THIS REACTION IS AN EXAMPLE THAT FITS THE BRONSTED-LOWRY DEFINTION

In this ionization reaction, obviously HI is the acid. HI transfers or donates its proton to water. Thus, water is the base in this reaction because it accepts the proton. The conjugate base of HI is I⁻.

The Lewis Definition

The scientist G.N. Lewis put forward a more elaborate theory regarding acids and bases. According to him, a **Lewis acid** is a species that can accept a pair of electrons from another species. He defined **Lewis base** as any species that can donate a pair of electrons to another species. For a thorough understanding of this concept, let's look at a typical Lewis acid-base reaction. The reaction between ammonia (NH_3) and boron trichloride (BCl_3) is shown:

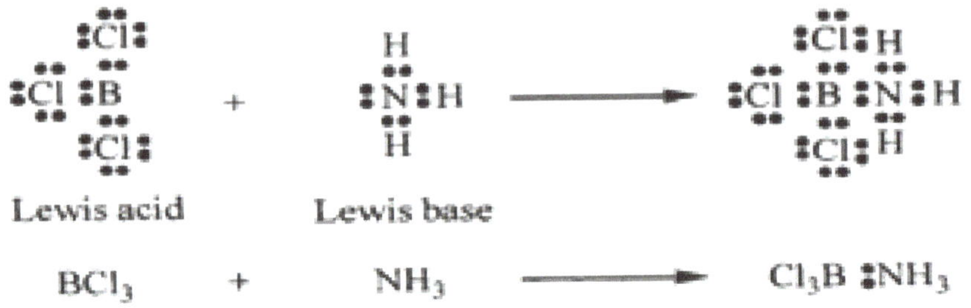

In this reaction, the electron acceptor is boron trichloride (Lewis acid) and the electron donor is ammonia (Lewis base). The new bond that is formed between the acid and the base is a coordinate covalent bond.

C. WATER AUTO-IONIZATION

Usually pure water is considered to be a nonelectrolyte. Nevertheless, it actually can conduct small amounts of electricity. This is because of the self-ionization of water. Since the species that act as the acid and the base are one and the same, we can describe it as follows:

A proton is grabbed from one water molecule, and is accepted by another water molecule. The resulting products are hydronium and hydroxide ions.

$$H_2O \; (l) \;\; + \;\; H_2O \; (l) \;\; \rightleftharpoons \;\; H_3O^+ \; (aq) \;\; + \;\; OH^- \; (aq)$$

The equilibrium expression (K_w) is written as:

$$K_w = [H_3O^+][OH^-] = 1\times10^{-14} \text{ at } 25°C$$

K_w is more correctly called the ion-product constant for water, which is actually the equilibrium value of the ion product.

D. THE CONCEPT OF pH

In order to describe the acidity of a solution, scientists have devised the pH scale. The **pH** is defined as the negative log of the hydrogen-ion concentration.

$$pH = -\log [\,H^+\,]$$

Example 10-1

What is the pH of a solution having a $1 \times 10^{-2}\,M$ hydrogen-ion concentration?

Solution:

The formula for pH is $pH = -\log [\,H^+\,]$. Substituting in this formula,

$$pH = -\log (1 \times 10^{-2}) = 2$$

The pH of this solution is 2.

We can also find pH if we know the hydroxide-ion concentration.

$$pOH = -\log [OH^-]$$

Since $pH + pOH = 14$, if we know the pOH, the pH can be easily calculated or vice versa.

Example 10-2

Find the pH of solution X, if it has a hydroxide-ion concentration of $1 \times 10^{-8}\,M$.

Solution:

Since the hydroxide-ion concentration is $1 \times 10^{-8}\,M$, the pOH is 8. Since we know that $pH + pOH$ is 14,

$$pH = 14 - 8 = 6$$

The pH value of solution X is 6.

E. STRONG AND WEAK ACIDS AND BASES

Strong Acids and Bases

Strong acids such as HNO_3, HCl, and HI dissociate almost completely. If we were asked to predict the direction of such a dissociation reaction, we should say that the direction of reaction favors the dissociation of the acid. The dissociation of HI is shown below:

$$HI\ (aq)\ +\ H_2O\ (l)\ \longrightarrow\ H_3O^+\ (aq)\ +\ I^-\ (aq)$$

Since there is complete dissociation for every mole of HI present, equal numbers of hydronium ions are formed. You may be wondering whether protons can be supplied by the water molecules that are present. Usually this supply is negligible (the self-ionization of water is extremely low) compared to the concentration of the strong acid present. But this may not be always the case. Think about an instance when the proton contribution of water is significant in an acidic solution such as that of hydrogen iodide. When you have a strong acid solution which is very dilute, water does contribute protons significantly compared to that of the strong acid present.

Now let's consider a strong base such as potassium hydroxide. Let's say the solution is 1×10^{-3} M. Since KOH is a strong base, it dissociates completely. So we can confidently say that the concentration of hydroxide-ion formed is also 1×10^{-3} M. Just like the strong acid, we can ignore the possibility of hydroxide-ion formation from water, since the self-ionization of water is negligible. Since the OH⁻ concentration is 1×10^{-3}, the pOH is 3. From this, we can say that the pH of this solution is close to 11, since pH + pOH = 14.

A pH value below 7 is acidic, a pH value above 7 is basic, and a pH value 7 is neutral.

Table 10-1

SOME EXAMPLES OF STRONG ACIDS

Sulfuric acid	H_2SO_4
Nitric acid	HNO_3
Hydrochloric acid	HCl
Hydrobromic acid	HBr
Hydroiodic acid	HI
Perchloric acid	$HClO_4$
Chloric acid	$HClO_3$

SOME EXAMPLES OF STRONG BASES

Lithium hydroxide	LiOH
Sodium hydroxide	NaOH
Potassium hydroxide	KOH
Cesium hydroxide	CsOH
Calcium hydroxide	$Ca(OH)_2$
Strontium hydroxide	$Sr(OH)_2$
Barium hydroxide	$Ba(OH)_2$

Weak Acids and Bases

Weak acids and bases cannot dissociate completely. They undergo the same type of dissociation as that of strong acids and bases, but the extent of dissociation is very small compared to strong acid or strong base dissociations.

Acid-ionization Constant (K_a)

A typical way to represent the dissociation of a weak acid is shown below:

$$HA\ (aq)\ +\ H_2O\ (l)\ \rightleftharpoons\ H_3O\ (aq)\ +\ A^-$$
weak acid

In this reaction, the protons from the weak acid are transferred to the water molecules. The acid-ionization constant (K_a) of this reaction is shown below:

$$\text{Acid-ionization constant, } K_a\ =\ \frac{[H_3O^+][A^-]}{[HA]}$$

We encounter weak acids every day. An example is carbonated water that contains dissolved carbon dioxide, and is called carbonic acid. Fruits like lemons and oranges contain citric acid which is also a weak acid. The list goes on and on.

Percentage Ionization

Percentage ionization is the percentage expression of the degree of ionization. What is the degree of ionization of a weak acid? Degree of ionization is the fractional amount of the weak acid that gets ionized.

Example 10-3

Find the degree of ionization of 0.1 M solution of acetic acid (CH_3COOH). Also find the pH of the solution.

(The acid-ionization constant of acetic acid is 1.8×10^{-5})

Solution:

$$CH_3COOH\ (aq)\ \rightleftharpoons\ H^+(aq)\ +\ CH_3COO^-\ (aq)$$

We will logically dissect the events that lead to the dissociation. At first we do not have any H^+ and CH_3COO^- ions. Let's say we have a unit volume (a liter) of acetic acid and $x\ M$ (mol/L) of it was ionized. We can represent the equation as follows:

	$CH_3COOH\ (aq) \rightleftharpoons$	$H^+(aq)\ +$	$CH_3COO^-\ (aq)$
Initial	0.1 M	~ 0	~ 0
At equilibrium	$(0.1 - x)\ M$	$x\ M$	$x\ M$

With the concentrations at equilibrium we can substitute the concentrations in the acid-ionization constant expression.

$$\text{Acid-ionization constant, } K_a = \frac{[H^+][CH_3COO^-]}{[CH_3COOH]}$$

$$= \frac{(x)\,(x)}{(0.1 - x)}$$

$$= 1.8 \times 10^{-5}$$

Even though this has to be solved using a quadratic equation, we can skip that elaborate process by making some chemically acceptable assumptions. Since the acid-ionization constant is very small, we can assume the same with the value of x. So the expression changes as follows. For the MCAT, you won't be given problems that require extensive calculations. The problems will test mostly concepts, and when calculations are involved the numbers will usually be manageable ones.

$$\frac{(x)^2}{(0.1 - x)} \text{ becomes } \frac{(x)^2}{0.1} = 1.8 \times 10^{-5}$$

Solving for x you will get roughly $1.34 \times 10^{-3} = 0.00134\ M$.

$$\text{Degree of ionization} = \frac{0.00134}{0.1} = 0.0134$$

The question also asks for pH of the solution.

$$pH = -\log[H^+]$$

The hydrogen ion concentration is $0.00134\ M$. By substituting in the pH formula you should get the pH of the solution as approximately 2.87. For the purposes of the MCAT, you need not be so accurate. You can use estimation and the shortcut $p[X \times 10^{-Y}] = (Y-1).(10-X)$. Thus for this example $p(1.3 \times 10^{-3}) = (3-1).(10-1.3) = 2.87$. Voila! Time saved, points earned.

Base-ionization Constant (K_b)

Just like the acid-ionization constant, there is also the base-ionization constant. Consider the ionization of ammonia in water.   NH3 (aq) + H20 (l)

$$NH3\ (aq) + H20\ (l) \rightleftharpoons NH_4^+(aq) + OH^-(aq)$$

For the above reaction, we can write the base-ionization constant (K_b) as follows:

$$\text{Base-ionization constant, } K_b = \frac{[NH_4^+][OH^-]}{[NH_3]}$$

F. POLYPROTIC ACIDS

Some acids have two or more protons that can be released upon dissociation. Such acids are called polyprotic acids. For example, phosphoric acid (H_3PO_4) can lose up to three protons in aqueous solution.

Sulfuric acid is a polyprotic acid that can lose two protons in solution. The first ionization is complete because sulfuric acid is a strong acid.

$$H_2SO_4 (aq) \longleftrightarrow H^+(aq) + HSO_4^- (aq) \quad \text{Dissociation constant } K_{a1} = \text{very large}$$

The second proton comes off as depicted by the next equation. In this case, an equilibrium exists because hydrogen sulfate ion (HSO_4^-) is not as strong as H_2SO_4.

$$HSO_4^- (aq) \longleftrightarrow H^+(aq) + SO_4^{2-}(aq) \quad \text{Dissociation constant } K_{a2} = 1.2 \times 10^{-2}$$

It is clear from this example that the second dissociation constant is always lower than the first dissociation constant. Thus, it is easier to remove a proton from an uncharged species H_2SO_4 than from a charged species (HSO_4^-).

Based on the Bronsted-Lowry definition of acids and bases, an acid is a proton donor and base is a proton acceptor. A species (charged or uncharged) that can gain or lose a proton is called amphoteric or amphiprotic species. For example, (bicarbonate ion) HCO_3^- can donate a proton acting as an acid. The same species can accept a proton acting as a base. Hence, amphoteric species can act as an acid or a base depending on the surrounding conditions.

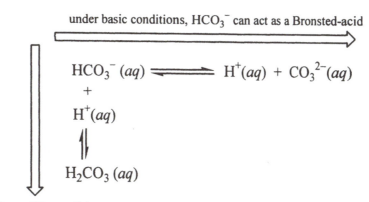

G. ACIDIC AND BASIC SALTS

Salt solutions can be acidic, neutral, or basic. Let's consider a salt solution of NaF. NaF dissolves in water to form sodium and fluoride ions.

$$NaF(s) \xrightarrow[H_2O]{} Na^+(aq) + F^-(aq)$$

While the sodium ion is not reactive to water, the fluoride ion is reactive to water (fluoride is the conjugate base of a weak acid, HF). The fluoride ion can act as a base by accepting a proton from H_2O by the process of hydrolysis. The reaction is shown below.

$$H_2O(l) + F^-(aq) \rightleftharpoons HF(aq) + OH^-(aq)$$

The increased presence of hydroxide ions (notice the formation of hydroxide ions as one of the products of the hydrolysis reaction) makes the solution basic. This strategy can be used to predict whether a salt solution is acidic, basic, or neutral.

1. A salt of a strong base and a strong acid gives a neutral aqueous solution.
    e.g.: NaCl is a salt of a strong acid (HCl) and a strong base (NaOH).
2. A salt of a weak acid and a strong base gives a basic aqueous solution.
    e.g.: NaCN is a salt of a weak acid (HCN) and a strong base (NaOH).
3. A salt of a weak base and a strong acid gives an acidic aqueous solution.
    e.g.: NH_4NO_3 is a salt of a weak base (NH_3) and a strong acid (HNO_3).

H. BUFFERS

A buffer is a solution which can maintain a constant pH. If we add an acid or a base to a buffer solution, it can resist the change in pH to a certain extent. You have to remember that we are talking about small additions of acid or base, and such changes will not alter the buffer-pH much. But if we add a large quantity of acid or base to a buffer, obviously there will be significant change in its pH.

Buffers are conjugate acid-base mixtures. Buffer systems are very important for all types of organisms. The bicarbonate buffer system present in our body plays an important role in maintaining a reasonably constant blood pH. They are usually made of a weak acid with its conjugate base, or it can also be a mixture of a weak base with its conjugate acid. Consider the theory behind the working of a buffer system. Regardless of the type of buffer, both component species in a buffer system are in a state of equilibrium. Consider a weak acid-conjugate base buffer. A perfect example is a mixture of acetic acid and its salt. We can write the equation as follows:

$$CH_3COOH + H_2O \rightleftharpoons H_3O^+ + CH_3COO^-$$

Let's say we are adding some acid into this buffer system. What happens to it? Well, as the acid is added, an increase in H_3O^+ is imperative. So the backward reaction is favored or in other words, the reaction proceeds to the left. This consumes the increased H_3O^+ and the system will try to attain equilibrium again. This process restores or maintains the pH, and that is exactly the function of a buffer system.

Consider what happens when we add a strong base (for example, KOH) to the same buffer system. The extra added

OH$^-$ ions will consume the H$_3$O$^+$. As this happens, the reaction shifts to the right. So more and more acetic acid will ionize restoring the hydrogen ion concentration, and thereby the pH of the solution is maintained.

I. TITRATION CURVES

Acid-base titrations are reactions by which we can determine the amount of acid or base present in a solution. This is done by reacting the solution with a base or acid (of known concentration), and by measuring the volume of the known acid or base used up in the process. The reaction data is usually plotted with the volume of the substance (concentration known) in the x-axis, and the pH of the solution in the y-axis. The graph is called a titration curve.

Take a look at the first titration plot (Figure 1) given. You will see a steep region in the plot. The center of this steep region is called the equivalence point. The **equivalence point** denotes the point at which equivalent amounts of acid and base have reacted. To know the equivalence point, we usually add an indicator which will change its color close to the equivalence point. We can use the following relation to equate the amount of acid or base present in a solution against the volume of acid or base added whose concentration is known.

$$N_1V_1 = N_2V_2$$
where N$_1$ is the normality of the unknown acid or base,
N$_2$ is the normality of the known base or acid,
V$_1$ is the volume of unknown acid or base, and
V$_2$ is the volume of the known base or acid.

Indicators

An indicator is usually used to detect the equivalence point in an acid-base reaction or titration. The most common indicators used are weak organic acids or bases that change color in response to a change from acidic to basic medium or vice versa. The pH at which the color change occurs is characteristic of each indicator. For an acid-base reaction, the indicator is chosen based on the pH at which the equivalence point is expected to occur. Consider the hypothetical dissociation reaction of an indicator represented by HIn.

$$HIn \rightleftharpoons H^+ + In^-$$
yellow   blue
color   color

Let's consider a scenario in which the indicator is in an acidic solution. Acidic solution means there is excess H$^+$. So the equilibrium will shift to the left (LeChâtelier's principle), and the predominant species will be HIn making the indicator show yellow color. On the other hand, in a basic solution, the equilibrium will shift favoring the forward reaction and the predominant species will be In$^-$ (blue color). Because HIn (acid form) and In$^-$ have different colors, this can indicate the equivalence point of acid-base reactions. You might be thinking that the dissociation of the indicator used might affect the pH of the tested solution. But this is negligible because only a tiny amount of the indicator is needed to show a visible color change.

Indicator	Approx. pH Range of Color Change	Color Change
Thymol blue	1.2-2.8	Red to Yellow
Methyl Orange	3.2-4.4	Red to Yellow
Cresol Red	7.1-8.9	Yellow to Red
Thymol Blue	8.0-9.7	Yellow to Blue
Phenophthalein	8.3-10.0	Colorless to Pink
Alizarin Yellow	10.0-12.0	Yellow to red

Table 10-2 Some Common Indicators

Titration of a Strong Acid with a Strong Base

Consider the titration reaction involving HCl against NaOH. Let's say that we have 50 ml of a 0.1 M solution of HCl, titrated with 0.1 M solution of NaOH. As we add NaOH into the solution of HCl, initially the pH increase will not be very drastic. The pH increases slowly. When a certain amount of NaOH is added, the change in pH becomes more drastic and the plot becomes very steep, as indicated in the plot (Figure 10-1). At this steep region, the equivalence point is reached. Can you guess the pH at the equivalence point? If you guessed 7, you are right. At the equivalence point of this titration you have a salt which is neutral, and hence the pH is 7.

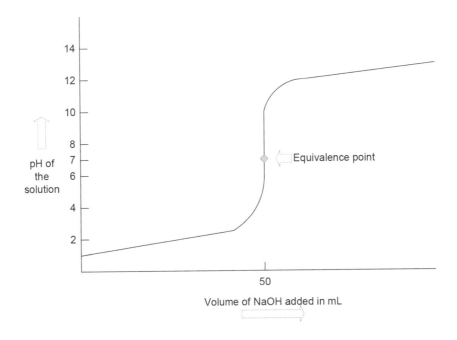

Figure 10-1

Titration of a Weak Acid with a Strong Base

The curve of a weak acid-strong base titration is different from that of the plot we learned for the strong acid-strong base titration. Unlike the previous curve, this plot will have a region which has buffering properties. Besides that, the equivalence point will be above the pH value 7. The general shape of the curve is shown in Figure 10-2.

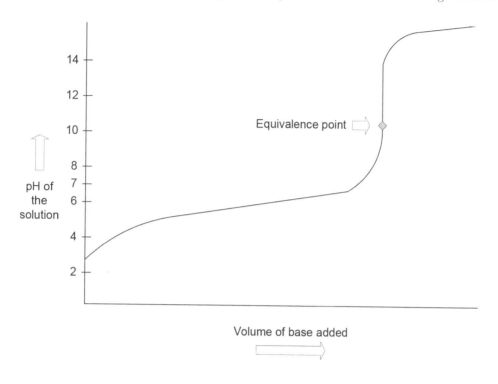

Figure 10-2

Titration of a Weak Base with a Strong Acid

The trend seen in the weak base-strong acid titration curve is somewhat similar to that of the weak acid-strong base curve. At first, as we add the acid, the pH slowly decreases. Then the decrease in pH becomes drastic, as you can see in Figure 10-3.

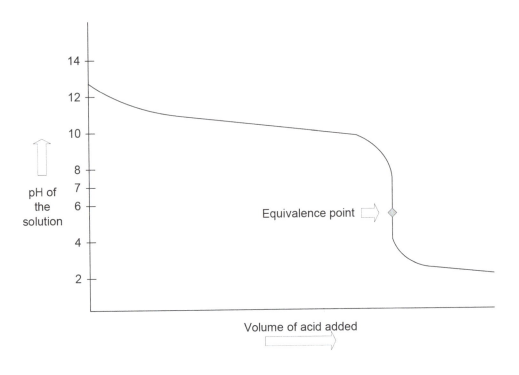

Figure 10-3

CHAPTER 10 PROBLEMS

1. If the pH of a solution is 2.5, what is the concentration of H_3O^+ in that solution?

    A. 2.9×10^{-1}
    B. 3.2×10^{-3}
    C. 3.8×10^{-2}
    D. 6.3×10^{-5}

2. NaCl solution is most likely:

    A. acidic.
    B. basic.
    C. neutral.
    D. cannot be predicted.

3. Which of the following is not a polyprotic acid?

    A. H_2SO_4
    B. $H_2PO_4^-$
    C. H_3AsO_4
    D. None of the above

4. Based on the equation,

$$pOH = pK_b + \log \frac{[\text{conjugate acid}]}{[\text{base}]}$$

which of the following is not valid?

A. $\log K_b = \log[OH^-] + \log \frac{[\text{conjugate acid}]}{[\text{base}]}$

B. $\log K_b = \log[OH^-] - \log \frac{[\text{base}]}{[\text{conjugate acid}]}$

C. $\log K_b + \log[OH^-] = \log \frac{[\text{conjugate acid}]}{[\text{base}]}$

D. None of the above are valid.

5. Which of the following species has the highest pK_a value?

    A. $H_2PO_4^-$
    B. H_3PO_4
    C. HPO_4^{2-}
    D. All the above species have almost the same pK_a values, since they all have the same type of phosphate anionic counterpart.

Questions 6-10 are based on the following passage.

Passage 1

Strong acids and bases ionize completely in aqueous solutions. Weak acids and bases ionize only partially in aqueous solutions. An acid-base reaction is shown below. A titration was done by adding a base to a known concentration and fixed volume of an acid. The reaction follows:

Reaction 1

$$HClO_4\,(aq) + NaOH\,(aq) \rightarrow NaClO_4\,(aq) + H_2O\,(l)$$

The dissociation of a weak acid can be represented as:

$$HA\,(aq) \longrightarrow H^+\,(aq) + \bar{A}$$

Chemists often use Henderson-Hasselbalch equation to calculate the pH of solutions containing a weak acid of known pKa, provided that the other concentrations are known. Henderson-Hasselbalch equation is:

$$pH = pKa + \log \frac{[A^-]}{[HA]}$$

This equation is also used to calculate the buffering capability of solutions. It is roughly estimated that a given buffer is most likely to be effective at pH levels between $(pKa + 1)$ and $(pK_a - 1)$.

6. The net ionic equation of Reaction 1 is:

A. $H^+ (aq) + OH^- (aq) \longrightarrow H_2O\ (l)$

B. $Na^+ (aq) + ClO_4^- (aq) \longrightarrow NaClO_4\ (aq)$

C. $H^+ (aq) + ClO_4^- (aq) + Na^+(aq) + OH^-(aq)$
$\longrightarrow Na^+ (aq) + ClO_4^- (aq) + H_2O\ (l)$

D. Perchloric acid is a weak acid and cannot ionize completely, so that net ionic equation cannot be written.

7. The titration curve of the acid-base reaction (Reaction 1) is best represented by:

A.

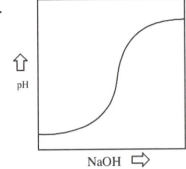

B.

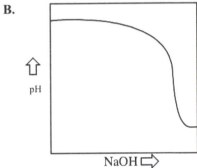

C.

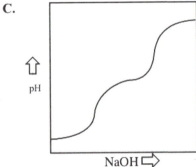

D.

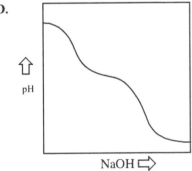

8. What are the base-to-acid ratios corresponding to the lower and upper limits of pH values which make the best buffer?

    A.   10 and 1
    B.   100 and 1
    C.   0.01 and 10
    D.   0.1 and 10

9. What is the pH of a $3.2 \times 10^{-4} \, M$ solution of HCl?

    A.   2.7
    B.   3.5
    C.   4
    D.   4.4

10. The pH at which the base and the acid concentrations are equal in a buffer system is called the:

    A.   equivalence point.
    B. pK_a.
    C.   neutralization point.
    D.   non-buffering zone.

Section 4
CONTENT REVIEW PROBLEMS

1. Which of the following is NOT a solution?

    A.   Bronze, an alloy of copper and tin
    B.   The Earth's atmosphere
    C.   The ocean
    D.   A muffin with raisins in it

2. When no more of a solute will dissolve in a solvent, it is a(n):

    A.   unsaturated solution
    B.   saturated solution
    C.   supersaturated solution
    D.   common ion solution

3. Sugar is added to water until no more will dissolve. The solution is then heated to boiling and more sugar is added until no more will dissolve. When more sugar dissolves in the 100°C water, the solution created is a(n):

    A.   unsaturated solution.
    B.   saturated solution.
    C.   supersaturated solution.
    D.   common ion solution.

4. Sugar is added to water until no more will dissolve. The solution is then heated to boiling and more sugar is added until no more will dissolve. The solution is then quickly cooled back to room temperature. Once it returns to room temperature, it is a(n):

    A.   unsaturated solution.
    B.   saturated solution.
    C.   supersaturated solution.
    D.   common ion solution.

5. A supersaturated solution of sucrose in water is prepared. Then, a single sugar crystal is dropped into the solution. This will cause:

    A.   precipitation of the sugar.
    B.   boiling of the solution.
    C.   the solution to become even more supersaturated.
    D.   the solution to become unsaturated.

6. Molarity is defined as:

    A.   kg / L
    B.   gram equivalent weights / L
    C.   mole / kg
    D.   mole / L

7. Molality is defined as:

    A.   kg / L
    B.   gram equivalent weights / L
    C.   mole / kg
    D.   mole / L

8. A 2.5 molar solution of sulfuric acid is:

    A.   1.25 N
    B.   2.5 N
    C.   5.0 N
    D.   7.5 N

9. A 0.02 M solution of nitric acid is:

    A.   0.01 N
    B.   0.02 N
    C.   0.04 N
    D.   0.08 N

10. A 2.4 N solution of sulfuric acid is:

    A.   1.2 M
    B.   2.4 M
    C.   4.8 M
    D.   24 M

11. Consider the following hypothetical reaction:

$$A_2B_3 \, (s) \rightarrow 2 \, A^{3+} \, (aq) + 3 \, B^{2-} \, (aq)$$

What is the K_{sp} expression for this reaction?

    A. $[A^{3+}]^2[B^{2-}]^3 / [A_2B_3]$
    B. $[A^{3+}][B^{2-}] / [A_2B_3]$
    C. $[A^{3+}][B^{2-}]$
    D. $[A^{3+}]^2[B^{2-}]^3$

12. Consider the following hypothetical reaction:

$$A_2B_3(s) \rightarrow 2\ A^{3+}(aq) + 3\ B^{2-}(aq)$$

If the K_{sp} for this reaction is 1.08×10^{12}, what is the molar solubility?

A. 1×10^2
B. $1 \times 10^{2.4}$
C. 2×10^{11}
D. 1.08×10^{12}

13. Consider the following hypothetical reaction:

$$A_2B_3(s) \rightarrow 2\ A^{3+}(aq) + 3\ B^{2-}(aq)$$

If the molar solubility for this reaction is 100 mole / L, what is the K_{sp}?

A. 1×10^2
B. $1 \times 10^{2.4}$
C. 2×10^{11}
D. 1.08×10^{12}

14. When the ion product of a solution is greater than the K_{sp}:

A. the solution is unsaturated.
B. the ions in solution must immediately precipitate out.
C. the solution is saturated.
D. the solution is supersaturated.

15. A saturated solution of $A(B)_2$ is prepared. Then, XB is added. Which of the following is true?

A. X must precipitate out of solution.
B. A must precipitate out of solution.
C. B must precipitate out of solution.
D. Both $A(B)_2$ and XB must precipitate out of solution.

16. Which of the following is NOT true?

A. Salts of alkali metals are generally soluble.
B. Nitrates are generally insoluble.
C. Silver halides are generally insoluble.
D. Sulfides are generally insoluble.

17. Which of the following is *least* likely to be a strong electrolyte?

A. H_2SO_4
B. KCl
C. CaS
D. NaOH

For questions 18 – 25 give the structure of the named ion.

18. Acetate

19. Cyanide

20. Chlorite

21. Permanganate

22. Phosphate

23. Peroxide

24. Chromate

25. Hypochlorite

26. Which of the following is an Arrhenius base?

A. NaOH
B. NH_3
C. HCl
D. $AlCl_3$

27. Which of the following is a Lewis acid?

A. HCl
B. $AlCl_3$
C. NaOH
D. NH_3

28. Which of the following is a Brønsted base?

A. HCl
B. $AlCl_3$
C. NaOH
D. NH_3

29. Which of the following is the conjugate base of acetic acid?

    A. CH_3COOH
    B. HOH
    C. CH_3COO^-
    D. NaOH

30. Which of the following is the conjugate acid of HPO_4^{2-}?

    A. H_3PO_4
    B. $H_2PO_4^-$
    C. HPO_4^{2-}
    D. PO_4^{3-}

31. Which of the following is the conjugate base of HPO_4^{2-}?

    A. H_3PO_4
    B. $H_2PO_4^-$
    C. HPO_4^{2-}
    D. PO_4^{3-}

32. Which of the following is the correct expression for K_w?

    A. $[H_3O^+][OH^-] / [H_2O]^2$
    B. $[H_3O^+][OH^-] / [H_2O]$
    C. $[H_3O^+][OH^-]$
    D. $[H_3O^+]^2[OH^-]^2$

33. What is the approximate pH of a solution whose $[H^+] = 3 \times 10^{-6}$?

    A. 3
    B. 5.5
    C. 6
    D. 7

34. What is the approximate pOH of a solution whose $[OH^-] = 3 \times 10^{-6}$?

    A. 3
    B. 5.5
    C. 6
    D. 7

35. What is the pH of a solution whose pOH is 3.75?

    A. 10.25
    B. 9.25
    C. 7
    D. 3.75

36. A solution is heated to 80°C and the pH is lowered to 4. Which of the following is true?

    A. The solution is basic.
    B. The pOH is 10.
    C. The pOH is greater than 10.
    D. The pOH is less than 10.

37. Which of the following is a strong acid?

    A. CH_3COOH
    B. $HClO_4$
    C. NaOH
    D. CH_3CHO

38. Each of the following is a strong base EXCEPT:

    A. KOH.
    B. CsOH.
    C. $Fe(OH)_3$.
    D. $Sr(OH)_2$.

39. A student prepares a solution of 0.3 M acetic acid. What is the approximate pH of the solution? ($K_a = 1.8 \times 10^{-5}$)

    A. 6
    B. 5.2
    C. 4.2
    D. 2.87

40. A student carries out a titration of HCl and NH_3. The equivalent point is likely to be:

    A. below pH 7.
    B. at pH 7.
    C. above pH 7.
    D. at the point where the slope of the titration curve is the flattest.

41. A student carries out a titration of CH_3COOH and NaOH. The salts formed include:

    A. a weak acid and a spectator ion.
    B. two spectator ions.
    C. a weak base and a spectator ion.
    D. a weak base and a weak acid.

42. In a titration curve starting with a weak acid and adding NaOH, the part of the curve where the slope is closest to 0 is the point at which:

    A. $[HA] = [A^-]$ for the weak acid
    B. $[NaOH] = [OH^-]$
    C. the moles of acid = moles of base.
    D. the pH is closest to 7.

43. In a titration curve starting with a weak acid and adding NaOH, the part of the curve where the slope is the biggest is the point at which:

    A. $[HA] = [A^-]$ for the weak acid
    B. $[NaOH] = [OH^-]$
    C. the moles of acid = moles of base.
    D. the pH is closest to 7.

44. In the titration of H_3PO_4 with NaOH, for the point at which $[HPO_4^{2-}] = [H_2PO_4^-]$ which of the following is true?

    A. pH = 7.00
    B. This is the second equivalence point.
    C. The slope of the titration curve is relatively close to 0.
    D. Twice as many moles of NaOH have been added as moles of H_3PO_4 initially present.

45. Which of the following is true in the middle of the buffer region of a titration curve?

    A. pH ≈ 7
    B. pH = pK_a
    C. pOH ≈ 7
    D. The curve is at its equivalence point.

46. A titration begins with 2 mole of CH_3COOH in 2 L of water. A student slowly adds NaOH to the solution. After 1 mole of NaOH has been added:

    A. the solution is at the equivalence point.
    B. the pH ≈ 7.
    C. the titration curve is past the buffer region.
    D. the solution is at the half-equivalence point.

47. The function of a buffer is primarily to:

    A. lower the pH.
    B. lower the pOH.
    C. lock the pH close to 7.
    D. resist changes in pH.

48. When selecting an indicator, a student should select a compound for which:

    A. its equivalence point is close to the equivalence point of the titration.
    B. its half-equivalence point is close to the half-equivalence point of the titration.
    C. its half-equivalence point is close to the equivalence point of the titration.
    D. the effect of the indicator on the pH of the titration curve will be maximized.

49. Given the following reaction, which equation is true?

$$NH_3 \text{ (aq)} + H_2O \text{ (l)} \rightarrow NH_4^+ \text{ (aq)} + OH^- \text{ (aq)}$$

    A. $K_b = [NH_4^+][OH^-] / [NH_3]$
    B. pH = log $[H^+]$
    C. pOH = log $[OH^-]$
    D. $K_b = [NH_4^+][OH^-] / [NH_3][H_2O]$

50. A room temperature aqueous solution of NaF and $CH_3COO^-Na^+$ would most likely have a pH that:

    A. is near 7.
    B. is below 7.
    C. is above 7.
    D. cannot be determined without more information.

SECTION 5
THERMODYNAMICS AND KINETICS

Thermodynamics, thermochemistry, kinetics, and equilibrium make this upcoming section one of the more challenging ones on the whole MCAT. Nonetheless, you'll need to invest heavily in prepping this material, as these topics ends up getting a lot of cross-disciplinary treatment on the MCAT.

Things like the effect of Gibbs free energy, catalysts, and Le Châtelier's principle are key concepts not just in passages dealing strictly with general chemistry, but in many biology and biochemistry topics as well. The MCAT is likely to ask you about the effect of temperature on a reaction in glycolysis or the Krebs cycle, or the free energy change associated with peptide bond formation, and so on.

As such, you may benefit from completing this section and then immediately moving over to the Biology and Biochemistry Content Review book, and completing the bioenergetics chapters there. By doing that work back-to-back, you can help solidify the kind of interdisciplinary learning that the MCAT will reward.

CHAPTER 11
Thermodynamics

A. INTRODUCTION

In this chapter, the review will mainly focus on the laws of thermodynamics and their implications. The discussion includes concepts such as enthalpy, entropy, specific heat, heat capacity, Gibbs free energy, spontaneity of reactions, and related aspects. We have many ideas to discuss. So buckle up!

What is Thermodynamics?

In our busy modern life, we often forget about the fundamental aspects of today's life that make it so unique. Everyday we use machines and gadgets, big and small, which depend on some type of energy. We harvest the available energy and use it in many ways. But how is this done? We use natural energy sources such as coal, petroleum products, and nuclear energy. The question is, what are the fundamental principles regarding the harvesting of energy from these sources? It is by chemical reactions that we make use of the hidden energy available from these sources. What we learn from thermodynamics is the dynamics of energy (heat) transfer during chemical changes. In this chapter, we will review the various aspects of thermodynamics and the related principles.

B. THE FIRST LAW OF THERMODYNAMICS

According to the **first law of thermodynamics**, energy is neither created nor destroyed, which also implies that the total energy present in the whole universe is constant. Based on this law, we can say that the energy is just taken from one form and converted to another form. This is exactly what we are doing when we are burning fuels such as gasoline to get sufficient energy to run the internal combustion engine, or when we are using nuclear reactions to turn the turbines of a nuclear power plant to make electricity.

Basic Aspects of Thermodynamics

First, let's talk about internal energy. **Internal energy** of a substance is the total energy present in the particular quantity of that substance. For a chemical reaction or a physical change of reactants, the change in internal energy (ΔE) of the reactants is expressed as follows:

Change in internal energy,

ΔE = Final internal energy (E_{final}) − Initial internal energy ($E_{initial}$)

$$\Delta E = Q + W$$

Here, Q represents the heat and W represents the work done.

Based on the above equation, these conventions are followed:

> When heat is absorbed by a system, heat (Q) is positive.
> When heat is given off by a system, heat (Q) is negative.
> When work is done on a system, work (W) is positive.
> When work is done by a system, work (W) is negative.

C. ENDOTHERMIC AND EXOTHERMIC REACTIONS AND HESS'S LAW

The change in heat for chemical reactions at constant pressure is called **enthalpy change**, denoted by ΔH. The change in enthalpy (ΔH) of a reaction is represented as shown below:

$$\Delta H = H_{products} - H_{reactants}$$

If the reaction is **endothermic**, the change in enthalpy is positive. In an endothermic reaction, the enthalpy of the reactants is less than the enthalpy of the products. So the reaction is accomplished by supplying energy to the reaction. On the other hand, the change in enthalpy is negative if the reaction is **exothermic**. Energy is released in this case. Also it is worth remembering that in an exothermic reaction, the enthalpy of the reactants is greater than the enthalpy of the products. Hence, if we have the enthalpy data, we can predict whether the reaction is endothermic or exothermic.

Hess's Law

According to the **law of heat summation** put forth by Henri Hess, we can find the total enthalpy of a reaction by adding the enthalpy changes of the individual steps in a reaction. It doesn't really matter if the reaction occurs in many steps or in one step. As long as the enthalpy values that we sum up are correct, we will get the overall enthalpy change.

> *Law of heat summation: The total enthalpy of a reaction can be derived by adding the enthalpy changes of the individual steps in the reaction.*

Example 11-1

Calculate the ΔH of the reaction between HCl and fluorine, forming HF and chlorine. The enthalpies of the related reactions are also given.

$$2\ HCl\ (g)\ +\ F_2\ \longrightarrow\ 2\ HF\ (l)\ +\ Cl_2\ (g)$$

		ΔH
(Reaction 1)	$HCl\ (g)\ +\ 1/4\ O_2\ (g)\ \longrightarrow\ 1/2\ H_2O\ (l)\ +\ 1/2\ Cl_2\ (g)$	-37.1 kJ/mol
(Reaction 2)	$2\ HF\ (l)\ \longrightarrow\ H_2\ (g)\ +\ F_2\ (g)$	$+1200$ kJ/mol
(Reaction 3)	$H_2\ (g)\ +\ 1/2\ O_2\ (g)\ \longrightarrow\ H_2O\ (l)$	-285.8 kJ/mol

Solution:

	ΔH
$2\,HCl\,(g)\ +\ 1/2\,O_2\,(g)\ \longrightarrow\ H_2O\,(l)\ +\ Cl_2\,(g)$	$-\,74.2$ kJ/mol
$H_2\,(g)\ +\ F_2\,(g)\ \longrightarrow\ 2\,HF\,(l)$	$-\,1200$ kJ/mol
$H_2O\,(l)\ \longrightarrow\ H_2\,(g)\ +\ 1/2\,O_2\,(g)$	$+\,285.8$ kJ/mol
Overall reaction: $2\,HCl\,(g)\ +\ F_2\ \longrightarrow\ 2\,HF\,(l)\ +\ Cl_2\,(g)$	$-\,988.4$ kJ/mol

The individual reactions that are given have to be reversed if necessary, so that the sum of the sub-reactions will add up to the overall equation. Reaction 1 should be multiplied by 2. The second and third reactions should be reversed. This applies to the corresponding enthalpy values as well. That means, if the reaction is reversed the sign of the corresponding change in enthalpy should also be reversed. The enthalpy of the overall reaction is −988.4 kJ/mol.

D. THE SECOND AND THIRD LAWS OF THERMODYNAMICS

The Second Law of Thermodynamics

We learned how to predict the mode of a reaction in terms of whether the reaction will be endothermic or exothermic. In this section, we will explore the dynamics and the factors that influence the spontaneity of reactions. For that, we have to be familiar with the term "entropy."

Entropy (S) is the measure of how disordered a system is. The entropy is dependent on the prevailing conditions such as pressure and temperature. From the MCAT point view, the values of entropy and related aspects that you will be dealing with are at standard state. The standard state refers to 1 atm and 25°C.

Entropy of a system is the measure of disorder or randomness of the system.

Let's talk more about entropy. The higher the disorder is, the greater the entropy of that system. In terms of the phases of matter, think about which phases will have a higher entropy. We can generalize that the gas phase of a substance has higher entropy than its liquid phase, and the liquid phase has higher entropy than its corresponding solid phase. Thus, as the temperature increases the entropy increases. The change in entropy (ΔS) is equal to the final entropy minus the initial entropy.

$$\Delta S = S_{final} - S_{initial}$$

According to the **second law of thermodynamics**, there is an overall natural tendency toward disorder. You have to understand that we are talking about the overall entropy. Do not confuse this with the fact that we sometimes look at individual systems or reactions and categorize them as having either increasing entropy or decreasing entropy. But the overall entropy of all the events together is increasing.

Example 11-2

Predict whether the entropy is increasing or decreasing for the following change.

$$CO_2 \ (s) \longrightarrow CO_2 \ (g)$$

Solution:

The question asks whether the entropy of the system is increasing or decreasing for the above written equation. Your response should be that there is an increase in entropy. Why? As we discussed, the change in phase is the key aspect to watch here. Carbon dioxide is changing from its solid form to gaseous form. Hence, the randomness of the system is increasing. So the entropy is increasing.

Example 11-3

Predict whether the entropy of the system is increasing as the reaction given below goes to completion.

$$2 \ C_2H_2 \ (g) \ + \ 5 \ O_2 (g) \longrightarrow 4 \ CO_2 \ (g) \ + \ 2 \ H_2O \ (g)$$

Solution:

The reaction shown above is the combustion reaction of acetylene. This reaction is made use of in welding, commonly called the "acetylene torch." Tremendous amount of heat is liberated as a result of this reaction and is used for welding purposes. As you can see from the equation, the number of moles of the reactants is greater than the number of moles of the products. Thus, as the reaction proceeds, there is a decrease in the number of moles of gas. If you predicted a decrease in entropy, your answer is correct.

The exam will test your understanding of the **zeroth law of thermodynamics**. The zeroth law states that if two thermodynamic systems are each in thermal equilibrium with a third, then all three are in thermal equilibrium with each other. Any two systems are said to be in the relation of thermal equilibrium if they are linked by a wall permeable only to heat, and do not change over time.

The Third Law of Thermodynamics

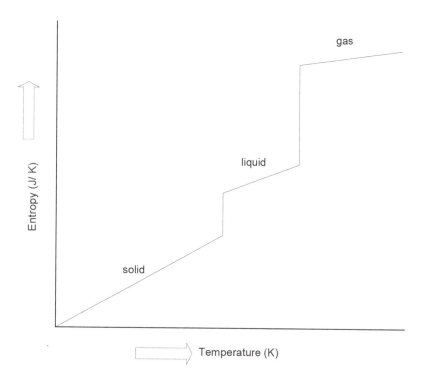

Figure 11-1 Entropy versus temperature

Let's state the **third law of thermodynamics**. The law states that pure and perfect crystalline substances have an entropy of zero at 0 kelvin. What does that mean? It means that a pure crystalline substance will have perfect order at absolute zero temperature. An increase in temperature will destroy this zero entropy. By looking at the graph (Figure 10-1), it is clear that an increase in temperature increases the entropy.

E. GIBBS FREE ENERGY

Free energy denoted by the letter G is a thermodynamic quantity, with which we can predict the spontaneity of a reaction. The change in free energy (ΔG) is related to the changes in enthalpy and entropy, and temperature as indicated by the equation:

$$\Delta G = \Delta H - T\Delta S$$

Here, ΔG represents the change in free energy, ΔH represents the change in enthalpy, ΔS represents the change in entropy, and T represents the temperature.

How Can We Predict Spontaneity?

On the basis of free energy change we can predict the spontaneity of a reaction. You should be able to manipulate the above mentioned equation, and once you have found the free energy change, you can do the prediction using the following guidelines.

If ΔG is positive, the reaction generally is nonspontaneous. If ΔG is negative, then the reaction is generally spontaneous. The changes in free energy and spontaneity depend on the change in enthalpy as well as the change in entropy. Besides these two important factors, the temperature at which the reaction takes place also plays a major role in dictating the spontaneity of reactions. Take a look at Table 10-1.

ΔG	ΔH	ΔS
Spontaneous at all temperatures	–	+
Spontaneous at low temperatures	–	–
Spontaneous at high temperatures	+	+
Nonspontaneous at all temperatures	+	–

Table 11-1

F. TEMPERATURE

We use the term temperature quite a lot in chemistry, but how can we define it? Students often get confused with the terms temperature and heat. Even though temperature and heat are related, they are not the same. Let us consider two objects that are at different temperatures; a hot object and a cold object. Let's say we kept them in close proximity for some time. The heat passes from the hot object to the cold one, until they reach equilibrium. So it is the heat (energy) that passes from the hot object to the cold one resulting in a change in temperature.

The common scales used to denote temperature are the Celsius scale and the Kelvin scale (K). The SI unit of temperature is actually kelvin (K). The Celsius and the Kelvin scales can be easily converted back and forth, and are related by the following simple relations:

$$K = {}^{\circ}C + 273.15$$
$$\text{or}$$
$${}^{\circ}C = K - 273.15$$

The other temperature scale that we are more familiar with is the Fahrenheit scale. Temperature denoted in degree Celsius can be converted to degree Fahrenheit using the following relation:

$$F = ({}^{\circ}C \times 1.8) + 32$$

You are expected to know these conversions for the MCAT.

CHAPTER 11 PRACTICE QUESTIONS

1. A bomb calorimeter is a device used to determine the energy changes associated with reactions. The calorimeter measures the heat absorbed or evolved during a reaction. Which of the following is true with respect to a bomb calorimeter?

    A. The measurements are done at constant volume.
    B. The measurements are not done at constant volume, because we cannot keep the volume constant.
    C. Theoretically work is done during the reaction in a bomb calorimeter.
    D. None of the above.

2. Consider the figure shown below in which ice is melted to form water. Which of the following is true regarding this conversion?

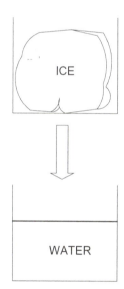

    A. Entropy is decreased.
    B. Entropy is increased.
    C. Entropy is not affected since the change does not constitute an actual reaction, but only a change in physical state of H_2O.
    D. Randomness is decreased.

3. If the change in free energy of a reaction is zero at constant temperature and pressure, what is true regarding such a system?

    A. The reaction is spontaneous.
    B. The reaction is nonspontaneous.
    C. The reaction is at its equilibrium state.
    D. Cannot be predicted.

4. Mercury sulfide can be converted to mercury by heating while exposed to air. What is probably true about this reaction?

$$HgS\ (s)\ +\ O_2\ (g)\ \longrightarrow Hg\ (l)\ +\ SO_2\ (g)$$

    A. The reaction is nonspontaneous.
    B. The reaction is endothermic.
    C. O_2 acts as the catalyst.
    D. None of the above can be ascertained without further data.

5. All the following are false regarding entropy, except:

    A. the entropy of a pure substance at 0 K is greater than 1.
    B. the entropy of a pure substance at 0 K is between 0 and 1.
    C. the entropy of a pure substance at 0 K is 0.
    D. the entropy of a pure substance at 0 K is a negative number.

CHAPTER 12
Kinetics and Equilibrium

A. INTRODUCTION

Different chemical reactions occur at different rates. Some reactions occur very fast, whereas some others take years and years to complete. A better understanding of chemical kinetics (the study of reaction rates) and equilibrium enables chemists to optimize the production of desirable products. This exploration of chemical kinetics has increased the understanding of biochemical pathways and other pharmaceutical endeavors. We will also discuss catalysts and their effects on reactions.

B. RATE OF REACTION

The rate of a reaction depends on many factors such as the concentration of reactants, the temperature at the time of the reaction, the states of reactants, and catalysts. The **rate of a reaction** is defined as the change of reactant or product concentration in unit time. If we were to define the rate of a reaction in terms of the reactants, we should define the rate as the rate of disappearance of reactants. If we were to define the rate in terms of the products formed, we should define it as the rate of appearance of products.

For further exploration of this concept, let's look at a hypothetical reaction. In the hypothetical representative reaction shown below, the small letters denote the coefficients of the corresponding capital letter reactants or products. In this reaction, A and B are reactants, and a and b their coefficients respectively. X and Y are the products, and x and y their coefficients respectively.

$$a \text{ A} + b \text{ B} \longrightarrow x \text{ X} + y \text{ Y}$$

For this reaction, we can represent the rate in terms of the disappearance of each reactant or appearance of each product. The numerators are the concentrations of either the reactant or the product, and Δt represents the elapsed time.

$$\text{Rate} = -\frac{\Delta[A]}{\Delta t}$$

We can also represent it in terms of reactant B. That looks the same as the rate in terms of concentration of A. In order to express it in terms of B's concentration, substitute the numerator with the concentration of B. The minus sign convention indicates that the rate is expressed in terms of the rate of disappearance (decreasing concentration) of the reactants.

$$\text{Rate} = -\frac{\Delta[B]}{\Delta t}$$

Also shown below are the representations of the rate in terms of the products:

$$\text{Rate} = \frac{\Delta[X]}{\Delta t} \qquad\qquad \text{Rate} = \frac{\Delta[Y]}{\Delta t}$$

Rate Law

Rate law is an expression that we can find experimentally, which relates the concentration of reactants and the rate of a reaction. Let's consider the same hypothetical equation:

$$a\,\text{A} + b\,\text{B} \longrightarrow x\,\text{X} + y\,\text{Y}$$

For this reaction, we can write the rate as follows:

$$\text{Rate} = k\,[A]^a\,[B]^b$$

Here, k is the rate constant,
a and b are the corresponding exponential values, and
[A] and [B] are the concentrations of reactants A and B.

Note that the rate constant and the exponents of a reaction are found experimentally. For questions related to finding the actual rate expression of a reaction, you will be given the relevant experimental data. We will look at some examples to familiarize ourselves with this concept.

We mentioned the exponent values (for this reaction, we represented them as m and n) in the rate law. Those exponents represent the order with respect to a particular reactant, or by adding all the exponents, you will get the overall order of the reaction. For our hypothetical reaction, the reaction order with respect to reactant A is m. The order with respect to reactant B is n. The overall order of the reaction is m+n. That is one way to determine the order of a reaction. Chemists categorize them as first order, second order, etc. You may have heard of zero order. In some reactions, even if a reactant appears in the balanced equation of a reaction, it may not appear in the experimentally found rate expression. The reason for this is that the particular reactant that does not appear in the rate expression has an exponent of 0. So the order with respect to that reactant is zero.

Example 12-1

From the given experimental data, determine the rate law of the hypothetical reaction indicated below:

$$\text{P} + 2\,\text{Q} \longrightarrow \text{PQ}_2$$

Experiment	Initial concentration of P	Initial concentration of Q	Initial Rate of product formation
1	0.20 M	0.20 M	0.012 M/min
2	0.20 M	0.40 M	0.048 M/min
3	0.40 M	0.40 M	0.096 M/min

Solution:

The rate of the reaction will be of the form shown. Assume that the rate law of the reaction is:

$$\text{Rate} = k\,[\,P\,]^m\,[\,Q\,]^n$$

The plan is to find out the actual values of m and n from the given data. Let's do it step by step.

Look at the given experimental data. If we compare Experiments 1 and 2, we can see that the concentration of Q is doubled in Experiment 2. But the concentration of P is kept constant. With these changes, we see the quadrupling of the rate. That means the exponent of Q is 2. At this point we can rewrite the rate law as follows:

$$\text{Rate} = k\,[\,P\,]^m\,[\,Q\,]^2$$

Now compare Experiments 2 and 3. Here the concentration of Q is kept constant, but the concentration of P is doubled. The rate is doubling because of this change. So the exponent of P is 1. We can now write the completed rate law of the reaction.

$$\text{Rate} = k\,[\,P\,]\,[\,Q\,]^2$$

C. TRANSITION STATE

From our earlier discussions, we know that exothermic reactions release energy and endothermic reactions consume energy. Here, we will plot the potential energy diagrams of exothermic and endothermic reactions. Before we do that, we will discuss the concept of a transition state. Consider the hypothetical reaction shown below:

$$A + B \longrightarrow X + Y + \text{heat energy}$$

Can you say what type of reaction this is? It is an exothermic reaction. For reactions to proceed, there should be breaking of bonds and formation of bonds. For many reactions, the stability barrier that originally made the reactant molecules stable should be overcome. This is achieved by the formation of an energy-state that has higher energy than the reactants and the products. This high-energy state is often referred to as a **transition state**. These transition states have a relatively short life span, and once this highly unstable transition state is formed, it quickly disintegrates to form the products. For a reaction to reach this transition energy level, a certain amount of energy is required. This energy is called the **activation energy** or the energy of activation.

In the diagram (Figure 12-1), the activation energy depicted in both (a) and (b) are for the forward reactions.

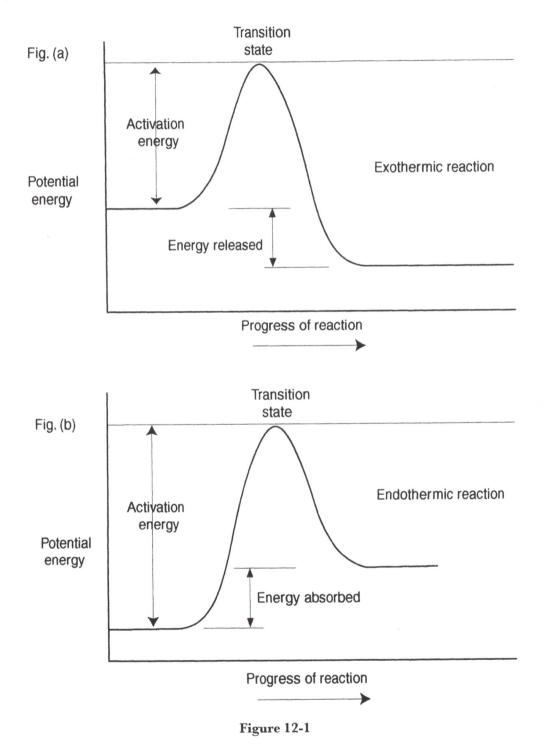

Figure 12-1

D. TEMPERATURE EFFECTS

The rate of a reaction depends on the prevailing temperature. Hence, the rate law is dependent on the temperature at which the reaction takes place. The reactants must attain a high energy form (transition state) in order for the reaction to occur. For this, the activated reactive species must collide (with feasible orientation) with each other with a minimum kinetic energy which is greater than that of the reactants. This kinetic energy depends on the temperature of the system in which the reaction takes place. At a particular temperature, some of the reactants will attain the activation energy to undergo the reaction. If we increase the temperature, more reactant molecules will attain this energy. More reactants attaining the required energy level means more reaction is taking place.

A mathematical relationship was introduced by Arrhenius. The expression relating the rate constant and the energy of activation is:

$$k = Ae^{-E_a/RT},$$

where k is the rate constant of the reaction,
E_a is the activation energy,
R is the gas constant (8.31 J/mol•K), and
T is the temperature.

There is no need to memorize this equation, but you should understand how to work with the equation conceptually.

E. CATALYSTS

We all have heard of catalysts. In lay terms we know that catalysts speed up reactions. But the question is how do they accomplish this? Consider the formal definition of a catalyst.

A catalyst is a chemical substance that can increase the rate of a reaction. Even if the catalyst is involved in the reaction, by the end of the reaction you will get the catalyst intact. In other words, the catalyst retains its identity. If a substance changes its identity and does not have the original nature after the reaction has occurred, it is not a catalyst, but a reactant.

As we said earlier, the **activation energy** is the minimum energy required by the reactants to reach the transition state. A catalyst lowers the activation energy of a reaction. Thus it provides a lower energy pathway for the reaction to occur. So the transition state bump in the potential energy diagram (see Figure 12-2) is lowered in a catalyzed reaction, compared to the corresponding uncatalyzed reaction.

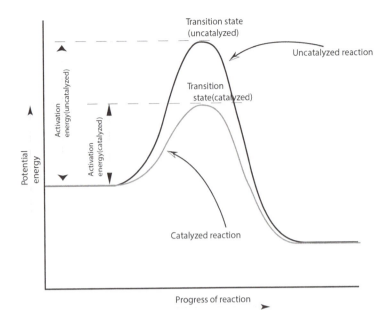

Figure 12-2

Catalysts are often classified on the basis of the phases (solid, liquid, and gas) in which they exist during a chemical reaction. If a catalyst exists in the same phase as the reactants of a reaction, then it is called a homogeneous catalyst. If a catalyst's phase is different from that of the reactants of a reaction, then it is called a heterogeneous catalyst.

F. EQUILIBRIUM

Many reactions are reversible. **Reversible reactions** are reactions in which there are both forward and backward reactions. Consider an experiment in which two reactants have been mixed. At first, the reaction proceeds with considerable rate in the forward direction (forward reaction favored). Before the reaction goes on to completion, the backward reaction takes place. Then again the forward reaction takes place, followed by the backward reaction and so on. These uneven back-and-forth directional changes take place until the reaction mixture reaches the equilibrium. At the equilibrium, the rate will be the same for both forward and backward reactions.

The Equilibrium Constant

We already talked about the rate of a reaction and its general expression. For reactions involving simple one-step mechanisms, we can easily write the rates of forward and backward reactions. Examine a one-step hypothetical reaction represented by the equation (balanced) given below:

$$a\,\text{A} + b\,\text{B} \longrightarrow c\,\text{C} + d\,\text{D}$$

The **equilibrium constant** of a reversible reaction is equal to the ratio of the product of the concentrations of the products raised to their corresponding coefficients, to the product of the concentrations of the reactants raised to their corresponding coefficients. Keep in mind that the coefficients are taken from the balanced equation. To further clarify this concept, take a look at the mathematical expression for equilibrium constant (K_c) can be calculated as:

$$K_c = [C]^c[D]^d \ / \ [A]^a[B]^b$$

The best way to find out the equilibrium constant of a particular reaction at a given condition is to do it experimentally. Equilibrium constant depends on temperature, and hence it differs with change in temperature. You should also ask yourself this question. Does the initial concentration of the reactants dictate the equilibrium constant? The answer is no.

We can also explore the meaning of equilibrium constant in terms of forward and backward reactions. A small value (less than one) for the equilibrium constant indicates that the forward reaction is not favored. A value greater than one for the equilibrium constant indicates that the forward reaction is favored.

Factors that Affect Equilibrium

The equilibrium of a reaction is affected by factors such as changes in concentration, pressure, and temperature. The likely resulting changes in equilibrium can be predicted on the basis of Le Châtelier's principle which can be stated as follows:

If we change the conditions (factors such as the ones mentioned above) of a reaction system in equilibrium, the system will shift in such a way as to reduce the imbalance caused by the stress. This is Le Châtelier's principle.

Based on this principle, we will look at some of the factors that affect the equilibrium of reactions.

Effect of Temperature

What is your first instinct when you think of a reaction scenario in which the temperature is changed? It is true that the reaction rate will change. The forward and reverse rates for almost all reactions will increase with increasing temperatures. But, not all reaction rates of all reactions invariably favor the forward reaction at higher temperatures. Though many reactions speed up with the increase in temperature, consider the reaction given below:

$$N_2 \ (g) \ + \ 3 \ H_2 \ (g) \ \rightleftharpoons \ 2 \ NH_3 \ (g) \ + \ heat$$

The reaction between nitrogen and hydrogen to give ammonia is an exothermic reaction. The reaction produces heat energy during the forward reaction. For this reaction at equilibrium, if we increase the temperature, it will only facilitate the backward reaction. Now we will consider another reaction.

$$C \ (s) \ + \ H_2O \ (g) \ + \ heat \ \rightleftharpoons \ CO \ (g) \ + \ H_2 \ (g)$$

For this reaction, we are supplying heat. So what kind of reaction is it? It is an endothermic reaction. If we subject this reaction in equilibrium to an increase in temperature, the forward reaction will be favored. We can generalize our observations as follows:

An increase in temperature favors endothermic reactions. An increase in temperature decreases the reaction rate, if the reaction is exothermic.

Effect of Pressure

The effects of pressure are significant in reactions involving gases. Think about what happens when we increase the partial pressure of reactants or products in an equilibrium. When the pressure is increased, the equilibrium no longer exists. Consider the reaction given below.

$$N_2 \, (g) \;+\; 3 \, H_2 \, (g) \;\rightleftharpoons\; 2 \, NH_3 \, (g)$$

The direction of reactions can be predicted based on Le Châtelier's principle. For the above reaction, if the pressure of the system is increased the forward reaction is favored. Why is the forward reaction favored? The reason is that the forward reaction will result in fewer moles of gas, thereby decreasing the strain caused by the increased pressure. This influence of pressure will not affect the reaction if the total number of moles of gaseous reactants and the total number of moles of gaseous products are equal, or if an increase in the pressure within a reaction vessel due to the addition of an inert gas does not influence the individual partial pressures of reactants and products. The influence of pressure is not seen with reactants or products which are either in their solid or liquid state because they are considered incompressible.

CHAPTER 12 PRACTICE QUESTIONS

1. Choose the correct equilibrium expression for the following reaction.

$$N_2\,(g) + 3\,H_2\,(g) \rightleftharpoons 2\,NH_3\,(g)$$

    A. $K = \dfrac{[\,NH_3]}{[\,N_2\,]\,[\,H_2\,]}$

    B. $K = \dfrac{[\,N_2\,]\,[\,H_2\,]^3}{[\,NH_3]^2}$

    C. $K = \dfrac{[\,N_2\,]\,[\,H_2\,]}{[\,NH_3]}$

    D. $K = \dfrac{[\,NH_3]^2}{[\,N_2\,]\,[\,H_2\,]^3}$

2. Based on the given data, what is the rate law of the following hypothetical reaction?

$$X + Y \rightarrow Z$$

Concentration of X	Concentration of Y	Initial Rate
0.02	0.02	2.0×10^{-5}
0.02	0.04	4.0×10^{-5}
0.04	0.04	1.6×10^{-4}
0.04	0.08	3.2×10^{-4}

    A.   Rate = k [Y]
    B.   Rate = k [X] [Y]
    C.   Rate = k [X]^2 [Y]
    D.   Rate = k [X] [Y]^2

3. Which of the following factors will affect the rate of a reaction?

    A.   The concentration of reactants
    B.   Temperature
    C.   The state of reactants
    D.   All the above

4. Figure 1 represents the potential energy diagram of a reaction. Pick the true statement regarding this reaction.

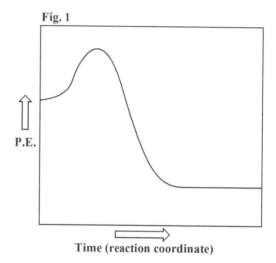

Fig. 1

P.E.

Time (reaction coordinate)

    A.   The reaction requires no activation energy, since it is spontaneous.
    B.   There is a net absorption of energy by the reaction.
    C.   Reactants have lower energy than that of the products.
    D.   None of the above.

5. Which of the following is true regarding catalysts?

    A.   Catalysts can change the rate of a reaction.
    B.   Catalysts increase the activation energy.
    C.   Catalysts are often consumed completely by the reactants.
    D.   All the above.

Questions 6-13 are based on the following passage.

Passage 1

At this point of advancements in science, chemists have a good understanding of the kinetics of reactions. They can predict the effects of changes in pH, temperature, and concentration in chemical reactions.

In a cylinder, there is a reaction mixture of hydrogen and iodine. The hydrogen and the iodine react to form hydrogen iodide.

$$H_2 (g) + I_2 (g) \rightarrow 2HI (g) \qquad \text{(Reaction 1)}$$

The industrial production of ammonia is done by a process called Haber process. The reaction occurs as shown below, and is usually done in the presence of an iron catalyst.

$$N_2 (g) + 3H_2 (g) \rightarrow 2 NH_3 (g) \qquad \text{(Reaction 2)}$$

$$\Delta H = -92 \text{ kJ}$$

6. If the reverse reaction of Reaction 1 is endothermic, what is the sign of ΔH of the reaction in which HI is on the product side?

    A. Positive
    B. Negative
    C. Neither positive nor negative, because the reaction is reversible
    D. Cannot be predicted, because more data is required regarding the individual enthalpy values

7. Which of the following is most likely to occur, if we remove H_2 from the reaction mixture in Reaction 1?

    A. The reaction will proceed to the right.
    B. The reaction will suddenly reach equilibrium.
    C. The reaction will proceed to the left.
    D. No apparent effect will be observed.

8. If the pressure applied to Reaction 1 is decreased, what is the most likely effect?

    A. The equilibrium will shift toward the left.
    B. The equilibrium will shift toward the right.
    C. There will be no effect on the equilibrium.
    D. The volume of the system will decrease.

9. A student researcher conducted experiments on the effects of changes in the conditions on reactions. The student did the experiments with Reaction 2, by increasing the pressure in the cylinder where the reaction mixture was present. Which of the following are completely true regarding the experiment?

    I. The reaction will shift toward the right, because there are more moles of gas on the product side.
    II. The reaction will shift toward the left, because there are more moles of gas on the reactant side.
    III. The reaction will have increased production of ammonia, because there are more moles of gas on the reactant side.

    A. I only
    B. II only
    C. III only
    D. II and III only

10. Which of the following best explains the theory behind the predictions of the effects of increasing the concentrations of reactants or products in a reaction system?

    A. Dalton's law
    B. Markovnikov's principle
    C. De Broglie principle
    D. Le Châtelier's principle

11. If 70 g of nitrogen is reacted with hydrogen, how many grams of ammonia will be produced ? (The weight of hydrogen used = 10 g)

    A.   42.5 g
    B.   57 g
    C.   85 g
    D.   17 g

12. In Reaction 2 for the production of ammonia from nitrogen and hydrogen, what is most likely to be true about entropy?

    A.   Entropy increases and is positive
    B.   Entropy decreases and is negative
    C.   Entropy increases and is negative
    D.   Entropy increases and is equal to zero

13. In the Haber process for the production of ammonia, what can you say about the spontaneity of the reaction with the available information in the passage?

    A.   The reaction is definitely spontaneous.
    B.   The reaction is definitely nonspontaneous.
    C.   The reaction is endothermic, and definitely spontaneous.
    D.   Cannot be predicted accurately without further data.

Section 5

CONTENT REVIEW PROBLEMS

1. The first law of thermodynamics asserts that:

    A.   the entropy of the universe is always increasing.
    B.   a crystal lattice with zero vibrational energy is at 0 K.
    C.   matter is conserved.
    D.   energy is conserved.

2. A system starts with 100 J of internal energy. It then does 50 J of work and 150 J of heat flows into it. The system now has:

    A.   -100 J
    B.   150 J
    C.   200 J
    D.   300 J

3. A system starts with 100 J of internal energy. It then does 100 J of work and 50 J of heat flows into it. The system now has:

    A.   -50 J
    B.   50 J
    C.   150 J
    D.   250 J

4. A reaction in which heat is given off as a product would have a:

    A. $\Delta G < 0$.
    B. $\Delta G > 0$.
    C. $\Delta H < 0$.
    D. $\Delta S > 0$.

5. A reaction in which heat is put in as a reactant would have:

    A. $\Delta G < 0$.
    B. $\Delta H > 0$.
    C. $\Delta H < 0$.
    D. $\Delta S > 0$.

6. A reaction which is spontaneous must have:

    A. $\Delta G < 0$.
    B. $\Delta H > 0$.
    C. $\Delta H < 0$.
    D. $\Delta S > 0$.

7. A reaction in which 2 moles of liquid and 1 mole of gas are converted into 1 mole of solid and 3 moles of gas would have:

    A. $\Delta G < 0$
    B. $\Delta H > 0$
    C. $\Delta S < 0$
    D. $\Delta S > 0$

8. In a given reaction, the $\Delta H = -674$ kJ/mole. If the stoichiometric coefficients of the reaction are doubled, the new ΔH would be:

    A.   -337 kJ
    B.   -674 kJ
    C.   -1348 kJ
    D.   +674 kJ

9. The second law of thermodynamics asserts that:

    A.   the entropy of the universe is always increasing.
    B.   a crystal lattice with zero vibrational energy is at 0 K.
    C.   matter is conserved.
    D.   energy is conserved.

10. A phase change of sublimation would involve:

    A.   a decrease in enthalpy.
    B.   an increase in entropy.
    C.   a Gibbs free energy that is always negative.
    D.   high pressure and high temperature.

11. The third law of thermodynamics states that:

    A. $S_{universe}$ is always increasing.
    B.   a crystal lattice with zero vibrational energy and zero entropy is at 0 K.
    C.   matter is conserved.
    D.   energy is conserved.

12. Which of the following describes a process that is always spontaneous?

    A. ΔH is negative, ΔS is negative
    B. ΔH is positive, ΔS is negative
    C. ΔH is negative, ΔS is positive
    D. ΔH is positive, ΔS is positive

13. Which of the following describes a process that is spontaneous at high temperatures?

    A. ΔH is negative, ΔS is negative
    B. ΔH is positive, ΔS is negative
    C. ΔH is negative, ΔS is positive
    D. ΔH is positive, ΔS is positive

14. Which of the following describes a process that is never spontaneous?

    A. ΔH is negative, ΔS is negative
    B. ΔH is positive, ΔS is negative
    C. ΔH is negative, ΔS is positive
    D. ΔH is positive, ΔS is positive

15. Which of the following describes a process that is spontaneous at low temperatures?

    A. ΔH is negative, ΔS is negative
    B. ΔH is positive, ΔS is negative
    C. ΔH is negative, ΔS is positive
    D. ΔH is positive, ΔS is positive

16. Which of the following is closest to the temperature at which °F and °C are equal?

    A. -80
    B. -40
    C. 0
    D. 100

17. A sample of solid has its temperature increased from 50°C to 150°C. In Kelvin, the temperature went from:

    A. 50 K to 150 K
    B. 323 K to 423 K
    C. 223 K to 323 K
    D. -223 K to -123 K

For questions 18-25 consider the following reactions:

1) $CH_4(g) + 2O_2(g) \rightarrow CO_2(g) + 2H_2O(l)$
$\Delta H = -900$ kJ/mol

2) $C(s) + O_2(g) \rightarrow CO_2(g)$
$\Delta H = -400$ kJ/mol

3) $H_2(g) + 1/2\, O_2(g) \rightarrow H_2O(l)$
$\Delta H = -300$ kJ/mol

18. Which of the listed reactions are exothermic?

    A. 2 only
    B. 1 and 2 only
    C. 2 and 3 only
    D. 1, 2, and 3

19. Reaction 1 involves what change in entropy?

    A. Increase
    B. No change
    C. Decrease
    D. Cannot be determined without knowing the temperature

20. Reaction 3 is:

    A. always spontaneous.
    B. never spontaneous.
    C. spontaneous at low temperatures.
    D. spontaneous at high temperatures.

21. Calculate the ΔH for the following reaction:
$2CO_2(g) + 4H_2O(l) \rightarrow 2CH_4(g) + 4O_2(g)$

    A. -1800 kJ
    B. -900 kJ
    C. +900 kJ
    D. +1800 kJ

22. Calculate the ΔH for the following reaction:
$CH_4(g) + 2O_2(g) + C(s) + O_2(g) \rightarrow 2CO_2(g) + 2H_2O(l)$

    A. -400 kJ
    B. -900 kJ
    C. -1300 kJ
    D. $+500$ kJ

23. Calculate the ΔH for the following reaction:
$C(s) + O_2(g) + H_2O(l) \rightarrow CO_2(g) + H_2(g) + 1/2\ O_2(g)$

    A. $-100\ kJ$
    B. $-700\ kJ$
    C. $+100\ kJ$
    D. $+700\ kJ$

24. What is the $\Delta H°_{formation}$ of water?

    A. $-300\ kJ$
    B. $-150\ kJ$
    C. $+300\ kJ$
    D. $+600\ kJ$

25. What is the ΔH of the following reaction:
$C(s) + 2H_2(g) \rightarrow CH_4(g)$

    A. $+200\ kJ$
    B. $-100\ kJ$
    C. $-1300\ kJ$
    D. $-1600\ kJ$

26. Given the following hypothetical reaction:
$A_2B\ (aq) + C(s) \rightarrow 2A^+(aq) + BC(s)$
the rate law is:

    A. $R = k[A^+]^2[BC]$
    B. $R = k[A_2B][C]$
    C. $R = k[A^+]^2 / [A_2B]$
    D. Unknown

Use the following hypothetical reaction and rate data provided to answer questions 27 – 31.
$A_2B\ (aq) + C(s) \rightarrow 2A^+(aq) + BC(s)$

	$[A_2B]_1$	$[C]_1$	R_1
1	0.3	0.2	6×10^{-5}
2	0.6	0.2	1.2×10^{-4}
3	0.9	0.4	7.2×10^{-4}

27. With respect to $[A_2B]$ the reaction is:

    A. zero order.
    B. first order.
    C. second order.
    D. third order.

28. The overall reaction is:

    A. zero order.
    B. first order.
    C. second order.
    D. third order.

29. With respect to $[C]$ the reaction is:

    A. zero order.
    B. first order.
    C. second order.
    D. third order.

30 The value of k is:

    A. 1.5×10^{-3}.
    B. 5×10^{-3}.
    C. 2.5×10^{-2}.
    D. 6×10^{-2}.

31. The units for k are:

    A. $L^2 / mol^2 \cdot s$
    B. $L / mole \cdot s$
    C. $1 / M \cdot s$
    D. s / M^2

32. The activation energy is:

    A. the energy required to reach the transition state.
    B. the energy difference between the reactants and the products.
    C. only positive in an endothermic reaction.
    D. only positive in an exothermic reaction.

33. The Arrhenius equation is usually expressed as:
$k = Ae^{-Ea/RT}$. Given this equation, if the temperature increases,

    A. the reaction rate decreases for an exothermic reaction.
    B. the value of $e^{-Ea/RT}$ increases.
    C. the equilibrium position of the reaction shifts to the right.
    D. the reaction rate decreases.

34. The Arrhenius equation is usually expressed as: $k = Ae^{-Ea/RT}$. Given this equation, if the E_a increases,

    A.   the reaction rate decreases only for an exothermic reaction.

    B.   the value of $e^{-Ea/RT}$ increases.

    C.   the equilibrium position of the reaction shifts to the right.

    D.   the reaction rate decreases.

35. Adding a catalyst to an exothermic reaction at equilibrium will:

    A.   have no effect on activation energy.

    B.   speed up the reaction rate only if the temperature remains constant.

    C.   speed up the reaction rate.

    D.   have no effect.

36. A catalyst will:

    A.   only reduce the activation energy of the forward reaction, not shift the equilibrium position.

    B.   shift the equilibrium position of a reaction to the left.

    C.   reduce the activation energy of the reverse reaction.

    D.   shift the equilibrium position of a reaction to the right.

37. What is the equilibrium expression for the following hypothetical reaction?
$A_2B(g) + C(s) \rightarrow A(l) + BC(g) + B(g)$

    A. $R = k[A_2B][C]$

    B. $K_{eq} = [BC][B] / [A_2B]$

    C. $K_{eq} = [A][BC][B] / [A_2B][C]$

    D.   It must be experimentally determined.

38. What is the equilibrium expression for the following hypothetical reaction?
$2XY_2(aq) + E_2F(l) + Q(s) \rightarrow 2XY_2E(s) + FQ(aq)$

    A. $K_{eq} = [FQ] / [XY_2]^2$

    B. $K_{eq} = [XY_2E]^2[FQ] / [XY_2]^2[E_2F][Q]$

    C. $K_{eq} = k[XY_2]^2[E_2F][Q]$

    D.   It must be experimentally determined.

For questions 39 – 50 use the following hypothetical reaction:

$A_2B(g) + 2CD(g) + F(s) \rightleftharpoons AFD_2(g) + ABC(g) + CF(s)$

$\Delta H = -300$ kJ/mol

39. What is the equilibrium expression for this reaction?

    A. $K_{eq} = [AFD_2][ABC][CF] / [A_2B][CD]^2[F]$

    B. $K_{eq} = [A_2B][CD]^2 / [AFD_2][ABC]$

    C. $K_{eq} = [AFD_2][ABC] / [A_2B][CD]^2$

    D.   It must be experimentally determined.

40. Before reaching equilibrium, this reaction is:

    A.   exothermic.

    B.   endothermic.

    C.   neither exo- nor endothermic.

    D.   both exo- and endothermic.

41. Before reaching equilibrium, in this reaction:

    A. $\Delta S > 0$.

    B. $\Delta S < 0$.

    C. $\Delta S = 0$.

    D.   It must be experimentally determined.

42. Before reaching equilibrium, this reaction is spontaneous:

    A.   always.

    B.   never.

    C.   at high temperatures.

    D.   at low temperature.

43. If the system is at equilibrium and more F(s) is added, the equilibrium will:

    A.   shift left.

    B.   shift right.

    C.   not shift.

    D.   cannot be determined.

44. If the system is at equilibrium and more $AFD_2(g)$ is added, the equilibrium will:

    A. shift left.
    B. shift right.
    C. not shift.
    D. cannot be determined.

45. If the system is at equilibrium and more $CD(g)$ is added, the equilibrium will:

    A. shift left.
    B. shift right.
    C. not shift.
    D. cannot be determined.

46. If the system is at equilibrium and the temperature is increased, the equilibrium will:

    A. shift left.
    B. shift right.
    C. not shift.
    D. cannot be determined.

47. If the system is at equilibrium and the pressure is decreased, the equilibrium will:

    A. shift left.
    B. shift right.
    C. not shift.
    D. cannot be determined.

48. If the system is at equilibrium and a catalyst is added, the equilibrium will:

    A. shift left.
    B. shift right.
    C. not shift.
    D. cannot be determined.

49. If the system is at equilibrium and the temperature is decreased, the equilibrium will:

    A. shift left.
    B. shift right.
    C. not shift.
    D. cannot be determined.

50. If the system is at equilibrium and the pressure increased while more $ABC(g)$ is added, the equilibrium will:

    A. shift left.
    B. shift right.
    C. not shift.
    D. cannot be determined.

This page intentionally left blank.

SECTION 6
ELECTROCHEMISTRY AND RADIOACTIVITY

Congratulations! You've made it to the final section of your MCAT general chemistry review. In this final section, we address the last two major topics included on the MCAT: electrochemistry and radioactivity.

These are both important topics on the MCAT, although the former is quite a bit more important than the latter. You certainly do need to be familiar with radioactivity, especially as it pertains to diagnostic technologies and lab techniques (e.g. radiolabeling molecules). But having said that, radioactivity is not as important as the other topics addressed so far.

By contrast, electrochemistry is critically important. The concepts contained in this chapter are relevant to biology topics such as the operation of the nerve cell and by extension to various neuron- and brain-based passages in the Psychological Foundations sections. Many students often come to the MCAT with a weak background in electrochemistry (my theory is that lots of students had a professor who would drop the lowest exam grade and since electrochem was the last test in the semester, students just don't bother studying for it). If you find yourself in that position, invest some extra time in the following chapter.

CHAPTER 13

Electrochemistry

A. INTRODUCTION

Electrochemistry is the study of chemical reactions that result in the production of electric current, and chemical reactions that occur when subjected to electric current. Electrochemical applications are part of everybody's day-to-day life. Energy storing batteries that we use for TV remotes, flashlights, automobiles are a few examples. Electroplating is another achievement among many others. In this chapter, our discussion will revolve around two types of electrochemical cells - the electrolytic cell and the galvanic cell.

B. ELECTROLYTIC CELL

In an electrolytic cell, electric current drives the chemical reaction. The chemical reaction involved in an electrolytic cell is nonspontaneous. Electric current is used to drive the reaction. This process is called **electrolysis** and hence the name, electrolytic cell. The reaction involves the transfer of electrons and thus it is a redox reaction. For further understanding of the functioning of an electrolytic cell, we will look at an example of an electrolytic cell involving the electrolysis of molten sodium chloride. Molten sodium chloride is a good conductor of electricity. The melting point of NaCl is around 800°C.

The cell contains molten sodium chloride into which two electrodes are immersed, as shown in Figure 13-1. One electrode is connected to the positive terminal of the battery, and the other is connected to the negative terminal of the battery. The electrode that is connected to the positive terminal of the battery is the anode. The other electrode is the cathode. **Reduction** occurs at the cathode, and **oxidation** occurs at the anode. When the current starts flowing the reaction starts, as described below:

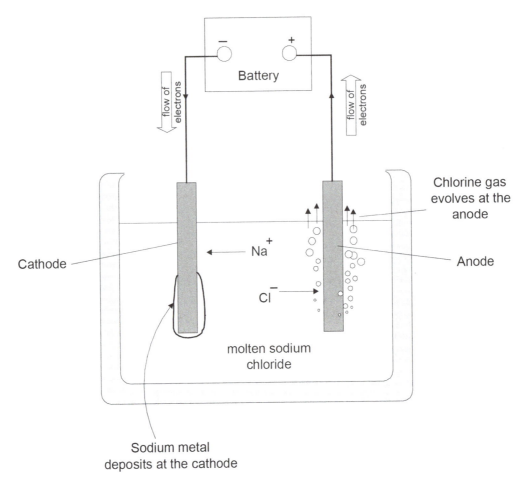

Figure 13-1 Electrolytic cell set up showing the electrolysis of molten NaCl

As the reaction proceeds, the sodium ions (Na^+) are reduced to sodium (Na) at the cathode, and the sodium metal is deposited at the cathode. On the other hand, the chloride (Cl^-) ions are oxidized at the anode forming chlorine gas (Cl_2). The half-reactions and the overall reaction are represented below:

$$Cl^-(l) \longrightarrow \tfrac{1}{2}Cl_2(g) + e^- \qquad \text{Anode}$$

$$Na^+(l) + e^- \longrightarrow Na(l) \qquad \text{Cathode}$$

$$\overline{Na^+(l) + Cl^- \longrightarrow Na(l) + \tfrac{1}{2}Cl_2(g)} \qquad \text{Overall reaction}$$

C. FARADAY'S LAW

According to **Faraday's law**, the amount of substance that undergoes oxidation-reduction reaction at the electrodes is directly proportional to the amount of electric current that the reaction is subjected to. Faraday constant is equal to the charge of one mole of electrons, and is numerically equal to 96,500 coulombs. You probably remember coulombs from your physics undergraduate courses. The unit coulomb is related to the unit **ampere** (*SI* unit of current) that is discussed in your physics content review book.

$$\text{amperes x seconds} = \text{coulombs}$$
$$\text{current x time} = \text{charge}$$

D. GALVANIC CELL

A galvanic cell is also known as a voltaic cell. The major difference between an electrolytic cell and a galvanic cell is that the reaction in a galvanic cell is spontaneous, and the reaction produces electric current. The batteries that we use in TV remotes and flash lights are galvanic cells. Galvanic cells convert the stored chemical energy into electrical energy for usage.

A galvanic cell has two half-cells. Each half-cell consists of a metal electrode immersed in a solution containing the same ions. The two half-cells are connected by a wire as shown in Figure 13-2. As we mentioned earlier, the galvanic cell produces electric current. Thus the voltage developed can be measured by setting a voltmeter along the connecting wire, as seen in the figure.

Here, we will look at a cell setup which uses zinc and copper as the electrodes. In addition to the electrodes, the two containers which hold the appropriate solutions, and the connecting wire, there is a salt bridge which connects the two solutions. The **salt bridge** is usually dipped into the solutions of the two half-cells. It contains a gel in which an electrolyte is present. The electrolyte present in the salt bridge will neutralize the buildup of ionic charge in the cells; a buildup which will otherwise slow down and stop the reaction from proceeding.

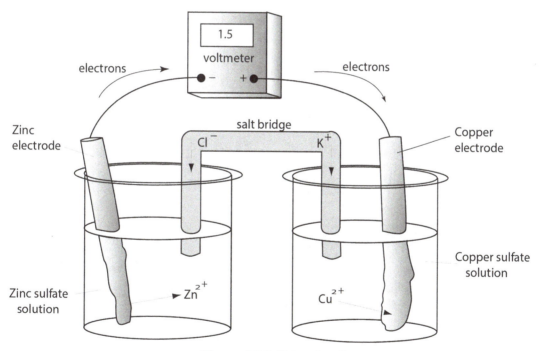

Figure 13-2 Galvanic cell

In the zinc half-cell, a zinc electrode is immersed in zinc sulfate solution. In the copper half-cell, a copper electrode is immersed in copper sulfate solution. The two electrodes are connected by a wire through which there will be flow of electrons resulting from the reaction. The half-reactions are shown below:

$$Zn\ (s) \longrightarrow Zn^{2+}\ (aq)\ +\ 2e^- \qquad \text{(Oxidation half-reaction)}$$

$$Cu^{2+}\ (aq)\ +\ 2e^- \longrightarrow Cu\ (s) \qquad \text{(Reduction half-reaction)}$$

$$Cu^{2+}\ (aq)\ +\ Zn\ (s) \longrightarrow Cu\ (s)\ +\ Zn^{2+}\ (aq) \qquad \text{(Overall reaction)}$$

The process of **oxidation** occurs at the **anode** and the process of **reduction** occurs at the **cathode**. So the first half-reaction (oxidation half-reaction) occurs at the anode, and second half-reaction (reduction half-reaction) occurs at the cathode. The overall reaction can be obtained by adding the two half reactions. Here, the zinc electrode is the anode, and the copper electrode is the cathode. In a galvanic cell, the anode is the negative electrode and the cathode is the positive electrode. As far as electron flow is concerned, the flow is always from the anode to the cathode.

Let's take a look at Figure 13-2 again. Notice the irregular edges of the electrodes. Why is that so? The reason is simple. As the reaction proceeds, zinc is stripped away from the zinc electrode, and thus it becomes thinner and thinner until the reaction stops (when it is at equilibrium). On the other hand, the copper electrode becomes thicker and thicker due to the deposition of metal copper on the copper electrode.

The half-reactions are often represented by the notation shown below. By convention, the oxidation reaction is written on the left of the symbol denoting the salt bridge, and the reduction reaction is written on the right side of the salt bridge symbol.

$$\underset{\text{Anode half-reaction}}{Zn \mid Zn^{2+}} \parallel \underset{\text{Cathode half-reaction}}{Cu^{2+} \mid Cu}$$

$$\parallel \text{ denotes salt bridge}$$

Note: See Table 13-2 at the end of this chapter for electrolytic versus galvanic cell comparison.

E. STANDARD ELECTRODE POTENTIALS

Before we discuss standard electrode potential, we will talk about electromotive force (emf). The **electromotive force** of a cell is the potential difference between the two electrodes. This can be measured using a voltmeter. The maximum voltage of a cell can be calculated using experimentally determined values called **standard electrode potentials**. By convention, the standard electrode potentials are usually represented in terms of reduction half-reactions. The standard electrode potential values are set under ideal and standard-state conditions (1 atm and 25°C). From the MCAT point of view, you can assume that the conditions are standard, unless stated otherwise. Table 1 shows a list of standard electrode potentials (in aqueous solution) at 25°C.

The standard electrode potential at the above mentioned standard state conditions is denoted by $E°$. For the MCAT, the values of the standard electrode (reduction) potentials will be given to you if you are required to solve such a question. Don't memorize those values. The standard electrode potentials are based on an arbitration with reference to a standard hydrogen electrode. The standard hydrogen electrode potential is considered to be 0 volt based upon the half reaction shown in table 13-1.

Table 13-1

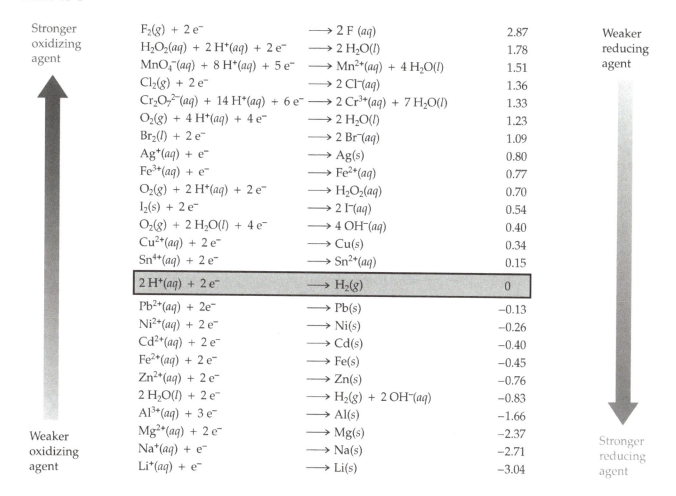

$F_2(g) + 2\,e^-$	$\longrightarrow 2\,F^-(aq)$	2.87
$H_2O_2(aq) + 2\,H^+(aq) + 2\,e^-$	$\longrightarrow 2\,H_2O(l)$	1.78
$MnO_4^-(aq) + 8\,H^+(aq) + 5\,e^-$	$\longrightarrow Mn^{2+}(aq) + 4\,H_2O(l)$	1.51
$Cl_2(g) + 2\,e^-$	$\longrightarrow 2\,Cl^-(aq)$	1.36
$Cr_2O_7^{2-}(aq) + 14\,H^+(aq) + 6\,e^-$	$\longrightarrow 2\,Cr^{3+}(aq) + 7\,H_2O(l)$	1.33
$O_2(g) + 4\,H^+(aq) + 4\,e^-$	$\longrightarrow 2\,H_2O(l)$	1.23
$Br_2(l) + 2\,e^-$	$\longrightarrow 2\,Br^-(aq)$	1.09
$Ag^+(aq) + e^-$	$\longrightarrow Ag(s)$	0.80
$Fe^{3+}(aq) + e^-$	$\longrightarrow Fe^{2+}(aq)$	0.77
$O_2(g) + 2\,H^+(aq) + 2\,e^-$	$\longrightarrow H_2O_2(aq)$	0.70
$I_2(s) + 2\,e^-$	$\longrightarrow 2\,I^-(aq)$	0.54
$O_2(g) + 2\,H_2O(l) + 4\,e^-$	$\longrightarrow 4\,OH^-(aq)$	0.40
$Cu^{2+}(aq) + 2\,e^-$	$\longrightarrow Cu(s)$	0.34
$Sn^{4+}(aq) + 2\,e^-$	$\longrightarrow Sn^{2+}(aq)$	0.15
$2\,H^+(aq) + 2\,e^-$	$\longrightarrow H_2(g)$	0
$Pb^{2+}(aq) + 2\,e^-$	$\longrightarrow Pb(s)$	−0.13
$Ni^{2+}(aq) + 2\,e^-$	$\longrightarrow Ni(s)$	−0.26
$Cd^{2+}(aq) + 2\,e^-$	$\longrightarrow Cd(s)$	−0.40
$Fe^{2+}(aq) + 2\,e^-$	$\longrightarrow Fe(s)$	−0.45
$Zn^{2+}(aq) + 2\,e^-$	$\longrightarrow Zn(s)$	−0.76
$2\,H_2O(l) + 2\,e^-$	$\longrightarrow H_2(g) + 2\,OH^-(aq)$	−0.83
$Al^{3+}(aq) + 3\,e^-$	$\longrightarrow Al(s)$	−1.66
$Mg^{2+}(aq) + 2\,e^-$	$\longrightarrow Mg(s)$	−2.37
$Na^+(aq) + e^-$	$\longrightarrow Na(s)$	−2.71
$Li^+(aq) + e^-$	$\longrightarrow Li(s)$	−3.04

Stronger oxidizing agent (↑) ... Weaker oxidizing agent

Weaker reducing agent ... Stronger reducing agent (↓)

Finding the emf of a Cell

The emf of a cell can be calculated from the standard electrode potentials of the half-reactions. In order to find the emf, we have to look at the two half-reactions involved in the reaction. Then, set up the two half-reactions so that when they are added we will get the net reaction. Once we have set the equations properly and assigned the proper potentials to those half-reactions, we can add the standard electrode potentials. A common mistake that students make is that they forget the fact that the standard electrode potentials are given in terms of reduction reactions. Redox reactions involve both oxidation and reduction. If one half-reaction is reduction, the other should be oxidation. So we must be careful about the signs of the half-reaction potentials, before we add the two half-reaction potentials to get the emf value. Do the next example.

Example 13-1

Calculate the emf of the cell, based on the following net reaction.

$$Cu^{2+}\,(aq) \; + \; Zn\,(s) \longrightarrow Cu\,(s) \; + \; Zn^{2+}\,(aq)$$

Standard Electrode Potentials of the half-cells

Half-reaction	E^o (volts)
$Zn^{2+}(aq) + 2e^- \longrightarrow Zn(s)$	$^-0.76$
$Cu^{2+}(aq) + 2e^- \longrightarrow Cu(s)$	0.34

Solution:

First, we have to write the half-reactions as indicated below.

$$Zn(s) \longrightarrow Zn^{2+}(aq) + 2e^- \qquad \text{(Oxidation half-reaction)}$$

$$Cu^{2+}(aq) + 2e^- \longrightarrow Cu(s) \qquad \text{(Reduction half-reaction)}$$

From Table 13-1, we can take the standard electrode potential values. The cell containing the copper electrode has a standard potential value of 0.34 V. For the other half-cell, the reaction is oxidation. Since the value given in the table is in terms of reduction half-reactions, we have to reverse the sign of the standard electrode potential given. The correct value for the oxidation half-cell is +0.76 V instead of –0.76 V. Now, you can add the two values to get the emf of the whole setup.

$$emf = 0.34 + 0.76 = 1.10 \text{ V}$$
$$\text{The answer is 1.10 V.}$$

	ELECTROLYTIC CELL	GALVANIC CELL
Spontaneity?	Nonspontaneous	Spontaneous
Cathode	Negative electrode	Positive electrode
Anode	Positive electrode	Negative electrode
Oxidation	Anode	Anode

Table 13-2 Electrolytic cell and Galvanic cell - a comparison

F. THE FREE ENERGY-EMF RELATION

The change in free energy (ΔG) is the maximum amount of energy that is available to do useful work. In an electrochemical cell, this free energy is equal to electrical work which is equal to the product of the number electrons, the Faraday constant, and the electrochemical cell's emf.

$$\Delta G^{\circ} = -nFE^{\circ}_{cell}$$

In this equation, n is the number of equivalents of electrons transferred in the reaction, F is the Faraday constant (96,500 coulombs), and E^{0}_{cell} (cell's emf). From this equation, we can deduce that if the emf is positive, the corresponding change in free energy (ΔG) will be negative. In other words, if the emf is positive the reaction is most likely to be spontaneous. On the other hand, if the emf of a cell is negative, the ΔG will be positive indicating a nonspontaneous reaction.

Example 13-2

Calculate the standard free energy change at 25°C for the redox reaction in Example 12-1. (Faraday constant = 96,500 coulombs)

Solution:

$$Cu^{2+}\ (aq)\ +\ Zn\ (s)\ \longrightarrow\ Cu\ (s)\ +\ Zn^{2+}\ (aq)$$

From the previous example, we know that the emf of this reaction is 1.10 V. The formula for ΔG in terms of the potential difference is:

$$\Delta G^{\circ} = -nFE^{\circ}_{cell} \qquad \text{(coulombs x volts = joules)}$$

Here, the number of electrons transferred is 2. This number is obtained by examining the balanced equation and evaluating the change in oxidation numbers. For example, copper ions with +2 oxidation state changed to copper (solid) with an oxidation state of 0. In other words, each half-reaction involves two electrons

$$\Delta G^{\circ} = -nFE^{\circ}_{cell} = -2 \times 96{,}500 \times 1.10\ V = -2.12 \times 10^{5}\ joules$$

Notice that the change in free energy is negative and this indicates that the reaction is likely to be spontaneous.

CHAPTER 13 PRACTICE QUESTIONS

1. Given below is the standard electrode potential $(E°)$ of the following redox reaction. Predict the most feasible event, if the reaction occurred spontaneously.

$$Zn^{2+} (s) + Sn (s) \longrightarrow Zn (s) + Sn^{2+}$$

$$E° = {}^-0.62 \ V$$

    A. Zn^{2+} was reduced.

    B.   Sn was oxidized.

    C.   Zn lost electrons.

    D.   Ether was used as the solvent medium.

2. What is the standard electrode potential of Reaction 1 given that:

Reaction 1

$$4Pb (s) \longrightarrow 4Pb^{2+}(aq) + 8e^-$$

    A. -0.13 V

    B. $+0.13$ V

    C. $+0.26$ V

    D. $+0.52$ V

3. The standard potential E^v is related to equilibrium constant K by the following relation:

$$-nFE° = -RT \ln K$$

In a reaction occurring at standard state conditions, if the concentrations of the products are greater than that of the reactants, which of the following is true?

    A. K is negative.

    B. E^v is negative.

    C.   The reaction is nonspontaneous.

    D.   None of the above

4. In an electrolytic cell, 5 A of current passes for about 3.5 minutes. The amount of electric charge equals:

    A.   17.5 coulombs.

    B.   85.7 coulombs.

    C.   1050 coulombs.

    D.   96500 x 5 x 3.5 coulombs.

Questions 5-10 are based on the following passage.

Passage 1

Table 1	
Half-reaction	E^0 (V)
$F_2 + 2\bar{e} \rightarrow 2\bar{F}$	+2.87
$Cl_2 + 2\bar{e} \rightarrow 2\bar{Cl}$	+1.36
$Ag^+ + \bar{e} \rightarrow Ag$	+0.80
$Cu^{2+} + 2\bar{e} \rightarrow Cu$	+0.34
$2H^+ + 2\bar{e} \rightarrow H_2$	0.00
$Pb^{2+} + 2\bar{e} \rightarrow Pb$	-0.13
$Ni^{2+} + 2\bar{e} \rightarrow Ni$	-0.25
$Cr^{3+} + 3\bar{e} \rightarrow Cr$	-0.74
$Zn^{2+} + 2\bar{e} \rightarrow Zn$	-0.76
$Mg^{2+} + 2\bar{e} \rightarrow Mg$	-2.38
$Na^+ + \bar{e} \rightarrow Na$	-2.71
$K^+ + \bar{e} \rightarrow K$	-2.92
$Li^+ + \bar{e} \rightarrow Li$	-3.05

By comparing standard reduction potentials, we can compare the reduction and oxidation powers of elements or ionic species. Some standard reduction potential values are given in Table 1.

5. Which of the following processes is most likely to be a spontaneous process?

    A.   Oxidation of copper
    B.   Reduction of chlorine
    C.   Oxidation of fluoride ion
    D.   Reduction of zinc ion

6. What is the overall cell potential for a cell which is formed with Ni/Ni^{2+} and Ag/Ag^+ half-cells?

    A.   +1.85 V
    B.   +0.55 V
    C.   −1.85 V
    D.   +1.05 V

7. In a galvanic cell, usually a salt bridge is used. What is the most likely purpose of this?

    A.   To conduct electricity
    B.   To prevent corrosion
    C.   To regulate electricity
    D.   To maintain neutrality in the half-cells

8. Which of the following will act as an oxidizing agent the most?

    A. Na^+
    B. Ag^+
    C. Cl_2
    D. Pb^{2+}

9. Which of the following species has the highest oxidation potential?

    A.   Cr
    B.   K
    C.   Cu
    D.   Ag

10. The process of corrosion is a redox reaction. Consider the rusting of the body panel of automobiles. Certain parts of the object that are undergoing corrosion act as if they were half cells. For the corrosion of iron, iron is changed to Fe^{2+} ions. Which of the following best represents the area where this change occurs?

    A.   Cathode
    B.   Anode
    C.   Both anode and cathode
    D.   Cannot be predicted without more data

CHAPTER 14

Radioactivity

A. INTRODUCTION

This is the last chapter in the general chemistry review. In this chapter, we will discuss the different aspects of radioactivity. Radioactivity is a nuclear phenomenon. It results from natural nuclear instability or externally induced nuclear instability. We will limit our discussion of nuclear chemistry to the basic aspects of radioactivity involving radioactive emissions such as alpha emission, beta emission, gamma rays, positron emission, and electron capture. We will also review other ideas such as the half-lives of radioactive substances and the mass-energy equation.

B. NUCLEAR STABILITY

The nucleus is not involved in normal chemical reactions. In radioactivity, it is the nucleus that undergoes the change. Nuclear forces are extremely strong forces that hold the nuclear particles together. These forces make the nucleus very stable. Remember that the protons are positively charged and can exert repulsive forces among themselves. It has been found out that there are certain predictable behavioral patterns in elements as the atomic number increases. As the atomic number increases, the neutron-to-proton ratio increases and as more and more protons are present in the nucleus, the stabilizing forces are not sufficient to keep the nucleus stable. Thus the stability of the nucleus decreases as the neutron-to-proton ratio increases.

C. RADIOACTIVE DECAY

Atoms with unstable nuclei can undergo radioactive decay to become atoms which are more stable than their parent atoms. In the process, different types of particles are emitted. We will discuss some of the important ones that you have to know from the MCAT point of view.

Alpha emission:

Alpha emission (α) is a low-penetrating emission. It is actually a helium nucleus and is often represented as

$$^4_2\text{He}$$

The format of alpha decay of is given below:

$$\begin{smallmatrix}A\\Z\end{smallmatrix}X \rightarrow \begin{smallmatrix}A-4\\Z-2\end{smallmatrix}Y + \begin{smallmatrix}4\\2\end{smallmatrix}\alpha$$

As you can see, the resulting atom has both mass number and atomic number changed. The atomic number decreases by 2, and the mass number decreases by 4.

Beta emission:

Beta particles (β^-) are emissions having medium level penetration. They are fast traveling electrons. As a result of beta emission, the resulting atom will have an increase in the atomic number by 1. There is no change in the mass number. In the process, there is also a proton formation from the neutron inside the nucleus, along with the electron formation. In the following example, thorium-234 decays to protactinium-234 by emitting a beta particle.

$$^{234}_{90}Th \longrightarrow {}^{234}_{91}Pa + {}^{0}_{-1}e$$

Positron emission:

Positron emission (β^+) is the positive counterpart of an electron emission. A positron has the exact mass of an electron, but has a positive charge. During this event, a proton is converted to a neutron and a positron. The product of a positron decay will have an atomic number less than that of the decayed atom by one unit. There is no change in mass number.

Electron capture:

As a result of electron capture, a proton is converted into a neutron. The electron is usually captured from the innermost shell of the atom. The atomic number of the product will be one less than that of the original atom. There is no change in mass number.

Gamma emission:

Gamma (γ) emissions or gamma rays, as they are commonly referred to, are highly penetrating and dangerous emissions. They are high frequency electromagnetic rays. Gamma rays travel at the speed of light. The resulting product atom has the same atomic and mass numbers as those of the parent atom from which the gamma rays are emitted. Gamma rays have no charge.

D. HALF-LIFE

All radioactive elements do not decay at the same pace. They have drastically different rates of decay. The radioactive decay time is expressed in terms of half-life period. The **half-life** of a radioactive substance is the time required for the decay of half the substance present in a sample of that substance. Regardless of the amount of a particular radioactive substance we have, it takes the same time (half-life) to complete the decay of half the number of nuclei in that sample.

The half-life of a radioactive substance is the time required for the complete decay of exactly half the amount of that substance.

Example 14-1

Calculate the amount of time (in years) it takes for the decay of 75% of a given sample of carbon-14. Carbon-14 has a half-life of approximately 5700 years.

Solution:

After the first 5700 years of decay, 50% of the original sample is left. After 5700 more years, 50% of that sample will have decayed, which means that there is now 25% of the original intact sample. This is the amount of time that the question is asking for. To be clear about our analysis, let's rephrase what we have said. We have 25% of the original sample left at this point. Thus the decay of 75% of the original sample is complete. So the answer is 5700 x 2 = 11400 years.

M = mass number of the parent nucleus undergoing decay.

Z = atomic number of the parent nucleus undergoing decay.

TYPE OF DECAY	MASS NUMBER OF THE DAUGHTER NUCLEUS	ATOMIC NUMBER OF THE DAUGHTER NUCLEUS
Alpha decay	M – 4	Z – 2
Beta⁻ decay	M	Z +1
Beta⁺ decay (Positron)	M	Z – 1
Electron capture	M	Z – 1
Gamma decay	M	Z

Table 14-1 Summary of changes in the parent nucleus due to different decay modes.

CHAPTER 14 PRACTICE QUESTIONS

1. Radium-226 can undergo radioactive decay to form Radon-222. Which of the following is the most likely type of particle that is emitted?

    A. Beta particle
    B. Alpha particle
    C. Gamma particle
    D. Positron

2. Consider the radioactive-decay equation given below. What is the most likely identity of X?

$$^{22}_{11}Na \rightarrow \ ^{22}_{10}Ne \ + \ X$$

    A. Alpha particle
    B. Beta particle
    C. Positron
    D. Neutron

3. Which of the following emissions travels at the speed of light?

    A. Gamma ray
    B. Beta particle
    C. Alpha particle
    D. Antineutrino

4. Which of the following has the highest penetrating power?

    A. Alpha particles
    B. Beta particles
    C. Gamma rays
    D. All the above have the same penetrating power

5. Substance X has a radioactive half-life of 12 years. How much time must have elapsed if only 9 grams is left from an original sample of 150 grams?

    A. 12 years
    B. 24 years
    C. 36 years
    D. 48 years

Questions 6-11 are based on the following passage.

Passage 1

In nuclear reactions, significant changes occur in the composition of the nuclei of the atoms involved. These reactions usually release tremendous amounts of energy. One of the reasons for the nuclear changes can be attributed to the stability of the nucleus.

The formation of the nucleus from the subatomic particles- neutrons and protons, results in the release of energy. The mass of these individual particles in the nucleus is greater than that of the actual nucleus that is formed. This loss of mass is due to the change of mass into energy. The energy-mass relation can be represented in terms of the equation:

$$E = mc^2,$$

where m represents the mass, and c represents the speed of light (3×10^8 m/s).

If the nucleus of an atom is not stable, it can get transformed into another nucleus. A plot of the number of neutrons versus the number of protons is often used to assess the stability trends of elements. If the number of protons and neutrons are equal, the nucleus is considered to be reasonably stable. As the atomic number increases, the trend changes.

Isotopes of elements having atomic numbers above ≈83 are unstable atoms. These unstable atoms can undergo disintegrations. The half-lives of some radio-active elements are shown in Table 1.

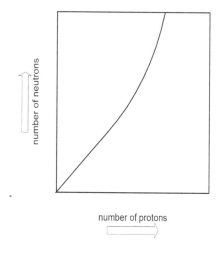

number of neutrons

number of protons

TABLE 1

atom	half-life
Carbon 14	5.73×10^3 years
Uranium 238	4.47×10^9 years
Radon 222	3.82 days
Radium 226	1.6×10^3 years
Krypton 89	3.2 minutes

6. If a sample of ^{226}Ra disintegrates to 3% of its original quantity, how many half-lives have passed?

    A. 2
    B. 3
    C. 4
    D. 5

7. ^{234}Th undergoes radioactive decay. If the thorium nucleus emitted a β-particle during its decay, what is the identity of the element that is formed?

    A. ^{234}Pa
    B. ^{234}Ac
    C. ^{234}Ra
    D. ^{232}U

8. All the following are true EXCEPT:

    A. α-particles are positively charged.
    B. β-particles are negatively charged.
    C. γ rays can be deflected by an electric field.
    D. There are radioactive emissions in which the mass number is not affected.

9. Which of the following is true regarding radioactivity?

    A. As the atomic number increases, eventually the neutron-proton ratio values become ≤ 1.
    B. As the atomic number increases, eventually the neutron-proton ratio values become ≥ 1.
    C. As the atomic number increases, eventually the proton-neutron ratio values become ≥ 1.
    D. None of the above

10. When a helium nucleus is formed, there is always some degree of loss of mass. If the loss of mass equals 3.1×10^{-5} kg during the formation of one mole of it, what is the binding energy?

    A. 3.1×10^{-5} J
    B. 1.8×10^{19} J
    C. 9.3×10^3 J
    D. 2.8×10^{12} J

11. The most probable set of particles that were given off during the series of nuclear changes from ^{232}Th to ^{224}Ra are:

    A. two alpha particles and one beta particle.
    B. one alpha particle and two beta particles.
    C. one alpha particle and three beta particles.
    D. two alpha particles and two beta particles.

Section 6

CONTENT REVIEW PROBLEMS

1. Which of the following is true of all electrochemical cells?

    A. Oxidation occurs at the anode.
    B. Oxidation occurs at the anode if the reaction is spontaneous.
    C. Oxidation occurs at the cathode.
    D. Electrons flow to the anode if the anode is the positive electrode.

2. Which of the following is true of all electrochemical cells?

    A. Current flows to the cathode.
    B. Electrons flow to the cathode.
    C. The cathode is positive if the reaction is non-spontaneous.
    D. Electrical current drives a chemical reaction.

3. Which of the following is true of all electrochemical cells?

    A. Cations migrate away from the cathode.
    B. Anions migrate away from the anode.
    C. Cations migrate to the cathode.
    D. Current flows to the cathode.

4. Which of the following is true of all electrochemical cells?

    A. Electrons flow from cathode to anode.
    B. Current flows to the electrode where reduction will be taking place.
    C. Cations migrate from cathode to anode.
    D. Current flows from cathode to anode.

5. Which of the following is true of all electrochemical cells?

    A. Anions migrate to the anode.
    B. Electrons flow from the electrode where reduction takes place to the electrode where oxidation takes place.
    C. Cations migrate to the anode from the cathode.
    D. Current flows from the electrode where oxidation takes place to the anode.

6. Which of the following is true of all electrochemical cells?

    A. Reduction is spontaneous and whether the cell is galvanic depends on the anode potential.
    B. Reduction occurs at the cathode
    C. Concentration of electrolytes increases as the reaction proceeds.
    D. None of the above.

7. Which of the following is true of all electrochemical cells?

    A. Electrons flow from cathode to anode.
    B. Oxidation occurs at the electrode to which electrons flow.
    C. Reduction occurs at the electrode to which current flows.
    D. None of the above.

8. Which of the following is true of a galvanic cell?

    A. Electrons flow to the anode.
    B. A voltmeter hooked up to a voltaic cell will give a negative reading.
    C. The anode is the negative electrode.
    D. The salt bridge allows the ions that form from one electrode to migrate to the other half-cell.

9. Which of the following is true of a galvanic cell?

    A. The cathode is negative.
    B. A spontaneous chemical reaction is used to generate current.
    C. Current flows to the cathode.
    D. Once equilibrium is established, the voltage will stabilize at its maximum value.

10. Which of the following is true of a galvanic cell?

    A. In the absence of a salt bridge, current will stop flowing sooner.
    B. The cathode is the negative electrode.
    C. Electrons flow from the electrode where oxidation takes place to the anode.
    D. The voltage asymptotically approaches infinity.

11. Which of the following is true of an electrolytic cell?

    A. The negative voltage means that reduction takes place at the anode.
    B. Current flows from anode to cathode.
    C. A non-spontaneous chemical reaction occurs due to applied voltage.
    D. The cell will not function if it does not obey Faraday's law.

12. Which of the following is true of an electrolytic cell?

    A. The emf of the cell is positive.
    B. The cations migrate from the cathode to the anode.
    C. A salt bridge is necessary to prevent the buildup of excessive positive charge in one of the half-cells.
    D. The anode is the positive electrode.

13. A cell is constructed with a E° of +1.5 V and 2 e^-/mole transferred. ΔG is: (use 10^5 for Faraday's constant)

    A. +300 kJ
    B. +300 J
    C. -300 J
    D. -300 kJ

For questions $14 - 17$ consider the following hypothetical reaction:

$3A^+(aq) + B(s) \rightarrow 3A(s) + B^{3+}(aq)$
$E^\circ = -2.5$ V

14. What is the Gibbs free energy change for this reaction? (use 10^5 for Faraday's constant)

    A. +750 kJ
    B. +250 kJ
    C. -250 kJ
    D. − 750 kJ

15. The reaction depicted is:

    A. spontaneous and a galvanic cell.
    B. spontaneous and an electrolytic cell.
    C. nonspontaneous and a galvanic cell.
    D. nonspontaneous and an electrolytic cell.

16. In the reaction depicted, a researcher constructs a system in which all of the stoichiometric coefficients have been doubled. This would create:

    A. $E^\circ = -1.25$ V
    B. $E^\circ = -2.5$ V
    C. $E^\circ = -5.0$ V
    D. $E^\circ = +2.5$ V

17. In the reaction depicted, a researcher constructs a system in which all of the stoichiometric coefficients have been doubled. This would create:

    A. $\Delta G = +375$ kJ
    B. $\Delta G = +750$ kJ
    C. $\Delta G = +1500$ kJ
    D. $\Delta G = -750$ kJ

For questions 18 – 25 use the following table of half reactions:

Half-reaction	E°
$Ag^+ + e^- \rightarrow Ag$	+0.80V
$Cu^{2+} + 2e^- \rightarrow Cu$	+0.34V
$2H^+ + 2e^- \rightarrow H_2$	0.00V
$Zn^{2+} + 2e^- \rightarrow Zn$	-0.76V
$Na^+ + e^- \rightarrow Na$	-2.71V

18. The reactions depicted in the table above are:

    A. reductions.
    B. oxidations.
    C. spontaneous.
    D. nonspontaneous.

19. What is the voltage of the following reaction:
$Ag \rightarrow Ag^+ + e^-$?

    A. +0.80 V
    B. 0.00 V
    C. -0.80 V
    D. Cannot be determined

20. What is the voltage of the following reaction:
$2 Zn^{2+} + 4 e^- \rightarrow 2 Zn$?

    A. -0.76V
    B. -1.52V
    C. +0.76V
    D. +1.52V

21. What is the voltage of the following reaction:
$2 Na \rightarrow 2 Na^+ + 2 e^-$?

    A. +2.71V
    B. +5.42V
    C. -2.71V
    D. -5.42V

22. The following reaction is:
$Ag^+ + e^- \rightarrow Ag$

    A. nonspontaneous.
    B. spontaneous.
    C. oxidation.
    D. only usable in a galvanic cell.

23. The following reaction is:
$2 Zn \rightarrow 2 Zn^{2+} + 4e^-$

    A. nonspontaneous.
    B. a reduction.
    C. only possible in a galvanic cell.
    D. characterized by a negative ΔG.

24. What is the voltage of the following reaction?
$2 Ag^+ + Cu \rightarrow 2 Ag + Cu^{2+}$

    A. +1.14V
    B. +0.46V
    C. -0.46V
    D. -1.14V

25. A student wishes to construct an electrolytic cell. He chooses the following as his anode half-reaction:
$Na \rightarrow Na^+ + e^-$

Which of the elements listed in the table could be used as the cathode?

    A. Silver
    B. Zinc
    C. Hydrogen
    D. None of them

26. Which of the following correctly characterizes α emission?

    A. The parent nucleus has its atomic number decrease by 2.
    B. The parent nucleus has its atomic mass increase by 4.
    C. The parent nucleus has its atomic number increase by 2.
    D. The emitted particle is a helium atom.

27. Which of the following correctly characterizes α emission?

    A. It would be the cause of a ^{14}C atom decaying into a ^{12}C atom.
    B. The emitted particle is a helium nucleus.
    C. The charge of the emitted particle is -2.
    D. It occurs after electron capture.

28. Which of the following correctly characterizes β⁻ emission?

    A. It is the result of electron capture.
    B. It creates an ionized molecule with a +1 charge.
    C. The atomic weight of the parent nucleus remains unchanged.
    D. The atomic number of the parent nucleus decreases by 1.

29. Which of the following correctly characterizes β⁺ emission?

    A. The atomic number of the parent nucleus changes by +1.
    B. It is the result of electron capture.
    C. The atomic weight of the parent nucleus changes by -1.
    D. It is the antiparticle of an electron.

30. Which of the following correctly characterizes γ emission?

    A. The particle emitted has a mass of 9.1 x 10^{-31}.
    B. The atomic number of the parent nucleus changes by +1.
    C. The atomic number of the parent nucleus changes by -1.
    D. The atomic number and the atomic mass of the parent nucleus remain unchanged.

For questions 31-35 consider the following theoretical decay:

Step 1: $^{209}Po \rightarrow Z + ^{205}Pb$
Step 2: $^{205}Pb + X \rightarrow ^{205}Tl$
Step 3: $^{205}Tl \rightarrow ^{4}\alpha + \beta^{+} + Q$
Step 4: $Q \rightarrow 2\ ^{4}\alpha + A$

31. In the decay mechanism above, what is A?

    A. ^{193}Pb
    B. ^{193}W
    C. ^{209}W
    D. ^{209}Pb

32. In the decay mechanism above, what is Q?

    A. ^{201}Au
    B. ^{201}Pt
    C. ^{209}Pt
    D. ^{209}Au

33. In the decay mechanism above, what is X?

    A. A positron
    B. An electron
    C. A photon
    D. A neutrino

34. In the decay mechanism above, what is Z?

    A. an electron
    B. a γ ray
    C. a β⁺ particle
    D. an α particle

35. What type of reaction is step 2?

    A. Positron decay
    B. β⁻ decay
    C. γ decay
    D. Electron capture

ORGANIC CHEMISTRY

SECTION 7

GENERAL CONCEPTS AND STEREOCHEMISTRY

The current version of the MCAT places organic chemistry in an odd position. On the one hand, organic chemistry is the least important science on the new test. It comprises something like a dozen questions on a 230 question test. And yet many of the foundational principles from organic chemistry will inform a lot of the biochemistry, general chemistry, and even biology tested on the exam.

As such, your preparation of organic chemistry should focus very heavily on a few areas: general principles (things like nomenclature, molecular structure, etc.), stereochemistry, and lab techniques. The MCAT has very strongly de-emphasized the memorization of lots and lots of "named" reactions and reaction mechanisms. As such, your college classes in orgo were probably taught in a way that didn't prepare you well for the MCAT – most undergrad orgo classes tend to bombard you with reactions which you memorize and then promptly forget the day after the test.

For the purposes of this review book, we have tried to strike a balance: we move briskly through the organic chemistry content, but we also still present to you all of the various classic reactions just so you have a chance to see them. Aside from the specific reactions mentioned in the outline at the very beginning of this book (see Chapter 1), you should NOT spend time memorizing the reactions you'll find throughout. Instead, look at *why* the reaction is proceeding the way it is, rather than simply memorizing *what* is happening.

Finally, in Chapter 1 we emphasized the importance of lab techniques. Arguably this is the most important part of any science review book for the MCAT. Most of your experience on Test Day will involve reading passages based on experiments, so you must be comfortable with the "language of the lab".

CHAPTER 15
General Concepts

A. INTRODUCTION

Organic chemistry is the study of carbon compounds. Carbon can form a wide array of compounds, because of its size and ability to form covalent bonds with other carbon atoms. In addition, carbon can form bonds with many other elements. This property of carbon increases the facility of forming multitudes of different compounds. The particular electronegativity of carbon also plays a key role in its versatility. In this chapter, we will review some of the fundamental aspects of carbon atom and the main types of hybridizations involving carbon compounds.

B. THE CARBON ATOM

Electrons are found in regions around the nucleus in an atom, and those regions are called **orbitals**. The orbitals can be defined and differentiated by size, shape, and orientation. **Valence electrons** are electrons that are found in the outermost shell. The carbon atom has four valence electrons. These valence electrons are involved in chemical reactions and bonding.

The electronic configuration:

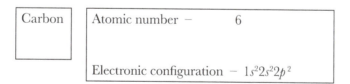

Carbon	Atomic number – 6
	Electronic configuration – $1s^2 2s^2 2p^2$

C. BONDING AND HYBRIDIZATION

Ionic bond – An Ionic bond is formed between an electropositive and electronegative atom (ion), or generally we can define it as an attractive force between a positive and a negative ion (e.g., KCl).

Covalent bond – A covalent bond is formed by the sharing of a pair of electrons between two atoms. Carbon compounds generally contain covalent bonds.

For a more detailed discussion of this topic see, chapter 5 in the general chemistry section of this book.

Orbital Hybridization

The six electrons of a carbon atom are distributed in the orbitals as follows:

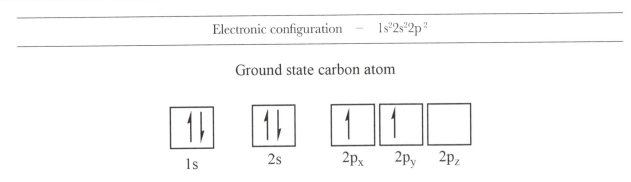

Electronic configuration $-$ $1s^2 2s^2 2p^2$

Ground state carbon atom

sp³ Hybridization

The carbon atoms of alkanes (e.g., methane, ethane) are sp^3 hybridized. In order to form the four bonds in methane, a carbon atom needs four half-filled orbitals. In order to have more free half-filled orbitals, the carbon atoms undergo hybridization.

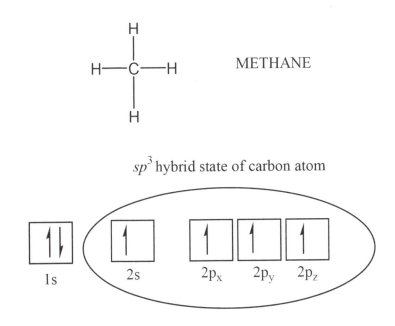

The hybridization results in one half-filled $2s$ orbital, and three half-filled $2p$ orbitals (a total of four half-filled orbitals). These unpaired electrons form the sp^3 hybridized carbon, which can form the four covalent bonds in the methane molecule. The four sp^3 hybrids are directed to the corners of a tetrahedron with bond angles of 109.5^0.

sp² Hybridization

In carbon-carbon double bonds, the carbons undergo another type of hybridization called sp^2 hybridization. In this hybridization, only one $2s$, and two $2p$ orbitals are involved. The C=C contains a sigma (σ) bond and a pi (π) bond. The pi bond is formed by unhybridized $2p$ orbital overlap. The three equal hybrids lie in an xy-plane with bond angles of 120°.

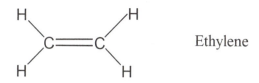

Ethylene

sp^2 hybrid state of carbon atom

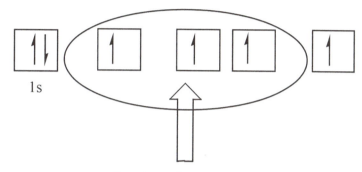

One 2s and two 2p orbitals

sp Hybridization

Yet another hybridization called *sp* hybridization exists in carbon-carbon triple bonds. An *sp* hybridized carbon atom is bonded only to two other atoms. In this type of hybridization, one 2s orbital and one 2p orbital are involved. A carbon-carbon triple bond contains one sigma bond and two pi bonds.

HC $\equiv$ CH   Acetylene

sp hybrid state of carbon atom

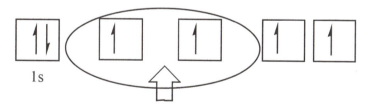

One 2s and one 2p orbitals

Resonance

Resonance is an important aspect in organic chemistry. Though we represent definite Lewis structures of molecules, in reality the electrons are not localized. They are shared and delocalized by the atoms in a molecule to have the most stable electron distribution. This is called **resonance**. Resonance promotes stability.

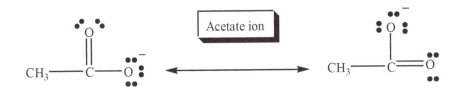

D. FUNCTIONAL GROUPS

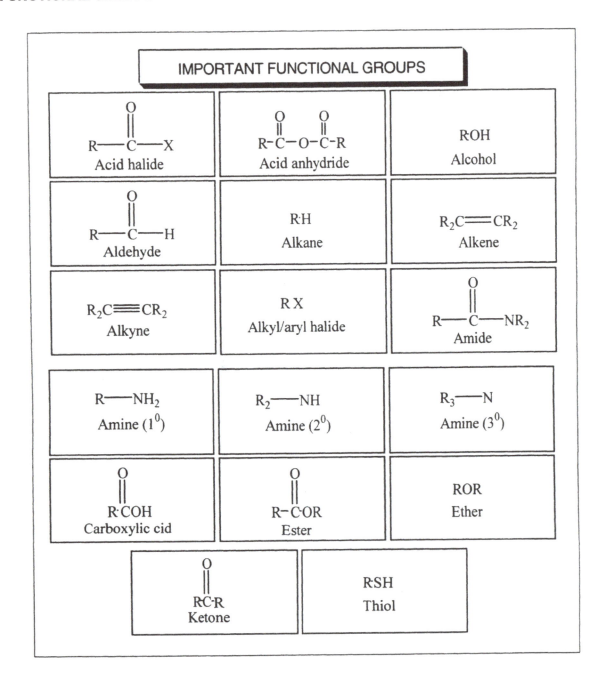

CHAPTER 15 PRACTICE QUESTIONS

1. The carbon indicated by the arrow has which of the following hybridizations?

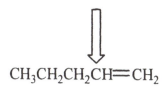

$$CH_3CH_2CH_2CH{=}CH_2$$

    A.   *sp* hybridization
    B.   *sp²* hybridization
    C.   *sp³* hybridization
    D.   *sp³d²* hybridization

2. In acetylene, how many sigma bonds are present between the two carbons?

    A.   One
    B.   Two
    C.   Three
    D.   Four

3. The triple bond of 2-propyne contains:

    A.   one sigma bond and one pi bond.
    B.   one sigma bond and two pi bonds.
    C.   two sigma bonds and one pi bond.
    D.   three sigma bonds.

4. Which of the following represents the arrangement of the *sp³* hybrid orbitals in methane?

    A.   Planar
    B.   Tetragonal planar
    C.   Tetrahedral
    D.   Bipyramidal

5. How many electrons are actually involved in the carbon-carbon bond of acetylene?

    A.   2
    B.   3
    C.   4
    D.   6

6. Which of the following best represents the hydrogen-carbon-hydrogen bond angles in methane?

    A.   90°
    B.   109.5°
    C.   120°
    D.   180°

7. Which of the following bonds indicated by the arrows has the shortest bond length?

    A.   a
    B.   b
    C.   c
    D.   d

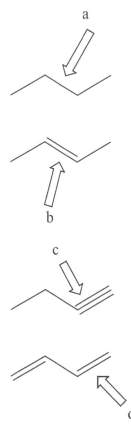

Figure for Question 7

8. The carbon-hydrogen bond in propane can be best described as:

    A.   an ionic bond.
    B.   a covalent bond.
    C.   a hydrogen bond.
    D.   a dipole-dipole bond.

CHAPTER 16

Alkanes

A. INTRODUCTION

Hydrocarbons are compounds containing only carbon and hydrogen. They are classified into **aliphatic** and **aromatic hydrocarbons**. Aliphatic hydrocarbons can be divided into three major groups – **alkanes**, **alkenes**, and **alkynes**. Alkanes come under saturated hydrocarbons, because they have carbon-carbon single bonds. Alkenes and alkynes are unsaturated hydrocarbons, since they have carbon-carbon double and triple bonds, respectively.

B. PROPERTIES OF ALKANES

Alkanes have the general molecular formula C_nH_{2n+2}. Hence, if we know the number of carbons present in an alkane, we can calculate the number of hydrogens in it or vice versa. Methane is the first member of the alkane family. It has a molecular formula of CH_4. Natural gases which are found in petroleum deposits contain gases such as methane, ethane, and propane. They are the first three members of the alkane family.

ALKANES WITH 1-12 CARBON ATOMS

Methane	CH_4	Heptane	C_7H_{16}
Ethane	C_2H_6	Octane	C_8H_{18}
Propane	C_3H_8	Nonane	C_9H_{20}
Butane	C_4H_{10}	Decane	$C_{10}H_{22}$
Pentane	C_5H_{12}	Undecane	$C_{11}H_{24}$
Hexane	C_6H_{14}	Dodecane	$C_{12}H_{26}$

Methane is a colorless, odorless gas. Ethane, propane, and butane are also gases, with butane having the highest boiling point among these. What kind of trend can we see from these observations? As the number of carbons and hydrogens increases, the boiling point increases. Each carbon in an alkane is sp^3 hybridized.

Physical Properties

At room temperature, the first four members of the alkane family are gases. The straight chain alkanes from pentane and up are liquids, and octadecane (18 carbons) and up in the alkane family are solids. As the number of carbons increases, the boiling point increases. Branched alkanes have lesser boiling points than their unbranched or less branched isomeric counterparts. The reason for this is that the unbranched molecules have more intermolecular interactions than the branched ones.

C. STRAIGHT CHAIN, BRANCHING, ALKYL GROUPS

Butane (C_4H_{10}) and the other alkanes above it can exhibit **constitutional isomerism**. If the alkane is unbranched and has a straight chain, it is called *n*-alkane. For example, the straight chain pentane is called *n*-Pentane.

n-Pentane $CH_3CH_2CH_2CH_2CH_3$

n-Butane $CH_3CH_2CH_2CH_3$

Constitutional (structural) isomers are isomers with the same molecular formula, but are different in terms of the order in which the atoms are connected.

Butane has two possible isomers: *n*-butane and isobutane

n-Butane

$CH_3CH_2CH_2CH_3$

Isobutane

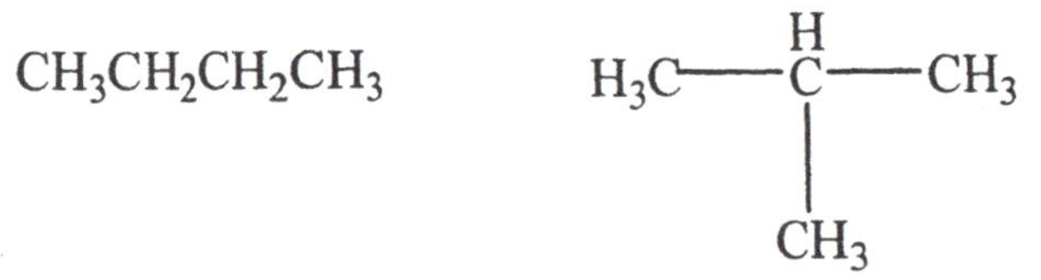

Pentane has three isomers: *n*-pentane, isopentane, and neopentane

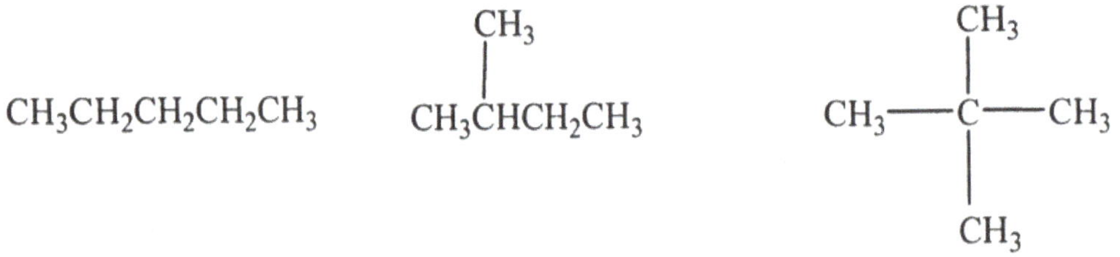

n-Pentane   Isopentane   Neopentane

The only way to find the number of possible isomers is by drawing out the structures sequentially and systematically, starting from the straight chain compound. There is no simple general formula to calculate the number of possible isomers of an alkane.

Alkyl Groups

Alkyl groups are groups which lack one hydrogen atom compared to its parent alkane. For example, the methyl group is CH_3—, which lacks one hydrogen atom with respect to its parent alkane, methane (CH_4). Similarly, ethyl group $(C_2H_5—,)$ lacks one hydrogen atom compared to ethane (C_2H_6).

Some common alkyl groups

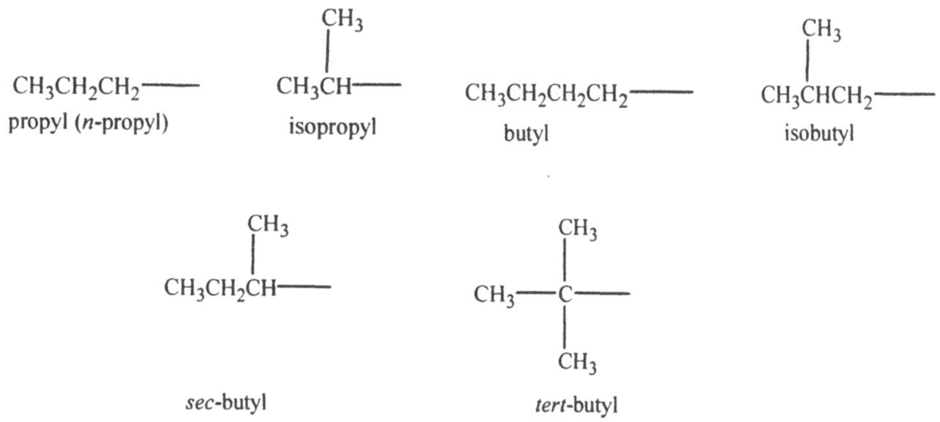

$$CH_3CH_2CH_2——$$
propyl (*n*-propyl)

$$\overset{\displaystyle CH_3}{\underset{\displaystyle }{|}}$$
$$CH_3CH——$$
isopropyl

$$CH_3CH_2CH_2CH_2——$$
butyl

$$\overset{\displaystyle CH_3}{\underset{\displaystyle }{|}}$$
$$CH_3CHCH_2——$$
isobutyl

$$\overset{\displaystyle CH_3}{\underset{\displaystyle }{|}}$$
$$CH_3CH_2CH——$$

sec-butyl

$$CH_3—\overset{\displaystyle CH_3}{\underset{\displaystyle CH_3}{\overset{|}{\underset{|}{C}}}}—$$

tert-butyl

D. THE IUPAC NAMING OF ALKANES

Main rules and strategies for the IUPAC naming of alkanes

1. Write out the expanded structural formula, if it is not given in the expanded form.
2. Find the longest carbon chain.
3. Then identify the alkyl or other substituents that are connected to this long chain.
4. The numbering of carbons should start from the specific end of the long chain, so that the numbers assigned for the substituents are the lowest.

$$\underset{1}{H_3C} - \underset{2}{HC} - \underset{3}{H_2C} - \underset{4}{H_2C} - \underset{5}{H_2C} - \underset{6}{CH_3}$$

with CH_3 branch on carbon 2

2-methyl hexane

4-ethyl-2-methyl heptane

2,2-dimethyl-4-ethyl heptane

E. CYCLOALKANES

Cycloalkanes are cyclic compounds with ring structures. The general molecular formula of a cycloalkane is C_nH_{2n}.

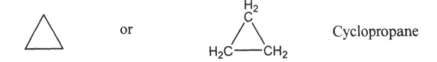

or   Cyclopropane

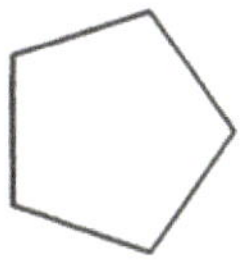

Cyclopentane

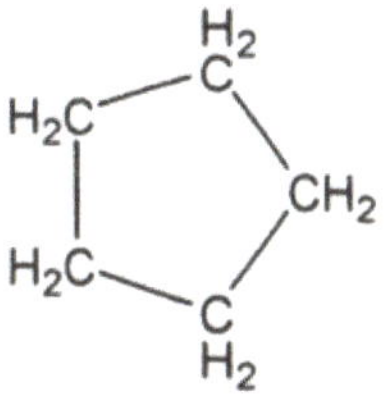

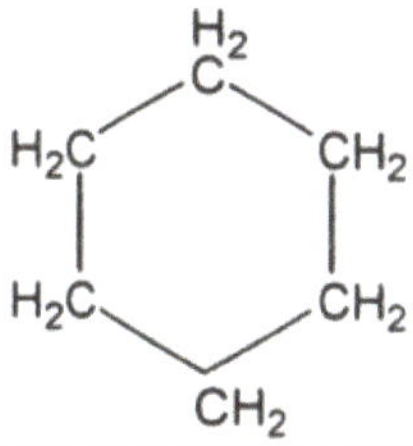

Cyclohexane

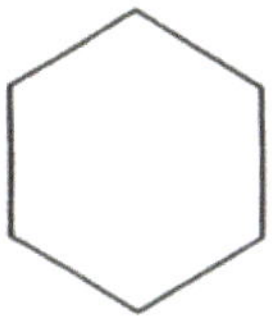

F. REACTIONS OF ALKANES

Combustion

Hydrocarbons undergo combustion reactions in the presence of oxygen to form carbon dioxide and water as products. Combustion reactions are very exothermic giving out energy, as they burn in the presence of oxygen.

Sample reaction 16-1

$$CH_4 + 2O_2 \rightarrow CO_2 + 2 H_2O \qquad \Delta H^0 = -890 \text{ kJ}$$

Halogenation

The **halogenation reaction** can be generalized as follows:

$$RH \quad + \quad X_2 \rightarrow RX \quad + \quad HX$$

In this substitution reaction, the halogen (fluorine, chlorine, bromine, iodine) substitutes one hydrogen atom in the alkane, forming hydrogen halide and alkyl halide as the products. The reactivity of halogens in the halogenation reactions is as follows:

Fluorine > Chlorine > Bromine > Iodine

Fluorine is the most reactive among halogens in halogenation reactions, and iodine is the least reactive.

Free Radical Substitution

While free radical reactions are not as important to the new MCAT, a familiarity with these reactions will help your understanding of organic chemistry for test day. Halogenation reactions occur via a mechanism called **free radical substitution**. There are three main steps in the free radical mechanism. They are:

1. initiation
2. propagation
3. termination.

The overall reaction of chlorination of methane.

$$CH_4 + Cl_2 \rightarrow CH_3Cl + HCl$$

(1) Initiation

This step involves the dissociation of the halogen molecule (e.g., chlorine molecule) into two chlorine atoms. Even though the total reaction is exothermic, initially energy should be supplied for the reaction to proceed.

(2) Propagation steps

During the propagation step, the hydrogen atom is abstracted from methane by a chlorine atom. This is followed by the reaction between the methyl radical and the chlorine molecule.

(3) Termination

The termination steps involve the combination of the radicals.

$$:\!\overset{..}{\underset{..}{Cl}}\!\cdot \;+\; CH_3\!\cdot \;\longrightarrow\; CH_3\!:\!\overset{..}{\underset{..}{Cl}}\!:$$

$$:\!\overset{..}{\underset{..}{Cl}}\!\cdot \;+\; :\!\overset{..}{\underset{..}{Cl}}\!\cdot \;\longrightarrow\; Cl_2$$

$$\cdot CH_3 \;+\; CH_3\!\cdot \;\longrightarrow\; H_3C\!-\!CH_3$$

Reactivity

Primary, Secondary, and Tertiary Carbons

A carbon which is attached directly to only one other carbon is called a primary (1^0) carbon. If it is attached directly to two other carbons, it is a secondary (2^0) carbon. A carbon is called a tertiary (3^0) carbon, if it is directly attached to three other carbons.

Though alkanes are not so reactive, they can undergo some reactions by forming intermediates. These intermediates can be alkyl radicals, carbocations, or carbanions. Alkyl radicals are intermediates of free radical reactions. Carbocations (carbonium ions) are species with a positive charge on one of the carbon atoms. A carbanion has a negative charge on one of its carbon atoms. Some major trends are given below:

Carbocation/Alkyl radical stability
$3^0 > 2^0 > 1^0 >$ methyl

Carbocation/Alkyl radical reactivity
$3^0 < 2^0 < 1^0 <$ methyl

Carbanion stability
$3^0 < 2^0 < 1^0 < \text{methyl}$

Carbanion reactivity
$3^0 > 2^0 > 1^0 > \text{methyl}$

G. CONFORMATION AND STABILITY OF ALKANES

Conformations

Alkanes can have different conformations. By analyzing the structure of ethane, we can define certain aspects regarding its conformations. **Conformations** are different arrangements of the atoms in a molecule, as a result of rotation around a single bond.

STAGGERED CONFORMATION

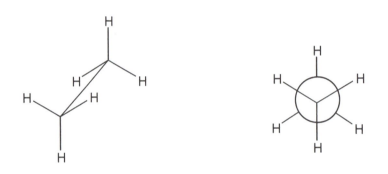

SAWHORSE REPRESENTATION   NEWMAN PROJECTION

Figure 16-1

In **staggered conformation**, the torsional angle is 60^0. In **eclipsed conformation**, each carbon-hydrogen bond is aligned with the carbon-hydrogen bond of the next carbon.

ECLIPSED CONFORMATION

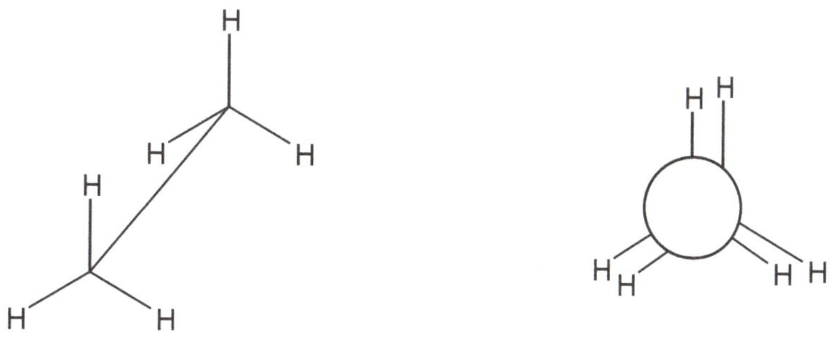

SAWHORSE REPRESENTATION   NEWMAN PROJECTION

Figure 16-2

In eclipsed conformations, the torsional angle is $0°$. In staggered conformations, the torsional angles can either be $60°$ (**gauche**) or $180°$ (**anti**). The anti conformation is more stable than the gauche conformation. We should also consider the fact that in this analysis of staggered conformation, the ethane molecule looks the same in the Newman projections, whether it is gauche or anti. Reason: There are no substituents other than just hydrogens. To denote the positional significance, the hydrogens are indicated in bold in the diagrams shown in Figure 16-4.

Eclipsed

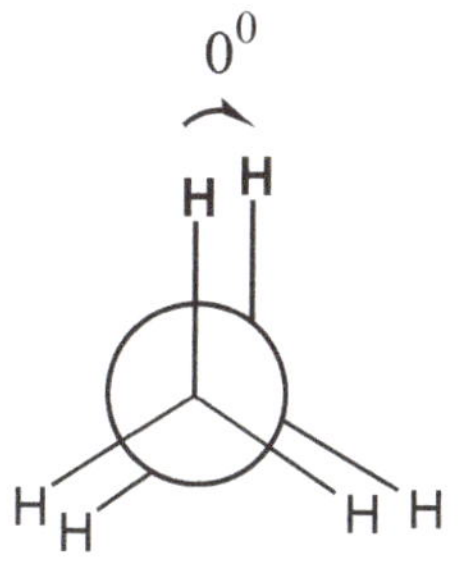

ANGLE OF TORSION
IS 0^0

Figure 16-3

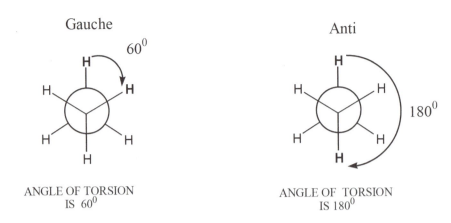

Figure 16-4

Conformation and Stability in Cycloalkanes

According to Baeyer strain theory, the stability of a cycloalkane is based on how close its angles are to 109.5°. The closer the angle is to 109.5°, the more stable the cycloalkane. Deviation from this angle can cause angle strain. An increase in the angle strain means a decrease in the stability of the molecule.

Conformations of Cyclohexane

Cyclohexane has a non-planar structure that makes it almost free from ring strain. The most important conformations that it can have include **chair conformation** and **boat conformation**. The chair conformation is more stable than the boat conformation. The boat conformation can sometimes be more stable than it usually is, by a slight rotation in the C-C bonds and is called the **skew boat conformation**. Nevertheless, the chair conformation is the most stable cyclohexane form.

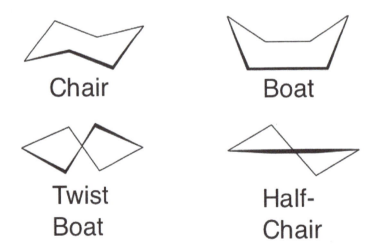

Relative energy levels of the conformations of cyclohexane

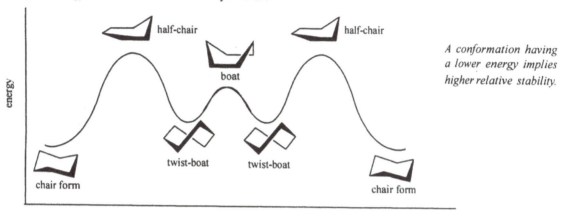

A conformation having a lower energy implies higher relative stability.

Based on the energy diagram of cyclohexane, the following inference can be made regarding the stability of the conformations:

chair conformation >twist boat conformation > boat conformation > half-chair conformation

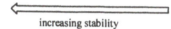

increasing stability

In the chair form of cyclohexane, there are two different kinds of carbon-hydrogen bonds. Of the twelve carbon hydrogen bonds in a cyclohexane, six bonds are pointed up or down and are called axial bonds. The remaining six carbon-hydrogen bonds are pointed at an angle out of the ring and are called equatorial bonds. Each carbon atom in the ring is attached to one hydrogen atom by an axial bond, and to the other hydrogen atom by an equatorial bond.

(a) axial position

(e) equatorial position

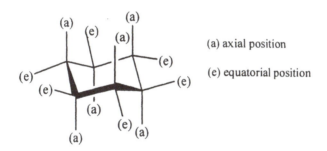

When ring flipping occurs between conformers, equatorial groups become axial, and axial groups become equatorial.

Experimental analysis has confirmed that among the two chair conformations of methylcyclohexane, 95% of the molecules have their methyl group in the equatorial position. In other words, the methyl group being in the equatorial position is more stable than methyl group in the axial position. The lower stability of the axial position can be attributed to the fact that there is an increased steric hindrance because of the proximity of the axial methyl group to the axial hydrogens that are attached to carbon atoms 3 and 5. This interaction called 1,3-diaxial interaction results in steric strain. This accounts for the increased relative stability of the conformation when the methyl group is in the equatorial position.

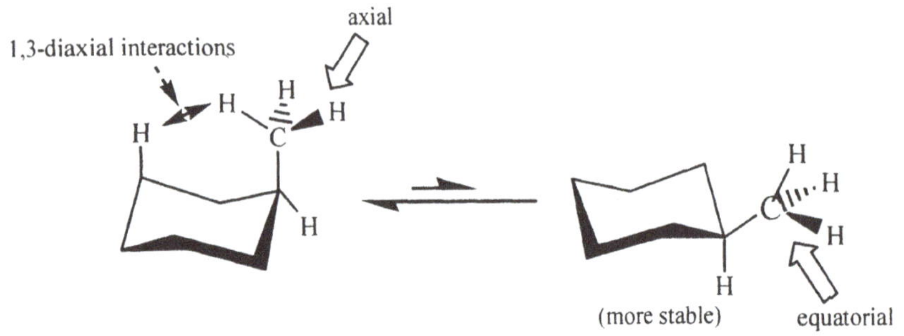

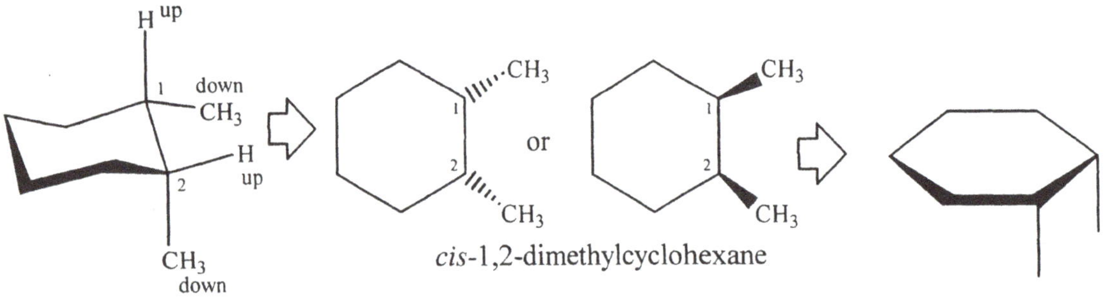

cis-1,2-dimethylcyclohexane

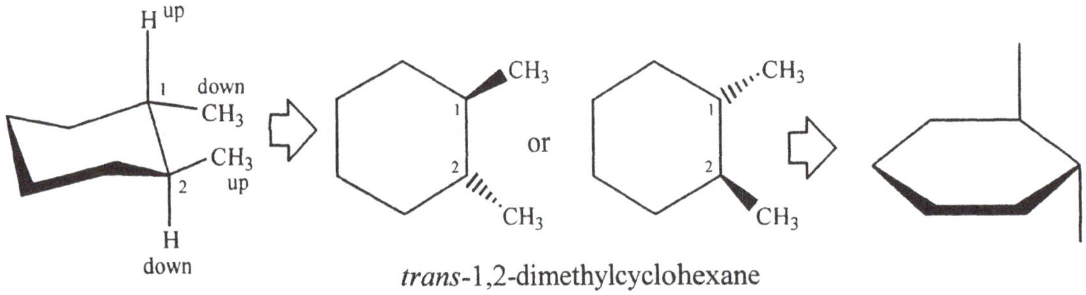

trans-1,2-dimethylcyclohexane

Example 16-1

The *cis*-geometric isomer of 1,3-dimethylclohexane is more stable than its *trans*-isomer. Why?

Solution:

To understand why the *cis*-geometric is more stable, let's draw the possible chair forms of 1,3-dimethylclohexane.

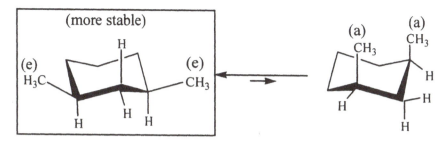

cis-1,3-dimethylcyclohexane

trans-1,3-dimethylcyclohexane

When the two methyl substituents are in 1,3 positions, the *cis*-isomer can have both substituents in equatorial position. In the *trans*-isomer, one methyl group must always be axial.

CHAPTER 16 PRACTICE QUESTIONS

1. A student is assigned to identify an unknown compound in an organic chemistry class. She is sure that the compound contains only carbon and hydrogen atoms. In addition, the unknown compound is a saturated hydrocarbon. If there are fourteen hydrogens in a molecule of this unknown compound, and it does not have a ring structure, what is the most likely number of carbons in this compound?

    A. 3
    B. 6
    C. 7
    D. 14

2. Which of the following represents the general formula of an alkane?

    A. C_nH_{2n+2}
    B. C_nH_{2n}
    C. C_nH_{2n-2}
    D. C_nH_n

3. n-Butane and isobutane are best described as:

    A. stereoisomers.
    B. anomers.
    C. diastereomers.
    D. constitutional isomers.

4. Choose the correct name of the following compound from the choices given below.

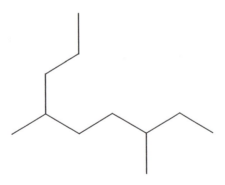

    A. 2-propyl-5-methyl heptane
    B. 3-methyl-6-propyl heptane
    C. 3,6-dimethyl nonane
    D. 4,7-dimethyl nonane

5. In the combustion reaction of butane, how many moles of carbon dioxide are formed, if one mole of butane undergoes complete combustion in a controlled environment in the presence of excess oxygen?

    A. one
    B. two
    C. four
    D. eight

6. Which of the following represents secondary carbons?

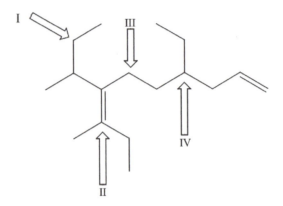

    A. I and II only
    B. I and III only
    C. II and IV only
    D. I, II, III and IV

7. Carbonium ions have:

    A. a positive charge.
    B. a negative charge.
    C. no charge.
    D. either a positive or a negative charge.

8. The gauche conformation is a form of:

    A. eclipsed conformation.
    B. anti-conformation.
    C. staggered conformation.
    D. none of the above conformations.

9. In cycloalkanes which of the following bond angles will have the least angle strain?

    A. 90°
    B. 110°
    C. 125°
    D. 180°

10. Which of the following alkanes has the highest boiling point?

I

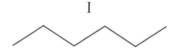

II

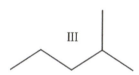

III

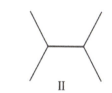

IV

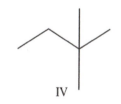

    A. I
    B. II
    C. III
    D. IV

Questions 11-15 are based on the following passage.

Passage 1

Hydrocarbons are compounds composed of carbon and hydrogen atoms. Alkanes are hydrocarbons. As the number of carbons increases in straight-chain alkanes, there is a steady gradation of properties which can be easily compared and predicted. The properties of branched alkanes vary considerably and are hard to predict because of other intervening forces that come into play. The boiling points of a few alkanes are given below:

methane	−161.6° C
propane	−88.6° C
pentane	36.1° C
hexane	68.7° C
octane	125.6° C
3-methylpentane	63.3° C

11. Which of the following intermolecular forces are important with respect to alkanes?

    A. Hydrogen bonding
    B. Dipole-dipole electrostatic forces
    C. Ionic forces
    D. Van der Waals forces

12. The melting point of butane is closest to:

    A. 37.5° C.
    B. 55.1° C.
    C. 24° C.
    D. −138° C.

13. Alkenes can undergo free radical substitution reactions with halogens. Which of the following best represents a chain propagation step during the free radical chlorination of methane?

A. $Cl_2 \longrightarrow 2 \; :\!\overset{\cdot\cdot}{\underset{\cdot\cdot}{Cl}}\!\cdot$

B. $\cdot CH_3 + :\!\overset{\cdot\cdot}{\underset{\cdot\cdot}{Cl}}\!\cdot \longrightarrow CH_3Cl$

C. $\cdot CH_3 + Cl_2 \longrightarrow CH_3Cl + :\!\overset{\cdot\cdot}{\underset{\cdot\cdot}{Cl}}\!\cdot$

D. $\cdot CH_3 + \cdot CH_3 \longrightarrow CH_3CH_3$

14. What is the most likely boiling point of 2,3-dimethylbutane?

    A. 58° C
    B. 63.3° C
    C. 68.7° C
    D. 75.8° C

15. The total number of possible structural isomers of heptane is:

    A. three.
    B. seven.
    C. nine.
    D. twelve.

CHAPTER 17
Stereochemistry

A. INTRODUCTION

Stereochemistry is the study of the three-dimensional structures of compounds. In this chapter, we will discuss the various concepts in stereochemistry starting with some simple terms such as isomers. What are isomers? **Isomers** are compounds with the same molecular formula, but with different arrangements of atoms. Stereochemistry takes us further into the intricacies of isomerism in terms of three-dimensional perspectives. Furthermore, stereochemistry helps us understand the differences in activities of molecules that are structurally rather close. In many compounds, the slightest changes in the three-dimensional form of molecules make them active or inactive. This concept is especially important in many biologically significant molecules. Stereochemistry has taken us deep into the secrets of many naturally occurring molecules in our body.

Constitutional isomers have the same molecular formula but different arrangements. Look at the examples shown in Figure 17-1. They are constitutional isomers.

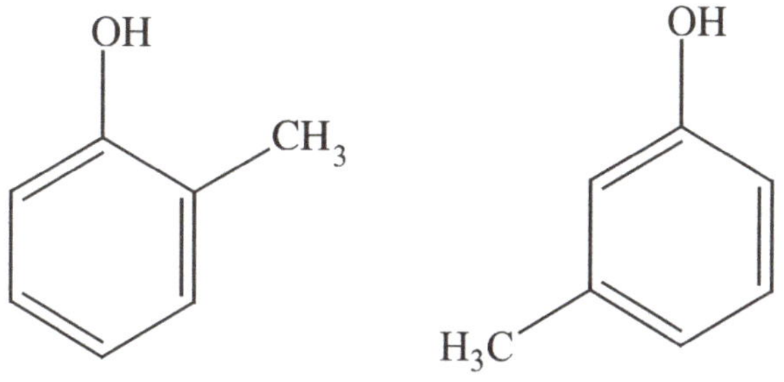

Figure 17-1

B. STEREOISOMERS

Isomers with atoms having the same order of bonding, but different spatial arrangements, are called **stereoisomers**. Stereoisomers which are non-superimposable mirror images are called **enantiomers**. **Diastereomers** are stereoisomers that are not mirror images.

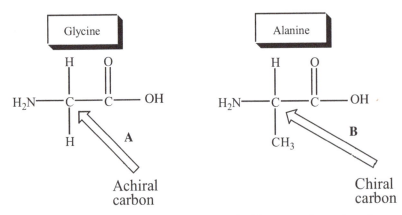

Figure 17-2 In glycine, the carbon indicated by the arrow is achiral because the carbon has two hydrogens (two of the same substituents) attached to it. That is not the case in alanine, and thus the carbon indicated by the arrow is chiral.

A carbon which is sp^3 hybridized (tetrahedral structure) with four different substituents is called a **chiral carbon**. If the carbon doesn't have four different substituents or say at least the carbon has two of the same substituents, then it is an **achiral carbon**.

Enantiomers

Enantiomers are compounds with same molecular formula and are nonsuperimposable mirror images. Look at the example shown in Figure **17**-3.

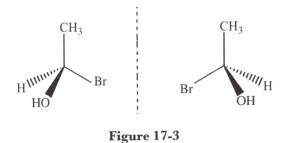

Figure 17-3

Diastereomers

Diastereomers have the same molecular formula, but they do not have a mirror-image relationship to each other. Study the examples in Figure 17-4.

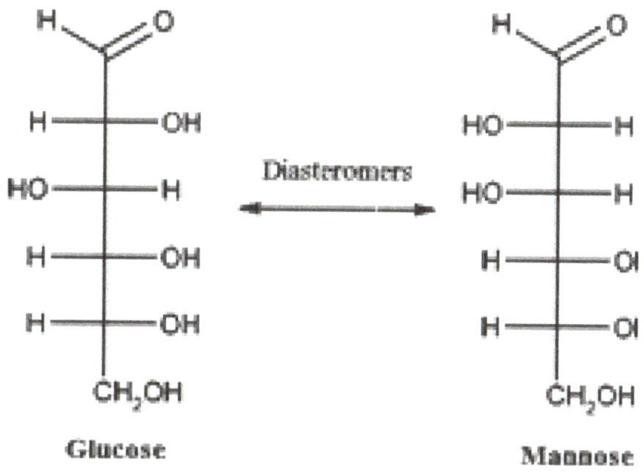

Figure 17-4

C. OPTICAL ACTIVITY

The molecular structure and the geometry of a compound dictate many of its properties. The structure of certain molecules makes them capable of rotating the plane of polarized light. In order to make use of this phenomenon, we must have a source of plane polarized light. When light waves are passed through polarizing materials, the electric field vector of the processed light oscillates in one plane. This is plane polarized light.

To examine the chiral properties, experimenters pass plane polarized light through solutions of chiral compounds. The rotation of light is noted with a detector. If the rotation perceived by an observer looking through the solution toward the source of light is clockwise, a positive (+) sign is used to denote the optical activity. For counterclockwise rotation, a negative (−) sign is used to denote the optical activity. The positive rotation is often referred as *d* (**dextrorotatory**) and negative rotation as *l* (**levorotatory**).

Some Generalizations Regarding Optical Activity

Consider two solutions – A and B. Solution A contains a pure enantiomer, and solution B contains the enantiomer of the compound in solution A. Let's say that solution A exhibited positive rotation.

Since the solution A containing a pure enantiomer exhibits positive rotatory properties, its enantiomer will have negative rotatory properties. What can we conclude about these compounds? Well, we can be certain that both compounds present in the solutions A and B are chiral, since they exhibit optical activity.

The specific rotation [α] of a compound at a given wavelength is denoted by

$$[\alpha] = \frac{\alpha}{c\, l}$$

where α is the observed rotation, c is the concentration in g/ml, and l is the length (in decimeters) of the polarimeter tube (the optically active solution is taken in the polarimeter tube for the analysis) that is used.

Properties of Enantiomers and Diastereomers

Enantiomers have identical physical properties. So they cannot be distinguished based on their melting points, boiling points, and densities. But enantiomers do differ in terms of optical activity. Enantiomers rotate place polarized light with the same magnitude, but in opposite directions. Because enantiomers have identical physical properties, separation of enantiomers using conventional methods such as simple distillation and recrystallization is not possible. Enantiomers react the same way with achiral molecules, but react differently with chiral molecules. This difference in reactivity of enantiomers toward chiral molecules is utilized in separating enantiomers. The process is called resolution. In one form of resolution, the enantiomeric mixture is reacted with a chiral molecule to form a pair of diastereomers. Because diastereomers have different physical properties, they can easily be separated. Diastereomers usually have different solubilities. Followed by the separation of the diastereomers that are formed, the original reaction is reversed to get the original enantiomer corresponding to the diastereomer.

D. CONFIGURATIONS

Before we look at configurations, we need to study chirality and associated ideas.

Chirality and Achirality

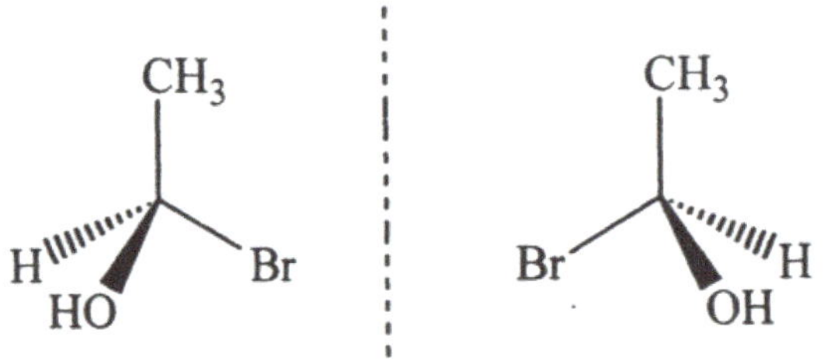

Figure 17-5

If a molecule does not have a plane of symmetry, it is chiral. A chiral molecule is not superimposable on its mirror image. The structures represented in Figure 5 are mirror images. These mirror images are non-superimposable. The molecules depicted in Figure 19-5 are chiral.

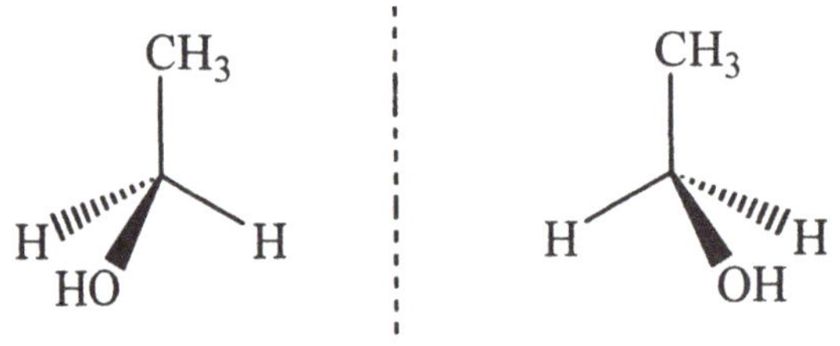

Figure 17-6

We will now consider Figure 17-6. The mirror images of the molecule depicted are superimposable. Hence it is an achiral molecule. Notice that two of the atoms attached to the central carbon atom are the same, namely the hydrogen atoms.

Achirality can also be recognized by looking at the molecular structure. When we are analyzing the structure of a molecule, we should look and determine whether there is any plane of symmetry in the molecule. Plane of symmetry reflects achirality.

The figure given below shows a stereoisomer of tartaric acid. Notice that this compound has two chiral (stereogenic) centers. But, there is a plane of symmetry and thus the molecule itself is achiral and optically inactive. Such compounds that contain one or more stereogenic centers, but are achiral, are called meso compounds. Hence, having a stereogenic center or chiral carbon does not always lead to chirality of the entire molecule.

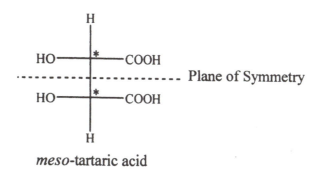

meso-tartaric acid

Absolute Configuration

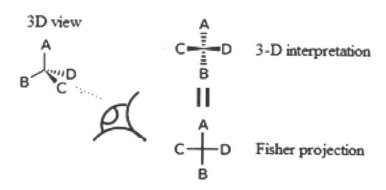

In a Fischer projection, the horizontal lines represent bonds that are toward you, and the vertical lines represent bonds that are pointing away from you.

Absolute configuration is the arrangement of substituents around the stereogenic center of a chiral molecule. The Fischer projection and the absolute configuration of a sample chiral carbon are shown in Figure 17-7.

R-S System of Representation

The *R-S* system of representation is a convenient and essential way of looking at molecules. The *R-S* convention is done by prioritizing the substituents that are bonded to the chiral carbon.

The following rules will familiarize you with the *R-S* naming of compounds.

1.   The orientation of the molecule should be in such a way that the lowest priority group is pointing away from you.

2. First, prioritize each group that is bonded to the chiral carbon. The priority is based on atomic number. The higher the atomic number of the atom that is connected to the chiral carbon, the higher the priority of that group. For example, if the four groups connected to the chiral carbon are CH_3, H, OH, and Br, then the bromine atom (atomic number 35) has the highest priority. This is followed by the oxygen atom (atomic number 8) of the hydroxyl group, then the carbon atom of the methyl group, followed by the hydrogen atom (atomic number 1). It is important to realize that the priority is determined by the atomic number of the atom that is directly connected to the chiral atom.

3. If two groups that are attached to a chiral carbon are isotopes (same atomic number, different mass numbers), the heavier isotope takes precedence.

4. If two groups have the same atom connected to a chiral carbon, then the next atom along the chain determines the priority. If that too fails (if it is the same atom), then go to the next highest priority atom to determine which group has higher priority. For example, $-CH_2F$ has a lower priority than $-CH_2I$. If the groups contain unsaturations such as double or triple bonds, consider that the atoms on both ends are duplicated depending on the number of bonds.

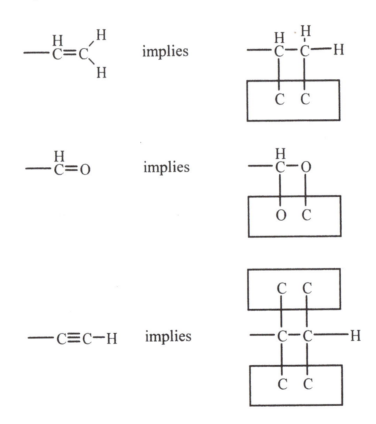

5. After prioritizing, draw an arrow starting from the first priority group to the third priority group through the second priority group. This is illustrated in the example given below.

6. If the arrow points in the clockwise direction, the configuration of that chiral carbon is *R*. If the arrow points in the counterclockwise direction, the configuration of that chiral carbon is *S*.

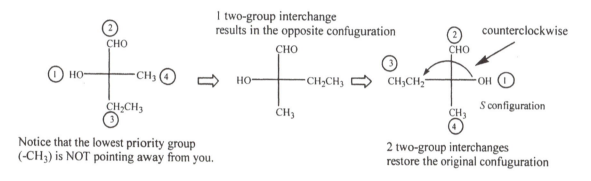

Notice that the lowest priority group
(H) is pointing away from you.

If the given orientation of a molecule shows the lowest priority group pointing toward the viewer, the orientation should be changed so that the lowest priority group points away from the viewer. In a Fischer projection, if the lowest priority group is attached to a vertical bond (the one that points up or down), the molecule should be viewed from another angle so that the lowest priority group points away from the viewer. This can be achieved by doing 2 two-group switches or interchanges. If only 1 two-group interchange is done, the opposite configuration results. See the example given below.

Notice that the lowest priority group
(-CH₃) is NOT pointing away from you.

2 two-group interchanges
restore the original confuguration

Example 17-1

Find the absolute configuration of the molecule shown below in terms of *R-S* notation.

$$HO\text{---}\overset{\overset{\displaystyle H}{|}}{\underset{\underset{\displaystyle H_3C}{}}{C}}\text{---}CH_2CH_3$$

Solution:

First, we have to think about the order of priority of the substituents. The order is as follows:

$$OH > CH_2CH_3 > CH_3 > H$$

We can simplify the structure by looking at the three substituents that determine the configuration. Let's redraw them as shown below:

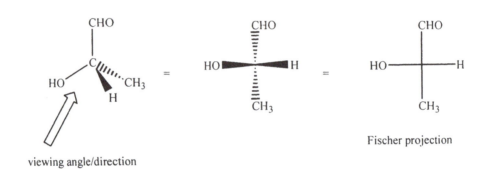

Since the direction of priority is clockwise, the configuration is R.

Some sample conversions to Fischer projection

Example 17-2

Draw the S configuration of the compound shown in Example 1.

Solution:

For S configuration, the direction of priority should be counterclockwise. So the structure can be best represented as follows:

Counterclockwise

CHAPTER 17 PRACTICE QUESTIONS

1. What is the best term that can be used to express the relationship between the two structures shown?

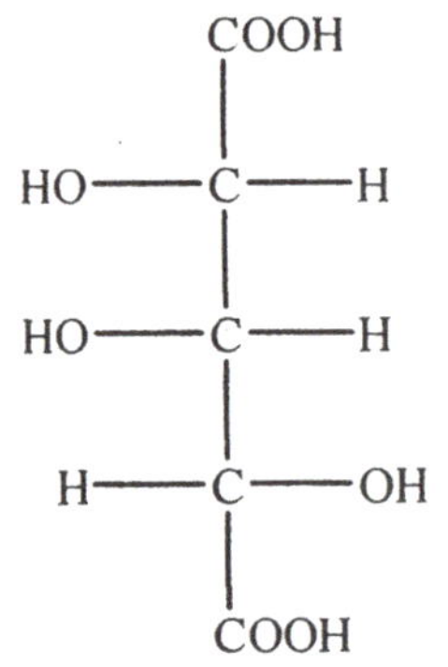

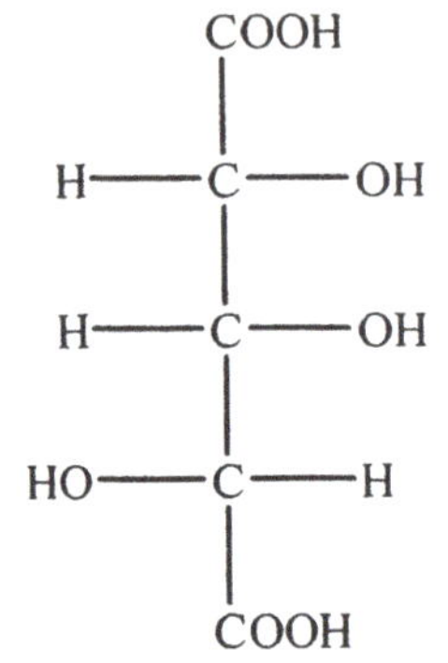

$$
\begin{array}{c}
\text{COOH} \\
| \\
\text{HO}-\text{C}-\text{H} \\
| \\
\text{HO}-\text{C}-\text{H} \\
| \\
\text{H}-\text{C}-\text{OH} \\
| \\
\text{COOH}
\end{array}
$$

$$
\begin{array}{c}
\text{COOH} \\
| \\
\text{H}-\text{C}-\text{OH} \\
| \\
\text{H}-\text{C}-\text{OH} \\
| \\
\text{HO}-\text{C}-\text{H} \\
| \\
\text{COOH}
\end{array}
$$

    A.   Diastereomers
    B.   Enantiomers
    C.   Meso compounds
    D.   Anomers

2. What is the best term that can be used to express the relationship between the two structures shown?

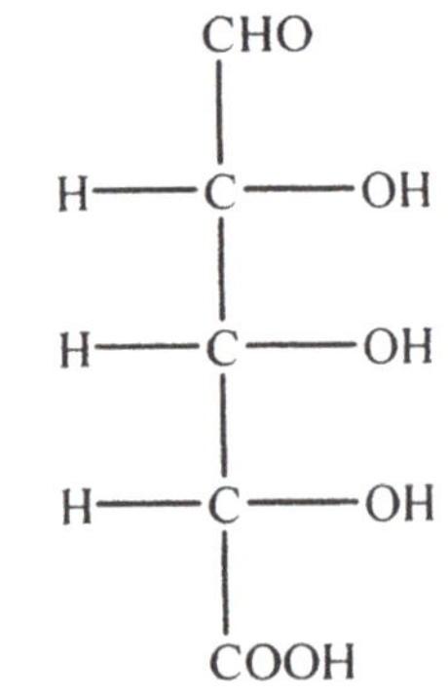

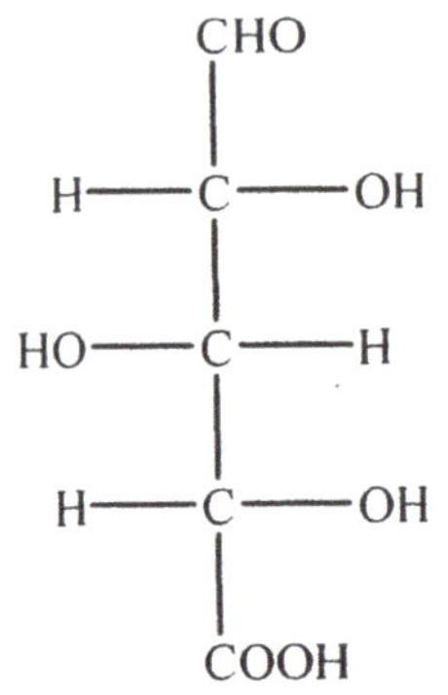

$$
\begin{array}{c}
\text{CHO} \\
| \\
\text{H}-\text{C}-\text{OH} \\
| \\
\text{H}-\text{C}-\text{OH} \\
| \\
\text{H}-\text{C}-\text{OH} \\
| \\
\text{COOH}
\end{array}
$$

$$
\begin{array}{c}
\text{CHO} \\
| \\
\text{H}-\text{C}-\text{OH} \\
| \\
\text{HO}-\text{C}-\text{H} \\
| \\
\text{H}-\text{C}-\text{OH} \\
| \\
\text{COOH}
\end{array}
$$

    A.   Diastereomers
    B.   Enantiomers
    C.   Identical compounds
    D.   None of the above

3. The structure shown is that of 2,3,4-trihydroxy glutaric acid. Choose the correct enantiomer of this compound.

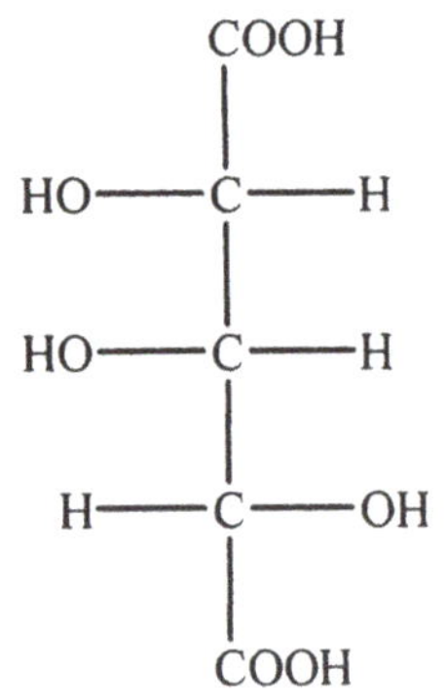

$$
\begin{array}{c}
\text{COOH} \\
| \\
\text{HO}-\text{C}-\text{H} \\
| \\
\text{HO}-\text{C}-\text{H} \\
| \\
\text{H}-\text{C}-\text{OH} \\
| \\
\text{COOH}
\end{array}
$$

A.

```
        COOH
         |
HO——————C——————H
         |
HO——————C——————H
         |
 H——————C——————OH
         |
        COOH
```

B.

```
        COOH
         |
 H——————C——————OH
         |
 H——————C——————OH
         |
 H——————C——————OH
         |
        COOH
```

C.

```
        COOH
         |
 H——————C——————OH
         |
 H——————C——————OH
         |
HO——————C——————H
         |
        CHO
```

D.

```
        COOH
         |
 H——————C——————OH
         |
 H——————C——————OH
         |
HO——————C——————H
         |
        COOH
```

4. All are equivalent structures or representations of the compound given, except:

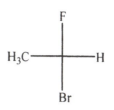

A.
```
        CH₃
         |
  F——————+——————Br
         |
         H
```
CH_3 top, F left, Br right, H bottom

B.
```
         H
         |
  Br——————+——————F
         |
        CH₃
```

C.
```
         H
         |
  Br——————+——————CH₃
         |
         F
```

D. All the above are equivalent structural representations.

5. What is the name of Compound X?

```
         F
         |
  H——————+——————Br
         |
        CH₃
```
Compound X

A. (S)-1-bromo-1-fluoromethane
B. (R)-1-bromo-1-fluoromethane
C. (S)-1-bromo-1-fluoroethane
D. (R)-1-bromo-1-fluoroethane

6. Which of the following are true?

I. Diastereomers are stereoisomers.

II. All stereoisomers are enantiomers.

III. All enantiomers are stereoisomers.

      A.   I and II only

      B.   I and III only

      C.   II and III only

      D.   I, II, and III

7. A sawhorse representation of a compound is given below. Which of the following is true about this structure?

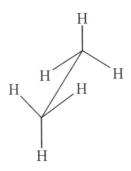

      A.   The compound has an eclipsed conformation.

      B.   The compound has a staggered conformation.

      C.   The compound has a *cis*-configuration.

      D.   None of the above

A. INTRODUCTION

Alkyl halides are organic compounds with the general formula RX, where R denotes the alkyl group and X denotes the halogen.

B. NOMENCLATURE

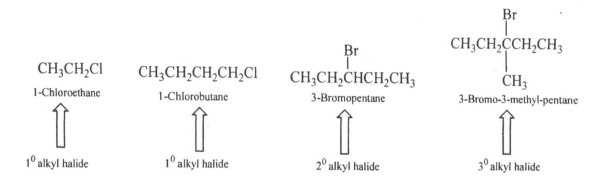

CH_3CH_2Cl	$CH_3CH_2CH_2CH_2Cl$	$CH_3CH_2CHCH_2CH_3$ (Br)	$CH_3CH_2CCH_2CH_3$ (Br, CH₃)
1-Chloroethane	1-Chlorobutane	3-Bromopentane	3-Bromo-3-methyl-pentane
1^0 alkyl halide	1^0 alkyl halide	2^0 alkyl halide	3^0 alkyl halide

We can classify alkyl halides as primary (1^0), secondary (2^0), and tertiary (3^0) alkyl halides. The general formulas for these are as follows:

Primary alkyl halide	RCH_2X
Secondary alkyl halide	R_2CHX
Tertiary alkyl halide	R_3CX

C. PROPERTIES OF ALKYL HALIDES

Alkyl halides have large dipole moments since the carbon-halogen bond is polar. They also have reasonably high boiling points because of the polarity and the high molecular weights.

Alkyl halides are generally insoluble in water. Density of alkyl halides increases as the atomic weight of the halogen present increases. The heavier the halogen is, the higher the density.

Increasing order of density $\Longrightarrow$

$$RF \quad < \quad RCl \quad < \quad RBr \quad < \quad RI$$

D. SYNTHESIS OF ALKYL HALIDES

From Alcohols

Alkyl halides can be prepared from alcohols. The following examples show some representative reactions. The conversion of an alcohol to an alkyl halide is an example of a **nucleophilic substitution** reaction.

Sample reaction 18-1

$$CH_3CH_2OH \xrightarrow{HCl} CH_3CH_2Cl$$

Ethyl Alcohol   Ethyl chloride

Sample reaction 18-2

$$\overset{\displaystyle OH}{\underset{\displaystyle CH_3CHCH_2CH_3}{|}} \xrightarrow{SOCl_2} \overset{\displaystyle Cl}{\underset{\displaystyle CH_3CHCH_2CH_3}{|}}$$

2-Butanol   2-Chlorobutane

From Alkanes

Alkyl halides can be synthesized from alkanes. In this reaction, one of the alkane's hydrogen atoms is substituted with a halogen atom. The reaction occurs by free radical mechanism.

Sample reaction 18-3

$$RH \xrightarrow{Cl_2} RCl \quad + \quad HCl$$

Alkane   Alkyl halide

From Alkenes

Alkyl halides can be prepared from alkenes.

Sample reaction 18-4

$$\underset{\text{Ethylene}}{CH_2{=}CH_2} + \underset{\text{Hydrogen halide}}{HX} \longrightarrow \underset{\text{Ethyl halide}}{CH_3\text{-}CH_2X}$$

Sample reaction 18-5

Markovnikov addition of hydrogen and bromine

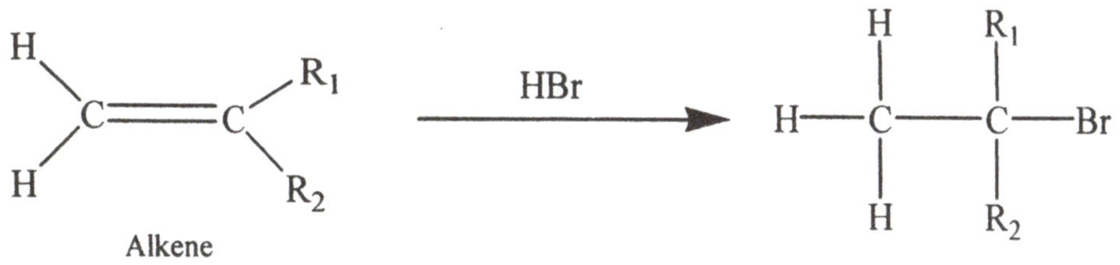

E. REACTIONS OF ALKYL HALIDES

Nucleophilic Substitution Reactions

In this section, we will discuss the two major substitution reactions – S_N1 and S_N2 reactions. In nucleophilic substitution reactions involving alkyl halides as the substrate, a Lewis base (nucleophile) substitutes the halogen present in the alkyl halide. We will discuss nucleophilic reactions in which alkyl halides react with nucleophiles. A general representation can be done as follows:

$$\underset{\text{(Alkyl halide)}}{RX} \xrightarrow[\text{(Nucleophile)}]{Nu^-} \underset{\text{(Substitution product)}}{RNu} + X^-$$

The S_N2 Reaction

S_N2 stands for bimolecular nucleophilic substitution reaction. Consider the reaction between methyl iodide and sodium hydroxide.

$$CH_3I + NaOH \longrightarrow CH_3OH + NaI$$

This reaction follows S_N2 mechanism. Experimentally, it has been confirmed that the rate of this reaction depends on both the alkyl halide and the nucleophile (OH⁻) involved. The reaction rate is written as follows:

$$Rate = k \, [CH_3I] \, [OH^-]$$

The Mechanism of S_N2 Reaction

We will look at the mechanism involved in the reaction between methyl iodide and sodium hydroxide. The S_N2 reaction proceeds via a five-coordinate transition state. This transition state has weak (the weak bonds are indicated by the dotted lines in the mechanism) carbon-iodine and carbon-oxygen bonds. Even though these two are weak bonds, the other three bonds involving the central carbon atom are complete bonds. As the leaving group detaches, there is an inversion of configuration (in chiral molecules) at the carbon where the leaving group was attached.

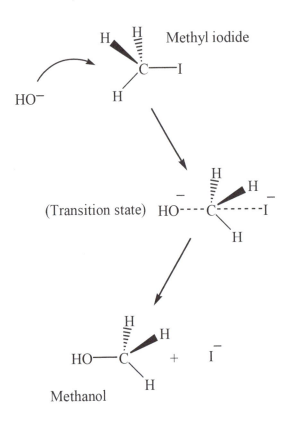

Figure 18-1 The mechanism of SN2 reaction

In S_N2 reactions, the nucleophilic attack occurs opposite (backside attack) to the side where the leaving group is present. This type of nucleophilic approach is thermodynamically favored since the backside attack minimizes the electrostatic repulsions between the nucleophile and the leaving group involved. If substituents (especially bulky ones) are present on the carbon where the nucleophilic attack occurs, this can hinder the S_N2 process. Hence, primary alkyl halides are the most reactive among alkyl halides with respect to S_N2 reactions.

S_N2 reactivity: Methyl > Primary > Secondary > Tertiary

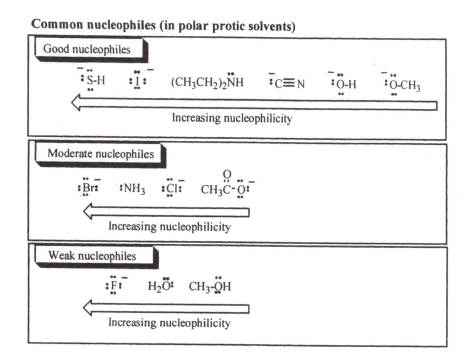

As mentioned earlier, the nucleophile and its concentration can influence the rate of S_N2 reactions. So the rate is different for different nucleophiles. Nucleophilicity or the strength of a nucleophile depends on how efficiently it can make the leaving group leave from the alkyl halide or any other substrate involved in a S_N2 reaction. Some generalizations can be made regarding nucleophiles. Along a period (in the periodic table), as basicity decreases, nucleophilicity decreases (e.g., $F^- < RO^- < R_2N^- < R_3C^-$). Along a group, as basicity decreases, nucleophilicity increases (e.g., $F^- < Cl^- < Br^- < I^-$).

Nucleophilicity can also be compared among species having the same nucleophilic atom. A negatively charged conjugate base of a neutral species (conjugate acid) is more nucleophilic than its corresponding neutral species. For example, HO^- is a better nucleophile than H_2O.

A leaving group plays an important role in both substitution and elimination reactions. A good leaving group has a weak, polarized carbon-leaving group (C-X) bond. It should be stable on its own once it leaves the substrate, regardless of whether it stays as an ion or a neutral species. Sometimes solvation helps a leaving group to achieve this. Halides are good leaving groups. The order of leaving group ability is $F < Cl < Br < I$. In general, the less basic the species is, the better the leaving group. Other good leaving groups include mesylate and tosylate

The S$_N$1 Reaction

S$_N$1 stands for unimolecular nucleophilic substitution reaction. Let's consider a typical S$_N$1 reaction.

$$(CH_3)_3CI \quad \xrightarrow{\quad H_2O \quad} \quad (CH_3)_3COH \quad + \quad HI$$

tert-Butyl iodide   *tert*-Butyl alcohol

The rates of S$_N$1 reactions depend only on the substrate (alkyl halide) concentration. The nucleophile does not influence the reaction rate of a typical S$_N$1 reaction.

The reaction rate is represented as follows:

$$Rate = k \, [\, (CH_3)_3CI \,]$$

The Mechanism of S$_N$1 Reaction

In this two-step reaction, shown in figure 18-2, the alkyl halide loses its halide leaving group to form a carbocation intermediate and a halide ion. During the second step, the carbocation reacts with the nucleophile to form the final product. Since the carbocation formed is planar, the nucleophile can attack the electrophilic carbon from either side. Thus an S$_N$1 reaction can result in partial of full racemization.

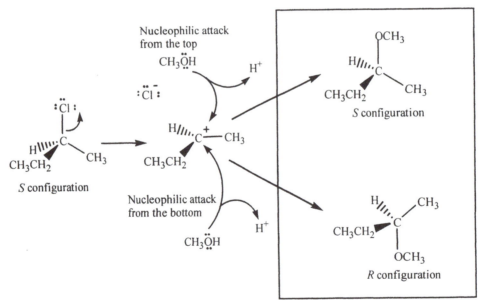

Figure 18-2 The mechanism of S$_N$1 reaction

S$_N$1 reactivity: Methyl < Primary < Secondary < Tertiary

A S$_N$2 reaction is favored when the alkyl halide involved is a primary or a secondary alkyl halide. A S$_N$1 reaction is favored when the alkyl halide involved is a tertiary or a secondary alkyl halide. In many cases, it is hard to predict the mode of reaction with secondary alkyl halides – it can either be S_N1 or S_N2, depending on certain other aspects such as the solvent used. The S_N1 reaction being favored by tertiary halides is understandable, because of the carbocation intermediate that is formed during the S_N1 process.

Polar solvents increase the rate of both types of substitution reactions. Polar solvents which have high dielectric constants can stabilize the transition state and this is highly useful in S_N1 reactions. In S_N2 reactions, the solvent effects are slightly different. Here what matters is whether the solvent is aprotic. Protic polar solvents such as water and carboxylic acids can undergo hydrogen bonding which in turn can interact with the nucleophile. This can decrease the rate of S_N2 reactions. So it is better to use aprotic polar solvents when we are dealing with S_N2 reactions. Dimethyl sulfoxide (DMSO) is a polar aprotic solvent.

$$H_3C{-}\overset{\displaystyle H_3C}{\underset{}{}}S{=}O \quad DMSO$$

Quite often nucleophilic reactions compete with elimination reactions. Next, we will review elimination reactions.

Elimination reactions

There are two types of elimination reactions in general – E1 and E2 reactions. We will first consider an E2 reaction.

The E2 reaction

The E2 reaction mechanism can generally be represented as shown. In the mechanistic representation shown, B stands for the base and X stands for the halogen.

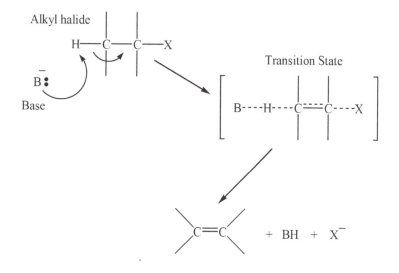

Figure 18-3 *The mechanism of E2 reaction*

The steps involved in an E2 reaction are the breaking of the carbon-hydrogen bond, the carbon double bond formation, and the breaking away of the carbon-halogen bond.

The rate of the E2 reaction is: Rate = k [RX] [base]

So the reaction rate depends on both the substrate (RX) and the base involved.

In an elimination reaction, the major product formed is the most stable alkene. Usually, the most stable alkene is the most substituted alkene. The increased stability of more highly substituted alkenes can be attributed to the **electronic effect**.

The E1 Reaction

Study the mechanism of E1 reaction, shown in figure 18-4 for a tertiary substrate.

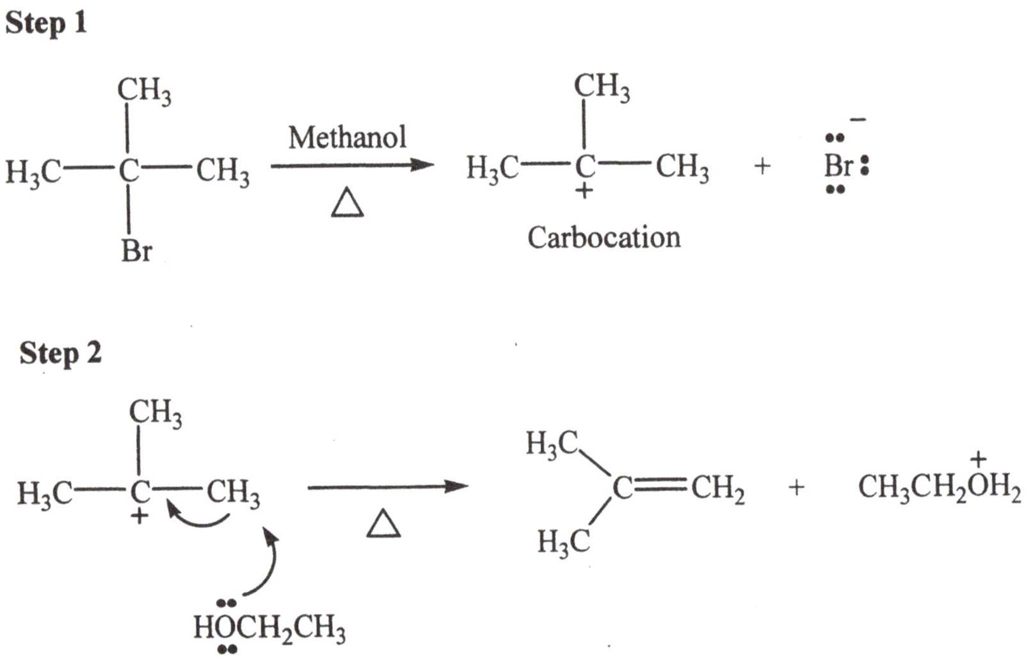

Step 1

Step 2

Figure 18-4 the mechanism of E1 reaction

In step (1), the alkyl halide forms (slow step) the carbocation and the halide ion. In step (2), the base abstracts the proton to form the product (alkene).

E1 reactivity: Methyl < Primary < Secondary < Tertiary
(Slowest)   (Fastest)

Substitution versus Elimination

Sometimes it is hard to predict the product of a reaction involving nucleophiles or bases. Why? Well, the reaction mechanisms are influenced by many factors. Different combinations of factors result in different outcomes. Even though this is the case, let's boil down some of the factors that we can rely on for reasonably judging the outcome of reactions. We will consider some conditions that favor substitution over elimination, and vice versa. The two key factors that we look for are the type of substrate that is undergoing the reaction, and the extent of nucleophilicity or basicity of the anion involved in the reaction.

1. Higher temperatures usually favor elimination over substitution. To be more precise, we can say that elimination is more favored than substitution reactions if the reaction occurs at a high temperature. The latter is more accurate because both types of reactions are favored by an increase in temperature, but elimination is more favored.

2. Strong bases guide or dictate elimination over substitution in most cases. In general, E2 type of elimination is favored under such conditions. Strong nucleophiles will favor substitution reactions, particularly S_N2 reactions.

3. If there is less hindrance or less bulky substituents at the carbon where the leaving group is present, substitution (S_N2) is favored over elimination (E2). Remember that in S_N2 reactions, the transition intermediate is a species in which both the leaving group and the incoming nucleophile are attached to the carbon, where the substitution is taking place.

4. Alkyl halides (tertiary), because of their bulky substituents, mostly prefer elimination rather than substitution provided that a strong base is present. Mild bases can make substitution to predominate even in tertiary alkyl halides. Can you think of a reason why tertiary alkyl halides prefer to undergo elimination? The reason is steric hindrance to the nucleophilic approach.

Note: We have been discussing a number of reactions, both substitution and elimination in terms of alkyl halides. This surely doesn't mean that only alkyl halides undergo these types of reactions.

Nucleophilic Substitution in Alkyl Halides - S_N1 vs S_N2 comparison

	S_N1	S_N1
Molecularity	Unimolecular (First order)	Bimolecular (Second order)
Rate	Rate = k [RX]	Rate = k [RX] [Nu]
Stereochemical aspect	Racemization	Inversion of configuration
Rearrangement?	Yes; Carbocation formation	No; No carbocation formation
Rate dependency	Rate independent of nucleophile	Rate dependent on nucleophile
Solvent effect	Best: Polar protic	Best: Polar aprotic
Reactivity	$RX < R_2X < R_3X$	$R_3X < R_2X < RX$
Reactivity of alkyl halides	$RF << RCl < RBr < RI$	$RF << RCl < RBr < RI$

Table 18-1

CHAPTER 18 PRACTICE QUESTIONS

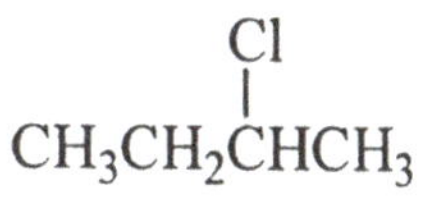

$$\overset{\overset{\displaystyle Cl}{|}}{CH_3CH_2CHCH_3}$$

1. The compound shown can be best described as a:

    A.   primary alkyl halide.
    B.   secondary alkyl halide.
    C.   tertiary alkyl halide.
    D.   primary alkenyl halide.

2. Which compound will have the highest boiling point?

    A.   1-Chloroethane
    B.   1,1-Dichloroethane
    C.   1,1,1-Trichloroethane
    D.   Cannot be predicted

3. Alcohols can react with hydrogen halides to form alkyl halides. Which of the following alcohols is the most reactive toward hydrogen halides?

    A. CH_3CH_2OH

    B. 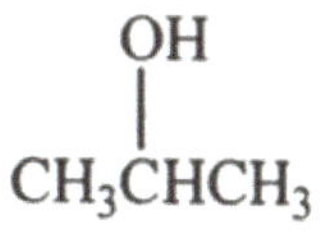 $\overset{\overset{\displaystyle OH}{|}}{CH_3CHCH_3}$

    C. CH_3OH

    D. $(CH_3)_3COH$

4. Which of the following is true regarding alkyl halides?

    A.   Relative to other organic molecules, alkyl halides have low boiling points because of their polarity.
    B.   Alkyl fluorides have lower densities than comparable alkyl bromides.
    C.   Alkyl halides are completely soluble in water.
    D.   None of the above

Questions 5-9 are based on the following passage.

Passage 1

Alkyl halides undergo substitution reactions and a variety of other reactions as well. The type of reaction that occurs depends on a variety of factors. The structural integrity of the alkyl group to which the halogen is attached plays an important role in determining the type of product that is likely to result. A reaction involving *t*-butyl bromide is given:

$$(CH_3)_3CBr \xrightarrow{\text{Ethyl alcohol/}\ H_2O} \text{Products}$$

5. Which of the following best represents the increasing rate of bimolecular substitution reaction for the following alkyl halides?

CH_3CH_2Br	= Compound A
CH_3Br	= Compound B
$(CH_3)_3CBr$	= Compound C
$(CH_3)_2CHBr$	= Compound D

    A.   A < B < C < D
    B.   C < D < B < A
    C.   C < D < A < B
    D.   B < A < D < C

6. Which of the following is true regarding substitution reactions?

    A.   Tertiary alkyl halides always undergo substitution by S_N2 mechanism.
    B.   Only alkyl halides can undergo substitution reaction by S_N2 mechanism.
    C. S_N2 reactions involve the formation of a carbocation intermediate.
    D.   None of the above

7. Consider the reaction given in the passage. Which of the following compound is produced as a result of that particular reaction?

A. 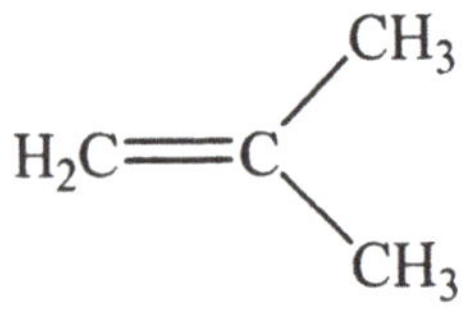 H_2C=C $\begin{array}{l} CH_3 \\ CH_3 \end{array}$

B. $(CH_3)_3COH$

C. $CH_3CH_2OC(CH)_3$

D. All the above are possible products.

8. Which of the following is characteristic of a typical S_N2 reaction?

    A. Rate = k [alkyl halide]
    B. Inversion of configuration
    C. Carbocation intermediate
    D. Unimolecular mechanism

9. Which of the following is the most reactive by substitution mechanism?

    A. CH_3I
    B. CH_3F
    C. CH_3Cl
    D. All are equally reactive.

Section 7

CONTENT REVIEW PROBLEMS

1. Which of the following solutions would NOT show rotation of plane polarized light?

    A.   2.0 M (R)-2-iodobutane
    B.   2.0 M (R)-2-iodobutane and 0.20 M (S)-2-iodobutane
    C.   2.0 M (S)-2-iodobutane
    D.   2.0 M (R)-2-iodobutane and 2.0 M (S)-2-iodobutane

2. A compound with three chiral carbons would have how many possible stereoisomers?

    A.   3
    B.   6
    C.   8
    D.   30

3. 2-butene and cyclobutane are:

    A.   cis-trans isomers.
    B.   structural isomers.
    C.   enantiomers.
    D.   tautomers.

4. Isomers that require no bond breaking to interconvert are:

    A.   conformational.
    B.   configurational.
    C.   structural.
    D.   tautomers.

5. Isomers that have the same bond connectivity, require bond-breaking to interconvert, but are not mirror images of each other are what kind of isomers?

    A.   Enantiomers
    B.   Conformational
    C.   Constitutional
    D.   Diastereomers

6. The hallmark of geometric (cis-trans) isomers is:

    A.   a mirror image relationship.
    B.   fundamentally different chemical properties.
    C.   alternate arrangements around a double bond.
    D.   chair and boat arrangements.

7. The enantiomer or mirror image of trans-2-butene would be:

    A.   cis-2-butene.
    B.   trans-2-butene.
    C.   cyclobutane.
    D.   boat conformation butene.

8. Each of the following would be optically inactive EXCEPT:

    A.   a solution of 0.01 M (S)-2-chlorobutane.
    B.   a solution containing 1.5 M of the R and 1.5 M of the S configurations of a molecule with one stereocenter.
    C.   a solution containing 2 M trans-2-butene but only 1 M cis-2-butene.
    D.   a solution containing a single molecule with two stereocenters and an internal plane of symmetry between the two stereocenters.

9. A cyclohexane molecule is more stable if:

    A.   it is in boat conformation with its larger substituents in axial positions.
    B.   it is in chair conformation with its larger substituents in axial positions.
    C.   it is in boat conformation with its larger substituents in equatorial positions.
    D.   it is in chair conformation with its larger substituents in equatorial positions.

10. Consider the following reaction:

This reaction gives a retention of:

    A. relative but not absolute configuration.
    B. relative and absolute configuration.
    C. absolute but not relative configuration.
    D. neither relative nor absolute configuration.

11. Which of the following compounds has the greatest number of π bonds?

    A. $C_{10}H_{22}$
    B. $C_{10}H_{20}$
    C. $C_{10}H_{18}$
    D. $C_{10}H_{16}$

12. Which of the following compounds has the greatest number of σ bonds?

    A. $C_{10}H_{22}$
    B. $C_{10}H_{20}$
    C. $C_{10}H_{18}$
    D. $C_{10}H_{16}$

13. The carbon atom in formaldehyde:

    A. possesses sp hybridization.
    B. possesses sp^2 hybridization.
    C. has four σ bonds.
    D. has two σ and two π bonds.

14. The molecule 1,2 ethynediol has:

    A. sp^2 hybridization around both carbons.
    B. sp^3 hybridization around one carbon.
    C. a total of five σ bonds
    D. a total of four π bonds.

15. A common Lewis acid reagent is BF_3. This molecule has:

    A. tetrahedral molecular geometry.
    B. trigonal pyramidal molecular geometry.
    C. sp^3 hybridization.
    D. trigonal planar molecular geometry.

16. A molecule with multiple resonance forms will demonstrate:

    A. molecular instability as the molecule oscillates between different resonance forms.
    B. increased ionization.
    C. decreased acidity.
    D. increased stability.

17. Compared to a triple bond, a resonance form comprised of one single and one double bond will be:

    A. more stable.
    B. shorter.
    C. more planar.
    D. longer.

18. The molecule C_8H_{16} is:

    A. octane.
    B. cyclononane.
    C. octene.
    D. heptane.

19. As the branching in an alkane increases:

    A. the boiling point decreases.
    B. the boiling point increases.
    C. molecular weight increases.
    D. molecular weight decreases.

20. Consider the following reaction:

$:\ddot{C}l\cdot + CH_3:H \qquad\qquad H:\ddot{C}l: + \cdot CH_3$

This represents:

    A.   an initiation step.
    B.   a propagation step.
    C.   a termination step.
    D.   an S_N2 reaction.

21. Consider the following reaction:
$CH_3I + NaOH \rightarrow CH_3OH + NaI$
This reaction demonstrates:

    A.   first-order kinetics.
    B.   second-order kinetics with respect to the base.
    C.   a two-step reaction mechanism.
    D.   second-order kinetics.

Consider the following reaction for Questions 22-23

$CH_3I + NaOH \rightarrow CH_3OH + NaI$

22. This reaction demonstrates:

    A.   an intermediate with a charged carbon species.
    B.   faster reaction rate in a polar protic solvent.
    C.   a transition state but no intermediate.
    D.   slower reaction rate than would be present with a more substituted carbon.

23. This reaction demonstrates:
    A.   a one-step mechanism.
    B.   a less favorable energy profile than if fluorine were the leaving group.
    C.   a rate law of $R = k[CH_3I]$
    D.   a carbocation intermediate.

24. Which of the following would favor an S_N1 reaction mechanism?

    A.   A methyl substrate
    B.   Resonance stabilization of the carbocation.
    C.   A polar aprotic solvent
    D.   A leaving group with an unstable lone pair.

25. Which of the following would favor an S_N1 reaction mechanism?

    A.   Inductive destabilization of the leaving group
    B.   A polar protic solvent
    C.   A substrate with little steric hindrance
    D.   A one-step reaction mechanism

SECTION 8
OXYGEN-CONTAINING COMPOUNDS

The term "oxygen containing compounds" covers a huge swath of organic chemistry, so understandably this section is one of the most extensive in the book, with five full chapters. As you work through the following chapters it is critically important that you keep in mind our general advice from the start of the previous section.

The MCAT's concern when it comes to organic chemistry is general principles, and how those principles tie into living systems. As such, you should move relatively briskly through these sections. Familiarize yourself with the nomenclature, the various functional groups, and their general properties. When reviewing the various reactions, don't worry about memorizing *what* the exact steps are, but *why* they are happening.

A. INTRODUCTION

Alcohols have the general formula **ROH**.

Some common examples of alcohols:

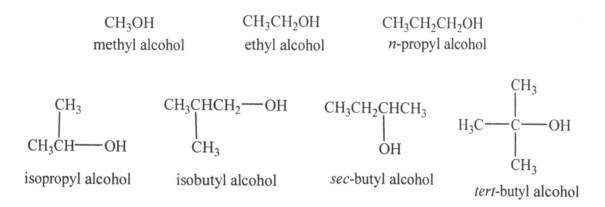

$$CH_3OH$$
methyl alcohol

$$CH_3CH_2OH$$
ethyl alcohol

$$CH_3CH_2CH_2OH$$
n-propyl alcohol

isopropyl alcohol

isobutyl alcohol

sec-butyl alcohol

tert-butyl alcohol

B. PROPERTIES OF ALCOHOLS

Boiling Point

One of the most important properties of alcohols is their ability to form hydrogen bonds. Since alcohols can form hydrogen bonds, they have very high boiling points. Consider the following comparative analysis to clarify this idea.

> The boiling point of ethane (C_2H_6) is $-88.7\ ^0$ C.
> The boiling point of propane (C_3H_8) is $-42.2\ ^0$ C.
> The boiling point of ethanol (C_2H_5OH) is $78\ ^0$ C.

Note the drastic difference in their boiling points.

By the above comparison, it is clear that some extra forces (here mainly H bonds) are working to increase the boiling points of alcohols.

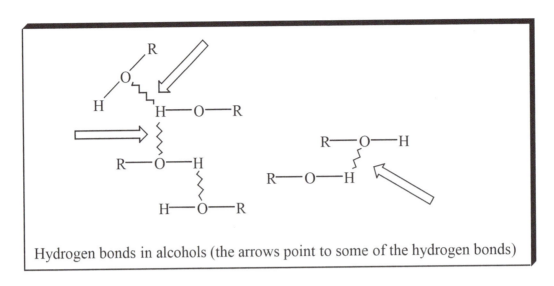

Hydrogen bonds in alcohols (the arrows point to some of the hydrogen bonds)

Figure 19-1

Solubility in H₂O

Low-molecular weight alcohols are soluble in water. The hydrogen bond formation plays a key role in the solubility of alcohols in water. In other words, hydrogen bonds enhance the solubility of alcohols in H_2O. As the number of carbons increases, the solubility of alcohols decreases as they become more and more similar to hydrocarbons with longer and longer nonpolar hydrocarbon chains.

Acidity of Alcohols

Alcohols are weakly acidic. In fact, they are weaker in acidity than water. Alcohols have K_a values around 10^{-17}.

Alcohols give off the acidic hydrogen to form **alkoxide ions**. Alkoxide ion is the conjugate base of alcohols and they are strong bases.

$$R\!-\!OH \xrightarrow{\ \ OH^-\ \ } R\!-\!O^- \ + \ H_2O$$

Alcohol   Alkoxide ion   Water

Among alcohols, primary alcohols are the most acidic, and tertiary alcohols are the least acidic.

Relative acidity: 3° alcohols < 2° alcohols < 1° alcohols

C. SYNTHESIS OF ALCOHOLS

Acid-Catalyzed Reaction

Sample reaction 19-1

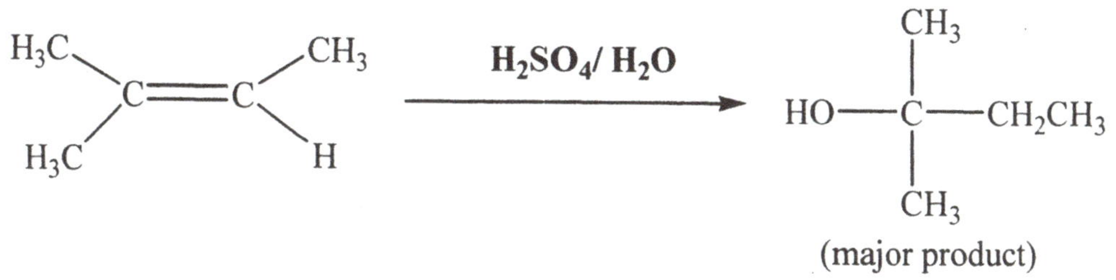

$$H_3C-C(CH_3)=C(CH_3)(H) \xrightarrow{H_2SO_4/H_2O} HO-C(CH_3)(CH_3)-CH_2CH_3$$
(major product)

Alkenes react with aqueous acidic solutions to form alcohols. The reaction intermediate is a **carbocation**. Hence, there is a possibility of rearrangement of the intermediates in such acid-catalyzed reactions. The reaction follows the **Markovnikov's rule**. Keep in mind that a tertiary carbocation is more stable than a secondary carbocation, which in turn is more stable than a primary carbocation.

Hydroboration-Oxidation

Sample reaction 19-2

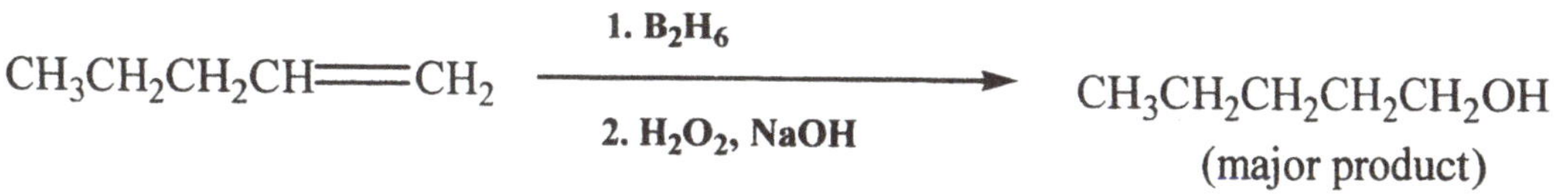

$$CH_3CH_2CH_2CH=CH_2 \xrightarrow[\text{2. } H_2O_2,\ NaOH]{\text{1. } B_2H_6} CH_3CH_2CH_2CH_2CH_2OH$$
(major product)

Oxidation followed by hydroboration of alkenes results in alcohols. The reaction occurs in an **anti-Markovnikov** fashion. Notice that hydrogen, instead of attaching to the carbon with the highest number of hydrogens, attaches to the carbon with the least number of hydrogens.

Oxymercuration-Demercuration

Sample reaction 19-3

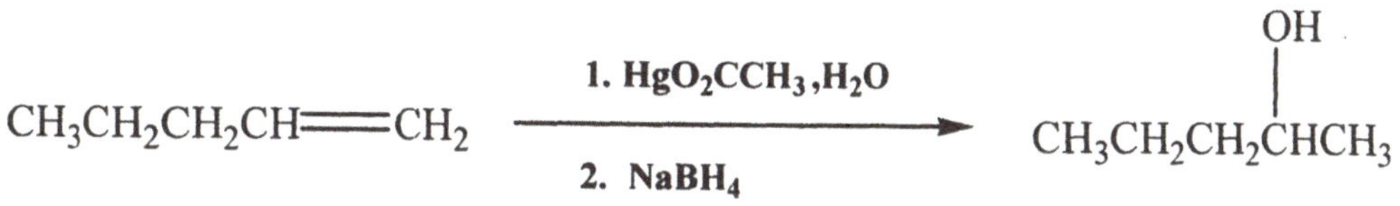

$$CH_3CH_2CH_2CH=CH_2 \xrightarrow[\text{2. } NaBH_4]{\text{1. } HgO_2CCH_3,\ H_2O} CH_3CH_2CH_2CH(OH)CH_3$$

Alkenes can be converted to alcohols by **oxymercuration-demercuration**. The addition of H and OH is in accordance with the **Markovnikov's rule**. There is no rearrangement in this reaction.

From Epoxides

Preparation of an alcohol from an epoxide is shown below. The epoxide (ethylene oxide) ring opens when the nucleophile attacks the carbon-oxygen bond. Note the fact that the nucleophilic carbon is supplied by the Grignard reagent (methyl magnesium bromide).

Sample reaction 19-4

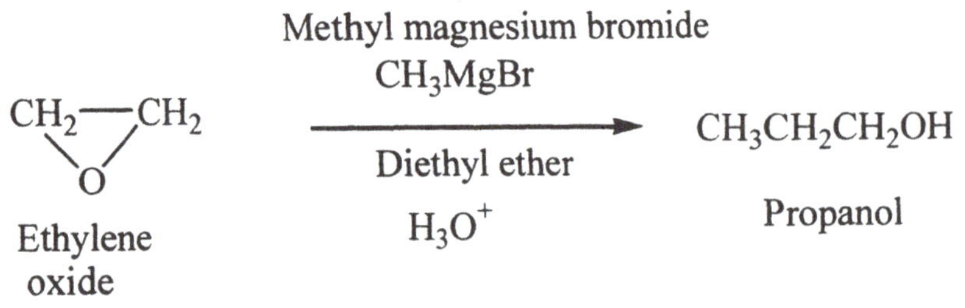

Alcohols can also be produced from aldehydes and ketones via Grignard reagents. Other methods to synthesize alcohols include the reduction of aldehydes and ketones. These reactions will be discussed later in the section.

D. REACTIONS OF ALCOHOLS

Formation of Alkoxides

Alcohols when treated with Group I metals like sodium and potassium result in alkoxides.

Sample reaction 19-5

$$\underset{\text{Methanol}}{2\ CH_3OH} \xrightarrow{2\ Na} \underset{\text{Sodium methoxide}}{2\ CH_3ONa} + 2\ H_2$$

Formation of Alkyl Halides

Sample reaction 19-6

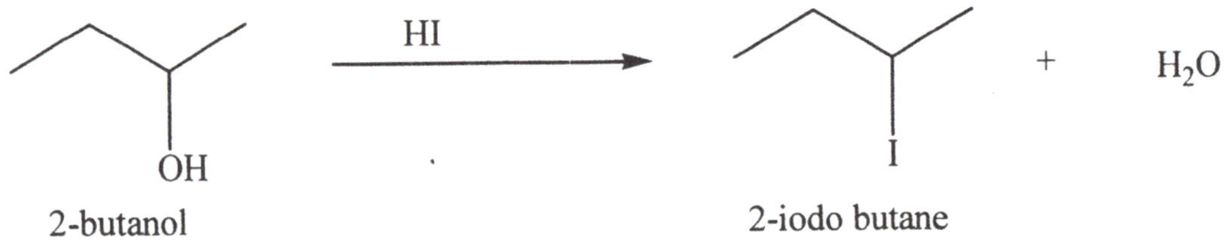

Sample reaction 19-7

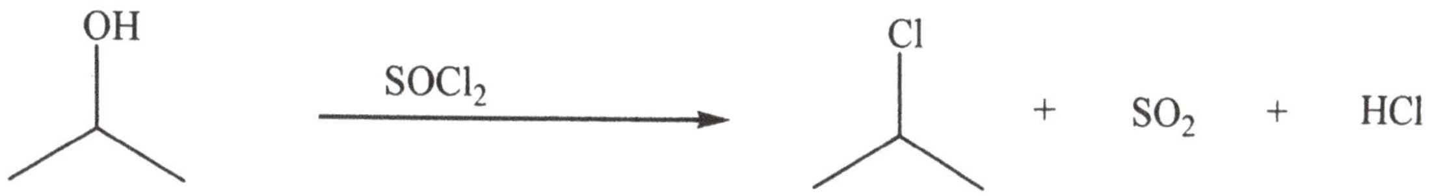
OH
$SOCl_2$
Cl
+ SO_2 + HCl

Oxidation of Alcohols

Primary alcohols can be oxidized to aldehydes by reagents like pyridinium dichromate (PDC), and pyridinium chlorochromate (PCC).

Sample reaction 19-8

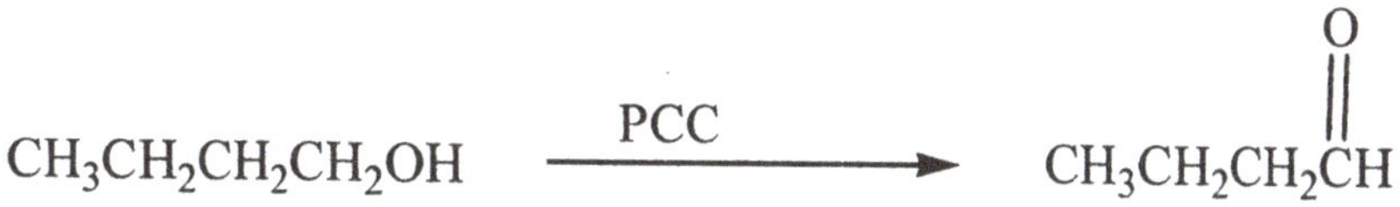
$CH_3CH_2CH_2CH_2OH$
PCC
O
$CH_3CH_2CH_2CH$

Butanol   Butanal (aldehyde)

Secondary alcohols can also be oxidized. The product is a ketone.

Sample reaction 19-9

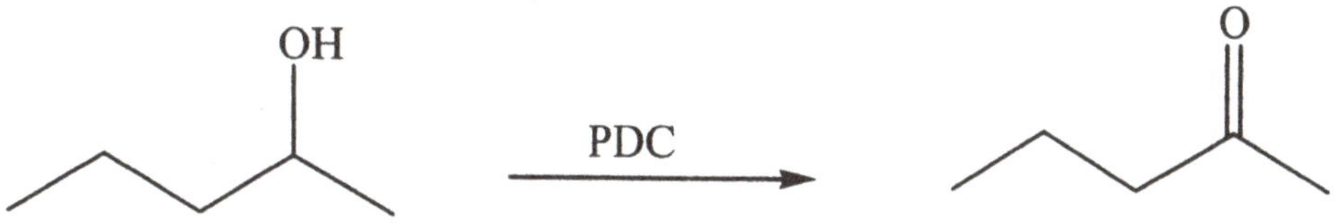
OH
PDC
O

2-Pentanol   2-Pentanone

Since tertiary alcohols do not have a hydrogen atom in the carbon carrying the hydroxyl group, they cannot be easily oxidized.

Strong oxidizing agents can oxidize alcohols to carboxylic acids. We can use potassium permanganate or chromic acid to do this conversion.

Sample reaction 19-10

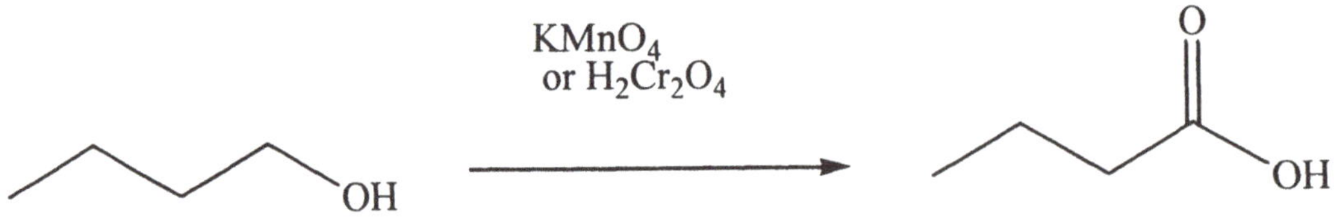

Primary alcohol → Carboxylic acid

Primary alcohol [oxidization] → Aldehyde [oxidization] → Carboxylic acid

Secondary alcohol [oxidization] → Ketone

Acid-Catalyzed Dehydration

Alcohols undergo acid-catalyzed dehydration reactions to form alkenes. The reaction is accomplished by the formation of a carbocation intermediate. Thus there is the possibility of rearrangement in the process. First, we will take a look at the mechanism of this reaction.

Mechanism of Acid-Catalyzed Dehydration of Alcohols

Sample reaction 19-11

$$(CH_3)_3COH \xrightarrow{\ H_3O^+ / heat\ } (H_3C)_2C = CH_2$$

The alcohol is protonated.

Step (1)

$$(CH_3)_3C\ \ddot{\underset{\cdot\cdot}{O}}H \xrightarrow{\ H_3O^+\ } (CH_3)_3C\overset{+}{\underset{H}{\ddot{O}}}{}^{\nearrow H} + H_2O$$

The formation of a carbocation.

Step (2)

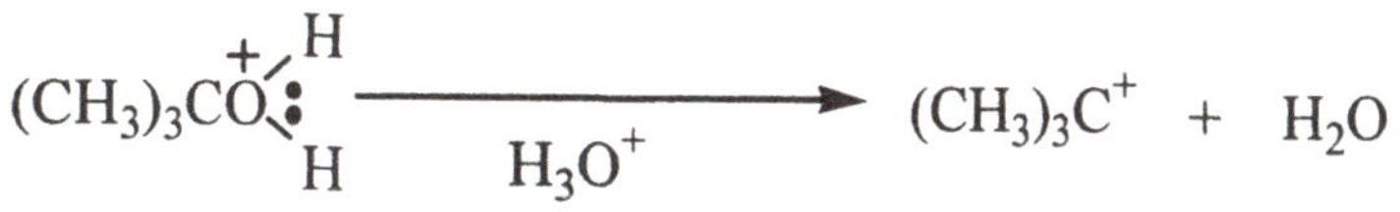

$$(CH_3)_3CO\!\!\!\overset{+}{\underset{H}{\overset{H}{\cdots}}} \xrightarrow{H_3O^+} (CH_3)_3C^+ \ + \ H_2O$$

The formation of a double bond.

Step (3)

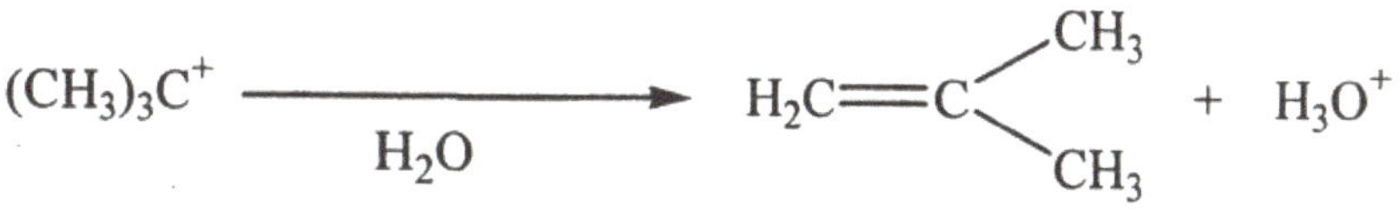

$$(CH_3)_3C^+ \xrightarrow{H_2O} H_2C\!\!=\!\!C\!\!\overset{CH_3}{\underset{CH_3}{\diagdown}} \ + \ H_3O^+$$

Rearrangement – An Example

Organic chemists have conducted experiments to understand the formation of multiple products in acid-catalyzed reactions such as that of 3,3-dimethyl-2-butanol. Let's consider the acid-catalyzed dehydration reaction of 3,3-dimethyl-2-butanol and explore the possibility of rearrangement.

$$(CH_3)_3CCHOHCH_3 \quad \text{3,3-Dimethyl-2-butanol}$$

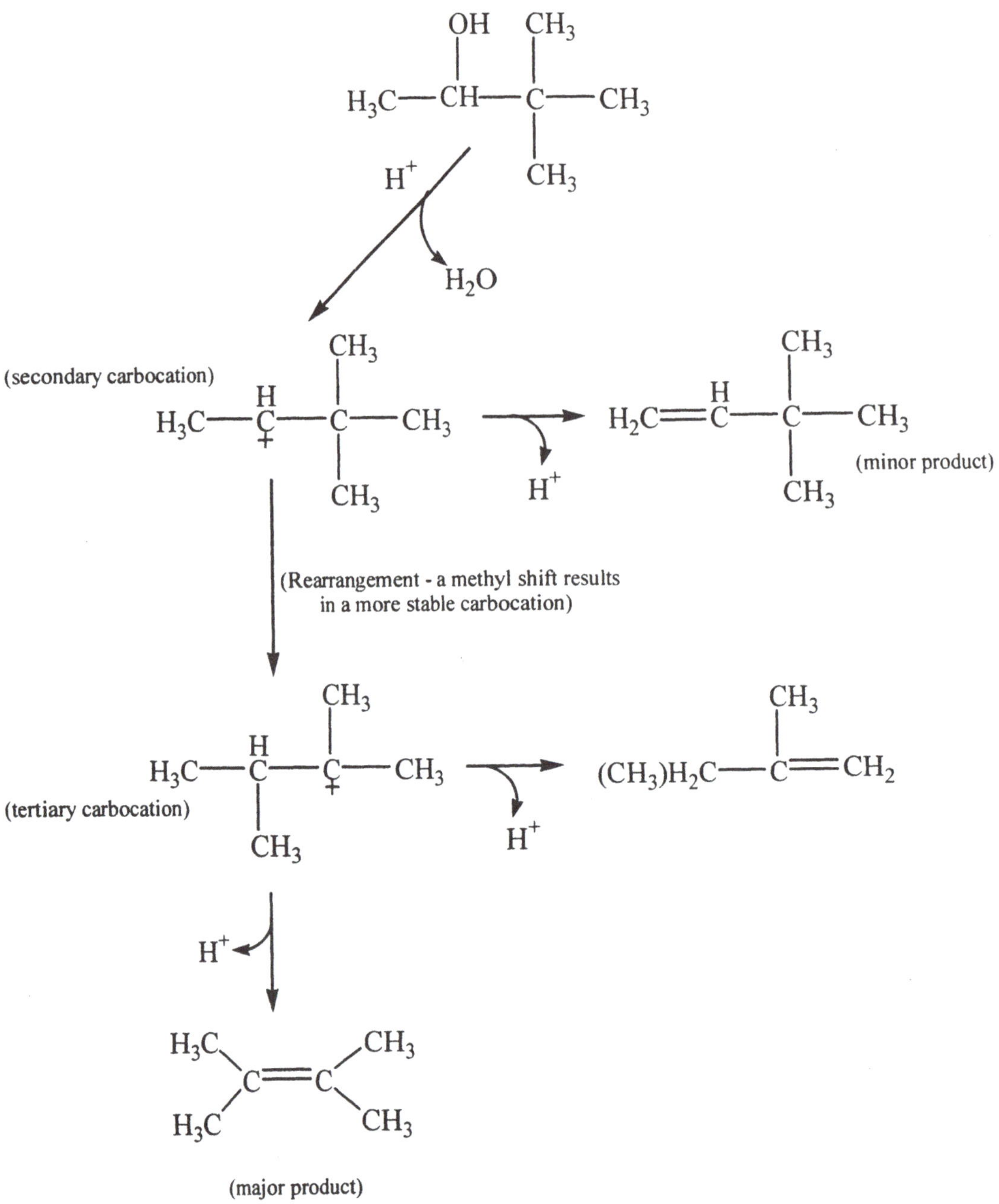

Figure 19-2

The major product formed in this reaction is 2,3-dimethyl-1-butene. Notice (Figure 2) the rearrangement that occurs in this reaction. The rearrangement results in a more stable carbocation (A tertiary carbocation is more stable than a secondary carbocation).

CHAPTER 19 PRACTICE QUESTIONS

1. The higher boiling points exhibited by alcohols with respect to comparable alkanes and ethers are primarily due to:

    A.   ionic bonds.
    B.   covalent bonds.
    C.   hydrogen bonds.
    D.   none of the above.

2. The conjugate base of alcohols are generally called:

    A.   alkyl ions.
    B.   alcoholic ions.
    C.   alkoxide ions.
    D.   vinyl ions.

3. Which of the following is a possible way of making alcohols?

    A.   Hydroboration-oxidation of alkenes
    B.   Acid catalyzed hydration of alkenes
    C.   Oxymercuration-demercuration of alkenes
    D.   All the above

4. An organic chemist synthesized and isolated the compound below. If this compound undergoes oxymercuration-demercuration reaction, the major product is most likely:

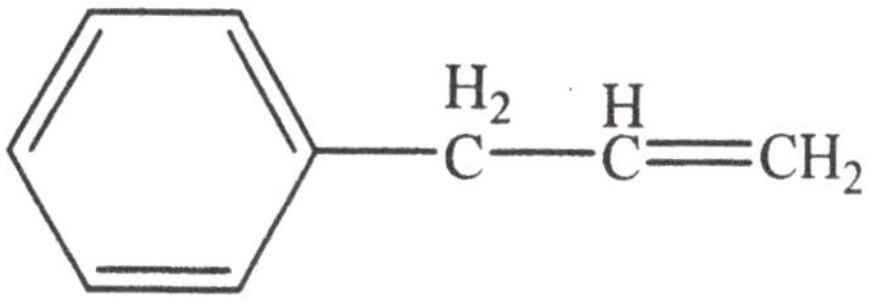

A. $-CH_2CH_2CH_2OH$

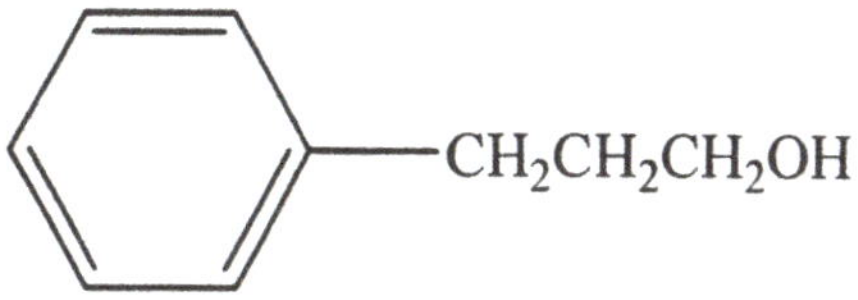

B. $-CH_2\overset{\overset{\textstyle OH}{|}}{C}HCH_3$

C. $-CH_2CH_2CHO$

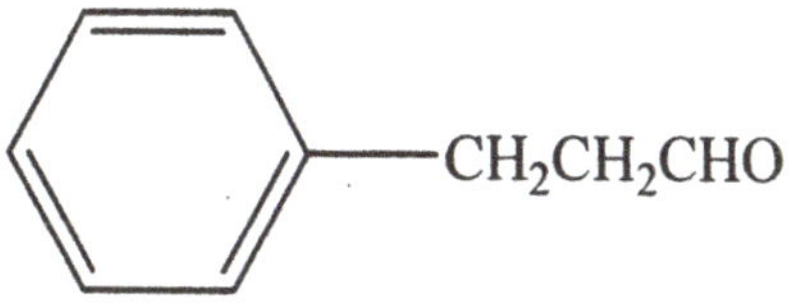

D. $-CH_2CH_2COOH$

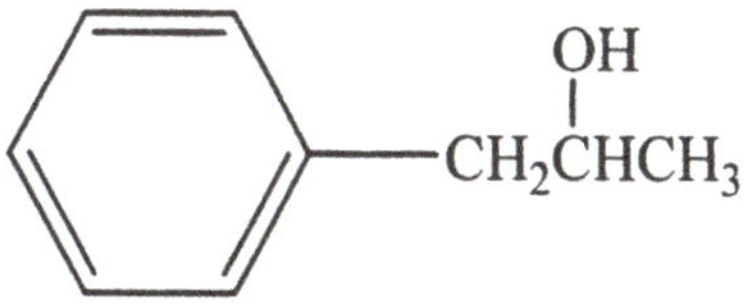

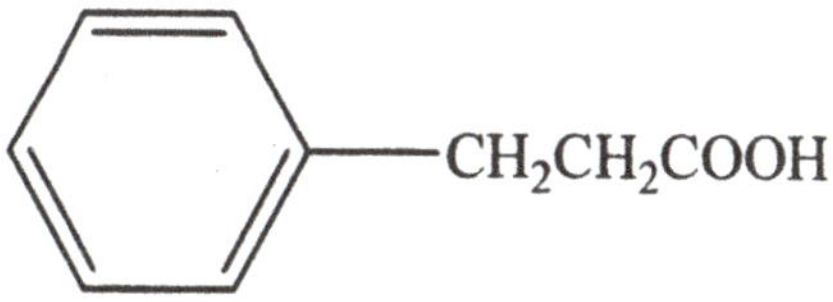

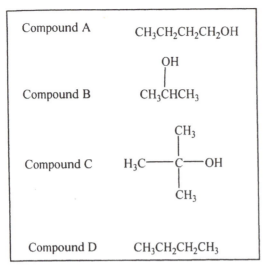

Table X (Question 5)

5. From Table X, the most acidic compound is:

   A. Compound A.
   B. Compound B.
   C. Compound C.
   D. Compound D.

6. Direct oxidation of which of the following can result in a carboxylic acid?

   A. Secondary alcohol
   B. Tertiary alcohol
   C. Primary alcohol
   D. All the above

7. Choose the correct product formed as a result of the reduction of a ketone.

   A. A primary alcohol
   B. A secondary alcohol
   C. A tertiary alcohol
   D. None of the above

8. The major product of the reaction shown is:

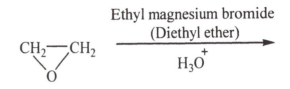

   A. a four-carbon ketone.
   B. a four-carbon halohydrin.
   C. a two-carbon aldehyde.
   D. a four-carbon alcohol.

9. Identify Compound B from the sequence of reactions.

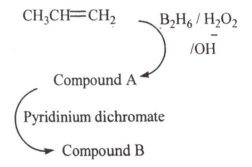

   A. Propanol
   B. Propanal
   C. Acetone
   D. Formaldehyde

10. Reduction of the organic compound shown results in:

   A. a ketone.
   B. a primary alcohol.
   C. a carboxylic acid.
   D. an ester.

Questions 11-15 are based on the following passage.

Passage 1

Alcohols are of tremendous use for the synthesis of a wide variety of organic compounds. They also have some very unique properties. Alcohols are in fact slightly weaker acids than water, and have pK_a values between 16 and 18.

An alcohol can lose its acidic hydrogen to form an alkoxide ion.

Reaction 1

$$2\ CH_3CH_2OH \xrightarrow{\quad 2\ Na \quad} 2\ NaOCH_2CH_3$$

11. The alcohol shown is:

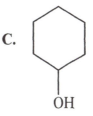

    A.   *cis*-2-ethylcyclohexanol.
    B.   *cis*-2-ethylcycloctanol.
    C.   *cis*-1-ethyl-2-hydroxycyclopentane.
    D.   *trans*-2-ethylcyclohexanol.

12. Which of the following is the most acidic?

    A. $(CH_3)_3COH$
    B. NH_3
    C. $(CH_3)_2CHOH$
    D. CH_3OH

13. In Reaction 1, predict the identity of the other product, if any.

    A. H_2O
    B. O_2
    C. H_2
    D.   No other products are produced.

14. Which of the following is the most reactive alcohol towards sodium?

    A. CH_3OH

    B. $(CH_3)_3COH$

    C.

    D. $H_3C-CH-CH\begin{smallmatrix}CH_3\\ \\CH_3\end{smallmatrix}$ (with OH on second carbon)

15. Which of the following can be used to make propanol directly by oxidation?

    A. CH_3CH_2CHO

    B. CH_3CH_2COOH

    C. $CH_3\overset{\overset{\displaystyle O}{\|}}{C}CH_3$

    D.   None of the above

CHAPTER 20

Carbonyl Compounds

A. INTRODUCTION

Aldehydes and **ketones** are compounds containing the acyl group. The carbonyl group present in them is polar because of the electronegativity of oxygen. It is noteworthy to mention that the carbonyl group in aldehydes and ketones are very reactive.

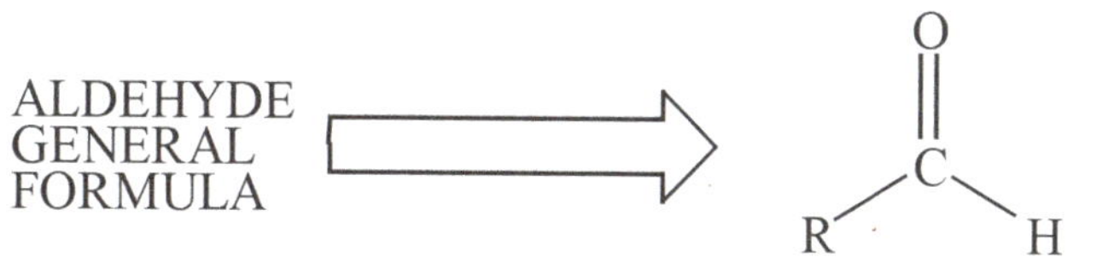

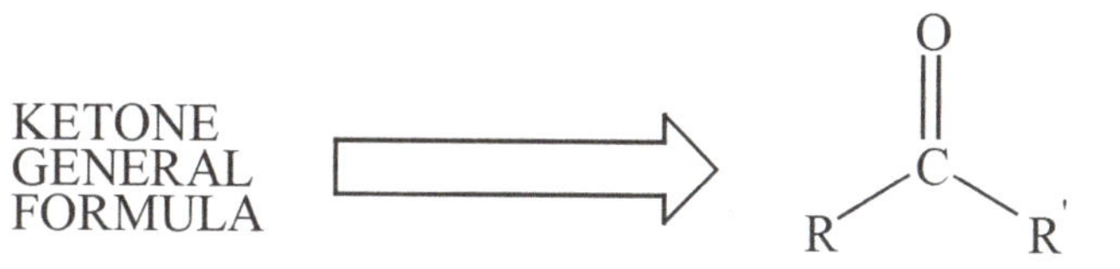

ALDEHYDE
GENERAL
FORMULA ⟹

$$\begin{array}{c} O \\ \parallel \\ R \diagup C \diagdown H \end{array}$$

KETONE
GENERAL
FORMULA ⟹

$$\begin{array}{c} O \\ \parallel \\ R \diagup C \diagdown R' \end{array}$$

$$\begin{array}{c} \delta^- \\ :\!O\!: \\ \parallel \\ R \diagup \overset{+}{\underset{\delta^+}{C}} \diagdown \end{array}$$

ACYL GROUP

$$\begin{array}{c} \delta^- \\ :\!O\!: \\ \parallel \\ \diagup \overset{+}{\underset{\delta^+}{C}} \diagdown \end{array}$$

CARBONYL GROUP

The partial negative charge on the oxygen is because of its higher electronegativity compared to carbon. This gives the carbonyl carbon a partial positive charge.

B. ALDEHYDES AND KETONES

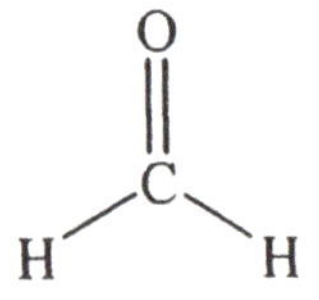

Methanal
(formaldehyde)

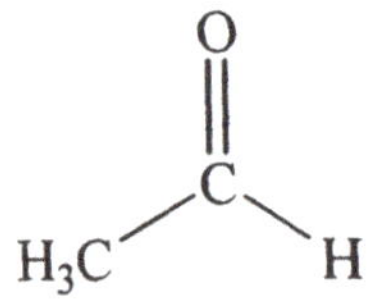

Ethanal
(acetaldehyde)

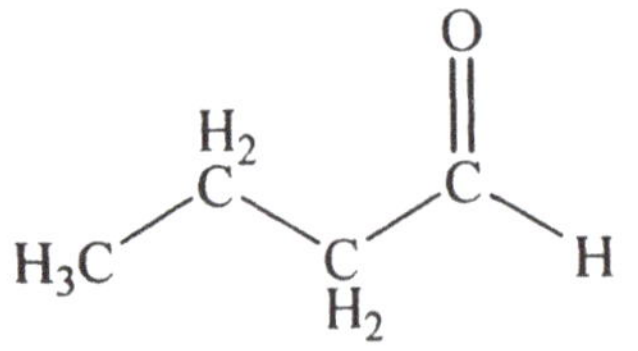

Butanal
(butanaldehyde)

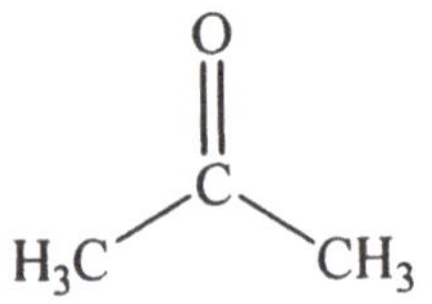

Acetone

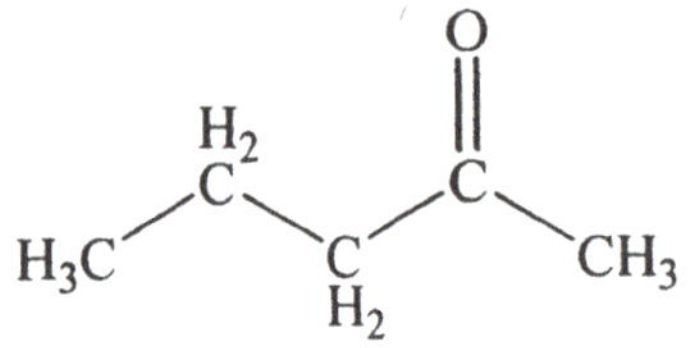

2-pentanone

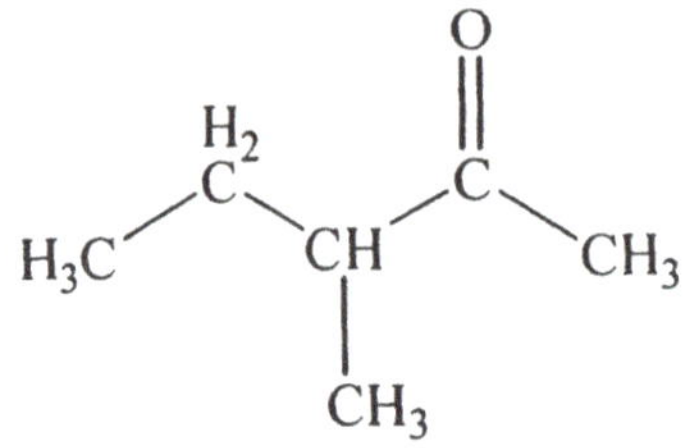

3-methyl-2-pentanone

Properties of Aldehydes and Ketones

The carbonyl group present in aldehydes and ketones make them polar in nature. Both aldehydes and ketones have higher boiling points than comparable hydrocarbons. Aldehydes and ketones do not form hydrogen bonds themselves. Hence, they have lower boiling and melting points compared to alcohols with comparable molecular weights. Finally, aldehydes and ketones have higher solubility in water than hydrocarbons, but less solubility than alcohols. Even though aldehydes and ketones cannot undergo hydrogen bonding themselves, they can undergo hydrogen bonding with water molecules.

C. SYNTHESIS OF ALDEHYDES AND KETONES

From Alcohols

Aldehydes can be prepared by the oxidation of primary alcohols. Oxidizing agents such as pyridinium chlorochromate (PCC) or pyridinium dichromate (PDC) can be used for such conversions.

Sample reaction 20-1

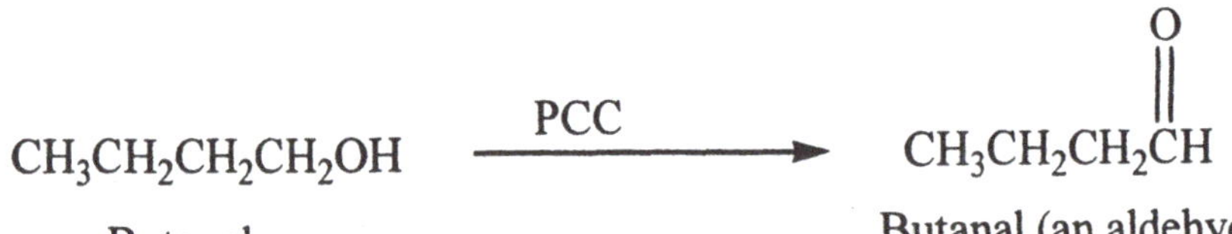

$CH_3CH_2CH_2CH_2OH \xrightarrow{\text{PCC}}$

Butanol

$CH_3CH_2CH_2\overset{\overset{\displaystyle O}{\|}}{C}H$

Butanal (an aldehyde)

Oxidation of secondary alcohols results in ketones.

Sample reaction 20-2

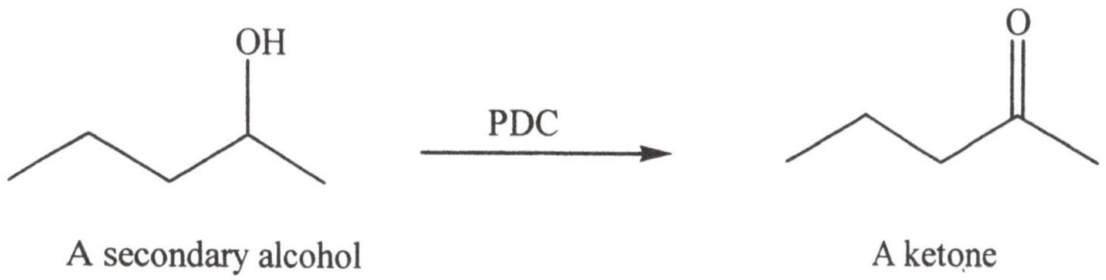

OH

PDC →

O

A secondary alcohol   A ketone

From Alkenes by Ozonolysis

Aldehydes and ketones can be prepared by the ozonolysis of alkenes.

Sample reaction 20-3

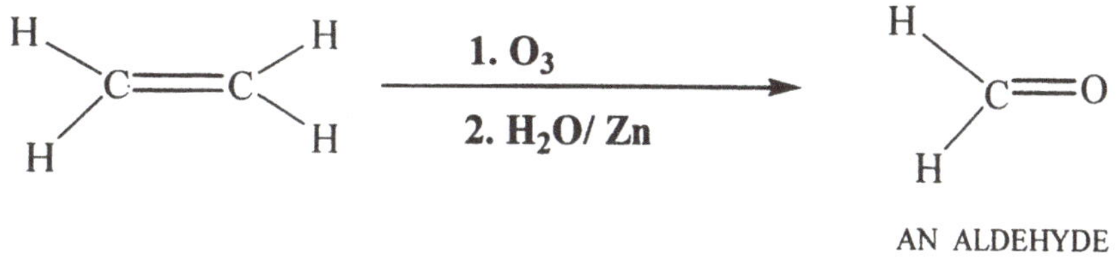

H₂C=CH₂ → **1. O₃** **2. H₂O/ Zn** → H₂C=O

AN ALDEHYDE

Sample reaction 20-4

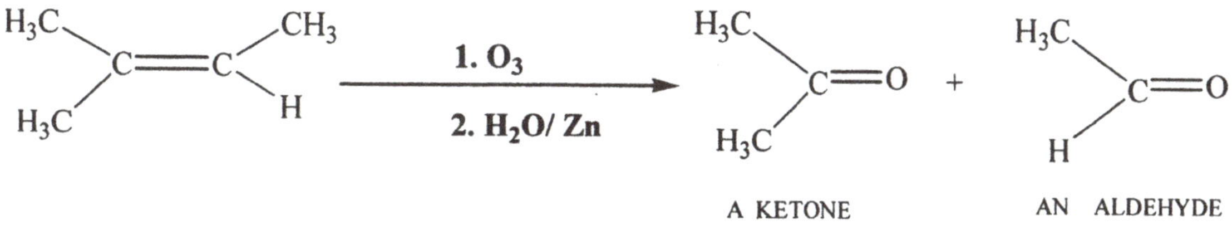

(H₃C)₂C=C(CH₃)H → **1. O₃** **2. H₂O/ Zn** → (H₃C)₂C=O + (H₃C)(H)C=O

A KETONE   AN ALDEHYDE

D. NUCLEOPHILIC ADDITION TO THE CARBONYL GROUP

The carbon of the carbonyl group is an electrophile. Thus it is susceptible to nucleophilic attack. During most addition reactions of alkenes, it is an electrophile that attacks the pi system. But in an addition reaction involving a carbonyl group, we see that the attack on the carbonyl carbon is made by a nucleophile. Think about why this is the case? One reason for this is the polar nature (due to electronegativity of the oxygen atom) of the carbonyl group. Furthermore, the resonance capability of the carbonyl group also enhances this type of reactive property. A generalized nucleophilic attack is shown below in Figure 20-1.

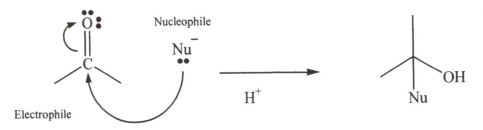

Figure 1

E. REACTIONS OF ALDEHYDES AND KETONES

Formation of Carboxylic Acids

Aldehydes can be oxidized to carboxylic acids using oxidizing agents such as potassium permanganate.

Sample reaction 20-5

$$RCHO \xrightarrow{\text{KMnO}_4} RCOOH$$

Sample reaction 20-6

$$CH_3CH_2-\overset{\overset{\text{O}}{\|}}{C}-H \xrightarrow[\text{/ dil. H}_2\text{SO}_4]{\text{Na}_2\text{Cr}_2\text{O}_7} CH_3CH_2-\overset{\overset{\text{O}}{\|}}{C}-OH$$

Sample reaction 20-7

$$R-\overset{\overset{\text{O}}{\|}}{C}_{\diagdown H} + 2[Ag(NH_3)_2]^+_{(aq)} + H_2O_{(l)} \longrightarrow R-\overset{\overset{\text{O}}{\|}}{C}_{\diagdown O^-} + 3NH_4^+{}_{(aq)} + NH_{3(aq)} + 2Ag_{(s)}$$

Tollens Reagent

With Grignard Reagents

Aldehydes and ketones react with Grignard reagents to form alcohols.

Grignard reagents are organometallic compounds. These reagents can be prepared from organic halides by reacting with magnesium.

$$RBr \xrightarrow{\text{Mg}} RMgBr$$

$$CH_3Br \xrightarrow{\text{Mg}} CH_3MgBr$$

Formaldehyde reacts with Grignard reagents to form primary alcohols.

Sample reaction 20-8

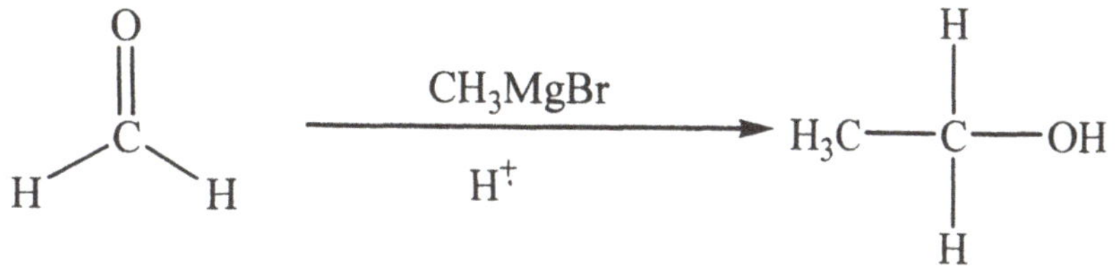

Other aldehydes react with Grignard reagents to form secondary alcohols.

Sample reaction 20-9

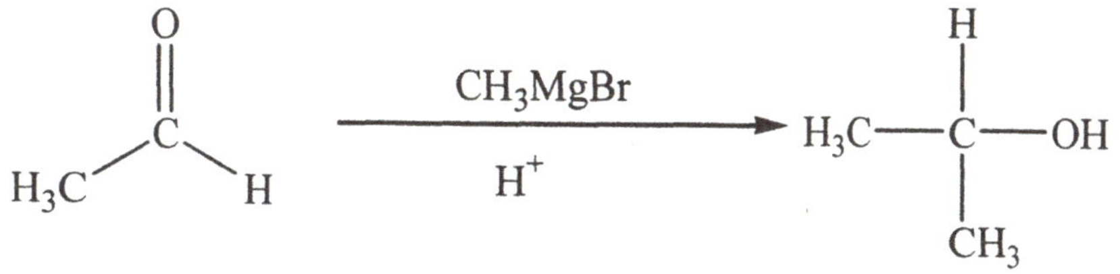

Aldehyde

2-Propanol

Ketones give tertiary alcohols.

Sample reaction 20-10

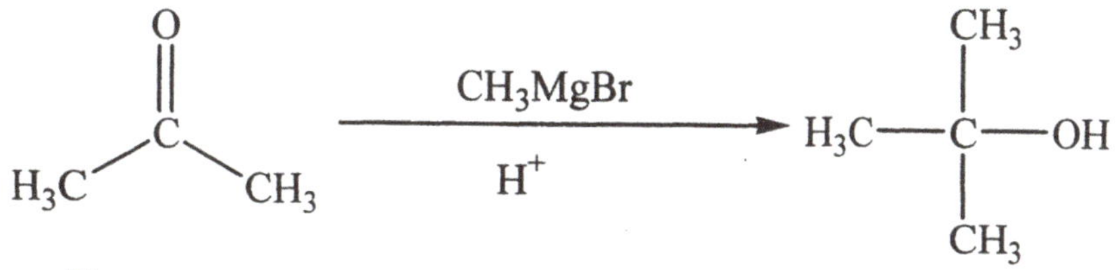

Ketone

Tertiary alcohol

Aldol Addition and Condensation

In aldol addition reactions, a carbon-carbon bond is formed between the carbonyl carbon of one aldehyde molecule and the α-carbon of another aldehyde molecule. The product is a β-hydroxy aldehyde. After the nucleophilic addition of the enolate ion to the carbonyl group, removal of water of the β-hydroxy aldehyde can occur resulting in an α,β-unsaturated aldehyde. Study Sample reactions 20-11 and 20-12.

Sample reaction 20-11

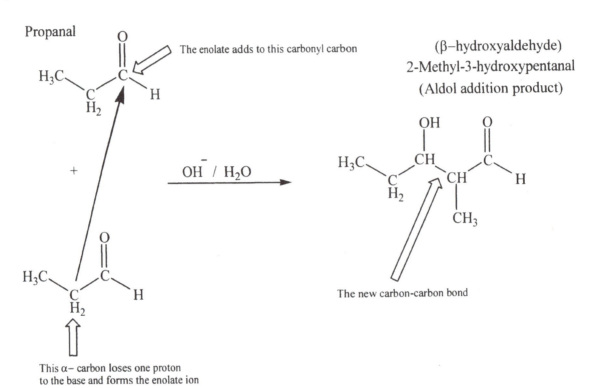

Sample reaction 20-12

The addition product upon heating will undergo elimination (dehydration) to form the α,β-unsaturated aldehyde.

α,β–Unsaturated aldehyde
(aldol condensation product)

Reduction Reactions

Conversion to Alcohols

Aldehydes and ketones can be reduced to alcohols using reducing agents such as lithium aluminum hydride ($LiAlH_4$), and sodium borohydride ($NaBH_4$).

Sample reaction 20-13

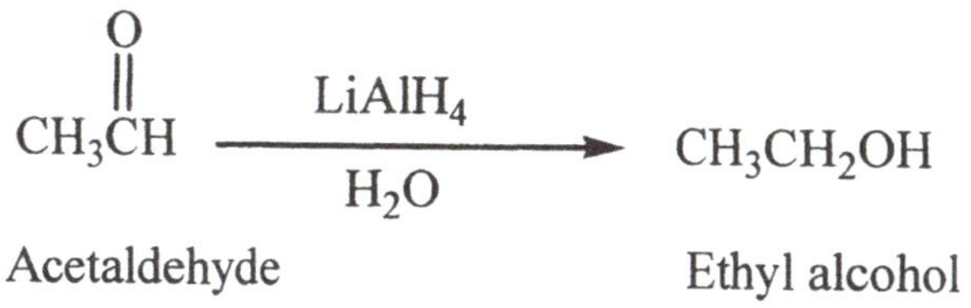

$$CH_3\overset{\overset{\displaystyle O}{\|}}{C}H \xrightarrow[H_2O]{LiAlH_4} CH_3CH_2OH$$

Acetaldehyde   Ethyl alcohol

Sample reaction 20-14

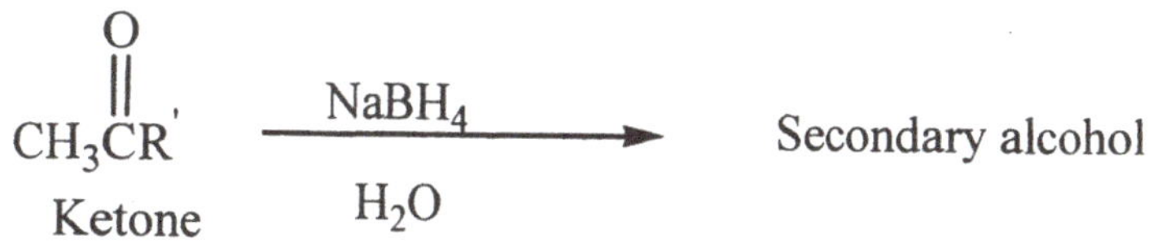

$$CH_3\overset{\overset{\displaystyle O}{\|}}{C}R' \xrightarrow[H_2O]{NaBH_4} \text{Secondary alcohol}$$

Ketone

Conversion to Hydrocarbons

The carbonyl groups of aldehydes and ketones can be converted to methylene groups by Clemmensen and Wolff-Kishner reduction reactions.

Sample reaction 20-15

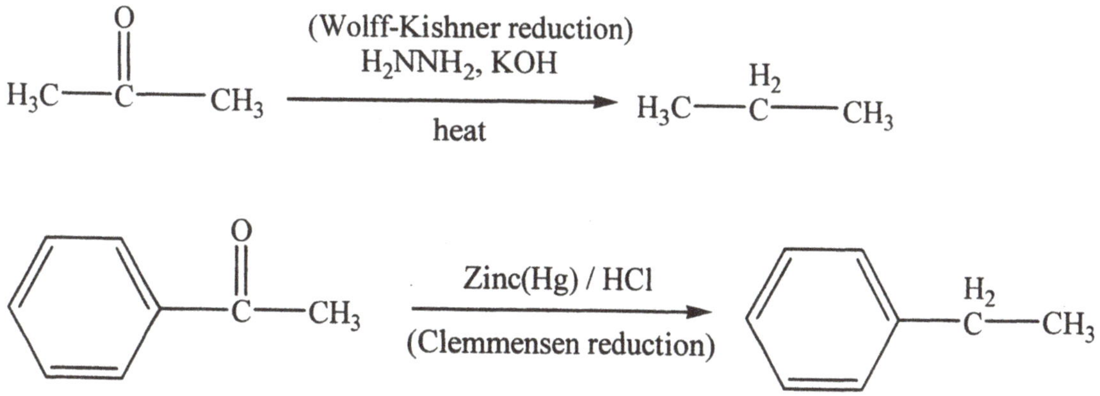

$$H_3C-\overset{\overset{\displaystyle O}{\|}}{C}-CH_3 \xrightarrow[\text{heat}]{\substack{\text{(Wolff-Kishner reduction)} \\ H_2NNH_2,\ KOH}} H_3C-\overset{\overset{\displaystyle H_2}{}}{C}-CH_3$$

$$\text{Ph}-\overset{\overset{\displaystyle O}{\|}}{C}-CH_3 \xrightarrow[\text{(Clemmensen reduction)}]{Zinc(Hg)\ /\ HCl} \text{Ph}-\overset{\overset{\displaystyle H_2}{}}{C}-CH_3$$

F. ACETALS

Aldehydes can undergo reactions with alcohols under acidic conditions. The product of this nucleophilic addition reaction is called a **hemiacetal**. A hemiacetal is formed by the nucleophilic addition of alcohol to the carbonyl carbon. A hemiacetal can react with one more mole of alcohol to form an **acetal**.

In monosaccharides (e.g., glucose, fructose), the cyclic ring structure is formed by the intramolecular reaction between the carbonyl and the hydroxyl groups within the same molecule. Glucose (an aldohexose) forms a cyclic hemiacetal by the intramolecular reaction between the aldehyde group of carbon 1 and the hydroxyl group of carbon 5.

FORMATION OF CYCLIC STRUCTURE OF GLUCOSE

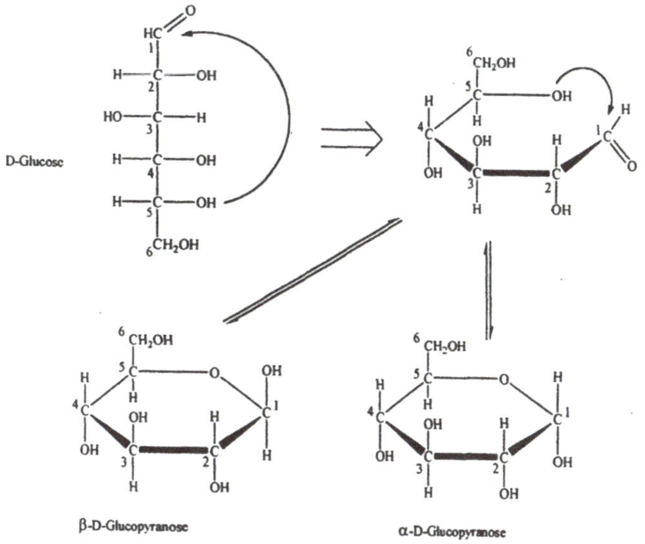

D-Glucose

β-D-Glucopyranose

α-D-Glucopyranose

CHAPTER 20 PRACTICE QUESTIONS

1. Propanal is treated with ethyl magnesium halide (with diethyl ether and H_3O^+). Which of the following is true regarding this reaction?

    A. A five-carbon ether is the major product.
    B. A five-carbon secondary alcohol is the major product.
    C. A five-carbon ketone is the major product.
    D. None of the above are true.

2. The structure shown below represents:

$$\underset{CH_3CH_2CHOCH_2CH_3}{\overset{\overset{\displaystyle OH}{|}}{}}$$

    A. a ketal.
    B. a hemiacetal.
    C. an acetal.
    D. a hemiketal.

3. The Baeyer-Villiger reaction is a very useful synthesis reaction. An example is the reaction of acetone with peroxyacetic acid to give an ester and a carboxylic acid. This reaction can be generalized as:

    A. a reduction reaction.
    B. an oxidation reaction.
    C. a hydrolysis reaction.
    D. an isomerization reaction.

4. Predict the aldol addition product of the structure shown below.

$$CH_3CH_2CH_2CH_2CH_2CHO$$

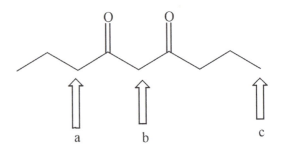

5. Which of the following carbons indicated by arrows has the most acidic protons?

    A. a
    B. b
    C. c
    D. No acidic protons are present, since ketones cannot be acidic.

6. The structure represented below can be most appropriately called an:

$$CH_3CH=C\overset{\displaystyle O^-}{\underset{\displaystyle CH_3}{\Big\langle}}$$

A. alkenyl ion.
B. acyl ion.
C. alkoxide cation.
D. enolate ion.

7. Predict the aldol condensation product (major product) of the following compound.

A.

B.

C.

D.

8. Which of the following is the conjugate base of a ketone?

A.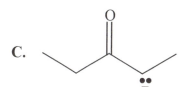

B.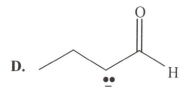

C.

D.

9. A student is trying to prove the identity of a compound that she synthesized. She knows that the compound is a methyl ketone. Which of the following qualitative tests can be used to prove the identity of the synthesized compound as a methyl ketone?

A. Ignition test
B. Potassium permanganate test
C. Beilstein test
D. Iodoform test

10. The chromic acid test can be used for the identification of:

A. aldehydes and ketones.
B. aldehydes only.
C. ketones only.
D. carboxylic acids only.

Questions 11-16 are based on the following passage.

Passage 1

Students of an organic chemistry class conducted several experiments with aldehydes and ketones. Some of the reactions are summarized below:

Experiment 1

Acetophenone was reacted with Reagent A. The product was ethyl benzene.

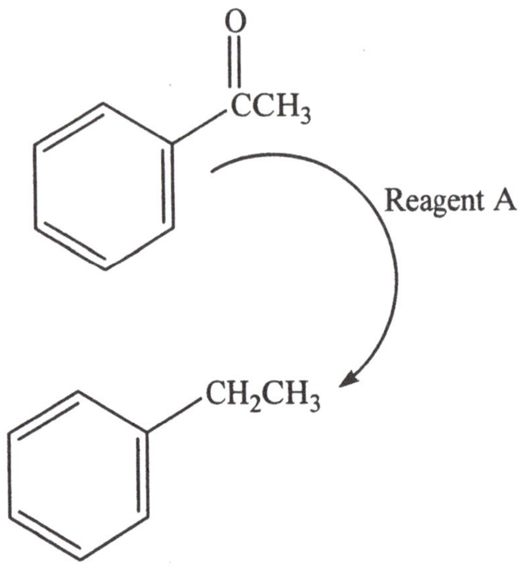

Experiment 2

Propanal had an acid-catalyzed reaction with alcohol.

$$CH_3CH_2CHO \xrightarrow[\text{HCl}]{\text{(excess) } CH_3OH} CH_3CH_2CH(OCH_3)_2$$

Experiment 3

$$CH_3CH_2CHO \longrightarrow CH_3CH_2\overset{\overset{\displaystyle OH}{|}}{C}HCH_3$$

Experiment 3 involved merely the analysis of a conversion. Students were asked to discuss a method to accomplish this synthesis reaction.

Experiment 4

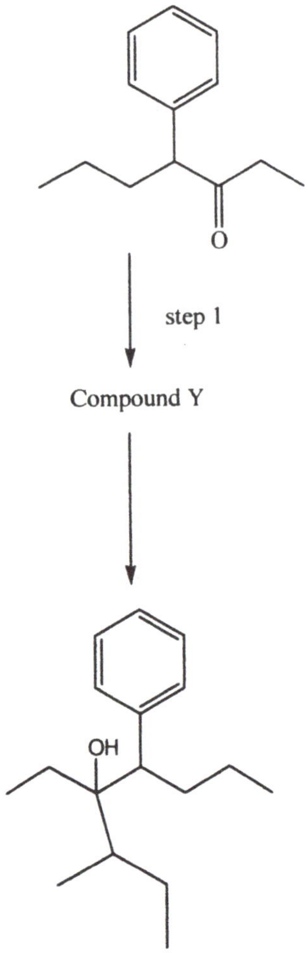

11. Which of the following best represents the general name of the product formed in Experiment 2?

    A. Hemiacetal
    B. Acetal
    C. Ketal
    D. Hemiacetal

12. The conversion presented in Experiment 1 is:

    A. an oxidation reaction.
    B. a reduction reaction.
    C. a dehydrohalogenation reaction.
    D. a dehydrogenation reaction.

13. Which of the following Grignard reagents will serve the purpose for the reaction in Experiment 4?

    A. $(CH_3)_3CMgBr$

    B. $CH_3CH_2CH_2CH_2MgBr$

    C. $CH_3CH(MgBr)CH_3$

    D. 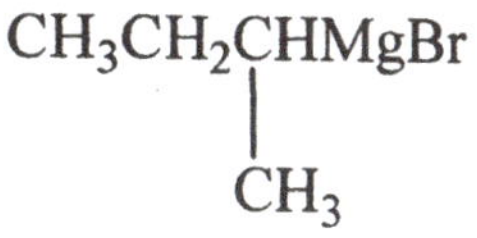 $CH_3CH_2CHMgBr$
                 |
                CH_3

14. In Experiment 3, which of the following is a possible scenario?

    A.   Reaction is possible, because propanal can be directly oxidized to form the product indicated.

    B.   Reaction is not possible, because you cannot convert an aldehyde to a secondary alcohol.

    C.   Reaction is possible, if the reactant is treated with an appropriate Grignard reagent followed by hydrolysis.

    D.   Reaction is not possible, because aldehyde carbonyls are nucleophilic and are thus unreactive.

15. Which of the following is not an organometallic compound?

    A. $H_3CC\equiv CNa$

    B. CH_3CH_2MgBr

    C.

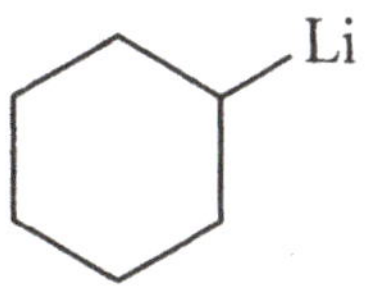

    D. $KOCH_2CH_3$

16. In our body, toxic chemicals are metabolized in the liver. One such process involves the production of acetaldehyde from ethanol. This conversion is best described as:

$$\text{Ethanol} \underset{\substack{\text{alcohol} \\ \text{dehydrogenase}}}{\rightleftharpoons} \text{Acetaldehyde}$$

    A.   a dehydrogenation reaction.
    B.   a hydrogenation reaction.
    C.   an oxidation reaction.
    D.   a reduction reaction.

CHAPTER 21

Carboxylic Acids

A. INTRODUCTION

Carboxylic acids are compounds with the general formula **RCOOH**.

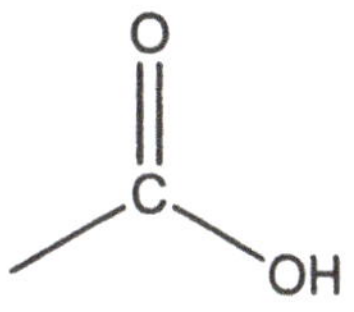

Carboxyl group

Formic acid
(Methanoic acid)

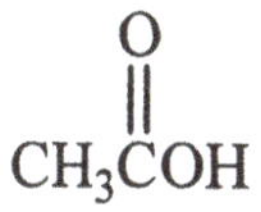

Acetic acid
(Ethanoic acid)

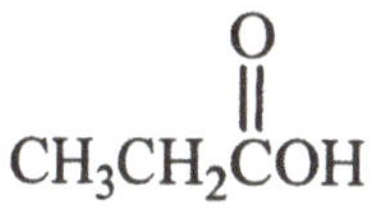

Propanoic acid

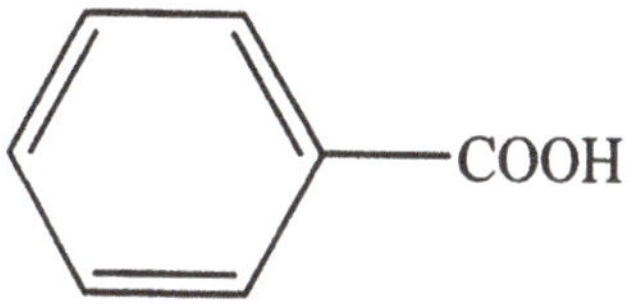

Benzoic acid

B. PROPERTIES OF CARBOXYLIC ACIDS

It is clear from the name that carboxylic acids are acidic. The hydrogen of the carboxyl group (-COO**H**) is acidic. The strength of these acids can be explained in terms of the relative stabilities of their conjugate bases. The weaker the conjugate base is, the stronger the acid. Keep in mind the fact that carboxylic acids are weak acids.

Acetic acid   Acetate ion

The K_a of acetic acid is to the order of 10^{-5}.

The acidity of a carboxylic acid is influenced by its substituents. Substituents which are very electronegative, especially when they are attached to the α-carbon, increase the acidity of carboxylic acids. As the number of electronegative substituents increases, so does the acidity. This increase in acidity is because of the increased stability of the carboxylate ion formed, as a result of the presence of the electronegative substituent. This effect is due to what is known as **inductive effect**. Because of the electron withdrawing effect of the substituent, the charge is dispersed and the ion (carboxylate ion) is stabilized. Study the following gradation of increasing acidity to reinforce the point just made.

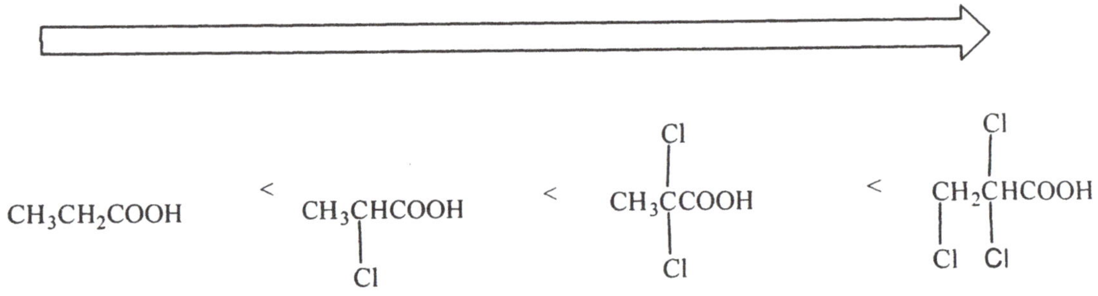

INCREASING ACIDITY

Carboxylic acids can undergo extensive hydrogen bonding. So they have higher boiling points than alkanes or even alcohols. Carboxylate ions are resonance stabilized (Figure 23-1). The negative charge in the carboxylate anion is shared by both the oxygens.

Figure 21-1

C. SYNTHESIS OF CARBOXYLIC ACIDS

By Oxidation

Carboxylic acids can be prepared by the oxidation of primary alcohols, and aldehydes. An oxidizing agent such as $KMnO_4$ can accomplish these conversions.

Sample reaction 21-1

$$CH_3CH_2CH_2OH \xrightarrow[\text{2. } H_3O^+]{\text{1. } KMnO_4/OH^-} CH_3CH_2COOH$$

From Grignard Reagents

Another way to synthesize carboxylic acids is to react Grignard reagents with CO_2. The Grignard reagent acts as a nucleophile toward the carbon dioxide. In an acidic medium the carboxylate entity formed is converted to carboxylic acid. Grignard reagents can be prepared by reacting alkyl halides with magnesium.

Sample reaction 21-2

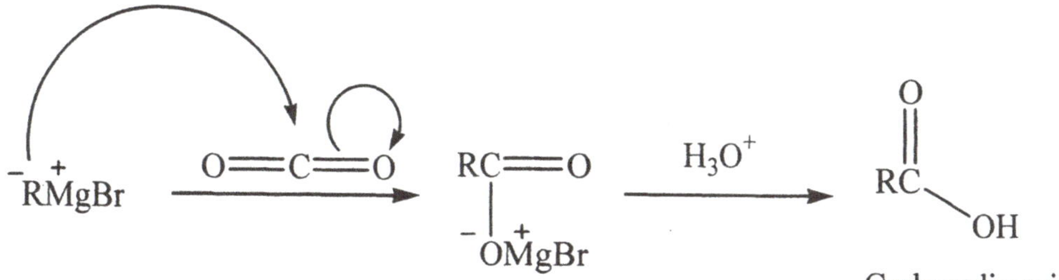

Carboxylic acid

From Alkyl Halides via Nitriles

Primary or secondary alkyl halides can be converted into nitriles (alkyl cyanide) by nucleophilic substitution. The nitriles formed can in turn be converted to carboxylic acids by hydrolysis.

Sample reaction 21-3

$$CH_3CH_2Cl \xrightarrow{NaCN} CH_3CH_2CN \quad + \quad NaCl$$

$$:\!C\!\!\equiv\!\!N\!: \quad \text{Cyanide ion}$$

The cyanide ion is negatively charged and the negatively charged carbon atom has nucleophilic character. The reaction usually occurs via S_N2 mechanism. The nitrile formed can be hydrolyzed to a carboxylic acid.

$$CH_3CH_2C\!\!\equiv\!\!N \xrightarrow[\text{heat}]{H_2O, \, H^+} CH_3CH_2COOH$$

D. REACTIONS OF CARBOXYLIC ACIDS

Esterification

Carboxylic acids and alcohols can react in the presence of an acid catalyst. The products formed are an ester and water.

Sample reaction 21-4

$$\text{RCOOH} + \text{R'OH} \xrightarrow{\text{H}_2\text{SO}_4} \text{RCOOR'} + \text{H}_2\text{O}$$

RCOOH — Carboxylic acid
R'OH — Alcohol
RCOOR' — Ester
H_2O — Water

Decarboxylation

In a decarboxylation reaction, the carboxylic acid loses carbon dioxide. The process usually requires heat to progress.

Sample reaction 21-5

$$\text{HOOCCH}_2\text{COOH} \xrightarrow{\text{Heat}} \text{CO}_2 + \text{CH}_3\text{COOH}$$

HOOCCH$_2$COOH — Malonic acid
CO_2 — Carbon dioxide
CH$_3$COOH — Acetic acid

CHAPTER 21 PRACTICE QUESTIONS

1. An alkyl magnesium halide is reacted with carbon dioxide under very low pH (acidic conditions). Which of the following are true regarding this reaction?
 I. Carbon dioxide acts as the nucleophile in this reaction
 II. Carboxylic acid is one of the products
 III. Grignard reagent acts as the nucleophile

    A. I only
    B. II only
    C. I and III only
    D. II and III only

2. Predict the major product (compound B) from the series of reactions shown.

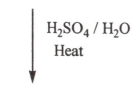

Compound A

H_2SO_4 / H_2O
Heat

Compound B

    A. A four carbon carboxylic acid
    B. A four carbon alkene
    C. A five carbon carboxylic acid
    D. A five carbon aldehyde

3. Predict the identity of Compound X from the reaction shown.

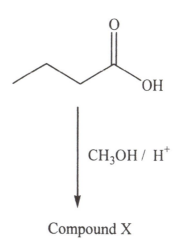

Compound X

    A. Butyl methanoate
    B. Butanaldehyde
    C. Methyl butanoate
    D. Butanol

4. Which of the following has the highest boiling point?

    A. Pentanoic acid
    B. Pentanol
    C. Pentane
    D. Pentanone

5. Which of the following is true regarding the acidity of Compounds A and B?

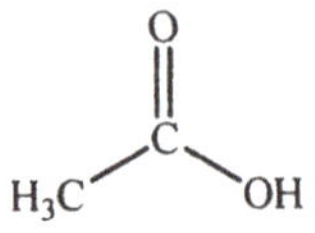

Compound A

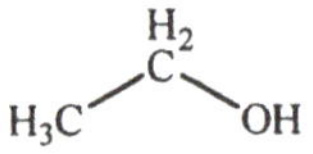

Compound B

A. Compound B is more acidic, because ethoxide is resonance stabilized.
B. Compound A is less acidic, because acetate is resonance stabilized.
C. Compound B is less acidic, because ethoxide is resonance stabilized.
D. Compound A is more acidic, because acetate is resonance stabilized.

6. Predict the most acidic compound from the choices shown?

A.

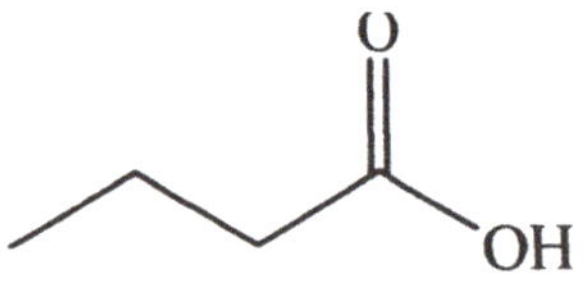

B.

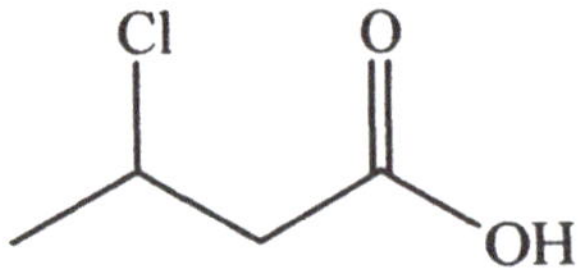

C.

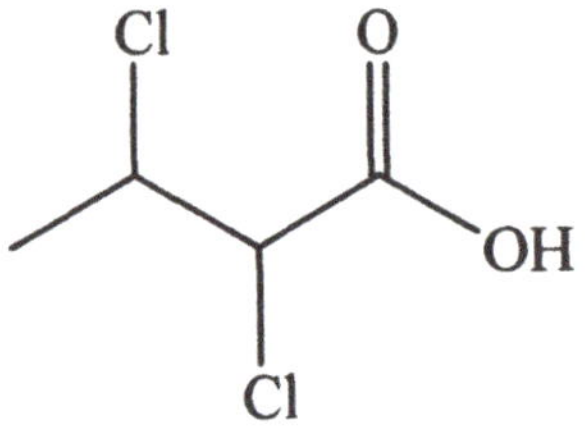

D.

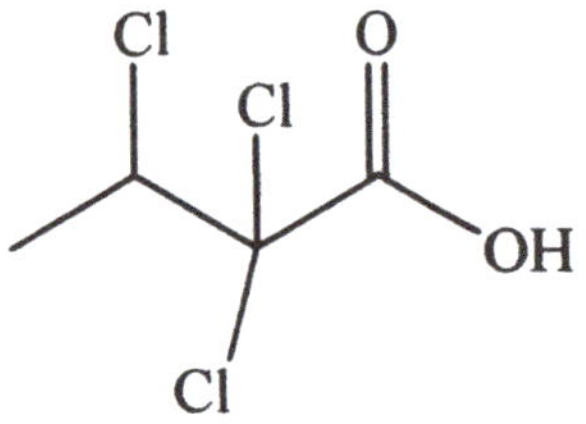

7. The product of the reaction shown is:

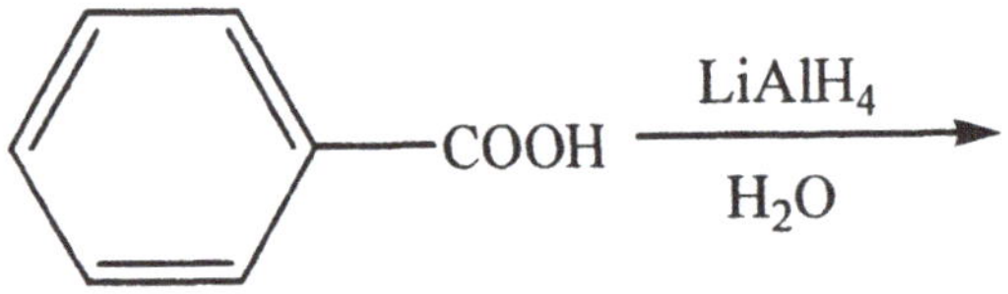

A. toluene.
B. benzene.
C. benzophenone.
D. benzyl alcohol.

8. The general formula RCOOH indicates what functional group?
A. Alkane
B. Aldehyde
C. Ester
D. Carboxylic acid.

9. Which of the following compounds has the highest boiling point?

   A.   Propanal
   B.   Propanoic acid
   C.   Propanone
   D.   Propane

10. The name of the structure shown is:

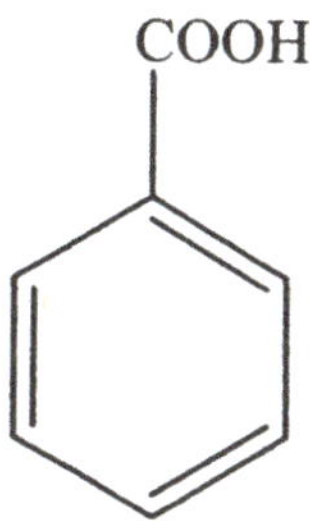

COOH

   A.   benzaldehyde.
   B.   benzoic acid.
   C.   phenyl ethanoic acid.
   D.   heptanoic acid.

Questions 11-16 are based on the following passage.

Passage 21.1

The sequence of reactions shown were done in a lab.

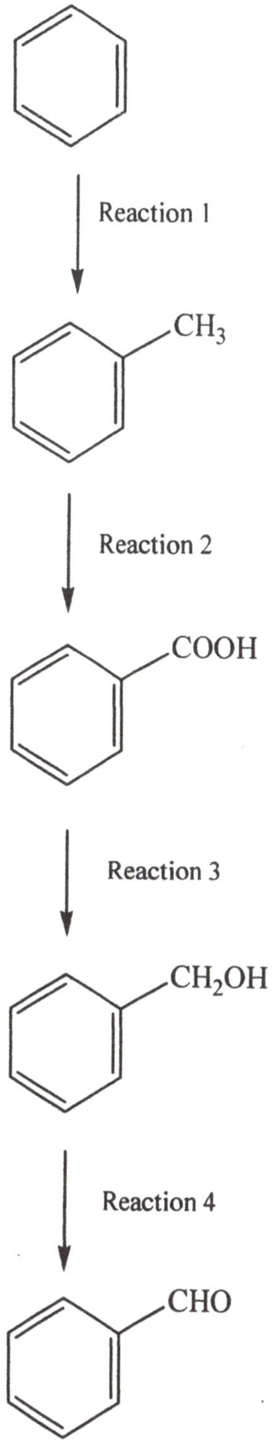

323

Some of the reactions were done to synthesize compounds that were used to conduct other reactions. The experiments were also used to analyze the efficiency of these reactions.

11. All the statements given below are true, except:

    A. CH_3COOH can undergo hydrogen bonding.

    B.   The melting points of carboxylic acids are higher than those of comparable alcohols.

    C.   The carbonyl groups in carboxylic acids are more electrophilic than that of ketones.

    D.   In carboxylic acids, resonance is possible.

12. Which of the following is true about the conversion involved in Reaction 2?

    A.   The conversion is an oxidation reaction, and can be accomplished by using $LiAlH_4$.

    B.   The conversion is a reduction reaction, and can be accomplished by using $LiAlH_4$.

    C.   The conversion is an oxidation reaction, and can be accomplished by using $KMnO_4$.

    D.   The conversion is a reduction reaction, and can be accomplished by using $KMnO_4$.

13. If the product of Reaction 2 were converted to an ester, which of the following reagents should be used for this conversion to be done most easily?

    A. $NaBH_4/H_2O$
    B.   Alcohol/HCl
    C.   Thionyl chloride/heat
    D.   Ether/HCl

14. Formaldehyde can be converted to formic acid. What is the correct hybridization of the carbon atom in the formic acid?

    A. sp
    B. sp^3
    C. sp^3d
    D. sp^2

15. Which of the following compounds has the highest pK_a value?

    A. FCH_2CH_2COOH
    B. F_2CHCH_2COOH
    C. $FCH_2CH_2(CH_3)CH_2COOH$
    D. FCH_2COOH

16. From the following compounds, choose the compound that is the most acidic?

    A. CH_3COOH

    B. $HC\equiv CH$

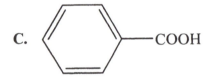

    C.   —COOH

    D. $NaOCH_3$

CHAPTER 22
Acid Derivatives

A. INTRODUCTION

Acid chlorides, anhydrides, amides, esters, and ketoacids are some examples of acid derivatives. An acid derivative has an acyl group which is attached to a functional group. If the functional group attached to the acyl group is a hydroxyl group, then it is a carboxylic acid.

Acid derivative

The acyl group is circled.

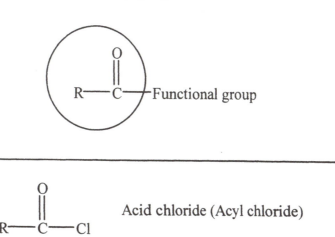

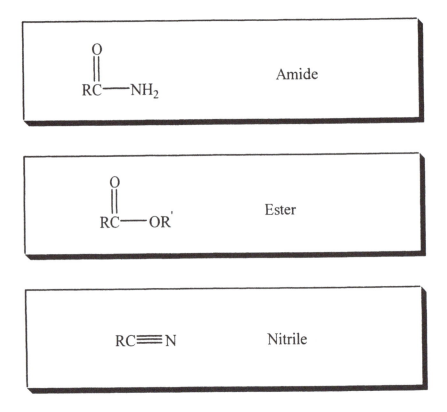

A nitrile is also considered as a carboxylic acid derivative, even though it has no acyl group.

An acid derivative can be converted to the corresponding carboxylic acid by hydrolysis.

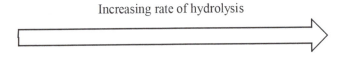

This hydrolysis reaction occurs by **nucleophilic substitution**.

Increasing rate of hydrolysis

Amide < Ester < Acid anhydride < Acid chloride

B. ACYL HALIDES

An acid chloride can be prepared by using thionyl chloride and the corresponding carboxylic acid.

Sample reaction 22-1

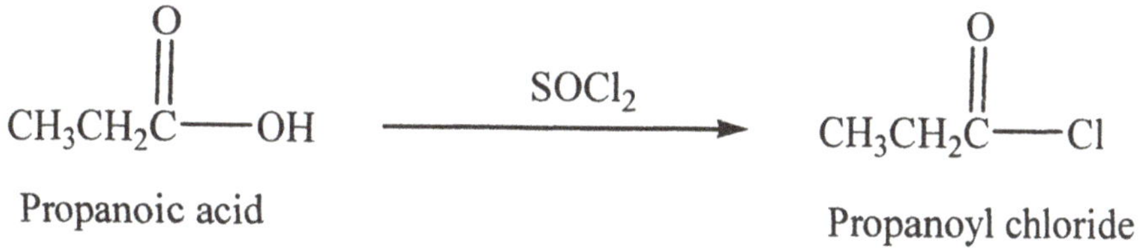

$$CH_3CH_2\overset{\overset{\displaystyle O}{\|}}{C}\!-\!OH \quad \xrightarrow{\text{SOCl}_2} \quad CH_3CH_2\overset{\overset{\displaystyle O}{\|}}{C}\!-\!Cl$$

Propanoic acid   Propanoyl chloride

Reactions of Acid chlorides

Acid chlorides form amides when reacted with amines or ammonia.

Sample reaction 22-2

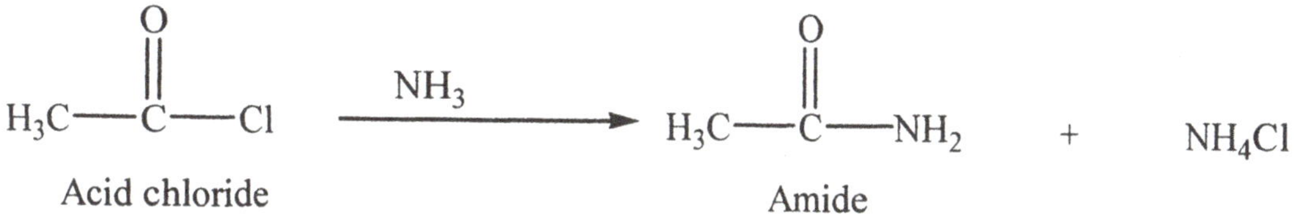

$$H_3C\!-\!\overset{\overset{\displaystyle O}{\|}}{C}\!-\!Cl \quad \xrightarrow{\text{NH}_3} \quad H_3C\!-\!\overset{\overset{\displaystyle O}{\|}}{C}\!-\!NH_2 \quad + \quad NH_4Cl$$

Acid chloride   Amide

Acid chlorides react with alcohols to form esters.

Sample reaction 22-3

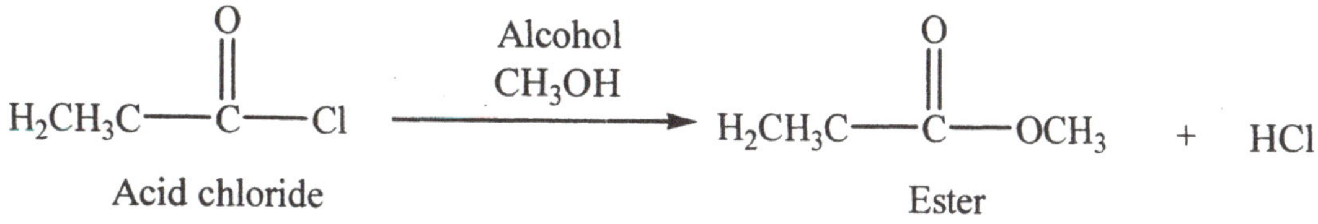

$$H_2CH_3C\!-\!\overset{\overset{\displaystyle O}{\|}}{C}\!-\!Cl \quad \xrightarrow[\text{CH}_3\text{OH}]{\text{Alcohol}} \quad H_2CH_3C\!-\!\overset{\overset{\displaystyle O}{\|}}{C}\!-\!OCH_3 \quad + \quad HCl$$

Acid chloride   Ester

C. ANHYDRIDES

Acid anhydrides have important commercial uses. One of the acid anhydrides of such importance is acetic anhydride.

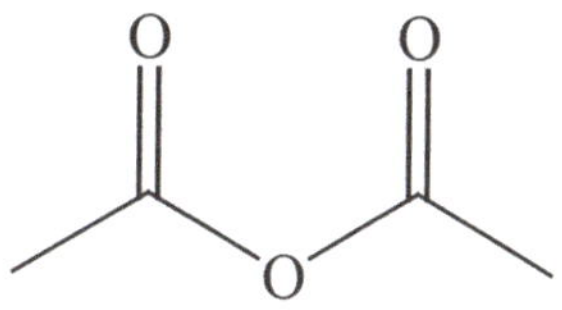

Acetic anhydride

Acetic anhydride can be synthesized by reacting a compound called ketene with acetic acid.

Sample reaction 22-4

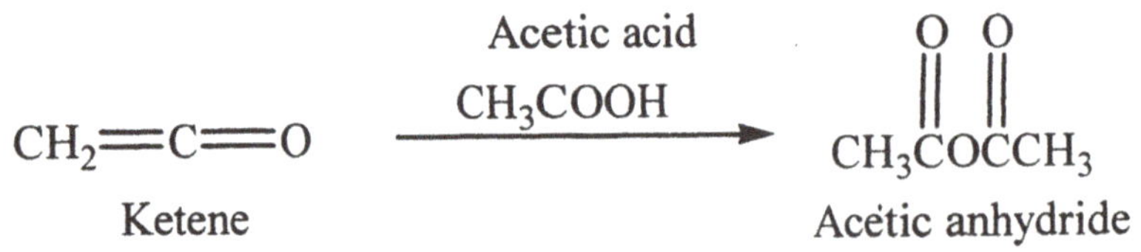

$$CH_2{=}C{=}O \xrightarrow[\text{CH}_3\text{COOH}]{\text{Acetic acid}} CH_3COCCH_3$$

Ketene   Acetic anhydride

Cyclic anhydrides such as succinic anhydride, maleic anhydride, and glutaric anhydride can be prepared by heating the corresponding dicarboxylic acids. The reaction results in intramolecular dehydration and ring formation. Study the following example.

Sample reaction 22-5

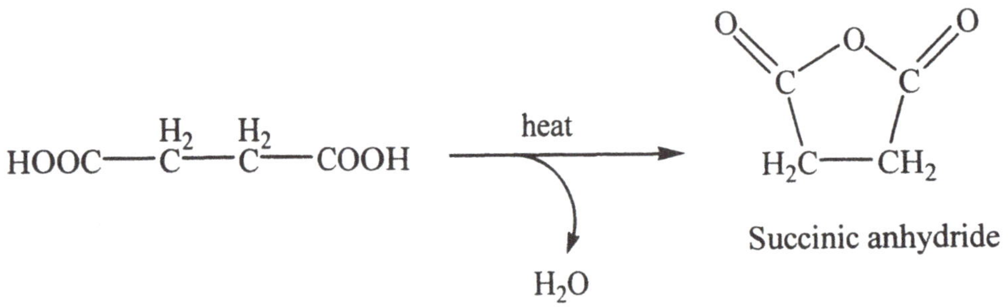

Succinic anhydride

Reaction Involving Acid Anhydrides

Acid anhydrides react with alcohols to form esters and carboxylic acids. A general equation representing this type of reaction is shown in the next sample reaction.

Sample reaction 22-6

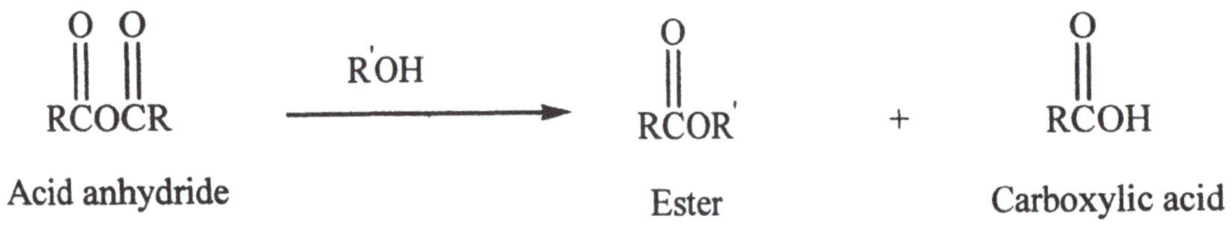

Acid anhydride   Ester   Carboxylic acid

D. AMIDES

Amides can be synthesized from acid chlorides by reacting with ammonia.

Sample reaction 22-7

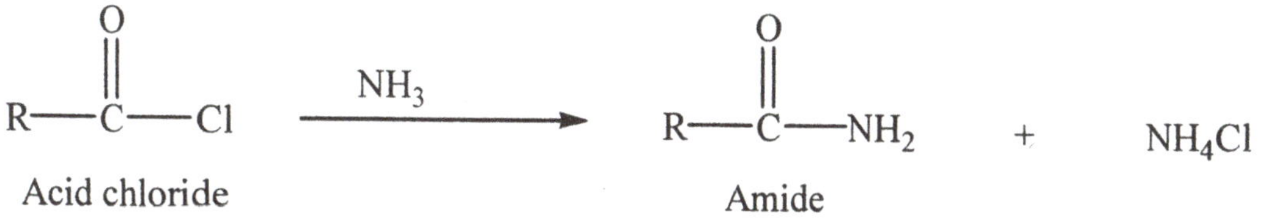

$$R-\overset{\overset{\displaystyle O}{\parallel}}{C}-Cl \xrightarrow{\quad NH_3 \quad} R-\overset{\overset{\displaystyle O}{\parallel}}{C}-NH_2 \quad + \quad NH_4Cl$$

Acid chloride   Amide

Hydrolysis of Amides

In the hydrolysis reaction of an amide in the presence of acids or bases, the products formed are carboxylic acid and amine. This is a nucleophilic acyl substitution reaction.

E. ESTERS

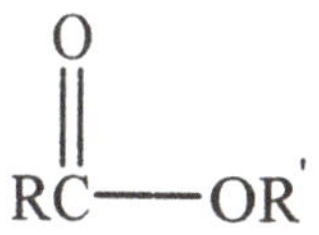

$$RC\overset{\overset{\displaystyle O}{\parallel}}{}-OR'$$

Esters are compounds having the general structure shown above. They have moderate dipole moments, resulting in intermolecular attractive forces. For this reason, they have higher boiling points than the corresponding hydrocarbons of comparable weights. But compared to alcohols, esters have lower boiling points, since they cannot form hydrogen bonds among themselves (Reason: No hydroxyl group). Esters can have hydrogen bonds with other hydroxyl containing compounds such as water and carboxylic acids.

Synthesis of Esters

Esters can be synthesized by reacting carboxylic acids with alcohols, in the presence of acid catalysts.

Sample reaction 22-8

$$RCOOH \quad + \quad R'OH \xrightarrow{\quad H_2SO_4 \quad} RCOOR' \quad + \quad H_2O$$

Carboxylic acid   Alcohol   Ester   Water

Reactions of Esters

Reduction

Esters can be converted to alcohols by reacting with reducing agents such as lithium aluminum hydride.

Sample reaction 22-9

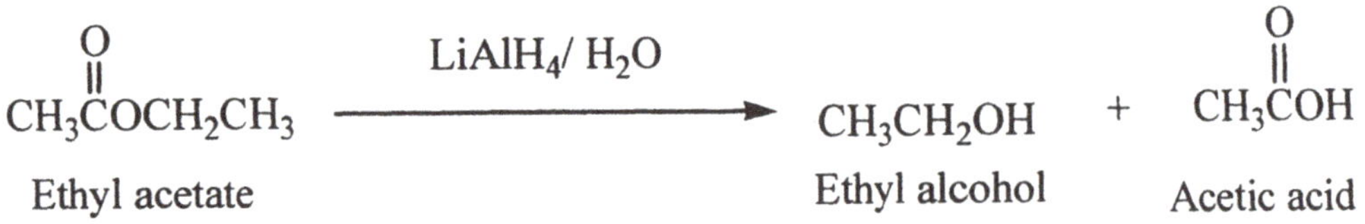

$$CH_3\overset{\overset{\displaystyle O}{\|}}{C}OCH_2CH_3 \xrightarrow{\quad LiAlH_4/\ H_2O \quad} CH_3CH_2OH \ + \ CH_3\overset{\overset{\displaystyle O}{\|}}{C}OH$$

Ethyl acetate   Ethyl alcohol   Acetic acid

Esters with Grignard Reagents

Esters can react with Grignard reagents (two equivalents) to form tertiary alcohols. See the following example.

Sample reaction 22-10

$$CH_3\overset{\overset{\displaystyle O}{\|}}{C}OCH_2CH_3 \ + \ 2CH_3MgBr \longrightarrow CH_3\underset{\underset{\displaystyle CH_3}{|}}{\overset{\overset{\displaystyle OH}{|}}{C}}CH_3 \ + \ CH_3CH_2OH$$

Saponification

The hydrolysis of esters in the presence of bases is called **saponification**.

Sample reaction 22-11

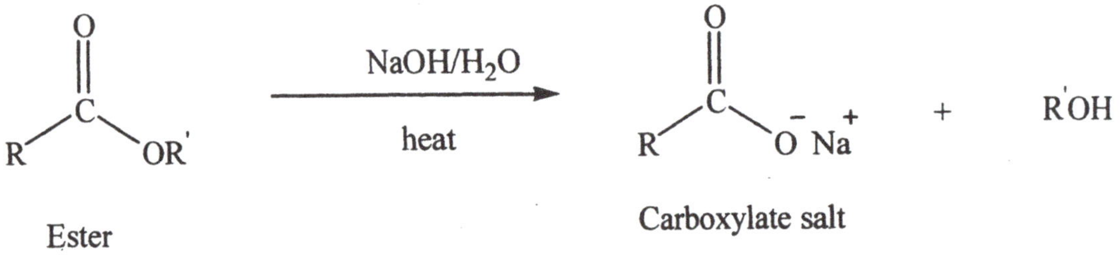

$$R\overset{\overset{\displaystyle O}{\|}}{\underset{\displaystyle OR'}{C}} \xrightarrow[\text{heat}]{\quad NaOH/H_2O \quad} R\overset{\overset{\displaystyle O}{\|}}{\underset{\displaystyle O^-\ Na^+}{C}} \ + \ R'OH$$

Ester   Carboxylate salt

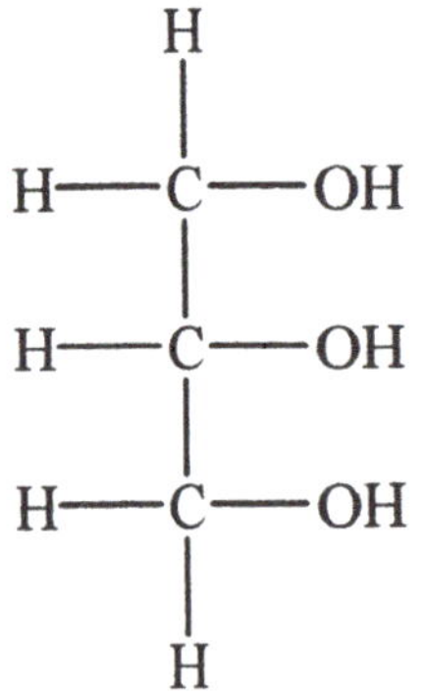

$$
\begin{array}{c}
H \\
| \\
H\!-\!\!-\!C\!-\!\!-OH \\
| \\
H\!-\!\!-\!C\!-\!\!-OH \qquad \text{Glycerol} \\
| \\
H\!-\!\!-\!C\!-\!\!-OH \\
| \\
H
\end{array}
$$

Fats are carboxylic acid esters of glycerol. When these esters are hydrolyzed, carboxylic acids with long hydrocarbon chains called fatty acids are formed, along with the parent alcohol (glycerol).

$$
\begin{array}{c}
\overset{\displaystyle O}{\overset{\|}{C}} \\
\end{array}
$$

Fat (triacyl glycerol)

CHAPTER 22 PRACTICE QUESTIONS

1. Which of the following most readily undergoes hydrolysis among the acid derivatives given below?

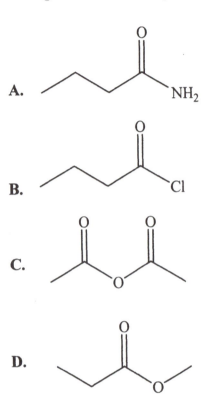

A.

B.

C.

D.

2. Which of the following is the major product of the reaction of an acid chloride with an alcohol?

    A.   An ester
    B.   An aldehyde
    C.   A ketone
    D.   An alkane

3. The reaction of an ester with Grignard reagent (excess) in the presence of an aqueous acid results in:

    A.   a primary alcohol.
    B.   a secondary alcohol.
    C.   a tertiary alcohol.
    D.   no reaction at all, because esters are not reactive with Grignard reagents.

4. Name the compound shown.

    A.   Methyl propanoate
    B.   Ethyl butanoate
    C.   Propionic anhydride
    D.   Propyl ethanone

5. Predict the product of the reaction shown.

    A.   Ortho-methylbenzyl acetate
    B.   Para-methyl benzoic acid
    C.   Para-methylbenzyl acetate
    D.   Para-methylethylbenzoate

6. The most likely product of an acyl chloride reaction with ammonia is:

    A.   a carboxylic acid.
    B.   an amide.
    C.   an anhydride.
    D.   an azide.

CHAPTER 22: ACID DERIVATIVES

7. All the following reactions can be used for the preparation of carboxylic acids, except:

      A.   ester hydrolysis.
      B.   nitrile hydrolysis.
      C.   by the reaction of Grignard reagent with carbon dioxide.
      D.   by the reduction of aldehydes.

CHAPTER 23
Ethers and Phenols

A. INTRODUCTION TO ETHERS

Ethers are compounds with the general formula ROR' (e.g., $CH_3CH_2OCH_2CH_3$).

B. PROPERTIES OF ETHERS

Ethers are polar molecules. Compared to alcohols, ethers have very low boiling points mainly because they cannot form hydrogen bonds (intermolecular). The boiling points of ethers are close to alkanes of comparable weights. Ethers are not very reactive.

C. REACTIONS OF ETHERS

Synthesis of Ethers

Simple ethers can be prepared by acid-catalyzed intermolecular dehydration of alcohols.

Sample reaction 23-1

$$2 \ C_2H_5OH \ \xrightarrow[\text{heat}]{H_2SO_4} \ C_2H_5OC_2H_5$$

An ether can also be prepared by the nucleophilic substitution of an alkyl halide by an alkoxide. The reaction is an example of S_N2 reaction. The reaction is called Williamson ether synthesis (Sample reaction 25-2).

Sample reaction 25-2

$$CH_3CH_2CH_2ONa \quad + \quad CH_3CH_2Cl \longrightarrow CH_3CH_2CH_2OCH_2CH_3 \quad + \quad NaCl$$

Sodium propoxide   Propyl ethyl ether

A primary alkyl halide

It is best to use primary alkyl halides in this type of reaction. Other halides most likely undergo elimination rather than substitution reaction.

Cleavage of Ethers

Ethers are cleaved when reacted with hydrogen halides to form alkyl halides and water. A sample reaction is shown:

Sample reaction 23-3

$$CH_3CH_2OCH_3 \xrightarrow[\text{heat}]{2\ HI} CH_3I \quad + \quad CH_3CH_2I \quad + \quad H_2O$$

Basicity of Ethers

Ethers are weakly basic. The basicity is due to the presence of the unshared electrons that are present on the oxygen atom of ethers.

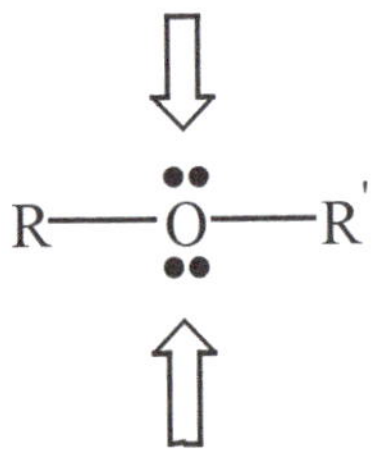

$$R \overset{\bullet\bullet}{\underset{\bullet\bullet}{O}} R'$$

D. EPOXIDES

Epoxides are three-membered cyclic ethers. Epoxides can be synthesized by the oxidation of corresponding alkenes with peroxy acid.

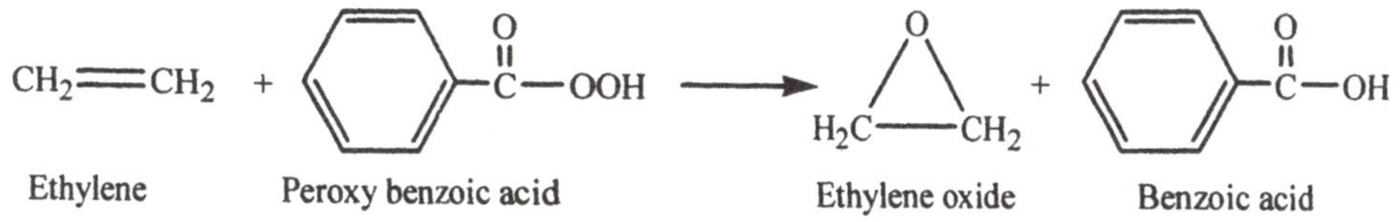

Ethylene   Peroxy benzoic acid   Ethylene oxide   Benzoic acid

Some Reactions of Epoxides

Epoxides can undergo acid or base-catalyzed ring-opening reactions. If the epoxide used in the reaction is symmetric, the product will be the same under both conditions. But the products will be different, if the epoxide is asymmetric.

Under Acid-Catalyzed Conditions

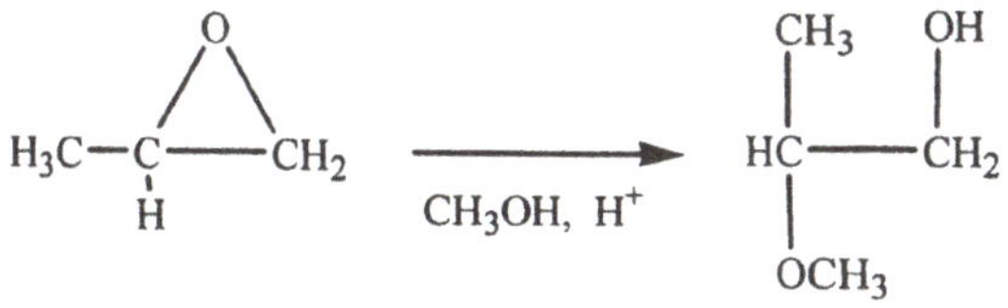

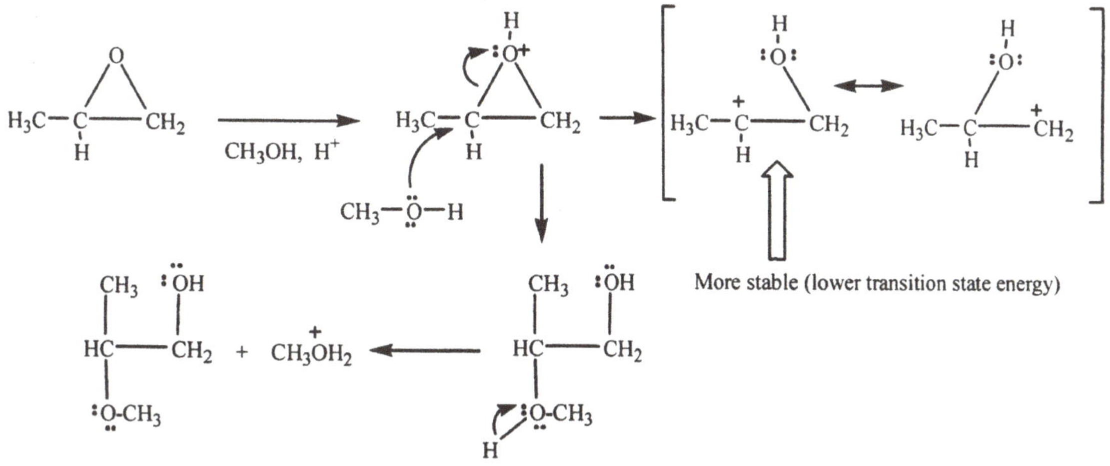

More stable (lower transition state energy)

Under acidic conditions, the nucleophilic attack is directed to the protonated epoxide ring. The nucleophile adds to the more highly substituted carbon in the epoxide ring. This is because in the protonated epoxide, the positive charge is shared by the ring-carbon atoms attached to the oxygen. The positive charge is more stabilized when it is on the more highly substituted carbon (stronger electrophile), and thus the attack of the nucleophile is preferentially on the more substituted carbon under acidic conditions.

Under Basic Conditions

In a base-catalyzed ring opening of an epoxide, the nucleophilic attack is on the less substituted (less hindered) carbon atom in the epoxide ring. The mechanism is shown below.

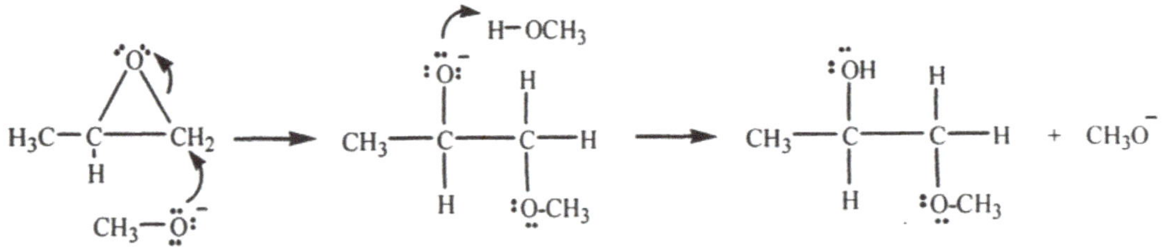

E. INTRODUCTION TO PHENOLS

Phenol is a compound which has a hydroxyl group attached to a benzene ring. Although phenols have similar properties to alcohols (one aspect of similarity is that both phenols and general alcohols have the hydroxyl group), phenols are unique because of their aromatic ring.

Phenol

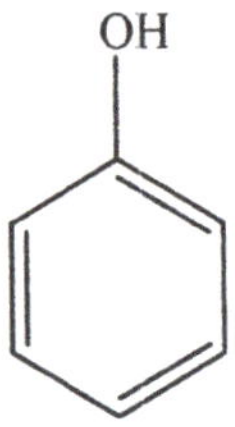

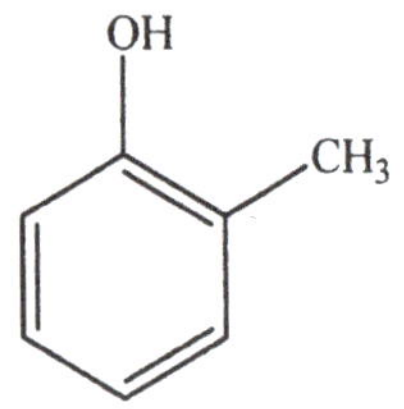

o-Cresol

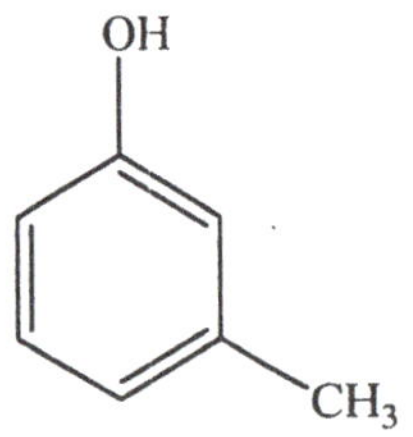

m-Cresol

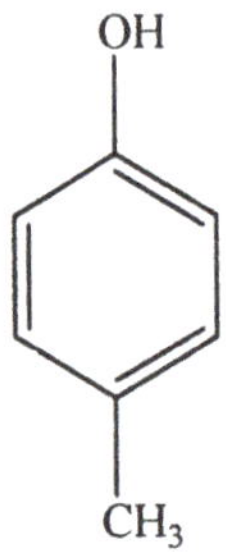

p-Cresol

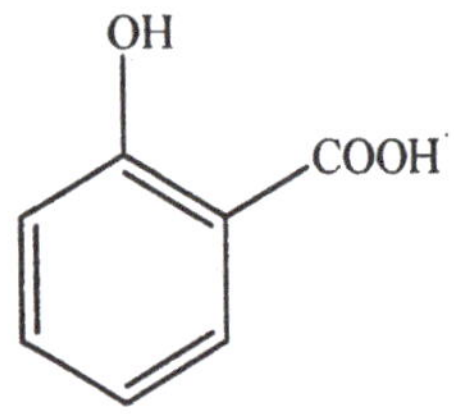

Salicylic acid
(*o*-hydroxybenzoic acid)

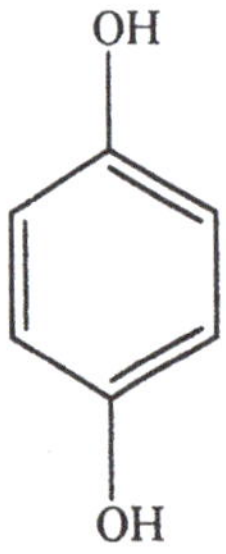

Hydroquinone
(1,4-Benzenediol)

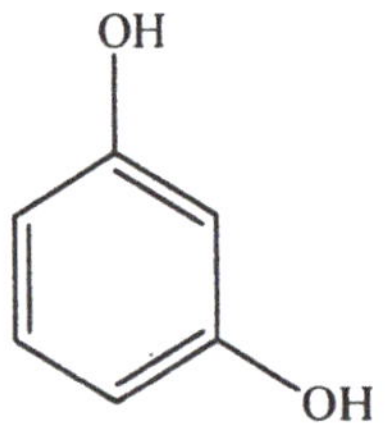

Resorcinol
(1,3-Benzenediol)

F. PROPERTIES OF PHENOLS

Hydrogen bonding is significant in phenols, because of the presence of the hydroxyl group. Phenols can form hydrogen bonds with other phenol molecules and water. Hence the boiling and melting points are relatively high for phenols. Phenols are acidic. In terms of acidity, phenols are between carboxylic acids and alcohols.

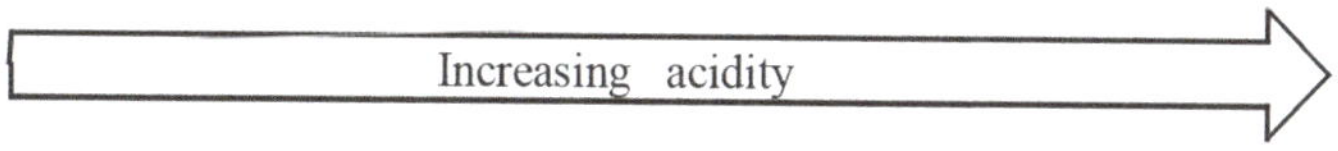

Increasing acidity

ALCOHOLS < PHENOLS < CARBOXYLIC ACIDS

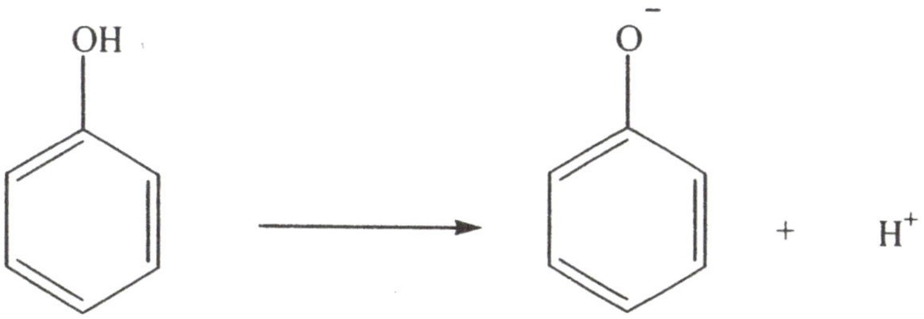

Phenol   Phenoxide anion

It is important to analyze the fact that the phenoxide ion's negative charge is stabilized by the delocalization of the electrons into the benzene ring. This is one of the reasons for phenols' increased acidity compared to alcohols. In alkoxide ions negative charge is localized in the oxygen atom (not delocalized).

G. ACIDITY OF PHENOLS

When a phenol has a strongly electron-withdrawing substituent group, the acidity of the phenol is increased. The reason for this increase is the electron-withdrawing group's ability to delocalize the negative charge, more than the phenoxide ion itself.

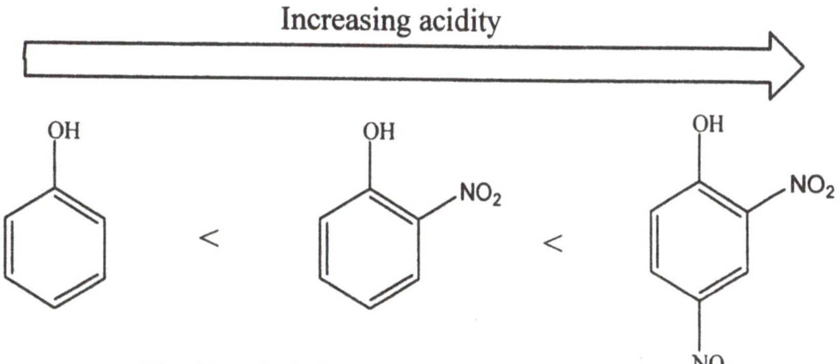

Increasing acidity

The effect of substituents on the acidity of phenol

On the contrary, electron-donating substituents decrease the acidity of phenols.

H. REACTIONS OF PHENOLS

Formation of Quinones

Oxidation of phenols results in compounds called quinones. They are conjugated, and they contain two carbonyl groups (dicarbonyl). See the example below:

Sample reaction 23-4

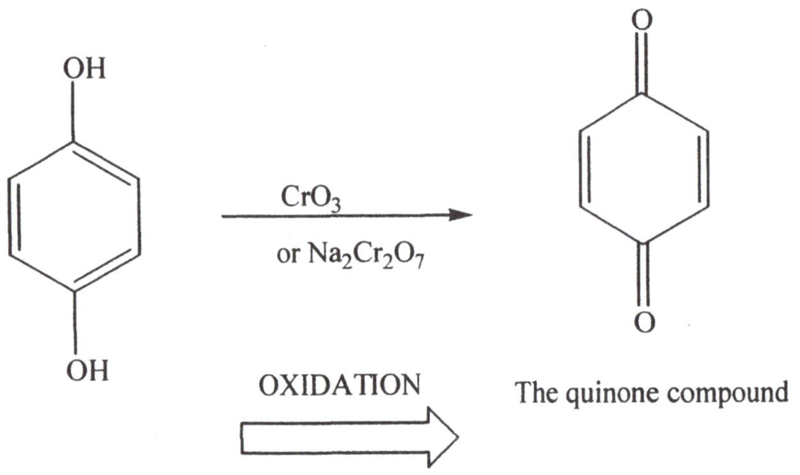

The quinone compound

Electrophilic Aromatic Substitution

Certain compounds (electrophilic) can react with phenols (nucleophilic). The nucleophilic activity can be either in the aromatic ring or the oxygen in the hydroxyl group. Examples of electrophilic aromatic substitution include nitration, halogenation, Friedel-Crafts reactions (alkylation and acylation), and sulfonation. The halogenation example shown below is a polysubstitution reaction involving bromine. The polysubstitution usually occurs when polar solvents are used.

Sample reaction 23-5

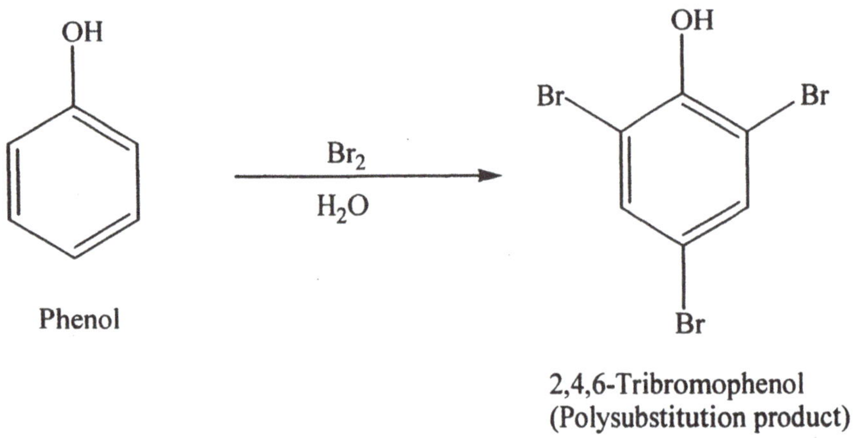

Phenol

2,4,6-Tribromophenol
(Polysubstitution product)

Monobromination can be achieved by using nonpolar solvents.

Sample reaction 23-6

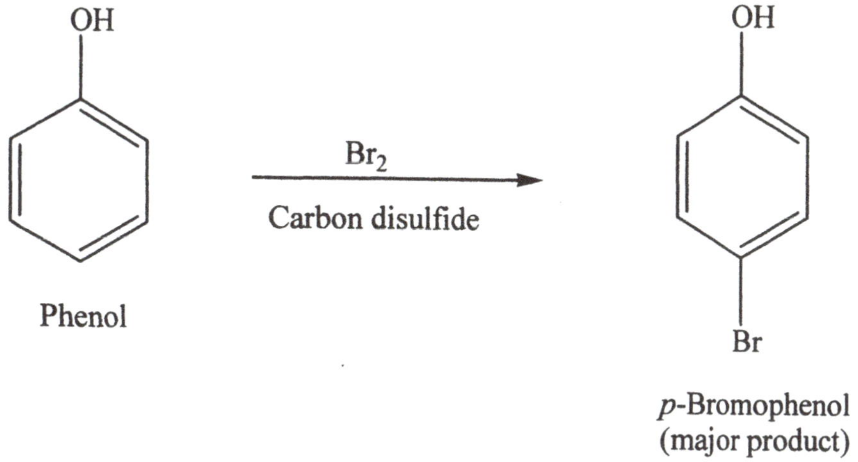

OH

Phenol

Br_2

Carbon disulfide

OH

Br

p-Bromophenol
(major product)

CHAPTER 23 PRACTICE QUESTIONS

1. All the reactions described below cannot prepare ethers, except:

    A.   Williamson synthesis.
    B.   dehydrogenation of alkenes.
    C.   decarboxylation of carboxylic acids.
    D.   Clemmensen reaction.

2. In terms of boiling point, ethers most resemble which of the following types of compounds?

    A.   alcohols
    B.   water
    C.   carboxylic acids
    D.   alkanes

3. Which of the following regarding ethers is true?

    A.   They are polar.
    B.   They are relatively less reactive.
    C.   They can be used as solvents in reactions.
    D.   All the above

Questions 4-8 are based on the following passage.

Passage 1

Consider the following synthesis reaction.

Reaction 1

$$CH_3CH_2CH_2ONa + RCl \longrightarrow$$

$$CH_3CH_2CH_2OR + NaCl$$

where R represents an alkyl group

4. Which of the following is true regarding ethers?
    I.   Ethers are not very reactive.
   II.   Ethers are extremely reactive.
  III. Ethers are flammable.
  IV. Ethers have higher boiling points than alcohols.

    A.   I and III only
    B.   II and III only
    C.   II, III, an IV only
    D.   I and IV only

5. The reaction sequence shown in the passage is most likely to be effective if the reaction runs by an S_N2 mechanism. Which of the following is the best suited alkyl halide to conduct this reaction most efficiently?

    A. CH_3Cl

    B. $CH_3\overset{\displaystyle CH_3}{\underset{\displaystyle |}{C}}HCl$

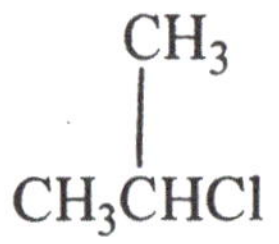

    C. $H_3C-\overset{\displaystyle CH_3}{\underset{\displaystyle CH_3}{\overset{\displaystyle |}{\underset{\displaystyle |}{C}}}}-Cl$

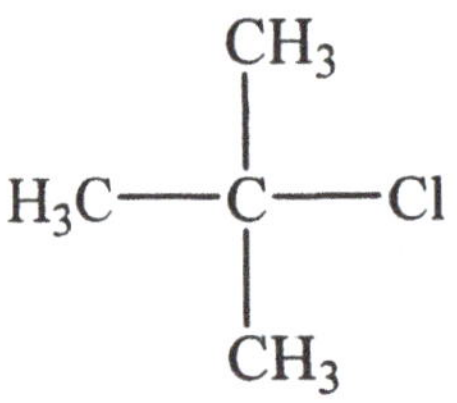

    D.

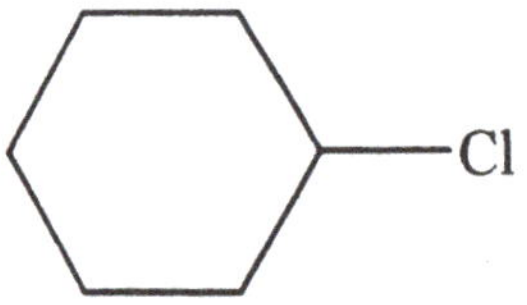

6. All the following alkyl halides can undergo elimination by the reaction represented in Experiment 1, except:

A. 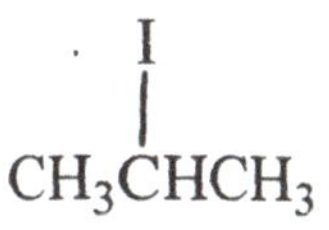

B. $(CH_3)_3CI$

C. 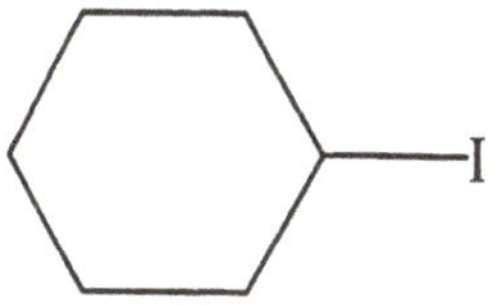

D. 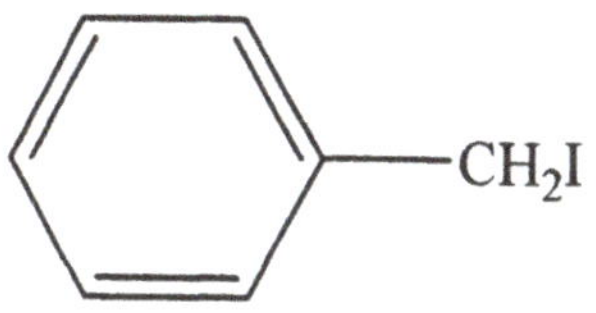

7. Predict the major product (Compound M) of the following reaction.

$$CH_3OCH_3 \xrightarrow{\text{conc.HBr}} \text{Compound M}$$

A. CH_3Br
B. CH_3OBr
C. CH_3OBrCH_3
D. No reaction occurs.

8. Which of the following is not an ether?

A. 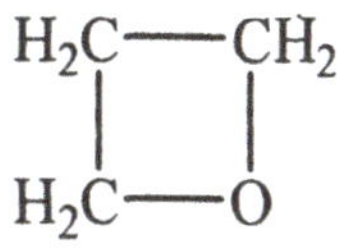

B. 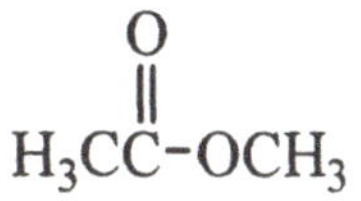

C. 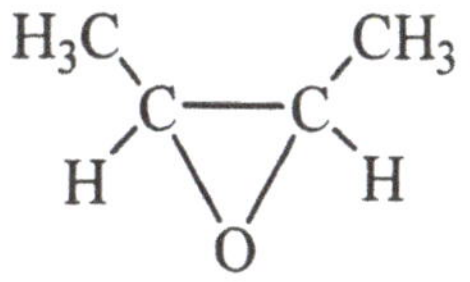

D. $(CH_3)_2CHOCH_2CH_3$

9. The product of the reaction sequence shown below is:

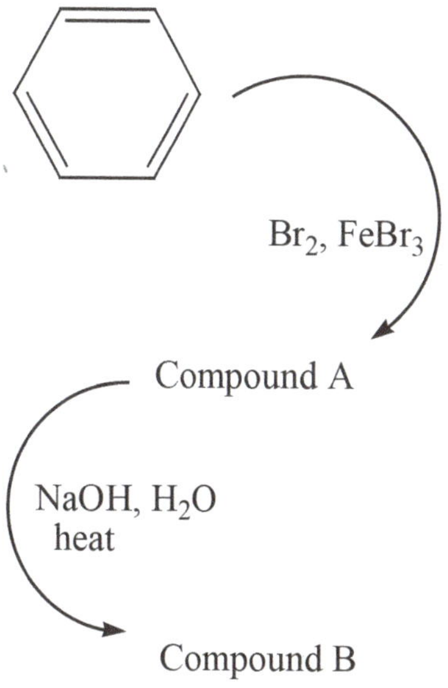

A. meta cresol.
B. phenol.
C. toluene.
D. styrene.

10. The reaction of phenol with Br_2 / H_2O can lead to all the following products in relatively significant quantities, except:

    A.   *ortho*-Bromophenol.
    B.   *meta*-Bromophenol.
    C.   2,4,6-Tribromophenol.
    D.   all the above are formed in significant amounts.

11. Which of the following compounds can have significant amounts of intramolecular hydrogen bonding?

    A.   *ortho*-nitrophenol
    B.   *para*-nitrophenol
    C.   phenol
    D.   *para*-hydroxy benzaldehyde

Section 8

CONTENT REVIEW PROBLEMS

1. A mixture of equimolar amounts of a primary alcohol, a tertiary alcohol, and a mild oxidizing agent will likely produce:

    A.   aldehydes and possibly some carboxylic acids, but no ketones.

    B.   aldehydes and ketones but no carboxylic acids.

    C.   carboxylic acids, but no aldehydes or ketones.

    D.   ketones but no aldehydes or carboxylic acids.

2. The IUPAC prefix and suffix for –OH groups are, respectively:

    A.   hydroxyl- and -ol.

    B.   hydroxyl- and -one.

    C.   carboxy- and -one.

    D.   carboxy- and –ol.

3. The boiling points of alcohols are:

    A.   lower than the analogous alkanes due to increased dispersion forces.

    B.   higher than the analogous alkanes due to increased dispersion forces.

    C.   higher than the analogous alkanes due to increased molecular polarity.

    D.   lower than the analogous alkanes due to increased molecular polarity.

4. 3-pentanol can be converted to 3-penantone by:

    A. CrO_3 .

    B.   PCC.

    C. $K_2Cr_2O_7$.

    D.   Any of the above.

5. Which of the following gives the correct order of boiling points listed in increasing order?

  I. Ethanol

  II. Butanol

  III. Pentanol

    A.   III < II < I

    B.   I < III < II

    C.   II < I < III

    D.   I < II < III

6. The hydrogen α to a carbonyl carbon is:

    A.   resonance stabilized.

    B.   likely to convert to the tautomeric form.

    C.   slightly acidic.

    D.   slightly less acidic.

7. The enolate ion:

    A.   is a cation that is resonance-stabilized by the oxygen in the carbonyl group.

    B.   is stabilized only through induction.

    C.   in an anion formed by the departure of an α hydrogen.

    D.   is the intermediate in the electrophilic attack on the carbonyl carbon.

8. Which of the following is NOT true?

    A.   The carbon in a carbonyl is electrophilic.

    B.   The oxygen in a carbonyl is electron-withdrawing.

    C.   A resonance structure created with a carbonyl puts a negative charge on the oxygen.

    D.   The π electrons in a carbonyl group are delocalized.

9. The product of a reaction between pentanal and an excess of propanol in the presence of acid is:

    A.   a hemiacetal.

    B.   an acetal.

    C.   a hemiketal.

    D.   a ketal.

10. The first step in aldol condensation is:

    A. removing a terminal hydrogen.
    B. protonating the carbonyl oxygen.
    C. forming an enolate anion.
    D. resonance stabilizing the attacking alcohol.

11. The conversion between 2-propanone and 2-propen-2-ol is:

    A. tautomerization.
    B. a resonance shift.
    C. conformational change.
    D. inversion of stereochemistry.

12. In a keto-enol tautomerization, the equilibrium vastly favors the ketone form. This is because:

    A. the enol is resonance stabilized.
    B. the enol is the kinetic product of a reaction.
    C. the ketone places more electron density around a carbon.
    D. the ketone is thermodynamically more stable.

13. Which of the following is most susceptible to nucleophilic attack?

    A. Hexane
    B. Hexanone
    C. Hexanol
    D. Hexanal

14. Which molecule has the most acidic α hydrogen?

    A. Benzaldehyde
    B. Benzaldehyde with an electron-withdrawing group oriented para.
    C. Benzaldehyde with an electron-withdrawing group oriented ortho.
    D. Propanone.

15. Which of the following correctly characterizes aldol condensation?

    A. It is a dehydration reaction.
    B. It is a cleavage reaction.
    C. It is an electrophilic acyl substitution reaction.
    D. It requires an acid catalyst in the first step.

16. The cyclic form of an amide and a ester are, respectively:

    A. lactone, lactam
    B. lactam, lactone
    C. lactam, anhydride
    D. anhydride, lactone

17. To increase the acidity of a carboxylic acid, a chemist could:

    A. add electron donating groups.
    B. reposition an electron withdrawing group farther from the carboxylate.
    C. add electron withdrawing groups.
    D. reposition an electron donating group closer to the carboxylate.

18. In nucleophilic acyl substitution:

    A. the carbonyl oxygen is converted to an alcohol.
    B. the aldehyde carbon is converted to a carboxylic acid.
    C. the leaving group must be a stronger nucleophile than the attacking group.
    D. the carbonyl is converted to a single bond and then reforms.

19. To reduce a carboxylic acid to a primary alcohol, an experimenter can use:

  I. $NaBH_4$
  II. LAH
  III. PCC

    A. I only
    B. II only
    C. I and II only
    D. II and III only

20. Which of the following is a soap?

    A. $CH_3O^-Na^+$
    B. $CH_3CH_2COO^-Na^+$
    C. $CH_3(CH_2)_{15}COO^-Na^+$
    D. $CH_3(CH_2)_{15}COOH$

21. Reacting ethanoic acid with butanol in acid could yield:

    A. ethyl butanoate.
    B. butyl ethanoate.
    C. ethyl butyl anhydride.
    D. ethanamide.

22. Combining an amine and a carboxylic acid can create an amide. Which of the following amines would react most readily to form an amide?

    A. Methylamine
    B. Benzylamine
    C. Dibutylamine
    D. Tributylamine

23. Which of the following correctly ranks the carboxylic acid derivatives in order of increasing reactivity?

    A. acyl halide < anhydride < amide
    B. amide < anhydride < ester
    C. ester < acyl halide < anhydride
    D. amide < ester < acyl halide

24. A researcher carries out a reaction to convert ethyl ethanoate to propyl ethanoate. This reaction:

    A. is a transesterification.
    B. must not be acid-catalyzed.
    C. will produce amides and carboxylic acids as side products.
    D. is too unfavorable to carry out.

25. Carrying out an esterification reaction in water is likely to result in:

    A. poor yield due to the low solubility of the reagents.
    B. poor yield of the product due to hydrolysis back to the parent compounds.
    C. high yield due to the stability of the ester bond.
    D. high yield as long as the reaction is carried out under high pressure.

SECTION 9
BIOLOGICAL MOLECULES

With the MCAT's increased focus on biological and living systems, the biological molecules portion of your organic chemistry prep is one of the most important. This is often in contrast to most college orgo courses – typically professors spend a lot of time focusing on simple alkanes and endless variations of reactions involving functional groups in molecules that aren't very biologically relevant. Often the discussion of sugars, fats, and proteins is relegated to the end of the course, sometimes with no coverage at all. Unfortunately, this does a real disservice to the MCAT student who will be facing a test that is certain to include passages and questions about biological molecules. Such passages will tend to fit more under the biochemistry umbrella, but some will have a more organic chem "feel" to them.

To solidify your understanding of this material, it is very strongly suggested that after working your way through this section of the book that you then move over to the Next Step MCAT Content Review: Biology and Biochemistry book and review the relevant portions of that book as well. Looking at these molecules in multiple passes from multiple points of view will help tremendously.

CHAPTER 24
Amines, Amino Acids, and Proteins

A. INTRODUCTION

Amines are derivatives of ammonia. The alkyl derivatives of ammonia are called **alkyl amines**, and the aryl (aromatic) derivatives of ammonia are called **aryl amines**. These nitrogen-containing compounds are unique for their basicity.

Ammonia
NH_3

$R\overset{\bullet\bullet}{N}H_2$	$R_2\overset{\bullet\bullet}{N}H$	$R_3\overset{\bullet\bullet}{N}$
Primary amine	Secondary amine	Tertiary amine
	R= alkyl or aryl group	

B. STRUCTURE AND PROPERTIES OF AMINES

The carbon to which the nitrogen is attached in an alkyl amine is sp^3 hybridized, and in aryl amines it is sp^2 hybridized. The nitrogen in the amines is sp^3 hybridized. As you have probably noticed, the nitrogen present in an amine has an unshared electron pair. In alkyl amines, the substituents attached to the nitrogen atom are arranged in a pyramidal manner around the nitrogen. In aryl amines, this pyramidal mode is more flat compared to alkyl amines. Moreover, the unshared pair of electrons in aryl amines has the advantage of delocalization into the pi electrons in the aromatic ring.

Physical Properties

Amines are somewhat polar. But the polarity is not as high as that of alcohols. As the figure below indicates, the amines have intermediate boiling points.

Keep in mind that we are comparing the boiling points of amines with alkanes and alcohols of comparable weight. Among amines only primary and secondary amines can form hydrogen bonds. Smaller amines are soluble in water.

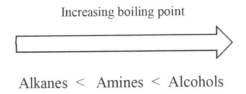

Increasing boiling point

Alkanes < Amines < Alcohols

C. SYNTHESIS AND REACTIONS OF AMINES

Alkylation Method

Amines can be prepared by the alkylation of ammonia. In this array of reactions (Figure 24-1), the amines nucleophilically attack the alkyl halides. As shown below, the first reaction yields a primary amine. Primary amines yield secondary amines which in turn yield tertiary amines, and tertiary amines yield quaternary ammonium salts.

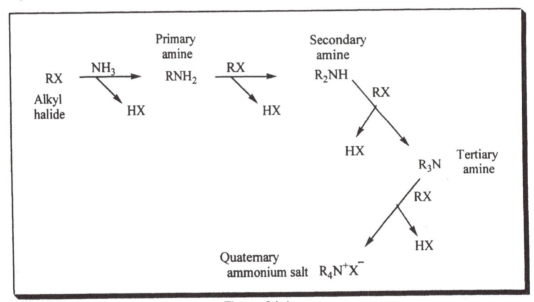

Figure 24-1

Reactions of Amines

Formation of Amides

Amines can react with acid chlorides to form **amides**. A representative reaction is shown in sample reaction 24-1. The reaction proceeds by nucleophilic addition to the carbonyl group by the amine.

Sample reaction 24-1

$$CH_3CH_2NH_2 \quad + \quad CH_3CH_2CH_2\overset{\overset{\displaystyle O}{\|}}{C}Cl \quad \longrightarrow \quad CH_3CH_2CH_2\overset{\overset{\displaystyle O}{\|}}{C}NHCH_2CH_3$$

Amine   Acid chloride   -HCl   Amide

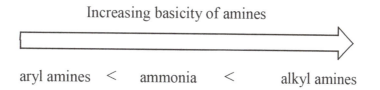

Acyl chloride   **R'**NH$_2$ The tetrahedral intermediate   Amide

D. BASICITY OF AMINES

Amines are weakly basic compounds. Alkyl amines are more basic than ammonia, and aryl amines are less basic than ammonia.

Increasing basicity of amines

aryl amines   <   ammonia   <   alkyl amines

E. AMINO ACIDS AND PEPTIDES

Proteins are polymers of amino acids. Proteins are extremely important since they have a wide range of biological significance. They serve as nutrients, enzymes, cellular products of genes by translation (reflects the hereditary information), building material of muscles and other biologically important structures.

Amino Acid Structure

Amino acids are the monomeric units of proteins. The general structure of an amino acid is as follows:

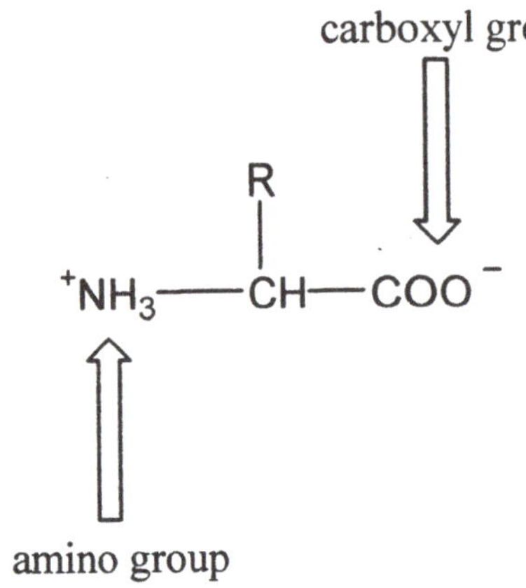

carboxyl group

$$^+NH_3 - CH - COO^-$$

amino group

In the above diagram representing an amino acid, the characteristic amino and carboxyl groups are indicated by the arrows. Amino acids combine with other amino acids to form **peptides**.

Peptide Bond

An *amido* linkage formed between two amino acids is called **peptide bond**. The figure below shows the peptide bond between the amino acids, alanine and serine.

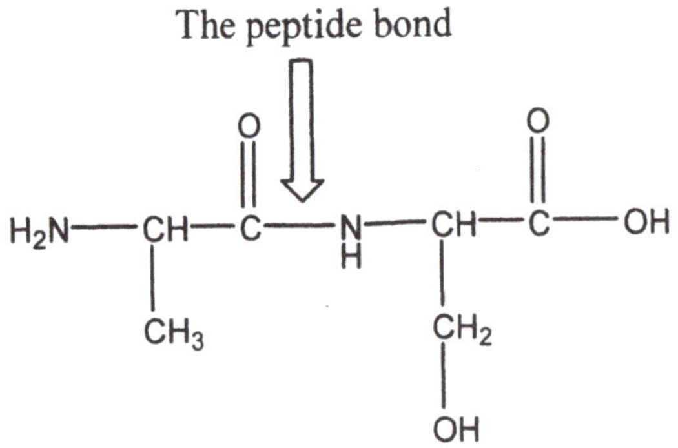

The peptide bond

$$H_2N - CH - C - N - CH - C - OH$$

Figure 24-3

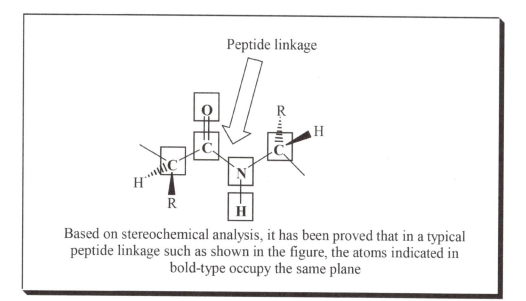

The four atoms present in a peptide bond can form two resonance structures.

Peptide linkage

Based on stereochemical analysis, it has been proved that in a typical peptide linkage such as shown in the figure, the atoms indicated in bold-type occupy the same plane

Figure 24-4

Peptides

Dipeptide	– contains two amino acids.
Tripeptide	– contains three amino acids.
Tetrapeptide	– contains four amino acids.
Pentapeptide	– contains five amino acids.
Polypeptides	– contain many amino acids.
Proteins	– contain fifty or more amino acids.
	(classifications slightly vary)

Alpha and Beta Amino Acids

Amino acids can be classified as α, β, γ, and so on. If the amino group is attached to the carbon next to the carboxylic carbon, the amino acid is an α–amino acid. If it is attached to carbon next to the α–carbon, the amino acid is a β–amino acid. In practice, the name "amino acid" is often used to refer solely to the α-amino acids that are the building blocks of proteins

$$^+NH_3-\underset{\alpha}{\overset{\overset{\textstyle R}{|}}{CH}}-COO^- \quad \alpha\text{–amino acid}$$

$$^+NH_3\,\underset{\beta}{CH_2}\underset{\alpha}{\overset{\overset{\textstyle R}{|}}{CH}}-\!\!-COO^- \quad \beta\text{–amino acid}$$

F. PROPERTIES OF AMINO ACIDS

Amino acids possess a dipolar nature. They are **amphoteric**, since they have both acidic and basic functional groups. Dipolar ions are often referred as **zwitterions**. In certain pH ranges, the amino acids exist predominantly as zwitterions, with a net charge of zero.

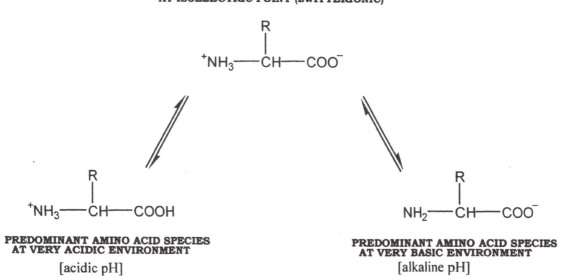

G. CLASSIFICATION OF AMINO ACIDS

On the basis of the R groups present in the amino acids, they can be classified into various groups. There are about 20 important amino acids that are found in proteins.

HYDROPHIC AMINO ACIDS

1. Nonpolar amino acids with aliphatic R groups

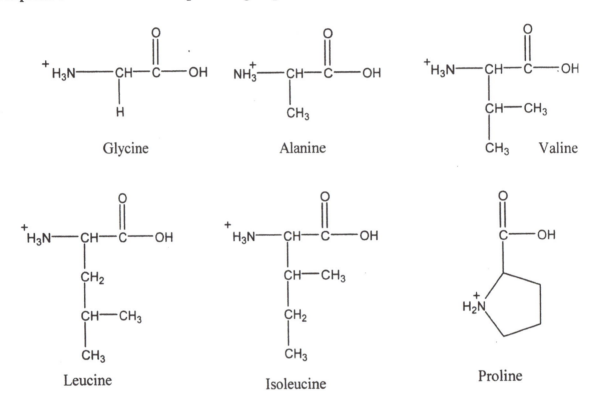

2. Nonpolar amino acids with aromatic R groups

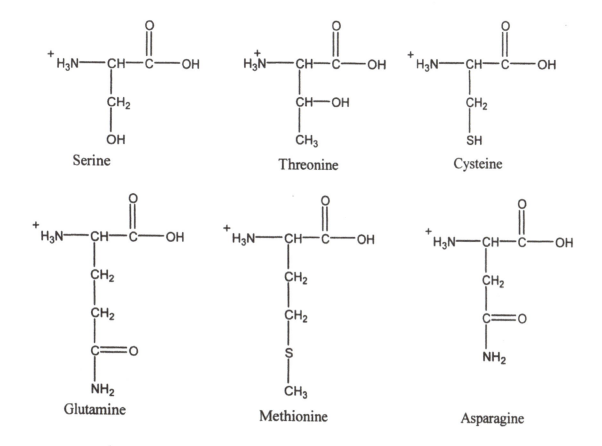

HYDROPHILIC AMINO ACIDS

1. Polar amino acids

2. Acidic amino acids

Aspartate

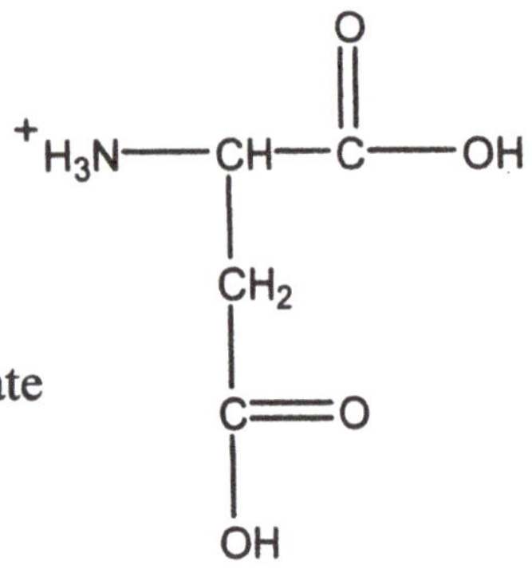

Glutamate

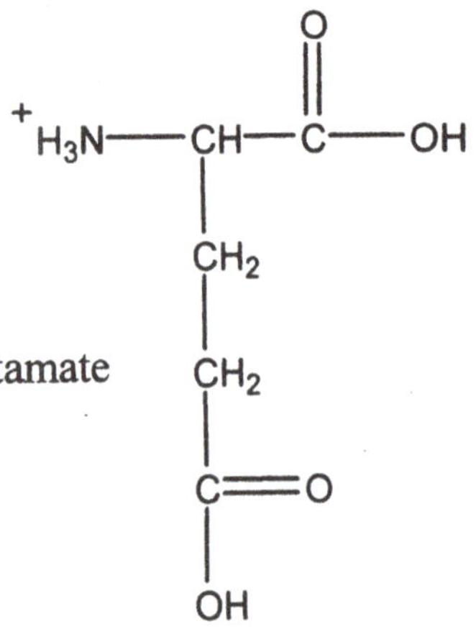

HYDROPHILIC AMINO ACIDS

3. Basic amino acids

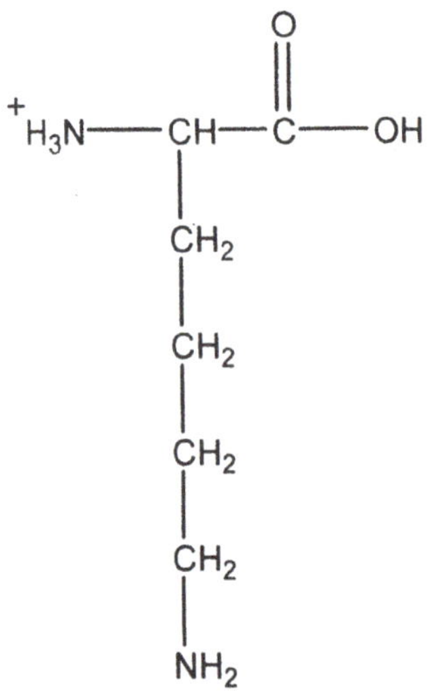

Lysine

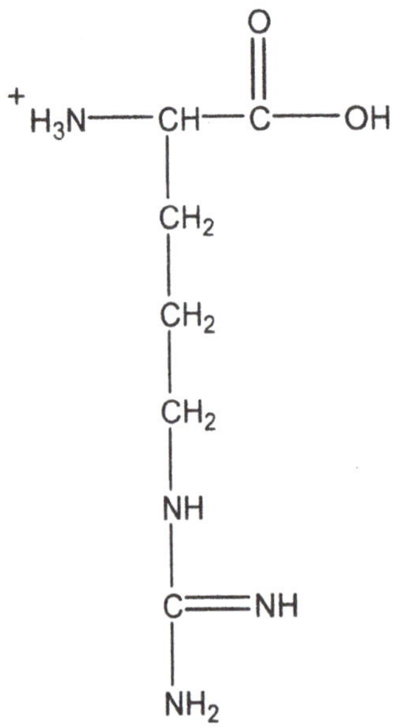

Arginine

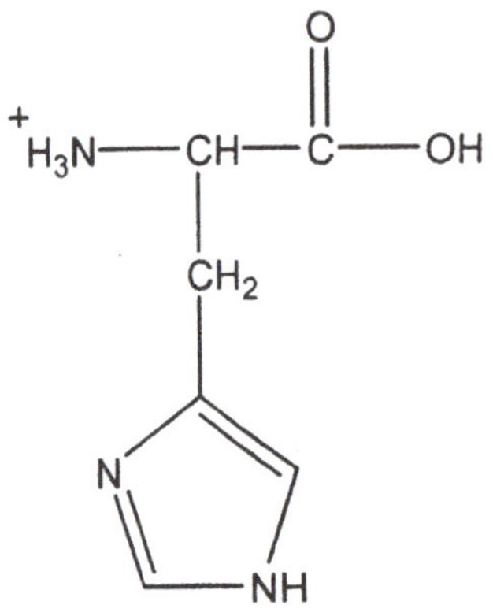

Histidine

Amino Acids and pK$_a$

Amino acids have ionizable groups. Each ionizable group has its own pK$_a$ value, which is the pH at which half of that particular ionizable group is in the dissociated state and the other half in the undissociated state. For the MCAT you should be familiar with the concept of isoelectric point. **Isoelectric point** of an amino acid is the pH at which the net charge of the amino acid is zero. Amino acids can sometimes act as acids or bases. They are therefore referred to as being amphoteric molecules.

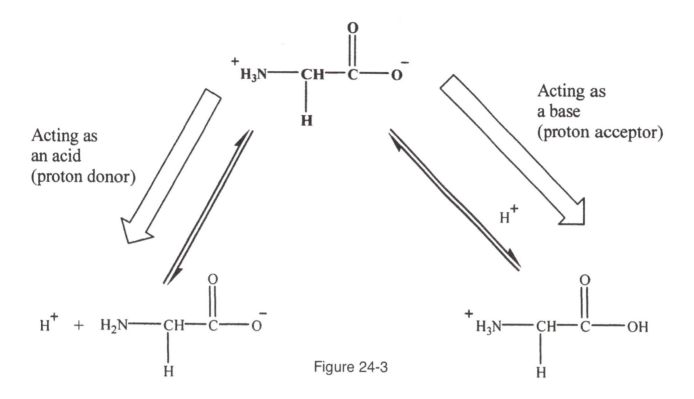

Figure 24-3

The amino acid shown in the above example is glycine. The amphoteric species is shown on top (bold faced).

H. PROTEINS

The structure of proteins can be classified into primary, secondary, tertiary, and quaternary structures, according to the level of complexity of the proteins.

Primary Structure of Proteins

The simple **sequence of amino acids** in a protein is called the **primary structure** of the protein. These sequences of amino acid chains can bend, fold, and bond to form more complex structures of proteins, which can be described in terms of secondary, tertiary, and quaternary structures. Figure 24-4 shows a tetrapeptide with amino acids: alanine, lysine, glycine, and phenylalanine.

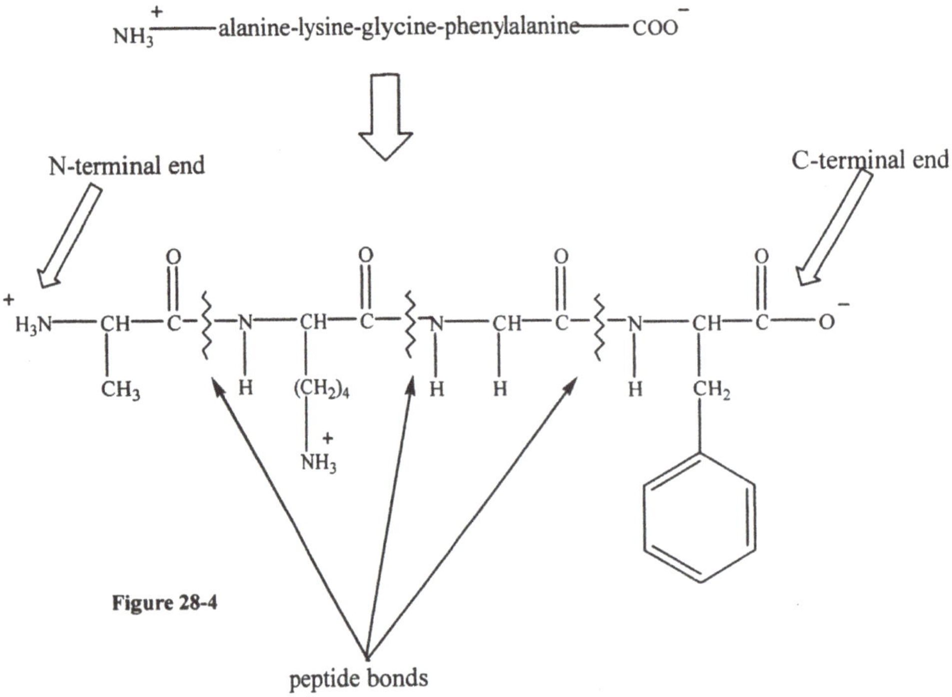

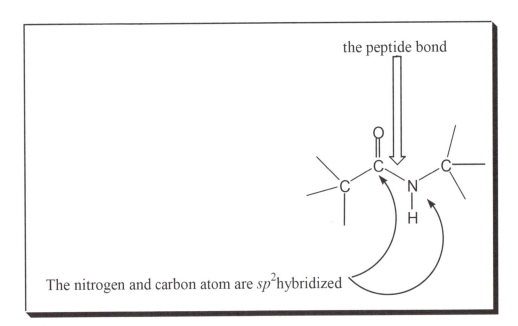

Figure 28-4

A peptide chain has an amino acid with the free (without a peptide bond) amino group on one end (the **N-terminal end**), and an amino acid with free (without a peptide bond) carboxylic group on the other end (the **C-terminal end**).

Figure 24-5

Secondary Structure of Proteins

The two main types of secondary structural arrangements are the α-helix and the β-pleated sheet. Generally, these conformations generate the secondary structure of proteins.

1. Alpha-helix

The α-helical structure or conformation is one of most important aspects of the secondary structure of proteins. This conformation of peptide chain has interactions within its chains by hydrogen bonding. A simple arrangement can be described as a helical structure in which the long polypeptide chain is wound around the long axis. The side chains (R groups) of the amino acids extend out of the helical backbone. Figure 24-6 shows right- and left-handed α-helical structures.

2. Beta-pleated sheet

These represent the sheet-like arrangement of the polypeptide chains. The hydrogen bonds are found between the adjacent polypeptide chains. The polypeptide chains involved in the pleated sheet structure can be either parallel or antiparallel. Hydrogen bonds stabilize the β-pleated sheet (see Figure 24-7).

Tertiary Structure of Proteins

The tertiary structure of proteins is the three dimensional arrangement of the polypeptide chain. Tertiary structure depicts the way in which the secondary structure folds to form the three dimensional form. Different kinds of bonds or interactions are responsible for the maintenance of the tertiary structure. They include hydrophobic forces, hydrogen bonds, disulfide bonds, salt bridges, and van der Waal forces.

Disulfide bonds: These are bonds formed by two cysteines.

Hydrophobic bonding: are weak interactions between hydrophobic side chains of the hydrophobic amino acids in the protein.

Quaternary Structure of Proteins

Some proteins can be complex, when they contain multiple subunits of polypeptide structural entities. The way in which three-dimensional subunits interact to form the complete functional protein is called the quaternary structure of a protein. This level of hierarchy is possible only if the protein has multiple units. An example is hemoglobin.

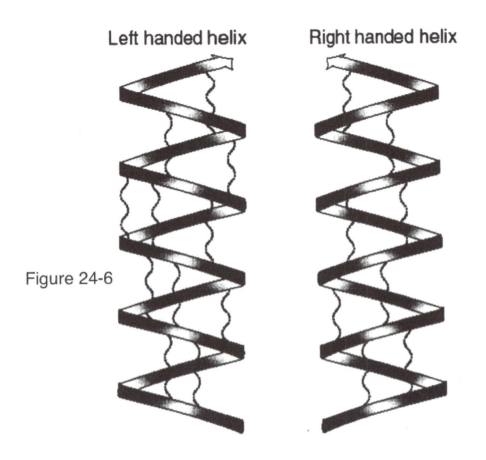

Figure 24-6

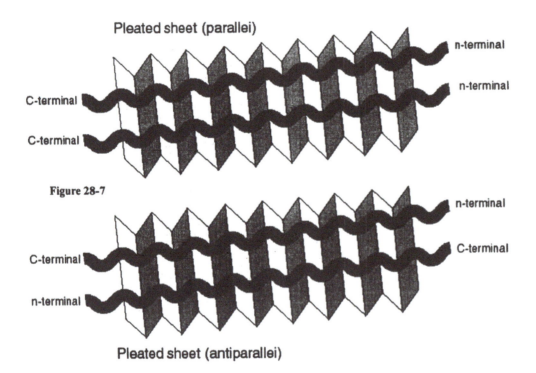

Figure 24-7

Denaturation of Proteins

Proteins can be denatured in many ways. A common example that we all have seen is the denaturation of egg albumin when we cook them. In this case, the denaturing agent is the temperature. Most biologically significant proteins are extremely heat sensitive. An increase in temperature can disrupt hydrogen bonds as well as hydrophobic interactions in proteins. This is one reason why we cannot survive in extreme (hot or cold) temperatures because at extreme temperatures, the proteins and other sensitive chemicals in our body denature and cease to function. Besides temperature changes, pH changes can also affect proteins. Other denaturing agents include detergents, oxidizing agents, reducing agents, UV light, and pressure.

Generally, protein denaturation includes the complete or partial unfolding of the polypeptide chain, cleavage of disulfide linkages, and breakage of noncovalent interactions. Denaturation is sometimes reversible. The reversing process is called **renaturation**.

CHAPTER 24 PRACTICE QUESTIONS

1. Arrange the following compounds in increasing order of boiling points?

Compound A $CH_3CH_2CH_2COOH$

Compound B $CH_3CH_2CH_2CH_3$

Compound C $CH_3CH_2CH_2CH_2OH$

Compound D $CH_3CH_2CH_2CH_2NH_3$

    A. A < B < C < D
    B. B < D < C < A
    C. B < C < D < A
    D. B < D < A < C

2. Which of the following compounds has the greatest basicity?

    A. $CH_3CH_2CH_2NH_2$

    B. NH_3

    C. 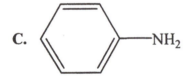 —NH_2

    D. $(CH_3CH_2)NH$

3. All the following are nitrogen-containing compounds, except:

    A. aniline.
    B. quaternary ammonium salt.
    C. oxime.
    D. ester.

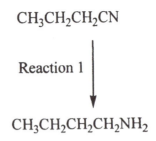

$$CH_3CH_2CH_2CN$$

$$\downarrow \text{Reaction 1}$$

$$CH_3CH_2CH_2CH_2NH_2$$

4. The conversion involved in Reaction 1 can be best characterized as:

    A. oxidation.
    B. dehydrogenation.
    C. isomerization.
    D. reduction.

Questions 5-10 are based on the following passage.

Passage 1

Amines range from simple structures to very complex structures. Some simple amines and their K_b values are given below.

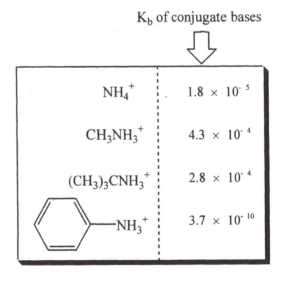

K_b of conjugate bases

NH_4^+	1.8×10^{-5}
$CH_3NH_3^+$	4.3×10^{-4}
$(CH_3)_3CNH_3^+$	2.8×10^{-4}
—NH_3^+	3.7×10^{-10}

There are a wide variety of naturally occurring amines. Amines include caffeine, morphine, cocaine, quinine, and amphetamines, just to name a few. Amines are also biologically important. Some of the biologically important amines include thiamine, adrenaline, acetylcholine, and riboflavin.

Gamma-aminobutyrate is an amine and a neurotransmitter. It has mainly an inhibitory function and is extensively found as a neurotransmitter in the Purkinje cells of the central nervous system.

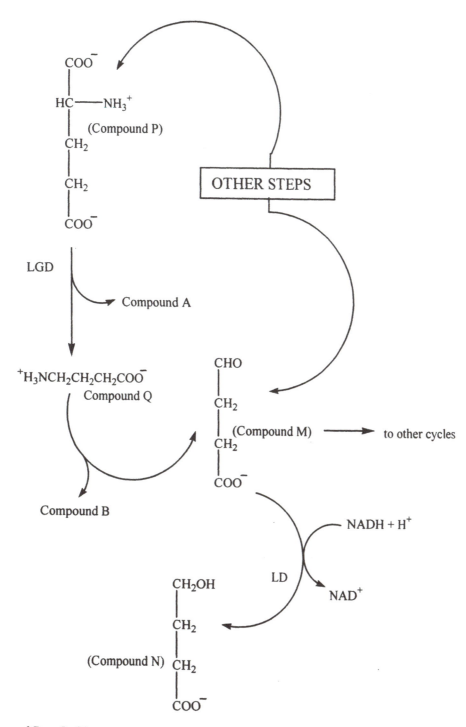

Compound P - L-Glutamate
Compound Q - γ-Aminobutyrate

5. Which of the following is the most acidic?

   A. CH_3NH_2
   B. $CH_3CH_2NH_2$
   C. $(CH_3)_2NH$
   D. CH_3OH

6. All the following can undergo hydrogen bonding themselves, except:

   A. aniline.
   B. triethylamine.
   C. ammonia.
   D. methylamine.

7. The conjugate acid of which of the following is the most acidic?

   A. Methylamine
   B. Ammonia
   C. *tert*-Butylamine
   D. Aniline

8. The conversion of glutamate to aminobutyrate is best described as:

   A. a neutralization reaction.
   B. a decarboxylation reaction.
   C. a deamination reaction.
   D. an amination reaction.

9. The conversion of Compound M to Compound N is done by the process of:

   A. oxidation.
   B. transamination.
   C. inversion of configuration.
   D. reduction.

10. γ-Aminobutyrate can be best described as a:

    A. primary amine.
    B. secondary amine.
    C. tertiary amine.
    D. peptide.

11. Which of the following is a basic amino acid?

    A. Valine
    B. Tryptophan
    C. Arginine
    D. Threonine

12. All the following amino acids are optically active, except:

    A. valine.
    B. proline.
    C. glutamic acid.
    D. glycine.

13. At a particular pH, the amino acid glutamic acid has a net charge of zero. When this pH is achieved, it is said to be at glutamic acid's:

    A. isobaric point.
    B. isomeric point.
    C. isotonic point .
    D. isoelectric point.

14. Which of following groups are not present in any of the common amino acids?

    A. Amino group
    B. Carbonyl group
    C. Aldehyde group
    D. All the above groups are present

15. Amino acids can be bonded to each other covalently by means of:

    A. hydrogen bonds.
    B. dipole-dipole interactions.
    C. phosphodiester linkages.
    D. peptide linkages.

16. Proteins are made of:

    A. monosaccharides.
    B. sugars.
    C. lipids.
    D. amino acids.

17. Which of the following will certainly not affect the structure of a protein?

    A. Proteases
    B. Strong bases
    C. Strong acids
    D. All the above can have some effect on the structure of proteins.

18. Which amino acid is responsible for the formation of disulfide bonds?

    A. lysine
    B. phenylalanine
    C. tryptophan
    D. cysteine

Questions 19-24 are based on the following passage.

Passage 1

Amino acids play an essential role in the physiological processes in our body. They are the main building blocks of the principal structures in our body. Amino acids themselves or in combination with carbohydrates, lipids, etc., form an intricate system of physiologically important structures and functional domains without which life as we know it cannot exist.

From a biological point of view with respect to life forms, only 20 amino acids are important, even though many more are found in nature. Most amino acids are optically active. With the functional groups and their chemical behavior, we can predict certain properties of amino acids such as ionization properties. Amino acids join together to form peptides. Table-1 shows the pKa values of some amino acids.

	-COOH	NH_3^+	Side chain
Alanine	2.3	9.7	
Arginine	2.2	9.0	12.5
Cysteine	2.0	10.3	8.2
Glutamate	2.2	9.7	4.3
Glycine	2.3	9.6	
Serine	2.2	9.2	
Threonine	2.1	9.1	
Tryptophan	2.8	9.4	
Tyrosine	2.2	9.1	10.1
Lysine	2.2	9.0	10.5

Table 1

Aspartic acid

19. Which of the following are true regarding amino acids?

  I. Amino acids have carboxyl groups.
  II. Amino acids have high melting points.
  III. Some amino acids can have a net positive charge.
  IV. Some amino acids can have a net negative charge.

    A. I, III and IV only
    B. I, II and III only
    C. I, III and IV only
    D. I, II, III and IV

20. Which of the following represents the pH at which there is no net movement of the amino acid when subjected to an electric field?

    A. pH at pK_a
    B. pH at pK_b
    C. pH at isoelectric point
    D. There is no such pH for amino acids because some amino acids are acidic, some are basic, and some are neutral.

21. Which of the following represents a peptide bond?

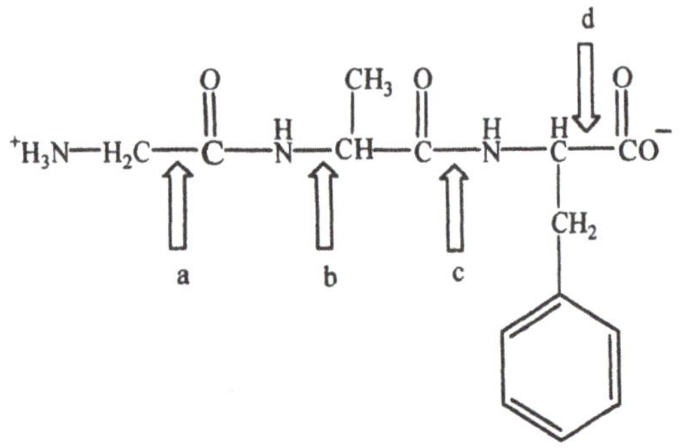

    A. a
    B. b
    C. c
    D. d

22. In our body, some amino acids are changed into metabolic intermediates which can enter metabolic cycles. One such example is given below. The example shows the conversion of serine into pyruvate which can be converted to acetyl CoA and enter the Krebs cycle. Compound Y can be best described as:

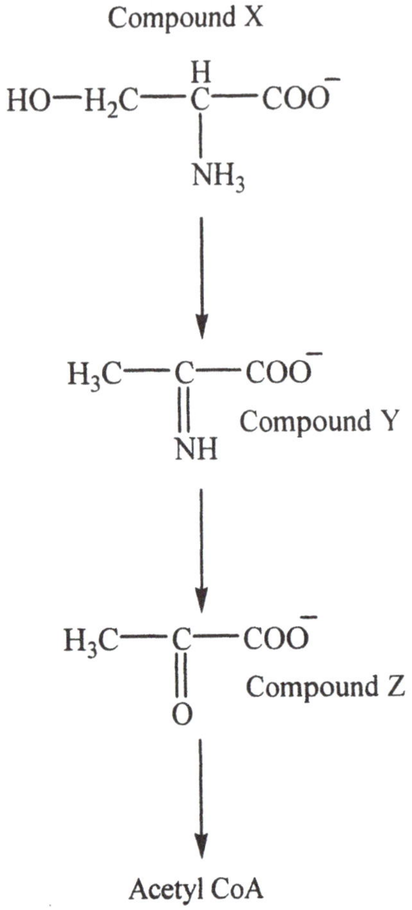

    A. an amide.
    B. an imine.
    C. a phenol.
    D. an imidazole.

23. Which of the following amino acids will migrate toward the positive electrode when subjected to an electric field at a pH of 7.0?

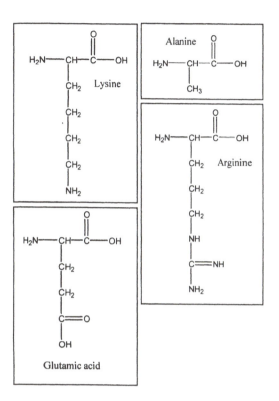

- A. Alanine
- B. Arginine
- C. Lysine
- D. Glutamic acid

24. All the following are not basic amino acids, except:

- A. glutamate.
- B. aspartate.
- C. alanine.
- D. lysine.

A. INTRODUCTION

Carbohydrates, commonly known as sugars, are the most abundant group of biomolecules in nature. Our daily regimen of foods includes different forms of carbohydrates. Potatoes, rice, bread, pasta are carbohydrate-rich sources of food. There are different types of carbohydrates. The simplest units are called **monosaccharides**. A **disaccharide** contains two monosaccharides. A **polysaccharide** contains many monosaccharide subunits.

B. MONOSACCHARIDES

Based on the number of carbons, monosaccharides can be called trioses (three carbons), tetroses (four carbons), pentoses (five carbons), hexoses (six carbons), heptoses (seven carbons), octoses (eight carbons), and so on.

Monosaccharides contain many hydroxyl groups and a carbonyl group. If a monosaccharide contains an aldehyde group, it is called an **aldose** sugar. If a monosaccharide contains an keto group, it is called an **ketose** sugar.

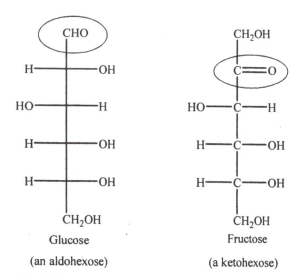

Figure 25-1 Glucose is an aldose sugar. Fructose is a ketose sugar.

Glyceraldehyde

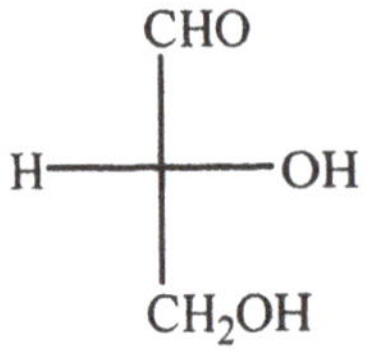

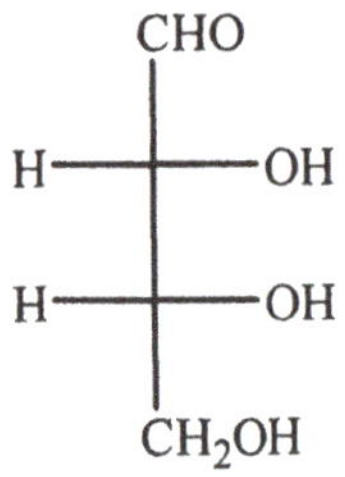

$$
\begin{array}{c}
CHO \\
H{-}{-}OH \\
CH_2OH
\end{array}
$$

Erythrose

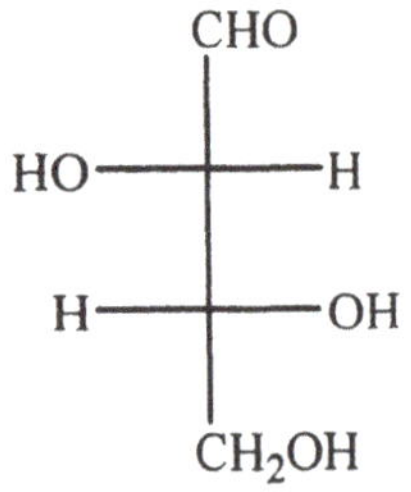

$$
\begin{array}{c}
CHO \\
H{-}{-}OH \\
H{-}{-}OH \\
CH_2OH
\end{array}
$$

Threose

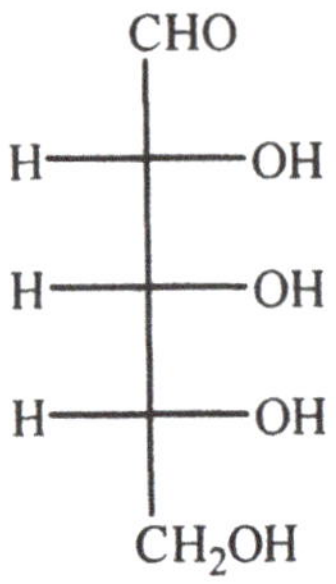

$$
\begin{array}{c}
CHO \\
HO{-}{-}H \\
H{-}{-}OH \\
CH_2OH
\end{array}
$$

Ribose

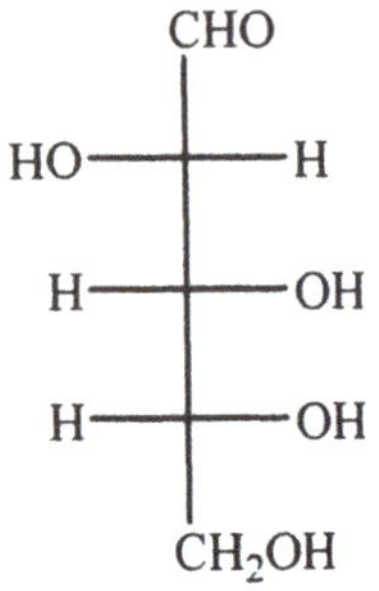

$$
\begin{array}{c}
CHO \\
H{-}{-}OH \\
H{-}{-}OH \\
H{-}{-}OH \\
CH_2OH
\end{array}
$$

Arabinose

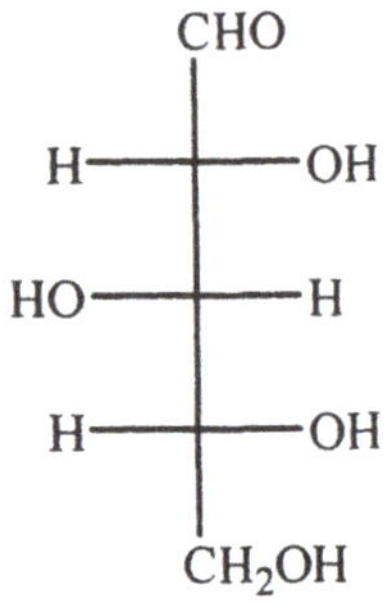

$$
\begin{array}{c}
CHO \\
HO{-}{-}H \\
H{-}{-}OH \\
H{-}{-}OH \\
CH_2OH
\end{array}
$$

Xylose

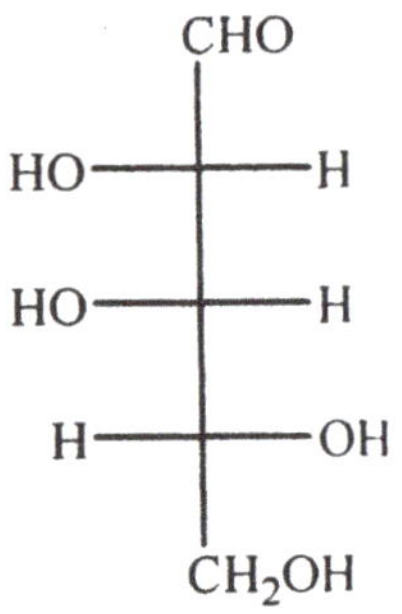

$$
\begin{array}{c}
CHO \\
H{-}{-}OH \\
HO{-}{-}H \\
H{-}{-}OH \\
CH_2OH
\end{array}
$$

Lyxose

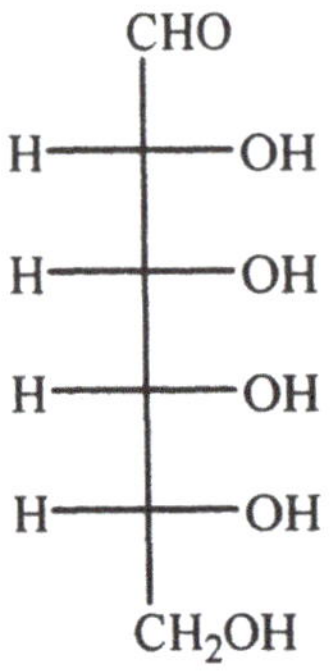

$$
\begin{array}{c}
CHO \\
HO{-}{-}H \\
HO{-}{-}H \\
H{-}{-}OH \\
CH_2OH
\end{array}
$$

Allose

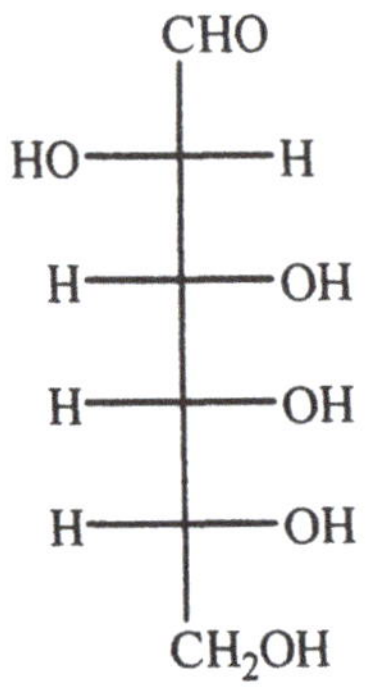

$$
\begin{array}{c}
CHO \\
H{-}{-}OH \\
H{-}{-}OH \\
H{-}{-}OH \\
H{-}{-}OH \\
CH_2OH
\end{array}
$$

Altrose

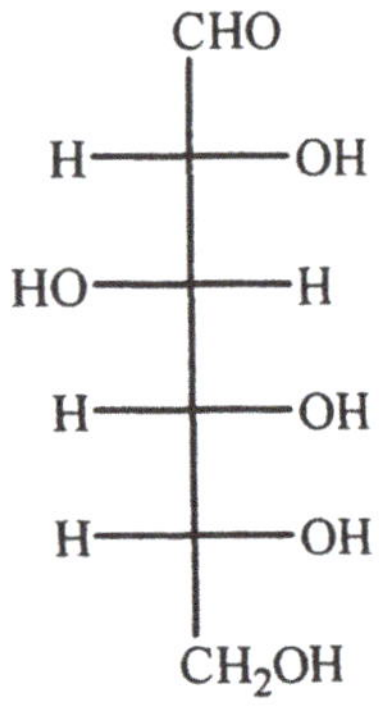

$$
\begin{array}{c}
CHO \\
HO{-}{-}H \\
H{-}{-}OH \\
H{-}{-}OH \\
H{-}{-}OH \\
CH_2OH
\end{array}
$$

Glucose

$$
\begin{array}{c}
CHO \\
H{-}{-}OH \\
HO{-}{-}H \\
H{-}{-}OH \\
H{-}{-}OH \\
CH_2OH
\end{array}
$$

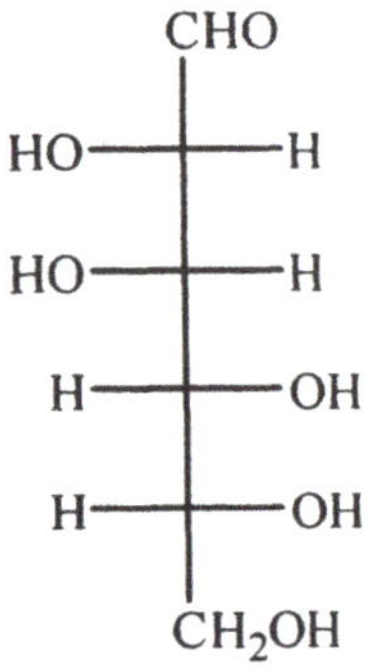

Mannose

$$
\begin{array}{c}
CHO \\
HO{-}{-}H \\
HO{-}{-}H \\
H{-}{-}OH \\
H{-}{-}OH \\
CH_2OH
\end{array}
$$

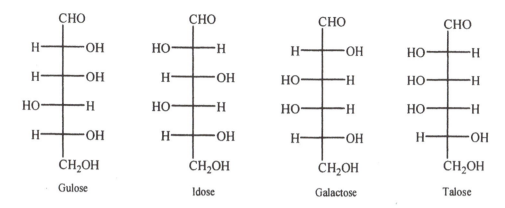

Figure 25-2 D-aldose sugars

C. CONFIGURATIONS OF MONOSACCHARIDES

Monosaccharides have chiral centers and thus exhibit optical activity. Let's explore the structure of glyceraldehyde. In the three-dimensional representation, the dotted wedges indicate the bonds that extend backwards from the chiral carbon (away from you or into the plane of the page); and the solid wedges indicate the bonds that are projected toward you (out of the plane of the page). In stereochemistry, Fischer projections are an important way to represent the spatial orientation of molecules. In Fischer projection representation, the bonds that are pointed backward (away from you or into the page) are indicated by vertical lines, and the bonds that extend toward you (out of the page) are represented by horizontal lines. For a more detailed approach, refer to the stereochemistry chapter.

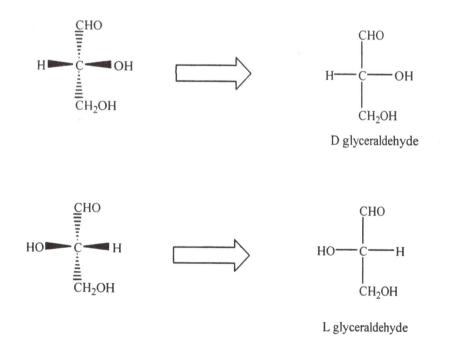

Figure 25-3

By convention, the carbonyl group is always drawn on top. With that as the standard, we can describe the structure of D-glyceraldehyde as follows:

D-glyceraldehyde has a hydroxyl group represented on the right side of the chiral carbon. L-Glyceraldehyde has a hydroxyl group represented on the left side of the chiral carbon. To determine whether a sugar structure shown is L or D, we have to locate the chiral carbon that is farthest from the carbonyl group, and see whether the hydroxyl group is on the right or on the left of the chiral carbon.

D. CYCLIC STRUCTURE OF HEXOSES

Glucose

Glucose is a six-carbon aldohexose. The straight chain hexose structures can become cyclic. When aldehydes and ketones undergo reactions with alcohols, hemiacetals or hemiketals are formed. In aldohexoses, the cyclic structure is formed when the hydroxyl group in the fifth carbon reacts (nucleophilic addition) with the carbonyl carbon of the aldehyde group. The product formed is a hemiacetal. The cyclization is represented in Figure 25-4.

A few facts worth remembering

1. The six-membered (hemiacetal) ring formed is called the **pyranose** ring.
2. The oxygen in the ring is from the hydroxyl group involved in the ring closure.
3. The carbon which is denoted as "carbon 1" in the cyclic structure is the carbonyl carbon of the straight chain (the aldehyde group).
4. Notice that the cyclic structure can go either way in the sense that the resulting cyclic structure can either be an alpha- or a β-anomer.
5. The carbon number '1' shown in the cyclic structure is called the anomeric carbon.
6. In aqueous solutions, the α- and β-anomers can interconvert, and the process is termed mutarotation.

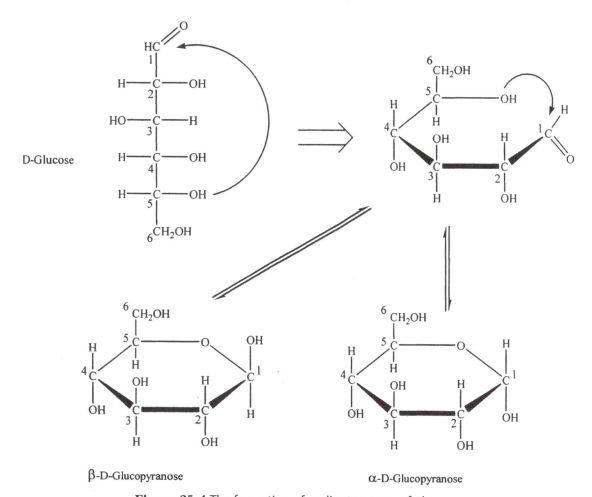

D-Glucose

β-D-Glucopyranose

α-D-Glucopyranose

Figure 25-4 The formation of cyclic structures of glucose

Fructose

Fructose is a ketohexose sugar. The cyclic structure formed is called a hemiketal, and the five membered ring that is formed is called **furanose** ring. The straight chain structure and the cyclic structures of fructose are shown in Figure 25-5.

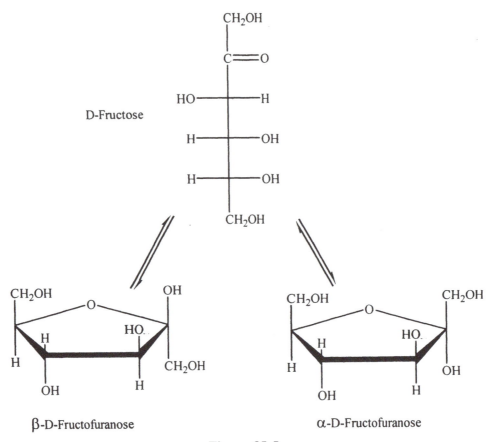

Figure 25-5

Epimers are any two isomeric sugars which differ in their configurations only at one of the chiral carbon atoms. Glucose and mannose are epimers. Glucose and galactose are also epimers.

E. OXIDATION OF MONOSACCHARIDES

Monosaccharides can be oxidized. Benedict's reagent (oxidizing agent) can accomplish this by reacting with the aldehyde group of the open-chain form. Thus aldose and ketose sugars are reducing sugars. In fact, all monosaccharides are reducing sugars. Some disaccharides can be oxidized by Benedict's reagent.

BENEDICT'S TEST FOR REDUCING SUGARS

[red precipitate]

Copper(I) oxide

$$RCHO \quad + \quad 2Cu^{2+} \quad \xrightarrow{\overset{-}{OH}} \quad RCOOH \quad + \quad Cu_2O \quad + \quad H_2O$$

OXIDATION

Benedict's reagent is reduced in the process to cuprous oxide.

F. DISACCHARIDES

Disaccharides are sugar units containing two monosaccharides linked by a covalent bond called a **glycosidic bond**. Maltose, sucrose, and lactose are examples of disaccharides. Maltose is formed by the linkage of two glucose molecules by a glycosidic bond. Sucrose is a combination of glucose and fructose. Lactose is composed of glucose and galactose. The hydrolysis of disaccharides gives their corresponding monosaccharide subunits.

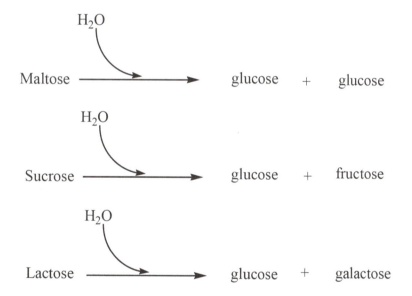

$$\text{Maltose} \xrightarrow{H_2O} \text{glucose} + \text{glucose}$$

$$\text{Sucrose} \xrightarrow{H_2O} \text{glucose} + \text{fructose}$$

$$\text{Lactose} \xrightarrow{H_2O} \text{glucose} + \text{galactose}$$

HYDROLYSIS OF DISACCHARIDES

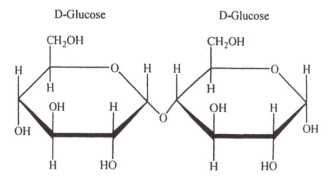

Figure 25-6 The structure of maltose

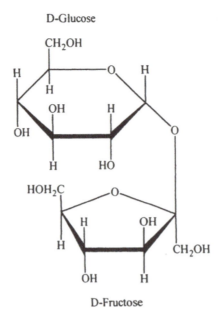

Figure 25-7 The structure of sucrose

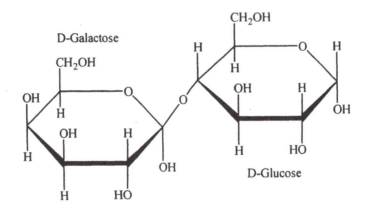

Figure 25-8 The structure of lactose

Polysaccharides

Polysaccharides are polymers of monosaccharides. Starch, glycogen, and cellulose are examples of polysaccharides. Polysaccharides can be homogeneous in terms of its fundamental unit (monosaccharide). If more than one type of monosaccharide is present in a polysaccharide, then it is called a heteropolysaccharide.

Starch

Starch is composed of two types of polymer structures derived from α-glucose, a linear polymer form called **amylose**, and a branched polymer form called **amylopectin**. Figure 25-9 shows the two types of glucose polymers involved in the formation of starch. The amylose has α(1->4) linkages of glucose subunits, and the amylopectin has α(1->6) and α(1->4) linkages.

Glycogen

Glycogen is a polysaccharide found in most animals as a storage medium of carbohydrate. It is stored mainly in the skeletal muscles and the liver. We can say that starch is to plants as glycogen is to animals. In other words, the animal carbohydrate storage medium is glycogen, and the plant carbohydrate storage medium is starch. The structure of glycogen is mostly like that of the amylopectin structures found in starch, only with more branching.

Cellulose

Cellulose is a polysaccharide found in plants. But unlike starch and glycogen, the monosaccharide units that build up the cellulose are β-glucose units. Also the polysaccharide chains found in the cellulose structure are unbranched. In addition, the linkages in cellulose units are β-linkages instead of α-linkages. This type of β-linkage is the reason why humans cannot digest cellulose. To be more precise, the enzymes that we have do not work on such linkages. Some herbivores such as cattle have cellulose digesting bacteria in their stomachs which digest the foods containing cellulose. Once the bacterial enzymes break the cellulose structures into simple sugars, then the animal can use them for its metabolic needs.

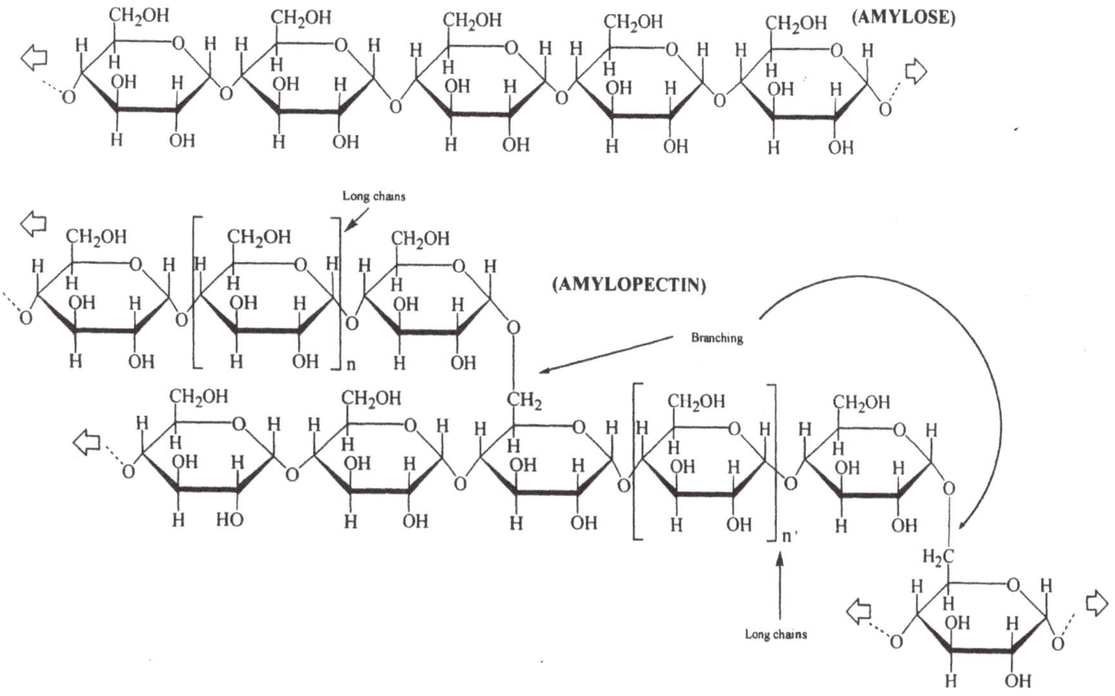

Figure 25-9 The glucose polymers that are involved in the formation of starch

CHAPTER 25 PRACTICE QUESTIONS

1. All the following are monosaccharides, except:

    A. galactose.
    B. glucose.
    C. ribose.
    D. maltose.

2. What is the name of the structure drawn below?

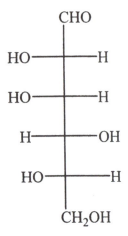

    A. D-glucose
    B. L-mannose
    C. D-galactose
    D. D-ribose

3. A lab technician making a fresh sugar solution noticed that the optical activity of the sugar solution changed after the solution had been standing for several hours. This change in optical activity is best explained by the phenomenon called:

    A. Tyndall effect.
    B. Brownian movement.
    C. optical anomaly.
    D. mutarotation.

4. Which of the following is NOT a disaccharide?

    A. Maltose
    B. Sucrose
    C. Glycogen
    D. Lactose

5. The structure shown below is that of a monosaccharide. How many optical isomers are possible for this structure?

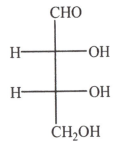

    A. 2
    B. 4
    C. 6
    D. 9

Questions 6-11 are based on the following passage.

Passage 1

The structures of some monosaccharides are drawn below.

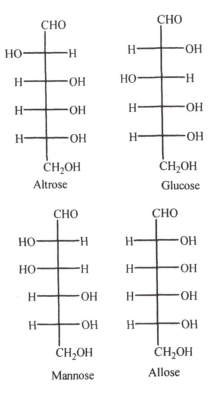

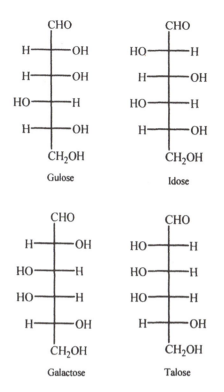

Gulose   Idose

Galactose   Talose

6. All the following are monosaccharides, except:

    A.   sucrose.
    B.   fructose.
    C.   glucose.
    D.   galactose.

7. The structure given below is:

CH₂OH

O

HO———H

H———OH

H———OH

CH₂OH

    A.   glucose.
    B.   ribose.
    C.   fructose.
    D.   maltose.

8. Which of the following statements are true regarding the two structures (Compounds I and II) drawn below?

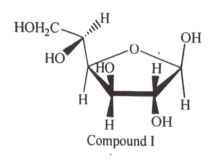

Compound I

Compound II

Statement (1) - Compound I is glucose.
Statement (2) - Compound II is glucose.
Statement (3) - Compound I is fructose.
Statement (4) - Compound II is fructose.

    A.   Statements 1 and 2
    B.   Statements 2 and 3
    C.   Statements 3 and 4
    D.   Statements 2 and 3

9. Glucose and mannose are:

    A.   anomers.
    B.   epimers.
    C.   enantiomers.
    D.   non-superimposable mirror images.

10. The structure of a disaccharide is shown below. The bond indicated by the arrow is called:

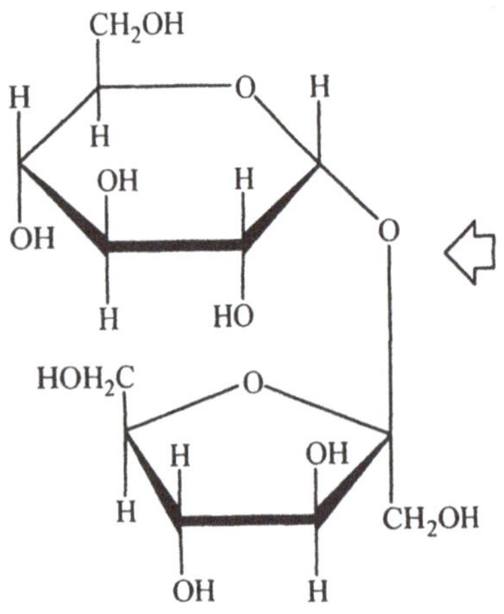

    A.   a glycosidic linkage.
    B.   a peptide linkage.
    C.   a glucose linkage.
    D.   an ester linkage.

11. The two stereogenic structures shown below are best related by the term:

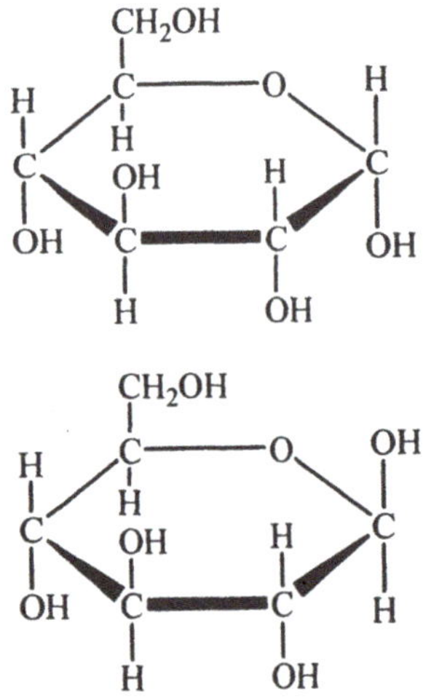

    A.   enantiomers.
    B.   resonance structures.
    C.   anomers.
    D.   mesomers.

CHAPTER 26
Lipids

A. INTRODUCTION

Lipids are a group of compounds which are hydrophobic, and have nonpolar groups predominantly. They can also contain polar groups. Lipids are important to living beings. Fats, a form of lipid, are used to store energy in organisms. Lipids are found in a wide variety of capacities; as hormones, as part of membranes, and as cofactors. Lipids are water insoluble. This makes them different and unique for their roles as biomolecules. Examples of lipids include waxes, steroids, and prostaglandins.

B. FATTY ACIDS

Fatty acids are carboxylic acids with long hydrocarbon chains. If the hydrocarbon chain in a fatty acid is saturated (no carbon-carbon double bonds), then it is called a **saturated fatty acid**. If there are (one or more) carbon-carbon double bonds in the hydrocarbon chain of a fatty acid, then it is called an **unsaturated fatty acid**. As the length of the hydrocarbon chain increases, the lipid solubility of fatty acids increases, and the water solubility decreases. Fats and oils are derivatives of fatty acids.

Table 26-1

Saturated Fatty Acids	
$CH_3(CH_2)_{12}COOH$	Myristic acid
$CH_3(CH_2)_{14}COOH$	Palmitic acid
$CH_3(CH_2)_{16}COOH$	Stearic acid

Unsaturated Fatty Acids	
$H_3C(H_2C)_7HC=CH(CH_2)_7COOH$	Oleic acid
$H_3C(H_2C)_4HC=CHCH_2CH=CH(CH_2)_7COOH$	Linoleic acid
$H_3CH_2CHC=CHCH_2CH=CHCH_2CH=CH(CH_2)_7COOH$	Linolenic acid

Table 26-2

C. TRIACYLGLYCEROLS

Triacylglycerols are esters of fatty acids. **Fats** or **triglycerides** are triacylglycerols. In a triacylglycerol, a glycerol molecule is linked with three fatty acids by ester linkages. The structure of glycerol is shown below:

GLYCEROL

$$\begin{array}{l} H_2C\!-\!OH \\ | \\ HC\!-\!OH \\ | \\ H_2C\!-\!OH \end{array}$$

The fatty acids that are present in fats are mostly straight-chain fatty acids (saturated and unsaturated), with even number of carbon atoms. According to the number of fatty acids esterifying the glycerol's hydroxyl groups, the glyceride formed could be a monoglyceride, a diglyceride or a triglyceride. Glycerides with long chain fatty acids are insoluble in water.

TRIACYLGLYCEROL

Figure 26-1

A diagrammatic representation of a triglyceride (triacylglycerol) is shown in Figure 26-1. In the figure, the vertical bar represents glycerol and the horizontal bars represent the fatty acids. The fatty acids (1, 2, and 3) present in a triacylglycerol molecule can be the same three fatty acids, or can be different fatty acids.

Fats can be solid or liquid. This physical property is a direct effect of the fatty acid substituents that are present in them. When fats are in their liquid state they are commonly called oils. Broadly we can generalize that solid fats mainly contain saturated fatty acids, and liquid fats mainly contain unsaturated fatty acids. We should not confuse this generalization with the fact that the naturally occurring fats and oils contain many different types of fatty acids, both saturated and unsaturated. The physical properties of fats are mostly a function of the fatty acids that are present in them. For example, human stored fat contains predominantly oleic acid (an unsaturated fatty acid) which constitutes about 47 % of the total fatty acid content. It also contains palmitic acid, linoleic acid, stearic acid, myristic acid, and other fatty acids in decreasing amounts respectively.

D. STEROIDS

A steroid has a drastically different structure from that of fats. **Steroids** are lipids having a particular fused-ring structure; a ring structure which has three six-carbon rings and a five-carbon ring. All steroids have this basic unit in their structures. Steroids include a wide variety of molecules, including cholesterol and its derivatives such as steroid hormones, and have tremendous biological significance. The steroid hormones include adrenocorticoid hormones and sex hormones.

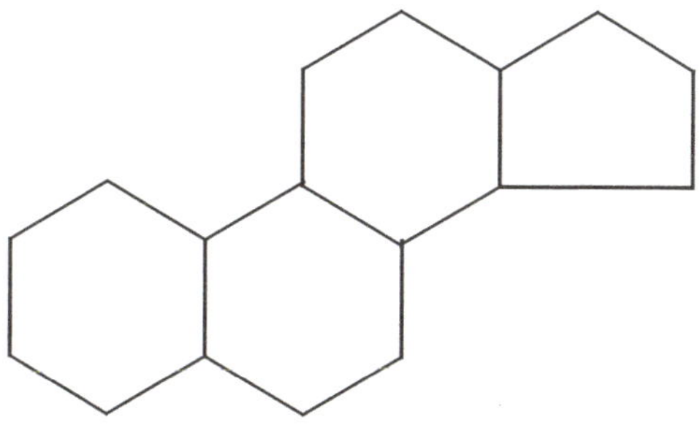

The fused ring of steroids

Cholesterol

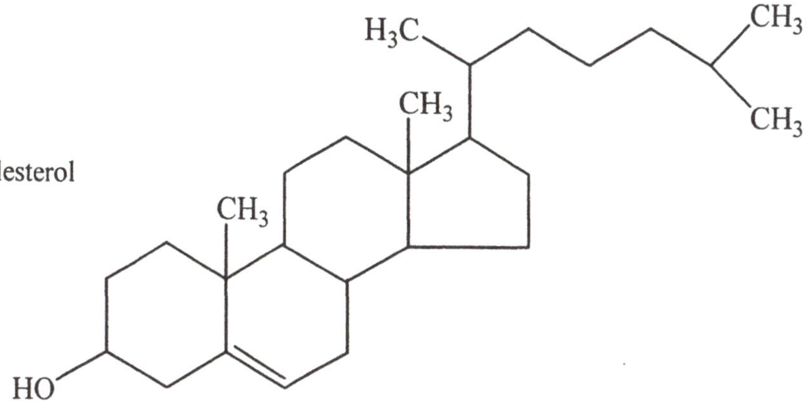

Adrenocorticoid hormones

Cortisone

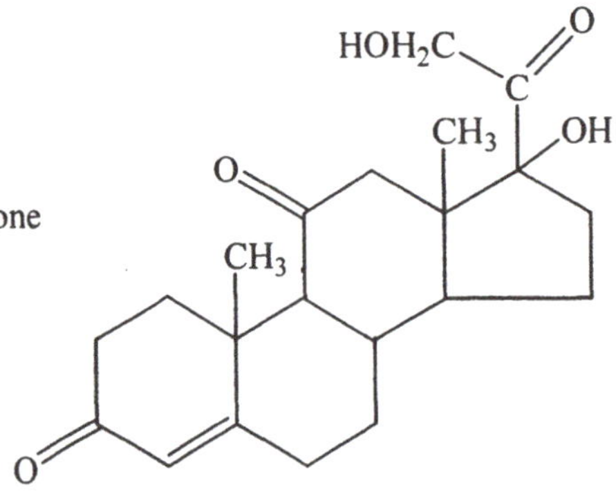

Aldosterone

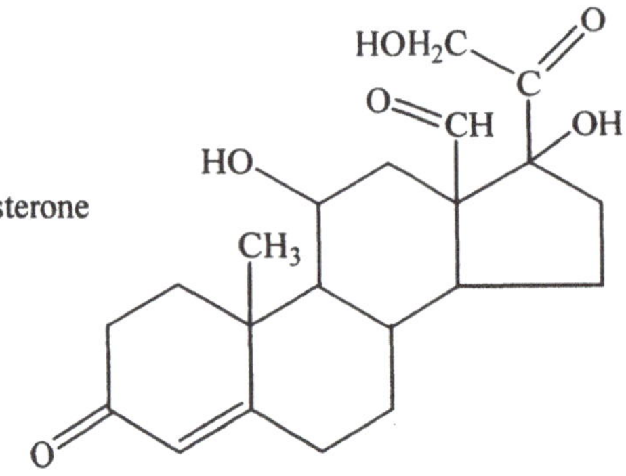

Sex hormones

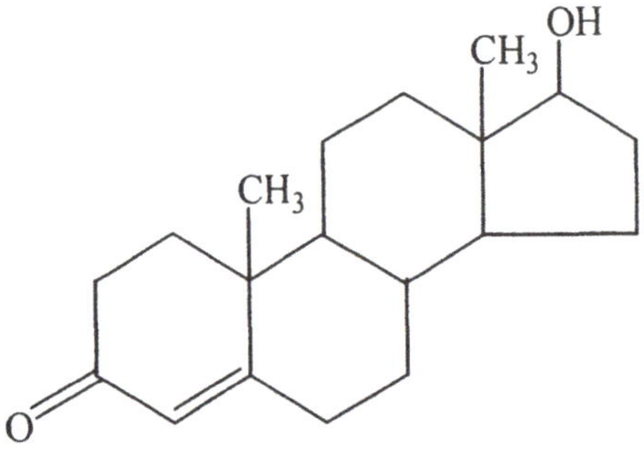

Testosterone

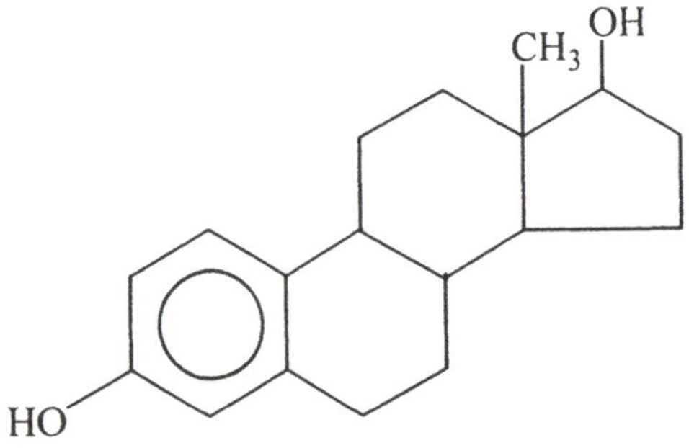

Estradiol

Notice that all these compounds have the fused-ring structure that we mentioned earlier. In fact, cholesterol acts as the starting material for the synthesis of steroid hormones. The steroid hormones play a very important role in the proper development and functioning of our body. The structures given above are just for reference and understanding the general structural integrity of steroids. You don't have to memorize them.

CHAPTER 26 PRACTICE QUESTIONS

1. If 1 mole of triglyceride is subjected to complete hydrolysis by using a lipase enzyme, the products formed are:

    A.   3 moles of glycerol and 1 mole of fatty acid.

    B.   1 mole of glycerol and 3 moles of fatty acid.

    C.   1 mole of glycerol and 1 mole of fatty acid.

    D.   2 moles of cholesterol.

2. Which of the following is NOT a steroid?

    A.   Vitamin D

    B.   Testosterone

    C.   Estradiol

    D.   All the above are steroids.

Section 9

CONTENT REVIEW PROBLEMS

1. All naturally occurring amino acids in animals are:

    A.   the L configuration.
    B.   the D configuration.
    C.   the + configuration.
    D.   the − configuration.

2. All naturally occurring sugars in animals are:

    A.   the L configuration.
    B.   the D configuration.
    C.   the + configuration.
    D.   the − configuration.

3. The key difference between the D and L designations as opposed to the R and S designations is that:

    A.   *R* and *S* configuration can only be determined experimentally using a polarimeter.
    B.   D and L configuration can only be determined experimentally using a polarimeter.
    C.   *R* and *S* is absolute configuration determined in the abstract, D and L is based on which glyceraldehyde molecule was the precursor.
    D.   D and L relate to the rotation of plane-polarized light such that all D molecules rotate light the same way, whereas *R* and *S* share no such correspondence.

4. A D-sugar must have:

    A.   *R* configuration at the first carbon in the chain.
    B.   *R* configuration at the next-to-last carbon in the chain.
    C.   *S* configuration at the first carbon in the chain.
    D.   *S* configuration at the next-to-last carbon in the chain.

5. Each of the following amino acids has a basic side chain EXCEPT:

    A.   histidine.
    B.   valine.
    C.   arginine.
    D.   lysine.

6. Which of the following amino acids has an acidic side chain?

    A.   Glutamate
    B.   Methionine
    C.   Leucine
    D.   Tryptophan

7. Which of the following amino acids has a polar side chain?

    A.   Valine
    B.   Alanine
    C.   Isoleucine
    D.   Serine

8. Which of the following amino acids has a non-polar side chain?

    A.   Histidine
    B.   Aspartic Acid
    C.   Phenylalanine
    D.   Threonine

9. Histidine is unique in that it side chain is the only one that has:

    A.   a nitrogen in a cyclic group.
    B.   a pK_a near physiological pH allowing it to act amphoterically.
    C.   a double-bonded nitrogen.
    D.   an aromatic ring.

10. Which of the following amino acids are most likely to be found folded into the center of a protein, away from water?

    A.   Valine and isoleucine
    B.   Threonine and tyrosine
    C.   Alanine and aspartic acid
    D.   Tryptophan and arginine

11. Which of the following amino acids include a sulfur residue in the side chain?
  I. Methionine
  II. Threonine
  III. Cysteine

    A. II only
    B. III only
    C. I and III only
    D. I, II, and III

12. What is the net charge on glycine at a pH of 12?

    A. -2
    B. -1
    C. 0
    D. +1

13. What is the net charge on glycine at physiological pH?

    A. -1
    B. 0
    C. +1
    D. +2

14. To calculate the pI of valine:

    A. subtract the pK_a of the amino group from the pK_a of the acid group.
    B. subtract the pK_a of the acid group from the pK_a of the amino group.
    C. find the pH at which the titration curve for valine has a slope that is the closest to zero.
    D. average the pK_a of the amino group and the acid group.

15. If an amino acid is placed in an electrophoretic gel in which the pH is greater than the pI, the amino acid will migrate:

    A. towards the negative electrode.
    B. towards the cathode.
    C. towards the anode.
    D. nowhere.

16. Aspartic acid has pK_as of 9.8, 3.9, and 2.1 for its three functional groups. If subjected to electrophoresis and pH = 7, aspartic acid will migrate:

    A. towards the negative electrode.
    B. towards the cathode.
    C. towards the anode.
    D. nowhere.

17. When being synthesized in a cell, the cell synthesizes proteins from:

    A. left to right.
    B. amino terminal to carboxy terminal.
    C. carboxy terminal to amino terminal.
    D. introns.

18. The free energy of a dipeptide is higher than that of the two individual amino acids. How is this reaction able to proceed spontaneously in cells?

    A. Peptide bond formation is coupled with expenditure of stored energy.
    B. The resonance in a peptide bond creates additional stability.
    C. The peptide bond is the thermodynamically favored product.
    D. Peptide bond formation is created under kinetic rather than thermodynamic control.

19. The resonance of the peptide bond creates:

    A. a partial positive charge on the oxygen in the amide bond.
    B. a partial negative charge on the nitrogen in the amide bond.
    C. triple-bond character in the carbonyl bond.
    D. significant rigidity as the double-bond character prevents rotation.

20. Naturally occurring glucose in animal cells:

   A. has 6 carbons and is in the D configuration.
   B. has 6 carbons and is in the L configuration.
   C. has 5 carbons and is in the D configuration.
   D. has 5 carbons and is in the L configuration.

21. Two hexose sugars have the same molecular formula, same connectivity between the atoms, and only differ in the absolute configuration at the last two chiral carbons. These sugars are:

   A. enantiomers.
   B. epimers.
   C. diastereomers.
   D. constitutional isomers.

22. Which of the following is true about the molecule below?

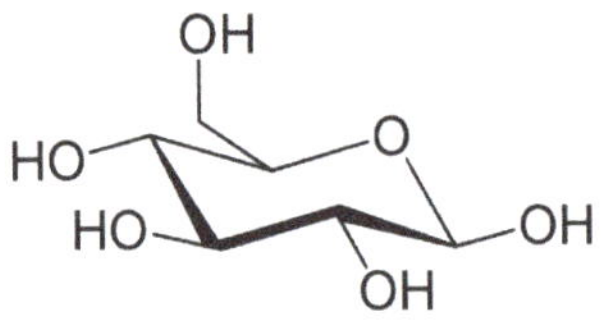

   A. It is an α furanose.
   B. It is a β pyranose.
   C. Polymers made from this molecule are the predominant form used in animals.
   D. It is a pentose.

23. To convert the molecule below into the opposite anomer:

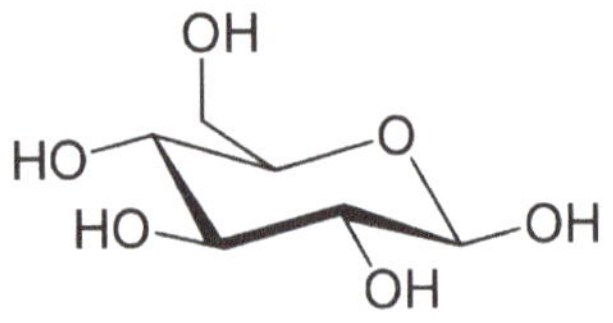

   A. mutarotation must occur to generate the β anomer.
   B. the molecule must change conformations.
   C. the molecule must form a different structural isomer.
   D. the ring must be broken open so mutarotation can occur.

24. Which of the following functional groups in sugars will NOT give a strongly positive Benedict's test?

   A. Acetals
   B. Hemi-acetals
   C. Aldehydes
   D. Ketones

25. An unsaturated fatty acid is liquid at room temperature whereas its saturated analog is a solid. This is due to:

   A. The increased polarity around the double bond in the unsaturated fat creates a slight molecular dipole which raises the boiling point.
   B. The saturated molecule has more hydrogens and thus a higher molecular weight.
   C. The straight-chain nature of the saturated fatty acid allows for better packing and thus a higher melting point.
   D. The unsaturated fatty acid includes electron-donating Lewis acid functional groups and thus can have intramolecular acid-base interactions.

This page intentionally left blank.

SECTION 10
LAB TECHNIQUES

As has been mentioned earlier, the MCAT will consist largely of passages that describe an experiment or some sort of experimental set up. This is true across all three of the science sections on the exam.

The good news is that much of what you encounter will be familiar to you. As a premed, you've taken tons of lab courses, so you've personally carried out a lot of the lab techniques the MCAT will want you to know. There's no better way to familiarize yourself with distillation, gel electrophoresis, or gas chromatography than to simply do it yourself.

Nevertheless, you shouldn't take this chapter for granted just because you have first-hand knowledge of lab techniques. Take the time to review this chapter thoroughly. If you would like to get the additional emphasis that comes from repetition, go to the Next Step MCAT Content Review: Physics and Math book and review the chapters there on experimental design.

CHAPTER 27

Separation, Purification, and Analysis

A. INTRODUCTION

For the MCAT, we should be familiar with the basic features of separation and purification of organic compounds. In this chapter, we will review some of the techniques that are commonly used by organic chemists.

B. EXTRACTION

Simple extraction involves the mixing of the organic solution with water in a separating funnel. Thorough mixing of the two phases (organic and aqueous) is done, and then the mixture is allowed to settle for some time until the two phases separate. Then the lower layer can be poured into another flask. This procedure can separate water soluble impurities such as inorganic salts, low molecular weight carboxylic acids, and alcohols. Similarly, extraction can be done with dilute aqueous acids to remove organic bases, and with dilute aqueous bases to remove organic acids.

C. CRYSTALLIZATION

Organic compounds (solids) can be purified by a method called crystallization. **Crystallization** works by dissolving the material to be purified in a solvent (under hot conditions), followed by slow cooling of the solution. If the impurities are also soluble just like the substance we are purifying, obviously the purification will not be that effective. After the crystallization by slow cooling is completed, the crystals are collected by vacuum filtration. Then the crystals are dried.

Qualities of the Solvent Used for Crystallization

(i) The compound that is purified should be soluble in the selected solvent, only at high temperatures. At low temperatures, the compound should be insoluble.

(ii) The solvent used should have a relatively low boiling point. The boiling point of the selected solvent should not be higher than the melting point of the compound to be purified.

Solubility depends on the polarities of the solute and the solvent. According to the principle "like dissolves like," if the solute is polar, the solvent required should be polar too. On the other hand, if the solute is nonpolar, a nonpolar solvent should be used.

Some of the solvents commonly used for crystallization include acetone, chloroform, methanol, benzene, diethyl ether, carbon tetrachloride, and water.

D. DISTILLATION

Distillation is a technique that can be employed if the compounds to be separated have reasonably different boiling points. Distillation involves boiling of the mixture to vaporize it. This is followed by condensation to get the distillate. The distillates are eventually collected in the order of their condensation. There are different types of distillations.

Simple distillation is used to separate compounds, which have boiling points that sufficiently differ (difference of about $>50^0$C).

Vacuum distillation is used for the separation of compounds that have very high boiling points, or that are heat sensitive.

Fractional distillation is used for the separation of compounds that have very close boiling points.

E. CHROMATOGRAPHY

Chromatography is a popular and widely used method of purification. **Chromatography** is based on the differences in the adsorption and the solubility of the compounds to be separated. It involves two phases – a stationary phase and a moving (mobile) phase. The moving phase actually carries the compounds along the stationary phase. Depending on the interactions between the compounds and the stationary phase, the compounds get held up or slowed down by the stationary phase.

Thin-layer Chromatography (TLC)

Thin-layer chromatography is used for the separation of small quantities of the desired compound, especially for qualitative analysis. It is a widely used technique. In TLC, the liquid (mobile) phase is allowed to run along a layer of adsorbent. This thin layer of adsorbent (usually alumina or silica gel) is usually coated on a plate. After the sample (mixture dissolved in a solvent) is put onto the plate (usually a spot of sample is placed at the bottom of the plate), the plate is held vertically with a small amount of the solvent just touching the bottom of the plate. Due to capillary action, the solvent will ascend up the plate.

The sample will be separated between the various phases. The separation occurs as a result of differences in the rate of migration of the individual components of the sample. This is because of the difference in the affinities of the solute with respect to the two phases. **As a rule of thumb, the greater the polarity of the compound (component) is, the lesser the rate of upward mobility of that compound.** This generalization is based on the fact that the stationary phase used is highly polar. Polar substances bind strongly to the stationary phase. Also, the moving phase generally used is less polar with respect to the adsorbent. The separated and migrated components will appear as a series of spots on the plate. If the components are colorless, certain reagents are used to make the spots visible. Choosing the correct solvent is extremely important, and is best achieved by experience. Sometimes the best choice of solvent can be attained only by trial and error.

R_f value is the ratio of the distance traveled by a compound to the distance traveled by the solvent.

Using known R_f values of compounds under the same conditions, we can make sure that the desired compound is present in the mixture and can be separated. R_f value is a constant (under specific conditions) for a given compound, and if the TLC is done exactly under the same conditions specified, we can be reasonably sure about the identity of the compound. Keep in mind that it is always safe to make sure of the identity of a compound with other qualitative analysis as well.

In addition to the function of identifying compounds, TLC is also used to monitor the progression of reactions, and to test the authenticity or the effectiveness of other separation techniques.

Gas Chromatography (GC)

As the name implies, a gas phase (moving phase) and a liquid phase (stationary phase) are involved in gas-liquid chromatography. **Gas chromatography** is usually employed for the separation of volatile compounds. The device used for this is called a gas chromatograph. Usually a syringe is used to inject the sample into the device, and the sample injected is readily turned into vapor form. This vaporized form of the sample is carried along the flow of an inert gas. The sample is passed through a column containing the adsorbent (liquid-stationary phase). The column is the site where the separation of the components occurs. The separated samples as they emerge from the column are detected using a detection device.

The maintenance of the correct temperature of the column is extremely important for an efficient separation of the components. The choice of the stationary liquid phase is also important, and so is the maintenance of an optimum rate of flow of the sample through the column. The latter can be maintained by controlling the flow of the carrier gas. This technique is highly sensitive. Hence, it can be used to detect compounds even if very little of the compound is present (as long as it is on the order of micrograms).

Technological developments in the field of identification of compounds using infrared and NMR techniques have revolutionized the ease with which we can analyze and identify even the most complex structures in organic chemistry. For the MCAT, we should be familiar with the techniques and the basic principles that are used in this field.

F. INFRARED (IR) SPECTROSCOPY

Infrared spectroscopy is a widely used tool to identify and analyze compounds. As you know, the infrared radiation is part of the electromagnetic spectrum. The IR has wavelengths between those of the visible light and the microwaves. From the analytical point of view, only a portion of the entire infrared range is actually useful for the spectroscopic analysis.

In order to analyze organic compounds, certain properties at the molecular level are put to use in the infrared spectroscopy. In this technique, the infrared light is passed through organic compound samples. By doing this, some of the frequencies are absorbed by the sample and the other frequencies simply pass through. The percentage absorbance or transmittance is plotted against the frequency or, to be more precise, the wave number. The wave number (cm^{-1}) is the reciprocal of wavelength expressed in centimeters. The plot can be used to analyze the structure of a compound by identifying the peaks that are characteristic to the groups present in the compound.

For example, the carbonyl group (>C=O) shows absorbance close to $1700\ cm^{-1}$ in the IR spectrum. The peaks around this value indicate the presence of carbonyl group in the compound that is analyzed. By knowing the IR values, we can predict the structure of a compound. Our discussion from the MCAT point of view will be limited to some of the common and important IR peaks. Other very complex IR spectra can only be interpreted by skilled and experienced professionals.

Vibrational Modes

Chemical bonds have characteristic natural frequencies with which they vibrate (bending and stretching) in certain specific energy levels. The special range of frequencies used in IR spectrometry is within the range of the natural vibrational frequencies of the bonds in organic compounds. By looking at the peaks, we can tell whether a particular functional group is present or absent in the compound that we are analyzing. The bonds present in the molecules of the sample vibrate when they absorb characteristic frequencies.

Molecules are always in a state of vibration. The bonds present in molecules have their own unique stretching and bending modes. Let's consider a hypothetical molecule A, which is non-linear, and has n atoms per molecule. Then, theoretically molecule A will have $3n - 6$ modes of vibration. But this does not mean that the vibrational modes strictly follow this rule. Some of the vibrational modes have frequencies that do not coincide with the frequencies of the IR that we use. We will consider the vibrational modes of the methylene group.

STRETCHING VIBRATIONS

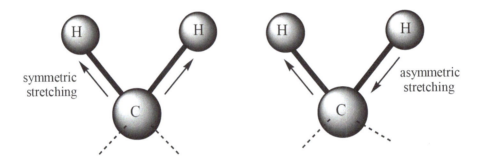

Figure 27-1 The stretching vibrational modes of a methylene group. The two drawings show stretching vibrations – symmetric (on the left) and asymmetric on the right.

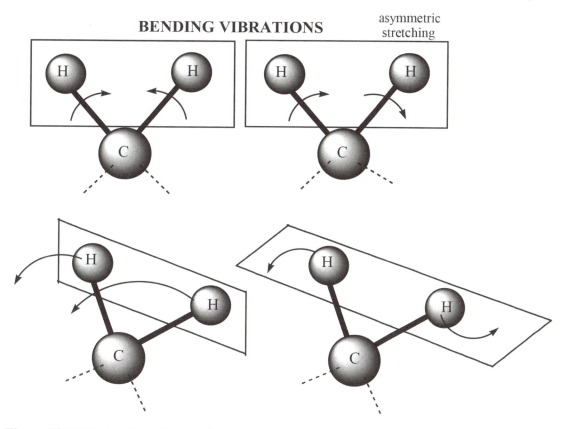

Figure 27-2 The bending vibrational modes of methylene group. The top two diagrams from the left are scissoring and rocking modes. The bottom two diagrams show wagging and twisting modes.

Besides the fundamental vibrational frequencies, overtones and combination tones can appear in the IR spectrum. For example, the overtone of a carbonyl group can appear close to 3400cm^{-1} (the carbonyl peak is close to 1700 cm^{-1}). Combination frequencies are peaks that appear when two frequencies intermingle, resulting in two weak frequencies.

SOME IR ABSORBANCES

TYPE OF BOND	ABSORBANCE (cm^{-1})
—OH (Alcohol)	3200-3600
—OH (Carboxylic acid)	2500-3300
—Aromatic ring	~1500, ~1600
—CH (Aromatic)	3000-3100
—CH (sp^3)	2850-3000
═CH (sp^2)	3000-3100
≡CH (sp)	~3300
Aldehyde	~2720, ~2820
-C≡N	2210-2260
Ethers	~1000, ~1300
Amines -NH	3300-3500
-C=O (Carbonyl)	~1715 (1640-1750)
-C=O (Ketone)	~1715 (1665-1725)
-C=O (Aldehyde)	~1715 (1660-1740)
-C=O (Amide)	~1690 (1630-1690)
-C=O (Ester)	~1735 (1735-1750)
-C=O (Acid)	~1710 (1700-1730)
-C=O (Acid)	~1710 (1700-1730)
$\diagdown$C=C$\diagup$ (Alkene)	1620-1680

Table 27-1

Example 27-1

Analyze the IR diagram shown below.

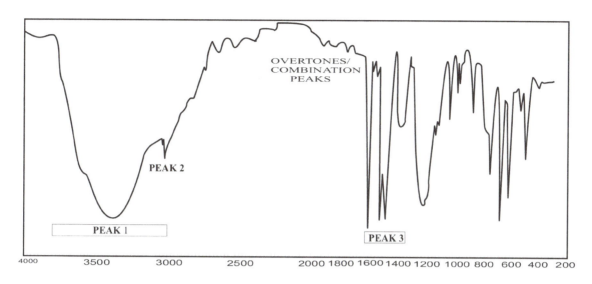

The given IR spectrum is that of phenol. Look at some of the important peaks that are present in this IR spectrum of phenol.

Analysis:

1. The peak 1 around 3400 cm^{-1} represents the peak caused by the -OH group.
2. The peak 2 at 3050 cm^{-1} represents the aromatic -CH.
3. The peak 3 denotes the benzene ring stretch.

Problem 27-1

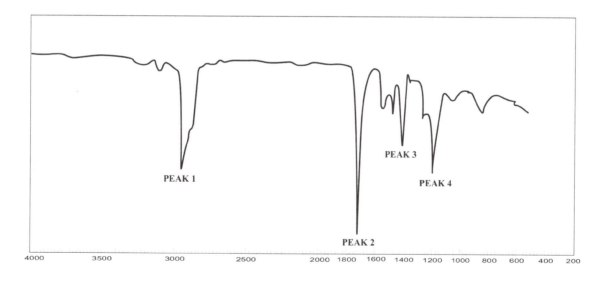

In the IR spectrum shown above, identify the most likely peak which represents the carbonyl group.

Solution:

The carbonyl peak is roughly around 1700 cm^{-1}. So Peak 2 indicated in the IR diagram is the correct answer.

G. NUCLEAR MAGNETIC RESONANCE (NMR) SPECTROSCOPY

Nuclear magnetic resonance spectroscopy (NMR) is a type of analysis with which we can identify the positions of certain atoms in a compound. Only those atoms which possess non-zero nuclear spins can exhibit NMR behavior. NMR spectroscopy is based on the magnetic properties exhibited by the nuclei of certain atoms. We will limit our discussion to the resonance spectroscopy involving the nuclei of hydrogen atoms, (proton NMR) since that is where the MCAT will focus. With proton NMR, we can find or recognize the characteristic groups in the unknown compound, to which the specific protons are attached. In addition, we can also identify the number of different types of equivalent protons in a compound that we are analyzing.

The Basics of Proton NMR

The neutrons and protons that make up atomic nuclei have an intrinsic quantum mechanical property referred to as spin. A non-zero nuclear spin gives rise to a non-zero nuclear magnetic moment. When hydrogen nuclei are exposed to a magnetic field, the nuclei will align themselves in coherence with the applied magnetic field as if they were tiny magnets. The alignment can be either along or opposite to the direction of the applied magnetic field. Among these two orientations, the one with the lower energy occurs when the alignment is along the direction of the field compared to the other orientation.

When sufficient energy (equal approximately to that found in the radio frequency region of the electromagnetic spectrum) is applied, the nuclei that are aligned along the magnetic field can reverse their orientation to align opposite to that of the applied magnetic field. The extent to which the nucleus is shielded from the magnetic field dictates the amount of energy required to change the orientation to a higher energy level. Based on this principle, we have to understand that depending on the extent of shielding they will absorb different frequencies. The energy that is absorbed is monitored and is recorded in the form of a NMR spectrum. Thus, protons in different regions of a molecule have different shifts (**chemical shifts**).

For the standard applied magnetic field, the absorption of frequencies differ only in terms of a few parts per million (ppm). In NMR spectroscopy, the relative standard molecule used is tetramethyl silane (TMS), and thus chemical shift (d) is measured in ppm relative to the proton signal of TMS, which is considered to have a standard arbitrary value of "0 ppm" and serves as the reference standard.

Figure 27-2

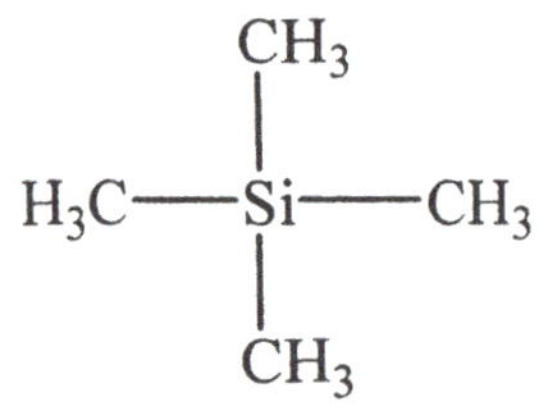

The reference compound used – Tetra-methyl silane

Spin-Spin Coupling

Spin-spin coupling results from the possibility of the coupling of the neighboring protons. Signals often appear as groups of peaks as a result of spin-spin coupling. This results in what is called **signal multiplicity**. The number of peaks in a signal is dictated by the following means. Consider this hypothetical situation. Let's say there are N_1 equivalent protons in set 1, and N_2 equivalent protons in the adjacent carbon (set 2). (Note: Equivalent protons do not split themselves.) If this is the case, signal 1 will have (N_2 + 1) peaks, and signal 2 will have (N_1 + 1) peaks. The intensities of a split pattern are symmetrical (bilaterally symmetrical). The relative intensities of the peaks in a signal follow a pattern. A singlet has only one peak. There is no splitting in singlets. So there is no relative ratio to compare with. A doublet has a 1 : 1 proportion of relative intensities. A triplet has 1 : 2 : 1 proportion of relative intensities. A quartet has 1 : 3 : 3 : 1 proportion of relative intensities, and so on.

The different types of equivalent protons reflect the total number of signals. In the NMR spectrum of a compound, the levels of intensities of the signals denote the proportion of equivalent protons present in the compound. For example, the intensity of a signal resulting from six equivalent protons will be greater than the intensity of a signal resulting from two equivalent protons. The intensity is equivalent to the areas under the signals, and is proportional to the number of protons creating that particular signal.

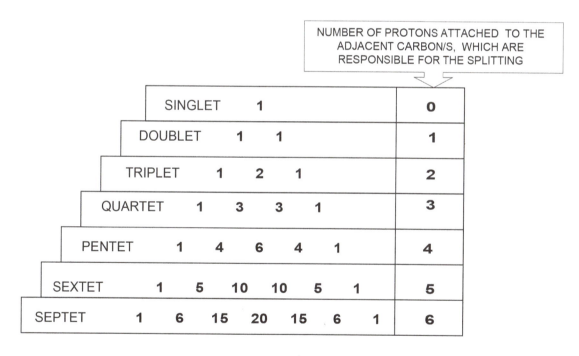

Figure 27-3 Relative intensities of the peaks

Proton Chemical Shifts

Table 27-2

Type of Proton	Chemical shift, δ (ppm)*
R-CH$_3$ (Primary)	0.9
R$_2$-CH$_2$ (Secondary)	1.3
R$_2$-CH (Tertiary)	1.5
-HC=CH (Vinyl)	4.5 - 6
—C≡CH (Acetylenic)	2 - 3
Ar-H (Aromatic)	6 - 8.5
Ar-CH (Benzylic)	2 - 3
C=CHCH$_3$ (Allylic)	1.6
-CHX (Halides)	2 - 4.5
-CHOH (Alcohol)	3.4 - 4
-CHOR (Ether)	3.4 - 4
-CHCOOH (Carboxylic)	2 - 2.6
-CHCOOR (Ester)	2 - 2.2
RCH=O (Aldehyde)	9 - 10
-CHOH (Hydroxyl)	1 - 5.6
-Ar-OH (Phenolic hydroxyl)	4 - 12
-CHCOOH (Carboxylic acid)	10 - 12
R-NH$_2$ (Amino)	1 - 5

*Approximate values with respect to TMS

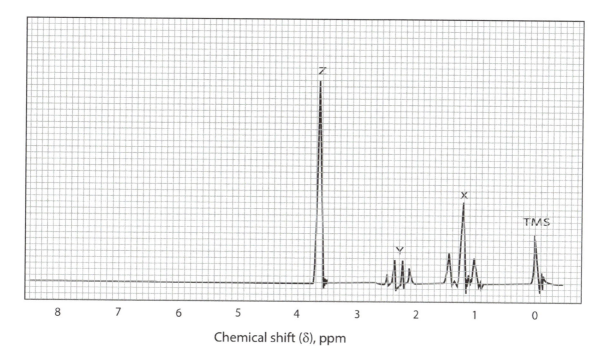

Figure 27-4 The NMR spectrum of methyl propionate

Look at the NMR spectrum of methyl propionate given in Figure 32-4.

$$CH_3—O—\overset{\overset{\displaystyle O}{\|}}{C}—\overset{H_2}{C}—CH_3 \qquad \text{Methyl propionate}$$

In the NMR spectrum, the signal at 0 ppm represents tetramethyl silane (standard). There are three distinct signals (sets of peaks). Altogether, there are 8 peaks – a set of three just after 1 ppm, a set of four just after 2 ppm, and a single peak around 3.5 ppm, totaling eight peaks. The set X is a triplet. The set Y is a quartet, and the set Z is a singlet. Sometimes it is hard to recognize the peaks distinctly because of interference between the nuclei, especially when there are multiple number of peaks.

In methyl propionate, there are three different types of protons denoted by X, Y, and Z. In the NMR spectrum, the set X is represented by the triplet in the nmr spectrum, the set Y is denoted by the quartet, and the set Z is denoted by the singlet.

CHAPTER 27 PRACTICE QUESTIONS

1. All the following are true regarding the process of crystallization, except:

    A. the solvent used should easily dissolve the compound when cold.

    B. minimum amount of solvent should be used.

    C. crystallization process is generally used when there aren't many impurities in the material purified.

    D. hexane is a good solvent that can be used to purify hydrocarbons.

2. Distillation is a very widely used technique for purifying compounds. Which of the following processes is involved?

    A. Vaporization is involved
    B. Boiling is involved
    C. Condensation is involved
    D. All the above

Questions 3-8 are based on the following passage.

Passage 1

A set of qualitative experiments were conducted in an organic chemistry lab.

Experiment 1

Chemist 1 treated cyclohexene with 1% aq. $KMnO_4$. One of the products was a *cis*-glycol.

Experiment 2

Chemist 2 conducted qualitative tests for some carbonyl compounds. Aldehydes and ketones gave a positive test for the reagent 2, 4-dinitro- phenyl hydrazine. The compound tested for the confirmation was propanone. The product formed as a result of this test involving propanone is shown below.

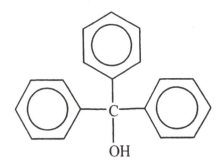

Experiment 3

In Experiment 3, three compounds were tested. These three compounds were treated with concentrated hydrochloric acid in the presence of zinc chloride ($ZnCl_2$). Compound A was ethyl alcohol, Compound B was *tert*-butyl alcohol, and Compound C was 2-propanol. The reactions were based on a unimolecular substitution mechanism.

Experiment 4

In Experiment 4, the chemists synthesized the following compound.

3. Based on Experiment 3, choose the true statement from the following choices.

    A. Compound A had the fastest reaction rate among the compounds tested.

    B. Compound B had the slowest reaction rate among the compounds tested.

    C. Compound C did not undergo the reaction.

    D. Compound A did not undergo the reaction.

4. In Experiment 2, which of the following IR peaks must have disappeared after the treatment of the compound with the reagent?

    A.   A broad IR band at 3400 cm^{-1}

    B.   A peak at 1700 cm^{-1}

    C.   A peak at 800 cm^{-1}

    D.   All the above peaks will be present for the product formed as a result of the reaction with the reagent.

5. Which of the following best describes the process involved in Experiment 1?

    A.   Reduction

    B.   Esterification

    C.   Oxidation

    D.   Dehydrohalogenation

6. Which of the following is true regarding Compounds A, B and C?

    A.   They all have carboxyl groups.

    B.   They all have double bonds.

    C.   They all have IR peaks close to 3400 cm^{-1}.

    D.   They all have the same reaction rate in terms of substitution reactions.

7. How many sets of ^{1}H-NMR signals are expected for Compound B?

    A.   2

    B.   3

    C.   4

    D.   10

8. Which of the following are true for the compound synthesized in Experiment 4?

  I. The compound is insoluble in H_2O.

  II. The compound is soluble in 5% aqueous solution of NaOH.

  III. The compound is an aromatic compound.

  IV. The compound is a strong base.

    A.   I and II only

    B.   I and III only

    C.   II and IV only

    D.   II and III only

Section 10

CONTENT REVIEW PROBLEMS

1. To extract hexanamine from organic solution, a chemist should extract with:

    A.   dilute HCl.
    B.   dilute $NaHCO_3$.
    C.   dilute NaOH.
    D.   distilled water.

2. To extract CO_3^- from organic naphthalene solution, a chemist can extract with:
 I. distilled water.
 II. carbon tetrachloride.
III. diethyl ether.

    A.   I only
    B.   II only
    C.   I and II only
    D.   II and III only

3. To extract pentanoic acid from organic solution, a chemist should extract with:

    A.   dilute HCl.
    B.   dilute $NaHCO_3$.
    C.   dilute H_2CO_3.
    D.   ether.

4. To extract phenol from organic solution, a chemist should extract with:

    A.   dilute HCl.
    B.   dilute NaOH.
    C.   dilute H_2CO_3.
    D.   dilute $NaHCO_3$.

5. In TLC, the motive force that moves the mobile phase is:

    A.   gravity.
    B.   high pressure.
    C.   capillary action.
    D.   electric potential.

6. A TLC separation is carried out with compounds X and Y. Compound X is more polar than compound Y. Therefore:

    A.   Compound Y will have a lower R_f.
    B.   Compound X will migrate further along the glass plate.
    C.   Compound X will have a lower R_f.
    D.   Compound Y will be more attracted to the glass plate.

7. A TLC separation is carried out with compounds X and Y. Compound X is more polar than compound Y. Therefore:

    A.   it will show less affinity for the silica.
    B.   it will dissolve more easily in the liquid mobile phase and move farther.
    C.   it will be insoluble in the liquid mobile phase and have an R_f value near 0.
    D.   it will show more affinity for the silica.

8. A chemist seeks to separate two compounds dissolved in an organic solvent. One compound is much more polar than the other and the chemist has a large volume of material to separate. As such, the chemist should:

    A.   carry out several simultaneous TLCs.
    B.   use a high pressure GC.
    C.   use a very large surface-area electrophoretic gel.
    D.   carry out a column chromatography.

9. In a column chromatography, the motive force that moves the mobile phase is:

    A.   gravity.
    B.   high pressure.
    C.   capillary action.
    D.   electric potential.

10. A chemist sets up a column chromatography apparatus with the column packed with silica beads. He then pours the solution in the top. The solution has compound X and compound Y dissolved in it. Compound X is more polar. The first fraction of liquid to exit the buret will:

    A.   largely consist of compound X.
    B.   largely consist of compound Y.
    C.   consist of equal amounts of X and Y.
    D.   depend on the relative molecular size of X and Y.

11. A chemist seeks to separate a large mixture of two amino acids, one with a negatively-charged side chain and one with a positively-ionized side chain. Which of the following would separate these compounds:

    A.   TLC.
    B.   mass spectroscopy.
    C.   centrifugation.
    D.   ion-exchange chromatography.

12. In high performance liquid chromatography, the motive force that moves the mobile phase is:

    A.   gravity.
    B.   high pressure.
    C.   capillary action.
    D.   electric potential.

13. A chemist sets up a chromatography apparatus by packing the buret with inert polymer beads that have many tiny pores in them. Which of the following is true about this set up?

    A.   A smaller molecule will move more quickly through the column.
    B.   The more highly polar molecule will move more slowly through the column.
    C.   A smaller molecule will move more slowly through the column.
    D.   The motive force is provided by capillary action.

14. A chemist sets up a chromatography apparatus by packing the buret with inert polymer beads that have many tiny pores in them. Which of the following is true about this set up?

    A.   This experimental setup will give the same results as a TLC but allows for larger samples.
    B.   This chromatography uses a pump to generate the pressure needed to carry out the experiment more quickly than would be possible with gravity alone.
    C.   This size-exclusion chromatography is used to separate molecules based on molecular size.
    D.   This is a form of ion-exchange chromatography based on the size difference between atomic and ionic radii.

15. A biologist has a solution composed of lysed bacterial cells and she wishes to separate a particular enzyme from the solution. She should carry out:

    A.   an affinity chromatography.
    B.   an ion-exchange chromatography.
    C.   a thin layer chromatography.
    D.   a mass spectroscopy.

16. Which of the following pairs of compounds would best be separated by a GC?

    A.   Two organic compounds of different polarities.
    B.   Two organic compounds with different pK_as.
    C.   An organic and inorganic compound with similar volatility but very different melting points.
    D.   Two organic compounds of different volatilities.

17. A simple distillation would be most appropriate to separate which two compounds?

    A. Three compounds with boiling points of 50°C, 150°C, and 155°C.
    B. Two compounds with boiling points of 35°C and 65°C.
    C. Two compounds with boiling points of 335°C and 465°C.
    D. Three compounds with boiling points of 150°C, 650°C, and 855°C.

18. An organic compound can most helpfully be analyzed by UV-Vis spectroscopy if it:

    A. has a highly conjugated electron system.
    B. consists solely of single bonds.
    C. includes –OH groups.
    D. is water soluble.

19. An organic compound can most helpfully be analyzed by UV-Vis spectroscopy if it:

    A. is polar aprotic.
    B. has at least one triple bond.
    C. is not water soluble.
    D. is an organometallic compound containing a transition metal.

20. Which of the following IR peaks would be most associated with a carbonyl group?

    A. $1735 - 1680$ cm^{-1}
    B. $3650 - 3200$ cm^{-1}
    C. $3150 - 2500$ cm^{-1}
    D. $2260 - 2220$ cm^{-1}

21. Which of the following IR peaks would be most associated with an –OH group?

    A. $1735 - 1680$ cm^{-1}
    B. $3650 - 3200$ cm^{-1}
    C. $3150 - 2500$ cm^{-1}
    D. $2260 - 2220$ cm^{-1}

22. Which of the following IR peaks would be most associated with an N-H bond?

    A. $1735 - 1680$ cm^{-1}
    B. $3650 - 3200$ cm^{-1}
    C. $3150 - 2500$ cm^{-1}
    D. $2260 - 2220$ cm^{-1}

23. The ^{1}H-NMR signal for butane would give:

    A. 1 signal.
    B. 2 signals.
    C. 3 signals.
    D. 4 signals.

24. The ^{1}H-NMR signal for butanal would give:

    A. 1 signal.
    B. 2 signals.
    C. 3 signals.
    D. 4 signals.

25. The ^{1}H-NMR signal for benzene would give:

    A. 1 signal.
    B. 2 signals.
    C. 3 signals.
    D. 4 signals.

This page intentionally left blank.

SECTION 11
SECONDARY TOPICS

The amount of material covered in a single year of intro organic chem is vast. Yet the amount directly tested on the MCAT is relatively small. There are certain orgo classics that are a staple of college classes, yet will only show up in a tangential way on the MCAT – in particular, the reactions of alkenes, alkynes, and aromatic compounds. We didn't feel comfortable leaving out these topics entirely, so we've included a final section we're calling "secondary topics".

If you're pressed for time, just skip this section entirely. Students who are trying to get their entire MCAT prep done in just a month or two shouldn't worry about these chapters at all. But if you've given yourself a longer prep timeline, say 3.5 to 4+ months then there is value in briefly reviewing the following chapters. Focus on the basic principles - nomenclature, reactions between nucleophiles and electrophiles, stability, etc.

Finally, we've included the chapter on phosphoric acid chemistry in this section, but it is a vitally important topic. The reason we've put under "secondary topics" is that the relevant chemistry is dealt with entirely under the biology and biochemistry headings. Phosphoric acid chemistry underlies DNA formation, ATP, and a host of other incredibly important biological molecules. Again, if you're pressed for time you can skip that chapter and just invest more heavily in the Next Step MCAT Content Review: Biology and Biochemistry book.

A. INTRODUCTION

Alkenes are hydrocarbon compounds that contain carbon-carbon double bonds. The first member of the alkene family is ethene (ethylene), similar to ethane of the alkane family in terms of the basic name, though the ending is -ene rather than -ane. The general molecular formula of alkenes is C_nH_{2n}.

B. NOMENCLATURE

Ethene (Ethylene) $CH_2=CH_2$
Propene (Propylene) $CH_2=CH-CH_3$

From the third member (butene) of the alkene family onward, there is a need to specify the location of the double bond to recognize the correct structure denoted by the name. When naming alkenes, the numbering should begin from the carbon chain end which gives the double bond position the lowest number.

Watch the numbering of carbons in the following examples.

$$\overset{1}{C}H_2 = \overset{2}{C}H\overset{3}{C}H_2\overset{4}{C}H_3 \qquad \text{1-Butene}$$

$$\overset{1}{C}H_2 = \overset{2}{C}H\overset{3}{C}H_2\overset{4}{C}H_2\overset{5}{C}H_3 \qquad \text{1-Pentene}$$

$$\overset{7}{C}H_3\overset{6}{C}H_2\overset{5}{C}H_2\overset{4}{C}H_2\overset{3}{C}H = \overset{2}{C}H\overset{1}{C}H_3 \qquad \text{2-Heptene}$$

$$\overset{7}{C}H_3\overset{6}{C}H_2\overset{5}{C}H_2\overset{4}{C}H_2\overset{3}{C}H = \overset{2}{C}H\overset{1}{C}H_3 \qquad \text{6-Methyl-2-heptene}$$
$$CH_3$$

C. ISOMERISM

The carbon atoms which contain the double bonds in alkenes are ***sp²* hybridized**. Each carbon-carbon double bond is made of one sigma and one pi bond.

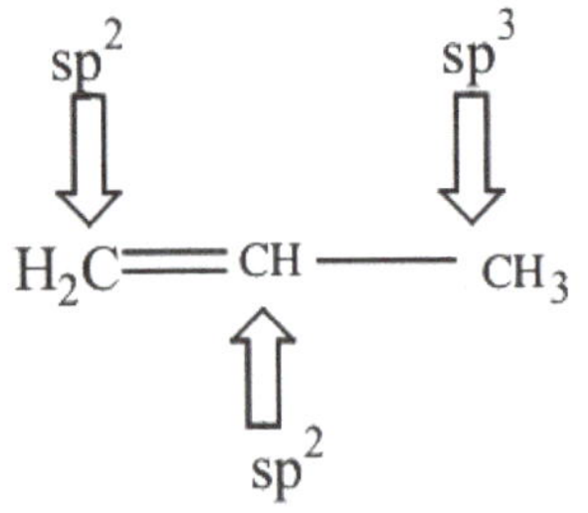

Isomerism

Any compound with a carbon-carbon double bond can exhibit cis-trans isomerism, provided that the carbons involved in the double bond do not have two of the same groups or atoms attached to each of them. 2-Butene is the simplest alkene that can have cis-trans isomerism. Trans isomers are generally more stable than their cis counterparts. Alkyl groups are mildly electron-donating toward the double bond. This can lead to polarity. For instance, *cis*-2-butene has a net dipole moment as shown in the diagram given below. On the other hand, in *trans*-2-butene the net dipole is zero since the dipole moments cancel out (the vector sum of the dipole moments is zero).

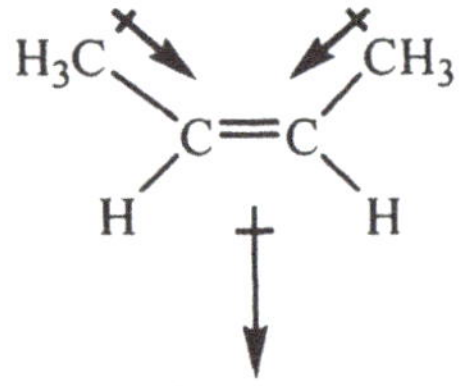

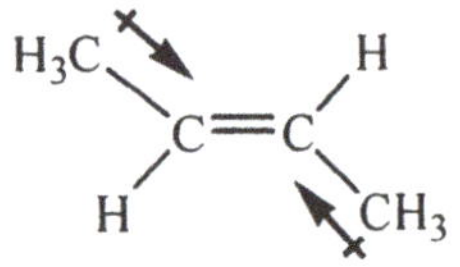

Both *cis* and *trans*-2-butene have van der Waals attractive forces. But, only the *cis*-isomer can have dipole-dipole interactions because it has a net dipole moment. Hence, *cis*-2-butene has a higher boiling point than *trans*-2-butene.

The E-Z System of Naming Alkenes

Sometimes we are not able to categorize alkenes into trans and cis isomers. The following example will reveal why that is the case.

For compounds such as the ones shown above, we have to prioritize the substituents, and that is the only way to name and identify these compounds. A new system was proposed by scientists, which categorizes these compounds under **E *(entgegen)***, and **Z (zusammen)** configurations. **E configuration** describes *opposite*, whereas **Z configuration** describes *same side*. Study the following examples to get familiarized with this system of naming alkenes. In order to recognize which substituent is higher or lower, you have to compare their atomic numbers. That means an atom with a higher atomic number takes precedence over an atom with a lower atomic number.

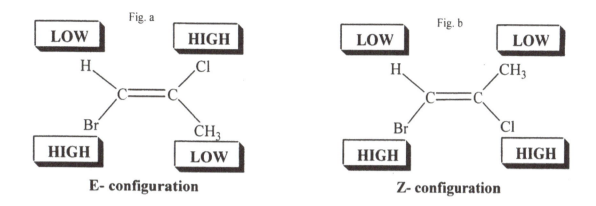

One key aspect to remember is that when we compare which substituent is higher or lower, we should compare the substitutions in the same carbon. In the above example, it is easy to see that on the left substitution, obviously bromine is higher (higher in the atomic number sense) than hydrogen. On the right side, chlorine is higher (atomic number:17) than carbon (atomic number: 6). So the compound shown in Fig. (a) has an **E configuration**, and the one shown in Fig.(b) has a **Z configuration**.

D. GENERAL PROPERTIES OF ALKENES

Just like alkanes, the melting and boiling points of alkenes increase with an increase in the number of carbons (increase in chain length). Carbon-carbon double bonds are shorter than carbon-carbon single bonds. Alkenes are insoluble in water, but are soluble in nonpolar solvents such as hexane, and ethers.

E. SYNTHESIS OF ALKENES

We can synthesize alkenes by processes such as dehydrogenation of alkanes, dehydrohalogenation of alkyl halides, and dehydration of alcohols.

From Alkanes

An alkene can be synthesized by the process of dehydrogenation (removal of hydrogen atoms), by heating an alkane up to about 700-750°C.

Sample reaction 28-1

$$CH_3\text{-}CH_3 \xrightarrow{750°} CH_2\text{=}CH_2 \quad + \quad H_2$$

Ethane   Ethylene   Hydrogen

From Alcohols

When alcohols undergo dehydration reactions, alkenes are generated. There is a chance of rearrangement of the carbocation intermediates to form more stable carbocation intermediates, whenever possible, resulting in the formation of more than one type of alkenes. The mechanisms of such rearrangements are discussed in Chapter 19.

Sample reaction 28-2

$$CH_3CH_2OH \xrightarrow[H_2SO_4, \text{ heat}]{} CH_2=CH_2 \quad + \quad H_2O$$

The only product in the above reaction is ethylene, since there is no rearrangement and more importantly, there is no need for rearrangement. This is because the intermediate formed in this reaction is a primary carbocation, and rearrangement cannot produce a more stable carbocation.

From Alkyl Halides by Dehydrohalogenation

Alkenes can be synthesized by reacting the corresponding alkyl halides with a suitable strong base that can abstract a proton from one of the carbon atoms, while the leaving group attached to the adjacent carbon leaves. The general mechanism is shown below.

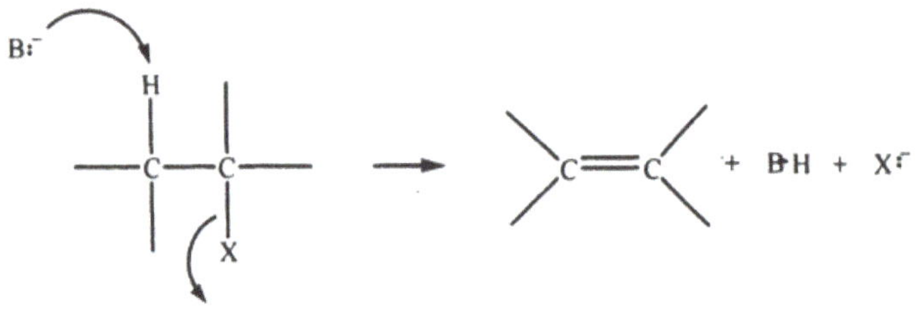

According to Zaitsev's rule, the major alkene product is the one that is the most highly substituted. Consider the following example involving 2-bromobutane with potassium hydroxide.

Sample reaction 28-3

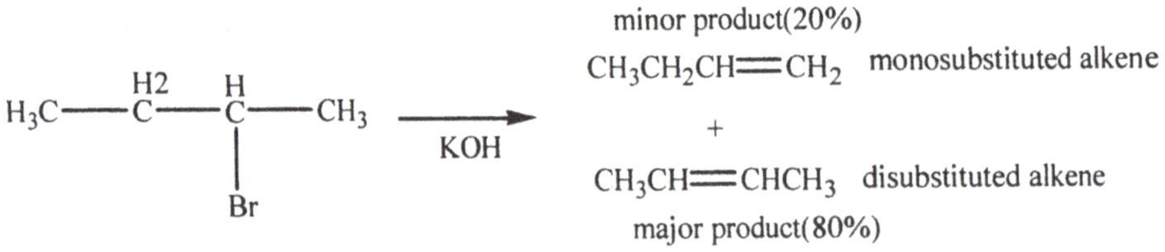

If bulky bases are used, the least substituted alkene may predominate as the product. In the next example, the base used is *tert*-butoxide ion. Since it is a bulky base it will preferentially abstract the less hindered hydrogen, leading to the formation of the least substituted alkene, also known as the Hofmann product.

Sample reaction 28-4

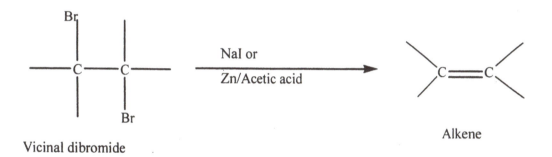

From Vicinal Dibromides by Dehalogenation

Vicinal dibromides have two bromines on adjacent carbon atoms. Vicinal dibromides can be converted to alkenes by reduction with zinc or iodide ion. A sample reaction is given below.

Sample reaction 28--5

Vicinal dibromide → NaI or Zn/Acetic acid → Alkene

F. REACTIONS OF ALKENES

Hydrogenation

In hydrogenation reactions, H_2 is added to the unsaturated (carbon-carbon double or triple bonds) bonds. The resulting product of hydrogenation of a pure alkene is an alkane.

$$CH_2{=}CHCH_2CH_2CH_2CH_3 + H_2 \longrightarrow CH_3CH_2CH_2CH_2CH_2CH_3$$

Usually, catalysts like platinum, palladium, or nickel are used for these types of hydrogenation reactions. Hydrogenation reactions are exothermic. Thus heat is generated as a result of hydrogenation and is called heat of hydrogenation.

The greater the substitution of the carbon-carbon double bond, the
smaller the heat of hydrogenation, and the higher the stability of the alkene.

Alkenes with Hydrogen Halides

Alkenes undergo electrophilic addition reactions with hydrogen halides, to form alkyl halides.

Sample reaction 28-6

$$CH_2=CH_2 \quad + \quad HX \longrightarrow CH_3\text{-}CH_2X$$

Ethylene   Hydrogen halide   Ethyl halide

In the process, the hydrogen halide attacks the double bond in the alkene, and the pi electrons in the double bond are transferred to the electrophile, resulting in a carbocation intermediate. This is followed by the formation of the alkyl halide.

$$CH_2=CH_2 \quad + \quad HX \longrightarrow CH_3\text{-}CH_2X$$

Ethylene   Hydrogen halide   Ethyl halide

(1)

Alkene   Hydrogen halide   Carbocation   Chloride ion

(2)

Carbocation   Chloride ion   Alkyl halide

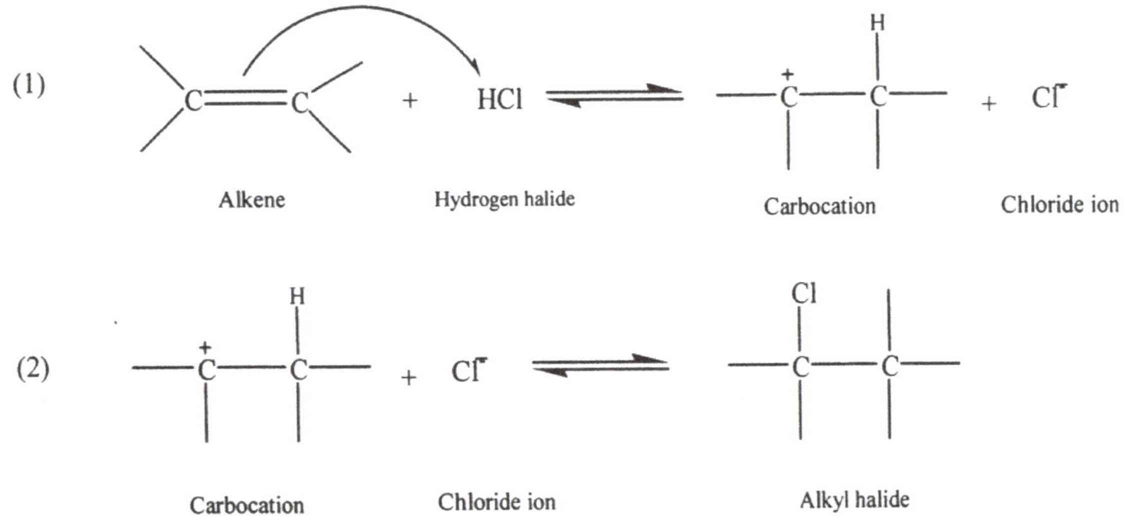

If the alkene used is not symmetrical, the possibility of different products from hydrogen halide addition is an issue. In such cases, the hydrogen from the hydrogen halide adds to the double-bonded carbon that already has the greater number of hydrogens. This is Markovnikov's rule. Based on this rule, we can predict the major product in such reactions. Consider the following reaction involving 2-methyl-2-butene with hydrogen bromide.

Markovnikov addition of hydrogen and bromine

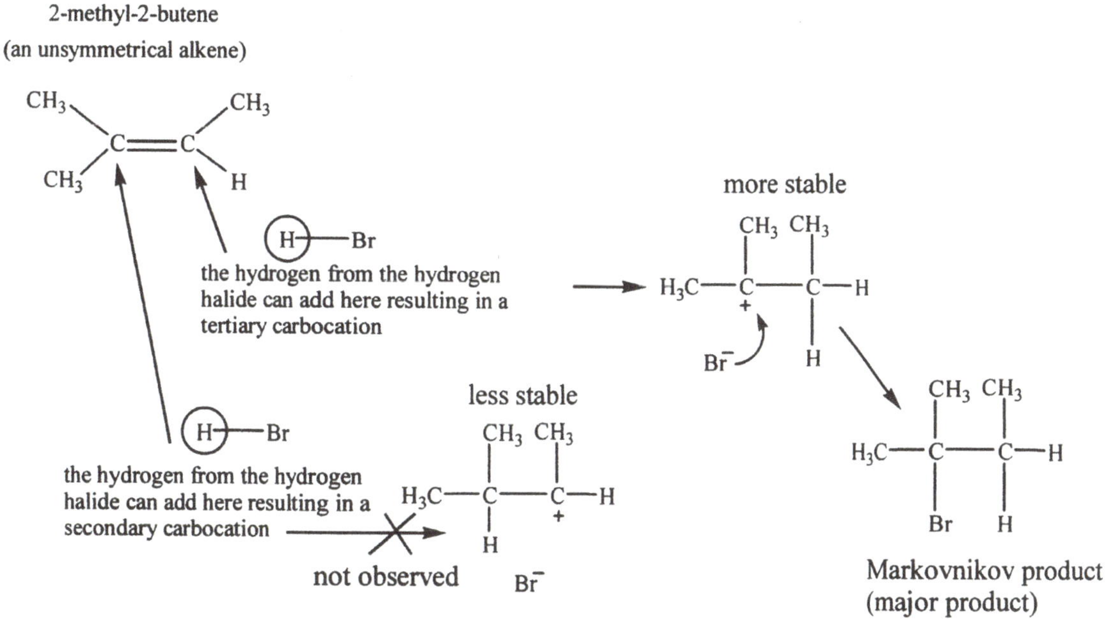
2-methyl-2-butene
(an unsymmetrical alkene)
H—Br
the hydrogen from the hydrogen halide can add here resulting in a tertiary carbocation
more stable
H—Br
the hydrogen from the hydrogen halide can add here resulting in a secondary carbocation
less stable
not observed
Markovnikov product (major product)

An example of a Markovnikov addition is shown below. Watch where the hydrogen and the bromine are added.

Sample reaction 28-7

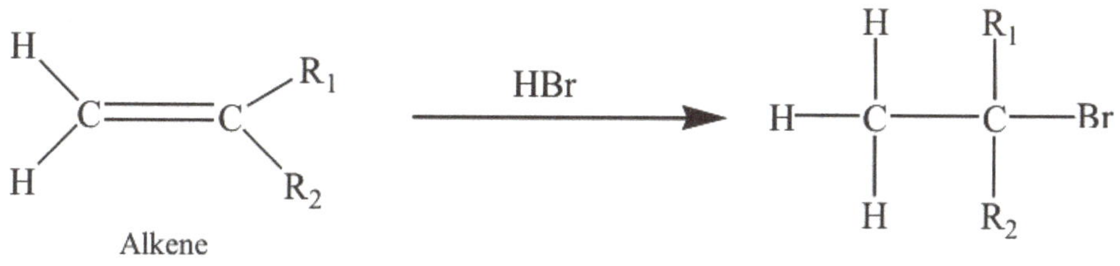
HBr
Alkene

Sample reaction 28-8

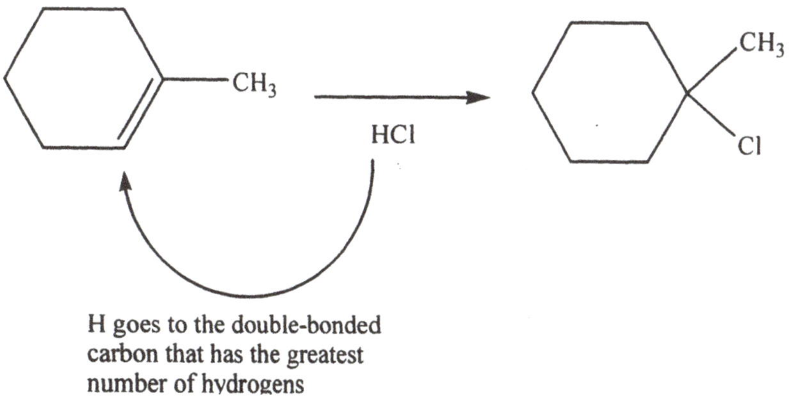
HCl
H goes to the double-bonded carbon that has the greatest number of hydrogens

NEXT STEP MCAT CONTENT REVIEW: CHEMISTRY AND ORGANIC CHEMISTRY

Anti-Markovnikov Addition

Hydrogen bromide in the presence of peroxides can add to an unsymmetrical alkene resulting in anti-Markovnikov products. The change in trend can be explained based on the mechanistic difference of HBr addition in the presence of peroxides. Peroxides can easily form free radicals, since the oxygen-oxygen bond in peroxides is weak. This type of addition is not seen with HCl or HI. The mechanism of HBr addition to an alkene in the presence of a peroxide is shown below.

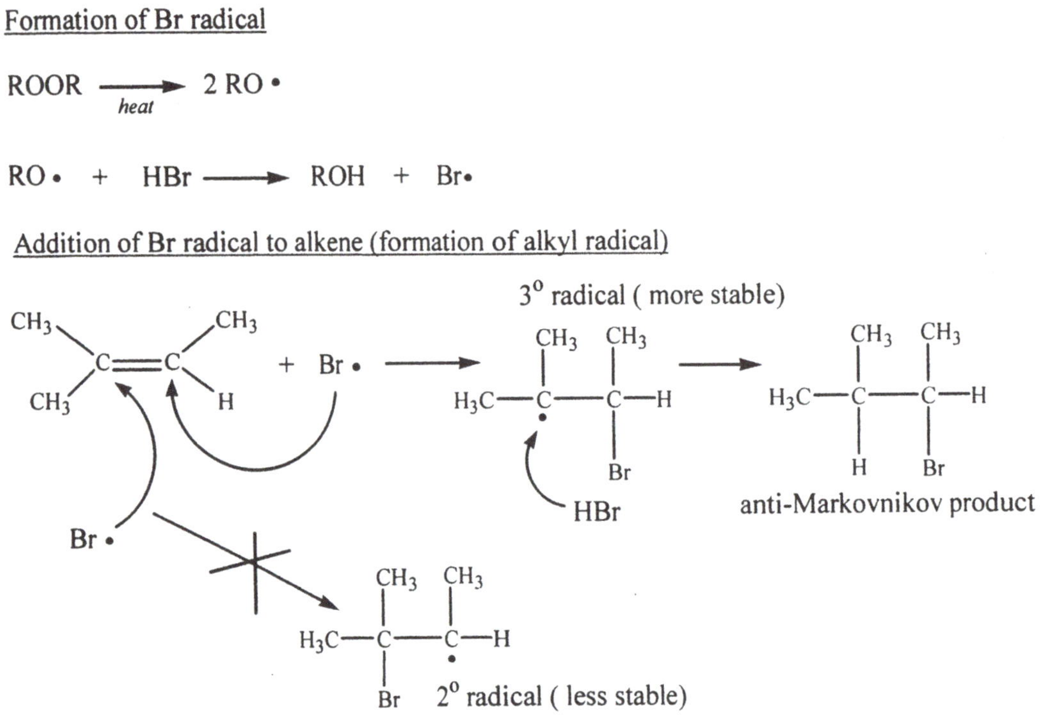

Formation of Br radical

$$ROOR \xrightarrow{heat} 2\,RO\cdot$$

$$RO\cdot \;+\; HBr \longrightarrow ROH \;+\; Br\cdot$$

Addition of Br radical to alkene (formation of alkyl radical)

Notice that when the bromine radical adds to the double-bonded carbon that contains the most number of hydrogens, the resulting alkyl radical is more stable (here, a tertiary radical is formed). Remember that free radical stability parallels carbocation stability. A tertiary radical is more stable than a secondary radical which is more stable than a primary radical.

Alkenes with Halogens

We will consider the reaction of ethylene with chlorine.

Sample reaction 28-9

The overall reaction:

$$CH_2{=}CH_2 \;+\; Cl_2 \longrightarrow ClCH_2CH_2Cl$$

The mechanism of the reaction:

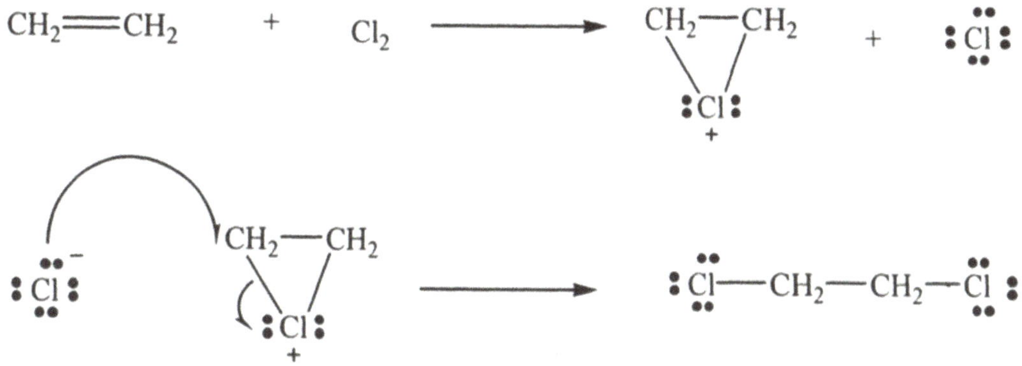

$$CH_2=CH_2 \quad + \quad Cl_2 \longrightarrow \quad \overset{CH_2-CH_2}{\underset{\overset{+}{\underset{\cdot\cdot}{Cl}}}{\diagdown\diagup}} \quad + \quad :\overset{\cdot\cdot}{\underset{\cdot\cdot}{Cl}}:$$

$$:\overset{\cdot\cdot}{\underset{\cdot\cdot}{Cl}}:^- \qquad \overset{CH_2-CH_2}{\underset{\overset{+}{\underset{\cdot\cdot}{Cl}}}{\diagdown\diagup}} \longrightarrow \quad :\overset{\cdot\cdot}{\underset{\cdot\cdot}{Cl}}-CH_2-CH_2-\overset{\cdot\cdot}{\underset{\cdot\cdot}{Cl}}:$$

This is an example of electrophilic addition of Cl_2 to an alkene. The mechanism of this reaction involves the following steps. In the first step, the ethylene reacts with chlorine to form the cyclic ethylene chloronium ion (intermediate) and chloride ion. Note that in this cyclic intermediate, the chlorine has a positive charge. This step is followed by the nucleophilic attack by a chloride ion on the chloronium ion. The reaction is enhanced by electron-donating substituents such as alkyl groups on the carbon-carbon double bond, since such groups can further stabilize the formation of the transition state which results in the formation of the chloronium ion.

Halogen addition is usually an *anti* addition process. See the next reaction that exemplifies this aspect.

Sample reaction 28-10

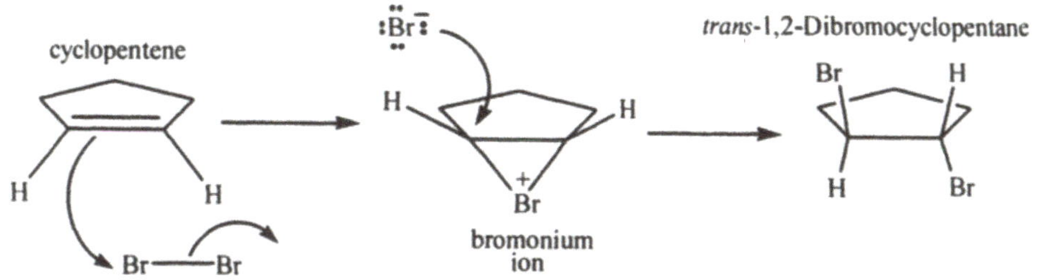

Alkenes with Halogens in Aqueous Medium

The organic product formed as a result of the reaction between an alkene and a halogen is called a halohydrin. An overall representative reaction is shown below:

Sample reaction 28-11

$$CH_2=CH_2 \quad + \quad Cl_2 \quad + \quad H_2O \longrightarrow HOCH_2CH_2CL \quad + \quad HCl$$

Ethylene   Chlorine   Halohydrin   Hydrogen chloride

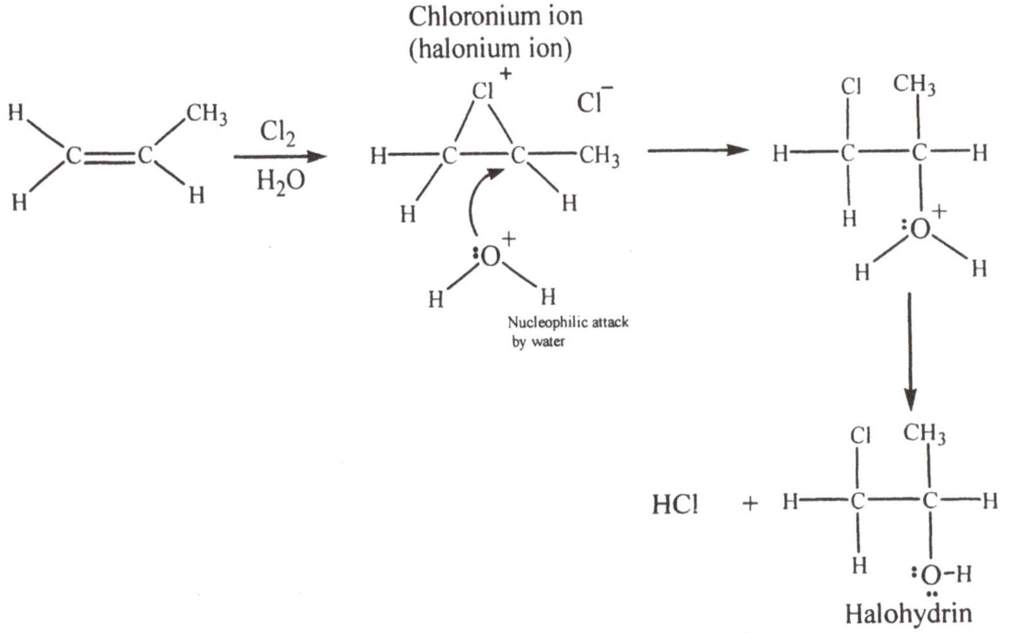
Chloronium ion
(halonium ion)
Nucleophilic attack by water
HCl
Halohydrin

Sample reaction 28-12

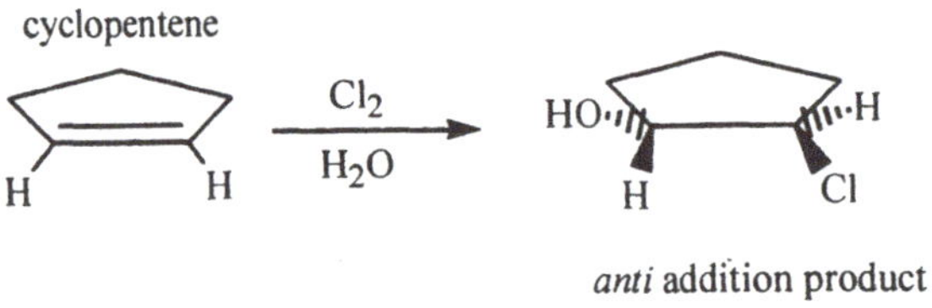
cyclopentene
anti addition product

Epoxidation

Sample reaction 28-13

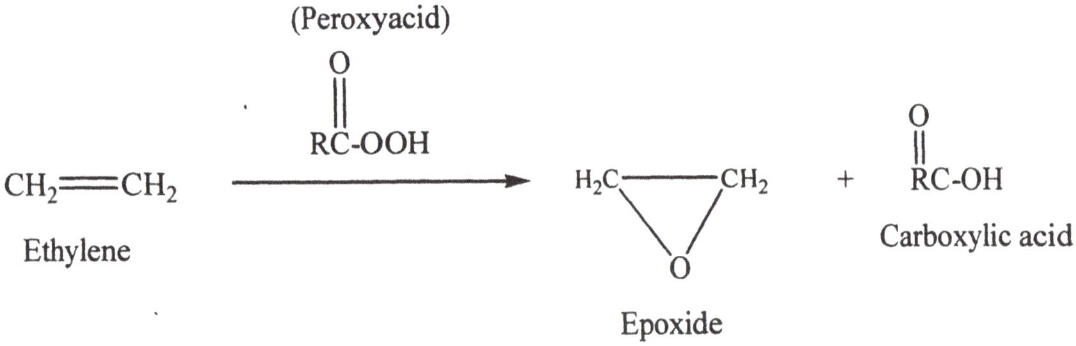
(Peroxyacid)
Ethylene
Epoxide
Carboxylic acid

Alkenes react with peroxy acids to form epoxides and carboxylic acids as products.

Ozonolysis

Alkenes react with O_3 (ozone) to form ozonides, which on hydrolysis with water form aldehydes or ketones or both, depending on the type of the reacting alkene. This is illustrated by the sample reactions.

Sample reaction 28-14

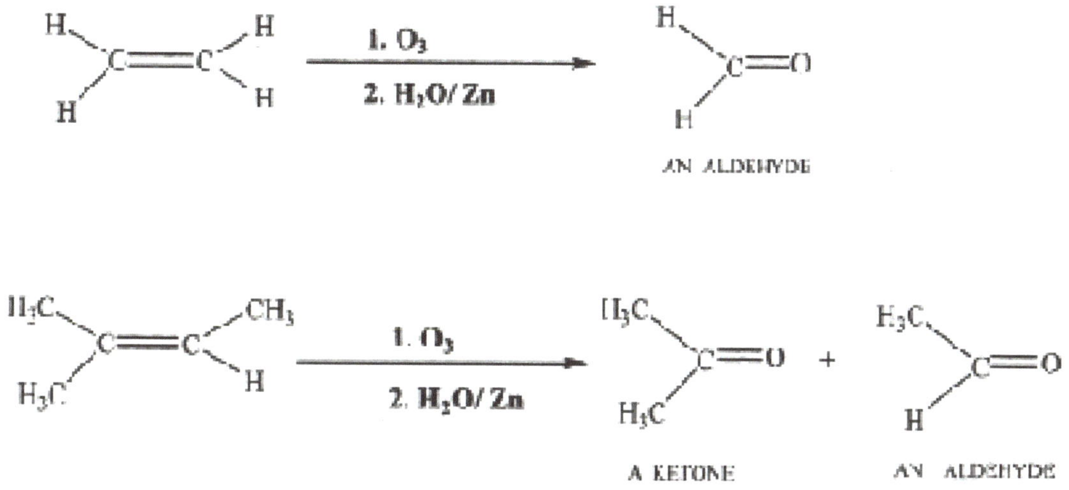

Hydroxylation using Osmium Tetroxide

Sample reaction 28-15

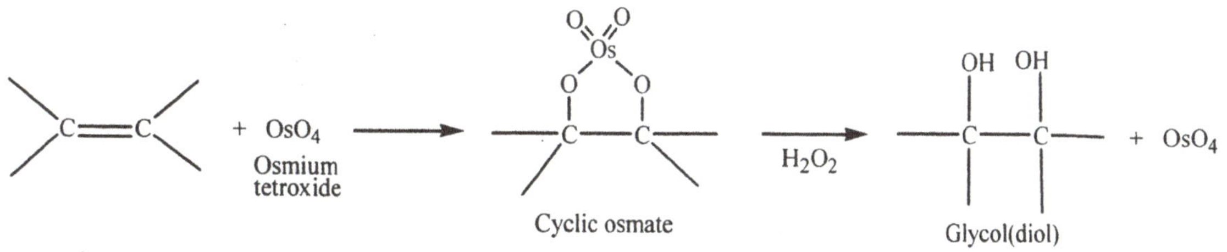

Osmium tetroxide can undergo reaction with alkenes to form a cyclic osmate, which in the presence of hydrogen peroxide results in a glycol (diol). Hydrogen peroxide oxidizes the osmium back to osmium tetroxide, while hydrolyzing the cyclic osmate to glycol. The predominant product is a *syn* addition product.

Acid Catalyzed Reaction

Sample reaction 28-16

$$H_3C-C(CH_3)=C(CH_3)(H) \xrightarrow{H_2SO_4/\ H_2O} HO-C(CH_3)(CH_3)-CH_2CH_3$$

(major product)

Alkenes react with aqueous acidic solutions to form alcohols. The reaction intermediate is a carbocation. There is a possibility of rearrangement of the intermediates. The reaction follows Markovnikov's rule.

Hydroboration-Oxidation

Sample reaction 28-17

$$CH_3CH_2CH_2CH{=}CH_2 \xrightarrow[\text{2. } H_2O_2,\ NaOH]{\text{1. } B_2H_6} CH_3CH_2CH_2CH_2CH_2OH$$

(major product)

Oxidation followed by hydroboration of alkenes results in alcohols. This reaction takes place in an anti-Markovnikov fashion. Notice that the hydrogen atom, instead of attaching to the carbon contained in the double bond with the highest number of hydrogen substituents, attaches to the carbon with the least number of hydrogen substituents.

Diborane (B_2H_6), a dimer of borane (BH_3), is usually used complexed together with tetrahydrofuran (THF) since diborane by itself is a toxic, and flammable gas. The reaction begins with borane adding to one of the double-bonded carbons resulting in an alkylborane. Because BH_3 is a strong electrophile it adds to the least highly substituted double-bonded carbon. This preference makes sense because in the transition state, the electron deprived boron pulls electrons from the pi cloud, resulting in a partial positive charge to the other carbon atom. This partial positive charge is better stabilized on the more highly substituted carbon. Hydrogen peroxide under basic conditions oxidizes the alkylborane to an alcohol. In effect, the addition in the hydroboration-oxidation is anti-Markovnikov.

Sample reaction 28-18

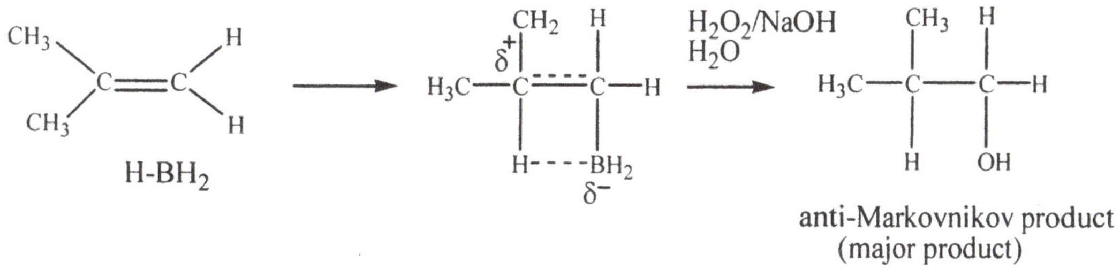

anti-Markovnikov product
(major product)

The addition of hydrogen and boron is simultaneous, and they must add to the same side of the double bond. Hence, this addition reaction involves *syn* addition or same-side addition. Study the next reaction.

Sample reaction 28-19

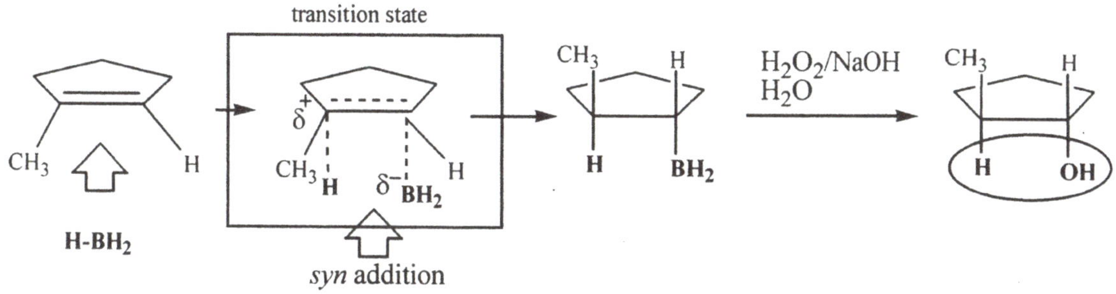

transition state

syn addition

Oxymercuration-Demercuration

Sample reaction 28-20

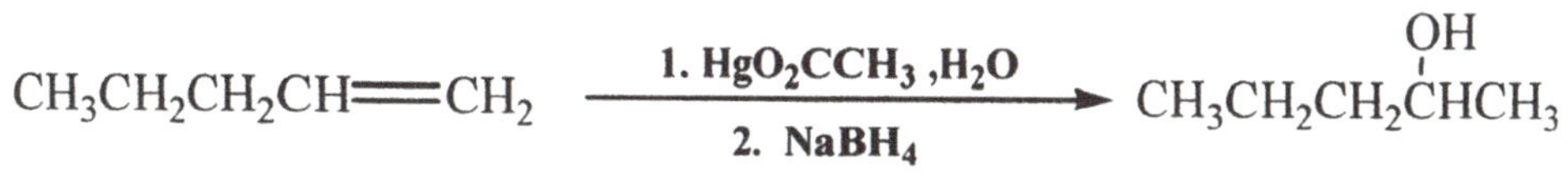

$$CH_3CH_2CH_2CH = CH_2 \xrightarrow[\text{2. NaBH}_4]{\text{1. HgO}_2\text{CCH}_3, \text{H}_2\text{O}} CH_3CH_2CH_2\overset{\overset{\displaystyle OH}{|}}{C}HCH_3$$

Alkenes can be converted into alcohols by oxymercuration-demercuration. The addition of H and OH is in accordance with the Markovnikov's rule. There is no rearrangement of the intermediates in this process.

In the oxymercuation process, the electrophilic addition of the mercuric species occurs resulting in a mercurinium ion which is a three-membered ring. This is followed by the nucleophilic attack of water and, as the proton leaves, an organomercuric alcohol (addition product) is formed. The next step, demercuration, occurs when sodium borohydride (NaBH$_4$) substitutes the mercuric acetate substituent with hydrogen. If an alkene is unsymmetric, oxymercuration-demercuration results in Markovnikov addition. The addition of mercuric species and is non stereospecific. Any stereochemistry set up in the formation of the organomercurial alcohols is scrambled by the reductive step. In the final hydrated product, syn addition is no more likely than anti addition. This reaction has good yield, since there is no possibility of rearrangement unlike acid-catalyzed hydration of alkenes.

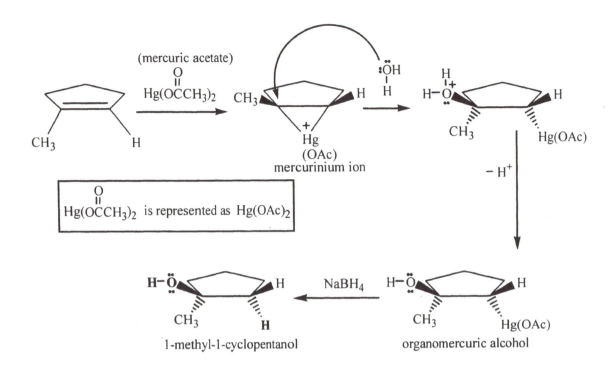

Sample reaction 28-21

The Diels-Alder Reaction

The Diels-Alder Reaction is an addition reaction involving an alkene and a diene. Let's look at the representative Diels-Alder reaction involving 1,3-butadiene and an alkene (dienophile means diene-lover). The reaction involves a cyclic transition state. The product is usually a cyclic addition product. Study the representative reaction given below. Pay close attention to how the new bonds are formed in relation to the reactants.

1,3-Butadiene   Alkene (dienophile)   The cyclic transition state   Cycloaddition product

Notice that the substituents in the alkene remain the same way in the product. In other words, *cis* substituents remain *cis* in the cycloaddition product. Hence, the Diels-Alder reaction is stereospecific.

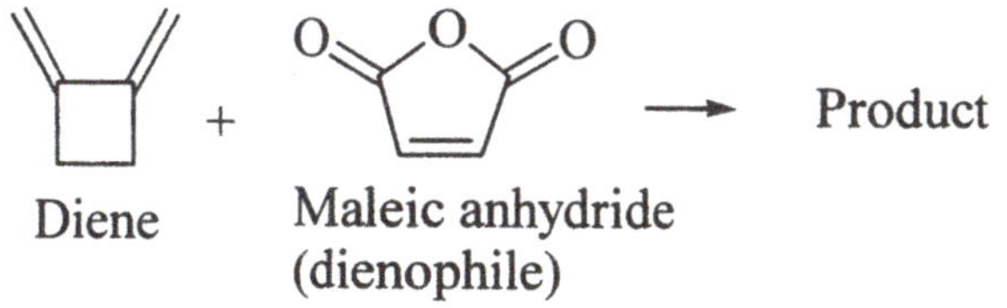

Diene   +   Maleic anhydride
                (dienophile) $\longrightarrow$ Product

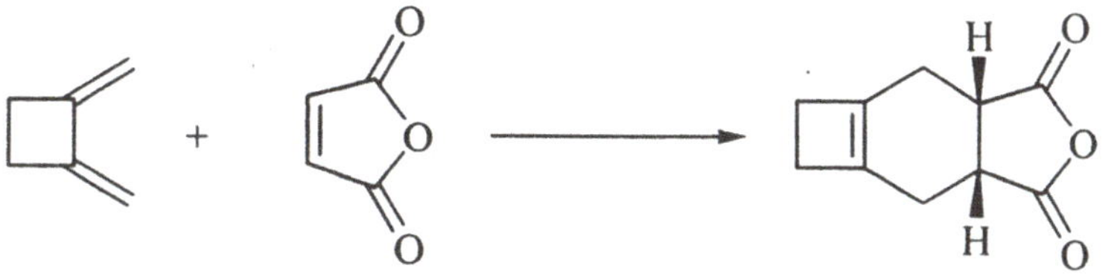

Diels-Alder product

Sample reaction 28-22

CHAPTER 28 PRACTICE QUESTIONS

1. All the following are possible products of the acid-catalyzed dehydration reaction of the compound shown below, except:

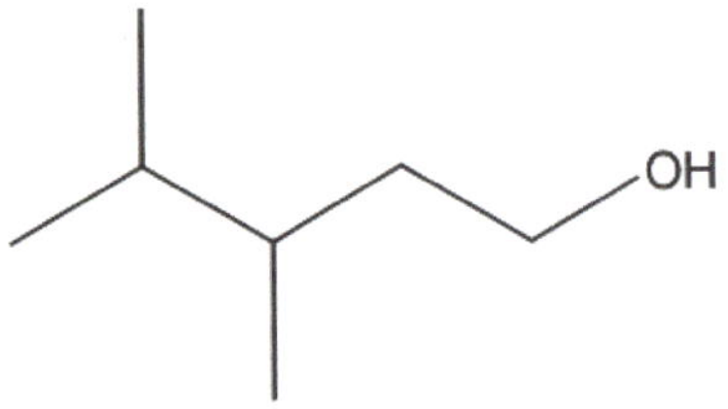

A.

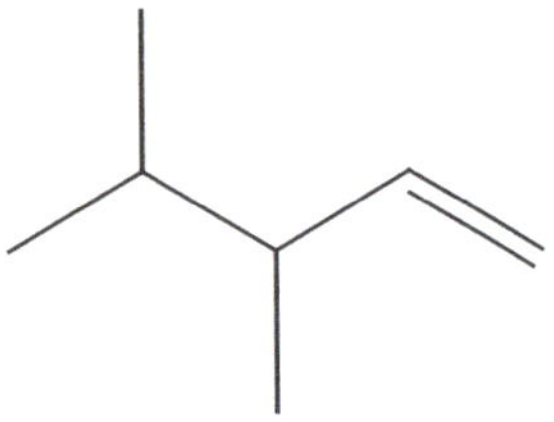

B.

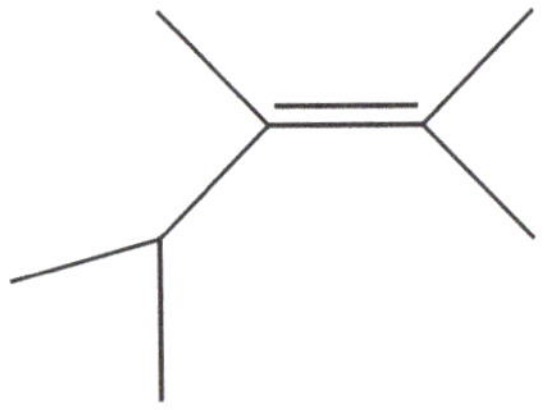

C.

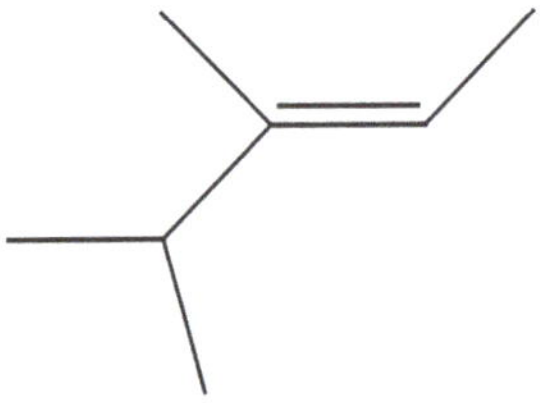

D.

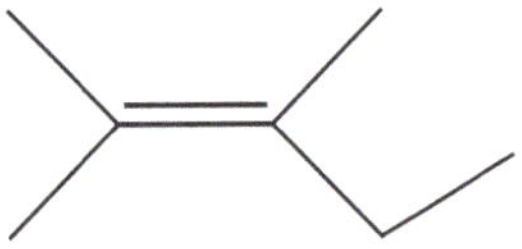

2. A student researcher calculated the number of moles of hydrogen used per mole for the hydrogenation of an unsaturated (only double bonds) aliphatic non-cyclic hydrocarbon compound. If the number of moles of hydrogen used for the complete hydrogenation of each mole of the hydrocarbon is eight, how many double bonds were there in the compound that was hydrogenated?

    A. two
    B. four
    C. eight
    D. sixteen

3. Choose the product of the following reaction.

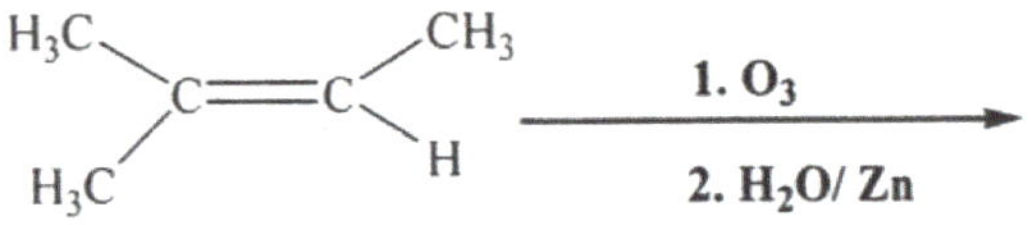

A. $CH_3CH_2CH_2CH_2CH_3$

B.

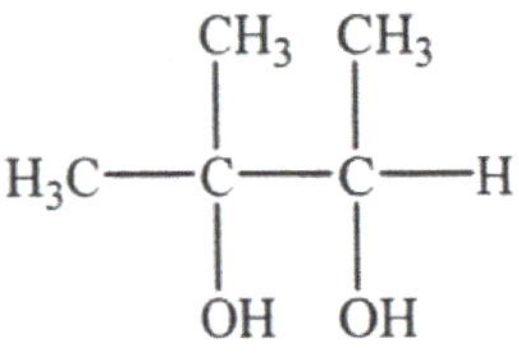

C.

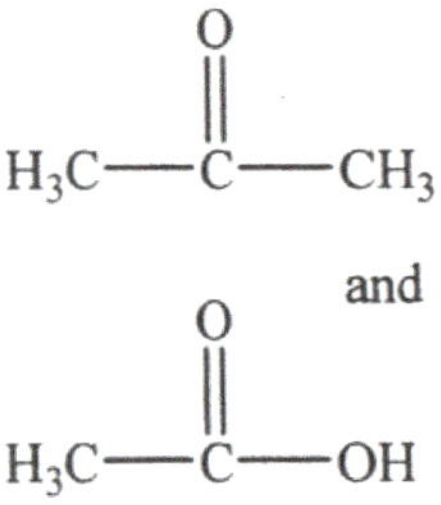

D.

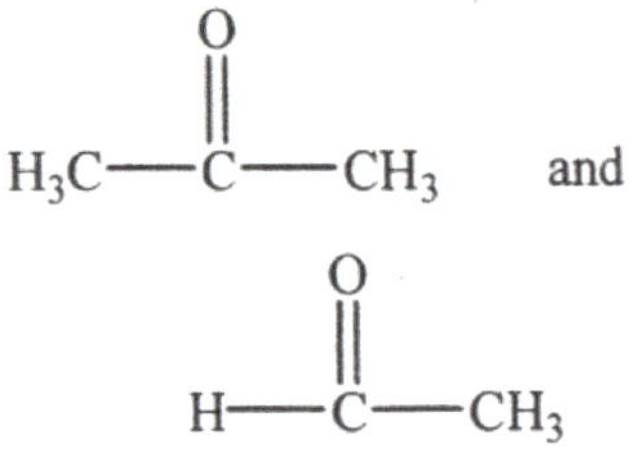

4. Which of the following is the most likely product of the reaction indicated below?

$$CH_3CH_2CH{=}CH_2 \xrightarrow{\;\;\;\;\;\;\;\;\;}$$
$$\underset{\overset{\|}{O}}{CH_3COOH}$$

A. $\underset{\underset{CH_3CHCHCH_3}{|\quad|}}{OHOH}$

B. $H_3CH_2CHC\overset{\displaystyle \diagup\diagdown}{\underset{O}{\quad}}CH_2$

C. $\underset{H_3C}{\overset{H_3C}{>}}C{=}O$

D. none of the above

5. Which of the following is the major product of the hydroboration-oxidation of 1-butene?

A. $CH_3CH_2CH_2CHO$

B. $CH_3CH_2CH_2OHCH_3$

C. $CH_3CH_2CH_2CH_2OH$

D. $CH_3CH_2CH\overset{\displaystyle \diagup\diagdown}{\underset{O}{\quad}}CH_2$

6. Which of the following compounds has the highest heat of hydrogenation?

    A. ethylene
    B. propene
    C. 1-butene
    D. 1-hexene

7. The major product that results in a reaction involving 1-propene with hydrogen bromide, in the presence of peroxides is:

    A. 1-bromopropane.
    B. 1,2-dibromopropane.
    C. 2-bromopropane.
    D. 1,3-dibromopropane.

8. Which of the following is true regarding a reaction of cis-2-pentene with $KMnO_4$?

    A. A *trans* diol will be formed.
    B. A *cis* diol will be formed.
    C. The reagent is not strong enough to oxidize *cis*-2-pentene.
    D. The double bond will be broken, and is followed by a ring closure or ring formation.

9. In the acid catalyzed dehydration reaction of an alcohol, which of the following aspects listed can definitely be true?

    A. There can be no rearrangement of the intermediate, regardless of the alcohol involved.
    B. There can be rearrangement involved, resulting in less stable intermediates from more stable intermediates.
    C. If possible, the major product is the most substituted product because of its higher stability.
    D. None of the above.

10. In the acid-catalyzed dehydration of alcohols to alkenes, which of the following are true?
   I. A carbanion intermediate is involved.
   II. A carbocation intermediate is involved.
   III. There is no intermediate involved.
   IV. Methyl shifts can occur in the interme-diates.
   V. Hydride shift can occur in the intermediates.

    A. I, IV and V only
    B. II, IV and V only
    C. III only
    D. II and V only

Questions 11-15 are based on the following passage.

Passage 1

The following synthesis reactions involving alkenes were done in a lab.

Reaction 1

$$H_2C{=}CH_2 \xrightarrow{H_2SO_4} CH_3CH_2OSO_3H$$

Reaction 2

$$(H_3C)_2C{=}CH_2$$
$$\downarrow KMnO_4 / H^+$$
(isolated)
$$[CH_3C{=}O] + CH_2O$$
$$\downarrow KMnO_4 / H^+$$
Product A

Reaction 3

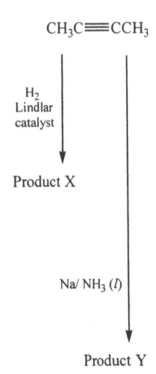

Reaction 4

$$CH_3C{\equiv}CCH_3$$

$$\downarrow \begin{array}{c} H_2 \\ \text{Lindlar} \\ \text{catalyst} \end{array}$$

Product X

$$\downarrow Na/ NH_3\ (l)$$

Product Y

11. Which of the following can be the oxidation product of an alkene?

    A. CH_3CH_2CHO
    B. $HOCH_2CH_2OH$
    C. $CH_3CH_2CH_2COOH$
    D.   All the above

12. Ethylene oxide in the presence of H_2O can be converted to ethylene glycol by oxidation. In the process, the ring in ethylene oxide is attacked by water. Which of the following best describes the role of water?

    A.   Electrophile
    B.   Nucleophile
    C.   Merely a solvent
    D.   No active part in the reaction other than being a spectator molecule

13. In Reaction 2, what is the identity of Product A?

    A.   Acetic acid
    B.   Carbon dioxide
    C.   Methane
    D.   None of the above

14. Products X and Y in Reaction 4 are best described as:

    A.   mirror images.
    B.   tautomers.
    C.   anomers.
    D.   geometrical isomers.

15. What is the correct name of the compound shown below?

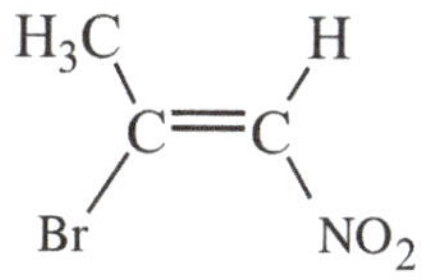

    A.   (E)-2-bromo-1-nitropropene
    B.   (Z)-2-bromo-1-nitropropene
    C.   (E)-2-bromo-1-nitrobutene
    D.   (Z)-2-bromo-1-nitrobutene

A. INTRODUCTION

Alkynes are hydrocarbons that contain carbon-carbon triple bonds. The general formula of alkynes is C_nH_{2n-2}.

$$HC\equiv CH \qquad \text{Acetylene}$$

In acetylene, the carbon is *sp* **hybridized**. The triple bond is composed of one sigma bond, and two pi bonds. The bond angle is $180°$. We should also realize that the sigma bonds are formed by *sp* hybrid orbitals, and the pi bonds are formed by the *p* orbitals.

If the triple bond in an alkyne is at the end of a carbon chain, it is called a terminal alkyne. If the triple bond is not at the end of a carbon chain, it is called an internal alkyne.

$$HC\equiv CCH_2CH_2CH_3 \qquad\qquad H_3CH_2CH_2CC\equiv CCH_2CH_3$$

A terminal alkyne   **An internal alkyne**

B. NAMING OF ALKYNES

The naming of alkynes is similar to that of alkenes.

sp hybridized

$$HC\equiv CH \qquad\qquad HC\equiv CCH_3 \qquad\qquad HC\equiv CCHCH_2CH_2CH_3$$

Ethyne (Acetylene)   **Propyne**   **3-methyl-1-hexyne**

(with CH_3 branch on the third carbon)

C. SYNTHESIS OF ALKYNES

Acetylene Synthesis by Adding H_2O to CaC_2 (calcium carbide)

Sample reaction 29-1

$$CaO \xrightarrow[\text{heat}]{C \text{ (Carbon)}} CaC_2 \xrightarrow{H_2O} HC \equiv CH \;+\; Ca(OH)_2$$

Calcium Oxide   Calcium carbide   Acetylene   Calcium Hydroxide

From Dihalogenoalkanes

Sample reaction 29-2

A representative reaction is given below:

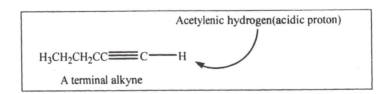

A dibromoalkane   KOH, C_2H_2OH Alkyne

From Acetylene

Higher alkynes can be synthesized from acetylene by reacting with $NaNH_2$ followed by treatment with the appropriate alkyl halide. Terminal alkynes can be deprotonated using strong bases such as sodium amide. Hydroxides or alkoxides are not strong enough to deprotonate an acetylenic hydrogen.

Acetylenic hydrogen(acidic proton)

$H_3CH_2CH_2CC \equiv C \text{---} H$

A terminal alkyne

Sample reaction 29-3

$$HC \equiv CH \quad + \quad NaNH_2 \quad \longrightarrow \quad HC \equiv C:^- Na^+ \quad + \quad NH_3$$

Acetylene   Sodium amide   Sodium acetylide   Ammonia

$$HC \equiv C:^- Na^+ \quad \xrightarrow{\overset{\delta^+ \quad \delta^-}{CH_3CH_2CH_2Br}} \quad HC \equiv CCH_2CH_2CH_3$$

1-Pentyne

D. REACTIONS OF ALKYNES

Hydrogenation

In the presence of catalysts such as palladium, platinum, or nickel, alkynes can be hydrogenated to the corresponding alkanes.

Sample reaction 29-4

$$HC \equiv CCH_2CH_2CH_3 \quad \xrightarrow{H_2 \ / \ Pt} \quad CH_3CH_2CH_2CH_2CH_3$$

1-Pentyne   Pentane

Alkynes can be hydrogenated to alkenes by using specific catalysts such as Lindlar palladium. This reaction is stereo-selective resulting in syn addition.

Sample reaction 29-5

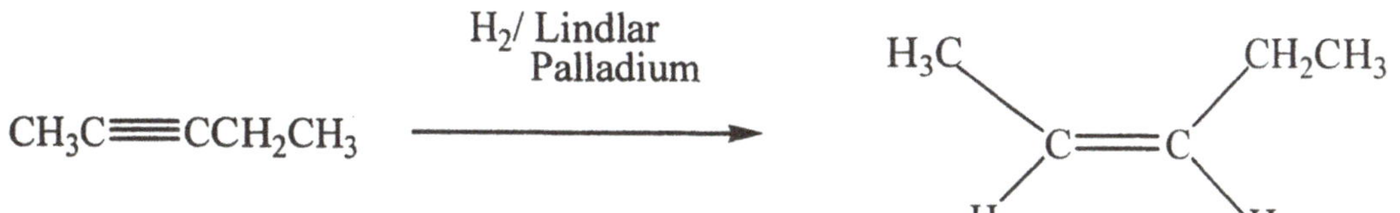

$$CH_3C \equiv CCH_2CH_3 \quad \xrightarrow{\underset{Palladium}{H_2/ \ Lindlar}} \quad$$

cis-2-pentene

2-Pentyne

An alkyne can be hydrogenated to a *trans*-alkene by hydrogenating the alkyne with sodium in liquid ammonia.

Sample reaction 29-6

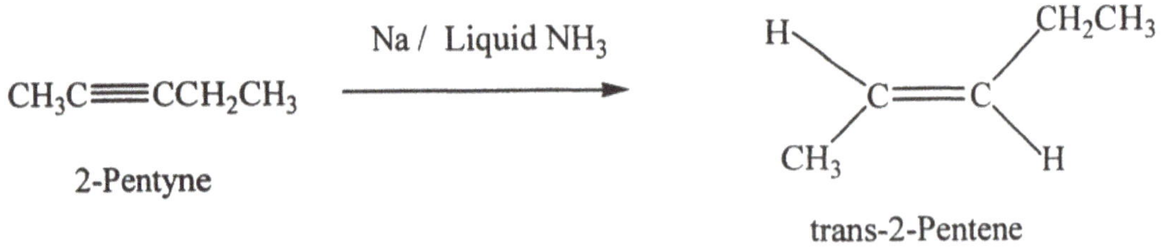

$$CH_3C\equiv CCH_2CH_3 \xrightarrow{\text{Na / Liquid } NH_3}$$

2-Pentyne

trans-2-Pentene

Acid-Catalyzed Hydration

Alkynes can undergo acid-catalyzed hydration reactions. The product is an **enol**, which is an unstable intermediate, and is immediately converted to a **ketone**. The formation of enol is based on Markovnikov addition (hydration).

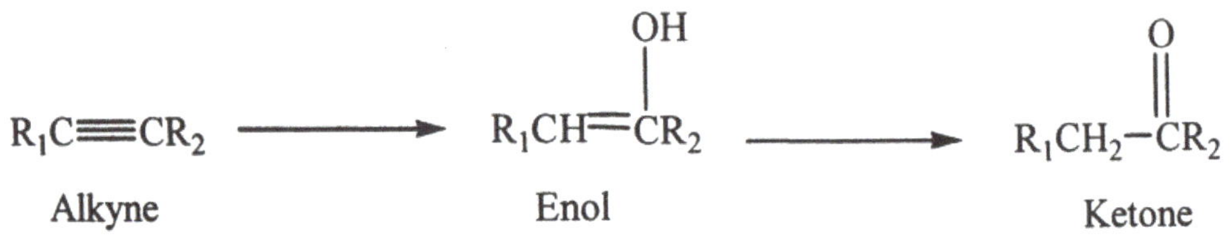

$$R_1C\equiv CR_2 \longrightarrow R_1CH=CR_2 \longrightarrow R_1CH_2-CR_2$$

Alkyne   Enol   Ketone

Sample reaction 29-7

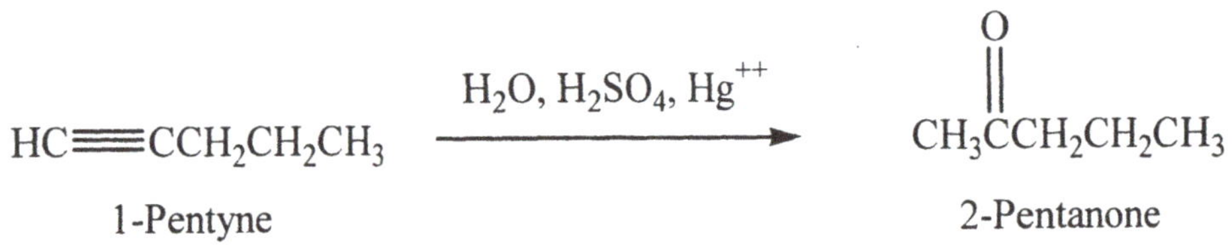

$$HC\equiv CCH_2CH_2CH_3 \xrightarrow{H_2O,\ H_2SO_4,\ Hg^{++}} CH_3CCH_2CH_2CH_3$$

1-Pentyne   2-Pentanone

Alkynes with Hydrogen Halides

Alkynes can undergo reactions with hydrogen halides. The reaction follows Markovnikov's addition of hydrogen and halogen to the triple bond. When two moles of hydrogen halide gets added to an alkyne, the reaction follows the same Markovnikov's pattern resulting in a geminal dihalide (two halogen atoms attached to the same carbon atom). Study the reactions given below.

Sample reaction 29-8

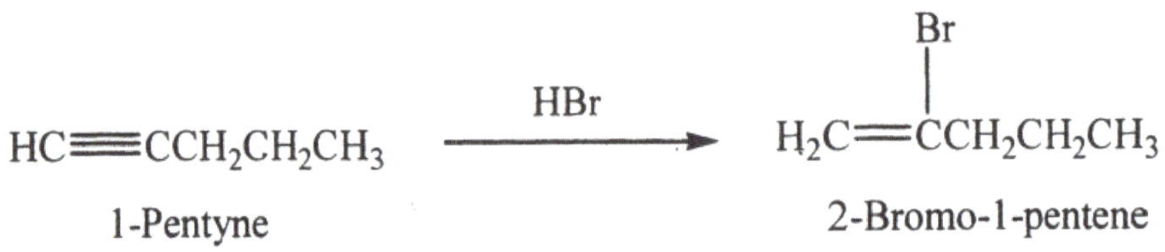

$$HC\equiv CCH_2CH_2CH_3 \xrightarrow{HBr} H_2C=CCH_2CH_2CH_3$$

1-Pentyne   2-Bromo-1-pentene

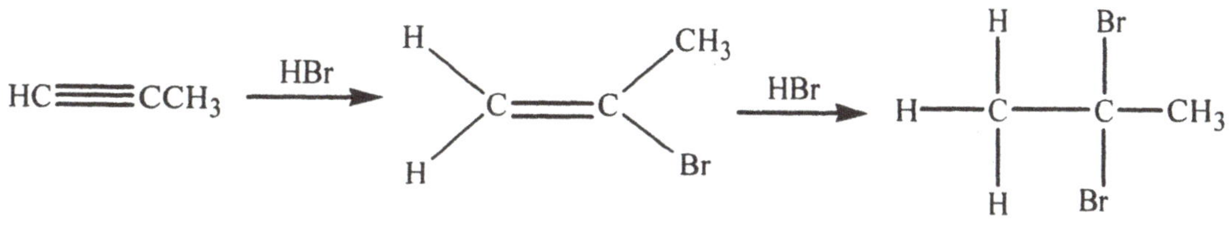

$$HC\equiv CCH_3 \xrightarrow{\text{HBr}} \quad \begin{array}{c} H \\ \end{array} C = C \begin{array}{c} CH_3 \\ Br \end{array} \xrightarrow{\text{HBr}} \quad H - C - C - CH_3$$

2,2-dibromopropane
(A geminal dihalide)

Alkynes with Halogens

Alkynes can undergo reactions with halogens forming di- and tetra-halogenated products.

Sample reaction 29-9

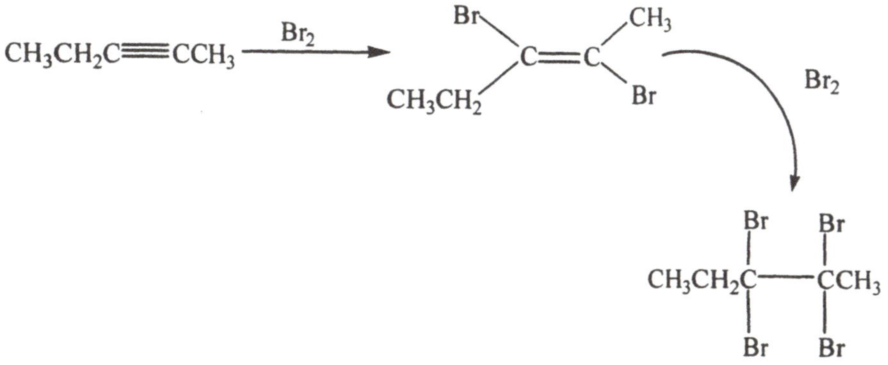

$$CH_3CH_2C\equiv CCH_3 \xrightarrow{\text{Br}_2} \quad \begin{array}{c} Br \\ CH_3CH_2 \end{array} C = C \begin{array}{c} CH_3 \\ Br \end{array} \xrightarrow{\text{Br}_2}$$

$$CH_3CH_2C - CCH_3$$

Ozonolysis

Alkynes can undergo ozonolysis. The products formed are carboxylic acids.

Sample reaction 29-10

$$H_3CC\equiv CCH_2CH_2CH_3 \xrightarrow{\text{1. O}_3 \quad \text{2. H}_3O^+} CH_3CH_2CH_2COOH + CH_3COOH$$

2-Hexyne

In this reaction, the products formed are butanoic acid and acetic acid. If a terminal alkyne is used, the products are carbon dioxide and a carboxylic acid. See the example given below.

$$CH_3C\equiv CH \xrightarrow{\text{O}_3 / \text{H}_3O^+} CH_3COOH + CO_2$$

Reaction Involving the Acidic Hydrogen in an Alkyne

The acidic hydrogen present in terminal alkynes can undergo reactions with Grignard reagents. A sample reaction is shown.

Sample reaction 29-11

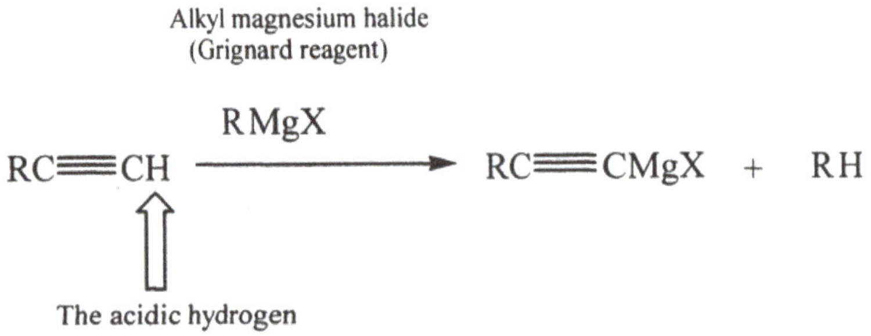

Alkyl magnesium halide
(Grignard reagent)

$$RC \equiv CH \xrightarrow{RMgX} RC \equiv CMgX \ + \ RH$$

The acidic hydrogen

Acetylide with Aldehydes and Ketones

Acetylides are strong bases and are good nucleophiles. So they can add to the carbonyl groups in aldehydes and ketones. The alkoxide ion that is formed during the reaction can be protonated to an alcohol by treating it with aqueous dilute acid.

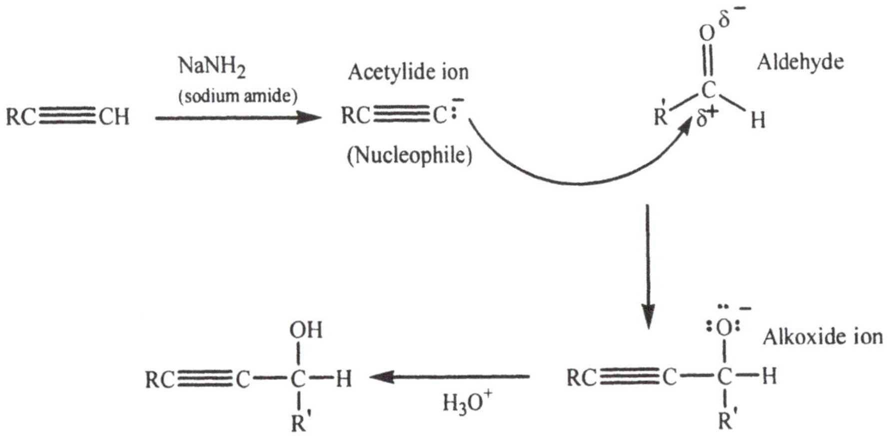

CHAPTER 29 PRACTICE QUESTIONS

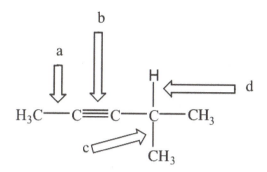

1. In the compound shown, which of the indicated bonds (arrows) have the shortest carbon-carbon bond?

    A. a
    B. b
    C. c
    D. d

2. If bottle A contains *cis*-2-butene, bottle B contains 1-propyne, and bottle C contains butane, identify the bottle that contains the compound with carbon-carbon bonds of the highest bond energy.

    A. Bottle A
    B. Bottle B
    C. Bottle C
    D. They all have equal bond dissociation energies.

3. Which of following compounds has the lowest pK_a value?

    A. Ethane
    B. Ethene
    C. Acetylene
    D. None of the above listed compounds are strong acids, and hence they do not have pKa values

$$CH_3CH_2C \equiv CCH_3$$

4. The compound shown above is treated with hydrogen in the presence of Lindlar catalyst. The major product is:

    A. pentanol.
    B. *cis*-2-pentene.
    C. pentane.
    D. *trans*-2-pentene.

5. 1-Butyne is treated with aqueous sulfuric acid in the presence of mercuric oxide as the catalyst. The major product is:

    A. 1-Butanone.
    B. 2-Butene.
    C. 2-Butanone.
    D. 1-Butanol.

6. Which of the following choices represents the product of ozonolysis of 3-hexyne?

    A. Propanone
    B. Propanal
    C. Hexanoic acid
    D. Propanoic acid

7. Double dehydrohalogenation of an alkyl vicinal dihalide can directly result in:

    A. a carboxylic acid.
    B. an alkyne.
    C. an alcohol.
    D. an ester.

8. The process by which an alkyne can be directly converted into an alkane is called:

    A. dehydrohalogenation.
    B. dehydration.
    C. hydrolysis.
    D. hydrogenation.

9. If liquid ammonia in the presence of sodium is added to an alkyne, the major product is:

    A. a *trans*-alkene.
    B. a *cis*-alkene.
    C. an aldehyde.
    D. a carboxylic acid.

10. Which of the following is true regarding alkynes?

    A.   Alkynes have generally higher boiling points than corresponding alkanes.

    B.   Alkynes have *sp* hybridized carbons.

    C.   Acetylene (an alkyne) can form salts called acetylides when exposed to strong bases.

    D.   All the above are true.

Questions 11-16 are based on the following passage.

Passage 1

Alkynes are hydrocarbons with carbon-carbon triple bonds in them. The simplest alkyne can be prepared by the process shown in Reaction 1.

Reaction 1

$$CaC_2 + 2\,H_2O \longrightarrow HC \equiv CH + Ca(OH)_2$$

Reaction 2

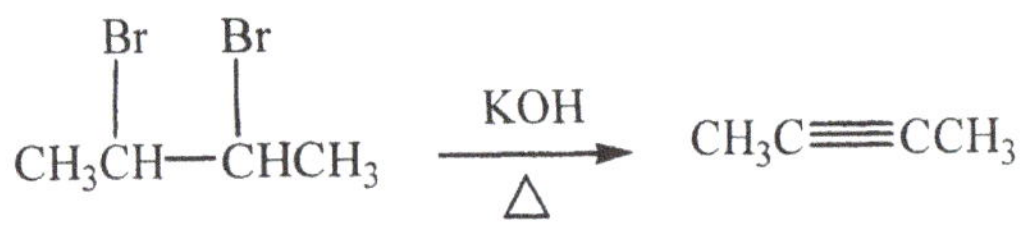

Also consider the following reactions.

Reaction 3

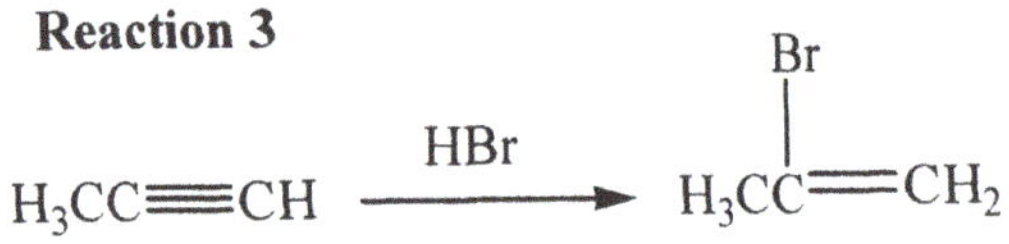

Reaction 4

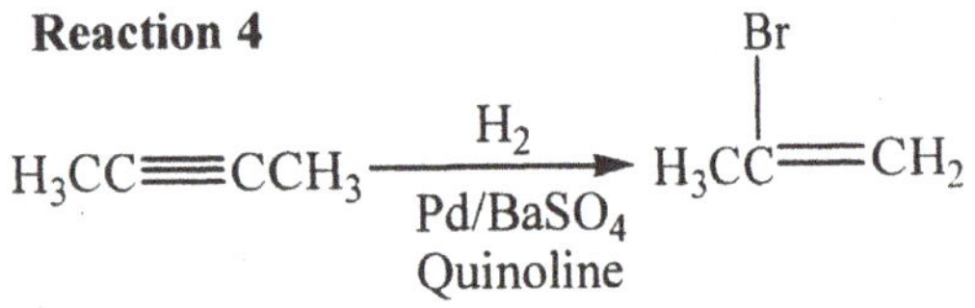

Quinoline is a heterocyclic amine.

11. The hybrid orbital that characterizes and differentiates alkynes from other simple hydrocarbons like alkanes and alkenes, is that alkynes have hybrid orbitals which have:

    A.   75% *p* character and 25% *s* character.

    B.   66% *p* character and 33% *s* character.

    C.   50% *p* character and 50% *s* character.

    D.   none of the above.

12. Reaction 3 is best described as:

    A.   a substitution reaction.

    B.   an addition reaction.

    C.   an elimination reaction.

    D.   a dehydrogenation reaction.

13. Which of the following sequences best describes a way to synthesize 1-hexyne from acetylene?

    A. **1.** NaNH$_2$/liq. ammonia
          2. *n*-propyl bromide

    B. **1.** NaNH$_2$/liq. ammonia
          2. *tert*-butyl bromide

    C. **1.** *n*-Propyl bromide
          2. NaNH$_2$/liq. ammonia

    D. **1.** NaNH$_2$/liq. ammonia
          2. *n*-butyl bromide

14. Lindlar catalyst is often used for the reduction of alkynes to alkenes. The catalyst consists of palladium which is deposited in a finely divided state of barium sulfate, which is subsequently treated with a heterocyclic amine called quinoline. Which of the following is the most likely function of quinoline?

    A.   To speed up the reaction so that the alkyne is completely converted to its most reduced form of hydrocarbon

    B.   To slow down the reaction, because the function of a catalyst is to slow down the reaction

    C.   To moderate the catalytic activity to facilitate a restrictive reduction

    D.   It acts as an oxidizing agent so that the alkyne is reduced.

15. Which of the following is the most likely structure of quinoline?

A.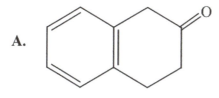

B.

C.

D.

16. Predict the major product of the reaction shown below.

$$H_3CH_2CC\equiv CCH_3 \xrightarrow[\text{Liquid NH}_3]{K}$$

A. $H_3CH_2CC\equiv CCH_2K$

B.

C.

D.

CHAPTER 30
Aromatic Compounds

A. INTRODUCTION

Aromatic compounds are compounds which have benzene rings in them. Aromatic hydrocarbons are also called arenes. Some compounds have structures which look like fused benzene rings. Such compounds are called **polycyclic aromatic compounds**.

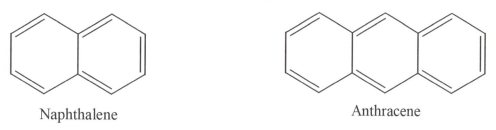

Benzene   Toluene

Polycyclic aromatic hydrocarbons

Naphthalene   Anthracene

B. BENZENE AND DERIVATIVES

Structure of Benzene

The formula of benzene is C_6H_6. The ring structure has alternate double and single bonds as shown in the diagrams below. According to the latest theories, benzene is in resonance between the two structural entities as shown below.

Benzene has a structure that is a hybridized form of these two structures.

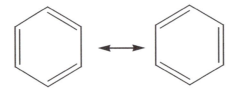

The hybridized structure is usually represented as shown below:

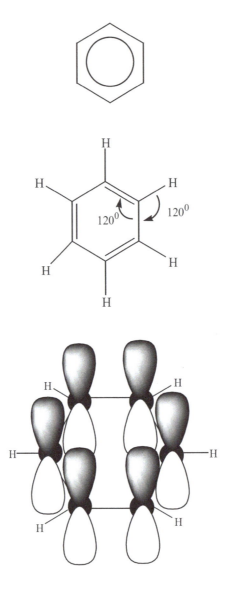

Figure 30-1

The six carbons in the benzene ring have a planar arrangement of a regular hexagon. The carbons are located at the vertices of the hexagon. The carbon-carbon bonds have the same length, and each bond angle is 120°. The hybridization is sp^2. The sigma bonds are formed by the sp^2 hybridized orbitals. However, the unhybridized $2p$ orbitals in each carbon overlap to form a cyclic pi system around the ring. The delocalization of these electrons creates the pi system in aromatic compounds. The electron cloud of the pi system occupies the regions above and below the ring as depicted in Figure 30-1.

Benzene Derivatives

Many derivatives of benzene are substituted derivative compounds. Some examples of such compounds are shown below:

SOME MONOSUBSTITUTED AROMATIC COMPOUNDS

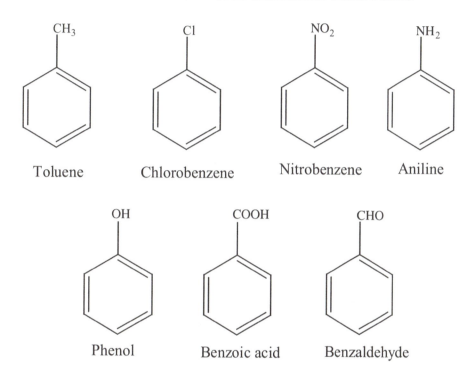

Toluene   Chlorobenzene   Nitrobenzene   Aniline

Phenol   Benzoic acid   Benzaldehyde

With respect to the substituent (the methyl group)
arrow (1) indicates the ortho position,
arrow (2) indicates the meta position,
arrow (3) indicates the para position.

o-Xylene   *m*-Xylene   *p*-Xylene

(Xylene is the general name of a dimethyl-substituted benzene)

C. PROPERTIES OF AROMATIC COMPOUNDS

Aromatic hydrocarbons are nonpolar, and are insoluble in water. They commonly undergo reactions like aromatic electrophilic substitution reactions and reduction reactions.

Aromaticity

Aromaticity of compounds is based on certain rules. According to Huckel's rule, the number of pi electrons present should be a number denoted by the formula 4n + 2, where n is 0, 1, 2, 3, ... Hence, for compounds to be considered aromatic the number of pi electrons should be 2, 6, 10, ... In addition, the structure should also have a cyclic pi system to be aromatic. Atoms in the ring must have unhybridized p orbitals. These unhybridized p orbitals must overlap resulting in a cyclic pi system. For this overlap, the structure must have planar (or nearly planar) configuration. In other words, the atoms related or involved in the pi bond should be in the same plane.

Test whether you can recognize the aromaticity of the structures in the examples that follow:

Tips for testing aromaticity

Step 1 – Count the number of pi electrons.
Step 2 – See whether there is a cyclic p orbital overlap.

Predict the aromaticity of the compounds given below:

Compound 1

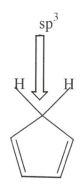

Number of pi electrons – 6
Cyclic overlap of p orbitals – Yes
Aromatic – Yes

Compound 2

1,3-Cyclopentadiene

Number of pi electrons – 4
Cyclic overlap of p orbitals – No
Aromatic – No

Compound 3

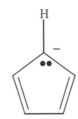

Cyclopentadienyl anion

Number of pi electrons – 6
Cyclic overlap of p orbitals – Yes
Aromatic – Yes

Some examples of heterocyclic aromatic compounds.

Pyridine

The nonbonded electron pair is in an sp^2 orbital which is perpendicular to the pi system and thus not part of the pi system. Since it has six pi electrons in a planar confirmation, it is aromatic.

Pyrrole

The nonbonded electrons occupy the unhybridized p orbital and thus are part of the cyclic pi system. With a total of six pi electrons, pyrrole is aromatic.

Furan

There are two lone pairs of electrons on the oxygen atom in Furan. One of the lone pairs occupies the sp^2 hybrid orbital, while the other pair occupies the unhybridized p orbital and forms the overlap with the pi electrons of the carbon atoms to form a continuous ring of six electrons. Hence, furan is aromatic.

D. REACTIONS OF AROMATIC COMPOUNDS

Benzene Stability

Benzene, unlike alkenes, will not react with halogens to form addition products.

This exemplifies the extra stability of the double bonds present in the benzene ring. However, benzene can undergo substitution reactions with halogens in the presence of a Lewis acid catalyst. The Lewis acid enhances the electrophilic nature of the halogen, thus enabling the reaction to proceed.

Electrophilic Substitution Reactions

One of the most characteristic reactions of benzene is the electrophilic substitution reaction, in which a hydrogen is replaced by an electrophile. In such reactions, the benzene acts as the nucleophile.

ELECTROPHILIC AROMATIC SUBSTITUTION REACTION

In a typical aromatic substitution reaction, the electrophile (means electron loving) accepts the electron pair from the pi system of benzene, resulting in a carbocation. This cation of benzene is called the **cyclohexadienyl cation**. Then, the cyclohexadienyl cation loses a proton forming the substitution product.

MECHANISM OF ELECTROPHILIC AROMATIC SUBSTITUTION

Nitration

Benzene can be nitrated by reacting with nitric acid (HNO_3). This is usually done in the presence of sulfuric acid (H_2SO_4).

Sample reaction 30-1

In this reaction, nitronium ion (NO_2^+) acts as the electrophile.

Friedel-Crafts Reactions

In Friedel-Crafts reactions, benzene is reacted with acyl or alkyl chlorides, in the presence of metal halides as catalysts. The metal halides act as Lewis acids in these reactions. The two types of Friedel-Crafts reactions are alkylation and acylation.

(1) Alkylation

In Friedel-Crafts alkylation, benzene is reacted with alkyl chlorides in the presence of metal halides ($AlCl_3$, $AlBr_3$) as catalysts. The catalyst serves as a Lewis acid and increases the electrophilicity of the alkyl halide. Alkylation is important for the synthesis of alkyl substituted derivatives of benzene. But there is a possibility of rearrangement of the intermediates resulting in undesired products. For example, if primary halides are used in alkylation, they can rearrange to form secondary or tertiary carbocations which are more stable intermediates. This can result in multiple products.

Sample reaction 30-2

| Benzene | Ethyl chloride | | Ethylbenzene | Hydrogen chloride |

The Mechanism of Alkylation Rearrangement

(2) Acylation

In Friedel-Crafts acylation reactions, benzene is reacted with acyl chlorides or acid anhydrides in the presence of metal halides (Lewis acids). The importance of acylation is that there is no rearrangement, unlike alkylation where there is a possibility of rearrangement of the cation intermediates.

The acyl halide forms a complex with the Lewis acid ($AlCl_3$), followed by the leaving of the halogen along with the Lewis acid. The resulting ion, called acylium ion, is resonance stabilized and is strongly electrophilic. The ion reacts with benzene to form an acylbenzene.

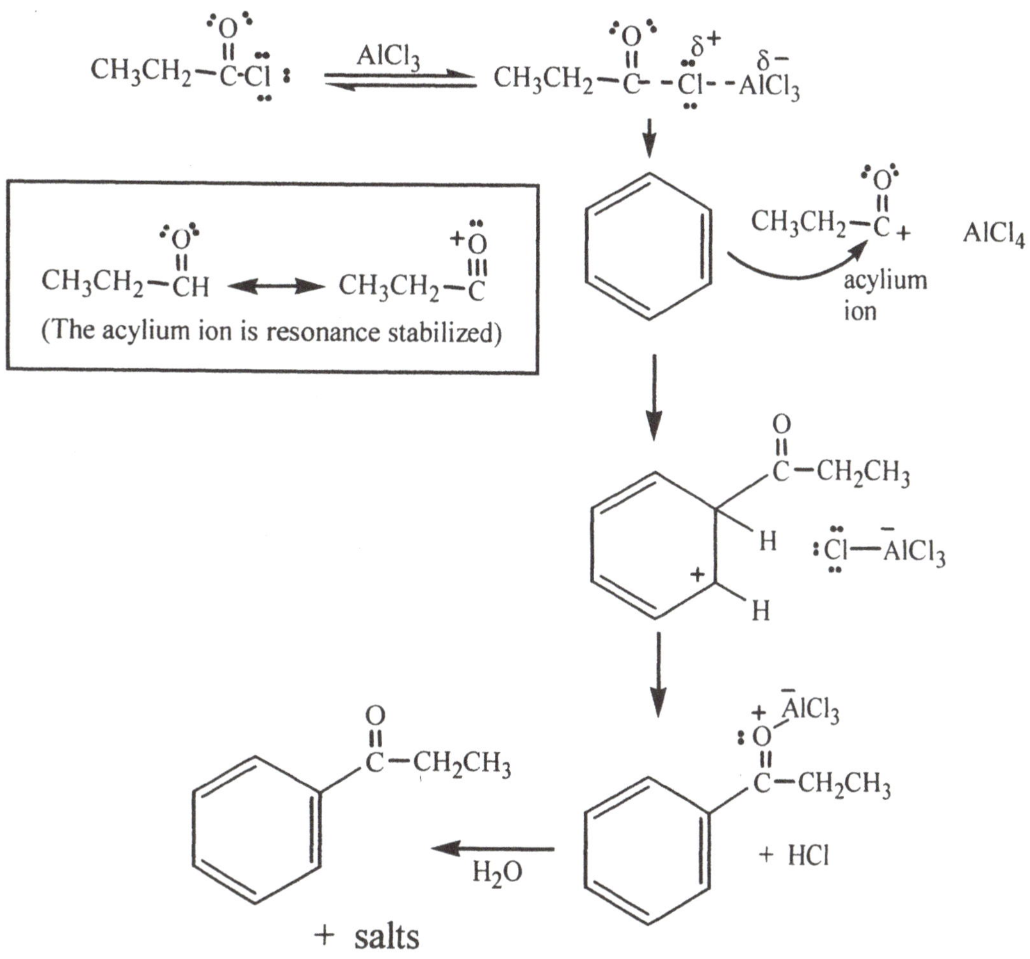

$CH_3CH_2-\overset{\overset{\textbf{:O:}}{\|}}{C}-\ddot{C}l: \quad \xrightleftharpoons{AlCl_3} \quad CH_3CH_2-\overset{\overset{\textbf{:O:}}{\|}}{C}-\overset{\delta+}{\ddot{C}l}--\overset{\delta-}{AlCl_3}$

$CH_3CH_2-\overset{\overset{\textbf{:O:}}{\|}}{CH} \longleftrightarrow CH_3CH_2-\overset{\overset{+\ddot{O}}{\|\|}}{C}$

(The acylium ion is resonance stabilized)

$CH_3CH_2-\overset{\overset{\textbf{:O:}}{\|}}{C}+ \quad AlCl_4$

acylium ion

$\overset{O}{\overset{\|}{C}}-CH_2CH_3$

:Cl—AlCl₃

$\overset{O}{\overset{\|}{C}}-CH_2CH_3$

+ HCl

$\overset{+\ \bar{A}lCl_3}{\overset{:O}{\|}}{\overset{\|}{C}}-CH_2CH_3$

$\overset{O}{\overset{\|}{C}}-CH_2CH_3$

H₂O

+ salts

Sample reaction 30-3

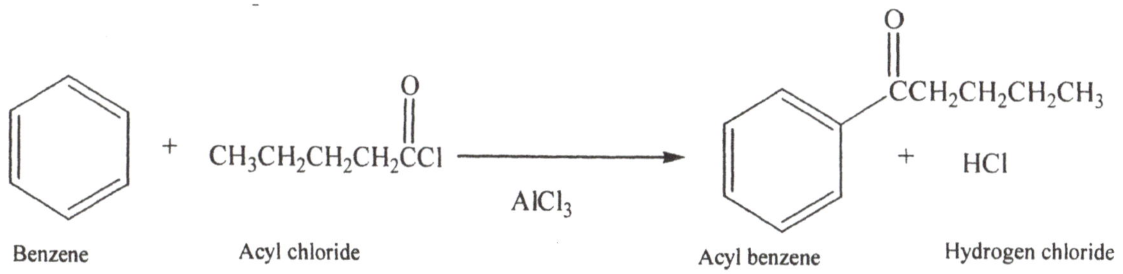

Benzene + $CH_3CH_2CH_2CH_2\overset{\overset{O}{\|}}{C}Cl$ $\xrightarrow{AlCl_3}$ $\overset{\overset{O}{\|}}{C}CH_2CH_2CH_2CH_3$ + HCl

| Benzene | Acyl chloride | Acyl benzene | Hydrogen chloride |

Acyl products that are formed can be reduced by reactions such as Clemmensen or Wolff-Kishner reductions.

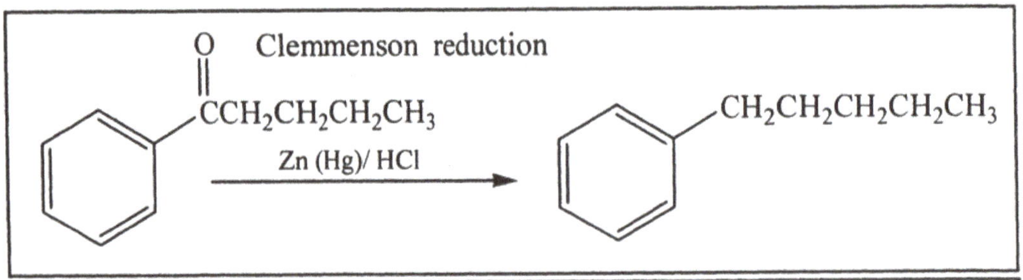

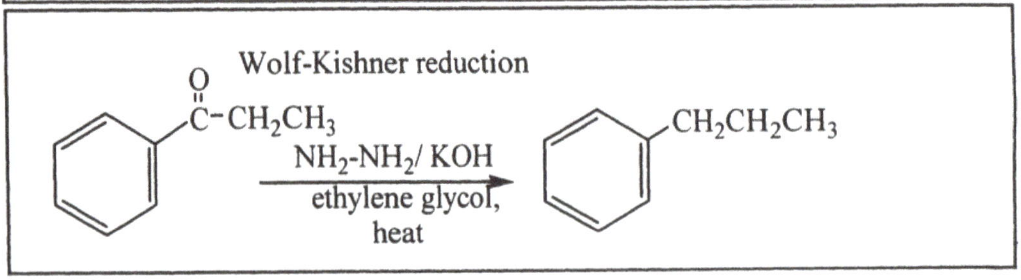

Sample reaction 30-4

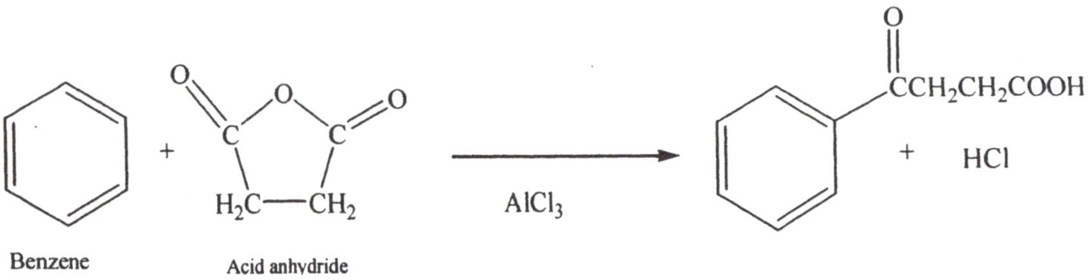

Benzene   Acid anhydride

Halogenation

Sample reaction 30-5

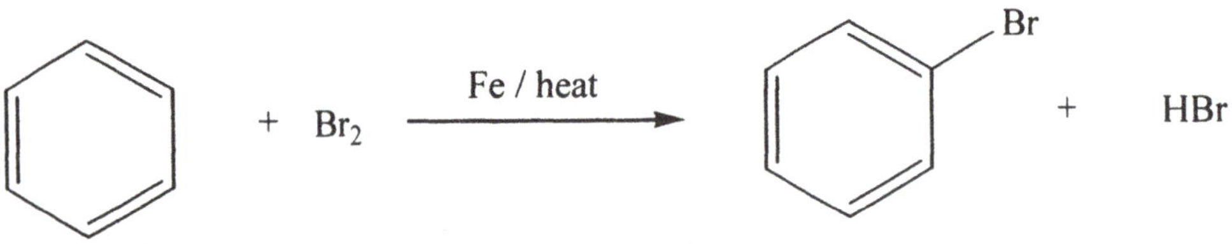

Benzene can be halogenated in the presence of Fe. In this reaction, the iron(III) bromide acts as the catalyst, which is formed from the iron and the bromine. The iron(III) bromide complex that is formed acts as the electrophile which attacks the benzene.

Sulfonation

Benzene can be sulfonated by heating with sulfuric acid.

Sample reaction 30-6

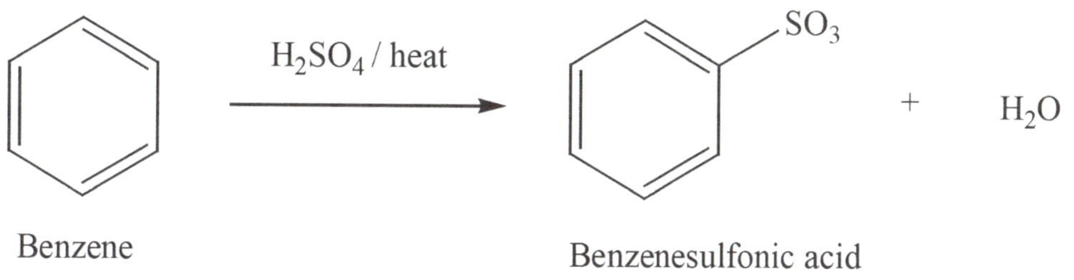

Benzene   Benzenesulfonic acid

E. DIRECTIVE EFFECTS OF SUBSTITUENTS

Consider the reaction of benzene with an electrophile (E).

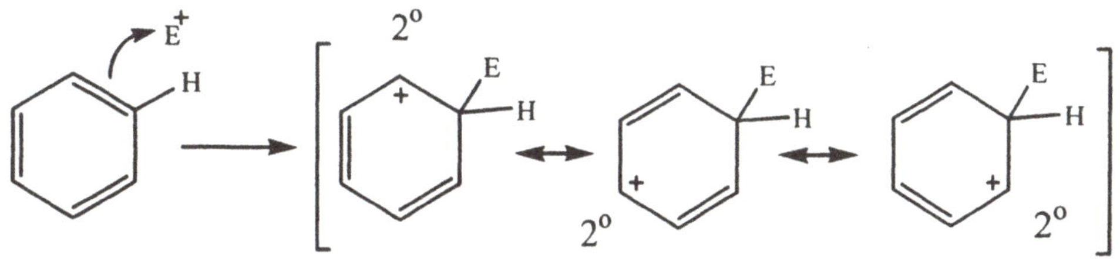

Notice that the positive charge is spread only on secondary carbons, and thus all resonance structures are equally stable.

In aromatic substitution reactions, the groups already present in the benzene ring can significantly influence the place of electrophilic attack of the incoming substituent. In other words, the substitution is influenced by the groups that are already present in the benzene ring. There are two types of groups – **activators** and **deactivators**. The groups that are activators cause the ring to be increasingly more reactive than benzene. The groups that are deactivators cause the ring to be decreasingly less reactive than benzene.

Activating Groups

As mentioned above, the activators increase the reactivity of the ring relative to benzene. In addition, the substitution primarily occurs in the ortho and para positions of the ring relative to the activating group. For this reason, activators are also called **ortho/para directors**. Let us analyze this with an example. In the following reaction, phenol is nitrated. Notice that phenol contains a hydroxyl group (-OH) which is an ortho/para activator. So the substitution occurs at ortho and para positions with respect to the -OH group.

Sample reaction 30-7

Phenol   Ortho-Nitrophenol   Para-Nitrophenol

Now let's us consider an electrophilic attack on toluene.

Ortho attack on toluene

Because the attack on the ortho or para attack results in more stable cation intermediates, those intermediates are formed faster and thus the resulting products from those intermediates are the predominant products.

Para attack on toluene

most favorable

Meta attack on toluene

By observing the resonance forms of the cation intermediates, it is clear that ortho and para attacks are favored. This is because ortho and para attacks have the possibility of spreading or sharing the positive charge by a tertiary carbon. Notice that when the attack is at the meta position, the positive charge is only shared by secondary carbons. A positive charge is better stabilized when it is on a tertiary carbon than on a secondary carbon. The methyl substituent is electron-donating and activates the benzene ring toward electrophilic attack, and the activation is more towards the ortho and para positions than the meta positions. In other words, alkyl groups are electron-donating substituents that are ortho-para directing by donating the electron density and thereby inductively stabilizes the intermediate.

Alkyl groups are electron-donating substituents, but it might seem counterintuitive to think at groups like -OH (hydroxyl) and -OCH$_3$ (methoxy) are also ortho/para activators since oxygen is a highly electronegative atom. This is because the oxygen atom that is bonded to the ring carbon has lone electrons or nonbonding electrons. As a result, the positive charge on the carbon atom in the intermediates formed from ortho and para attacks is stabilized through resonance. In other words, such groups can also donate electron density because of the presence of nonbonded electrons.

Deactivating Groups

Deactivators make the ring less reactive than benzene. There are two types of deactivators – **ortho/para** and **meta deactivators**.

1) Ortho/para deactivators

Some deactivators direct the incoming substituents primarily to the ortho and para positions. Halogens (Fluorine, chlorine, bromine, iodine) are ortho/para deactivators. They are electron withdrawing substituents through inductive effect. Furthermore, they have nonbonded electrons that can donate electron density by resonance. Because of the high electronegativity of halogens, they pull the electron density away from the ring, making the ring less susceptible to electrophilic substitution (deactivating property). Halogen substituents have nonbonded electrons which can be donated to a positively charged carbon in the intermediates resulting from ortho and para attacks. Hence, halogens are ortho, para-directing, and deactivating substituents.

Ortho attack

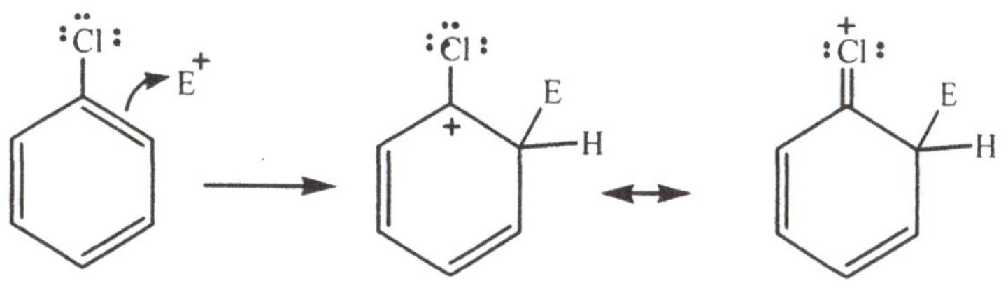

Para attack

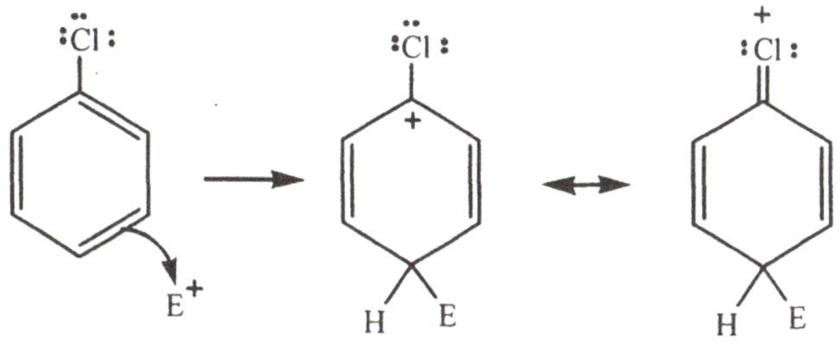

2) Meta deactivators

The meta deactivating groups direct the incoming substituents to the meta position. These groups are strongly electron-withdrawing groups. Consider the following example.

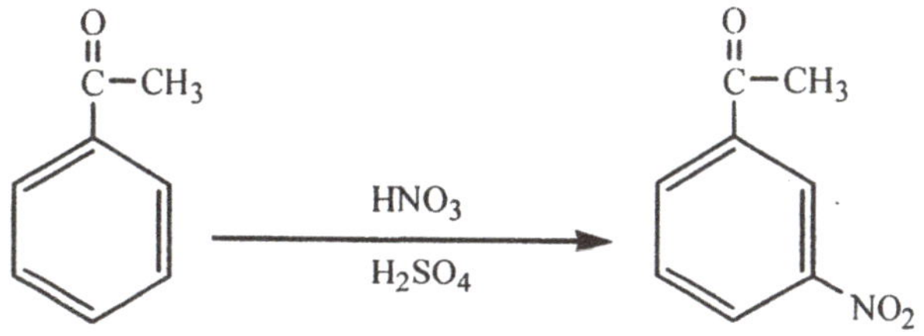

Major product
(meta substitution)

The substituent acyl group has a highly polarized carbon-oxygen double bond.

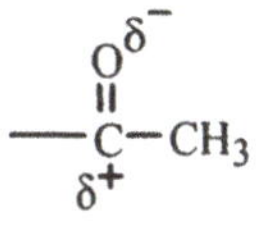

The positively charged carbon withdraws electron density from the benzene ring inductively. This accounts for the deactivation (less reactivity than benzene) of the ring toward electrophilic substitution.

Ortho attack

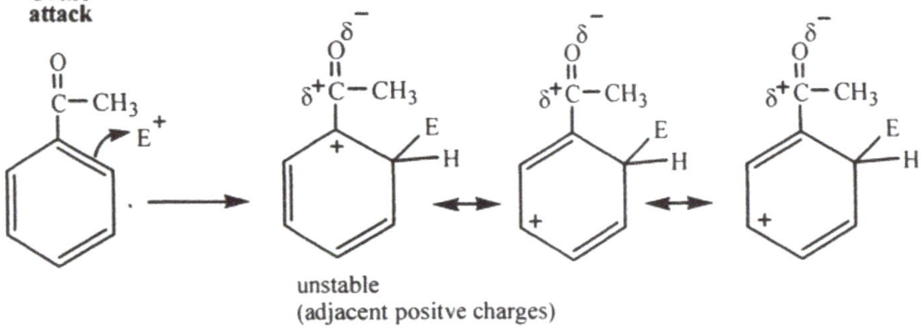

unstable
(adjacent positve charges)

Para attack

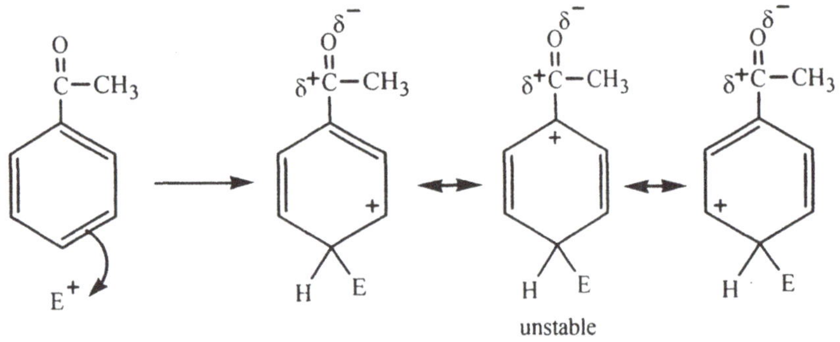

unstable

Meta attack

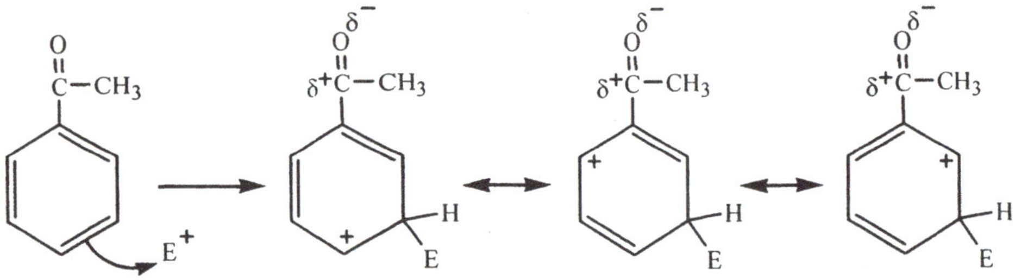

Both ortho and para attacks result in an intermediate that has adjacent positively charged (polarized) atoms, making it a highly unstable (higher energy) form. On the other hand, meta substitution doesn't result in an intermediate with positively charged atoms adjacent to each other. Thus, meta substitution results in the most stable (lower energy) intermediates. This accounts for the predominance of meta substitution products if acyl or similar groups are present in the ring.

ORTHO, PARA DIRECTORS	
Activating	**Deactivating**
-OH -OR -NH$_2$ -R -Ar -NHR -NR$_2$ $\overset{\displaystyle O}{\overset{\|}{-OCR}}$	Halogens (-X)

META DIRECTORS (Deactivating)

-CN
-CO$_2$R
-NO$_2$
-SO$_3$H
+NR$_3$
-CHO
-CO$_2$H
-SO$_2$OR
-CF$_3$

$\overset{\displaystyle O}{\overset{\|}{-CCl}}$

$\overset{\displaystyle O}{\overset{\|}{-CR}}$

Table 30-1

CHAPTER 30 PRACTICE QUESTIONS

1. Which of the following compounds is commonly known as xylene?

A.

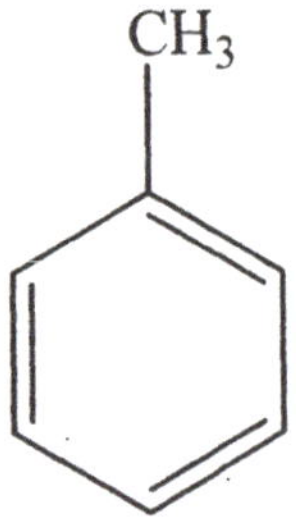

CH_3

B.

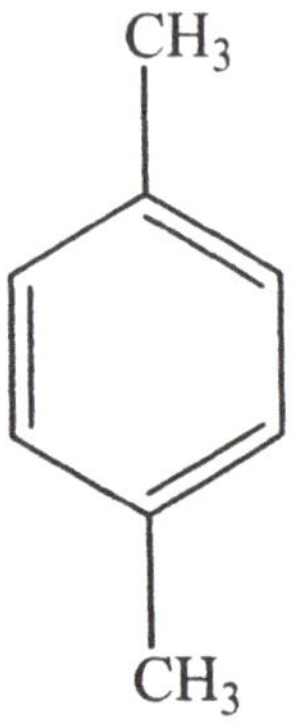

CH_3

CH_3

C.

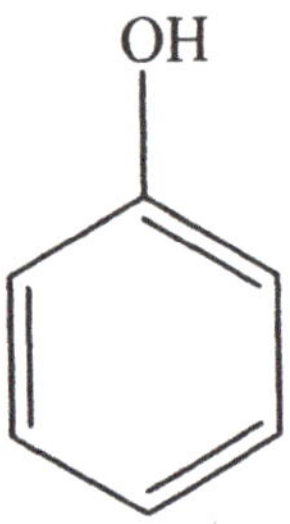

OH

D.

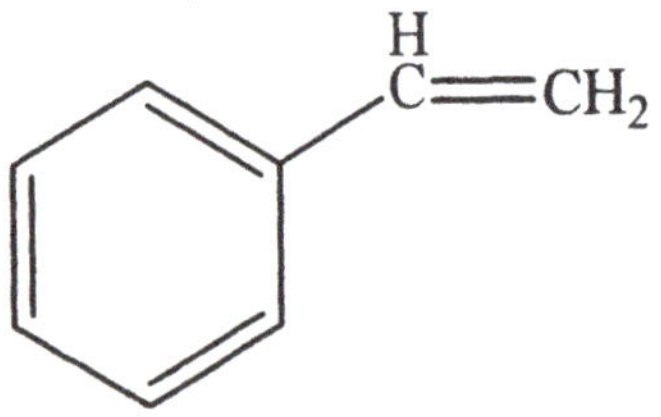

$\overset{H}{C}=CH_2$

2. The carbons in the benzene ring are:

    A.   *sp* hybridized.
    B. sp^2 hybridized.
    C. sp^3 hybridized.
    D.   not hybridized.

3. All the following are monosubstituted aromatic compounds, except:

    A.   phenol.
    B.   benzoic acid.
    C.   xylene.
    D.   toluene.

4. A compound can be aromatic, only if it has a certain number of pi electrons in its ring. All the following numbers can be attributed to the number of pi electrons and aromaticity, except:

    A.   two.
    B.   four.
    C.   six.
    D.   ten.

5. For the reaction involving benzene and nitric acid in the presence of sulfuric acid, which of the following is true?

    A.   The nitronium ion acts as the electrophile.
    B.   The reaction is an example of nucleophilic hydrogenation.
    C.   The reaction is an example of electrophilic addition reaction.
    D.   None of the above

6. What is the name of the reaction shown below?

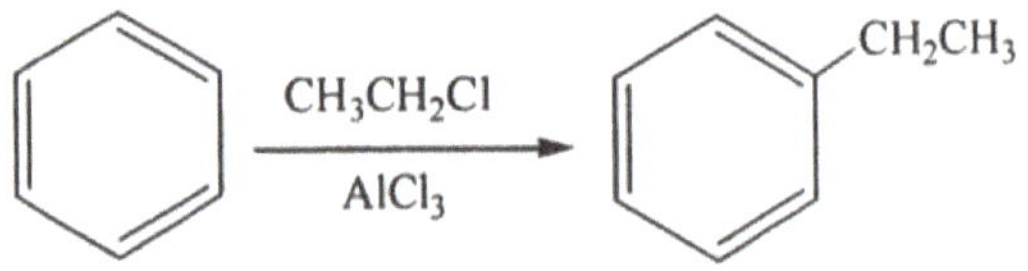

$$\text{benzene} \xrightarrow[\text{AlCl}_3]{\text{CH}_3\text{CH}_2\text{Cl}} \text{ethylbenzene } (CH_2CH_3)$$

    A.   Clemmensen reaction
    B.   Williamson synthesis
    C.   Raman synthesis
    D.   Friedel-Crafts reaction

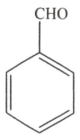

Reaction for Q. 7

Zn (Hg)/ HCl

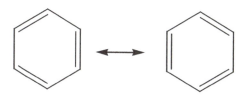

7. The reaction shown is commonly known as:

A. Clemmensen reduction.
B. Wolff-Kishner reaction.
C. Benedict's test.
D. Zaitsev reaction.

8. The group $-NO_2$ can be best described as:

A. an ortho/para activator.
B. a meta activator.
C. an ortho/para deactivator.
D. a meta deactivator.

9. Halogens can be best described as:

A. ortho/para activators.
B. meta activators.
C. ortho/para deactivators.
D. meta deactivators.

10. If the compound shown was reacted with nitric acid in the presence of sulfuric acid, which of the following is the major product?

A. A para substituted product
B. A meta substituted product
C. An ortho substituted product
D. No net reaction occurs

Questions 11-16 are based on the following passage.

Passage 1

The earliest predictions about the structure of benzene could not completely explain some of its properties. Later it was found that benzene has a cyclic structure which is commonly represented as follows:

These two structures are resonance structures of benzene. Benzene is also commonly represented as shown below:

A series of reactions were conducted using benzene and other aromatic compounds.

Reaction 1

In Reaction 1, benzene was reacted with *n*-propyl chloride in the presence of $AlCl_3$.

Reaction 2

Nitrobenzene was reacted with nitric acid and sulfuric acid. The reaction occurred as follows:

Compound A + Compound B + Compound C
(major product)

11. Which of the following is true regarding Reaction 1 described in the passage?

    A. It is a Friedel-Crafts acylation reaction.
    B. It is a reaction which results in a single product.
    C. $AlCl_3$ acts as a Lewis base.
    D. Rearrangement is possible.

12. An alkoxy group is best described as:

    A. an ortho, para-director, and an activating group.
    B. an ortho, para-director, and a deactivating group.
    C. a meta-director, and an activating group.
    D. a meta-director, and a deactivating group.

13. If phenol is reacted with bromine, the major product formed is:

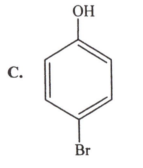

A.

B.

C.

D.

14. The reaction shown here is:

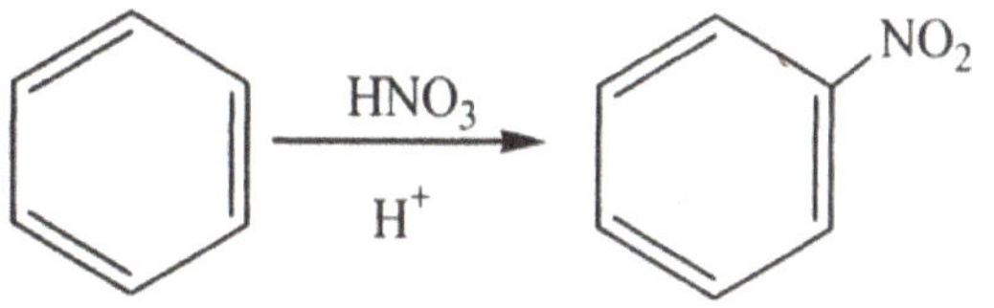

    A.   an electrophilic substitution reaction.
    B.   an electrophilic addition reaction.
    C.   a reduction-addition reaction.
    D.   an electrophilic elimination reaction.

15. The inscribed circle in the benzene ring represents:

    A.   the carbon chain in the cyclic ring.
    B.   the sigma-system of electrons.
    C.   the pi-system of electrons.
    D.   the eight pi-electrons in the cyclic system.

16. All the following are false about Reaction 2, except that:

    A.   Compound A is a meta product.
    B.   the major product is a 1,2 substituted product.
    C.   the major product is a para substituted product.
    D.   Compound C is a 1,3 substituted product.

CHAPTER 31

Phosphoric Acid Chemistry

A. INTRODUCTION

Phosphoric acid is H_3PO_4. It is an important molecule with respect to its part in a wide variety of biomolecules in our body such as adenosine triphosphate (ATP), deoxyribonucleic acid (DNA), and ribonucleic acid (RNA).

Phosphoric acid

B. DISSOCIATION OF PHOSPHORIC ACID

Phosphoric acid is a triprotic acid. That means it has three pKa values.

C. ESTERS AND ANHYDRIDES

Phosphoric acid can form esters with alcohols. It can form monoesters, diesters, and triesters. A general representation of the formation of phosphoesters is given below. R represents the alkyl group.

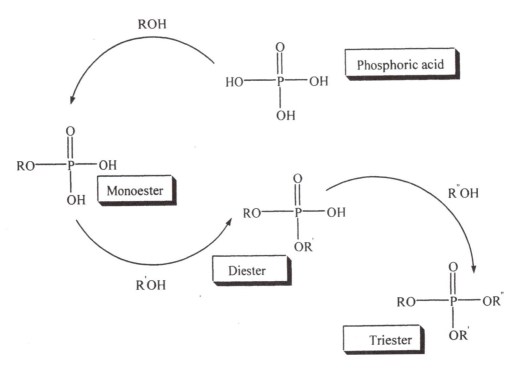

Figure 31-1

Besides esters, phosphoric acid forms anhydrides such as phosphoric anhydrides by reacting with themselves. One such combination is shown in Figure 31-2.

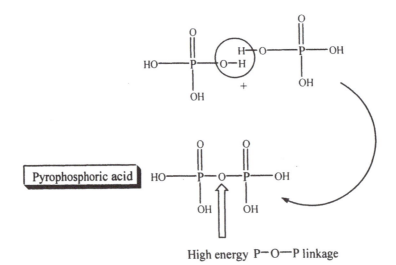

High energy P—O—P linkage

Figure 31-2

These anhydrides are biologically useful since the —P—O—P— linkages found in them are high-energy linkages, and are used by the body to store energy. When energy is required, the linkage is hydrolyzed to give off the stored energy which is in turn used for the metabolic processes in the body.

D. BIOLOGICAL SIGNIFICANCE OF PHOSPHORIC ACID

We cannot completely fathom the importance of phosphoric acid in the biological processes. It is a part of our genetic makeup in the sense that phosphoric acid is a part of the deoxyribonucleic acid (DNA) and the ribonucleic acid (RNA). The deoxyribose sugars in the DNA are connected using phosphoric acid entities by forming linkages called **phosphodiester bonds**. These phosphodiester bonds connect the 3' hydroxyl group of one sugar to the 5' hydroxyl group of the next sugar forming the backbone of the nucleic acids. See Figure 31-3.

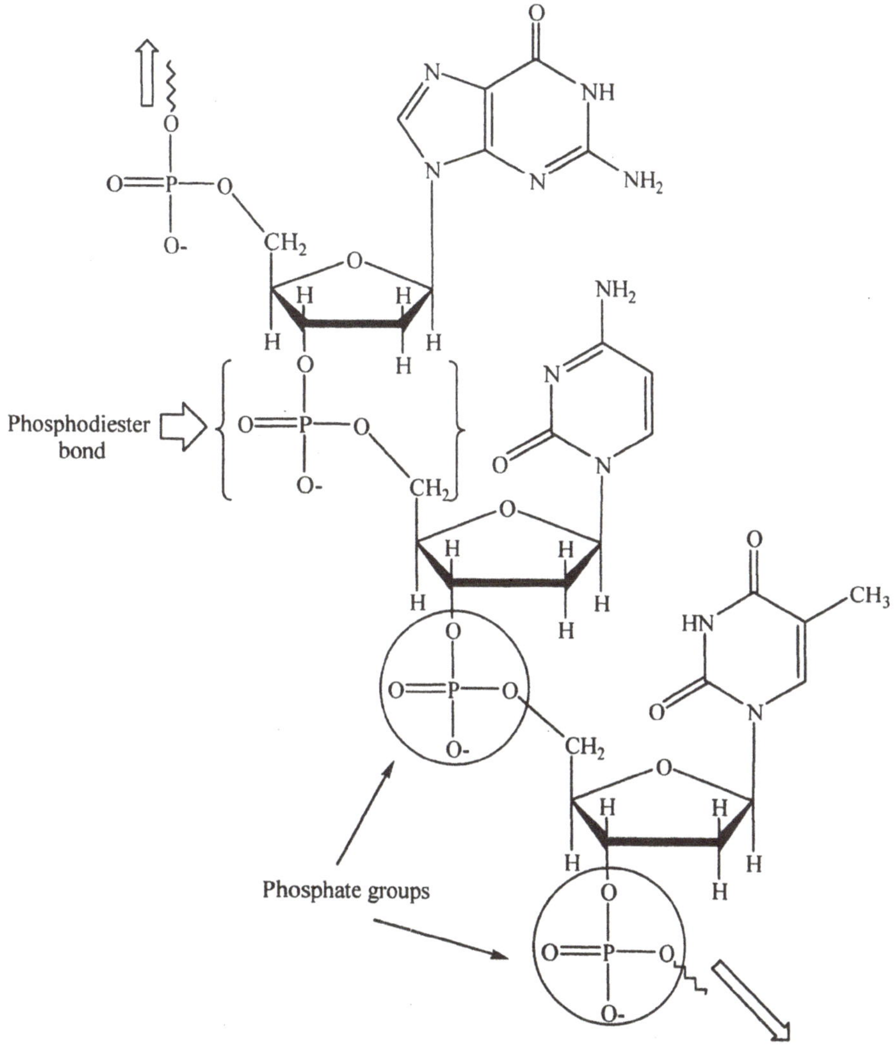

Figure 31-3 Part of a DNA backbone showing the phosphodiester bonds. The deoxyribose sugars are linked by the phosphate groups (indicated by the circles).

At normal biological pH range (7.35-7.45), the phosphate esters usually show a double negative charge. This property of the phosphate esters makes them generally water soluble, and thus perfect for the physiological environment in our body.

473

Another noteworthy biomolecule that contains the phosphate groups is ATP (adenosine triphosphate). ATP molecules act as one of the major energy currencies of living beings. It is a triphosphate ester. The formation of ATP from AMP (adenosine monophosphate) is shown in Figure 31-4.

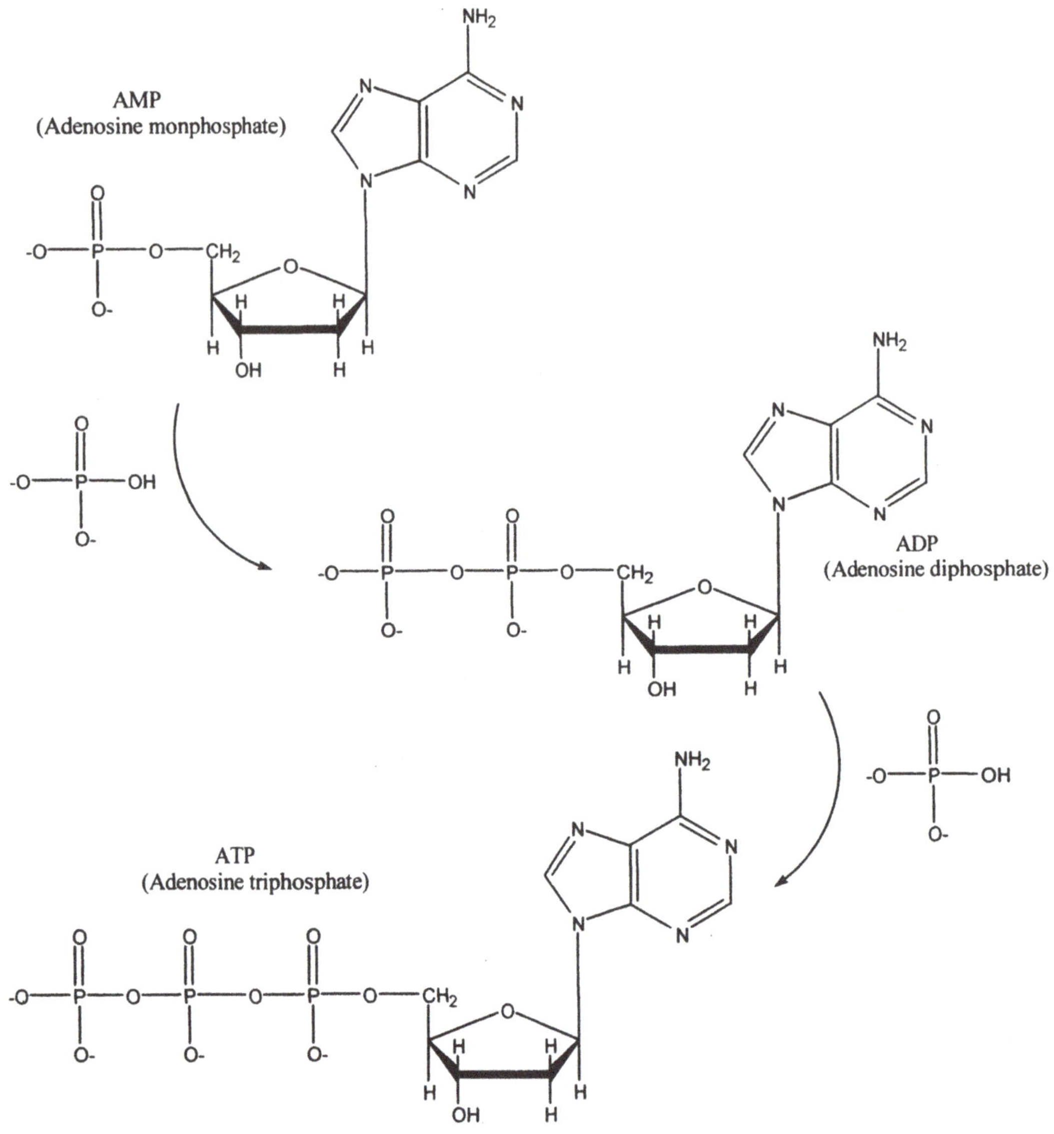

Figure 31-4 The formation of ATP from AMP

CHAPTER 31 PRACTICE QUESTIONS

Questions 1-7 are based on the following passage.

Passage 1

Phosphoric acid is an integral part of some of the most important biomolecules in our body.

Reaction 1

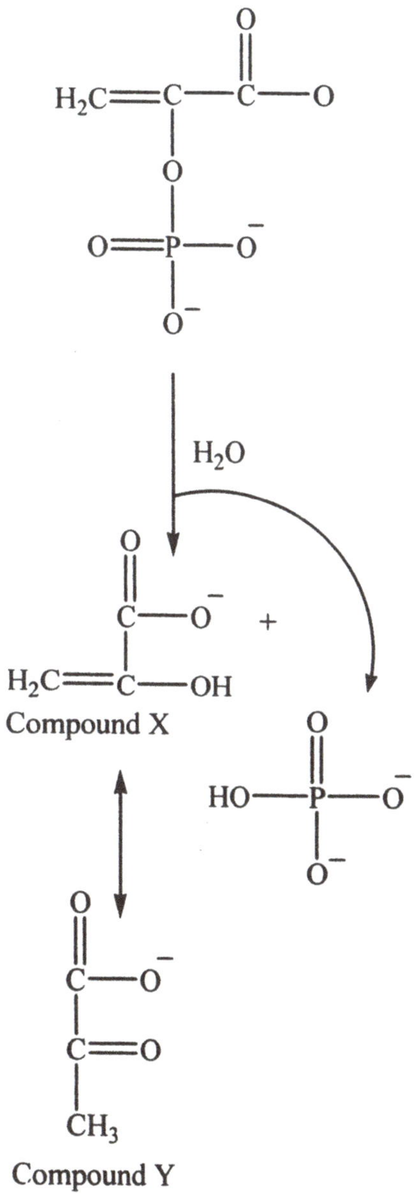

Compound X

Compound Y

Reaction 1 depicts the conversion of phosphoenol pyruvate to pyruvate.

Phosphate is a part of many high-energy compounds in biological systems. Examples include ATP (adenosine triphosphate) and GTP (guanosine triphosphate).

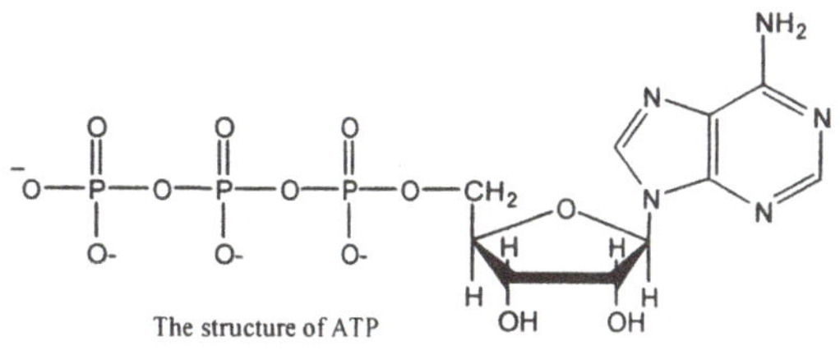

The structure of ATP

$$ATP \xrightarrow{H_2O} ADP + Pi$$

$$\Delta G = -31 \text{ kJ/mol}$$

1. The bond indicated by the arrow is a:

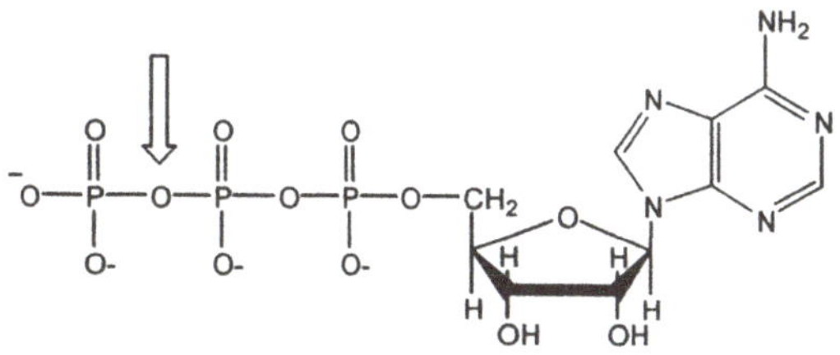

    A.   phosphate ketone bond.
    B.   phosphate anhydride bond.
    C.   phosphate ester bond.
    D.   *N*-glycosidic bond.

2. Reaction 1 can be best described as a:

    A.   reduction reaction.
    B.   dehydration reaction.
    C.   dehydrohalogenation reaction.
    D.   hydrolysis reaction.

3. The interconversion of Compounds X and Y is called:

    A.   resolution.
    B.   tautomerism.
    C.   Tyndall effect.
    D.   Brownian movement.

4. The bond indicated by the arrow is a:

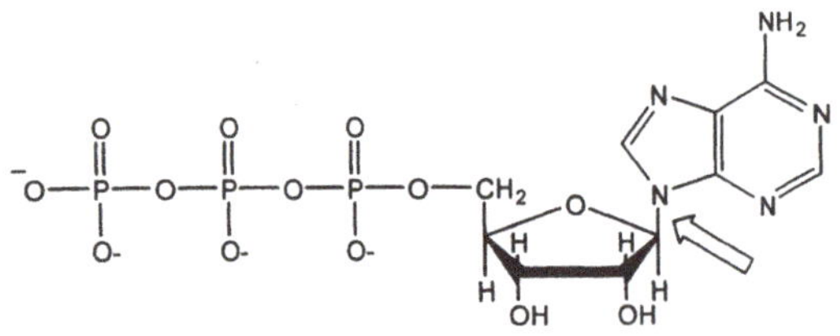

    A.   phosphate ketone bond.
    B.   phosphate anhydride bond.
    C.   phosphate ester bond.
    D.   *N*-glycosidic bond.

5. The phosphate anhydride bonds present in the ATP molecules are high-energy bonds. Which of the following is true regarding the hydrolysis of these bonds?

    A.   The products of hydrolysis have less energy than that of the reactants.
    B.   The products of hydrolysis have the same energy as that of the reactants.
    C.   The reactants of hydrolysis have less energy than that of the products.
    D.   None of the above

6. Choose the correct change in free energy in the following conversion. (The products have higher free energy than the reactants)

Adenosine + Phosphate –> AMP

    A.   −14 kJ/mole
    B.   −34 kJ/mole
    C.   +14 kJ/mole
    D.   −40 kJ/mole

7. Phosphoric acid is a:

    A.   monoprotic acid.
    B.   diprotic acid.
    C.   triprotic acid.
    D.   strong acid.

Section 11

CONTENT REVIEW PROBLEMS

1. What is the IUPAC name of the following molecule:

$CH_2CHCH_2CH_2CHCHCH_3$

    A.   1,5-heptadiene
    B.   2,5-heptadiene
    C.   2,6-heptadiene
    D.   5-methly-2-hexene

2. Which of the following is the same molecule as *cis*-2-butene?

    A.   E-2-butene
    B.   Z-2-butene
    C.   2-methyl-2-propene
    D.   2-methyl-1-propene

3. In an anti-Markovnikov addition reaction, which of the following is true?

    A.   The intermediate will rearrange to form the more stable primary radical.
    B.   The radical species formed is most stable on a secondary carbon.
    C.   The radical species formed is most stable on a tertiary carbon.
    D.   Unlike Markovnikov addition which requires a radical, anti-Markovnikov involves only the addition of a halide acid.

4. What is the name of the following functional group?

$H_2C\overline{\quad\quad}CH_2$
           O

    A.   Ether
    B.   Peroxide
    C.   Ester
    D.   Epoxide

5. What is the IUPAC name for the following molecule?

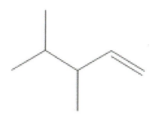

    A.   3,4-dimethyl-1-pentene
    B.   2-methyl-3-vinyl-butane
    C.   2-vinyl-3-methyl-butane
    D.   3,4-dimethyl-2-pentene

6. What is the common name for CHCH?

    A.   Ethyne
    B.   Ethene
    C.   Acetylene
    D.   Formaldehyde

7. In the molecule CH_3CCCH_3, the carbon atoms demonstrate:

    A.   sp hybridization only.
    B. sp^3 hybridization only.
    C.   sp and sp^2 hybridization.
    D.   sp and sp^3 hybridization.

8. Which of the following is true about a stereoselective reaction such as the hydrogenation of an alkyne to an alkene using a catalyst like Lindlar palladium?

    A.   The reaction only operates on one stereoisomer to produce a particular stereoisomer product.
    B.   The reaction favors the formation of one stereoisomer over the other.
    C.   The reaction would be nonspontaneous in the absence of the metal catalyst.
    D.   The product can be in the *cis* **or** *trans* form.

9. The acid-catalyzed hydration of an alkyne will produce products that are predominantly:

    A. ketones.
    B. enols.
    C. equal mixtures of ketone and enol.
    D. carboxylic acids.

10. The ozonolysis of an alkyne results in:

    A. one carboxylic acid and an alkane.
    B. one aldehyde and an alcohol.
    C. two primary alcohols.
    D. two carboxylic acids.

11. Which of the following is an example of a polycyclic aromatic hydrocarbon?

    A. Naphthalene
    B. Phenol
    C. Benzene
    D. Toluene

12. The planar shape of benzene results from:

    A. sharing electrons between the sp^2 hybridized orbitals.
    B. the additional stability that a planar conformation has over boat conformation for cyclic molecules.
    C. the $109.5°$ bond angles between the carbon atoms in the ring.
    D. delocalization of unhybridized p orbitals.

13. A benzene ring with an amino group on it is called:

    A. toluene.
    B. aniline.
    C. benzaldehyde.
    D. phenol.

14. A benzene ring with an aldehyde group on it is called:

    A. toluene.
    B. aniline.
    C. benzaldehyde.
    D. phenol.

15. A cyclic compound has 8 pi electrons in a conjugated system. As such, the molecule is:

    A. aromatic.
    B. antiaromatic.
    C. nonaromatic.
    D. unusually stable.

16. Which of the following is a heterocycle with one lone pair on the nitrogen atom that participates in the delocalization of pi electrons?

    A. Pyridine
    B. Furan
    C. Pyrrole
    D. D-glucose

17. The linkages between ribose sugars that form the backbone of DNA are:

    A. ethers.
    B. esters.
    C. aldehydes.
    D. anhydrides.

18. The high-energy phosphate linkages used in the body's primary energy molecule are:

    A. ethers.
    B. esters.
    C. aldehydes.
    D. anhydrides.

19. To form a nucleotide from a nucleoside, what must be carried out?

    A. Addition of a phosphate group
    B. Removal of a phosphate group
    C. Polymerization via phosphodiester bonds
    D. Addition of a nitrogenous base

20. ATP is formed from:
  I. An adenine molecule
 II. A hexose sugar
III. Three phosphate groups

      A.   I and II only
      B.   I and III only
      C.   II and III only
      D.   I, II, and III

FINAL EXAM

Chemistry and Organic Chemistry

CONTENT REVIEW

1. Acetaldehyde is the common name for:

    A.   methanal.
    B.   ethanal.
    C.   ethanol.
    D.   formalin.

2. Which of the following is considered a terminal functional group?

    A.   Aldehyde
    B.   Ketone
    C.   Ether
    D.   Ester

3. The name for the parent chain of the following molecule is:

    A.   butanoic acid.
    B.   propanol.
    C.   propanoic acid.
    D.   propanoate.

4. The following molecule would be named as a(n):

    A.   ester.
    B.   anhydride.
    C.   ketone.
    D.   ether.

5. A particular biological molecule has the following functional groups in its structure:

- CHO.
- NH_2.
- COOH.
- C – OH.
- CH_2Cl.

The suffix of this molecule would be:

    A.   – al.
    B.   – ol.
    C.   – oic acid.
    D.   – amide.

6. What is the name of the following molecule?

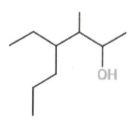

    A.   3-chloro-4-propyl-2-hexanol
    B.   4-chloro-3-propyl-5-hexanol
    C.   2-hydroxy-4-propyl-3-hexyl chloride
    D.   3-chloro-4-ethyl-2-heptanol

7. The conjugate base of oxalic acid is a major component of kidney stones. It is a molecule with a – COOH functional group on each end of the carbon chain. As such, its IUPAC name would include:

    A.   – dioic acid
    B.   – bioic acid
    C.   – oicoic acid
    D.   – oic acid

8. Which prefix serves as the common name for organic molecules with only one carbon?

    A. meth -
    B. form -
    C. acet -
    D. cis -

9. A student is given an organic structure and names the molecule 5-ethyl-3-butylhexane. The student should have named the molecule:

    A. 2, 4-diethyloctane.
    B. 3-butyl-5-ethylhexane.
    C. isodecane.
    D. 5-ethyl-3-methyl-nonane.

10. All of the following solutions would show optical activity EXCEPT:

    A. 2.0M solution of (R)-2-chlorobutane.
    B. 0.2M solution of (S)-2-chlorobutane.
    C. a solution of 2.0M (R)-2-chlorobutane and 2.0M (S)-2-chlorobutane.
    D. a solution of 2.0M (R)-2-chlorobutane and 0.2M (S)-2-chlorobutane.

11. The following molecules are:

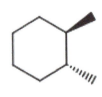 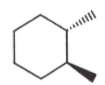

    A. diastereomers.
    B. enantiomers.
    C. geometric isomers.
    D. the same molecule.

12. L-(+)-tartaric acid and D-(-)-tartaric acid are:

    A. diastereomers.
    B. enantiomers.
    C. geometric isomers.
    D. the same molecule.

13. n-heptane and 2,3-dimethylpentane are:

    A. diastereomers.
    B. constitutional isomers.
    C. unrelated.
    D. epimers.

14. (S)-2-iodo-(R)-3-chlorobutane and (R)-2-iodo-(R)-3-chlorobutane are:

    A. diastereomers
    B. enantiomers
    C. geometric isomers.
    D. the same molecule.

15. If butane is drawn in a Newman projection with the front and rear methyl groups 180° apart, then the molecule is in its:

    A. gauche conformation.
    B. lower energy staggered form.
    C. higher energy staggered form.
    D. eclipsed form.

16. Which of the following subshells is the lowest energy?

    A. 4s
    B. 4p
    C. 4d
    D. 4f

17. In the molecule ethane, the carbon atoms have an s orbital that is hybridized with:

    A. one p orbital
    B. two p orbitals
    C. three p orbitals
    D. no p orbitals

18. The hybridization around the boron atom in BH_3 is:

    A. sp.
    B. sp^2.
    C. sp^3.
    D. s^2p.

19. Two atomic orbitals may combine to form each of the following EXCEPT:

    A.   a hybridized orbital.
    B.   a bonding molecular orbital.
    C.   an antibonding molecular orbital.
    D.   a free radical orbital.

20. σ and π bonds are respectively formed by:

    A.   s-orbitals and p-orbitals.
    B.   p-orbitals and s-orbitals.
    C.   s-orbitals and sp^2 hybrid orbitals.
    D.   sp hybrid orbitals and s-orbitals.

21. A molecular orbital can hold what maximum number of electrons?

    A.   2
    B.   4
    C.   2 per σ and 2 per π
    D. $2n^2$

22. How many σ and π bonds, respectively, are present in 3-oxopenatoic acid?

    A.   13, 2
    B.   12, 4
    C.   15, 2
    D.   15, 4

23. Compared to triple bonds, double bonds are:

    A.   shorter.
    B.   stronger.
    C.   made up of more π bonds.
    D.   weaker.

24. Resonance energy is:

    A.   the additional energy saved by a molecule entering an unstable resonance state.
    B.   always greater than the energy of a single bond.
    C.   the sum of the differences in the energy levels between the contributing form that is the most stable and the one that is the least stable.
    D.   the energy difference between the resonance hybrid and the lowest energy form that contributes to the resonance hybrid.

25. The electronic geometries for CH_4, NH_3, and H_2O are, respectively:

    A.   tetrahedral, tetrahedral, tetrahedral.
    B.   tetrahedral, trigonal pyramid, bent.
    C.   pyramidal, trigonal pyramid, bent.
    D.   octahedral, tetrahedral, linear.

26. The molecular geometries for CH_4, NH_3, and H_2O are, respectively:

    A.   tetrahedral, tetrahedral, tetrahedral.
    B.   tetrahedral, trigonal pyramid, bent.
    C.   pyramidal, trigonal pyramid, bent.
    D.   octahedral, tetrahedral, linear.

27. Ammonia commonly may act as any of the following EXCEPT a(n):

    A.   Lewis base.
    B.   Brønsted base.
    C.   nucleophile.
    D.   electrophile.

28. Which of the following is the best leaving group?

    A. OH^-
    B. H_2O
    C. H^-
    D. I^-

29. CH_3CH_2CHO is treated with $LiAlH_4$ leading to:

    A. $CH_3CH_2CH_2OH$.
    B. CH_3CH_2COOH.
    C. $CH_3CH_2CH_3$.
    D. CH_3CHCH_2.

30. S_N2 reactions are favored by:

    A.   polar protic solvents.
    B.   tertiary substrates.
    C.   small, strong nucleophiles.
    D.   unstable leaving groups.

31. A benzene ring with hydroxyl groups on carbons 1 and 4 would be a quinone with the hydroxyl groups arranged:

    A.   ortho.
    B.   meta.
    C.   para.
    D.   staggered.

32. Compared to alkyl –OH groups, phenols are:

    A.   less acidic due to resonance stabilization.
    B.   more acidic due to resonance stabilization.
    C.   less acidic because the conjugate base destabilizes the resonance in the benzene ring.
    D.   more acidic because the benzene ring becomes susceptible to electrophilic aromatic substitution.

33. The functional group $-SO_3C_6H_4CH_3$ is:

    A.   a mesylate.
    B.   a tosylate.
    C.   used to deprotect ketone functional groups.
    D.   a cysteine side chain.

34. In its function in the electron transport chain, ubiquinone is converted to ubiquinol. This is a(n):

    A.   reduction reaction.
    B.   oxidation reaction.
    C. S_N1 mechanism reaction.
    D.   galvanic reaction.

35. The hydroxyl functional groups leads to molecules that, relative to their analogous alkanes have:

    A.   lower boiling points.
    B.   diminished hydrogen bonding.
    C.   lower melting points.
    D.   increased water solubility.

36. The hydrogen α to a ketone or aldehyde:

    A.   is less acidic than the analogous alkyl hydrogen.
    B.   is more acidic than the analogous alkyl hydrogen.
    C.   generates a 1700 cm^{-1} IR peak.
    D.   is bonded to a carbon with sp^2 hybridization.

37. In a carbonyl functional group the carbon is:

    A.   slightly negative.
    B.   nucleophilic.
    C.   sp hybridized.
    D.   electrophilic.

38. Which of the following will oxidize a primary alcohol into an aldehyde?

    A. $LiAlH_4$
    B. $Na_2Cr_2O_7$
    C.   PCC
    D. CrO_3

39. In a ketal, the central carbon is bonded to:

    A.   –OH, -R, -OH, -H
    B.   –OR, -R, -OR, -H
    C.   –OR, -R, -OH, -R
    D.   –OR, -R, -OR, -R

40. Which of the following would produce a geminal diol?

    A. $CH_3COCH_3 + H_2O_2$
    B. $CH_3COCH_3 + CH_3CH_2OH$
    C. $CH_3COCH_3 + H_2O$
    D. $CH_3COCH_3 + LiAlH_4$

41. The conversion between an enamine and an imine is a:

    A.   tautomerization.
    B.   reduction reaction.
    C. S_N2 reaction.
    D.   resonance reaction.

42. The conversion between ketone and an enol is:

    A.   tautomerization.
    B.   reduction reaction.
    C. S_N2 reaction.
    D.   resonance reaction.

43. The α hydrogen in a ketone is more acidic because:

    A.   hydride is a good leaving group.
    B.   the conjugate base is resonance stabilized.
    C.   the oxygen on a ketone can accept a hydrogen, thereby destabilizing the carbonyl double cond.
    D.   the negative charge can be destabilized between both oxygens in the functional group.

44. An aldol condensation product is a(n):

    A.   carbonyl alkene.
    B.   carbonyl alkane.
    C.   geminal diol
    D.   carboxylic acid.

45. A nucleophilic attack would proceed most rapidly on:

    A.   pentane.
    B.   2-pentone.
    C.   pentanal.
    D.   Both A and C.

46. The molecule $CH_3(CH_2)_{15}COO^-K^+$ would be classified as:

    A.   a carboxylic acid.
    B.   a soap.
    C.   a ketone.
    D.   a phospholipid.

47. Using a two-step reaction, a carboxylic acid may be converted to:

    A.   an ester.
    B.   an alkyne.
    C.   a protein.
    D.   an alkene.

48. A micelle is:

    A.   a structure with a hydrophilic interior.
    B.   formed from esters.
    C.   a self-aggregating organization of soap molecules.
    D.   thermodynamically unstable due to the decreased entropy of the spherical structure.

49. Rank the following molecules in order of increasing acidity:

    I. $CH_3CH_2CH_2COOH$
    II. $CH_3CH_2CHClCOOH$
    III. $CH_3CHClCF_2COOH$

    A.   III < II < I
    B.   III < I < II
    C.   I < II < III
    D.   II < III < I

50. What is the major product of the reaction between propanoic acid and methanol in acid?

    A.   Methyl propanoate
    B.   Propyl Methanoate
    C.   Methyl propyl anhydride
    D.   Methyl propyl ether

51. Which of the following will most readily form an amide bond when reacted with a carboxylic acid?

    A.   Tripropylamine
    B.   2-Butanol
    C.   Diphenylamine
    D.   Methylamine

52. In the presence of a very small amount of acid catalyst, a mixture of an amide and water will form:

    A.   a carboxylic acid and an amine.
    B.   an amide.
    C.   an anhydride and a diamine.
    D.   an ester and an amine.

53. The conversion of methyl methanoate to ethyl methanoate is:

    A.   impossible.
    B.   a hydrolysis reaction.
    C.   a redox reaction with ethane as the oxidizing agent.
    D.   transesterification.

54. β-lactams are all of the following EXCEPT:

    A.   a form of amide.
    B.   a ring structure with minimal ring strain.
    C.   more reactive than the straight-chain analog.
    D.   cyclic.

55. An esterification reaction carried out with a water solvent would:

    A.   likely produce very little product due to hydrolysis of the products.
    B.   proceed more quickly than if carried out in organic solvent.
    C.   require an acid catalyst.
    D.   produce the more stable anhydride rather than the desired ester product.

56. Which of the following amino acids is achiral?

    A.   Glycine
    B.   Cysteine
    C.   Aspartic Acid
    D.   Threonine

57. Which of the following pairs of amino acids both possess a sulfur atom?

    A.   Cysteine and Valine
    B.   Methionine and Lysine
    C.   Cysteine and Lysine
    D.   Cysteine and Methionine

58. Many synthetic fabrics are very long polymers made from repeating amide linkages. One such synthetic polymer is nylon. Nylon-6 is made through the combination of hexanedioic acid and:

    A.   2-aminohexane.
    B.   hexanol.
    C.   hexanediamine.
    D.   hexyl hexanoate.

59. At the pH of the blood, phosphoric acid predominantly exists as:

    A. $H_2PO_4^-$ and PO_4^{3-}
    B. H_3PO_4 and $H_2PO_4^-$
    C. $H_2PO_4^-$ and HPO_4^{2-}
    D. HPO_4^{2-} and PO_4^{3-}

60. In both the Gabriel and Strecker synthesis:

    A.   amino acids are produced in small quantities as a by-product.
    B.   a racemic mixture of amino acids are produced.
    C.   only amino acids with basic side chains may be produced.
    D.   multiple base-catalyzed steps are carried out.

61. A scientist analyzes a molecule using IR spectroscopy. He will most directly gain useful information about:

   A. the C-H bonds present in the molecule.
   B. the optical rotation of the molecule.
   C. the level of deshielding of its protons.
   D. functional groups on the molecule.

62. Because molecular oxygen does not change its dipole moment due to rotation or vibration:

   A. it cannot be analyzed using mass spectroscopy.
   B. it cannot be analyzed using distillation.
   C. it functions as a powerful oxidizing agent.
   D. it cannot be analyzed using IR spectroscopy.

63. Which of the following lists elements all of which could be analyzed using NMR?

   A. ^1H, ^2H, ^{12}C
   B. ^1H, ^4He, ^{13}C
   C. ^1H, ^2H, ^{13}C
   D. ^1H, ^4He, ^4Be

64. In proton NMR, the coupling between hydrogen atoms that are three bonds away from each other:

   A. results in splitting of the signal.
   B. has no effect.
   C. creates a larger area under the curve representing the signal.
   D. shifts the signal to the left on the plot.

65. In UV-Vis spectroscopy, electrons move from:

   A. the highest occupied molecular orbital to the lowest unoccupied molecular orbital, which must have relatively far apart energy levels.
   B. the lowest occupied molecular orbital to the highest unoccupied molecular orbital, which must have relatively far apart energy levels.
   C. the highest occupied molecular orbital to the lowest unoccupied molecular orbital, which must have relatively close energy levels.
   D. the highest occupied molecular orbital to the highest unoccupied molecular orbital, which must have relatively close energy levels.

66. (R)-2-butanol and (S)-2-butanol will have:

   A. different IR spectra.
   B. different ^1H-NMR spectra.
   C. identical optical rotations.
   D. identical IR spectra.

67. Relative to the analogous primary alcohol, the ^1H-NMR spectrum of a carboxylic acid would include a hydrogen peak that is:

   A. deshielded and shifted to the left.
   B. deshielded and shifted to the right.
   C. shielded and shifted to the left.
   D. shielded and shifted to the right.

68. Substances with which of the following boiling points would most likely require fractional distillation to separate?

   A. 45°C and 51°C
   B. 45°C and 95°C
   C. 14°C and 114°C
   D. -4°C and 31°C

69. Extraction of $CH_3(CH_2)_8COOH$ from organic solvent would most effectively be accomplished with:

    A. $CH_3(CH_2)_8COO^-Na^+$.
    B. NaOH.
    C. HCl.
    D. toluene.

70. Substances with which of the following pairs of boiling points would most likely require vacuum distillation to be separated?

    A. $38°C$ and $45°C$
    B. $75°C$ and $115°C$
    C. $-31°C$ and $15°C$
    D. $212°C$ and $242°C$

71. Chromatography is carried out on a silica gel with ether as the mobile phase. Which substance would elute first?

    A. Substance A with an R_f value of 0.12
    B. Substance B with an R_f value of 0.22
    C. Substance C with an R_f value of 0.25
    D. Substance D with an R_f value of 0.42

72. When extracting an organic compound from aqueous solution, most effective separation would occur by using:

    A. one wash with 10 mL of organic solvent.
    B. two washes with 5 mL of organic solvent.
    C. four washes with 2.5 mL of organic solvent.
    D. four washes with 2.5 mL of basic solvent.

73. At the end of an experiment, an extraction is carried out with ethyl iodide ($\rho = 1.9$) and salt water ($\rho = 1.1$). The organic layer is:

    A. not present in this experiment.
    B. the layer on top.
    C. the layer on bottom.
    D. mixed between the two solvents.

74. A student finds that at the end of an experiment, she has a flask filled with silica grit, methylamine, benzene, and phenol. To separate these four substances, she should carry out:

    A. filtration, acidic extraction, and distillation.
    B. filtration, TLC, and HPLC.
    C. basic extraction with $NaHCO_3$ and filtration.
    D. filtration, basic extraction with $NaHCO_3$, and distillation.

75. The silica plate in TLC and the gas eluent in HPLC are, respectively:

    A. stationary phase, stationary phase.
    B. stationary phase, mobile phase.
    C. mobile phase, mobile phase.
    D. mobile phase, stationary phase.

76. Which of the following gives the correct electron configuration for Fe^{3+}?

    A. $1s^22s^22p^63s^23p^63d^5$
    B. $1s^22s^22p^63s^23p^64s^23d^3$
    C. $1s^22s^22p^63s^23p^34s^23d^6$
    D. $1s^22s^22p^63s^23p^64s^5$

77. Each of the following is a possible set of numbers to describe an electron EXCEPT:

    A. $n = 3, l = 2, m_l = 0, m_s = -1/2$
    B. $n = 4, l = 0, m_l = 0, m_s = +1/2$
    C. $n = 2, l = 1, m_l = -1, m_s = -1/2$
    D. $n = 2, l = 2, m_l = 1, m_s = +1/2$

78. The principal quantum number 3 can hold a maximum of:

    A. 2 electrons.
    B. 9 electrons.
    C. 18 electrons.
    D. 20 electrons.

79. Each of the following elements only has paired electrons in its ground state EXCEPT:

    A.   helium.
    B.   neon.
    C.   magnesium.
    D.   sodium.

80. An electron moves from an $n = 2$ state to an $n = 4$ state. This is most likely accompanied by:

    A.   emission of a photon.
    B.   absorption of a photon.
    C.   movement from a d-orbital to an s-orbital.
    D.   forming a positive ion.

81. Which of the following isotopes is the *least* abundant in the Earth's crust?

    A. ^{14}Si
    B. ^{28}Si
    C. ^{29}Si
    D. ^{30}Si

82. The Heisenberg uncertainty principle asserts that:

    A.   it is impossible to exactly know both the position and energy level of an electron at the same time.
    B.   it is impossible to exactly know both momentum and position of an electron at the same time.
    C.   no two electrons may occupy the same four quantum numbers on the same atom.
    D.   the enthalpy change associated with a reaction can be found by summing the enthalpy changes of any acceptable steps that sum to the overall net reaction.

83. A hydrogen atom would need to absorb a photon with the shortest wavelength if its electron were to move from:

    A. $n = 5$ to $n = 2$.
    B. $n = 2$ to $n = 6$.
    C. $n = 1$ to $n = 2$.
    D. $n = 2$ to $n = 0$.

84. The following electron configuration most directly violates:

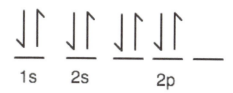

    A.   Hund's rule.
    B.   the Aufbau principle.
    C.   Heisenberg's Uncertainty principle.
    D.   the Right Hand Rule.

85. Oxygen and sulfur have similar chemical properties because they:

    A.   are in the same period.
    B.   have unfilled d-orbitals.
    C.   are in the same group.
    D.   are electronegative.

86. Sodium and potassium have very similar chemical properties but have different:

    A.   numbers of valence electrons.
    B.   sub-shells for their outermost electrons.
    C.   number of nucleons.
    D.   group.

87. Atomic radius increases with:
  I. increasing number of valence electrons for ions with the same nucleons.
  II. decreasing effective nuclear charge.
 III. increasing number of neutrons in the nucleus.

    A.   I only
    B.   II only
    C.   I and II only
    D.   II and III only

88. Which of the following correctly arranges electron affinity in increasing order?

    A. C < O < F
    B. F < Cl < Br
    C. Ca < K < Cs
    D. S < As < Sn

89. Silicon is a(n):

    A. metal.
    B. nonmetal.
    C. metalloid.
    D. halogen.

90. Going from left to right across the periodic table:

    A. electronegativity decreases.
    B. electron affinity decreases.
    C. atomic radius increases.
    D. atomic radius decreases.

91. Radiators designed to heat homes were typically made of coils of metal tubing. Metal was used because:

    A. it is malleable.
    B. it has good thermal conductivity.
    C. it has luster.
    D. it has a very high melting point.

92. The alkali earth metals:

    A. form divalent cations.
    B. form multiple different anions.
    C. are unique in having an atomic radius that decreases as you move down the group.
    D. make excellent oxidizing agents.

93. Complex ion formation is most often found with:

    A. alkali metals.
    B. transition metals.
    C. silicon.
    D. halogens.

94. The third period on the periodic table includes elements with how many valence electrons?

    A. 3
    B. 8
    C. An increasing number as atomic number increases
    D. The number cannot be determined according to the Heisenberg Uncertainty Principle

95. The carbon-carbon bond and the carbon-oxygen bond in ethanol are, respectively:

    A. covalent, non-polar covalent.
    B. covalent, ionic.
    C. covalent, polar covalent.
    D. polar covalent, covalent.

96. When a nitrogen atom forms bonds with hydrogen in an ammonium molecule, it has a formal charge of:

    A. -2.
    B. -1.
    C. 0.
    D. +1.

97. Which atom bears the negative formal charge in HSO_4^-?

    A. Hydrogen
    B. Sulfur
    C. Oxygen
    D. No atom as the negative charge is equally distributed among all six atoms in the molecule.

98. The resonance structure that makes up HCO_3^- includes which of the following as a major contributing structure?

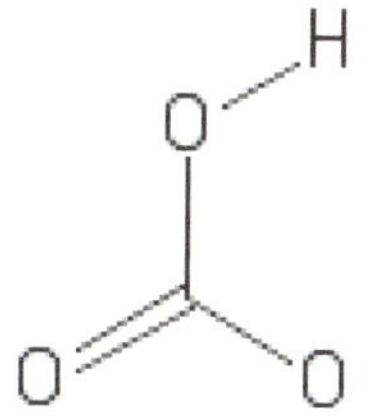

A)

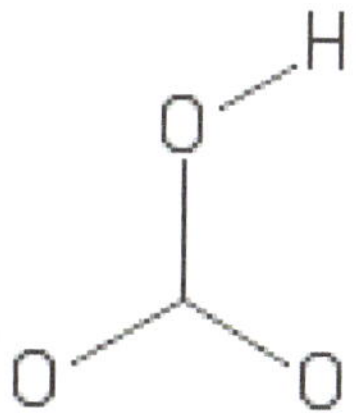

B)

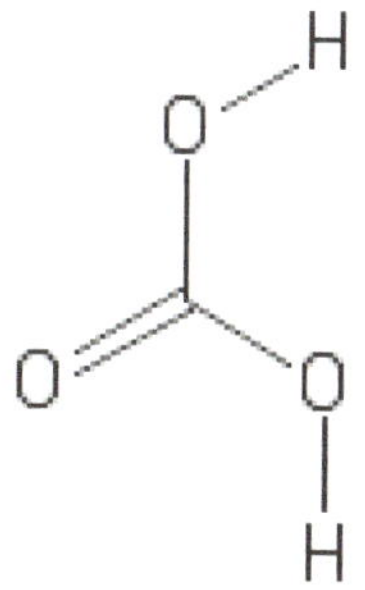

C)

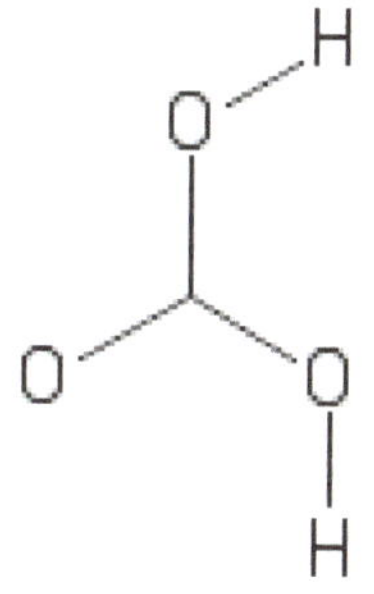

D)

99. Rank the following molecules in order of increasing boiling point:
   I. Propanal
   II. 1-Propanol
   III. NaCl

   A. III < II < I
   B. I < II < III
   C. III < I < II
   D. I < III < II

100. XeF_4 and CH_4 have the same number of atoms around the central atom yet XeF_4 shows square planar molecular geometry while methane does not. Why?

   A. Methane has tetrahedral geometry.
   B. Carbon has unfilled d-orbitals.
   C. Xenon is a noble gas.
   D. Xenon has lone pairs that orient themselves as far from each other as possible.

101. A carbon-chlorine bond is polar yet carbon tetrachloride is not. Why?

   A. Bond dipoles only exist between two atoms and are irrelevant to the formation of molecular dipole.
   B. The bond dipoles add as vectors and result in a net zero vector for the molecular dipole.
   C. Carbon tetrachloride has a very low boiling point given its molecular weight.
   D. The chloride atoms form intramolecular bridged intermediates preventing a molecular dipole from forming.

102. Hydrogen bonding is especially strong because:

   A. hydrogen is very electronegative, creating a strong attraction for the electrons on the F, O, or N with which it is hydrogen bonding.
   B. other intermolecular forces are limited as a function of Coulomb's law.
   C. the hydrogen atom is very small, allowing it get very close to the F, O, or N with which it is forming the hydrogen bond.
   D. it is central to the chemical nature of water and thereby to all biological systems on Earth.

103. When nitrogen in ammonia accepts a proton, it can be understood as acting as both a Lewis base and a Bronsted base when it forms:

    A.   an ionic bond with hydrogen.
    B.   a covalent bond with hydroxide.
    C.   a coordinate covalent bond with hydrogen.
    D.   an ionic bond with the cation salt of the acid.

104. Which of the following choices list atoms that can or always do violate the octet rule when forming stable compounds?

    A.   H, Be, S, Xe
    B.   H, Li, C, Au
    C.   C, N, F, Ne
    D.   He, B, O, K

105. The molecular weight for potassium chloride is closest to:

    A.   7.5 amu.
    B.   25 amu.
    C.   50 amu.
    D.   75 amu.

106. 147 grams of sulfuric acid would release approximately how many moles of protons?

    A.   1
    B.   2
    C.   3
    D.   4

107. The gram equivalent weight of hydrochloric acid is closest to:

    A.   1.
    B.   18.
    C.   36.
    D.   72.

108. The percent composition of carbon by mass for ethanol is closest to:

    A.   25%.
    B.   50%.
    C.   75%.
    D.   100%.

109. The reaction below can NOT be described as a:

$$H_2CO_3 + 2\,NaOH \rightarrow Na_2CO_3 + HOH$$

    A.   metathesis reaction.
    B.   neutralization.
    C.   double displacement reaction.
    D.   redox reaction.

110. The reaction below is a:
$$AgNO_3 + HCl \rightarrow HNO_3 + AgCl$$

    A.   metathesis reaction.
    B.   neutralization.
    C.   single displacement reaction.
    D.   redox reaction.

111. The number of reactants and products is typically the same in:

    A.   decomposition reactions.
    B.   synthesis reactions.
    C.   polymerization reactions.
    D.   double displacement reactions.

112. Galvanization helps protect steel with a zinc coating such that if the steel is exposed to the elements, the following reaction takes place instead of corrosion of steel:
$$2\,Zn + O_2 \rightarrow 2\,ZnO$$

This is a(n):

    A.   metathesis reaction.
    B.   neutralization.
    C.   double displacement reaction.
    D.   redox reaction.

113. A compound has the empirical formula CH_2O and the molar mass of 180 g/mole. The molecule's molecular formula is:

    A. CH_2O.
    B. $C_3H_6O_3$.
    C. $C_6H_{12}O_6$.
    D. $C_{10}H_{12}O_{10}$.

114. Consider the following hypothetical reaction:
$8 A_2 + BC_4 + 2 D \rightarrow D_2A_8 + 4 AC + BA_4$

A chemist mixes 20 moles of D with 8 moles of BC_4 and 60 moles of A_2. The limiting reagent is:

    A. A_2
    B. BC_4
    C. D
    D. Whichever product is formed the most quickly.

115. An experimenter determines a reaction to be second order. The reaction involves the combination of two reactants to form a single product. When she doubles the concentration of the first reactant, the reaction rate does not change. When she doubles the concentration of the second reactant, the reaction rate will:

    A. remain the same.
    B. double.
    C. quadruple.
    D. be cut in half.

116. A non-spontaneous reaction is one in which:

    A. the free energy of the products is higher than the reactants.
    B. the free energy of the reactants is higher than the products.
    C. heat is produced as a product.
    D. reactants which are gases are converted into products which are solids or liquids.

117. An experimenter determines that a reaction is third order. The reaction consists of two reactants forming two products. If the experimenter doubles the concentration of the first reactant:

    A. the reaction rate will remain unchanged.
    B. the reaction rate will double.
    C. any change in the reaction rate will depend on temperature.
    D. nothing can be concluded about the change in reaction rate without more information.

118. The liver's oxidation of ethanol to acetaldehyde functions approximately as a zero-order reaction. If a person drinks double the alcohol in the same period of time, the rate at which his body processes the alcohol will:

    A. be cut in half.
    B. remain unchanged.
    C. double.
    D. depend on the size of the liver and the history of alcohol consumption.

119. Each of the following will increase the rate of reaction EXCEPT:

    A. lowering the temperature of the reaction vessel containing a highly exothermic reaction.
    B. decreasing the pressure inside a reaction container in which liquid reactants are producing gaseous products.
    C. distilling off the product of an irreversible reaction as it occurs.
    D. adding more reactant to an aqueous reaction in which the ion product of the reactant is well below its K_{sp} value.

120. A battery is constructed with the following reaction:

Pb (s) + PbO_2 (s) + 2 H_2SO_4 (aq) → 2 $PbSO_4$ (s) + 2 H_2O

In an attempt to speed up the reaction, a researcher adds more Pb (s) to the reaction. This will:

    A.   speed up the reaction.
    B.   do nothing.
    C.   slow down the reaction.
    D.   push the Le Châtelier's equilibrium to the right.

121. Consider the following hypothetical reaction rate:

$R = k\ [C_6H_{12}O_6][O_2]^2$

Which of the following is true?

    A.   Doubling the concentration of O_2 will double the reaction rate.
    B.   The addition of compounds other than $C_6H_{12}O_6$ or O_2 will not affect the reaction rate.
    C.   The reaction is a third-order reaction with respect to oxygen.
    D.   This is a third-order reaction.

122. What is the reaction rate given the following experimental data?

Trial	[A]	[B_2]	Rate$_1$
1	2	1	2.4
2	4	1	4.8
3	6	2	28.8

    A. $R = k\ [A]^2[B_2]$
    B. $R = k\ [A][B_2]$
    C. $R = k\ [A][B_2]^2$
    D. $R = k\ [A]^2[B_2]^2$

123. A catalyst will alter a chemical reaction rate by:

    A.   being consumed in the course of the reaction.
    B.   being regenerated in the course of the reaction.
    C.   altering the free energy profile of the reaction to bring the energy state of the reactants to a higher level closer to the activation energy.
    D.   leaving the free energy state of the reactants and the products unchanged but lowering the energy difference between the reactants and the transition state.

124. A given set of reagents can produce two different products by two different pathways. If the reaction is carried out at room temperature for only a few minutes, what products will be observed?

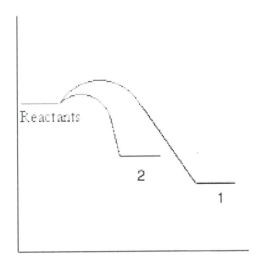

    A.   Predominantly product 1
    B.   Predominantly product 2
    C.   Equal concentrations of product 1 and 2
    D.   Unreacted reactants

125. Reactants are mixed and allowed to react overnight. The next morning the reaction vessel contains a mixture that is 88% products and 12% reactants. What can be said about this mixture?

    A. The reaction rate of the forward reaction is equal to the reaction rate of the reverse reaction.
    B. The reaction rate of the forward reaction is much higher than the reaction rate of the reverse reaction.
    C. This is an irreversible reaction.
    D. The ΔG for the forward reaction is negative whereas it's positive for the reverse reaction.

126. What is the equilibrium expression for this theoretical reaction:

A (s) + 3 B^- (aq) $\rightarrow$ AB (l) + B_2 (g)

    A. $[AB][B_2] / [A][B^-]^3$
    B. $[AB][B_2] / [B^-]^3$
    C. $[B_2] / [B^-]^3$
    D. $[AB][B_2] / B^-]^3$

127. Seltzer is simply H_2O with dissolved H_2CO_3. When a bottle of seltzer is opened, the taste changes as the seltzer reaches equilibrium with the atmosphere. Which of the following explains what is happening?

    A. As the seltzer warms up to room temperature, the increasing thermal energy in the liquid increases the pH.
    B. As the liquid of the seltzer is exposed to the atmosphere, N_2 dissolves into the seltzer because N_2 is by far the biggest component of the atmosphere.
    C. In response to the reduced pressure from opening the seltzer bottle, the H_2CO_3 is able to dissociate, lowering the pH and altering the taste.
    D. Opening the container reduces the pressure, allowing the H_2CO_3 to convert into CO_2 and H_2O, and the CO_2 escapes into the atmosphere.

128. A reaction is allowed to equilibrate overnight at it is found that the K_{eq} value is significantly less than 1. This means that:

    A. the reaction proceeded very slowly.
    B. the reaction vessel will contain equal concentrations of reactants and products.
    C. the reaction vessel will contain mostly products and very little reactants.
    D. the reaction vessel will contain mostly reactants and very little products.

129. A saturated solution of NaCl has some $CaCl_2$ added to it. This will:

    A. allow slightly more NaCl to dissolve.
    B. cause some NaCl to precipitate out of solution.
    C. raise the K_{sp}.
    D. lower the K_{sp}.

130. Given the following theoretical reaction, which of the following would decrease product formation?
AB_2 (g) + 2 C (g) $\rightarrow$ ABC_2 (g) + B (s)
ΔH = -53 kJ/mol

    A. Increased pressure
    B. Decreased temperature
    C. Increased [C]
    D. Increased [ABC_2]

131. Given the following theoretical reaction, which of the following would increase product formation?
AB_2 (g) + 2 C (g) $\rightarrow$ ABC_2 (g) + B (s)
ΔH = -53 kJ/mol

    A. Increased pressure
    B. Increased temperature
    C. Decreased [C]
    D. Increased [ABC_2]

132. Given the following theoretical reaction, which of the following would increase the concentration of $[AB_2]$?

$AB_2 (g) + 2 C (g) \rightarrow ABC_2 (g) + B (s)$

$\Delta H = -53 \text{ kJ/mol}$

    A. Increased pressure
    B. Decreased pressure
    C. Decreased temperature
    D. Increased [C]

133. A given substance has a K_b of 10^{-5}. Which of the following would most likely react with this substance?

    A. NH_3
    B. NaOH
    C. H_2CO_3
    D. $(CH_3)_3N$

134. Given that K_{eq} is 5×10^{-3} for the following reaction: $FeI (aq) + I_2 (g) \rightarrow FeI_3 (aq)$
Find the K_{eq} for this reaction:
$FeI_3 (aq) \rightarrow FeI (aq) + I_2 (g)$

    A. 2×10^{-4}
    B. 5×10^{-3}
    C. 2×10^2
    D. 5×10^3

135. In the pressure volume diagram below, the gas underwent cooling. The process depicted here could be:

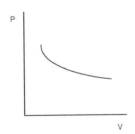

    A. isobaric.
    B. isovolumetric.
    C. isothermal.
    D. adiabatic.

136. A certain reaction is endothermic and has a ΔS value that is negative. This reaction is:

    A. always spontaneous.
    B. always non-spontaneous.
    C. spontaneous at low enough temperatures.
    D. spontaneous at high enough temperatures.

137. A certain reaction is exothermic and has a ΔS value that is negative. This reaction is:

    A. always spontaneous.
    B. always non-spontaneous.
    C. spontaneous at low enough temperatures.
    D. spontaneous at high enough temperatures.

138. A certain reaction is endothermic and has a ΔS value that is positive. This reaction is:

    A. always spontaneous.
    B. always non-spontaneous.
    C. spontaneous at low enough temperatures.
    D. spontaneous at high enough temperatures.

139. In the 1940's the army found it had a large surplus of sodium after World War II. To dispose of the sodium they dumped it in a remote lake. The process was filmed and the sodium can be seen spontaneously bursting into flame as it contacts the frigid water. This reaction has a K_{eq} that is:

    A. less than 0.
    B. less than 1.
    C. equal to 1.
    D. greater than 1.

140. The combustion of long straight-chain alkanes:

    A. has a ΔS value that is always positive.
    B. has a ΔS value that is always negative.
    C. releases more energy than corresponding molecules substituted with functional groups.
    D. proceeds quickly only at low temperature.

141. Given the following approximate bond energies (in kJ/mol) calculate the ΔH of the following reaction:

C – C	350
C – O	360
C – H	410
C – Cl	330
O – H	450
H – Cl	430

$CH_3CH_2Cl + H_2O \rightarrow CH_3CH_2OH + HCl$

    A.   - 790.
    B.   - 10.
    C.   + 10.
    D.   + 790.

142. Given the following approximate bond energies (in kJ/mol) calculate the ΔH of the following reaction:

C – C	350
C – O	360
C – H	410
C – Cl	330
O – H	450
H – Cl	430

$CH_3CH_2OH + HCl \rightarrow CH_3CH_2Cl + H_2O$

    A.   - 790.
    B.   - 10.
    C.   + 10.
    D.   + 790.

143. Given the following approximate bond energies (in kJ/mol) calculate the ΔH of the following reaction:

H – H	430 kJ/mol
C – O	360 kJ/mol
Cl – Cl	330 kJ/mol
C – Cl	330 kJ/mol
O – H	450 kJ/mol
H – Cl	430 kJ/mol

$HOCH_2CH_2OH + 4\ HCl \rightarrow CH_2ClCH_2Cl + 2\ H_2O + Cl_2 + H_2$

    A.   - 2320 kJ.
    B.   - 120 kJ.
    C.   + 120 kJ.
    D.   + 2440 kJ.

144. For a given compound, which of the following processes would have the largest positive ΔS?

    A.   freezing
    B.   condensation
    C.   evaporation
    D.   sublimation

145. A gas behaves most like an ideal gas under which of the following conditions?

    A.   high temperature, low pressure
    B.   high temperature, high pressure
    C.   low temperature, low pressure
    D.   low temperature, high pressure

146. An ideal gas is placed in a chamber of with flexible volume and kept at STP. 2 moles of gas are introduced into the chamber. The volume of the chamber is closest to:

    A.   11.2 L.
    B.   22.4 L.
    C.   44.8 L.
    D.   273 L.

147. An ideal gas with a molecular weight of 100 g/mole is kept at STP. It has a volume of 33.6 L. What is the approximate density of the gas in g/L?

    A.   3 g/L
    B.   4.5 g/L
    C.   22.4 g/L
    D.   3300 g/L

148. Helium and argon are kept in a sealed chamber. A pinhole opening is made in the chamber and the He and Ar are allowed to leak out. As time goes on:

    A.   the mole fraction of He and Ar will remain constant.
    B.   the mole fraction of both He and Ar will go down.
    C.   the mole fraction of He will increase and Ar will decrease.
    D.   the mole fraction of He will decrease and Ar will increase.

149. The kinetic molecular theory of gases and the ideal gas law assume each of the following EXCEPT:

    A.   the gas has a high temperature and a low pressure.
    B.   gas molecules have no size.
    C.   gas molecules experience no attraction to other gas molecules.
    D.   the collisions between the gas particles and the walls of the container are elastic.

150. Consider the following hypothetical reaction:
$2 A_2B_3 (s) \rightarrow 4 AB (g) + B_2 (g)$

If four moles of the reagent are placed into a two liter vacuum chamber and the reaction goes to completion, and the chamber is kept at 25°C what is the approximate pressure in the chamber?

    A.   12 atm
    B.   50 atm
    C.   120 atm
    D.   10,000 atm

151. According to the kinetic molecular theory of gases, if:

    A.   two gas samples are at the same absolute temperature, then the molecules of those two gases all have the same kinetic energy.
    B.   a gas particle collides with the walls of the container, it loses energy and transfers some energy to the container.
    C.   a gas's absolute temperature is raised to an infinitely high level, the gas will undergo nuclear fission as an elastic process.
    D.   two gas samples are at the same absolute temperature, then the samples have the average kinetic energy for their molecules.

152. The following distribution of particle velocities is observed in a sample containing three gases:

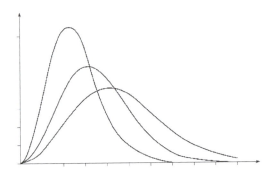

If the sample contains Ne, Ar, and Kr, which curve likely represents the Ne?

    A.   The far right curve
    B.   The far left curve
    C.   The middle curve
    D.   Cannot be determined without knowing the temperature

153. A chamber with a sample of three gases is kept at 298 K and 5 atm. The chamber contains 1 mole of O_2, 2 moles of N_2, and 5 moles of Ne. What is the partial pressure of the N_2?

    A.   0.625 atm
    B.   1.25 atm
    C.   3.125 atm
    D.   5 atm

154. A chamber with a sample of three gases is kept at 298 K and 5 atm. The chamber contains 1 mole of O_2, 2 moles of N_2, and 5 moles of Ne. What is the partial pressure of the Ne?

    A.   0.625 atm
    B.   1.25 atm
    C.   3.125 atm
    D.   5 atm

155. A sample of gas is subjected to a number of different experimental conditions. The experimenters are able to correctly predict whether the volume will increase or decrease for each of the following circumstances EXCEPT:

    A.   pressure is increased while temperature is also increased.
    B.   pressure is held constant while temperature is increased.
    C.   pressure is decreased while temperature is increased.
    D.   pressure is increased while temperature is decreased.

156. A 100 g water sample has 0.5 mole of a substance added. It is found that the boiling point increases to 107.68°C. The substance dissociates into how many particles in solution? (K_b = 0.512 K•kg/mol)

    A.   1
    B.   2
    C.   3
    D.   4

157. Considering only the three most common components, Earth's atmosphere could be considered:

    A.   a solution with a solvent of oxygen gas and solutes of nitrogen and carbon dioxide.
    B.   a colloidal suspension with oxygen molecules suspended in a nitrogen solvent.
    C.   a heterogeneous mixture with an uneven distribution of particulates suspended in a solvent of nitrogen and carbon dioxide.
    D.   a solution with a solvent of nitrogen gas and solutes of oxygen and water gas.

158. A chemist prepares a mixture of 10% v/v of ethanol dissolved in propanol. Will this mixture behave as an ideal solution?

    A.   Yes; ethanol and propanol are very structurally similar and so will obey Raoult's Law.
    B.   Yes; ethanol and propanol are very structurally similar and so will not obey Raoult's Law.
    C.   No; ethanol and propanol are very structurally similar and so will obey Raoult's Law.
    D.   No; ethanol and propanol are very structurally similar and so will not obey Raoult's Law.

159. The substance mixed into the water (discussed in question 156) would have which of the following effects on the melting point of the solution?

    A.   Melting point would increase due to the substance's enhancing the formation of a solid water lattice.
    B.   Melting point would decrease due to the substance's interfering with the formation of a solid water lattice.
    C.   Melting point would increase due to the substance's interfering with the formation of a solid water lattice.
    D.   Melting point would decrease due to the substance's enhancing the formation of a solid water lattice.

160. To get NaCl to dissolve into water, the Na^+ and Cl^- ions must be separated and then the H_2O molecules must be separated from each other to make room for the ions. The Na^+ and Cl^- ions can then interact with the water molecules. In this process:

    A. the first two steps are endothermic but the final step is exothermic resulting in an overall unfavorable reaction.

    B. each step is individually an unfavorable process but the overall process increases entropy, resulting in an unfavorable but irreversible process.

    C. the first two steps are endothermic but the final step is exothermic resulting in an overall favorable reaction.

    D. ΔG is negative as is ΔS.

161. When mixed with a basic solution, zinc can form a metal hydroxide, $Zn(OH)_2$ and then form a soluble complex ion, $Zn(OH)_3^-$. How would the complex ion formation affect the solubility in a basic solution?

    A. Decrease solubility because metal hydroxides themselves are generally insoluble but the complex ion formation allows for solubility.

    B. Decrease solubility because metal hydroxides themselves are generally soluble but the complex ion formation creates an insoluble complex.

    C. Increase solubility because metal hydroxides themselves are generally insoluble but the complex ion formation allows for solubility.

    D. Increase solubility because metal hydroxides themselves are generally soluble but the complex ion formation allows for solubility.

162. To make a simple sugar, a cook dissolves two cups of sugar in one cup of hot water at 80°C. What is the approximate percent composition by mass of sucrose in the resulting syrup solution? (note: 1 cup = 240 mL; density of water at 80°C = 0.98 g/mL; density of sucrose = 1.6 g/mL)

    A. 25%

    B. 50%

    C. 75%

    D. 100%

163. Which of the following solutions would display non-ideal behavior with a lower vapor pressure than predicted by Raoult's Law?

    A. Benzene and water

    B. Ethanol and methanol

    C. Dodecane and ammonia

    D. Nitric acid and water

164. The ΔH_{soln} of dissolving $Ca(Cl)_2$ in water is positive, indicating an unfavorable reaction, yet $Ca(Cl)_2$ will spontaneously dissolve in water. This is because:

    A. the calcium chloride is a highly organized salt and dissolving it in water creates a large enough increase in entropy to overcome the positive ΔG.

    B. dissolution reactions are determined by the relative values of the ion product and the K_{sp} rather than the sign of the ΔG.

    C. the reaction will become colder due to the positive ΔH indicating that the solution will experience melting point elevation.

    D. the ΔS is positive and large enough to overcome the unfavorable change in enthalpy.

165. A one liter solution of water has 0.5 mole of each of the following substances dissolved in it. Which of the following will result in the biggest decrease in vapor pressure?

    A. Glucose

    B. Glycine

    C. Sodium chloride

    D. Sodium sulfate

166. Consider the following hypothetical reaction:

AB_2 (s) → A^{2+} (aq) + 2 B^- (aq)

$K_{sp} = 8 \times 10^{-9}$

What would the molar solubility of AB_2 be in 0.01M solution of B^-?

    A. 2.7×10^{-5}
    B. 8×10^{-5}
    C. 1.2×10^{-3}
    D. 6.4×10^{9}

167. Which of the following is a Brønsted base?

    A. HNO_2
    B. NH_3
    C. HF
    D. $CH_3CH_2CH_3$

168. A solution of 2 L of water with 5×10^{-3} moles of HCl dissolved in it would have a pH that is approximately:

    A.   1.5.
    B.   2.5.
    C.   3.5.
    D.   4.5.

169. The molecular formula for chlorous acid is:

    A. $HClO_2$.
    B. $HClO_3$.
    C. $HClO_4$.
    D. ClO_2^-.

170. The molecular formula for perchloric acid is:

    A. $HClO_2$.
    B. $HClO_3$.
    C. $HClO_4$.
    D. ClO_3^-.

171. Which of the following is the strongest base?

    A. NH_3
    B. CH_3NH_2
    C. $(CH_3)_2NH$
    D. HSO_4^-

172. Each of the following is a strong acid EXCEPT:

    A.   HCl.
    B.   HF.
    C. HNO_3.
    D. H_2SO_4.

173. A buffer solution has its strongest buffering capacity when the pH of the solution is approximately equal to:

    A.   7.
    B.   the pK_a of the acid used in the titration.
    C.   the pK_b of the base used in the titration.
    D.   the pK_a of the buffer molecule.

174. In the blood plasma, the carbonic acid buffer system:

    A.   primarily acts to slow down the reaction between acids and bases in the blood.
    B.   serves to resist changes in pH when acid is added as a result of metabolism.
    C.   catalyzes the reaction between acid and base to help maintain a neutral pH.
    D.   prevents the pH from fluctuating from 7.00.

175. Consider the following titration curve:

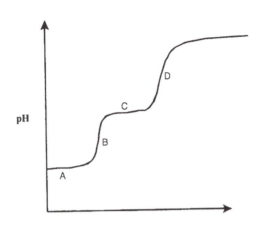

The second equivalence point is indicated by:

A. A.
B. B.
C. C.
D. D.

176. Consider the following titration curve:

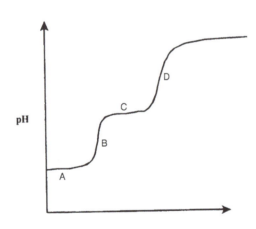

The point at which the pH is approximately equal to the pK_{a2} is indicated at point:

A. A.
B. B.
C. C.
D. D.

177. A 4.5 N solution of H_2SO_4 can be made by adding 2L of water to how many moles of H_2SO_4?

A. 2.25
B. 4.5
C. 9
D. 18

178. Consider the following hypothetical reaction:
$4\ HCl + 2\ CH_3CH_2OH \rightarrow 2\ H_2 + 2\ Cl_2 + H_2O_2 + CH_3CH_2CH_2CH_3$

In this reaction:

A. at least one hydrogen atom is being reduced.
B. the oxygen in the product has the same oxidation number as the oxygen in water.
C. the chlorine, as a halogen, has an oxidation number of -1 in both products and reactants.
D. the hydrocarbons are being oxidized.

179. Consider the following hypothetical reaction:
$4\ HCl + 2\ CH_3CH_2OH \rightarrow 2\ H_2 + 2\ Cl_2 + H_2O_2 + CH_3CH_2CH_2CH_3$

In this reaction:

A. hydrogen, as a relatively electropositive element, always has an oxidation number of +1.
B. at least one chlorine atom is being oxidized.
C. the chlorine atoms are oxidizing agents.
D. the hydrocarbons are being oxidized.

180. Consider the following hypothetical reaction:
$4 \, HCl + 2 \, CH_3CH_2OH \rightarrow 2 \, H_2 + 2 \, Cl_2 + H_2O_2 + CH_3CH_2CH_2CH_3$

In this reaction:

A. the chlorine atoms are oxidizing agents.
B. the oxygen atoms are in a product molecule that is more stable that their reactant molecule.
C. at least one oxygen atom is acting as a reducing agent.
D. hydrogen, as a relatively electropositive element, always has an oxidation number of +1.

181. Consider the following hypothetical reaction:
$4 \, HCl + 2 \, CH_3CH_2OH \rightarrow 2 \, H_2 + 2 \, Cl_2 + H_2O_2 + CH_3CH_2CH_2CH_3$

In this reaction:

A. the oxygen atoms are in a product molecule that is more stable that their reactant molecule.
B. the hydrocarbons are being oxidized.
C. the hydrochloric acid is acting as an Arrhenius base.
D. at least one carbon atom is acting as an oxidizing agent.

182. What is the oxidation number of boron in sodium borohydride?

A. -4
B. 0
C. +3
D. +4

183. Given the following electronic configurations, which would act as reducing agents?
I. $1s^2 2s^2 2p^6 3s^2 3p^6 4s^1$
II. $1s^2 2s^2 2p^6 3s^2 3p^5$
III. $1s^2 2s^2 2p^6 3s^2 3p^6$

A. I only
B. II only
C. I and II only
D. I and III only

184. Given the following electronic configurations, which would be very likely to be reduced?
I. $1s^2 2s^2 2p^6 3s^2 3p^6 4s^1$
II. $1s^2 2s^2 2p^6 3s^2 3p^5$
III. $1s^2 2s^2 2p^6 3s^2 3p^6$

A. I only
B. II only
C. I and II only
D. I and III only

185. Given a complex ion made up of many different atoms including the following, which atom would have its oxidation number determined last?

A. F
B. Na
C. O
D. Fe

186. A student carried out a series of reactions in which formaldehyde is converted to formic acid and then to methanol. The oxidation number of the carbon:

A. increases then decreases.
B. increases.
C. decreases.
D. decreases then increases.

187. A hypothetical metal, X, can form a number of different metal oxides. In which of the following compounds would the metal act as the strongest Lewis acid?

A. X_2O
B. XO
C. XO_2
D. X_2O_5

188. Dissolving Cl_2 in water may give the following reaction:
$H_2O + Cl_2 \rightarrow H^+ + Cl^- + ClOH$

This reaction is best described as a(n):

A. metathesis reaction.
B. decomposition reaction.
C. disproportionation reaction.
D. oxidation reaction.

189. Upon exposure to O_2 in the environment, many metals will corrode. One way to prevent steel from corroding is to coat it with zinc. Even if the zinc flakes off and exposes the underlying steel (which is mostly iron), the zinc will have a redox reaction with environmental oxygen before the iron will. This is because:

    A.   zinc has a more negative oxidation potential than iron, making it more favorable for zinc to accept electrons from O_2.

    B.   zinc has a more negative oxidation potential than iron, making it more favorable for zinc to donate electrons to O_2.

    C.   zinc has a more positive oxidation potential than iron, making it more favorable for zinc to accept electrons from O_2.

    D.   zinc has a more positive oxidation potential than iron, making it more favorable for zinc to donate electrons to O_2.

190. Consider the following list of reduction potentials and the following reaction:

$Mg^{2+} + 2e^- \rightarrow Mg$ $E° = -2.37$ V
$Zn^{2+} + 2e^- \rightarrow Zn$ $E° = -0.76$ V
$Cu^{2+} + 2e^- \rightarrow Cu$ $E° = +0.34$ V
$Ag^+ + e^- \rightarrow Ag$ $E° = +0.80$ V

$2 Ag^+ + Mg \rightarrow Ag + Mg^{2+}$

The reaction voltage is:

    A.   -3.97 V.
    B.   -3.17 V.
    C.   +3.17 V.
    D.   +3.97 V.

191. Consider the following list of reduction potentials and the following reaction:

$Mg^{2+} + 2e^- \rightarrow Mg$ $E° = -2.37$ V
$Zn^{2+} + 2e^- \rightarrow Zn$ $E° = -0.76$ V
$Cu^{2+} + 2e^- \rightarrow Cu$ $E° = +0.34$ V
$Ag^+ + e^- \rightarrow Ag$ $E° = +0.80$ V

$Cu + Zn^{2+} \rightarrow Zn + Cu^{2+}$

The reaction voltage is:

    A.   -1.1 V.
    B.   -0.42 V.
    C.   +0.42 V.
    D.   +1.1 V.

192. Consider the following list of reduction potentials and the following reaction:

$Mg^{2+} + 2e^- \rightarrow Mg$ $E° = -2.37$ V
$Zn^{2+} + 2e^- \rightarrow Zn$ $E° = -0.76$ V
$Cu^{2+} + 2e^- \rightarrow Cu$ $E° = +0.34$ V
$Ag^+ + e^- \rightarrow Ag$ $E° = +0.80$ V

$2 Ag^+ + Cu \rightarrow Ag + Cu^{2+}$

The reaction voltage is:

    A.   -1.26 V.
    B.   -0.46 V.
    C.   +0.46 V.
    D.   +1.26 V.

193. Consider the following list of reduction potentials:

$Mg^{2+} + 2e^- \rightarrow Mg$ $E° = -2.37$ V
$Zn^{2+} + 2e^- \rightarrow Zn$ $E° = -0.76$ V
$Cu^{2+} + 2e^- \rightarrow Cu$ $E° = +0.34$ V
$Ag^+ + e^- \rightarrow Ag$ $E° = +0.80$ V

Using only these four metals, to construct a battery with the maximum possible voltage, one should use a(n):

    A.   silver anode and magnesium cathode.
    B.   magnesium anode and silver cathode.
    C.   silver anode and copper anode.
    D.   copper anode and silver cathode.

194. Consider the following list of reduction potentials:

$Mg^{2+} + 2e^- \rightarrow Mg$ $E° = -2.37$ V

$Zn^{2+} + 2e^- \rightarrow Zn$ $E° = -0.76$ V

$Cu^{2+} + 2e^- \rightarrow Cu$ $E° = +0.34$ V

$Ag^+ + e^- \rightarrow Ag$ $E° = +0.80$ V

A student constructs a battery using a zinc cathode. To create a galvanic cell, he could use which of the following as the anode:

    A.   Mg.
    B.   Cu.
    C.   Ag.
    D.   Cu or Ag.

195. Which of the following is always true of both galvanic and electrolytic cells?

I.   Cations migrate to the cathode.
II.   The anode is the positive electrode.
III.   Current flows from cathode to anode.

    A.   I only
    B.   II and III only
    C.   I and III only
    D.   I, II, and III

196. A student wishes to double the voltage of a galvanic cell he has constructed. To do so, he replaces the anode and cathode with electrodes that are twice as big. Will this work?

    A.   Yes; voltage of a galvanic cell is determined by surface area, distance between the electrodes, and the permittivity of free space.
    B.   Yes; with twice as much space to react, the redox reactions at both electrodes can proceed at twice the speed.
    C.   No; doubling the electrode size can double the value of ΔG but will have no effect on voltage.
    D.   No; the voltage will remain the same but the current will double.

197. In an electrolytic cell:

    A.   cations migrate to the anode.
    B. ΔG is always positive.
    C.   current flows to the cathode.
    D.   electrons flow to the anode.

198. In a galvanic cell:

    A.   the anode is the negative electrode.
    B.   current flows to the cathode.
    C.   anions migrate to the cathode.
    D. ΔG is always positive.

199. In an electrochemical cell, the ΔG for the reaction is found to be +300 kJ/mole. The reaction involves the transfer of two electrons. The voltage of this cell is: (note: use 100,000 C/mole for Faraday's constant)

    A. -1.5×10^{-4} V.
    B. -1.5 V.
    C. $+1.5$ V.
    D. $+150,000$ V.

200. An atom is:

    A.   the smallest possible unit of matter.
    B.   the smallest unit that defines the chemical elements.
    C.   the smallest indivisible portion of matter.
    D.   the smallest unit that includes nucleons.

SOLUTIONS

Chemistry and Organic Chemistry

PROBLEMS

CHAPTER 2 SOLUTIONS

1. The answer is D. This question tests your understanding of the concept of mole. The student is preparing a solution using calcium hydroxide. The formula of calcium hydroxide is $Ca(OH)_2$. The formula weight of calcium hydroxide is 74.1 grams/mole. Here, the student added two moles of it. So the answer is 74.1 x 2 = 148.2 g.

2. The answer is D. The sample weighs 102 g. The molecular weight of NaCl is 58 g/mole. So the number of moles of NaCl present is roughly 1.75. Remember that 1 mole contains Avogadro's number of particles. Since 1.75 moles of NaCl is present, there are 1.75 x 6.0 x 10^{23} molecules of NaCl. Are we done at this point? No! The question asks for the total number of ions present in the sample. Since each sodium chloride molecule is composed of 2 ions, the total number of atoms in this sample equals 2 x 1.75 x 6.0 x 10^{23} = 21 x 10^{23}.

3. The answer is B. Gas discharge tubes are vacuum tubes with electrodes connected to very high voltages. Cathode rays are emitted from the cathode of the tube. A cathode ray consists of a beam of electrons. Since electrons are negatively charged, cathode rays will bend away from a negatively charged plate.

4. The answer is D. This question asks for a true statement from the choices. Let's look at each of those choices. Choice A is incorrect, because neutrons and electrons do not have the same mass. Choice B claims that the mass of a neutron is less than that of an electron. That is not true either. Protons are positive and neutrons are neutral. They cannot together make the nucleus neutral. In fact, the nucleus is positively charged, not electrically neutral. So Choice C is wrong. The last choice makes perfect sense. A proton is more massive than an electron.

5. The answer is B. The actual formula of butane is C_4H_{10}. But the question is not about butane's actual formula. The question asks for the empirical formula of butane. Empirical formula is the most simplified ratio of the actual formula. So the correct answer is C_2H_5.

6. The answer is C. The question is simply testing your understanding of a definition. The mass of a substance in one mole of it is numerically equal to its molecular weight.

7. The answer is A. Density is equal to mass per volume. Furthermore, the mass is equal to the product of the number of moles and molar mass. Equating these two equations we can get the answer. Using the letter notations given in the question, the expression of volume is given by Choice A.

8. The answer is D. The formula of sulfur dioxide is SO_2. The formula weight of SO_2 is 64 g/mole. This sample of SO_2 contains 1.5 moles of it. If we calculate the percentage mass of the oxygen, we can see that the oxygen's mass contribution is 50% in SO_2. So regardless of the amount of SO_2 present, half of its mass is due to the presence of oxygen and the other half is due to the presence of sulfur. Here we have 96 g of SO_2. Now, one half of 96 g gives 48 g.

9. The answer is A. The formula of carbon tetrachloride is CCl_4. The formula weight of CCl_4 is 154 g/mole. The percentage composition of Cl can be calculated as follows:

$$\% \text{ chlorine} = \text{mass chlorine} / \text{mass } CCl_4 \text{ x } 100\% = 142/154 \text{ x } 100\% = 92\%$$

10. The answer is C. In the question, the percentage compositions of nitrogen and oxygen are given. With that information, we have to find the formula of that compound. Just as discussed in our review, assume that we have 100 grams of this compound. If there are 100 grams, logically it should contain 63.6 grams of nitrogen and 36.4 grams of oxygen.

Step 1

$$\text{\# of moles of nitrogen} = 63.6/14 \approx 4.5 \text{ moles of nitrogen}$$
$$\text{\# of moles of oxygen} = 36.4/16 \approx 2.275 \text{ moles of oxygen}$$

Step 2

Divide every number of moles with the smallest number of moles calculated in Step 1. Here the smaller one is 2.275. Divide both mole numbers by 2.275. This will give you the simplest ratio between them.

$$\text{Nitrogen} \quad 4.5/2.275 \approx 2 \qquad \text{Oxygen} \quad 2.275/2.275 \approx 1$$

Since the ratio of nitrogen to oxygen is 2:1, the compound is N_2O.

11. The answer is B. Reaction 2 is a typical example of a combustion reaction.

12. The answer is C.

$$2C_2H_6 \; + \; 7O_2 \; \longrightarrow \; 4CO_2 \; + \; 6H_2O$$

Reaction 2

According to Reaction 2, two moles of ethane will react with 7 moles of oxygen to form 4 moles of carbon dioxide and 6 moles of water. In the question, it is given that 54 g of water was formed. This corresponds to 3 moles of water. From the equation, we can say that 1 mole of ethane must have reacted to form 3 moles of water. We can also say that 3.5 moles of oxygen must have reacted in the formation of 3 moles of water. The last step is the conversion of moles to grams. The corresponding quantities in grams are 30 g of ethane and 112 g of oxygen.

13. The answer is B. From the question, we can say that the empirical formula of dextrose is CH_2O. The molecular weight of dextrose is also given. Let's first calculate the weight of the empirical formula. Maybe the empirical formula represents the actual formula. The weight of the empirical formula is 30 g/mole. But the question says it is 180 g/mole. In this case, the molecular formula is not the same as the empirical formula. By dividing the actual weight by the empirical weight, we will get the coefficient with which we have to multiply the empirical formula to get the actual formula. The coefficient is $180/30 = 6$. So the molecular formula is $C_6H_{12}O_6$.

14. The answer is C. The formula of methane is CH_4. The molecular weight is 16 g/mole. We have 40 g of methane. That means we have 2.5 moles of methane. So the number of hydrogen atoms can be calculated.

$$6.0 \times 10^{23} \times 2.5 \text{ moles} \times 4 \text{ hydrogen atoms/mole} = 6.0 \times 10^{24} \text{ atoms}$$

CHAPTER 3 SOLUTIONS

1. The answer is A. The correct order of filling from $3s$ onward is $3s$, $3p$, $4s$, $3d$, and $4p$. For the MCAT, you must know the order of filling of subshells.

2. The answer is D. Inert gases (noble gases) have the completed outermost s and p subshells. Helium is an exception to this.

3. The answer is D. The atomic number of Kr (krypton) is 36. After the representation of Kr, how many electrons do we have? There are 14 more electrons. That adds up to an atomic number of 50. The atomic number 50 corresponds to the element Sn.

4. The correct answer is B. The maximum number of electrons that can occupy the principal energy level is calculated using the formula $2n^2$.

5. The answer is C. The statement "no two electrons of an atom can have the same set of four quantum numbers" is the Pauli exclusion principle.

6. The answer is C. The only correct statement in the set of choices is "the $5d$ subshell has higher energy than the $6s$ subshell." All other choices are wrong.

7. The answer is D. The question asks us to pick the species that is not isoelectronic (same number of electrons) with the noble gases. In order to solve this problem, you have to find the number of electrons present in them, and if it matches with the number of electrons in any of the noble gases, you can eliminate that choice. All the ions match with any of the noble gas in terms of the number of electrons, except Mg^+.

8. The answer is D. The nitrogen atom has a total of 7 electrons. The principal quantum number could be 1 or 2. With that alone, we cannot rule out any of the choices. The next quantum number given is the azimuthal quantum number, also known as the angular momentum quantum number. The angular momentum quantum number can have values from 0 to $n-1$, where n represents the principal quantum number. Since 2 denotes the maximum n value, we cannot rule out any of the choices yet. Look at the next quantum number, which is the magnetic quantum number. The magnetic quantum number can have values from $-l$ to $+l$, where l represents angular momentum quantum number. So the magnetic quantum number cannot be $+2$ for nitrogen.

9. The answer is A. This question tests your ability to recognize a given electronic configuration. The fastest way to approach this type of question is to look at the root element given. The atomic number of argon is 18. We can count 14 more electrons in the given configuration to get a total of 32 electrons. The atomic number 32 is that of germanium (Ge).

10. The answer is B. Osmium, silver, and radium can have the $4d$ subshell. Copper belongs to the 4th period and therefore cannot have a $4d$ subshell. All the other elements listed belong to the periods 5, 6 and 7.

CHAPTER 4 SOLUTIONS

1. The answer is B. Sulfur belongs to Group VIA (the representative elements). The inner transition elements are the group of elements that are in the two rows below the main section of the periodic table. The transition elements range from IB through VIIB including the collective group of elements under Group VIII (not the zero group). Choices A and B are ruled out. Sulfur is not classified as a metal. This rules out Choice D.

2. The answer is C. The Group IA metals are collectively called the alkali metals. The Group IIA metals are the alkaline earth metals. Among the choices, only strontium belongs to this group.

3. The answer is D. Electronegativity increases from left to right along the rows. For this question let's rephrase this trend. Electronegativity decreases from right to left along the columns, and from top to bottom.

4. The answer is B. The *f* block contains the inner-transition elements. The only element that is listed among the choices that is an inner-transition element is uranium.

5. The answer is C. Oxygen, nitrogen, and chlorine are diatomic gases. Neon is a noble gas (zero group element) which is stable on its own.

6. The answer is D. This question tests your knowledge of a periodic trend. Here, the trend of atomic radius is asked. Along a period as the atomic number increases, the atomic radius decreases. Down a group, the atomic radius increases.

7. The answer is A. This question is similar to the previous one. It is again just a matter of comparing the size of the atoms according to the periodic trend of the atomic radius.

8. The answer is D. All the trends listed as choices are wrong. Along a period from left to right, the atomic radius decreases. So Choice A is incorrect. Along a period from left to right, the ionization energy increases. This rules out Choice B. The electronegativity of elements decreases from right to left along a period. Since Choice C contradicts this, it is incorrect.

9. The answer is D. HF is a weak acid and all the other choices are strong acids. This rules out Choice A. Among the other choices, HI is the strongest acid because it can give off protons more easily than any of the other acids listed. The order of acidity is HI > HBr > HCl.

10. The answer is B. The given configuration is that of Group IVA (carbon family).

CHAPTER 5 SOLUTIONS

1. The answer is A. The central atom of the structure is sulfur. So draw the skeletal (structural) framework. In this structure, sulfur doesn't have the octet. So the next move is to introduce a double bond.

2. The answer is D. Let us look at the choices one by one. The water molecule is a bent molecule. So there is good reason to believe that it has a net nonzero dipole moment. In HCl, the hydrogen-chlorine bond is a polar bond, and thus there is clearly a separation of charge. This means it has a dipole moment. Oxygen is more electronegative than carbon. This creates a charge separation in the CO molecule. Thus the oxygen has a partial negative charge. So CO is a good candidate, having a net nonzero dipole moment. The CH_4 molecule has a tetrahedral structure and the small individual dipoles cancel out. So the net dipole of methane is zero.

3. The answer is B. The electronegativity difference between the nitrogen and the oxygen in NO_2 is not enough to cause an ionic interaction. Hence, it is not an ionic bond. The correct answer is covalent bond, because the bond is formed by the sharing of electrons between the nitrogen and the oxygen.

4. The answer is A. Ammonia (NH_3) and boron trifluoride (BF_3) can undergo a special type of covalent bonding, coordinate covalent bond. Even though this is a covalent bond, the electrons for the bond formation are supplied by one of the partners involved in the bonding. Boron has only three electrons in its outermost shell and they are already involved in the formation of the BF_3 molecule itself. There are no more electrons available from boron. But that is not the case with the nitrogen atom in NH_3. Two lone electrons are available from the nitrogen in NH_3 which make this bond formation possible.

5. The answer is A. To answer this question, we have to use our intuition. We do not have any specific data on any of the compounds listed as choices. But we can do an intelligent elimination. Choices B and D have the same zero dipole moment. Now it is just a matter of deciding which one of the remaining choices (A and C) is the answer. The electronegativity of fluorine is higher than that of bromine. So HF has the highest dipole moment.

6. The answer is B. BCl_3 can be drawn as shown below. The geometry is trigonal planar.

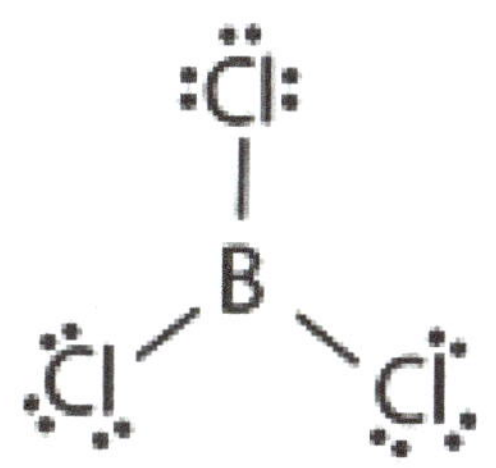

Boron trichloride

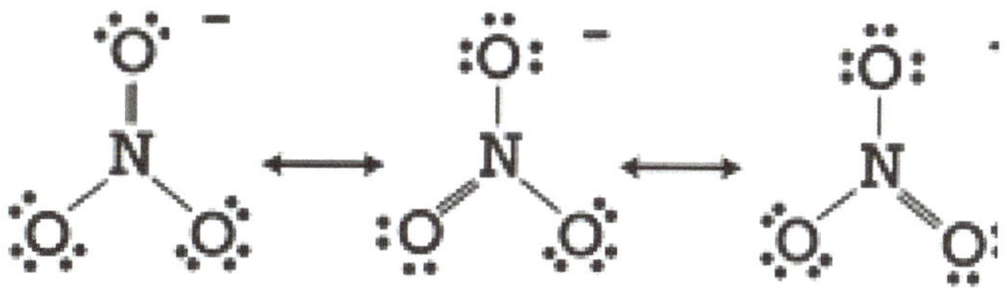

Nitrate resonance

7. The answer is D. If you draw the electron-dot structure of the CCl_4 molecule, you can see that there are four electron pairs around the central carbon atom. All these electrons form four carbon-chlorine bonds which make the molecular geometry - tetrahedral.

8. The answer is A. The Lewis structure of the nitrate ion is shown above . By analyzing the Lewis structure, the best prediction is that the nitrate ion is trigonal planar.

9. The answer is C. SF_6 has 6 equally repelling substituents surrounding the central atom. This results in an octahedral geometry.

10. The answer is D. All the statements (I, II, III, and IV) are correct. Let's see why this is the case. All the individual bonds in both compounds are dipoles. This makes items I and II correct. The question says that both molecules are tetrahedral. Hence, these individual bond dipoles cancel out to give a net zero dipole.

11. The answer is C. An ionic bond is formed mainly when there is a noticeable electronegativity difference between the atoms. Usually ionic bonds have the highest electronegativity difference. Choice A is incorrect. Covalently bonded atoms have lesser electronegativity difference. Among Choices B and C, nonpolar covalent bonds obviously have the least electronegativity difference. So our answer is C. Choice D is not true in this case. We do not need any more data to predict this general trend.

12. The answer is C. For Compound A, we should compare the atoms involved in the bond in question. Chlorine is more electronegative than boron. This rules out Choices B and D. For Compound B, the bond dipole should be directed toward the carbon atom. This rules out Choices A and D. So the only choice which has not been ruled out is C.

13. The answer is D. The question is not asking for the molecular geometry of water. It is actually asking for the electronic orientation or electronic geometry of water which is tetrahedral. The four electron pairs (two bonded pairs and two lone pairs) of the water molecule result in a tetrahedral geometry. Moreover, Choices A and B are essentially the same. If one is not correct, the other cannot be correct either.

CHAPTER 6 SOLUTIONS

1. The answer is D. This question tests your understanding of the general classification of reactions. The reaction is clearly not a combustion reaction. Combustion reactions occur in the presence of oxygen and involve release of heat. There is no indication of that in the given reaction. You might be tempted to select Choice C since the given reaction is a replacement reaction, but double-replacement reaction best describes the given reaction. In the reaction, the iodine is replaced with the chlorine, and the chlorine is replaced with the iodine.

2. The answer is C. Choices A, B, and D are all acid-base reactions, which when combined in equivalents, result in neutralization reactions . Choice C is the formation of a base $Al(OH)_3$, and not a neutralization reaction.

3. The answer is B. Let's start balancing the equation from the sulfate point of view. You have 3 sulfate groups in aluminum sulfate. It has to come from the sulfuric acid. So the coefficient is 3 for the sulfuric acid. Since there are 2 aluminums in aluminum sulfate, we can assign a coefficient of 2 to the aluminum hydroxide. The rest of the hydrogens and oxygens can be balanced with water.

The balanced equation should look like this:

$$3\ H_2SO_4 + 2\ Al(OH)_3 \longrightarrow 6\ H_2O + Al_2(SO_4)_3$$

4. The answer is B. First, we have to check whether the given reaction is balanced. Without the balanced equation, the calculations will be incorrect. As a matter of fact, the given reaction is not balanced. The balanced equation is this:

$$2\ NaCl + H_2SO_4 \longrightarrow Na_2SO_4 + 2\ HCl$$

Now we can work out our magic calculations. The question specifies the grams of HCl synthesized. The 73 grams converted to moles should give 2 moles. According to the equation, 2 moles of NaCl are required to synthesize two moles of HCl. All you have to do now is to convert moles to grams. The correct value is 117 grams of NaCl.

5. The answer is D. This is a straightforward definition-type question. The ions that are present in the solution sometimes do not actually participate in the reaction. By writing the complete ionic equation of such a reaction, we can see that the spectator ions on both sides of the equation are in the same state or form. We can cancel them out and get the net equation of the reaction. Spectator ions are not usually depicted in the net ionic equation.

6. The answer is D. This is also a definition-type question. Amphoteric substances can exhibit both acidic and basic properties depending on the environment that they are subjected to.

7. The answer is D. The reaction mentioned in this question is the rusting of iron. The balanced reaction should look like this:

$$4\,Fe + 3\,O_2 \longrightarrow 2\,Fe_2O_3$$

8. The answer is D. The question tests your understanding of the concept of mole. In Choice A, we have 32 g of O_2 which corresponds to 1 mole of oxygen, and 32 g of SO_2 which corresponds to half a mole. Choice A is not correct. In Choice B, we have 49 g of NO_2 which corresponds to a little more than 1 mole, and 40 g of NaOH which corresponds to 1 mole. So this may be our answer. Choice C is not correct, because we have 20 g of HF which is 1 mol, and 36 g of water which is 2 moles. So Choice C is incorrect. Choice D has 60 g of C_2H_6 which is 2 moles, and 156 g of C_6H_6 is also 2 moles. So D is a better choice than B.

9. The answer is B. To answer this question, you have to use your intuition. The reaction occurs by means of the heat supplied to the aluminum hydroxide, and it is a dehydration reaction. So the most plausible answer is water.

10. The answer is D. The reactant coefficients in a balanced equation cannot be used to determine the identity of the limiting reagent. Without comparing the amounts of reactants that are actually present, we cannot determine the identity of the limiting reagent. CO being a gas has nothing to do with being the limiting reagent for the given reaction. Choice C is not logical, because it is a product. The best answer is that we cannot determine the identity of the limiting reagent, if any, without any data regarding the amount of reactants used.

11. The answer is C. Look at the items one by one. Item I says that the second student had the highest yield of products. In Experiment 1, the first student used 40.5 g of Al and 80 g of Fe_2O_3. This translates to 1.5 moles of Al and roughly 0.5 moles of Fe_2O_3. Here Fe_2O_3 is the limiting reagent. What was the second student doing? Well, the second student increased the amount of Fe_2O_3 used, keeping the same amount of Al. Since Fe_2O_3 is the limiting reagent, an increase of Fe_2O_3 will increase the product yield. So the second student must have had more yield than the first student. The first and the third students have the same yield for aluminum oxide, because the amount of limiting reagent present is the same in both cases. So items I and III are true.

12. The answer is C. By increasing the amount of aluminum used by the first student, there will not be an increase in the yield because Fe_2O_3 is the limiting reagent. Hence, Choice A is not correct. The same reasoning rules out Choice B. Increasing the amount of Fe_2O_3 by the second student will increase the yield further, because we actually have unreacted Al left according to the amounts used in the experiment. Hence, if we further increase the amount of Fe_2O_3 used, it will increase the yield until the Al runs out. Choice D is wrong.

13. The answer is A. In the question, we are given that 80 g of Fe_2O_3 is used in the reaction mixture. How much of this actually reacted is another story. That is to be found out from the yield data. The amount of CO_2 produced is 22 g. Based on the balanced equation, we can infer that for every 3 moles of CO reacted, 3 moles of CO_2 are produced. So CO and CO_2 have a 1:1 ratio. If 22 g or 0.5 moles of CO_2 is produced, 0.5 moles of CO must have reacted.

14. The answer is B. Based on the question, we can say that about 0.5 moles of Fe_2O_3 and 0.5 moles of CO was present in the reacting mixture. Since the Fe_2O_3 to CO reacting ratio is 1:3, CO will completely react, and there will be some leftover unreacted Fe_2O_3 after the reaction is complete. So the limiting reagent is CO.

15. The answer is B. This question tests your understanding of the mole concept. Since we have excess amounts of Fe_2O_3, we do not have to worry about it. But, what you should consider is that the amount of CO present dictates the reaction. One mole of CO_2 contains Avogadro's number (6.02×10^{23}) of molecules. The reaction results in 0.1 moles of CO_2. So 0.1 moles of CO_2 contains 6.02×10^{22} molecules.

CHAPTER 7 SOLUTIONS

1. The answer is C. First, we should write the balanced equation. Without the balanced equation there is a good chance we might choose the incorrect answer.

$$2 \, NO \, (g) \; + \; O_2 \, (g) \longrightarrow 2 \, NO_2 \, (g)$$

According to the balanced equation, 2 liters of NO react with 1 liter of O_2 to give 2 liters of NO_2. According to the question, 4 liters of NO_2 were formed. By taking proportionality, we can say that 4 liters of NO and 2 liters of O_2 must have reacted so far.

2. The answer is B. Density is mass per unit volume. Since we know the density and the volume, we can find the weight of the gas. Since this represents 1 mole of the gas, that itself is its molecular weight.

$$\text{Molecular weight of the gas} = 1.8 \text{ g/L x } 45 \text{ L/mol} = 81 \text{ g/mol}$$

3. The answer is C. One mole of an ideal gas occupies 22.4 L at STP. From the density-volume-mass relationship, we can find the mass of 1 mole of this gas. We know both the density and the volume of the gas.

$$\text{Weight of the gas} = 1.4 \text{ g/L x } 22.4 \text{ L/mole} = 31.5 \text{ g/mole}$$

This molecular weight is closest to that of oxygen.

4. The answer is B. The objective of this question is to convert the given pressure value (in mmHg) to pascals. In order to do this, we should first convert the given value into atmospheres. Since one atm equals 760 mmHg, 1330 mmHg equals 1.75 atm. The conversion of atmospheres to pascals is given in the question. The conversion is: 1atm $= 10^5$ pascals. This gives B as the correct answer.

5. The answer is B. This is a simple conversion problem that every MCAT student should know and do without any reference. This conversion should come automatically

$$273 - 27 = 246 \text{ K}$$

6. The answer is A. The given quantity of CO_2 corresponds to 0.26 mole. This quantity of CO_2 will occupy 0.26 x 22.5 ≈ 5.9 L.

7. The answer is B. Gases behave the most ideally under conditions such as high temperature and low pressure. Choice D is wrong. The passage makes the behavior of gases very clear: They depend on the prevailing temperature and pressure.

8. The answer is C. By rearranging the ideal gas equation, we can find the correc ≈ nit of the gas constant.

9. The answer is A. The question is asking for effusion rates of SO_2 and O_2. The rate of effusion of a molecule is inversely proportional to the square root of its molecular weight. The problem should be solved as follows:

$$\frac{\text{Rate of } SO_2 \text{ effusion}}{\text{Rate of } O_2 \text{ effusion}} = \sqrt{\frac{\text{Mol. wt of } O_2}{\text{Mol. wt of } SO_2}} = \sqrt{\frac{32}{64}} \approx 0.7$$

10. The answer is B. A value of zero for both the *a* and *b* factors in the van der Waals equation of state would make the equation reduce to the ideal gas law. Thus, for a gas if both of those factors were zero then we would expect the gas to behave ideally.

11. The answer is D. The clues to answer this question have to be taken from the given data. What can we infer from the data given about halogens? The correction factor of fluorine is $1.170 \; L^2 \cdot atm/mol^2$. The correction factor of chlorine is $6.340 \; L^2 \cdot atm/mol^2$. By analyzing the trend, we can deduce that bromine must have a correction factor that is higher than that of chlorine. The only value that is higher than that of chlorine is $9.80 \; L^2 \cdot atm/mol^2$. Hence, the best choice is D. All units correspond to that of constant *a* and not of *b*.

12. The answer is D. According to Avogadro's principle, at a fixed T and P, two ideal gases should occupy the same volume and thus have the same number of moles present.

13. The answer is D. According to the kinetic-molecular theory, all the items are true.

CHAPTER 8 SOLUTIONS

1. The answer is D. The conversion of a gas to a solid is called deposition. Sublimation is the conversion of a solid to a gas. Condensation is the conversion of a gas to a liquid. Freezing is the conversion of a liquid to a solid.

2. The answer is B. Vaporization, sublimation, and melting require heat (consume heat). The only process listed which releases heat is condensation.

3. The answer is D. Potassium fluoride is an ionic compound. See the chapter for descriptions of all types of solids.

4. The answer is **C.** In order to answer this question we have to think in terms of ionic bonding. What enables the formation of an ionic bond in the first place? The electronegativity differences between the bonded atoms make ionic bonds possible. It is in fact the electrostatic forces that hold the atoms involved in an ionic bond.

5. The answer is B. To answer this question, we need to recall some basic aspects regarding phase diagrams. Just by knowing those, we can eliminate some of the choices right away. In Choices A and D, the phases are wrongly labeled. The phases are correctly labeled only in Choices B and C. This rules out Choices A and D. Water has some anomalous properties. Such properties make water unique. In fact, the solid-liquid segment in the phase diagram of water has a negative slope.

6. The answer is B. See the explanation for Question 5.

7. The answer is B. The question describes a phase change scenario based on the diagram given in the passage. Substance M will be a liquid at point A. If the pressure is decreased, the most likely phase change will be from liquid (the phase before the change) to gas.

8. The answer is C. This is a definition-type question. The point indicated by the X mark is called "triple point." At the triple point of a substance, the three phases coexist at equilibrium. Below this point, the solid to gas conversion or vice versa is direct without the intermediate liquid phase.

9. The answer is C. The critical temperature is defined to be the temperature above which a gas cannot be changed into a liquid. The choice that best reflects this idea is C.

10. The answer is A. In the phase diagram given in the passage, locate the segment XZ. This segment separates the liquid and the gas phases.

CHAPTER 9 SOLUTIONS

1. The answer is C. Normality of a solution is the number of equivalents of solute per liter of solution.

2. The answer is A.

$$\text{The number of moles of glucose} = \frac{270 \text{ g}}{180 \text{ }^{g}/_{mol}} = 1.5 \text{ moles}$$

$$\text{Molarity} = \frac{\text{moles of solute}}{\text{liters of solution}} = \frac{1.5 \text{ moles}}{1 \text{ liter}} = 1.5 \text{ M}.$$

3. The answer is D. First, we should calculate the molar mass of HCl which is 36.5 g/mole. We have a 2.5 molar solution of HCl. That means every liter of the solution will have 2.5 moles of HCl. Here we have 1.25 L of the solution, and a total of 3.125 moles of HCl. That comes closest to 3.125 x 36.5 = 114 g.

4. The answer is B. We can equate the diluted solution with the stock solution as follows:

(Molarity of solution made x Volume of solution made) is equal to (Molarity of the stock solution x Volume of the stock solution required). With this in mind, let's plug in the values that we know.

$$2 \text{ } M \text{ x } 30 \text{ ml} = 10 \text{ } M \text{ x Volume of the stock solution required}$$

We need not convert the milliliters into liters for this problem, because the molar units will cancel out.

$$\text{Volume of stock solution} = [2 \text{ M x } 30 \text{ ml}] / [10 \text{ M}] = 6 \text{ ml}$$

5. The answer is C. The quickest way to solve this problem is to calculate how many moles of NaCl are present in this solution. Then convert the number of moles to grams of NaCl. The correct answer is 5.1 g.

6. The answer is D. All the solubilities shown in the graph are endothermic. In fact most compounds (solids) dissolve endothermically. The graph shows that as the temperature increases, the solubility of the salts increases. In other words, as the temperature increases, more and more of the salt present is dissociated into ions. This is exactly how an endothermic process works.

7. The answer is D. The first step in answering this question is to find the molality of the solution. Then plug that number into the boiling-point-change equation given in the passage.

$$\text{Molality of the glucose solution} = \frac{315 \text{ g } C_6H_{12}O_6}{0.750 \text{ kg } H_2O} \times \frac{1 \text{ mol } C_6H_{12}O_6}{180 \text{ g } C_6H_{12}O_6} = 2.33 \text{ m}$$

$$\Delta T_b = K_b \text{ m} = (0.512^0 \text{ C/m})(2.33 \text{ m}) = 1.2^0\text{C}.$$

$$\text{The answer is } 100^0 \text{ C} + 1.2^0 \text{ C} = 101.2^0\text{C}.$$

8. The answer is B. The observed changes in colligative properties are less than what was theoretically predicted. This is because the ionization of salts in water is not as complete as we expect. Some of the oppositely charged ions stick together and function as a unit. So the number of particles (units) is lower than what we expect. As the concentration increases, the possibility of the oppositely charged ions sticking together is greater than that in dilute solutions.

9. The answer is D. This question is a bit tricky. You may have selected Choice A. But you have to understand what exactly is asked in the question. The question is not asking about the change in boiling point (ΔT). Instead, it asks what happens to the boiling point. It will not double; it will only increase slightly.

10. The answer is C. Choice C is the only true statement given. Looking closely at Choices A and B, you should realize that they represent the same relationship. Since you cannot have two correct answers, this rules out Choices A and B. Thus, such logical elimination-techniques can be used to solve many MCAT problems and save valuable time.

CHAPTER 10 SOLUTIONS

1. The answer is B. This question tests your understanding of the concept of pH. You also have to use some mathematical skill to answer this question, since you are not allowed to use a calculator.

$$pH = -\log [H^+]$$

To get the hydrogen ion (hydronium or H_3O^+) concentration, we have to take the antilog. If the pH were 2, the molar concentration would have been 10^{-2}. If the pH were 3, the molar concentration would have been 10^{-3}. Since the pH is 2.5, the best choice is 3.2×10^{-3}.

2. The answer is C. NaCl is a salt. Think about its source. NaCl is a salt of sodium hydroxide and hydrogen chloride. NaOH is a strong base and HCl is a strong acid. A salt solution of a strong acid and a strong base is neutral.

3. The answer is D. An acid which can furnish more than one proton per molecule of the acid is called a "polyprotic acid." Choices A, B and C are all polyprotic acids. So the reasonable choice is 'none of the above.' Note that the question asked for an acid which is not a polyprotic acid. You should make a habit of noting key words in the question, especially when the question stem contains words such as "not, except, increasing, decreasing."

4. The answer is C. To answer this question, you have to manipulate the given equation.

The given equation is:

$$pOH = pK_b + \log \frac{[\text{conjugate acid}]}{[\text{base}]}$$

$$pOH = -\log [OH^-]$$

$$pK_b = -\log [K_b]$$

$$-\log [OH^-] = -\log [K_b] + \log \frac{[\text{conjugate acid}]}{[\text{base}]}$$

$$\log [K_b] = \log [OH^-] + \log \frac{[\text{conjugate acid}]}{[\text{base}]}$$

$$\log [K_b] = \log [OH^-] - \log \frac{[\text{base}]}{[\text{conjugate acid}]}$$

5. The answer is C.

$$H_3PO_4 \xrightarrow{\ \ 1\ \ } H^+ + H_2PO_4^-$$

$$\downarrow 2$$

$$H^+ + PO_4^{3-} \xleftarrow[\ \ 3\ \ ]{} HPO_4^{2-} + H^+$$

The choices are phosphoric acid and its dissociation products (see above). In a polyprotic acid, such as H_3PO_4, almost invariably the first dissociation will be of the highest degree. So the highest pK_a is for HPO_4^{2-}. This is Choice C. For a comparison, the K_a values are given below. But as you know, we do not need them to answer this question.

$$H_3PO_4 \longrightarrow K_{a1} = 7.5 \times 10^{-3}$$

$$H_2PO_4^- \longrightarrow K_{a2} = 6.2 \times 10^{-8}$$

$$HPO_4^{2-} \longrightarrow K_{a3} = 3.6 \times 10^{-11}$$

6. The answer is A. The question asks for the net ionic equation of the given acid-base equation. The given reaction is a strong acid-strong base reaction.

7. The answer is A. For this question, we are looking for a strong acid-strong base curve. Why? Well, the answer is simple. In Reaction 1, we have a strong monoprotic acid ($HClO_4$) reacting against a strong base (NaOH). The only curve that satisfies this criterion is given in Choice A.

8. The answer is D. In this question, we are asked to analyze the upper and lower limit ratios of base-to-acid at the best buffering pH. How can we answer this question? Well, there are some clues in the passage. According to the passage, the effective pH range of a buffer system is between $pK_a - 1$ and $pK_a + 1$. What other relevant information do we have in the passage? The passage also gives us an equation with which we can relate the pH and the pK_a.

$$pH = pKa + \log([A^-] / [HA])$$

In order to have a pH value of $pK_a - 1$, the second half of the equation with the log should be negative 1. For this the base-acid ratio should be 0.1; $\log 0.1 = -1$. For the other criterion $pK_a + 1$, the log value should be +1. For this, the ratio should be 10.

9. The answer is B. The question asks for the pH of a solution of HCl. HCl is a strong acid, and strong acids completely ionize. So we don't have to worry about partial ionization such as in weak acids.

$$pH = -\log[H^+] = 3.2 \times 10^{-4} \approx 3.5$$

10. The answer is B. This is actually one way of defining pKa value. At the pKa value, the acid-base ratio is 1. So the best answer is Choice B. In addition, it is near the pKa value that the solution will have its best buffering capacity. So Choice D wrong.

CHAPTER 11 SOLUTIONS

1. The answer is A. "Bomb calorimeter" is a device used to determine the energy changes that are associated with reactions by measuring the amount of heat generated or absorbed by a reaction at constant volume. The changes (measurements) are made at constant temperature and constant volume. There is nothing true about Choice B. Keeping the volume constant is not an impossible task! This rules out Choice B. Choice C is wrong, since there is no change in volume, and theoretically there is no work done.

2. The answer is B. The figure shows the conversion of ice (*s*) to water (*l*). The process is melting. What happens when a solid is converted to its liquid form? There will be an increase in randomness. This rules out Choice D. Choice C doesn't make any sense. Since the randomness is increased, the entropy is increased.

3. The answer is C. The change in free energy (ΔG) is related to enthalpy and entropy by the following equation:

$$\Delta\Gamma = \Delta H - T\,\Delta S$$

In this question, the change in free energy is zero. This means that there is no <u>net</u> transfer of free energy. This in turn means that the forward and backward reactions are both equally favorable and thus the reacting system is in equilibrium.

4. The answer is D. This question tests your knowledge and ability to make reasonable judgments based on a limited amount of information. We are given only an equation and a description of that equation. Without further data on this reaction, we cannot be sure whether the reaction is exothermic or endothermic. We cannot say whether the reaction is spontaneous or nonspontaneous without pertinent data. Choice C is untrue.

5. The answer is C. According to the third law of thermodynamics, the entropy of a pure, crystalline substance at 0 K is zero.

CHAPTER 12 SOLUTIONS

1. The answer is D. The equilibrium constant is the equilibrium molar concentrations of the products raised to their corresponding coefficients, divided by concentrations of the reactants raised to their corresponding coefficients. The coefficients can be taken directly from the balanced equation of the reaction.

$$N_2 (g) + 3 H_2 (g) \rightleftharpoons 2 NH_3 (g)$$

The equilibrium expression is:

$$K = \frac{[NH_3]^2}{[N_2][H_2]^3}$$

2. The answer is C. From the given equation, we can write the general form of the rate as:

$$\text{Rate} = k [X]^m [Y]^n$$

Our next step is to find m and n using the given information. Examining the first and the second experiments shows that the concentration of X is kept constant, but the concentration of Y is doubled. When the concentration of Y is doubled, the rate also is doubled. So the order (n) with respect to Y is 1. Now compare experiments 2 and 3. In experiments 2 and 3, the concentration of Y is kept constant, but the concentration of X is doubled. This time, the rate is quadrupled. Hence, the order (m) with respect to X should be 2. So the correct expression is Rate = k [X]² [Y].

3. The answer is D. This question tests your basic understanding of the factors that affect the rate of reactions. All the listed factors can influence the rate of reactions.

4. The answer is D. This is the potential energy diagram of a reaction. For the MCAT, you should be familiar with diagrams of this type. Since the direction of the reaction-coordinate is indicated in the diagram, we can predict the potential energy level of the reactants and the products. The bump in the graph represents the activation energy of the reaction. So Choice A doesn't make any sense. According to Choice B, there is a net absorption of energy. But in contrast to this statement, there is a net release of energy. This prediction is based on the fact that the energy level of the products is below that of the reactants. This makes Choice C wrong. That leaves us with Choice D. In fact the diagram is that of an exergonic reaction.

5. The answer is A. Catalysts can change the rate of reactions, by decreasing the activation energy. Catalysts are not consumed by the reactants. If a substance is consumed in the process, it cannot be a catalyst.

6. The answer is B. According to the question, the reverse reaction of Reaction 1 is endothermic. This means the forward reaction is exothermic. For exothermic reactions, the ΔH is negative.

7. The answer is C. In the experiment, the hydrogen is removed. Such a change in concentration will upset the equilibrium. We have to approach this problem in terms of Le Châtelier's principle. Changes in the concentrations of reactants or products of this reaction will turn the system into a non-equilibrium state. The result will be an adjustment of the reaction mode to restore the system to equilibrium. So if we take H_2 away, the backward reaction will be favored for restoring the equilibrium.

8. The answer is C. The pressure is decreased in the system. Such a decrease in pressure will not change the reaction mode. Let's take a look at the reacting system.

$$H_2 \; + \; I_2 \; \rightleftharpoons \; 2HI \qquad \text{(Reaction 1)}$$

Both sides of the equation have equal number of moles, two on the reactant side and two on the product side. So the pressure change will not affect the reaction in this case.

9. The answer is C.

$$N_2\,(g) \; + \; 3H_2(g) \; \rightleftharpoons \; 2NH_3\,(g) \qquad \text{(Reaction 2)}$$

In Reaction 2, a pressure change will affect the reaction. Here, the pressure is increased and that will increase the forward reaction. In other words, the reaction shifts to the right. Item I says that the reaction shifts to the right. But for the wrong reason. According to the equation, we have more moles on the reactant side. So item I is not fully correct. Item II is also ruled out because the reaction shifts to the right. Item III makes perfect sense.

10. The answer is D.

11. The answer is B. There are 2.5 moles (70 g) of nitrogen. The amount of H_2 used should also be taken into account. According to the question, 10 g of hydrogen was used, which is equivalent to 5 moles. So the hydrogen acts as the limiting reagent. By the reaction of 5 moles of hydrogen with excess of nitrogen, the number of moles of ammonia produced should equal 10/3 moles. Now, it is a matter of converting moles to grams.

$$10/3 \text{ moles x } 17 \text{ g NH}_3 \,/\, 1 \text{ mole NH}_3 \approx 57 \text{ grams}$$

12. The answer is B. Entropy is a thermodynamic quantity which measures the randomness in a system. An increase in randomness means an increase in the entropy. In general, gas phase has a higher entropy than liquid phase, and liquid phase has a higher entropy than solid phase. But in this reaction, all the components are in their gas phases, and the reactant side has more of them. The production of ammonia causes the entropy to decrease because there is less randomness than before the reaction began.

13. The answer is D. We cannot predict the spontaneity of the reaction accurately based on the information given in the passage. The only fact that we know regarding the reaction is that it has a ∆H value of –92 kJ. Based on that alone, it is not possible to predict the spontaneity accurately.

CHAPTER 13 SOLUTIONS

1. The answer is C. A redox equation is represented in the question. The electrode potential of the reaction is also given. The question also says that the reaction occurred spontaneously. For the given direction of the reaction, the electrode potential is negative. So the reaction must have taken place in the opposite direction of what is given in the question and thus had a positive potential. A net positive potential means a negative free energy change. A negative free energy change denotes spontaneity. We can rewrite the equation:

$$Zn\ (s)\ +\ Sn^{2+}\ \longrightarrow\ Zn^{2+}\ (s)\ +\ Sn\ (s)$$

$$E^{o}\ =\ +0.62\ \ V$$

Now we have a positive voltage, where the zinc is oxidized and a tin ion is reduced. Oxidation of zinc means it is losing electrons. Recall that oxidation is losing electrons, and reduction is gaining electrons.

2. The answer is B. The voltage (standard potential) represents the electromotive force, which has nothing to do with the coefficients of the equation. In fact, the two reactions are same. One equation is the simplified version of the other. So the standard potential will remain the same.

3. The answer is D. Based on the given information in the question, we can say that E^{o} is directly related to K. The question also says that the product concentrations are greater than the reactant concentrations. So we can say that the equilibrium constant value is greater than 1. We can rule out Choice A, because there is no such thing as a negative concentration. So K cannot be negative anyway. Since we know that K is greater than 1, the natural logarithm of K will be positive. So from the equation, we can say that E^{o} cannot be negative, which rules out Choice B. Hence, the E^{o} value should be positive. Since we have a positive E^{o} value, the reaction is most likely to be spontaneous. Keep in mind the conditions at which the reaction occurs - standard state (1 atm, 25 °C).

4. The answer is C. Ampere is defined as the total amount of charge that flows per second.

$$ampere = coulombs/seconds$$

The charge in coulombs = 5 A x 3.5 min. x 60 s/ 1 min. = 1,050 coulombs.

5. The answer is B. For a reaction to be spontaneous, the electrode potential should be positive. Oxidation of copper has a negative electrode potential. That rules out Choice A. Oxidation of fluoride ion and reduction of zinc ion have negative electrode potentials, which rules out Choices C and D respectively. The reduction of chlorine represented below has a positive potential which indicates spontaneity.

$$Cl_2 + 2\,\bar{e} \longrightarrow 2\,Cl^- \quad \Longrightarrow \quad +1.36$$

6. The answer is D. The two half-reactions can be written as shown below:

$$Ni \longrightarrow Ni^{2+} + 2\,e^- \qquad +0.25$$
$$Ag^+ + \bar{e} \longrightarrow Ag \qquad +0.80$$
$$\overline{}$$
$$+1.05\ V$$

Now, it is just a matter of adding the individual potentials to get the overall potential. A word of caution: when you add the individual half-electrode potentials, make sure that the appropriate sign has been assigned to them.

7. The answer is D. Even though a salt bridge allows an electrical connection between the two half-cells in a galvanic cell, the function of a salt bridge is not to conduct electricity. So Choice A is ruled out. Choice B makes no sense. The salt bridge does not control the voltage. The function of a salt bridge is to maintain electrical neutrality in the half-cells so that excess buildup of charge will not occur in the half-cells. If excess charge builds up in the half-cells, the reaction will slow down and quickly die out.

8. The answer is C. The question asks for the best oxidizing agent. An oxidizing agent gets reduced in the process. So the oxidizing agent (species) should be able to accept electrons with ease. The most positive reduction potential is that of chlorine (Cl_2), which makes chlorine the best oxidizing agent among the choices.

$$Cl_2 + 2\,\bar{e} \longrightarrow 2\,Cl^- \quad \Longrightarrow \quad +1.36$$

9. The answer is B. The question asks for the species that has the highest <u>oxidation</u> potential. Oxidation is losing electrons. Thus all the half reactions should be considered in the oxidation sense. Since the table gives you reduction half-reactions, you have to reverse all the equations, and when you reverse the equations the sign of the potentials should also be reversed. The most positive value is that of the oxidation of potassium.

$Cr \longrightarrow Cr^{3+} + 3\,\bar{e}$		$+0.74\ V$
$K \longrightarrow K^+ + \bar{e}$		$+2.92\ V$
$Cr \longrightarrow Cr^{2+} + 2\,\bar{e}$		$+0.34\ V$
$Ag \longrightarrow Ag^+ + \bar{e}$		$+0.80\ V$

10. The answer is B. The process described in the question is Fe changing to Fe^{2+}, which is oxidation. Oxidation occurs at the anode and reduction occurs at the cathode.

CHAPTER 14 SOLUTIONS

1. The answer is B. We are asked to evaluate the radioactive change. The equation should look like this:

$$_{88}^{226}\text{Ra} \rightarrow \ _{86}^{222}\text{Rn} \ + \ _{2}^{4}\text{He}$$

Notice that the atomic and mass numbers decreased by 2 and 4 units, respectively. The helium nucleus shown in the equation is an alpha particle.

2. The answer is C. In the given radioactive decay, sodium is converted to neon. Notice that the atomic number decreased by one, but the mass number remained the same. The most likely particle that is emitted is a positron. A positron is a positively charged electron. The equation is shown below:

$$_{11}^{22}\text{Na} \rightarrow \ _{10}^{22}\text{Ne} \ + \ _{1}^{0}\text{e}^{+} \ + \ \gamma$$

A gamma particle is also emitted, but that information is not needed to answer this question.

3. The answer is A. This question tests your knowledge of common radioactive emissions. The only emission listed that is a high-energy electromagnetic radiation is the gamma ray. Electromagnetic rays travel at the speed of light. The only emissions that travel close to the speed of light are beta particles. But the best choice is gamma ray. So the answer is A. In addition to the greater speed, gamma rays have the highest penetrating power.

4. The answer is C. See the explanation for Question 3.

5. The answer is D. This question tests your knowledge of the concept of half-life. Half-life is defined as the amount of time for a radioactive substance to decay to half its initial quantity. Since the half-life of substance X is 12 years, it takes twelve years for substance X to decay to half its initial quantity. We have 9 grams of substance X present. The amount of substance X that was originally present is 150 grams. So it must have undergone radioactive decay for at least four half-lives. Write the decay mode, starting from the original amount present.

$$150 \Rightarrow 75 \Rightarrow 37.5 \Rightarrow 18.75 \Rightarrow 9.375$$

Each arrow indicates one half-life, for a total of four half-lives. Since one half-life is 12 years, the total time elapsed is 12 x 4 = 48 years. The exact answer is a little above 48 years. But the approximation is correct since the choices are far apart and no values higher than 48 are given.

6. The answer is D. Half-life is the amount of time required for a radioactive substance to disintegrate to half its initial quantity. The sample described in the question has disintegrated to 3% of its original quantity. The disintegration can be analyzed as follows:

$$100\% \Rightarrow 50\% \Rightarrow 25\% \Rightarrow 12.5\% \Rightarrow 6.25\% \Rightarrow 3.125\%$$

This means, at least 5 half-lives must have elapsed.

7. The answer is A. A beta particle is an electron. By the emission of a β-particle, the nucleus must have changed into protactinium (Pa) which has atomic number 91. Remember that a β emission decreases the atomic number by one.

8. The answer is C. Since alpha particles are positively charged and beta particles are negatively charged, Choices A and B are true. Gamma rays are not deflected because they have no charge. Choice D is also true.

9. The answer is B. According to the figure given in the passage, as the number of protons increases the neutron-proton ratio increases and becomes greater than or equal to one. (Clue: Look at the slope)

10. The answer is D. The mass loss can be equated with the binding energy. In essence, mass loss can be calculated using the equation $E = mc^2$.

$$\text{Energy} = (3.1 \times 10^{-5} \text{ kg})(3 \times 10^8 \text{ m/s})^2 = 2.8 \times 10^{12} \text{ kg} \cdot \text{m/s}^2 = 2.8 \times 10^{12} \text{ J}.$$

11. The answer is D.

$$^{232}_{90}\text{Th} \rightarrow \text{ ??? } + {}^{224}_{88}\text{Ra}$$

The question tests your ability to evaluate radioactive emissions by analyzing a given radioactive emission reaction. Notice that the atomic number decreased by 2 and the mass number decreased by 8. If two alpha particles were emitted, that would decrease the mass number to 224, because an alpha particle is a helium nucleus

$$^{4}_{2}\text{He}$$

It would also decrease the atomic number by 4. But apparently that is not the case here. The atomic number decrease by only 2. This can be accounted for if two β-particles were also emitted.

CHAPTER 15 SOLUTIONS

1. The answer is B. The carbon indicated by the arrow is a sp^2 hybridized carbon atom. Notice that the indicated carbon has a double bond and two single bonds. The double bond connects this carbon to the end-carbon. A hydrogen atom and the third carbon are attached to this carbon via single bonds.

2. The answer is A. Acetylene is the smallest member of the alkyne group. The carbon-carbon bond is a triple bond which contains one sigma bond and 2 pi bonds.

3. The answer is B. The triple bond of 2-propyne (an alkyne) contains one sigma bond and two pi bonds.

4. The answer is C. The sp^3 hybrid orbitals such as those seen in alkanes have a tetrahedral orientation.

5. The answer is D. This question also tests your basic knowledge of hybridization in carbon compounds. A triple bond means three bonds. Since there are three bonds, six electrons are involved in the bond.

6. The answer is B. Methane has a tetrahedral geometry. So the hydrogen-carbon-hydrogen bond angle is closest to 109.5°.

7. The answer is C. The triple bond is the shortest among the bonds indicated by the arrows. The only triple bond-bearing compound given is Choice C.

8. The answer is B. The carbon-hydrogen bond is a single covalent bond.

CHAPTER 16 SOLUTIONS

1. The answer is B. To answer this question, we can use the following clues from the question:

> i) The compound is composed of only carbon and hydrogen atoms.
> ii) It is a saturated hydrocarbon.
> iii) It does not have a ring structure.

So the compound is an alkane. Alkanes have the general formula C_nH_{2n+2}. Now this becomes a simple algebra problem. Since there are 14 hydrogens, $2n+2 = 14$.

$$\text{So, n} = \frac{14-2}{2} = 6.$$

2. The answer is A.

3. The answer is D. Constitutional isomers are compounds with the same molecular formula, but differ in the order with which the atoms are bonded. This definition matches the relationship between n-butane and isobutane.

4. The answer is C. First, we have to number the carbon chain to get the longest possible chain in the structure. The numbering should be done in such a way that the branches will have the smallest substituent number. The numbering is done as follows:

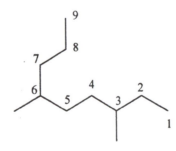

There are 9 carbons in the parent chain. So the parent chain is clear and the complete name ends with "nonane." This rules out Choices A and B. There are 2 methyl groups on carbons 3 and 6. So the compound is 3,6-dimethyl nonane.

5. The answer is C. Butane contains 4 carbon atoms and if one mole of butane is completely combusted, at least 4 moles of carbon dioxide will be formed provided that there is enough oxygen.

6. The answer is B. A secondary carbon atom should be attached to two other carbon atoms. The carbon atoms indicated by arrows I and III are secondary carbon atoms.

7. The answer is A. A carbonium ion is a special kind of a carbocation. A carbocation is a positively charged species.

8. The answer is C. Gauche conformation is a form of staggered conformation. The conformation is gauche if the relative separation of two substituents on adjacent atoms is 60°. The Newman representation of a gauche conformation is shown:

Gauche

ANGLE OF TORSION IS 60°

9. The answer is B. The angle closest to 109.5° is 110°. That is the most likely bond angle, having the least angle strain.

10. The answer is A. All the given choices are alkanes. Item I is an unbranched alkane. Items II, III, IV have increasing degrees of branching. Branching decreases the area of contact and thereby decreases the intermolecular interactions. So the unbranched alkane has the highest boiling point. Keep in mind that without actually measuring the properties, we can only compare compounds of comparable weights and number of carbons with reasonable accuracy.

11. The answer is D. The question asks for the type of force that is important with respect to alkanes. Alkanes cannot undergo hydrogen bonding. So Choice A is out. Choice B is generally not important in alkanes. Since there are no ionic bonds in an alkane, Choice C is wrong. The correct choice is van der Waals forces.

12. The answer is D. To answer this question you have to do some intuitive thinking based on the information given in the passage. Butane is a four-carbon alkane with the formula C_4H_{10}. It is a bigger molecule than propane, but a smaller molecule than pentane. So the boiling point of butane should be between propane and pentane. We are talking in terms of the relative boiling points. But the question asks for the melting point. So let's translate this idea in terms of melting point. Obviously, the melting point of a substance should be below its boiling point. So the answer cannot be either 37.5°C or 55.1°C. This rules out Choices A and B. Choice C is not a sensible answer because butane is a gas at 25°C.

13. The answer is C. Choice A is an initiation step. Choice B is a chain termination step. Choice D is also a chain termination step. The only choice which represents a chain propagation step is Choice C.

14. The answer is A. This question tests your knowledge of intermolecular forces and other interactions that give rise to some of the chemical and physical properties of compounds. Let's take a look at the compound 2,3-dimethylbutane. We do not have a clue about the precise properties of the compound asked in this question. But what we do know is the boiling point of one of its relatives. In the table given in the passage, we are told that the boiling point of 3-methylpentane is 63.3° C. If we compare these two compounds, we see that they have the same number of carbons and hydrogens – both are six-carbon alkanes. If the boiling point of 3-methylpentane is 63.3° C, then 2,3-dimethylbutane will have a boiling point lower than that. The only choice with a lower value is Choice A.

15. The answer is C. The only way to answer this question is to draw the possible isomers by trial and error. There is no choice other than drawing out the possible structures, starting from the straight chain form of heptane.

CHAPTER 17 SOLUTIONS

1. The answer is B. Enantiomers are non-superimposable mirror images. These compounds are enantiomers.

2. The answer is A. The two compounds are stereoisomers. To be precise, they are diastereomers. Diastereomers are not mirror images. Diastereomers are any two compounds that differ in at least one, but less than all, of their shared chiral centers. Hence, the two compounds given are not mirror images.

3. The answer is D. Choice D is the mirror image, choice C is a different molecule, and choices A and B are diastereomers.

4. The answer is C. A Fischer projection is a two-dimensional way of representing structures. To manipulate the Fischer projection, we should think in three-dimensional terms. This can be done by interchanging two pairs of substituents at a time. If only one pair is interchanged, we will not get the equivalent structure. Let's say we interchanged only one pair. This will result in its enantiomer. Such an example is Choice C which is the only non-equivalent structure.

5. The answer is D. The given structure is an ethane derivative, not a methane derivative. This rules out Choices A and B. In the Fischer projection, the horizontal lines represent the bonds extending out of the plane of the paper toward you. The vertical lines represent the bonds pointing into the plane of the paper (away from you). With this in mind, we can start the switching of groups as follows:

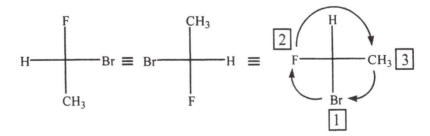

The switching is done so that the lowest ranking substituent (here, it is H) points away (into the plane of paper). The numbering or priority is based on decreasing atomic number. That means the substituent atom with the highest atomic number gets number 1, the next highest gets number 2, and so on. Since the order is clockwise, the configuration is R.

6. The answer is B. Only statements I and II are true. All enantiomers are stereoisomers, but not all stereoisomers are enantiomers. Diastereomers are also stereoisomers.

7. The answer is B.

CHAPTER 18 SOLUTIONS

1. The answer is B.

$$\underset{CH_3CH_2CHCH_3}{\overset{\overset{\displaystyle Cl}{|}}{}}$$

The halogen is attached to a secondary carbon atom and hence it is a secondary alkyl halide.

2. The answer is C. In general, as the number of carbons increases, the boiling point increases. But in this question, all the given choices are derivatives of the same alkane. In other words, they all have the same number of carbon atoms. The compound 1-chloroethane is monochlorinated, the compound 1,1-dichloroethane is dichlorinated, and the compound 1,1,3-trichloroethane is trichlorinated. As the number of Cl atoms increases, the attractive forces also increase, which means the boiling point increases.

3. The answer is D. The reactivity-trend of alcohols with hydrogen halides:

Tertiary alcohol > Secondary alcohol > Primary alcohol

4. The answer is B. The generalization in Choice A is not correct. Alkyl halides are generally insoluble in water. Choice C is wrong. The only reasonable choice is B.

5. The answer is C. The question asks for the order of reactivity of bimolecular substitution reactions. The general order of reactivity is:

Methyl halide > Primary halide > Secondary halide > Tertiary halide.

6. The answer is D. Choice A is not true because tertiary halides usually undergo substitution by an S_N1 mechanism. Choice B is too extreme by using the word "only". Choice C is not correct, because the S_N2 mechanism generally does not involve a carbocation intermediate, whereas the S_N1 mechanism does involve a carbocation intermediate. Hence, by elimination the answer is D.

7. The answer is D. For this reaction, Choices A, B, and C are possible products. Besides substitution, elimination is also possible, resulting in three products.

$$(CH_3)CBr \xrightarrow[\text{H}_2\text{O}]{\text{C}_2\text{H}_5\text{OH}} [\ (CH_3)_3\overset{+}{C}\ ]$$

carbocation
intermediate

$(CH_3)_3COH$

$CH_3CH_2OC(CH_3)_3$

$$H_2C{=}C\Big\langle{\text{CH}_3 \atop \text{CH}_3}$$

8. The answer is B. The inversion of configuration (at the stereogenic carbon involved in the substitution) is a characteristic of S_N2 reactions.

9. The answer is A. Among alkyl halides, alkyl fluorides have the lowest nucleophilic substitution rate. The fastest are alkyl iodides, followed by alkyl bromides and alkyl chlorides.

CHAPTER 19 SOLUTIONS

1. The answer is C. One of the most important properties of alcohols is their ability to undergo hydrogen bonding. The higher boiling points exhibited by alcohols when compared to similar alkanes and ethers are caused by the ability of alcohols to undergo hydrogen bonding.

2. The answer is C. A deprotonated alcohol group is known as an alkoxide ion.

3. The answer is D. All the listed processes are possible ways of making alcohols.

4. The answer is B. The oxymercuration-demercuration reaction converts an alkene to an alcohol. The hydration follows Markovnikov's rule and thus the hydrogen adds to the carbon atom with greater number of hydrogens.

5. The answer is A. Alcohols are much more acidic than alkanes. Among alcohols, primary alcohols are the most acidic ones. Compound A is a primary alcohol. Compound B is a secondary alcohol and Compound C is a tertiary alcohol.

6. The answer is C. Primary alcohols can be converted (oxidized) directly to carboxylic acids. Oxidation of secondary alcohols results in ketones. In some rare cases, secondary alcohols can be converted into carboxylic acids using very strong oxidizing agents, but generally that is not the case. Tertiary alcohols cannot be oxidized. So the best choice is C.

7. The answer is B. Reduction of a ketone usually results in a secondary alcohol.

8. The answer is D. When ethyl magnesium bromide is reacted with ethylene oxide, the carbon chain extends by two more carbons. The product is an alcohol with four carbon atoms.

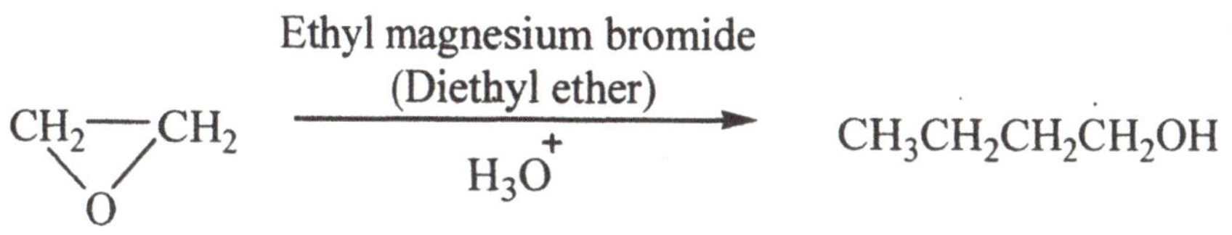

$$CH_2-CH_2 \quad \xrightarrow[\text{H}_3\text{O}^+]{\text{Ethyl magnesium bromide (Diethyl ether)}} \quad CH_3CH_2CH_2CH_2OH$$
$$\searrow_O\nearrow$$

9. The answer is B.

$$CH_3CH=CH_2 \searrow \quad B_2H_6 / H_2O_2$$
$$\text{I}$$

$$CH_3CH_2CH_2OH \quad \text{(Compound A)}$$

Pyridinium dichromate

$$CH_3CH_2CHO$$
(Compound B)

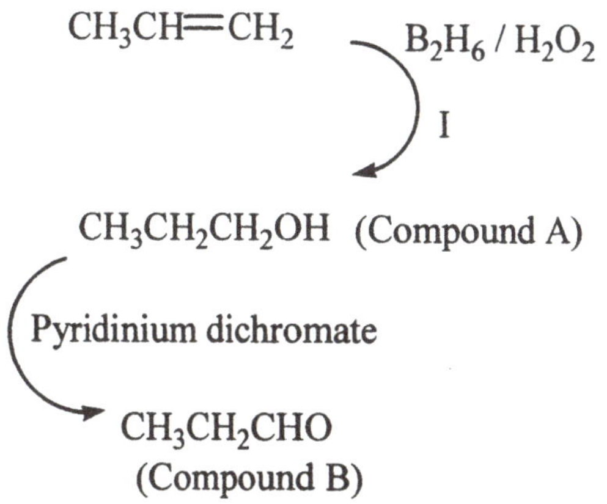

Reaction I sequence results in the alcohol shown above (Compound A). The alcohol formed is oxidized by pyridinium dichromate. The product formed is an aldehyde (propanal).

10. The answer is B. The given organic compound is an aldehyde. The reduction of an aldehyde results in a primary alcohol.

11. The answer is A. The numbering of carbon in the ring should be done as follows:

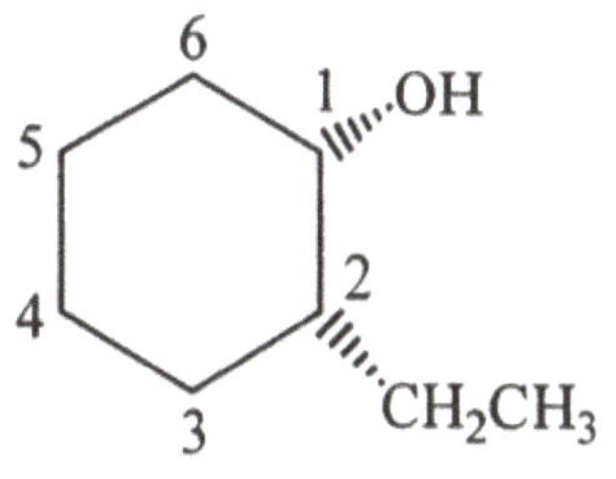

The substituents are *cis* to each other.

12. The answer is D. Primary alcohols are more acidic than secondary alcohols, and secondary alcohols are more acidic than tertiary alcohols. Ammonia is much weaker than any other compound in the remaining choices. In fact NH_3 has a pK_a of roughly 36. All the alcohols listed have pK_a values ranging from 16 through 18.

13. The answer is C. The complete reaction is shown below:

$$2\ CH_3CH_2OH \xrightarrow{\ 2\ Na\ } 2\ NaOCH_2CH_3\ +\ H_2$$

14. The answer is A. Primary alcohols are the most reactive alcohols toward metals. Methanol is a primary alcohol. The other choices are tertiary and secondary alcohols.

15. The answer is D. The question asks for a compound which can be directly converted to propanol by oxidation. If an aldehyde is oxidized, it is converted to a carboxylic acid. Oxidation of compounds in Choices B and C cannot produce an alcohol directly by oxidation.

CHAPTER 20 SOLUTIONS

1. The answer is B. Aldehydes can undergo nucleophilic addition reaction with Grignard reagents. The major product here is 3-pentanol which is a five carbon alcohol.

$$CH_3CH_2CHO \xrightarrow[\text{(ether)}]{CH_3CH_2MgBr/\ H_3\overset{+}{O}} CH_3CH_2CHOHCH_2CH_3$$

2. The answer is B.

$$\overset{\displaystyle OH}{\underset{\displaystyle CH_3CH_2CHOCH_2CH_3}{|}}$$

The product formed as a result of nucleophilic addition reaction between an alcohol and an aldehyde is called a hemiacetal. The given structure is a hemiacetal.

3. The answer is B. The reaction described in the question is an oxidation reaction.

4. The choice is A. The reaction can be written as follows:

$$2\ CH_3CH_2CH_2CH_2CH_2CHO$$

$$\searrow \overset{\displaystyle NaOH/\ H_2O}{\underset{\displaystyle \triangle}{}}$$

$$CH_3CH_2CH_2CH_2CH_2CHOHCH(CHO)CH_2CH_2CH_2CH_3$$

5. The answer is B. The carbonyl group can act as an electron-withdrawing group. This greatly increases the acidity of a carbonyl compound. Proximity to the carbonyl group is of very great influence in the case of acidity. In essence, carbonyl groups increase the acidity of protons that are connected to the adjacent carbon atoms. The closest protons influenced by the carbonyl group are indicated by the arrows a and b. Among these positions, the protons indicated by b are more acidic because they are influenced by the carbonyl groups from both sides.

6. The answer is D.

7. The correct answer is D.

8. The answer is C. The alpha proton adjacent to a carbonyl group is relatively acidic, and will be the atom to leave the ketone.

9. The answer is D. The iodoform test is used to identify methyl ketones. Methyl ketones give a positive iodoform test which is indicated by a yellow precipitate.

10. The answer is B. The chromic acid test is a qualitative test that can be used to confirm whether a given unknown compound is an aldehyde or not. Even though aldehydes give a positive response to this test, ketones do not. A sample reaction is shown below:

$$\underset{\text{CH}_3\text{CHO}}{} \xrightarrow[\text{H}_2\text{Cr}_2\text{O}_7 \,/\, \text{H}_2\text{SO}_4]{\text{(orange color)}} \text{CH}_3\text{COOH} \quad + \quad \underset{\text{(green precipitate)}}{\text{Cr}_2(\text{SO}_4)_3}$$

A green precipitate confirms a positive test.

11. The answer is B. The product that is formed in Experiment 2 is an acetal. When one mole of the given compound reacts with two moles of the alcohol, the product formed is an acetal. A simple acetal does not have the -OH group, whereas a hemiacetal has the -OH group.

12. The answer is B. This question tests your ability to judge the type of reaction presented. The conversion is a reduction reaction.

13. The answer is D.

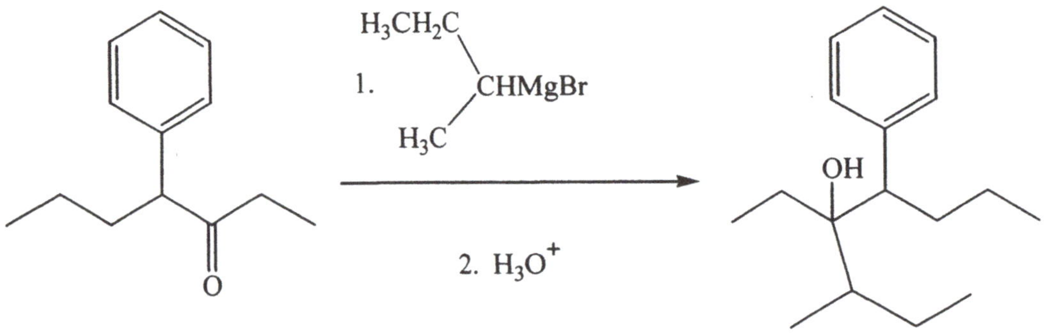

The compound shown in Experiment 4 can be converted to an alcohol by the addition of Grignard reagents. The proper Grignard reagent that should be used for this conversion can be found by comparing the reactant and the desired product.

14. The answer is C. In the experiment, 3-propanal is converted to 2-butanol. Direct oxidation is not an option because there aren't enough carbons in propanal to form an alcohol with four carbons. So Choice A is ruled out. Choice B is not completely true. With appropriate steps, the reaction is possible. One of the best ways to accomplish the reaction is to first treat the reactant with the appropriate Grignard reagent. Since Grignard reagents are nucleophilic, they can add to the carbonyl group. This extends the carbon chain. The product formed can be then hydrolyzed to form the alcohol.

$$\text{CH}_3\text{CH}_2\text{CHO} \xrightarrow{\text{CH}_3\text{MgBr}} \text{CH}_3\text{CH}_2\overset{\overset{\displaystyle \text{OMgBr}}{|}}{\text{C}}\text{HCH}_3 \xrightarrow{\text{H}_3\text{O}^+} \text{CH}_3\text{CH}_2\text{CH(OH)CH}_3$$

15. The answer is D. By definition, an organometallic compound should have a bond between a carbon atom and a metal atom. The only compound listed here which does not satisfy the definition is Choice D.

16. The answer is C. The conversion is an oxidation reaction.

CHAPTER 21 SOLUTIONS

1. The answer is D. An alkyl magnesium halide, aka a Grignard reagent, can react with carbon dioxide to form carboxylate salts. The description of the reaction mentioned in the question also says that the reaction occurred in acidic conditions. Under acidic conditions, the salt is converted to a carboxylic acid. So statement II is true. Furthermore, alkyl magnesium halide (Grignard reagent) acts as the nucleophile in the reaction. So statement III is true.

2. The answer is C. The first step results in n-butyl cyanide (Compound A). n-Butyl cyanide upon hydrolysis produces pentanoic acid.

3. The answer is C. Butanoic acid reacts with methanol in the presence of an acid catalyst to form methyl butanoate.

4. The answer is A. Alkanes and ketones have lower boiling points compared to carboxylic acids and alcohols. This aspect rules out Choices C and D. Comparing Choices A and B, we can say that carboxylic acid is a better choice since it can undergo extensive hydrogen bonding. In essence, carboxylic acids have higher boiling points than comparable alcohols.

5. The answer is D. Compound A is more acidic because it is a carboxylic acid. In general, carboxylic acids are more acidic than alcohols.

6. The answer is D. Substituents, especially electronegative ones, increase the acidity of carboxylic acids. Choice D has more substituents of this type than the other choices. So the carboxylic acid represented in Choice D is the most acidic.

7. The answer is D. LiAlH$_4$ is a very good reducing agent. The product is benzyl alcohol.

8. The answer is D. A carbonyl attached to an -OH group is a carboxylic acid.

9. The answer is B. Intermolecular forces will contribute to the BP of a molecule. Of all the molecules, the carboxylic acid will be polar due to the carbonyl group AND it will engage in hydrogen bonding. This additional intermolecular force will result in the highest BP of all the molecules listed.

10. The answer is B. The molecule shown is a carboxylic acid group attached to the aromatic benzene ring.

11. The answer is C. Choice A is true. Carboxylic acids can undergo hydrogen bonding. Choice B is also true and so is Choice D. Choice C is not true. In fact, the hydroxyl group makes its carbonyl group less electrophilic. In a ketone there is no hydroxyl group and that makes its carbonyl group more electrophilic than that of a carboxylic acid.

12. The answer is C. The conversion is an oxidation reaction. This rules out Choices B and D. LiAlH$_4$ is a reducing agent. So Choice A is wrong. KMnO$_4$ is a good oxidizing agent which can accomplish this conversion.

13. The answer is B. Esterification is commonly carried out by acid-catalyzed nucleophilic attack on a carboxylic acid, which is what we have in this question.

14. The answer is D. Formic acid is HCOOH.

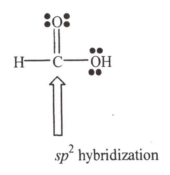

sp^2 hybridization

15. The answer is C. The question asks for the compound that has the highest pK$_a$ value. Highest pK$_a$ value means the weakest acid. The inductive effects become less and less pronounced as the electronegative substituents are farther away from the carboxylic group.

16. The answer is C. NaOCH$_3$ is basic. Carboxylic acids are much more acidic than alkynes. Choices B and D are ruled out. It is a tough call between Choices A and C. The carboxylic group of acetic acid is attached to an alkyl group. The carboxylic group of benzoic acid is attached to an aryl group. The sp^2 carbons in the benzoic acid ring are more electron withdrawing than the sp^3 carbon in the acetic acid. This makes benzoic acid more acidic than acetic acid.

CHAPTER 22 SOLUTIONS

1. The answer is B. Among the acid derivatives, the acyl chloride is the least stable and the most reactive compound toward hydrolysis.

2. The answer is A. Esterification is commonly carried out by acid-catalyzed nucleophilic attack on a carbonyl group, which is what we have in this question.

3. The answer is C. Esters can react with Grignard reagents to form tertiary alcohols. The intermediary compound formed is a ketone which reacts with the second Grignard reagent molecule to form the tertiary alcohol. A representative reaction is shown below:

$$CH_3COCH_3 \xrightarrow{CH_3MgBr} CH_3CCH_3$$

$$CH_3MgBr \text{ / } H_3O^+$$

$$(CH_3)_3OH$$

4. The answer is B. This is an ester. The carbonyl chai is four carbons long, meaning a butanoate suffix. The OR side chain is 2 carbons long, so the official IUPAC name will be ethyl butanoate.

5. The answer is C. Here we have a good nucleophile, the sodium acetate ion, and a good electrophile, the primary alkyl halide. We should expect the O⁻ to attach to the alkyl halide, resulting in an ester. This eliminates choice B. The carbonyl chain of the ester has 2 carbons, meaning it will be an acetate. Between choice A and C, only C correctly identifies the position of the methyl group on the benzene as para.

6. The answer is B. Do your checklist for MCAT reactions. Good nucleophile? Check, we have the ammonia. Good electrophile? Check, we have the acyl chloride. We will perform nucleophilic acyl substitution of the ammonia on the carbonyl carbon, resulting in an amide.

$$CH_3CCl \xrightarrow{NH_3} CH_3CNH_2$$
Amide

7. The answer is D. Choices A, B, and C describe possible ways of preparing carboxylic acids. Oxidation of an aldehyde can result in a carboxylic acid.

CHAPTER 23 SOLUTIONS

1. The answer is A. Williamson ether synthesis is a reaction, forming an ether from an organohalide and an alcohol. It involves the reaction of an alkoxide ion with a primary alkyl halide via an S_N2 reaction.

2. The answer is D. Alcohols, water, and carboxylic acids can undergo intermolecular hydrogen bonding. Ethers cannot undergo intermolecular hydrogen bonds. Alkanes cannot form intermolecular hydrogen bonds either. So the best conclusion is that ethers have boiling points similar to that of alkanes.

3. The answer is D. Ethers are polar. Hence, Choice A is true. Ethers are relatively less reactive and are widely used as solvents. Hence, Choices B and C are true.

4. The answer is A. It is true that ethers are not very reactive. Hence, statement I is true and statement II is false. Ethers are flammable. Hence, statement III is true. Ethers have very low boiling points compared to that of alcohols. Hence, statement IV is false.

5. The answer is A. The reaction given in the passage is called Williamson ether synthesis. By looking at the reaction we cannot answer this question. But a clue is given in the question. According to the question the reaction is most effective if it follows a S_N2 mechanism. Now we have something to hang on to. Since the reaction is mostly effective when followed by a S_N2 mechanism, the alkyl halide most appropriately used must be a primary alkyl halide. The only primary halide among the choices is methyl chloride.

6. The answer is D. In the Williamson ether synthesis, if the alkyl halide is either tertiary or secondary, there is a good chance that elimination reaction can prevail. However, this is not desired in this reaction. In fact, the compounds given in Choices A, B, and C can undergo elimination reaction. Only the compound in Choice D is exempt from undergoing elimination.

7. The answer is A. Ethers are usually not so reactive, but they will react with concentrated acids. This is exactly the type of reaction given in the question. Methyl bromide is the product formed, and the reaction is a nucleophilic substitution reaction.

8. The answer is B. All the compounds given are ethers except in Choice B. Choice B is an ester.

9. The answer is B.

Reaction 1 results in bromobenzene (Compound A). In Reaction 2, the bromobenzene formed is hydrolyzed to phenol.

10. The answer is B. Phenol has the hydroxyl group which is an ortho/para activator. So the substitutions are more likely to be in the ortho and para positions of the ring.

11. The answer is A. Only the ortho position will result in the nitro group and hydroxyl group being close enough to engage in such bonding.

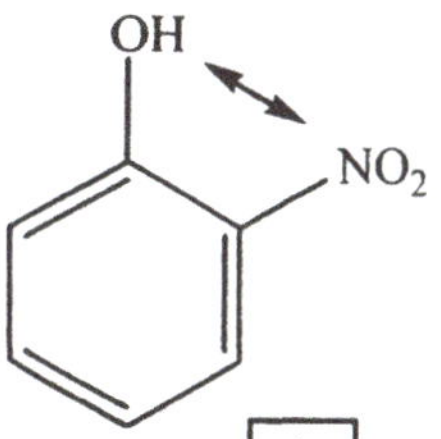

As you can see in the diagram, the intramolecular hydrogen bonding is most pronounced in ortho-nitrophenol because of the proximity of the -NO_2 group to the hydroxyl group.

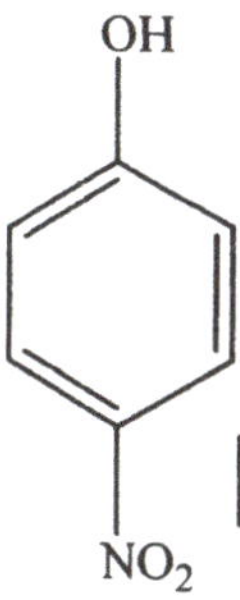

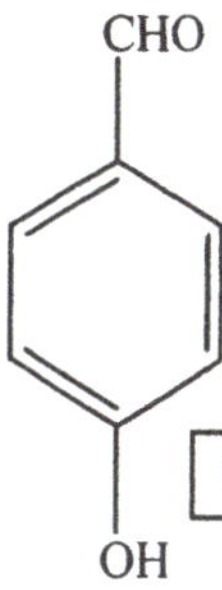

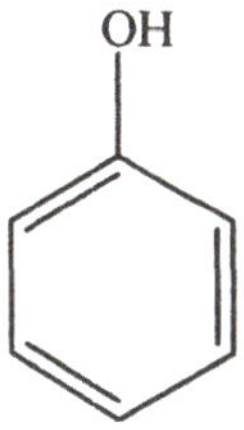

CHAPTER 24 SOLUTIONS

1. The answer is B. The lowest boiling point is likely to be exhibited by Compound B which is an alkane. The highest boiling point is attributed to Compound A which can undergo extensive intermolecular hydrogen bonding, followed by the alcohol, and trailed by Compound D.

2. The answer is D. In general, aryl amines are less basic than ammonia. Alkyl amines are more basic than ammonia. Among alkyl amines, secondary amines are generally more basic than primary amines.

3. The answer is D. Esters have the general formula RCOOR. There are no nitrogens in it.

4. The answer is D. The given reaction is a reduction reaction.

5. The answer is D. In general, alcohols (comparable) are more acidic than amines. In the choices, the only alcohol given is ethanol.

6. The answer is B. Tertiary amines cannot have hydrogen bonds themselves, because they have no nitrogen-hydrogen bond connections unlike the other compounds listed.

7. The answer is D. From the values in Table 1, we can compare the basicity of the compounds. It appears that the weakest base is the conjugate base of aniline, which also makes it the most acidic.

8. The answer is B. The conversion that is asked for in the question is accompanied by the loss of carbon dioxide (CO_2). This is a typical example of a decarboxylation reaction.

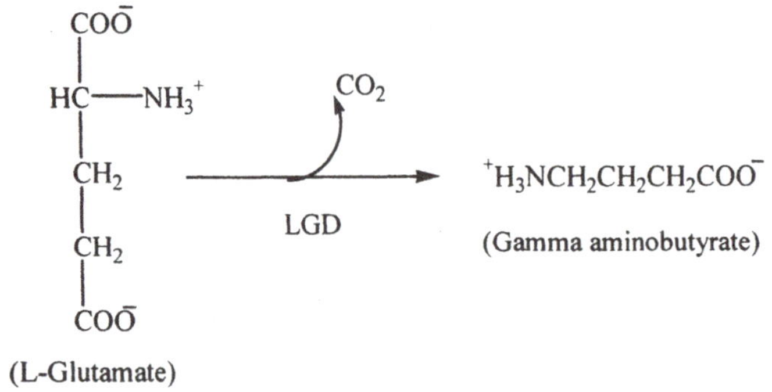

(L-Glutamate)

9. The answer is D. The conversion is best described as a reduction reaction.

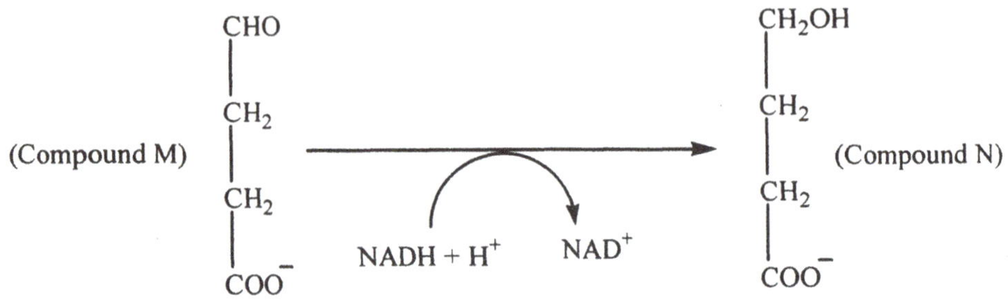

10. The answer is A. In the this molecule, the amino group is on the terminal carbon, the 4th carbon of the molecule. This makes it a primary amine.

11. The answer is C. Of all the amino acids listed, only arginine, with its amine and imine containing side chain, has a basic side chain.

12. The answer is D. All amino acids are optically active except glycine. Glycine has a simple structure and is achiral.

The structure of glycine.:

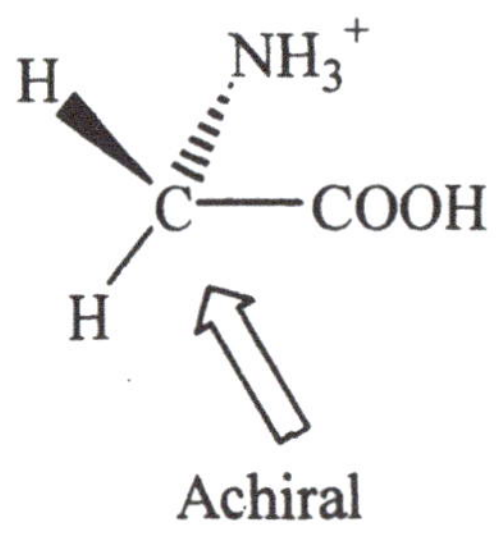

13. The answer is D. At a certain pH (unique for each amino acid), the net charge of an amino acid equals zero. When this pH is achieved, it is said to be at the amino acid's isoelectric point. At the isoelectric pH of an amino acid, the net movement of that particular amino acid will be zero when the amino acid is subjected to an electric field.

14. The answer is C. The general structure of an amino acid is shown below:

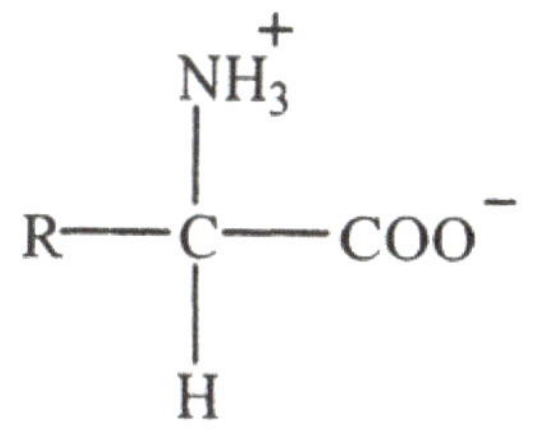

$$R\text{---}\underset{\underset{H}{|}}{\overset{\overset{+}{NH_3}}{\overset{|}{C}}}\text{---}COO^-$$

15. The answer is D. Amino acids are bound together when an amino group from one acid attached to the carbonyl group on another acid, resulting in an amide bond. This bond is known as a peptide bond when it occurs between amino acids.

16. The answer is D. Amino acids are the building blocks of proteins.

17. The answer is D. Proteases are enzymes that can affect the structural integrity of proteins. Strong bases and acids can also affect the structural mode of proteins.

18. The answer is D. Amino acids can engage in disulfide links of they contain sulfur. Of the amino acids listed, only cysteine has sulfur atoms in its structure.

19. The answer is D. All amino acids have at least one carboxyl group. Hence, statement I is true. Amino acids have high melting points since they can have multiple charges. This results in strong ionic interactions and hence much energy is required to break the ionic interactions between them. Thus it is hard to break the crystal lattice, and they have high boiling points. Hence, statement II is true. Depending on the pH and the particular amino acid's nature, amino acids can have either a net positive charge, a net negative charge, or a net zero charge. Hence, statements III and IV are true.

20. The answer is C. Amino acids will cease to move in isoelectric gel when they achieve a neutral zwitterion state and are no longer attracted to either electrode. This will happen when the pH of the gel is equal to its pI.

21. The answer is C. The **p**eptide bond is a covalent bond which connects amino acids in the formation of a peptide or the primary structure of a protein. The peptide link is formed between the amino group of one amino acid and the carboxyl group of the adjacent amino acid.

22. The answer is B. A carbon group double bonded to a nitrogen is known as an amine.

23. The answer is D. From the table, we can assess the behavior of amino acids by comparing the pKa values of the amino acids. At pH 7 only glutamate will have a net negative charge.

24. The answer is D. Amino acids with basic side chains are lysine, arginine, and histidine.

CHAPTER 25 SOLUTIONS

1. The answer is D. Galactose, glucose, and ribose are monosaccharides. Maltose is a disaccharide made of glucose units.

2. The answer is B. We can rule out Choices A and C, because the given sugar is not a D-sugar. Ribose is a 5-carbon sugar. So Choice D is also ruled out.

3. The answer is D. The synthesis of sugar probably resulted in mostly one form of the sugar. According to the question, there was a change in optical activity. This is due to a phenomenon called mutarotation. The sugar solution that was made mutarotated to form its corresponding anomer, which changed the observed optical activity. The mutarotation will continue until an equilibrium is established.

4. The answer is C. Glycogen is the only non-disaccharide listed. All the other molecules are disaccharides. In animals, carbohydrates are stored mainly in the form of glycogen. It is mostly stored in the liver and the skeletal muscles.

5. The answer is B.

$$\begin{array}{c} CHO \\ | \\ H\!\!-\!\!\!-\!\!-OH \\ | \\ H\!\!-\!\!\!-\!\!-OH \\ | \\ CH_2OH \end{array}$$

There are two chiral carbons in the given structure. So the number of possible optical isomers is $2^2 = 4$.

6. The answer is A. Fructose, glucose, and galactose are monosaccharides. The only choice that is not a monosaccharide is sucrose. Sucrose is a disaccharide formed by glucose and fructose.

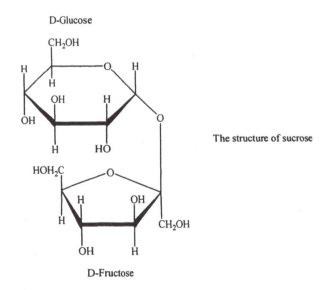

The structure of sucrose

7. The correct answer C. The given structure is not glucose. Ribose is a five-carbon sugar. The given structure is a six-carbon sugar. Maltose is a disaccharide. Further, the given structure is a ketose sugar, and the only ketohexose sugar listed is fructose.

8. The answer is A.

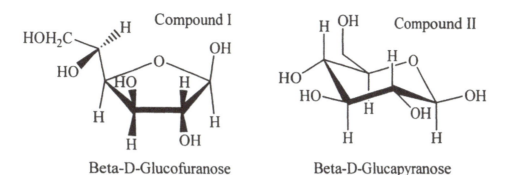

Beta-D-Glucofuranose   Beta-D-Glucapyranose

Statements 1 and 2 are true. Both given structures are glucose; one is in the furanose ring form, and the other is in the pyranose ring form. The five-membered ring of glucose is called glucofuranose. The six-membered ring of glucose is called glucopyranose.

9. The answer is B. Glucose and mannose are not anomers, nor are they are mirror images. So Choices A and C are ruled out. Choice D is not true. In fact, they are epimers. Epimers are isomeric sugars that differ in their configurations only at one of their stereogenic centers.

10. The answer is A. Disaccharides are formed by the combination or bonding of two monosaccharides by a linkage called the glycosidic linkage.

11. The answer is C. Anomers differ only in stereogenicity at the anomeric carbon. The structures of alpha-D-glucose and beta-D-glucose are drawn below. They are anomers.

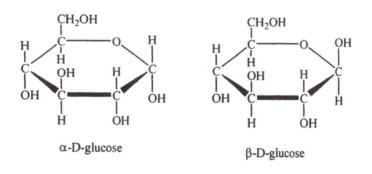

α-D-glucose   β-D-glucose

CHAPTER 26 SOLUTIONS

1. The answer is B. Triglycerides are triesters of glycerol. A triglyceride can be represented as follows:

As a result of hydrolysis, each mole of a triglyceride can give 1 mole of glycerol and 3 moles of fatty acids.

2. The answer is D. Steroids comprise a group of cyclical organic compounds whose basis is a characteristic arrangement of seventeen carbon atoms in a four-ring structure linked together from three 6-carbon rings followed by a 5-carbon ring and an eight-carbon side chain on carbon 17. All of these molecules are steroids.

CHAPTER 27 SOLUTIONS

1. The answer is A. Crystallization is based on solubility. Solutes are more soluble in hot liquids (solvents) than they are in cold liquids. If a saturated hot solution is allowed to cool, the solute is no longer soluble in the solvent and forms crystals of pure compound. Impurities are excluded from the growing crystals and the pure solid crystals can be separated from the dissolved impurities by filtration.

2. The answer is D. Distillation is used to purify a compound by separating it from a non-volatile or less-volatile material. When different compounds in a mixture have different boiling points, they separate into individual components when the mixture is carefully distilled.

3. The answer is D. According to the passage, the reactions in Experiment 3 are based on a unimolecular substitution mechanism. Based on this information, we can say that compound B has the fastest reaction rate. The second fastest is compound C. These observations rule out Choices A, B, and C. Compound A is a primary alcohol and is not likely to undergo a S_N1 reaction.

4. The answer is B. According to the passage, propanone is reacted with the reagent to form a product that lacks the carbonyl group. Note that the compound propanone is a ketone and contains a carbonyl group. But after the reaction, the carbonyl group is not present in the product formed. So the peak that disappeared is the carbonyl peak.

5. The answer is C. The conversion results in the formation of a glycol (an alcohol). Such a conversion is best described as an oxidation reaction.

6. The answer is C. Compounds A, B and C are alcohols. They don't have carboxyl groups. They have different reaction rates for substitution reactions. Since they are alcohols, they all have broad IR peaks around 3400 cm^{-1}.

7. The answer is A. The compound B is *tert*-butyl alcohol.

$$H_3C-\underset{\underset{CH_3}{|}}{\overset{\overset{CH_3}{|}}{C}}-OH$$

Even though there are three methyl groups, all the methyl groups are equivalent and so are their protons. So the methyl protons give rise to one peak. The hydroxylic proton will give rise to another peak, totaling two sets of NMR peaks.

8. The answer is B. Since the compound is insoluble in water, statement I is true. Since the compound is insoluble in 5% aqueous sodium hydroxide, statement II is false. Since the compound is an aromatic compound, statement III is true. The compound is not a strong base. Hence, statement IV is false.

CHAPTER 28 SOLUTIONS

1. The answer is B. Acid-catalyzed dehydration of the alcohol shown will result in a mixture of alkenes. All the given choices are alkenes. But Choice B is different, because it has 8 carbons. The parent alcohol has only 7 carbons. So Choice B is not possible as one of the products. All the other compounds given are possible products because of the rearrangement involved in this type of reaction.

2. The answer is C. The question asks for the number of double bonds present in the unsaturated alkene that undergoes complete hydrogenation. Each double bond to be converted to a saturated bond requires 2 hydrogen atoms. If 8 moles of hydrogen (hydrogen is diatomic) is used per mole of the compound, the compound should have 8 double bonds.

3. The answer is D. Ozonolysis is a two-step reaction sequence in which carbonyl groups are generated. The double bonded carbon atoms become the carbon of the carbonyl groups that are created.

4. The answer is B. In this reaction, 2-butene is reacted with peroxyacetic acid. This reagent converts the alkene into an epoxide, which is a compound that has a three-sided ring with an oxygen atom in the ring.

5. The answer is C. This reaction (hydroboration-oxidation) involves the conversion of 1-butene into an alcohol by hydration. The hydration follows anti-Markovnikov's rule. There is no rearrangement in this reaction.

$$CH_3CH_2CH{=}CH_2 \xrightarrow[\text{2. } H_2O_2/\ OH^-]{\text{1. } B_2H_6} CH_3CH_2CH_2CH_2OH$$

6. The answer is A. The heat of hydrogenation decreases as there are more and more substituents in the alkene group. Among the choices, the least amount of substitution is for ethylene.

7. The answer is A. The reaction between 1-propene and HBr in the presence of peroxides results in the addition of HBr into the alkene group. The addition follows anti-Markovnikov's rule. The reaction is shown below:

$$H_3CH_2C{=}CH_2 \longrightarrow H_3CH_2CCH_2Br$$

8. The answer is B. The treatment of an alkene with a strong oxidizing agent like $KMnO_4$ will result in the formation of a geminal diol.

9. The answer is C. Since the acid-catalyzed dehydration sequence may involve rearrangement depending on the alcohol involved, Choice A is wrong. Choice B is only partially correct. Even though it is true that there can be rearrangement, the process of rearrangement results in more stable intermediates rather than less stable intermediates. The major product is the most substituted product, because the most substituted product translates to higher stability.

10. The answer is B. Rearrangement is possible in acid-catalyzed dehydration of alcohols. The intermediate is a carbocation, not a carbanion. This eliminates statements I and III. Depending on the type of alcohol, the rearrangement may involve either methyl shift or hydride shift.

11. The answer is D. All the compounds listed in the choices can be synthesized by the oxidation of alkenes.

12. The answer is B.

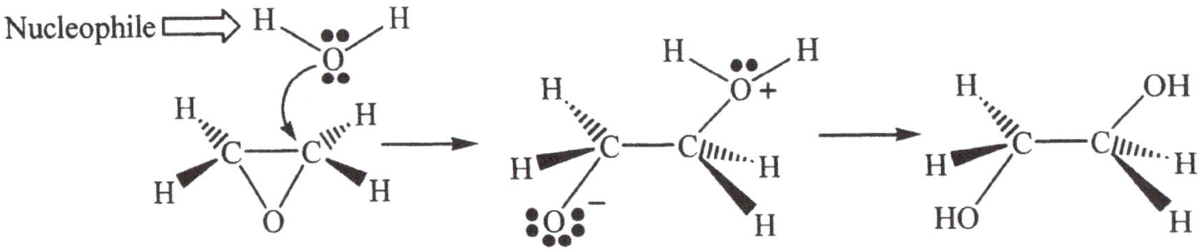

13. The answer is B. The oxidation of methanal will yield carbon dioxide.

14. The answer is D. Both of these reaction will result in an alkene. X will result in a cis alkene due to the syn addition of hydrogen while Y will result in a trans alkene after Birch reduction of an alkyne into a trans alkene.

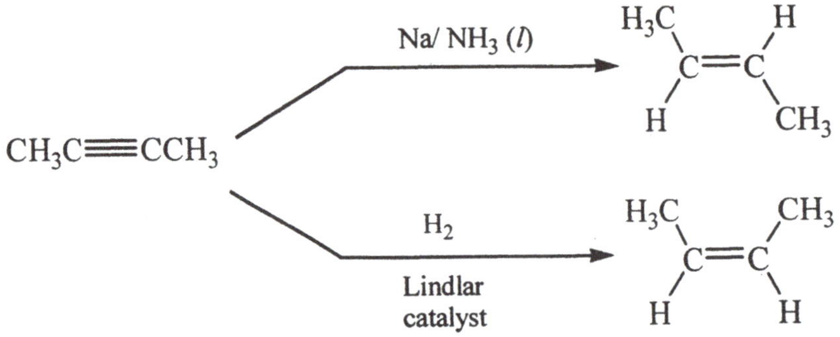

These two products are *cis-trans* isomers and are commonly called *geometric isomers.*

15. The answer is B.

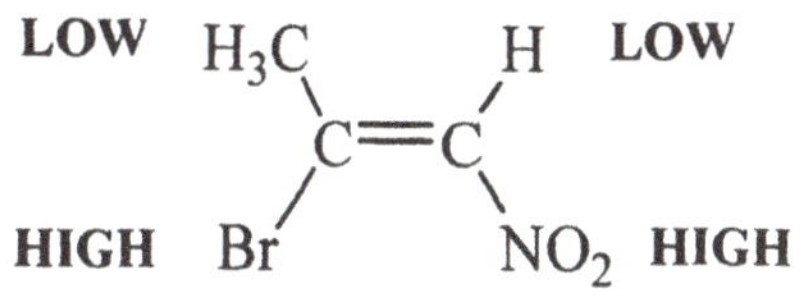

The given structure has Z-configuration. Recall that the priorities are based on the atomic number of the atom bonded to the double bonded carbon.

CHAPTER 29 SOLUTIONS

1. The answer is B. The shortest bond here is the triple bond.

2. The answer is B.

Bottle A – *cis*-2-Butene
Bottle B – 1-Propyne
Bottle C – Butene

Compare the carbon-carbon bonds that distinguish these compounds. *cis*-2-Butene is an alkene which has a carbon-carbon double bond. 1-Butyne is an alkyne and has a carbon-carbon triple bond and butane has carbon-carbon single bonds. The triple bonded carbon-carbon bonds have the highest bond dissociation energy. Bottle B contains 1-propyne.

3. The answer is C. Of the given choices, acetylene is the most acidic and has the lowest pK_a value.

4. The answer is B. Lindlar catalyst is a combination catalyst which does selective or restrictive hydrogenation of alkynes to alkenes. Furthermore, the product is a *cis*-alkene.

5. The answer is C. When 1-butyne is treated with sulfuric acid in the presence of mercuric oxide as catalyst, hydration occurs. The hydration follows Markovnikov's rule and forms a ketone. The reaction is given below:

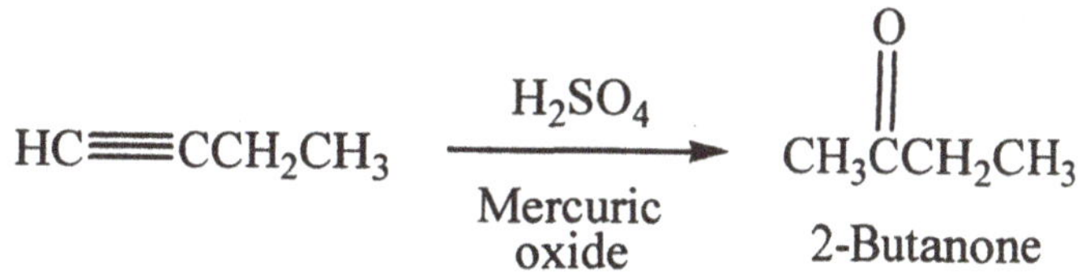

6. The answer is D. When 3-hexyne undergoes ozonolysis, propanoic acid is formed.

$$CH_3CH_2C{\equiv}CCH_2CH_3 \xrightarrow[\text{2. H}_2\text{O}]{\text{1. O}_3} CH_3CH_2COOH$$

7. The answer is B. The general structure of a vicinal dihalide:

$$R—\overset{\overset{\displaystyle H}{|}}{\underset{\underset{\displaystyle X}{|}}{C}}—\overset{\overset{\displaystyle H}{|}}{\underset{\underset{\displaystyle X}{|}}{C}}—R' \qquad X = \text{Halogen}$$

The double dehydrohalogenation (two dehydrohalogenations or eliminations) of vicinal dihalide results in an alkyne.

8. The answer is D. There is nothing there to dehydrate or dehydrohalogenate in an alkyne. This eliminates Choices A and B. Hydrolysis will not help the direct conversion of an alkyne to alkane. A simple hydrogenation is the best way to accomplish this conversion.

9. The answer is A. The liquid ammonia-sodium combination can be used to convert an alkyne to a *trans*-alkene. In essence, this reaction involves the restrictive hydrogenation of an alkyne to an alkene (*trans*-product).

10. The answer is D. Alkynes have higher boiling points than corresponding alkanes. So Choice A is true. Alkynes have *sp* hybridized carbons. So Choice B is true. Choice C is also true, since a terminal alkyne like acetylene can form acetylide ions when exposed to strong bases.

$$HC{\equiv}C\overset{..}{:}^{-} \qquad \text{(Acetylide ion)}$$

11. The answer is C. Alkynes are characterized by hybrid orbitals called *sp* orbitals. In the *sp* orbitals, there is 50% *s* character and 50% *p* character.

12. The answer is B.

Reaction 3

$$H_3CC{\equiv}CH \xrightarrow{\text{HBr}} H_3C\overset{\overset{\displaystyle Br}{|}}{C}{=}CH_2$$

Alkynes, just like alkenes, can undergo addition reactions. Reaction 2 is a typical example of an addition reaction.

13. The answer is D.

$$HC{\equiv}CH \xrightarrow[\text{Liq.NH}_3]{\text{NaNH}_2} HC{\equiv}\overset{+}{C}\,\overset{-}{Na} \xrightarrow[\text{bromide}]{n\text{-butyl}} HC{\equiv}C(CH_2)_3CH_3$$

14. The answer is C. Oxidizing agents oxidize other compounds; they do not reduce! This rules out Choice D. Choice B does not make any sense either. The alkyne is not being reduced to an alkane, but is being reduced to an alkene. This is not the most reduced form. Choice A is incorrect. The function of quinoline is to moderate the activity of the catalyst so that the double bonded alkenes that are formed will not undergo further reduction to form alkanes. Moreover, quinoline is not the actual catalyst.

15. The answer is D. According to the passage, quinoline is a heterocyclic amine.

Quinoline

16. The answer is D. The product of this catalytic conversion reaction is a *trans*-alkene. The combination of reagents (group I metal with liquid ammonia) used is unique in the sense that the product formed is a *trans*-product. The intermediate involved in this reaction, called the alkenyl radical, readily forms the resulting *trans*-product.

CHAPTER 30 SOLUTIONS

1. The answer is B. Dimethylated benzenes are called xylenes.

2. The answer is B.

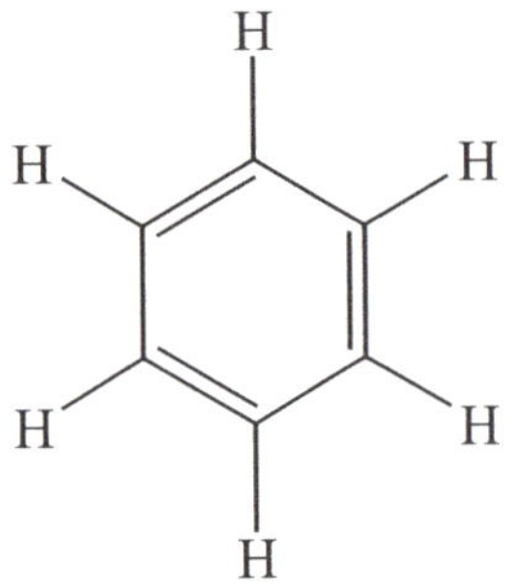

The carbons in the benzene ring are sp^2 hybridized.

3. The answer is C. See explanation for Question 1.

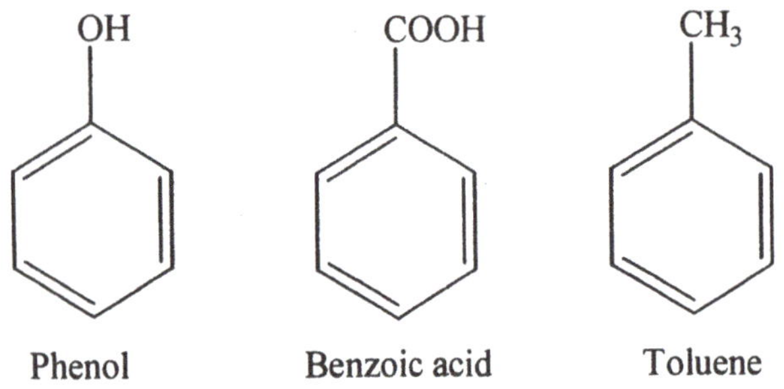
OH
COOH
CH_3
Phenol
Benzoic acid
Toluene

4. The answer is B. For a compound to be aromatic, it should have 4n+2 number of pi electrons. So the numbers satisfying the 4n+2 condition are 2, 6, 10, 14, ... Four is not in this series and that is the answer.

5. The answer is A. This reaction is an electrophilic aromatic substitution reaction. The product formed is nitrobenzene. In the reaction, nitronium ion acts as the electrophile which attacks the benzene to form the cyclohexadienyl intermediate, followed by the elimination of the proton to form nitrobenzene. The reaction mechanism follows:

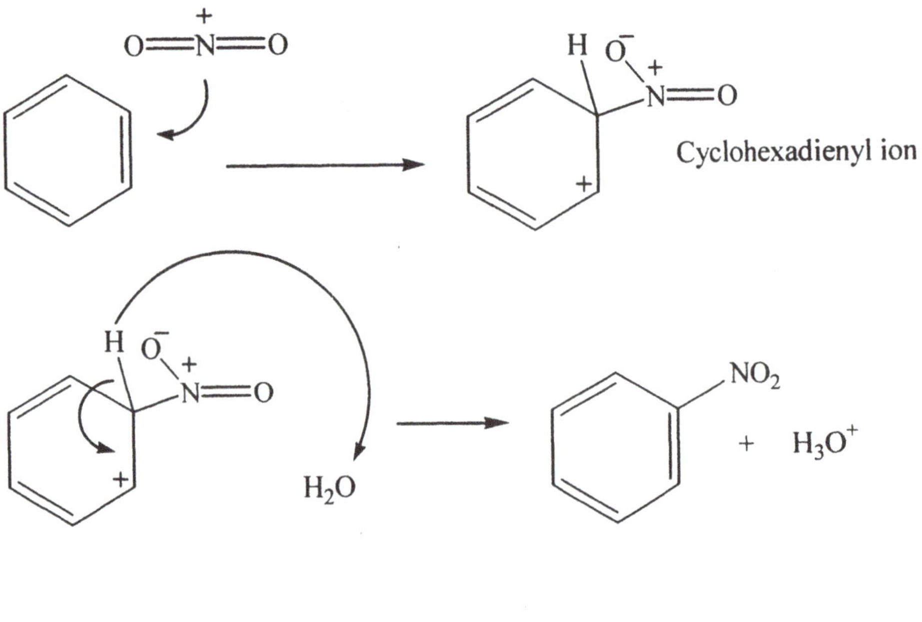
Cyclohexadienyl ion
H_2O
NO_2
+ H_3O^+

6. The answer is D. This reaction is best described as a Friedel-Crafts alkylation reaction.

7. The answer is A. This reaction is commonly called the Clemmensen reaction.

8. The answer is D. The nitro group ($-NO_2$) is a strongly electron withdrawing group, and thus a meta deactivating group. So it favors meta substitutions the most.

9. The answer is C. The regioselectivity of halogens favor ortho/para positions. Halogens are electron withdrawing entities that are ortho/para directing and also deactivating groups.

10. The answer is B. The -CHO group present in the ring is best described as a meta-directing group. So the most likely position of substitution is the meta position.

11. The answer is D. This reaction is a Friedel-Crafts alkylation reaction. This rules out Choice A. In an alkylation reaction, there is a possibility of rearrangement. The primary alkyl halide (*n*-propyl chloride) can form secondary carbocations by rearrangement. To avoid this type of rearrangement, chemists often use Friedel-Crafts acylation reactions which do not involve rearrangement. The carbonyl group in the acylation product can be easily reduced to get the desired hydrocarbon.

12. The answer is A. An alkoxy group can be represented as -OR, where R stands for an alkyl group. It is an ortho/para-directing group and also a good activating group.

13. The answer is C. The substituent -OH is an ortho/para activator. The resulting product is a bromine substitution product. The only choice that fits the reasoning is C.

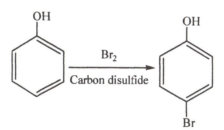

14. The answer is A. The reaction shown is neither an addition reaction, nor an elimination reaction. So the Choices B, C, and D can be ruled out. This is a typical electrophilic substitution reaction.

15. The answer is C. The inscribed circle stands for the pi-system of electrons present in the benzene ring. Let's be more precise: The circle represents the 6 pi electrons of the benzene ring. Choice D states "8 pi-electrons" which is wrong.

16. The answer is D. To answer this question, we have to think about the substituent; the nitro group. The nitro group is a meta deactivating group. So the substitution predominantly results in a meta-product (1,3 substituted). According to the passage, compound C is the major product.

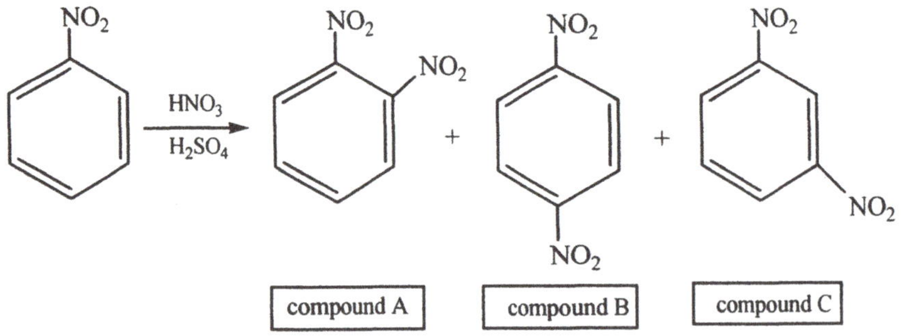

compound A   compound B   compound C

CHAPTER 31 SOLUTIONS

1. The answer is B. The indicated bond is best described as a phosphate anhydride bond.

2. The answer is D. The given reaction is a hydrolysis reaction.

3. The answer is B. The interconversion between the compounds X and Y is a typical example of tautomerism. Compound X is the enol form of pyruvate. Compound Y is the keto form of pyruvate. The interconversion of such forms is called tautomerism.

4. The answer is D. The bond indicated by the arrow is an example of N-glycosidic bond.

5. The answer is A. According to the passage, the hydrolysis of ATP has a negative change in free energy (ΔG). So it is sensible to say that the products have less energy than that of the reactants.

6. The answer is C. ATP is a higher energy-currency than AMP. So the hydrolysis of AMP will have a ΔG that is less negative than -31 kJ/mole (given in the passage). Moreover, the conversion represented in the question is the formation of AMP rather than the hydrolysis of AMP. This eliminates Choices B and D. According to the clue given in the question, the products have higher free energy than the reactants. This can give only a positive ΔG.

7. The answer is C. This is a four-carbon chain with an alkyne between the two middle carbons. This results in two sp-hybridized carbons and two sp^3 hybridized carbons.

SECTION 1 CONTENT REVIEW SOLUTIONS

1. **B.** The size of atoms ranges from 2.5×10^{-11} m (hydrogen), to 2.73×10^{-10} m (cesium). Generally, a unit (and prefix) are chosen that corresponds to the appropriate power of ten for the base unit. For atoms, the most commonly used unit is the angstrom Å, which is 10^{-10} m.

2. **D.** The charge of an electron is known as the elementary charge, whose magnitude has been measured to be $1.6021766208(98) \times 10^{-19}$ C and was first measured using Millikan's oil drop experiment.

3. **C.** Generally the most common isotope of an element will have a mass number close to the average atomic mass for that element on the periodic table. The atomic masses of carbon, oxygen and sulfur are 12.0107 amus, 15.9994 amus and 32.065 amus, respectively. The atomic mass of nitrogen is 14.0067 amus, therefore ^{15}N has a relatively low percent abundance.

4. **A.** Choice A is the definition of an atomic mass unit (amu).

5. **C.** Since an amu is 1/12 the mass of a ^{12}C atom, and since one mole of ^{12}C is 12 amus and has a mass of 12 g, then 1 gram will be one mole of amus or alternatively Avogadro's number of amus.

6. **C.** The rows of elements exhibit systematic or periodic changes in properties and are called periods.

7. **A.** Elements in the columns of the periodic table tend to have similar chemical properties and are sometimes called families or groups.

8. **B.** The number of protons is the atomic number and is the subscript to the left of the atomic symbol.

9. **A.** The mass number is the sum of the protons and neutrons for a particular isotope of an element and is the superscript to the left of the atomic symbol.

10. **C.** The most common definition of electronegativity was developed by Linus Pauling as the ability of an atom to attract electrons to itself in a chemical bond. The scale was defined based on a value of 4.0 for fluorine, the most electronegative element. If an element does not form compounds it doesn't have an electronegativity value. Oxygen is the most electronegative element in group VIA (group 16), having a value of 3.44, whereas Argon is the most electronegative Noble gas, having a value of 3.2. There are no known compounds of helium or neon.

11. **C.** The nucleus contains the two most massive subatomic particles, protons and neutrons. Electrons orbit the nucleus.

12. **C.** The proton and electron have relative charges of +1 and -1, respectively, whereas the neutron has no charge.

13. **D.** An anion is a negatively charged atom or group of atoms, resulting from the addition of additional electrons.

14. **A.** The Heisenberg uncertainty principle states that you can not simultaneously know the velocity and position of a moving object with great certainty. This is especially true for electrons that are moving at nearly the speed of light, therefore all we can do is predict the probability of finding an electron at a certain location in the atom. The Bohr model of the atom is consistent with Rutherford's gold foil experiment and choices B and D. While the Bohr model is similar to the model of the solar system, only the planets have elliptical orbits, no experiment has suggested that electrons have two dimensional elliptical orbits.

15. **B.** As seen on the Periodic Table, iron has an atomic number of 26.

16. **C.** The mass number is the sum of the protons and neutrons.

$$56 - 26 = 30 \text{ neutrons}$$

17. **A.** The charge must equal the total charge of the protons and electrons.

$$3+ = 26 - x$$
$$x = 23$$

18. **B.** Read carefully, this is not the same question as question 15. The charge of Fe^{3+} ion does not change the number of protons. If it is an iron atom, there must be 26 protons.

19. **C.** Nucleons are the subatomic particles located in the nucleus. The mass number tells us the number of nucleons.

20. **A.** As seen on the periodic table: the atomic number of hydrogen is 1 and its atomic mass is 1.00794 amus; the atomic number of helium is 2 and its atomic mass is 4.002602 amus; the atomic number of Boron is 5 and its atomic mass is 10.811 amus; and the atomic number of oxygen is 8 and its atomic mass is 15.9994 amus.

21. **B.** The atomic mass of potassium (element 19) is close to 39, therefore there are 39 - 19 = 20 neutrons.

22. **D.** Of the answer options, lithium is the only metal. Metals tend to form cations by loss of electrons.

23. **C.** The most electronegative element of the answer options is nitrogen.

24. **C.** The neutron to proton ratios are:
Ca, 1:1; Mg, 1:1; V, 28:23; Cr, 7:6.

25. **D.** The atomic number, or number of protons, determines the identity of the element.

26. **A.** The mass of an alpha particle is $6.64465675(29) \times 10^{-27}$ kg (4 amu), the mass of a neutron is $1.674927351(74) \times 10^{-27}$ kg (1 amu), the mass of a proton is $1.672621777(74) \times 10^{-27}$ kg (1 amu) and the mass of an electron is $9.10938291(40) \times 10^{-31}$ kg (0 amu). An alpha particle is essentially two protons and two neutrons. A free neutron is essentially a combination of a proton and an electron, into which it decays by beta emission and therefore a neutron is slightly more massive than a proton.

27. **B.** In terms of relative charge, an alpha particle has a 2+ charge, a proton has a +1 charge, a neutron has 0 charge and an electron has -1 charge.

28. **D.** For a particular element, the number of protons will always be the same. The number of neutrons (and therefore nucleons) can vary, depending upon the

isotope. The number of electrons can vary if the element forms a cation or anion.

29.   **A.** Nucleons are the subatomic particles in the nucleus, i.e. protons and neutrons, both have considerably more mass than an electron.

30.   **D.** For the stable isotopes of the light elements, the ratio of neutrons to protons is close to 1:1. As the number of protons in the nucleus increases the electrostatic repulsion of the positive charges of the protons, requires this ratio to increase, in order to maintain nuclear stability. Beginning with element 83 (Bi), there a no elements with stable isotopes, even though some may have very long half-lives.

31.   **C.** The number of atoms can be calculated by dividing the mass by the formula weight, times the number of atoms in the formula and finally times Avogadro's number. However, calculating the number of moles of atoms would allow you to answer this question, without unnecessary waste of time.

$NaCl$: [(100 g)/(58 g/mol)](2) = 3.4 moles of atoms
$CaCl_2$: [(80 g)/(111 g/mol)](3) = 2.2 moles of atoms
$MgCl_2$: (3 mol)(3) = 9 moles of atoms
$NaCl$: (4 mol)(2) = 8 moles of atoms

32.   **B.** The most efficient method to answer this question would be to calculate the moles of molecules, by dividing the mass by the formula weight. Note that NaCl and argon are not molecular compounds.

CO_2: (30 g)/(44 g/mol) = 0.68 moles
H_2O: (30 g)/(18 g/mol) = 1.7 moles

33.   **D.** Since each answer choice has one mole, the answer will simply be the formula with the most number of atoms.

34.   **C.** Multiply the number of moles by the formula weight, or atomic mass.

$NaCl$: (1 mol)(58 g/mol) = 58 g
H_2O: (2 mol)(18 g/mol) = 36 g
Ne: (3 mol)(20 g/mol) = 60 g
He: (4 mol)(4 g/mol) = 16 g

35.   **B.** For choices B and D, multiply the moles by the formula weight.

$CaCO_3$: (1.5 mol)(100 g/mol) = 150 g
$CaCl_2$: (1 mol)(111 g/mol) = 111 g

36.   **A.** The formula weight of water is 18 g/mol and its density is 1 g/cm^3, so the volume

1 mol(18 g/mol)(1 cm^3/g) = 18 cm^3

37.   **A.** The formula for methanol is CH_3OH.

(2 mol)(32 g/mol)(1 cm^3/0.792 g)
$\sim$ (64)/(8 x 10^{-1}) = 8 x 10^1 = 80 cm^3

38.   **A.** For an ideal gas there are 22.4 liters per mole.

(5.6 L)(1 mol/22.4 L)(1 L/0.9002 g)(6 x 10^{23} atoms/mol)
= 1.7 x 10^{23} atoms

39.   **A.** Convert the mass to moles by dividing by the formula weight and then multiply by 22.4 L/mol. However, simply calculating the moles will allow you to most efficiently determine the answer. Also note that the atomic mass increases as you go down the group, so for the pairs of noble gases with the same mass: the volume of Ne will be greater than the volume of Ar; and the volume of Kr will be greater than the volume of Xe, eliminating

choices B and D. So you really only need to calculate the moles of Ne and Kr.

Ne: (30 g)(1 mol/20 g) = 1.5 mol
Kr: (90 g)(1 mol/84 g) = 1.1 mol

40.   **B.** Planck's constant (6.6 x 10^{-33} m^2kg/s) is extremely small, so its inverse is extremely large.

10^2 x 6 x 10^{23} $\sim$ 10^{26}
1/(6.6 x 10^{-34}) $\sim$ 10^{33}
(100 g)(1 mol/4 g)(6 x 10^{23}) $\sim$ 10^{25}
(200 g)(1 mol/4 g)(2 p/He)(6 x 10^{23}) $\sim$ 10^{25}

41.   **A.** The atomic mass of sodium and chlorine are 23 g/mol and 35 g/mol, respectively. The percent sodium must be less than 50%, eliminating choices B and C.

(23/58) x 100 = 39 %

In the case of choice D, it is pretty close to 50%, so hopefully you could eliminate that answer option as well, without have to take the time to actually do the math.

42.   **C.**   C: 12 x 6 = 72 amu
H: 1 x 12 = 12 amu
O: 16 x 6 = 96 amu
FW = 180 amu

The carbon must be less than 50%, eliminating choice D.

(72/180) x 100 = 40 %

43.   **C.** Water has a higher density than oil. Oil floats on water.

44.   **D.** Standard temperature is 0°C. The density of neon gas at 0°C is 0.9 g/L. Water could be either a solid or a liquid at this temperature. The density of liquid water is close to 1.0 g/cm^3, whereas the density of ice is 0.917 g/cm^3. Ice floats on liquid water. The density of liquid methanol (mp -98 °C) at 0°C is 0.79 g/cm^3. Most organic compounds are less dense than water. The density of liquid deuterated water, also known as "heavy water", at 0 °C is 1.11 g/cm^3 and the density of heavy ice is 1.10 g/cm^3. Whichever phase of matter the heavy water is in at 0°C, it will have the most mass.

45.   **A.** Density is mass per unit volume. If the mass remains constant, for the density to decrease, the volume must increase.

46.   **B.** Density is the mass per unit volume, therefore kilograms per liter (kg/L) is an acceptable combination of units.

47.   **A.** The %C can be calculated by taking the atomic mass of carbon (12 amu), and divide by the formula weight of carbon dioxide (44 amu) and then multiplying by 100.

48.   **B.** The mass of an O_2 molecule (32 amu) is slightly greater than the mass of an N_2 molecule (28 amu). If the masses were the same, then the mass percentage would be the same as the volume percentage, but since O_2 has slightly more mass than N_2 we would expect a mass percentage slightly higher than the volume percentage. No calculation is really needed to answer this question.

49.   **A.** 1.251 g x (80/100) = 1.0008 g

50.   **C.** The symbol for the principal quantum number is n. The symbol for the azimuthal quantum number is l, and the symbol for the magnetic quantum number is m_l. The symbol for the spin quantum number

is m_s and the letter s is used to indicate the spherical shape of an orbital whose azimuthal quantum number is zero.

51.   **A.** The principal quantum number n indicates the relative distance that the electron shell is located from the nucleus and hence the size of the associated orbitals. The azimuthal quantum number l indicates the shape; the magnetic quantum number m_l indicates the orientation of an orbital (i.e. p_x, p_y or p_z); and the spin quantum number m_s describes the angular momentum of an electron in an orbital.

52.   **B.** See the explanation for question 51.

53.   **D.** See the explanation for question 51.

54.   **C.** See the explanation for question 51.

55.   **C.** The principal quantum number can have integer values starting with one and going up to infinity. The azimuthal quantum number depends upon the value of n and can have integer values ranging from zero up to the value of n - 1. The magnetic quantum number depends upon the l value and takes on integer values from negative l up to positive l. The spin quantum number is either +1/2 or -1/2.

In choice A, the l value violates the rules; in choices B and D, the m_l value violates the rules.

56.   **B.** Sodium is the first element in the third period, of the periodic table, so n = 3, which puts it in the s-block, s orbitals have l = 0 and m_l must equal zero.

57.   **A.** The values of l are given letter designations describing the shape of the orbital, where l = 0, 1, 2, and 3, correspond to s, p, d, and f, respectively.

58.   **A.** See the explanation for question 51.

59.   **D.** See the explanation for question 51.

60.   **B.** See the explanation for question 51.

61.   **C.** See the explanation for question 51.

62.   **C.** The number of orientations is determined by the possible m_l values. The d orbitals (l = 2) have possible m_l values of -2, -1, 0, +1, +2 and hence five different orientations, sometimes referred to as d_{xy}, d_{xz}, d_{yz}, $d_{z}2$ and $d_x2_{-y}2$.

63.   **A.** There is only one s orbital (l = 0) per shell, three p orbitals (l = 1), five d orbitals (l = 2) and seven f orbitals (l = 3). Only 2l + 1 correctly give the right number of orbitals.

64.   **C.** See the explanation for question 57.

65.   **A.** See the explanation for question 55.

66.   **D.** See the explanation for question 55.

67.   **B.** By definition, no two electrons in an atom can have the same set of four quantum numbers.

68.   **C.** Putting two electrons in the same orbital is energetically costly due to charge repulsion issues, and does not occur until all degenerate orbitals at a particular energy level have at least one electron.

69.   **C.** There are three types of orbitals, s, p and d. There is one s orbital, three p orbitals and five d orbitals, for a total of 9 orbitals, that can hold up to 18 electrons.

70.   **D.** There are four types of orbitals, s, p, d. and f. There is one s orbital, three p orbitals five d orbitals and seven f orbitals, for a total of 16 orbitals, which can hold up to 32 electrons.

71.   **B.** The Aufbau principle can be used to determine the order of relative energies.

You can also use the periodic table and the period numbers to determine the principal quantum numbers for the various orbitals (blocks of elements), but remember that the 3d orbitals are in the 4th period, and the 4f orbital are in the 6th period.

72.   **A.** Choice A correctly describes the Aufbau principle as the order that electrons are placed into the various orbitals based on their relative energies. Choices B and D are consequences of the Pauli exclusion principle. Choice C is Hund's rule.

73.   **C.** Metals are on the left side and nonmetals are in the top right hand corner of the period table. The metals and nonmetals are separated by a zig-zag line of elements with intermediate properties, called the metalloids. There are many more metals than nonmetals.

74.   **B.** Oxygen has six valence electrons, with an electron configuration of $[He]2s^22p^4$. Therefore, there should be four arrows, in the orbital diagram, representing the four valence electrons in the 2p orbitals. This eliminates choice A and D. Only choice B correctly follows Hund's rule.

75.   **A.** Neon, element 10, has a total of 10 electrons. Only choice A has a total of ten electrons, as indicated by the total of the superscripts of the letter designation for the orbitals.

76.   **D.** Chromium is element 24, so Cr^{2+} would have a total of 22 electrons in its electron configuration, eliminating choices A and C. For the ion, there should not be any electrons in the 4s orbital, making choice D the answer.

77.   **C.** Chromium has six valence electrons, which are indicated by the sum of the superscripts for the letter designations of the orbitals. Therefore, we can eliminate choice B. While choice A follows the Aufbau principle, chromium is an exception, because of the stability of the half-filled shell. Choice D would be an excited state.

78.   **B.** Placing an electron in the 5s orbital before completely filling the 3d orbitals does not follow the Aufbau principle, and therefore choice B must be an excited state.

79.   **C.** Nitrogen, phosphorus and arsenic are all in group 15 (group VA). Selenium is in group 16 (group VIA).

80.   **B.** The alkaline earth elements are in group IIA, whereas the alkali metals are in group IA, the halogens are in group VIIA and the noble gases are in group VIIIA.

81. **C.** Of the answer options, only the proton and the electron have charge. A proton is approximately 1900 times more massive than an electron.

82. **C.** Avogadro's number is 6.02 x 10^{23}, which corresponds to the mole. The atomic mass of the isotope ^{12}C is 12 g/mol, by definition. Choice A happens to be the number of hydrogen atoms in 1 g of H_2. Choices B and D are both 1/12 of a mole of carbon atoms.

83. **C.** Most of the halogens, group 17 or VIIA, are nonmetals, except for At, which is a metalloid, and Uus (element 117) whose properties are unknown due to its short half-life.

84. **A.** The hardest and highest melting metals are in the middle of the d-block, i.e. tungsten (group 6) has a melting point of 3422 °C, due to having half-filled shells for metallic bonding. The soft metals are on the edges of the metallic region of the periodic table. Metallic sodium (group 1) can be cut with a knife like butter and has a melting point of 98°C. The melting points of the other group 1 elements go down as you go down the group, with cesium having a melting point of 28°C., melting slightly above room temperature.

85. **B.** Fluorine is the most electronegative element (4.0), followed closely by oxygen (3.4) and then chlorine (3.2). Neon does not have an electronegativity value because it does not form bonds with other elements.

86. **B.** Lithium is the biggest second period element. There are three protons and two electrons in the n = 1 shell. The valence electron experiences an effective nuclear charge of +1, due to the shielding effects of the core electrons. Of the answer options the ratio of core electron charge to nuclear charge is greatest for lithium.

87. **C.** Atoms generally get smaller as you go up a group (column) and from left to right in a period (row).

88. **A.** In the periodic table atomic radii generally decrease from left to right in a period and increase from top to bottom in a group. Therefore, the largest atoms are in the lower left hand corner of the periodic table.

89. **D.** The first ionization energy is the energy required to remove a single electron from an atom, and usually the electron that is easiest to remove. The second ionization energy is the energy necessary to doubly ionize an atom.

$$A^+ (g) + h\upsilon \rightarrow A^{2+} (g) + e^-$$

Of the answer options, potassium cation K^+, has a stable closed shell electron noble gas configuration, and therefore would be the most difficult to ionize to a 2+ cation.

90. **D.** Electron affinity is the change in energy when an atom gains an electron in the gas phase to become an anion.

$$A (g) + e^- \rightarrow A^- (g)$$

Of the answer options neon, with it closed shell electron configuration, forms the least stable anion.

91. **A.** Electronegativity generally increases from left to right in a period and decreases from top to bottom in a group. Sodium and chlorine are separated the most in the periodic table and therefore have the biggest difference in electronegativity.

92. **A.** Atomic weight is the mass of an element and has units of atomic mass units (amu) or g/mol, whereas molecular weight (or formula weight), is the g/mol of a compound. Therefore using dimensional analysis, choice A is a calculation of moles.

$$\cancel{g} \div (\cancel{g}/mol) = mol$$

The other choices do not provide the appropriate unit.

93. **C.** Electrons located in shells underneath the valence shell mask some of the nuclear charge such that the effective nuclear charge is the sum of the number of protons minus the number of core, or inner shell, electrons.

94. **A.** Electron affinity is the energy associated with an atom gaining an electron to become negatively charged. A negative value indicates that energy is released when the atom gains an electron, because the negative ion is more stable than the neutral atom.

95. **A.** Linus Pauling assigned fluorine, the most electronegative element, an electronegativity of 4.

96. **C.** Ionization is when an electron is removed from an atom by adding enough energy for the electron to reach the n = ∞ level such that the atom becomes positively charged.

97. **A.** 100 g H_2O x 1 mol/18 g x 2 H/1 H_2O x 6 x 10^{23} atoms/mol = 67 x 10^{23} H atoms.

98. **B.** For water the H% = (2/18) x 100 = 11%.

99. **B.** You could assume a 100 g sample and calculate the whole number mole ratios of the elements. Alternatively, using the formulas provided in the answer, you could calculate the percentage of carbon.

C_2H_6O: %C = (24/46) x 100 = 52.0%
CH_4O: %C = (12/32) x 100 = 37.5%
$C_2H_4O_2$: %C = (24/58) x 100 = 41.0%
CH_2O: %C = (12/30) x 100 = 40.0%

100. **D.** If the electronegativity difference between two atoms is greater than 1.7, the bonding will be ionic, and if the difference is less than 1.7 the bonding will be primarily covalent.

SECTION 2 CONTENT REVIEW SOLUTIONS

1. **A.** An ionic bond is a result of the electrostatic attraction between oppositely charged ions. Alkali metal ions are cations with a 1+ charge (Li^+, Na^+, K^+, etc.) and halide ions are anions with a 1- charge (F^-, Cl^-, Br^-, etc.).

2. **D.** If there is a large difference in electronegativity between two elements, i.e. a metal and a nonmetal, then electrons will be transferred from the metal to the nonmetal, forming a positive cation and a negative anion, respectively, which have ionic bonding. See also the explanation for question 1.

3. **B.** While lithium and helium are a metal and a nonmetal, respectively, helium has a completed valence shell and does not form bonds of any kind.

4. **C.** Noble gases have completely filled valence shells. See also the explanation for question 3.

5. **A.** See the explanation for question 1.

6. **C.** Metals tend to have low electronegativities and lose their valence electrons to form positively charged cations. While carbon and iodine do have positive oxidation states, they both are nonmetals that tend to form anions as well, i.e. carbide and iodide. Gallium and beryllium are both metals and both tend to form cations, however, beryllium's electronegativity (1.57) is less than gallium (1.81) making the latter most likely to be a cation.

7. **C.** The most electronegative element will be the most likely to be an anion. The electronegativities of carbon, boron, chlorine and calcium are 2.55, 2.04, 3.16 and 1.0 respectively. Electronegativities tend to increase from left to right and bottom to top in the periodic table.

8. **B.** Potassium permanganate has K^+ cations and MnO_4^- anions. The bonding within the polyatomic ions, MnO_4^- and PO_4^{3-} is polar covalent bonding. See also the explanation for question 1.

9. **C.** See the explanation for question 8.

10. **A.** See the explanation for question 2.

11. **C.** See the explanation for question 2

12. **A.** The cation and anion simply combine in one step to form the ionic solid, due to electrostatic attraction, e.g.

$$Ca^{2+} (g) + O^{2-} (g) \rightarrow CaO (s)$$

13. **B.** There is only one step, which means the reaction is first order in both calcium and oxide ions, therefore it is second order overall. See also the explanation for question 12.

14. **C.** Covalent bonding occurs between nonmetal atoms with similar electronegativities such that pairs of electrons are shared between the atoms.

15. **A.** Carbon and oxygen are both nonmetals that form polar covalent bonds due to modest differences in electronegativities. For choices B and C, the elements are a metal and a nonmetal, with relatively large differences in electronegativities and ionic bonds. Ammonium and permanganate are a cation and an anion and form ionic bonds. See also the explanations for questions 1 and 2.

16. **C.** See the explanations for questions 1 and 14.

17. **A.** The electronegativities of carbon (2.5) and hydrogen (2.20) are very similar. The electronegativities of nitrogen, oxygen and fluorine are 3.0, 3.4 and 4.0, respectively.

18. **B.** See the explanation for question 17.

19. **A.** A polar covalent bond is formed between nonmetal atoms with modest differences in electronegativity, such that there is a bond dipole, where the atoms have partial positive and negative charges.

20. **D.** See the explanation for question 15.

21. **C.** Nitrogen has an atomic number of 7, with two electrons in the first (n = 1) shell and five electrons in the second shell, or outer valence shell. The group number also indicates the number of electrons in the valence shell of an element. Nitrogen is in group VA (group 15).

22. **B.** Elemental oxygen has six valence electrons and oxygen has two negative oxidation states, -1 (peroxide, O_2^{2-}) and -2 (oxide, O^{2-}).

23. **B.** The formula for the ammonium ion is NH_4^+. Nitrogen has five valence electrons and hydrogen has one valence electron, but since the ammonium ion has a +1 charge, the total number of valence electrons is eight. Alternatively, since nitrogen is more electronegative than hydrogen, we can formally assign nitrogen an oxidation number of -3, which would also give eight valence electrons and none from the hydrogen atoms, each with a +1 oxidation number.

24. **A.** Formal charge is determined by taking the number of valence electrons for an atom, subtract one for each covalent bond to that atom and subtract two for each lone pair of electrons on that atom. In this case, nitrogen has five valence electrons, there are three covalent bonds and one lone-pair, 5 - 3(1) - 1(2) = 0.

25. **C.** Oxygen is the most electronegative element in the formula.

26. **B.** 6 - 1(1) - 3(2) = -1
     See also the explanation for question 24.

27. **B.** 5 - 2(1) - 2(2) = -1
     See also the explanation for question 24.

28. **B.** A resonance structure typically involves switching the position of single and double bonds between atoms in which one of the atoms is involved in both types of bonds. In this case the oxygen atoms labeled A and B are both bonded to the same carbon atom and switching the position of the double bond (and a lone pair) represents two resonance structures.

29. **D.** The carbon-oxygen bonds involving the atoms labeled A and B are involved in a resonance structure and have the same bond order, 1.5 and would have a bond length somewhere between a C-O bond (143 pm) and a C=O bond (120 pm). While the bond order for the oxygen-hydrogen bond is only a single bond, the hydrogen atom is much smaller than nitrogen or oxygen and the O-H bond is the shortest (96 pm) of the answer choices.

30. **B.** The question provides the Lewis dot structure for nitrate (NO_3^-). For a molecule with one nitrogen and three oxygen atoms, there would be a total of 5 + 3(6) = 23 valence electrons. The structure shows 24 total

electrons, 4 bonds and 8 lone pairs. Hence the overall charge must be -1.

31.   **D.** The total number of valence electrons for the formula should be $2(5) + 4(1) = 14$. Only the structure shown in choice D has the proper number of valence electrons, four N-H bonds, a N-N bond and two lone pairs. The structure shown in choice A only has 10 electrons, four N-H bonds and one N-N bond. The structure in choice B only has 12 electrons, four N-H bonds and N=N bond. While the structure shown in choice C has 14 electrons, it violates the octet rule for the nitrogen atoms.

32.   **C.** $5 - 4(1) = +1$
See also the explanation for question 24.

33.   **C.** Sulfur will expand its octet forming a double bond with one oxygen and single bonds with the others.

34.   **B.** There are three resonance structures for nitrate involving two N-O and one N=O bonds.

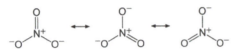

35.   **B.** The electronegativity of oxygen and chlorine are 3.44 and 3.16, respectively.

36.   **D.** See the explanation for question 23.

37.   **B.** In VSEPR theory, lone pairs, single bonds, double bonds and triple bonds each count as a single electron domain or region of electron density around a central atom. In this case there are three bonds to chlorine atoms, which minimizes their interactions by adopting a trigonal planar (Cl-B-Cl = 120°) molecular structure.

38.   **A.** It takes energy to break a stable chemical bond and energy is released when isolated atoms are combined to for stable bonds.

39.   **C.** Bond order increases as the number of pairs of electrons shared between atoms increases, causing a greater degree of attraction between the nuclei of the bonded atoms.

40.   **C.** In general the size of atoms decreases as you go from left to right in a row (period) of the periodic table, and increases as you go down a column (group). Hydrogen atoms are much smaller than the second period elements, so we can eliminate the combination of second period elements, choices B and D. Since oxygen is smaller than nitrogen, the O-H bond (96 pm) will be shorter than the N-H bond (101 pm).

41.   **D.** As bond order is related to the number of pairs of electrons shared by two atoms, there will be a greater attraction between two atoms as the number of shared pairs of electrons increases, which results in a greater bond dissociation energy.

42.   **D.** As bond order increase, bond length decreases. See also the explanation for question 40.

43.   **B.** See the explanation for question 38.

44.   **C.** Completely full shells correspond to 2, 8, 18, 32 electrons for the n = 1, 2, 3 and 4 shells, respectively.

45.   **C.** There are four single bonds, which would correspond to a tetrahedral molecular geometry.

46.   **B.** The molecular geometry is derived from a tetrahedral coordinate (electron domain) geometry for the three different sulfur-oxygen bonds and the lone pair on the central sulfur atom. When there are three bonds and one lone pair, the molecular geometry is a trigonal pyramid.

47.   **C.** See the explanation for question 46.

48.   **A.** The spatial geometry is the same as the molecular geometry and is determined by the location of atoms attached to a central atom. In this case there are three bonds, which is a trigonal planar structure. See also the explanation for question 37.

49.   **C.** The hybridization is determined by the number of s-bonds. There are four s-bonds to the carbon atom, hence we need a hybridization with four atomic orbitals, one s and three p orbitals.

50.   **B.** There are three s-bonds and one p-bond to the carbon atom. See also the explanation for question 48.

51.   **C.** The molecular geometry, in this case, is determined by the maximum angle (109°) between the four different coordinate regions of electron density, i.e. the four bonds to other atoms. See also the explanations for questions 46, 47 and 48.

52.   **B.** For example, the structure of ammonia ($:NH_3$).

53.   **C.** The lone pairs occupy more space than the bonding pairs. The coordinate structure is octahedral and having the lone pairs in opposition positions (180°) minimizes the electrostatic repulsions of the lone-pairs.

54.   **A.** The trigonal planar structure maximizes the angle (120°) between the bonds. A trigonal pyramidal structure would have a smaller angle (109°), which would be electrostatically unfavorable. Since there are only three regions of electron density around the central atom, the tetrahedral and trigonal bipyramidal structures are not appropriate, since they would correspond to coordinate structures with four and five domains, respectively.

55.   **A.** There are a total of five domains in the coordinate structure, which corresponds to a trigonal bipyramid, but since two of these positions are lone pairs, they will occupy the equatorial positions to minimize the lone pair-lone pair interactions. Therefore the molecular geometry is T-shaped with one substituent in an equatorial position and the other two substituents in axial positions.

56.   **A.** The H-O-H angle in water is slightly less than 109°.

57.   **D.** The coordinate geometry results from the two lone pairs and the two O-H bonds. See the explanations for questions 46, 47, 48 and 56.

58.   **D.** The O-C-O bond angle is 180°. There are only two C=O bonds and no lone pairs on the carbon. See also the explanations for questions 46 and 48.

59.   **B.** There are two Xe-F bonds and three lone pairs on the Xe. The coordinate structure is trigonal bipyramidal, with the lone pairs in the equatorial positions, maximizing the angles between the lone pairs (120°) and the fluorines are in axial positions, with a F-Xe-F angle of 180°.

60.   **D.** See the explanation for question 59.

61. **D.** An example of a square planar structure is XeF_4; an example of a square pyramidal structure is $XeOF_4$; and an example of a trigonal bipyramidal structure is PF_5.

62. **D.** In a single replacement reaction, an element reacts with a compound to form a new compound and an element. If the reactant element is a metal, it will replace the metal cation in the compound; if the reactant element is a nonmetal it will replace the nonmetal anion in the compound. A decomposition reaction is when a large compound is broken up into more than one compound. A double replacement is when two ionic compounds react and the combinations of cations and anions are switched, often resulting in the formation of a precipitate. There is no such thing as a triple replacement reaction.

63. **C.** A balanced chemical reaction provides the lowest whole number stoichiometric ratios of reactants and products such that there are the same number of atoms of each element on the reactant and product sides of the arrow. Choice B does not have enough oxygen atoms on the reactant side and choice D has too many oxygen atoms on the product side. Choice A is not the lowest whole number ratio.

64. **D.** In the balanced reaction (see the explanation for question 63), the stoichiometric ratio of CH_4 to O_2 is 1:2, therefore there needs to be eight moles of O_2 to completely react with all of the CH_4, e.g.

$$4 \text{ mol } CH_4 \times 2 \text{ } O_2/1 \text{ } CH_4 = 8 \text{ mol } O_2$$

Only three moles (6/2) of CH_4, e.g.

$$6 \text{ mol } O_2 \times 1 \text{ } CH_4/2 \text{ } O_2 = 3 \text{ mol } O_2$$

will be consumed. Therefore, CH_4 is in excess and O_2 is the limiting reagent.

65. **D.** Starting with the moles of the limiting reagent, and assuming no other reaction products are formed (i.e. carbon monoxide)

$$6 \text{ mol } O_2 \times 1 \text{ } CO_2/2 \text{ } O_2 \times 44 \text{ g/mol} = 132 \text{ g } CO_2$$

66. **C.** Choice A doesn't have enough hydrogen atoms on the product side and not enough oxygen atoms on the reactant side. Choice B doesn't have enough oxygen atoms on the reactant side and not enough hydrogen atoms on the product side. Choice D doesn't have enough oxygen atoms on the reactant side and not enough hydrogen on the product side.

67. **A.** See the explanation for question 66 for the balanced reaction. Starting with the moles of C_6H_6

$$4 \text{ mol } C_6H_6 \times 15 \text{ } O_2/2 \text{ } C_6H_6 = 30 \text{ mol } O_2$$

For the C_6H_6 to completely react we would only need 30 moles of O_2, and since there are 35 moles of O_2

$$35 \text{ mol } O_2 \times 2 \text{ } C_6H_6/15 \text{ } O_2 = 4.7 \text{ mol } C_6H_6$$

oxygen is in excess and C_6H_6 is the limiting reagent.

68. **C.** Starting with the limiting reagent (see the explanation for question 67)

$$4 \text{ mol } C_6H_6 \times 12 \text{ } CO_2/2 \text{ } C_6H_6 = 24 \text{ mol } CO_2$$

69. **B.** A combination reaction is when more than one compound reacts to form a single compound as a product. See also the explanation for question 62.

70. **C.** See the explanations for question 62 and 69.

71. **D.** See the explanation for question 62.

72. **C.** When balancing reactions involving ions, we just need to make sure the number of cations and anions are the same on both sides of the reaction. For choice A, there are more calcium ions on the reactant side than on the product side; for choices B and D, there are more silver and nitrate ions on the product side than on the reactant side.

73. **A.** The most efficient order for balancing combustion reactions is carbon, then hydrogen, and then oxygen.

74. **B.** This is a single replacement reaction which is also a REDOX reaction. Choice A is not the lowest whole number ratio; for choice C, there are more sulfate ions as reactants than products; for choice D, there are more copper ions as reactants than products.

75. **D.** This is a net ionic reaction for a REDOX reaction, where the spectator ions are not included. In this type of reaction we need to balance both the atoms and the charge. For choices A and C, there is more positive charge on the reactant side than on the products side; for choice B there is more positive charge on the products side than on the reactants side.

76. **D.** REDOX reactions can be balanced using half-reactions. The reduction half-reaction is

$$Au^{3+} \text{ } (\boldsymbol{aq}) + 3 \text{ e}^- \rightarrow Au \text{ (s)}$$

And the oxidation half-reaction is

$$Zn \text{ (s)} \rightarrow Zn^{2+} \text{ (aq)} + 2 \text{ e}^-$$

The number of electrons that are reactants and products must be the same, therefore we must multiply the reduction and oxidation half-reactions by factors of 2 and 3, respectively, which results in a transfer of six electrons.

77. **D.** A reactant that is oxidized has its oxidation number increase and electrons are products in the half-reaction. See also the explanation for question 76.

78. **C.** This is a REDOX reaction, but it can be balanced like any other reaction, by making sure that the number of atoms of each reactant and product are equal. For choices A and B, there are not enough aluminum or oxygen atoms as reactants. For choice D, there are not enough aluminum atoms as reactants.

79. **C.** The balanced oxidation and reduction half-reactions are

$$Al \rightarrow Al^{3+} + 3 \text{ e}^-$$
$$O_2 + 4 \text{ e}^- \rightarrow 2 \text{ } O^{2-}$$

To get the number of reactant and product electrons to be the same and to have charge balance, we need to multiply the oxidation by three and the reduction by four. Combining the half-reactions, gives the overall REDOX reaction

$$4 \text{ Al} + 3 \text{ } O_2 + 12 \text{ e}^- \rightarrow 4 \text{ Al}^{3+} + 6 \text{ } O^{2-} + 12 \text{ e}^-$$

Note that the Al^{3+} and O^{2-} combine to form 2 moles of the solid product Al_2O_3.

80. **C.** The oxidizing agent is the reactant that gets reduced. In this case the oxidation number for oxygen is going from 0 to -2, because the oxygen is removing electrons from the aluminum metal.

81. **B.** The molecular weight is $2(12) + 6(1) = 30$ g/mol.

$$90 \text{ g } C_2H_6 \times 1 \text{ mol}/30 \text{ g} = 3 \text{ mol } C_2H_6$$

82.   **C.** The balanced reaction is
$$2 C_2H_6 + 7 O_2 \rightarrow 4 CO_2 + 6 H_2O$$
See the explanation for question 81.
$$3 \text{ mol } \cancel{C_2H_6} \times 6 H_2O/2 \cancel{C_2H_6} = 9 \text{ mol } H_2O$$

83.   **C.** See the explanation for question 82. The molecular weight of water is $1(16) + 2(1) = 18$ g/mol.
$$9 \text{ mol } H_2O \times 18 \text{ g/mol} = 162 \text{ g } H_2O$$

84.   **C.** See the explanation for question 82.
$$9 \text{ mol } H_2O \times 6.02 \times 10^{23} \text{ molecules/mol}$$
$$= 5.42 \times 10^{24} \text{ molecules}$$

85.   **B.** The stoichiometric ratio is both the ratio for moles and molecules in a balanced reaction.
$$1.2044 \times 10^{24} \cancel{C_6H_6} \text{ molecules} \times 6 H_2O/2 \cancel{C_6H_6}$$
$$= 3.613 * 10^{24} \text{ molecule } H_2O$$

86.   **C.** See the explanation for question 81.
$$3 \text{ mol } \cancel{C_2H_6} \times 4 CO_2/2 \cancel{C_2H_6} \times 44 \text{ g/mol} = 264 \text{ g } CO_2$$

87.   **B.** The molar mass of oxygen (O_2) is 32 g/mol.
$$64 \text{ } \cancel{g} O_2 \times 1 \text{ mol}/32 \cancel{g} = 2 \text{ mol } O_2$$

88.   **B.** See the explanation for question 82 for the balanced chemical reaction. The ratio of C_2H_6 to O_2 is 2:7. There are 3 moles of C_2H_6 but only 2 moles of O_2. Therefore O_2 is the limiting reagent.
$$2 \text{ } \cancel{\text{mol}} \cancel{O_2} \times 6 H_2O/7 \cancel{O_2} \times 18 \text{ g/} \cancel{\text{mol}} = 31 \text{ g } H_2O$$

89.   **C.** See the explanation for question 83 for the theoretical yield of water.
$$\% \text{ yield} = (\text{actual/theo}) \times 100$$
$$(121/162) \times 100 = 75 \%$$

90.   **C.** See the explanation for question 82 for the balanced reaction.
$$121 \text{ } \cancel{g} \cancel{H_2O} \times 1 \text{ } \cancel{\text{mol}}/18 \text{ } \cancel{g} \times 4 CO_2/6 \cancel{H_2O} \times 44 \text{ g/} \cancel{\text{mol}}$$
$$= 197 \text{ g } CO_2$$

91.   **A.** See the explanation for question 82 for the balanced chemical reaction. The ratio of C_2H_6 to O_2 is 2:7.
$$1.2044 \times 10^{24} \text{ molecules } C_2H_6 = 2 \text{ mol } C_2H_6$$
$$96 \text{ g } O_2 = 3 \text{ mol } O_2$$
Elemental oxygen is the limiting reagent.

92.   **D.** $\% \text{ yield} = (\text{actual/theo}) \times 100$
$$(1/8) \times 100 = 12.5 \%$$

93.   **A.** $\% \text{ yield} = (\text{actual/theo}) \times 100$
$$66 = (\text{actual}/120 \text{ g}) \times 100$$
$$\text{actual} = 66(120/100) = 79 \text{ g}$$

94.   **D.** $\% \text{ yield} = (\text{actual/theo}) \times 100$
$$20 = (1 \text{ g/theo}) \times 100$$
$$\text{theo} = (1/20) \times 100 = 100/20 = 5 \text{ g}$$

95.   **A.** Unless the compound is a peroxide (O_2^{2-}) or elemental oxygen (O_2), oxygen always has an oxidation number of -2.

96.   **D.** The total charge of the molecule (or ion) must equal the total oxidation number for each atom in the formula. See also the explanation for question 95.
$$-2 = 1(S) + 3(-2)$$
$$S = +4$$

97.   **C.** See also the explanations for questions 95 and 96.
$$-1 = 1(Mn) + 4(-2)$$
$$Mn = +7$$

98.   **B.** Unless you have elemental hydrogen (H_2) or a metal hydride like NaH, the oxidation number of

hydrogen in a compound will be +1. See the explanations for questions 95 and 96. This is hydrogen peroxide.
$$0 = 2(+1) + 2(O)$$
$$O = -1$$

99.   **C.** This is an example of a Bronsted-Lowry acid-base reaction, in which the HI is the hydrogen ion donor (acid) and the alcohol is the hydrogen ion acceptor (base).

100.   **C.** Acetate (CH_3COO^-) has resonance forms in which the double bond between the carbon and oxygen moves between the two oxygens. Thus each oxygen has a 1.5 bond with carbon.

SECTION 3 CONTENT REVIEW SOLUTIONS

1.   **B.** Henry's law relates the solubility or concentration c of a gas in a particular solvent to the partial pressure of that gas. Choice A is Boyle's law, which is the inverse relationship between the pressure P and volume V of an ideal gas; choice C is Charles's law which is the direct relationship between volume and temperature T, in Kelvin, of an ideal gas; and choice D is Gay-Lussac's law which is the direct relationship between pressure P and temperature of an ideal gas.

2.   **A.** See the explanation for question 1.

3.   **C.** See the explanation for question 1.

4.   **D.** The ideal gas law relates the pressure P and volume V, to the number of moles n and temperature T in degrees Kelvin, with the gas constant being R = 0.0821 L•atm/mol•K.

5.   **D.** See the explanation for question 1. Choice A is Graham's law of effusion; and choice B is Avogadro's law, relating the number of moles n to the volume of a gas.

6.   **B.** Choice A is Dalton's law of partial pressures. See also the explanations for questions 1 and 5.

7.   **C.** See the explanations for questions 1 and 5.

8.   **A.** See the explanations for questions 1 and 6.

9.   **D.** According to the combined gas law
$$P_1V_1/T_1 = P_2V_2/T_2$$
If we assume $P_1 = V_1 = T_1 = 1$ and $P_2 = T_2 = 2$.
$$V_2 = P_1V_1T_2/T_1P_2 = (1)(1)(2)/(1)(2) = 1$$

10.   **D.** If we assume $P_1 = V_1 = T_1 = 1$ and $V_2 = 2$ and $P_2 = 1/2$
$$T_2 = P_2V_2T_1/P_1V_1 = (1/2)(2)(1)/(1)(1) = 1$$
See also the explanation for question 9.

11.   **C.** If we assume $P_1 = V_1 = T_1 = 1$ and $V_2 = 2$ and $T_2 = 1/2$
$$P_2 = P_1V_1T_2/T_1V_2 = (1)(1)(1/2)/(1)(2) = 1/4$$
See also the explanation for question 9.

12.   **A.** If the temperature increases, the pressure must increase, assuming the walls of the metal container are rigid such that the volume of the gas will not change significantly and the moles will not change because it is a closed container. R is the gas constant. See also the explanation for question 1.

13.   **B.** If the pressure remains constant, the moles can not leave the closed container and the gas constant does not change, then the volume must increase as the gas is heated.

14.   **A.** The pressure will decrease. See also the explanation for question 1.

15.   **D.** The prefix iso- means the same or constant, whereas the root of the word, -bar-, refers to pressure. One bar is approximately one atmosphere of pressure or 100 kPa.

16.   **B.** Rearranging the ideal gas law, PV = nRT, for the gas constant and inserting the appropriate units gives
$$R = PV/nT = atm•L/mol•K$$
$$1 L•atm = 101 J$$

The gas constant can have values of 0.0812 L•atm/mol•K or 8.31 J/mol•K.

17.   **D.** See the explanation for question 16.

18.   **A.** See the explanation for question 16.

19.   **A.** 1 L is equivalent to 10^{-3} m^3. See also the explanation for question 16.

20.   **C.** One atmosphere is equivalent to 101 kPa. See also the explanation for question 16.

21.   **B.** See the explanations for questions 16 and 19.

22.   **C.** An ideal gas is a theoretical substance that has no molecular volume and has no intermolecular forces of attraction, resulting in completely elastic collisions. Real gases that do have molecular volumes and intermolecular forces, will behave like ideal gases at high temperatures and low pressures.

23.   **A.** Pressure is the force per unit area and for gases results from molecular collisions that push on the walls of the container.

24.   **B.** Temperature is a measure of the average kinetic energy of a material.

25.   **B.** KE = 1/2 mV^2 and in terms of the Boltzmann constant k, KE = 3/2 kT. Setting these two equations equal gives
$$1/2 mv^2 = 3/2 kT$$
Solving for the velocity gives the root mean square velocity.
$$mv^2 = 3kT$$
$$v = [3kT/m]^{1/2}$$
Since the ideal gas law can be stated in terms of the kinetic molecular theory and the Boltzmann relationship, PV = nRT = NkT, where n is the number of moles and N is the number of molecules. We can rewrite the root mean square equation in terms of molecular weight M and the gas constant.
$$v = [3RT/M]^{1/2}$$
The key thing to remember is that the average velocity of a gas molecule is directly related to the temperature and inversely related to the molar mass.

26.   **B.** The relative rate R of effusion for two gases with different molar masses M_1 and M_2 is
$$R_1/R_2 = [M_2/M_1]^{1/2}$$
The ratio of the molar masses of H_2 and O_2 are 32:2 or 16:1, the root of which is 4:1. See also the explanation of question 25.

27.   **C.** At standard temperature and pressure both hydrogen gas and oxygen gas behave like ideal gases, and equal moles would have equal volumes.

28.   **A.** The partial pressure of N_2 will be 80% of the atmospheric pressure (1atm = 760 mmHg).
$$(80/100) 760 = 608 mmHg$$

29.   **A.** First we need to calculate the number of moles of each gas.
$$64 g O_2 \times 1 mol/32 g = 2 mol O_2$$
$$28 g N_2 \times 1 mol/28 g = 1 mol N_2$$
$$1 g H_2 \times 1 mol/2 g = 0.5 mol H_2$$
The partial pressure of O_2 is the mole fraction times the total pressure [1 atm = 760 mmHg = 101 kPa and 1 torr = 1 mmHg].
$$(2/3.5) \times 760 = 433 mmHg$$

30.   **B.** See the explanation for question 29.
         $(1/3.5) \times 760 = 217$ mmHg

31.   **C.** See the explanation for question 29.
         $(0.5/3.5) \times 760 = 109$ mmHg

32.   **C.** See the explanation for question 29.
         380 mmHg x 101 kPa/760 mmHg x 10^3 Pa/1 kPa
         = 5.5×10^4 Pa

33.   **B.** See the explanation for question 29.

34.   **B.** STP stands for standard temperature and pressure, which are 0 °C and 1 atm respectively.

35.   **D.** See the explanation for question 29; K = °C + 273; the volume of one mole of an ideal gas at STP is 22.4 L.

36.   **A.** See the explanation for question 34.

37.   **A.** The rate of effusion is directly related to the root mean square (RMS) of the speed of a gas, which is inversely related to the molar mass. Elemental hydrogen would have the fastest RMS of any gas and hence the greatest rate of effusion. See also the explanation for question 26.

38.   **A.** Graham's law is associated with the root mean square speed of a gas, which is related to the rate of diffusion. See the explanations for questions 1, 25 and 26.

39.   **A.** In the solid state, molecules are in contact with each other and are unable to undergo translational motion. In the liquid phase some of the intermolecular interactions are broken and translational motion becomes possible, however molecules are still in contact with other molecules. In the gas phase, the remaining intermolecular interactions are broken such that the molecules only make brief contact during momentary random collisions with other molecules.

40.   **B.** See the explanation for question 39.

41.   **D.** The only two elements that are liquids at 25°C are mercury and bromine. All other elements are gases or solids. All of the group 18 elements (Noble gases) are gases at room temperature. For the diatomic halogens, fluorine and chlorine are gases, bromine is a liquid and iodine is a solid (with a relatively high vapor pressure). This trend is due to increasing London (van der Waals) dispersion forces.

42.   **A.** Hydrogen bonding (HB) is a strongly directional interaction of a hydrogen atom that is polar-covalently bonded to nitrogen, oxygen or fluorine, with a lone-pair of electrons located on a nitrogen, oxygen or fluorine in a neighboring molecule. Dipole-dipole (DD) interactions are between molecules that have permanent molecular dipoles and tend to be weaker than hydrogen bonding interactions. London dispersion (LD) forces tend to be very weak attractions caused by the temporary formation of molecular dipoles due to the asymmetry of charge created by the movement of electrons. The strength of LD forces generally increases as the size and polarizability of the molecule increases. Induced dipole (ID) interactions result when an ion or a molecule with a permanent dipole distorts the electron cloud of a molecule without a dipole moment, causing a polarization that favors intermolecular interactions. The general trend in the strength of the intermolecular forces is HB > DD > ID > LD.

43.   **B.** See the explanation for question 42.

44.   **B.** Ionic bonding is the very strong electrostatic interaction of charged atoms or groups of atoms. See also the explanation for question 42.

45.   **B.** See the explanation for question 42.

46.   **A.** The strongest intermolecular force in both methane and carbon tetrafluoride is London dispersion. Both water and methanol can form hydrogen bonds, but water has an optimized ratio of covalently bonded hydrogen atoms to lone pairs, forming a more extensive hydrogen-bonding network than methanol. See also the explanation for question 42.

47.   **B.** See the explanations for questions 42 and 46. Methane (bp -162 °C) is smaller and less polarizable than carbon tetrafluoride (bp -128 °C).

48.   **C.** See explanations for questions 42, 46 and 47.

49.   **B.** Evaporation involves a phase change from the liquid state to the gas phase, at the surface of a liquid and can happen at any temperature. Heat of fusion is associated with the process in which a liquid becomes a solid. The reverse process is melting, which requires the same amount of heat per gram, as fusion. Heat of vaporization is associated with boiling, or its reverse process, which is condensation. The heat of sublimation is associated with a phase change of a solid directly to the gas phase.

50.   **A.** See the explanation for question 49.

51.   **A.** Bond polarity is related to the difference in electronegativities of the atoms involved in the bonding.

52.   **A.** The symmetrical structure of carbon tetrafluoride makes it the least polar.

53.   **D.** At standard pressure, water's melting point is 0 °C and its boiling point is 100 °C. In an open container, the liquid water might completely evaporate. In a closed container that is not completely filled with liquid, the vapor pressure will be reached and the system will come to equilibrium between the liquid and gas phase. In a closed container, completely filled with liquid water, it will all be liquid.

54.   **D.** K = °C + 273
At 1 atm and 0 °C, the water could be solid, liquid or a mixture of solid and liquid. See also the explanation for question 53.

55.   **D.** The water could be liquid, gas or a mixture of liquid and gas. See also the explanations for questions 53 and 54.

56.   **A.** See the explanation for question 39.

57.   **A.** Sound is transmitted by pressure waves in which matter is the medium in which the wave is propagated. In the solid state, the mater is in direct contact with other atoms, the wave is transmitted very quickly. In the gas phase, the atoms are not in direct contact and additional time is required for the collisions to occur. The liquid phase is an intermediate situation.

58.   **A.** Solids have a higher density than liquids, which have higher densities than gases. Volume per unit mass (cm^3/g) is the inverse of density (g/cm^3).

59.   **C.** See the explanations for question 25 and 26. Elemental nitrogen and oxygen are N_2 and O_2, with

molar masses of 28 and 32 amus respectively. Methane is CH_4 with a molar mass of 16 amu and neon has an atomic mass of 20 amu.

60. **C.** See the explanation for question 1.

61. **A.** See the explanation for question 1.

62. **D.** See the explanation for question 1.

63. **D.** The triple point is where all three phases of matter can exist simultaneously.

64. **A.** The critical point is where the material becomes a supercritical fluid.

65. **A.** At 1 atm and 300 K, the water will be liquid and raising the temperature (follow the horizontal dashed line to the right) will cause the liquid to change to gas at 373 K.

66. **C.** The initial pressure is slightly above the pressure for the triple point. At 273 K the water will be solid, if the pressure increases (follow the vertical dashed line up), eventually at a pressure of about 1 atm the solid will begin to melt (become liquid).

67. **D.** The initial pressure is slightly above the pressure for the triple point. At 273 K the water will be solid, if the pressure decreases (follow the vertical dashed line down), eventually at a pressure of about 0.004 atm the solid will begin to sublime (become gas).

68. **C.** Freezing is when a liquid becomes a solid; deposition is when a gas becomes a solid; melting is when a solid becomes a liquid; and evaporation is when a liquid becomes a gas.

69. **A.** Sublimation is when a solid becomes a gas; condensation is when a gas becomes a liquid; boiling is when a liquid becomes a gas at a pressure such that bubbles form inside the liquid; fusion is when a liquid becomes a solid.

70. **D.** See the explanation for question 68.

71. **C.** See the explanations for questions 68 and 69.

72. **B.** See the explanations for questions 68 and 69.

73. **A.** See the explanation for question 68.

74. **B.** Super cooling is when a pure liquid substance, such as water, is below its normal freezing point, but does not form the solid phase because the molecules are unable to orient themselves into the proper shape to form the crystalline solid.

75. **A.** The dissolution of non-volatile solutes increases the boiling point from the boiling point of the pure liquid, due to a decrease in the vapor pressure of the liquid, and is a colligative property.

76. **B.** Dissolving a solute depresses the freezing points of a liquid and is a colligative property.

77. **C.** See the explanation for question 75.

78. **B.** Colligative properties depend upon the total concentration of particles (molecules or ions) in solution. For NaCl the concentration of ions is 2 mol/kg; for $CaCl_2$ the concentration of ions is 2.4 mol/kg; for Na_2SO_4 the concentration of ions is 1.5 mol/kg; and for KCl the concentration of ions is 2 mol/kg.

79. **C.** The normal boiling point of water is 273 K. Multiplying the molality of ions in the solution by the boiling point elevation constant, gives

$$2 \times 1\ m \times 0.512\ °C/m = 1.24\ °C$$

80. **A.** The vapor pressure must go down compared with the pure liquid, eliminating choices B and D. The mole fraction of the solvent times the normal vapor pressure gives

$$10/12 \times 23.8\ torr = 19.8\ torr$$

81. **C.** See the explanations for questions 75 and 78.

$$1.86\ °C/m \times 0.5\ m \times 3 = 2.79\ °C$$

82. **B.** Osmotic pressure depends on the molarity M of the number of ions i produced in solution per formula unit and the temperature T, with the proportionality constant being the gas constant R = 0.0821 L•atm/mol•K.

83. **A.** See the explanation for question 82.

84. **D.** The van't Hoff factor i for a molecular compound is 1 and is essentially the number of ions per formula unit that are produced in solution when a soluble ionic compound dissolves.

85. **B.** Standard temperature is 0 °C or 273 K, the molarity is 1.5 mol/6 L and the van't Hoff factor for NaCl is 2.

$$P = MRTi$$
$$P = (1.5\ mol/6\ L)(0.0821\ L\ atm\ mol^{-1}K^{-1})(273\ K)(2)$$
$$= 11.2\ atm$$

86. **C.** Standard temperature is 273 K and standard pressure is 1 atm or 1 bar. See the explanation for question 15.

87. **B.** Standard temperature is 273 K and 100 atm is 100 bar

88. **C.** The critical point is denoted by the "•" at the intersection of the vertical and horizontal dashed lines.

89. **D.** The triple point is where all three phases of matter can exist simultaneously and is the intersection of the three solid lines separating the solid, liquid and gas phases.

90. **B.** K = °C + 273 = 273 - 68 = 205 K

91. **B.** Standard pressure is 1 atm or 1 bar. While the phase diagram does not show the data for temperatures below 200 K, presumably the solid line separating the gas phase from the solid phase could be extrapolated to lower temperatures.

92. **B.** The temperature must be slightly less than 200 K and -78.5 °C is 194.5 K.

93. **D.** See the explanation for question 89.

94. **B.** A supercritical fluid is a remarkable material that exists at very high temperatures and pressures, where the physical properties are similar to both the gas and liquid phases, i.e. it can effuse like a gas and dissolve solutes like a liquid. Essentially the liquid expands to fill the container.

95. **A.** See the explanation for question 94.

96. **B.** Real gases are most likely to behave like ideal gases at high temperatures and low pressures.

97. **A.** See the explanation for question 96.

98. **B.** Boiling is a process when bubbles form inside of the liquid, where the vapor pressure equals the external pressure on the surface of the liquid.

99. **B.** The number of moles is n = 14 g/28 g mol^{-1} = 0.5 mol; the temperature is 273 + 25 °C = 298 K; the gas constant is 0.0821 L•atm mol^{-1}•K^{-1}; and the volume is 2 L.

$$PV = nRT$$
$$P = (0.5 \text{ mol})(0.0821 \text{ L}\cdot\text{atm mol}^{-1}\cdot\text{K}^{-1})(298 \text{ K})/(2 \text{ L})$$
$$P = 6.1 \text{ atm}$$

100.   **C.** The normal boiling point of water is when the external pressure is 1.0 atm and the temperature is 100 °C, which is 273 + 100 °C = 373 K.

SECTION 4 CONTENT REVIEW SOLUTIONS

1.   **D.** Homogeneous solutions are evenly distributed mixtures (on the molecular level) and can be solids liquids or gases.

2.   **B.** For a given set of conditions a saturated solution is when the maximum amount of solute has dissolved in the solvent.

3.   **B.** The amount of solute that will dissolve in a solvent is often very temperature dependent.

4.   **C.** A supersaturated solution is a metastable situation in which more solute is dissolved in the solvent than normally would be present for a saturated solution.

5.   **A.** The seed crystal provides a surface with the right shape necessary for the solid to form and the solution will come to equilibrium between the solid and the saturated solution, by precipitating the excess sugar.

6.   **D.** Molarity is a concentration unit, defined as the moles of solute per liter of solution.

7.   **C.** Molality is also a concentration unit, and is defined as the moles of solute per kilogram of solvent.

8.   **C.** Normality is defined as the concentration of the reactive unit for a compound. Sulfuric acid (H_2SO_4) is a diprotic acid, and therefore there are twice as many hydrogen ions available to react with a base, as there are of the formula unit.

9.   **B.** Nitric acid (HNO_3) is a monoprotic acid, so there one to one ratio of hydrogen ions to formula units.

10.   **A.** The molarity of the H_2SO_4 formula unit will be half the normality.

11.   **D.** For equilibrium expressions, the concentration of products, raised to the appropriate stoichiometric powers, are divided by the concentration of the reactants, raised to their stoichiometric powers. However, pure solids and pure liquids do not appear in the expression.

12.   **A.** The molar solubility is the moles per liter of A_2B_3 that dissolves. If x is defined as the molarity of A_2B_3 that dissolves, then substituting this into the equilibrium expression, gives
$$1.08 \times 10^{12} = [2x]^2[3x]^3$$
Probably the most efficient method for solving this problem at this point would be to substitute the answer options in for the value of x. For choice A
$$[200]^2[300]^3$$
$$4 \times 10^4 \times 2.7 \times 10^7$$
$$10.8 \times 10^{11}$$
$$1.08 \times 10^{12}$$

13.   **D.** See the explanation for question 12.

14.   **D.** The ion product is the same as the equilibrium expression, except it is prior to the establishment of equilibrium. Another term for "ion product" is "reaction quotient". When the ion product is greater than the K_{sp} the solution must form a precipitate to reach equilibrium and therefore must be supersaturated.

15.   **C.** The equilibrium reaction is
$$AB_2 \text{ (s)} \leftrightarrow A^{2+} \text{ (aq)} + 2 \text{ B}^- \text{ (aq)}$$

Based on Le Chatelier's principle and the common ion effect, by adding a second compound containing B- cause the equilibrium to shift to the left and formation of a precipitate.

16. **B.** Based on the solubility rules, all nitrates are soluble.

17. **C.** To be a strong electrolyte, an ionic compound needs to be soluble in aqueous solution. Most sulfides are insoluble and calcium sulfide is not an exception to this rule.

For questions 18 – 25 give the formula of the named ion.
18. CH_3COO^-
19. CN^-
20. ClO_2^-
21. MnO_4^-
22. PO_4^{3-}
23. O_2^{2-}
24. CrO_4^{2-}
25. ClO^-

26. **A.** An Arrhenius base is a compound, that when added to water, increases the concentration of hydroxide ion. Sodium hydroxide (choice A) is a classic example of a strong Arrhenius base. Methanol (choice B) is a molecular compound and does not dissociate hydroxide. Hydrochloric acid (choice C) is a strong acid and aluminum chloride is a Lewis acid.

27. **B.** Lewis acids are electron pair acceptors. The aluminum in $AlCl_3$ does not formally have a completed octet.

28. **D.** A Bronsted-Lowry base is able to accept a hydrogen ion. Ammonia accepts H^+ to form ammonium ion, NH_4^+.

29. **C.** Choice A is the formula for acetic acid. When an acid loses its hydrogen ion and reacts with a base, if forms an ionic compound whose anion is the conjugate of the original acid and the cation comes from the base.

$$HC_2H_3O_2 + KOH \rightarrow KC_2H_3O_2 + H_2O$$
acid   base   c-base c-acid

30. **B.** A conjugate acid has one more hydrogen atom in its formula than the base from which it was formed.

31. **D.** A conjugate base has one less hydrogen atom in its formula than the acid from which it was formed.

32. **C.** The auto ionization reaction for water is
$$H_2O \; (l) \leftrightarrow H^+ \; (aq) + OH^- \; (aq)$$
The concentration of the pure water does not appear in the equilibrium expression.

33. **B.** The pH will be the -log of 3×10^{-6} M. Since the -log of 10^{-6} is 6, and since the concentration of hydrogen ion is slightly greater than 10^{-6} M, the pH must be between 5 and 6.

34. **B.** The pOH will be the -log of 3×10^{-6} M. Since the -log of 10^{-6} is 6. And since the concentration of hydrogen ion is slightly greater than 10^{-6} M, the pOH must be between 5 and 6.

35. **A.** $pH + pOH = 14$

36. **D.** The auto ionization of water is endothermic.
$$heat + H_2O \; (l) \leftrightarrow H^+ \; (aq) + OH^- \; (aq)$$

Heating the solution shifts the equilibrium to the right, increasing the K_w and decreasing the pK_w, but for pure water $[H^+] = [OH^-]$, so pH = pOH.

37. **B.** The strong acids are nitric acid (HNO_3), perchloric acid ($HClO_4$), sulfuric acid (H_2SO_4) and all the hydrohalic acids, (HCl, HBr and HI) except hydrofluoric acid (HF), which is a weak acid.

38. **C.** The strong bases have group 1 cations (Li^+, Na^+, K^+, Rb^+, and Cs^+) or group 2 cations (Ca^{2+}, Ba^{2+}, and Sr^{2+}), with $Be(OH)_2$ being an exception.

39. **D.** The pH will be lower than the pKa, which is slightly less than 5 (it's 4.74 using a calculator), eliminating choices A and B. The equilibrium expression is
$$K_a = [H^+][C_2H_3O_2^-]/[HC_2H_3O_2]$$
Which can be approximated and solved as
$$1.8 \times 10^{-5} = x^2/0.3$$
$$x^2 = 1.8 \times 3 \times 10^{-1} \times 10^{-5}$$
$$x^2 = 5.4 \times 10^{-6}$$
$$x = 2.3 \times 10^{-3} \; M = [H^+]$$
$$pH = -\log(2.3 \times 10^{-3}) = 2.6$$

40. **A.** At the equivalence point all of the ammonia (NH_3) will have been converted into the ammonium ion, which is a weak acid.

41. **C.** The products of this neutralization reaction will be water and sodium acetate. Sodium ion is the conjugate of a strong base and therefore it is a neutral ion. Acetate is the conjugate base of acetic acid.

42. **A.** If the slope is close to zero then it is in the buffer region, in which the concentration of the weak acid and conjugate base are close to being equal.

43. **C.** At the equivalence point for this titration where base is being added to acid, there will be a rapid increase in pH.

44. **C.** This is a buffer situation, such that the pH resists changes, hence a slope close to zero. The pK_{a2} for phosphoric acid is 7.21. Choices B and D are the same thing and hence neither can be the answer.

45. **B.** The Henderson-Hasselbalch equation is the logarithmic form of the equilibrium expression for a weak acid.
$$HA \; (aq) \leftrightarrow H^+ \; (aq) + A^- \; (aq)$$
$$pH = pK_a + \log[A^-]/[HA]$$
When $[A^-] = [HA]$, then $\log 1 = 0$, and $pH = pK_a$.

46. **D.** The sodium hydroxide will have neutralized half of the acetic acid and converted it into acetate. The titration is half way to the equivalence point.

47. **D.** A buffer is a solution that contains both a weak acid and its conjugate base, which can react with other acids or bases and minimize the change in pH.

48. **C.** Indicators are weak acids or bases that change color. The half equivalence point is the same as when the concentration of the weak acid and weak conjugate base are equal (maximum buffer capacity) and is the point in which the indicator will be a mixture of the colors of the acid and base forms of the indicator. This is the situation that should match the equivalence point of the titration.

49. **A.** Choice A is the hydrolysis equilibrium expression for the weak base, ammonia. For choices B and C, the negative sign is missing. For choice D, the

hydrolysis equilibrium expression does not include the pure liquid water.

50.   **C.** Sodium is the cation of the strong base, NaOH, and therefore Na^+ is neutral. Fluoride, F^-, is the conjugate base of the weak acid, hydrogen fluoride (HF), and acetate is the conjugate base of the weak acid, acetic acid ($HC_2H_3O_2$).

SECTION 5 CONTENT REVIEW SOLUTIONS

1.   **D.** The first law of thermodynamics states that energy can not be created or destroyed. The second law of thermodynamics states that energy, in the form of increasing entropy, is distributing itself as evenly as possible throughout the universe. The third law states that the entropy of a system would be zero at a temperature of absolute zero would, where all molecular motion would cease. The law of conservation of matter is not a thermodynamic law.

2.   **C.** If the system does work it must lose 50 J of energy and then the heat adds 150 J. The result is
$$100 - 50 + 150 = 200 \, J$$

3.   **B.** See also the explanation for question 2.
$$100 - 100 + 50 = 50 \, J$$

4.   **C.** A negative change in enthalpy (ΔH) indicates that the final state of the system has less energy than the initial state and that heat went into the surroundings.

5.   **B.** If ΔH is positive then heat goes into the system. See also the explanation for question 4.

6.   **A.** Negative changes in Gibbs free energy (ΔG) indicate that the products are more stable than the reactants and that the reaction will be spontaneous.

7.   **D.** Gases tend to have more entropy (disorder) than liquids, which have more entropy than solids. In this reaction, the entropy of the products will most likely be greater than the reactants, such that ΔS will be positive.

8.   **C.** When calculating the $\Delta H°$ for the reaction, using heats of formation, the enthalpy of formation for each species in the balanced reaction must be multiplied by the stoichiometric coefficients, and the reactants are subtracted from the products (Δ means final minus initial).

9.   **A.** See the explanation for question 1.

10.   **B.** Sublimation is when a solid goes directly to the gas phase. See the explanation for question 7.

11.   **B.** See the explanation for question 1.

12.   **C.** To be spontaneous, the Gibbs free energy must be negative.
$$\Delta G = \Delta H - T\Delta S$$
If the enthalpy change is negative and the entropy change is positive, ΔG will always be negative, regardless of the temperature. If the enthalpy change is positive and the entropy change is negative, then the reaction will always be nonspontaneous. If both the enthalpy change and the entropy change are positive, then the reaction will be spontaneous at high temperatures and nonspontaneous at low temperatures. If both the enthalpy change and the entropy change are negative, then the reaction will be spontaneous at low temperatures and nonspontaneous at high temperatures.

13.   **D.** See the explanation for question 12.

14.   **B.** See the explanation for question 12.

15.   **A.** See the explanation for question 12.

16.   **B.** A degree Celsius is slightly less than twice as big as a degree Fahrenheit and 0 °C = 32 °F. Therefore,
$$°C \times 9/5 + 32 = °F$$

17.   **B.** K = °C + 273
18.   **D.** Exothermic reactions have negative enthalpy (ΔH) changes.
19.   **C.** The liquid formed as a product would cause the products to have less entropy than the reactants. See also the explanation for question 7.
20.   **C.** The entropy change for this reaction is most likely negative and since the enthalpy change is negative, the reaction will only be spontaneous at low temperatures. See the explanations for questions 7 and 12.
21.   **D.** If reaction 1 is reversed and the stoichiometric coefficients are doubled, we will get the desired reaction. When a reaction is reversed the sign of the enthalpy will be changed and doubling the coefficients, double the enthalpy change.
22.   **C.** Combining reaction 1, with reaction 2, we get the overall reaction of interest.

$$CH_4(g) + 2\,O_2(g) \rightarrow CO_2(g) + 2\,H_2O(l)$$
$$C(s) + O_2(g) \rightarrow CO_2(g)$$
$$\Delta H = -900) - 400 = -1300 \text{ kJ}$$

23.   **A.** By combining reaction 2, with the reverse of reaction 3, we get the overall reaction of interest. Also see the explanation for question 21.

$$C(s) + O_2(g) \rightarrow CO_2(g)$$
$$H_2O(l) \rightarrow H_2(g) + 1/2\,O_2(g)$$
$$\Delta H = 300 - 400 = -100 \text{ kJ}$$

24.   **A.** The enthalpy of formation is the heat of reaction associated with making a compound from its elements in their standard states. Reaction 3 is the formation reaction for liquid water.
25.   **B.** By combining the reverse of reaction 1, with reaction 2 and doubling reaction 3, we get the reaction of interest. Also see the explanation for question 21.

$$C(s) + O_2(g) \rightarrow CO_2(g)$$
$$CO_2(g) + 2\,H_2O(l) \rightarrow CH_4(g) + 2\,O_2(g)$$
$$H_2(g) + 1/2\,O_2(g) \rightarrow H_2O(l)$$
$$\Delta H = -400 + 900 - 600 = -100 \text{ kJ}$$

26.   **D.** Without knowing the mechanism or measuring reaction rates, there is no way to know.
27.   **B.** Doubling the concentration (experiments 1 and 2) of A_2B results in a doubling of the rate, so the exponent for $[A_2B]$ in the rate law must be x = 1.

$$\text{Rate} = k[A_2B]^x\,[C]^y$$

28.   **D.** The reaction is first order in A_2B based on experiments 1 and 2. By comparing experiments 1 and 3, if the reaction was zero order in C, the rate of experiment 3 would be three times faster than experiment 1, but in fact reaction 3 is an additional four times faster than that, so it must be second order in C. The overall order is the sum of the orders of each reactant.
29.   **C.** See the explanation for question 28.
30.   **B.** The rate law is

$$\text{Rate} = k[A_2B]^1\,[C]^2$$

Substituting the concentrations and rate for experiment 1 into the rate law, gives

$$6 \times 10^{-5} = k\,[0.3][0.2]^2$$
$$6 \times 10^{-5} = k\,[1.2 \times 10^{-2}]$$
$$k = (6/1.2) \times 10^{-3}$$
$$k = 5 \times 10^{-3}$$

31.   **A.** The concentration unit is molarity (M - mol/L) and the unit for the rate is $M\,s^{-1}$.

$$k = [M\,s^{-1}]/[M][M]^2$$
$$k = s^{-1}\,M^{-2}$$
$$k = s^{-1}\,[\text{mol}/L]^{-2}$$

Which is equivalent to choice A.
32.   **A.** In the energy diagram shown below, in which reactant A is converted to product C, $\Delta G^{\neq}$ is the activation energy. The transition state is the high-energy species B, sometimes known as the activated complex.

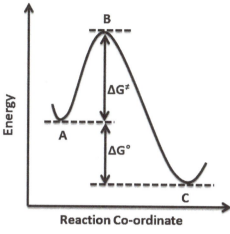

Reaction Co-ordinate

Reaction: A ⟶ C

33.   **B.** Since the temperature T is in the denominator of the exponent, increasing the temperature would cause the exponent to become less negative, thereby increasing the value of the rate constant.
34.   **D.** The exponent of the base of the natural logarithm is negative. If the value of E_a gets bigger, then k will have a smaller value and the reaction rate will be slower.
35.   **D.** The catalyst speeds up both the forward and reverse reactions, but does not affect the energy of the reactants and products. Therefore adding a catalyst has no effect on the concentrations at equilibrium.
36.   **C.** A catalyst reduces the activation energy of both the forward and reverse reactions.
37.   **B.** The equilibrium expression is the concentrations of products raised to their stoichiometric coefficients, divided by the concentrations of the reactants raised to their stoichiometric coefficients, which is equal to the equilibrium constant. Pure liquids and solids do not appear in the expression.
38.   **A.** See the explanation for question 37.
39.   **C.** See the explanation for question 37.
40.   **A.** Since ΔH is negative, heat is given off to the surroundings.
41.   **B.** There is the same number of moles of solid on both sides of the reaction, but more moles of gas are reactants than products, therefore the reactants have more disorder than the products, so the entropy change must be negative. See also the explanations for question 7.

42.   **D.** Since the enthalpy and the entropy changes are both negative, the reaction will be spontaneous at low temperatures and nonspontaneous at high temperatures. See also the explanations for questions 40, 41 and 12.

43.   **C.** Based on Le Chatelier's principle, adding a reactant should cause the equilibrium to shift to the right to lower the concentration of the reactants and re-establish equilibrium. However, in this case F is a pure solid that has no effect and does not appear in the equilibrium expression.

44.   **A.** Since AFD_2 is a gaseous product, the reaction rate in the reverse direction will temporarily increase, causing the reaction to shift towards the reactants to re-establish equilibrium.

45.   **B.** Since CD is a gaseous reactant, the reaction quotient Q will be less than the equilibrium constant K, the reaction will shift to the right to get Q to equal K. See also the explanation for question 43.

46.   **A.** Since the reaction produces heat, increasing the temperature will cause the reaction to shift to the left to absorb some of the heat.

47.   **A.** Since there are more gas phase moles of reactants than products, decreasing the pressure will cause the reaction to shift to the left to partially compensate for the pressure change.

48.   **C.** The position of the equilibrium is determined by the relative energy of the reactants and products. Adding a catalyst lowers the activation energy, increasing the rate at which the reaction reaches equilibrium, but does not have an effect on the concentration of reactants or products at equilibrium.

49.   **B.** Since heat is produced by the reaction, lowering the temperature will cause the reaction to shift to the right to produce heat to partially compensate for the stress. See also the explanation for question 46.

50.   **D.** Increasing the pressure would cause the reaction to shift to the right, whereas adding a product ABC (*g*) would cause the reaction to shift to the left. Since the stresses act in opposite directions, there is no way to predict the effect based on Le Châtelier's principle.

SECTION 6 CONTENT REVIEW SOLUTIONS

1.   **A.** The anode compartment attracts anions from the salt bridge, and is where oxidation occurs, regardless of whether the cell is Galvanic or electrolytic. Reduction occurs at the cathode and electrons flow from anode to cathode ("The red cat, is a fat cat") through a circuit involving an electrochemical cell.

2.   **B.** See the explanation for question 1. For choice A, it should be noted that current involves the flow of positive charge, which can be thought of as moving in the opposite direction of the electrons.

3.   **C.** Since the cathode is where reduction occurs, the compartment attracts positively charged ions (cations) from the salt bridge. Also see the explanation for question 1.

4.   **D.** See the explanations for questions 1 and 2.

5.   **A.** See the explanations for questions 1-3.

6.   **B.** See the explanation for question 1.

7.   **D.** See the explanation for question 1.

8.   **C.** The anode is the negatively charged terminal. For example, if a piece of zinc metal is an anode, two electrons will remain on the metal electrode when Zn^{2+} spontaneously goes into the aqueous solution. For a copper cathode, the positive Cu^{2+} (*aq*) ions in the solution are spontaneously attracted to the copper electrode, making it positive. As soon as the anode terminal is connected to the cathode terminal by a wire, the electrons flow through the wire from the anode to the cathode so that oxidation and reduction can occur.

9.   **B.** A Galvanic cell uses a thermodynamically spontaneous reaction involving the transfer of electrons from one species to another, to produce voltage and current. The voltage is produced under non-equilibrium conditions and will drop to zero once the reaction reaches equilibrium. See also the explanation for question 1.

10.   **A.** Some current will flow without a salt bridge, but there will quickly become an excess of cations in the cathode compartment and anions in the anode compartment, which will eventually stop any further flow of changes through the wire connecting the electrodes.

11.   **C.** A negative voltage indicates that the reaction is not spontaneous in the indicated direction. To make the reaction become spontaneous an external power supply can apply positive voltage, such that the total voltage is positive. Faraday's law concerns the production of a magnetic field by a moving charge and is not directly applicable to this question.

12.   **D.** Prior to application of an external positive voltage the charges of the terminals are determined based on the convention for a Galvanic cell, i.e. the anode is negative and the cathode is positive. When the external voltage is applied, the half reactions are reversed and the positively labeled terminal becomes the anode and the negatively labeled terminal becomes the cathode.

13.   **D.** $\Delta G° = -nFE°$
$$\Delta G° = -(2)(10^5)(+1.5) = -3 \times 10^5 \, J$$

14. **A.** The number of electrons transferred is n = 3.
$$\Delta G° = -nFE°$$
$$\Delta G° = -(3)(10^5)(-2.5) = +7.5 \times 10^5 \, J$$

15. **D.** Negative voltages correspond to a nonspontaneous reaction that requires greater than +2.5 V of external voltage under electrolytic conditions to cause the reaction to proceed in the direction indicated.

16. **B.** Voltages do not depend upon the amount of reacting species.

17. **C.** Voltages don't change, but free energies do change, because now the value of n has doubled.
$$\Delta G° = -nFE°$$
$$\Delta G° = -(6)(10^5)(-2.5) = +15.0 \times 10^5 \, J$$

18. **A.** Reduction half reactions have electrons as reactants and the oxidation number of the ion is reduced.

19. **C.** When a reduction half-reaction is reversed and becomes an oxidation, the sign of the voltage is switched.

20. **A.** See the explanation for question 16.

21. **A.** See the explanation for questions 16 and 19.

22. **B.** The voltage is +0.80 V because positive voltages correspond with spontaneous REDOX processes, which have negative Gibbs free energy changes. See also the explanation for question 13.

23. **D.** The reduction half-reaction for zinc has a voltage of -0.76 V. Therefore, the oxidation half-reaction has a voltage of +0.76 V, which is spontaneous and has a negative Gibbs free energy. See also the explanation for question 13.

24. **B.** The reduction half-reaction is
$$Ag^+ + e^- \rightarrow Ag$$
$$E° = +0.80 \, V$$
And the oxidation half-reaction is
$$Cu \rightarrow Cu^{2+} + 2e^-$$
$$E° = -0.34 \, V$$
with the overall REDOX process being the sum of the two half-reaction voltages.
$$E°_{overall} = E°_{red} + E°_{ox}$$
$$E°_{overall} = (+0.80) + (-0.34) = +0.46 \, V$$

25. **D.** The oxidation potential for sodium is +2.71 V, and none of the answer choices have negative reduction potentials that when added to the oxidation potential would produce a negative overall cell potential.

26. **A.** Since an a-particle has two protons and two neutrons, there must be two less protons in the nucleus and the mass of the parent isotope must go down by four amus. The emitted particle is an a-particle and will become a helium atom once it gains two electrons.

27. **B.** An alpha particle has two protons and two neutrons ($^4\alpha$), which is the same as a helium nucleus.

28. **C.** A beta negative is essentially an electron that has virtually no mass. Beta emission essentially converts a neutron into a proton and an electron, therefore the atomic number of the parent isotope increases. The beta particle comes from the nucleus and does not produce an ion, unlike the loss of a valence electron.

29. **D.** A positron (β^+) is the antimatter particle of a beta negative particle (β^-), which is essentially an electron.

30. **D.** A gamma (γ) particle is a photon of energy with no mass or charge.

31. **B.** The atomic number of Tl is 81 and must equal the atomic number of Q, plus the two protons in the a-particle plus the charge of the positron. Therefore Q is platinum. the mass number of the thallium isotope must equal the mass of the products
$$^{205}Tl \rightarrow {}^4\alpha + {}^0\beta^+ + {}^{201}Pt$$
Likewise, the A isotope must have an atomic number of 74 and is tungsten.
$$^{201}Pt \rightarrow 2\,{}^4\alpha + {}^{193}W$$

32. **B.** See the explanation for question 31.

33. **B.** $^{205}Pb + {}^0\beta^+ \rightarrow {}^{205}Tl$

34. **D.** $^{209}Po \rightarrow {}^4\alpha + {}^{205}Pb$

35. **D.** See the explanation for question 33.

SECTION 7 CONTENT REVIEW SOLUTIONS

1.   **D.** A solution containing equal concentrations of both the R and S stereoisomers is a racemic mixture and would not rotate plane-polarized light. Look very carefully at numbers in choice B; the concentrations are not equal.

2.   **C.** The number of stereoisomers is 2^n where n is the number of chiral centers.

3.   **B.** Geometric isomers have the same formula and similar connectivity, but different arrangements of atoms that can not be interconverted with one another by rotation around bonds; structural isomers have the same formula but different connectivity; enantiomers are geometric isomers that are mirror images of one another; tautomers are structural isomers that occur when a carbonyl compound has a hydrogen on the alpha carbon that forms an enol.

4.   **A.** Examples of conformational isomers are the boat and chair forms of cyclohexane.

5.   **D.** This is the definition of diastereomers.

6.   **C.** See the explanation for question 3. For example 1,1-dichloroethene and the cis- (Z) and trans- (E) isomers of 1,2-dichloroethene are geometric isomers.

7.   **B.** The mirror image can be rotated and then superimposed on the original structure, so the mirror image is the same structure and not an enantiomer. The compound 2-butene does not have a chiral carbon and as such the R and S designations are not appropriate.

8.   **A.** Choice B is a racemic mixture; for choice C, the cis- and trans-2-butene isomers are not optically active (no chiral carbon); and choice D describes a meso structure, which is not optically active.

9.   **D.** The chair conformation is thermodynamically more stable than the boat conformation, and equatorial positions are sterically less congested than axial positions.

10.   **B.** A relative configuration would be if a compound had a single chiral center and has two enantiomers, we would know that the two isomers are mirror images, but we would not know their absolute configurations (R or S) until we knew the actual formula and identified the priority of the groups around the chiral carbon for one of the isomers.

11.   **D.** A saturated hydrocarbon has a 2n+2 formula and for each double bond (or ring) we can remove two hydrogen atoms. Choice A is saturated; choice B could have one double bond; choice C could have two double bonds; and choice D would have three double bonds.

12.   **A.** The highest number of s-bonds would occur in a saturated hydrocarbon. See also the explanation for question 11.

13.   **B.** The Lewis structure for formaldehyde ($H_2C=O$) predicts a planar structure with three s-bonds (sp^2 hybridized) and one p-bond between the carbon and oxygen.

14.   **C.** The Lewis structure is

$$HO-C\equiv C-OH$$

There are two O-H σ-bonds, two O-C σ-bonds, one C-C σ-bond, and two p-bonds between the carbon atoms.

15.   **D.** BF$_3$ adopts a trigonal planar structure with three B-F s-bonds (sp^2 hybridized).

16.   **D.** Resonance leads to a more energetically stable bonding situation, as in benzene.

17.   **D.** Formally the bond order would be 1.5 for resonance between a double and single bond, which would have a longer bond distance than a bond order of 3.

18.   **C.** Since there are eight carbon atoms in the formula, choices B and D can be eliminated. Octane is a saturated hydrocarbon and would have a 2n+2 formula. Octene, with a single C=C bond would have the appropriate 2n formula.

19.   **A.** Linear alkanes have more degrees of freedom of motion, which increases the possibilities for intermolecular interactions, and results in higher boiling points than similar branched alkanes.

20.   **B.** An initiation step in a radical mechanism involves a reactant that forms a radical. A propagation step in a radical mechanism is one in which a radical is both a reactant and a product. A termination step in a radical mechanism is when one or more radicals combine to form products that are not radicals.

21.   **D.** This is the textbook S$_N$2 substitution reaction, a second order (overall) nucleophilic substitution, where in a single step the hydroxide attacks the carbon, forming a five coordinate carbon as the transition state, subsequently pushing the leaving group off the other side.

22.   **C.** See the explanation for question 21.

23.   **A.** See the explanation for question 21.

24.   **B.** An S$_N$1 substitution proceeds by way of a two-step mechanism in which the leaving group initially comes off the carbon, forming a carbocation, which then in a second step reacts with the nucleophile to form the product. Resonance stabilization of the intermediate would provide more time for the nucleophile to complete the reaction.

25.   **B.** The partially positive hydrogen of a polar-protic solvent would help stabilize the negatively charged leaving group, making it more likely to be displaced with the formation of the intermediate carbocation. See also the explanation for question 24.

SECTION 8 CONTENT REVIEW SOLUTIONS

1.   **A.** Mild oxidizing agents in non-aqueous solvents, tend to give incomplete oxidation (aldehydes) of primary alcohols. To from a ketone, there would have to be a secondary alcohol, so that after oxidation (loss of H_2) carbon atoms would end up on both sides of the carbonyl. The tertiary alcohol will be resistant to oxidation by a mild oxidizing agent.

2.   **A.** The prefix carboxy- is associated with organic acids (-CO_2H) and the suffix -one is used for ketones.

3.   **C.** The hydroxyl group of an alcohol produces a polar C-O bond due to differences in electronegativity. This often results in greater intermolecular forces, due to dipole-dipole interactions (and hydrogen bonding), which increases the boiling points of alcohols as compared with alkanes of similar molecular weight.

4.   **D.** Each of the answer choices are chromium based oxidizing agents, which are plenty strong enough to oxidize a secondary alcohol to a ketone, but, further oxidation of the ketone is unlikely.

5.   **D.** While the functional group remains the same in each compound, the molecular weight, and hence the London dispersion forces increases. The boiling points are: ethanol, 78°C; 1-butanol, 117°C; 1-pentanol, 137°C.

6.   **C.** The anion is stabilized by resonance with the carbonyl and the electronegativity of the oxygen atom.

7.   **C.** A ketone with a hydrogen atom on the alpha carbon can undergo tautomerization. The hydrogen atoms on the alpha carbons are modestly acidic and deprotonation would produce a negatively charged ion that would have similar resonance stabilization.

8.   **D.** Unless there is one or more additional p bonding functional groups within one bond of the carbonyl group, the p -bond will be localized between only two atoms, the carbon and the oxygen of the carbonyl.

9.   **B.** Initially, a hemiacetal will be formed, but in the presence of excess alcohol, further reaction will occur to form the acetal.

10.   **C.** The initial step in a base catalyzed aldol condensation involves the formation of an enolate, followed by reaction with another carbonyl compound, thereby forming a carbon-carbon bond.

11.   **A.** This is the textbook example of the tautomeriztion of acetone (propanone).

12.   **D.** The species that is lower in energy thermodynamically will always have a higher concentration at equilibrium. The only time this situation

might not be true is if the activation energy is high and the reaction has not yet reached equilibrium.

13.   **D.** Nucleophilic attack requires the molecule to have a site of unsaturation, thus eliminating hexane (choice A). The carbon of a carbonyl group would be much more electrophilic than the carbon of an alcohol, eliminating hexanol (choice C). The electron donating properties of the alkyl group of a ketone, reduces the electrophilicity of the carbonyl carbon as compared with an aldehyde.

14.   **D.** Benzaldehyde is more acidic than propanone, (pK_a = 14.9 and 19.2, respectively), however, it does not have a hydrogen atom on the carbon that is alpha to the carbonyl. The acidic hydrogen in benzaldehyde is directly attached to the carbonyl.

15.   **A.** Overall, an aldol condensation involves the reaction between a ketone capable of undergoing acid catalyzed tautomerization to form an enol (or enolate, when base catalyzed), followed by reaction with another carbonyl compound to form a carbon-carbon bond, and subsequent loss of water to form a conjugated enone.

16.   **B.** Both lactones and lactams are cyclic esters or amides, respectively, formed from organic acids that also have alcohol or amine functional groups. The -am suffix indicates the presence of a nitrogen atom in the structure, e.g. amines and amides. An anhydride is formed when two organic acids undergo dehydration, and are not necessarily cyclic structures.

17.   **C.** Electron withdrawing groups will increase the acidity by stabilizing the anion. Moving an electron-withdrawing group away from the carboxylate decreases the stabilizing effect. Electron-donating groups will have the opposite effect and destabilize the anion, making it less acidic.

18.   **D.** In this type of substitution, a nucleophile first attacks the carbonyl carbon, which pushes electron density out onto the oxygen atom, reducing the bond order, with subsequent loss of the leaving group and reformation of the carbonyl double bond.

19.   **B.** PCC stands for pyridinium chlorochromate, which is an oxidizing agent. Both sodium borohydride and lithium aluminum hydride are reducing agents, but LAH is a stronger reducing agent than sodium borohydride and is often used to produce primary alcohols from organic acids. However, sodium borohydride is a strong enough reducing agent to reduce an aldehyde to a primary alcohol.

20.   **C.** Soaps are a type of surfactant, generally having long hydrophobic alkyl groups that are attached to a carboxylate. Soaps can be produced from triglycerides (fats) by base catalyzed hydrolysis.

21.   **B.** This is a typical acid catalyzed esterification reaction. In order to get this question right you need to know the naming system for esters, i.e. the alcohol is the group associated with the -yl suffix and the organic acid will be the group associated with the -oate suffix.

22.   **A.** The primary amines would have the least steric congestion and therefore be better nucleophiles, in terms of reaction kinetics. Methyl amine is a better base than

benzyl amine (pK$_a$s of 3.38 and 4.86, respectively), because the inductive effect is reduced by the presence the aromatic ring system.

23.   **D.** The reactivity is determined by the bond strength. The acyl halide would be the most reactive because the halide is a good leaving group, followed by the alkoxide and then the amide, which correlates well with the multiple bond character between the carbonyl carbon and the leaving group.

24.   **A.** Converting one ester into another by reaction with an alcohol is transesterification, which can be either acid or base catalyzed. If water is present then a carboxylic acid can be produced by hydrolysis.

25.   **B.** Esterification is dehydration of an alcohol and an organic acid, and represents an equilibrium reaction with water as a product. If water is the solvent, the equilibrium will be shifted towards reactants and poor yields will result.

SECTION 9 CONTENT REVIEW SOLUTIONS

1.   **A.** All of the amino acids used to make proteins in higher animals are the L-isomers. There are a few D-isomers of amino acids that are produced by bacteria. The capital D and L designations are determined by relating the molecule to glyceraldehyde, and does not necessarily relate to the lowercase d and l (+ or -) designations with respect to the rotation of plane-polarized light.

2.   **B.** Naturally occurring sugars in plants and animals only adopt the D configuration.

3.   **C.** The R and S system is based on assigning the priority to the various groups attached to a chiral atom. See also the explanation for question 1.

4.   **B.** The Fischer projection of linear D-glucose and the ring structure of the a isomer are shown below.

When the carbonyl is placed at the top of the linear Fischer projection, if the chiral carbon furthest from the carbonyl (carbon 5) has its -OH group on the right, it will be R and defines this isomer as D-glucose. If the -OH on this carbon were on the left, it would be the L isomer.

5.   **B.** The structure of valine has an isopropyl side chain. All of the other choices have nitrogen atoms in the side chain that can undergo base hydrolysis.

6.   **A.** Glutamate is the deprotonated form of glutamic acid.

7.   **D.** Valine, alanine, and isoleucine, have alkyl side chains, which are nonpolar and hydrophobic. Serine's side chain is -CH$_2$OH, which makes it polar and can form hydrogen bonds with water.

8.   **C.** As the name implies, phenylalanine is similar to the structure of alanine, which has a methyl side chain, except that in phenylalanine, one of the hydrogen atoms of the methyl group has been replaced with a phenyl (C$_6$H$_5$) group.

9.   **B.** The key word is "unique". Other amino acids such as proline and tryptophan have nitrogen in cyclic groups. There are also other amino acids with aromatic groups as side chains, such as phenylalanine and tyrosine. Since the imidazole group is aromatic, the formal bond order for the nitrogen atoms in the ring is 1.5. The pK$_a$ of histidine is about 6, and therefore it can act as either an acid or a base under physiological pH conditions.

10.   **A.** Valine and isoleucine have isopropyl and sec-butyl side chains, which are hydrophobic. All the other pairs of amino acids have at least one hydrophilic amino acid.

11.   **C.** Methionine has a thioether (C-S-C) as part of its side chain, and cysteine has a thiol (C-S-H) group. Threonine has an alcohol (C-O-H) functional group as part of its side chain.

12.   **B.** Both the acid and the amino groups will be deprotonated.

13.   **B.** The acid will be deprotonated and the base will be protonated, therefore it is in its zwitterionic form.

14.   **D.** The pI, or the isoelectrtic point, is the pH where the acid form is deprotonated and the base form is protonated (the Zwitterion). This is the pH half way between the two pK_as and would be the first equivalence point in a titration.

15.   **C.** If the pH is greater than the pI (where the net charge is zero), then additional protons will be removed from the amino acid and the net charge will be negative. This will cause the amino acid to migrate towards the positive electrode, which is the anode, the electrode where oxidation occurs.

16.   **C.** Aspartic acid has an acidic side chain, therefore its net charge will be -1 at pH 7 (pH > pI, see the explanation for question15), and will be attracted to the positively charged electrode, which is the anode, the electrode where oxidation occurs.

17.   **B.** This is a direct result of the mechanism for enzyme catalyzed peptide bond formation, in which the nitrogen lone pair of the new amino acid (the smaller molecule) attacks the carbonyl carbon of carboxylic acid of the peptide.

18.   **A.** A thermodynamically unfavorable reaction can be driven by coupling it with other thermodynamically more favorable processes, such as the hydrolysis of ATP.

19.   **D.** The resonance involves pushing the lone pair of the nitrogen to form a double bond with the carbonyl carbon. This then requires that one of the bonding pairs of electrons between the carbon and oxygen be pushed towards the oxygen to form a carbon-oxygen single bond and an additional lone pair is created on the oxygen. As a result, the formal charges of the oxygen and nitrogen will be -1 and +1, respectively.

20.   **A.** Naturally occurring glucose is the D-isomer and it is a hexose ($C_6H_{12}O_5$). See the explanations for question 2 and 4.

21.   **C.** Diastereomers are stereoisomers that are not mirror images; enantiomers are stereoisomers that are mirror images; epimers are stereoisomers that differ at only one chiral center; and constitutional isomers have the same formula but different connectivity.

22.   **B.** A pyranose has a six-membered ring with oxygen as part of the ring. A furanose is a five-membered ring with oxygen as part of the ring. This is b-D-glucose, which when polymerized forms cellulose, which can not be digested by most animals. This molecule is a hexose, not a pentose, because there are six carbons in the formula, not five.

23.   **D.** An anomer is a special type of epimer (different at one chiral carbon) is a cyclic saccharide that differs at the hemiacetal/acetal group because of the orientation that the hydroxyl group of the linear form had when being attached the carbonyl, to close the ring.

24.   **A.** Benedict's test can be used to identify reducing sugars, i.e. any sugar that has an aldehyde (linear form) or a keto group that can isomerize to an aldehyde. All monosaccharides are reducing sugars, but some disaccharides, such as sucrose are not because of the formation of the acetal [$R_2C(OR')_2$] functional group, which does not readily isomerize to form an aldehyde.

25.   **C.** There is free rotation around carbon-carbon single bonds, whereas the restricted rotation around carbon-carbon double bonds reduces the degrees of freedom and restricts the ability of the molecule to undergo conformational changes. To become a solid, appropriate arrangements of molecular interactions must be possible to promote intermolecular interactions.

SECTION 10 CONTENT REVIEW SOLUTIONS

1.   **A.** The strong acid will convert the amine into its corresponding ammonium ion, which will be much more soluble in aqueous solution than the amine.

2.   **A.** Sodium carbonate is an ionic compound that is significantly soluble in water and naphthalene is a nonpolar aromatic organic compound, which is essentially insoluble in water. Carbon tetrachloride is a nonpolar solvent that would dissolve the naphthalene but not the sodium carbonate. Both naphthalene and sodium carbonate will probably dissolve to some extent in diethyl ether.

3.   **B.** Bicarbonate would be a strong enough base to deprotonate the organic acid, producing the negatively charged carboxylate, which would be much more soluble in the aqueous solution than in the organic solvent.

4.   **B.** Deprotonating the slightly acidic phenol with a strong base would produce the negatively charged phenoxide, which would be much more soluble in the aqueous solution than in the organic solvent.

5.   **C.** The mobile solvent must move up the TLC plate by capillary action.

6.   **C.** The solid support for TLC is typically silica gel, which is a fairly polar stationary phase that would interact more strongly with the polar compound. The retardation factor R_f is the ratio of the distance travelled by a given compound divided by the distance traveled by the solvent front.

7.   **D.** See the explanation for question 6.

8.   **D.** Column chromatography is most often used for preparative scale separations. The other options are generally used for small-scale separations.

9.   **A.** The solvent moves down the column due to its weight.

10.   **B.** The surface of silica is relatively polar and would interact with the polar compound, increasing its retention time as compared with the nonpolar compound that will move through the column faster by remaining in the mobile phase.

11.   **D.** Ion-exchange materials have cations (or possibly anions) attached to the solid support that can be swapped with another ion in the mobile phase, that has a greater affinity for the oppositely charge site on the stationary phase. For example a cation-exchange column would retain the amino acid with a positively charged side chain, and allow the amino acid with the negatively charged side chain to pass through the column with the mobile phase.

12.   **B.** HPLC uses a pump to create a high pressure to force the mobile phase through the stationary phase.

13.   **C.** Small molecules will enter the pores, while large molecules can not enter the pores. As a result the large molecules will move with the mobile phase faster than the small molecules.

14.   **C.** See the explanation for question 13.

15.   **A.** Affinity chromatography is a method of separating biochemical mixtures based on highly specific interactions between the substrate and the stationary phase, such as interactions between an antigen and an antibody, or between an enzyme and its substrates.

16.   **D.** In gas chromatography the compounds must be in the gas phase since the mobile phase is a carrier gas. Variations in volatility and temperature gradients in the column allow for the separations.

17.   **B.** Separation based on distillation requires that the boiling points of the compounds be sufficiently separated so that a relatively pure vapor is produced at a certain temperature. Compounds with high normal boiling points can be separated using vacuum distillation (choice A), but this requires special equipment. An azeotrope is a mixture of two compounds that boil at the same temperature and can not be separated by distillation. Melting points (choice D) are irrelevant to distillation.

18.   **A.** Conjugated organic p-systems tend to cause low energy electronic transitions (p --> p *), in the visible region of the spectrum. Compounds with single bonds tend to be colorless, as are alcohols. Water solubility is irrelevant.

19.   **D.** Most organic compounds are colorless and absorb light only in the UV region of the spectrum. Transition metal ions often have distinct colors, due to electronic d-d electronic transitions.

20.   **A.** Carbonyl (C=O) stretches for organic compounds such as ketones or aldehydes tend to be strong and sharp peaks in the $1735 - 1680$ cm^{-1} region.

21.   **B.** The hydroxyl (-OH) stretches in compounds such as alcohols or organic acids tend to be broad features in the $3650 - 3200$ cm^{-1} region for liquids or solids, due to hydrogen bonding.

22.   **C.** N-H stretches tend to be asymmetric broad features in the $3150 - 2500$ cm^{-1}, region due to hydrogen bonding.

23.   **B.** The two signals result from the chemically equivalent methyl groups (-CH$_3$) and the chemically equivalent methylenes (-CH$_2$-), appearing as a triplet and quartet due to spin-spin coupling.

24.   **D.** The structure of butanal is

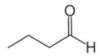

The four signals result from the methyl (-CH$_3$) and two methylenes (-CH$_2$-), as well as the aldehyde hydrogen.

25.   **A.** The symmetry of benzene makes all of the hydrogen atoms chemically equivalent.

SECTION 11 CONTENT REVIEW SOLUTIONS

1.   **A.** Note that the suffix of each of the answer options is -ene, therefore there must be one or more double bonds. In order to complete the octets for each of the carbon atoms, the structural formula should be

$$CH_2=CHCH_2CH_2CH=CHCH_3$$

This is a straight chain of seven carbon atoms, so it must have the prefix hept-, eliminating choice D. The lowest numbers that indicate the positions of the double bonds is 1, 5, not 2,6.

2.   **B.** In the older naming system, cis- means on the same side, while trans- means on opposite sides. Using the newer E-Z designations, the priority system is used to determine if the higher priority groups are zusammen, or entgegen, which are German words to together or opposite, respectively.

3.   **C.** Alkyl substituents are electron-donating groups and would help stabilize a radical intermediate with an incomplete octet in the case of anti- Markovnikov addition and the carbocation in the case of Markovnikov addition.

4.   **D.** Epoxides are a specific type of cyclic ether that has a three membered ring.

5.   **A.** The carbon-carbon double bond is part of the longest chain of five carbon atoms, so this is a pentene. Vinyl groups are side functional groups and we can eliminate choices B and C. The double bond takes priority and needs the lowest number to indicate its position. The first position is between the first and second carbon atoms. Once this is established the positions of the methyl groups must be 3 and 4.

6.   **C.** There must be a carbon-carbon triple bond, which using current IUPAC rules should be called ethyne, but historically has been called acetylene.

7.   **D.** This organic compound is 2-butyne, whose structural formula is

$$H_3C-C\equiv C-CH_3$$

The methyl groups are tetrahedral and sp³ hybridized, while the carbons that form the triple bond are linear and sp hybridized.

8.   **B.** Presumably one of the stereochemical forms interacts with the catalyst in an energetically more stable interaction than the other, due to steric interactions.

9.   **A.** The mechanism initially involves the formation of an unstable enol that rearranges to form a thermodynamically more stable ketone.

10.   **D.** Ozone is a strong oxidizing agent that when reacted with alkynes, forms products similar to the oxidative cleavage of alkynes by permanganate.

11.   **A.** All of the answer options are aromatic compounds, but only naphthalene has a structure with more than one ring, i.e. polycyclic.

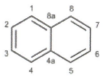

12.   **D.** It is the delocalized p system that results from the overlap of the p orbitals on each carbon atom that makes benzene so stable.

13.   **B.** The structures of toluene, aniline, benzaldehyde and phenol are shown from left to right, respectively.

14.   **C.** See the explanation for question 13.

15.   **B.** Since aromatic compounds are unusually stable and there can not be more than one correct answer, we can eliminate choices A and D. Aromatic ring systems have 2n+2 p electrons, where n is an integer. If an organic compound contains a non-planar ring system that is not aromatic, it is considered nonaromatic. Antiaromatic compounds are nonaromatic and are unstable compounds with 4n p electrons.

16.   **C.** Glucose and furan do not have nitrogen in their formulas, eliminating choices B and D. The structure of pyridine

does have a nitrogen in an aromatic ring, but the lone pair is not part of the aromatic p system, making it a very good Lewis base. The structure of pyrrole is

and the lone pair is part of the 2n+2 aromatic p system.

17.   **B.** The linkages are phosphate esters.

18.   **D.** The structure of ATP is

The phosphate groups in ATP are formed by the dehydration of hydrogen phosphates. Anhydride means without water.

19.   **A.** A nucleoside consists of a nucleic base and a sugar, such as deoxyribose. When a phosphate group is added, a nucleotide is formed.

20.   **B.** The structure of ATP (see question 18) consists of a triphosphate group attached to a pentose sugar (ribose), which is also attached to a purine base (adenine).

FINAL EXAM SOLUTIONS

1.   **B.** The formula for acetaldehyde is CH_3COH. With the new IUPAC naming system, since there are two carbons in the chain, with no carbon-carbon multiple bonds, the prefix is ethan- and the suffix is -al, indicating an aldehyde functional group. Methanal would only have one carbon, and is historically known as formaldehyde, a saturated aqueous solution of which is known as formalin. Ethanol is the alcohol, CH_3CH_2OH.

2.   **A.** A terminal functional group is on the end of a carbon chain. An aldehyde must be terminal, otherwise it is a ketone.

3.   **C.** The acid takes priority over the alcohol. The priority order is: alkyl ammonium ions > organic acids > acid chlorides > amides > nitriles > aldehydes > ketones > alcohols > thiols > alkenes > alkynes > alkanes. The prefix propan- is because there are three carbons in the chain. It is an organic acid (-ic acid) because of the R-CO_2H group, whereas the suffix -ate, would indicate the deprotonated R-CO_2^- anion.

4.   **B.** This is an anhydride formed from two molecules of acetic acid.

5.   **C.** See the explanation for question 3.

6.   **D.** See the explanation for question 3. The longest chain of carbon atoms is 7 and numbering with the -OH in the 2-position provides the lowest position numbers.

7.   **A.** The -CO_2H functional group is an organic acid, whose IUPAC naming has the suffix of -ic acid. Since there are two of the functional groups, the Greek prefix di- would be included.

8.   **B.** The prefixes for the number of carbon atoms in the longest chain of an organic compound are meth-, eth-, prop, but-, pent-, hex-, hept-, oct-, etc. The common name for methyl molecules is formyl.

9.   **D.** The longest chain of carbon atoms determines the prefix (see the explanation for question 8). In this case there are nine carbons in the longest chain, nonane, with a one carbon (methyl) and a two carbon (ethyl) side chains, whose positions should use the lowest possible numbers (3 and 5, not 5 and 7). The prefix -iso is no longer an IUPAC accepted method for nomenclature.

10.   **C.** To be optically active and rotate plane polarized light, the solution would need to contain a single stereoisomer, or unequal concentrations of the opposite isomers (enantiomers).

11.   **B.** If the molecule on the right is rotated 180° along a vertical axis so that the hash and wedge are pointed to the left, we would see that these two molecules are mirror images (enantiomers) of each other.

12.   **B.** The L and D designations indicate that these are the opposite stereoisomers (enantiomers) of tartaric acid. The + and - designations indicate that the isomers rotate plane polarized light in opposite directions, but does not necessarily indicate that the molecules are enantiomers or that a particular configuration (D or L) will rotate plane polarized light one way or the other.

13.   **B.** Both molecules have the formula C_7H_{16}, but the connectivity of carbon atoms is different, so they are

structural (constitutional) isomers. There are no chiral centers in these molecules.

14. **A.** The molecules are stereoisomers with the same formula, but are not mirror images of each other, hence they are diastereomers, not enantiomers.

15. **B.** Shown below are the Newman projections for the various conformations of butane. From left to right, we have the eclipsed conformation with a dihedral angle of 0° for the methyl groups; the gauche conformation; the eclipsed conformation with a dihedral angle of 120°; and the lowest energy anti configuration.

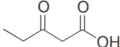

16. **A.** For a particular shell the order of energies for the subshells is s < p < d < f

17. **C.** The tetrahedral carbon atoms in ethane are sp^3 hybridized.

18. **B.** Boron trihydride (BH_3) adopts a trigonal planar structure and as a monomer the boron violates the octet rule.

19. **D.** A free radical is an atom or molecule with an unpaired electron, which may occupy a single atomic orbital.

20. **A.** Sigma bonds are formed by the direct overlap of orbitals, whereas pi bonds are formed by the sideways overlap of orbitals, which is not possible for a pure s atomic orbital.

21. **A.** Just like atomic orbitals, molecular orbitals can not hold more than two electrons with opposite spin quantum numbers.

22. **C.** The formula is $C_5H_8O_3$, whose structure is

There are seven C-H sigma bonds, one O-H sigma bond, four C-C sigma bonds and three C-O sigma bonds, for a total of fifteen sigma bonds. There are two C-O pi bonds in the two carbonyl groups.

23. **D.** Triple bonds are shorter, stronger and have more pi bonds than double bonds.

24. **D.** In benzene, the energy associated with alternating single and double bonds does not accurately represent the stability of the ring, because the sideways, delocalized pi bonding of the p-orbitals provides additional stability, which in Lewis theory is known as resonance.

25. **A.** The electronic geometry, also known as the coordinate, or electron domain structure and is comprised of bonds between a central atom and other atoms, as well as lone-pairs of electrons. Methane (CH_4) has four C-H bonds in a tetrahedral geometry, ammonia (NH_3) has three N-H bonds and a lone-pair in a tetrahedral geometry, and water (H_2O) has two O-H bonds and two lone-pairs in a tetrahedral geometry.

26. **B.** Molecular geometries are determined by the position of atoms bonded to a central atom. See also the explanation for question 25.

27. **D.** An electrophile must be electron deficient or have a site of unsaturation. The nitrogen in ammonia (NH_3) has a closed shell electron configuration, with the lone-pair of electrons allowing the molecule to be answer choices A, B and C.

28. **B.** The fact that H_2O is not charged makes it a better leaving group than an anion, which would have greater electrostatic forces of attraction with the carbon atom to which it was bonded.

29. **A.** LAH is a modest reducing agent, which is capable of reducing aldehydes to alcohols, but not strong enough to reduce the alcohol further. To produce an organic acid from an aldehyde, you would need to use an oxidizing agent.

30. **C.** A S_N1 mechanism would be favored in polar-protic solvents and if there were sterically demanding tertiary alkyl groups. Unstable leaving groups will disfavor substitution reactions. A good nucleophile will be more likely to form a bond to the carbon, rather than act as a base that would favor an elimination reaction.

31. **C.** The structure of hydroquinone is

When two functional groups are located in the 1,4 position of a benzene ring, the isomer is commonly referred to as a para isomer; 1,3 positions are known as meta isomers; and 1,2 positions are ortho isomers.

32. **B.** The negative charge of the phenoxide is stabilized by delocalization (resonance) into the benzene ring.

33. **B.** The structure of the tosylate group is

The mesylate group is similar, but has a methyl alkyl group. Tosylate groups are used to protect ketones. The side chain in cysteine is a thiol group, not a sulfoxide group.

34. **A.** Ubiquinone (or CoQ₁₀) is a ketone that can be reduced to the corresponding alcohol, ubiquinol.

35. **D.** Alcohols have significant solubility in aqueous solution due to hydrogen bonding. The hydrogen bonding would increase both the melting and boiling points.

36. **B.** The carbonyl stabilizes the carbanion that would form from the loss of a hydrogen ion, making these compounds relatively acidic. The C-H stretching vibration would be in the 2850-3000 cm^{-1} region of the IR spectrum, not the C=O region (around 1700 cm^{-1}). The carbonyl carbon is sp^2 hybridized and the **α** carbon would be sp^3 hybridized.

37. **D.** The oxygen is more electronegative than the carbon, such that the carbon would have a partial positive charge, which also means it is electron deficient and would be an electrophile, not a nucleophile. The hybridization of the carbon would be sp^2.

38.   **C.** LAH is a reducing agent. Under acidic conditions, sodium chromate and acidified chromium (VI) oxide are relatively strong oxidizing agents and will convert the alcohol into a carboxylic acid. PCC is a milder oxidizing agent, and will only oxidize the alcohol to an aldehyde.

39.   **D.** Addition of an alcohol to an aldehyde, first produces a hemiacetal and then an acetal, whereas addition of an alcohol to a ketone, first produces a hemiketal and then a ketal, as shown below.

40.   **C.** The word "geminal" means that the functional groups are on the same carbon atom. In this case the functional groups are two -OH groups (a diol). This would be accomplished by addition of water to a ketone. Reaction of peroxide to a ketone would probably lead to oxidation. Reaction between an alcohol and a ketone would lead to a hemiketal or ketal (see the explanation for question 39). Reaction of a ketone with LAH would lead to reduction.

41.   **A.** An imine ($R_2C=NR'$) is isoelectronic with a ketone ($R_2C=O$) and likewise can undergo tautomerization if a hydrogen atom is present on the alpha carbon.

42.   **A.** If there is a hydrogen atom on an alpha carbon, that hydrogen can be transferred to the oxygen of the carbonyl.

43.   **B.** If the hydrogen on the alpha carbon is removed as H^+, distributing the negative charge through the formation of an enolate, stabilizes the anion.

44.   **A.** The initial product of the self condensation of a carbonyl compound with a hydrogen on the alpha carbon, is the aldol (ald- for aldehyde and -ol for alcohol) product, in which the enol has reacted with the keto form to make a carbon-carbon bond, as seen below.

Aldol

Loss of water from the aldol product results in the commonly observed product containing a carbon-carbon double bond and a carbonyl, and enol (en- for an alkene and -ol for an alcohol).

45.   **C.** Pentane is unlikely to undergo nucleophilic substitution, eliminating choices A and D. The aldehyde is less sterically congested than the ketone.

46.   **B.** This molecule is the potassium salt of a long straight chain fatty acid, which represent the main components in surfactants or soaps.

47.   **A.** This is the classic esterification reaction between an organic acid and an alcohol, which is a dehydration equilibrium that produces an ester and water as products.

48.   **C.** The long chain organic carboxylates of soaps (see also the explanation for question 46) can form stable spherical structures in which the hydrophobic alkyl chains are attracted to one another due to intermolecular forces of attraction and the anionic hydrophilic carboxylate heads are on the outside. The interior of a micelle is therefore hydrophobic.

49.   **C.** The presence of highly electronegative halogens close to the carboxylic acid functional group, helps stabilize the conjugate anion, and makes the organic acid more acidic. Fluorine is more electronegative than chlorine.

50.   **A.** This is an esterification reaction between an alcohol and an organic acid (see the explanation for question 47). In the nomenclature for esters, the alcohol becomes the side chain (the initial portion of the name with the -yl suffix) attached to the oxygen of the ester and the organic acid is the main chain (with the -oate suffix).

51.   **D.** The primary amine is the least sterically congested nucleophile. An alcohol will not form an amide, it will form an ester, eliminating choice B.

52.   **A.** An amide is formed by the dehydration of an amine and an organic acid, while the reverse hydrolysis will convert an amide into an amine and an organic acid.

53.   **D.** Converting one ester into another by reacting an ester with an alcohol is transesterification. This reaction is not a REDOX reaction. Hydrolysis of an ester would form an organic acid and an alcohol.

54.   **B.** A beta lactam has a ring structure as seen below and 2-azetidinone, is the simplest beta lactam, with considerable ring strain, and as such is relatively reactive.

55.   **A.** See the explanation for question 47 and consider Le Chatelier's principle.

56.   **A.** Glycine ($NH_2CH_2CO_2H$) is the only amino acid that does not have an additional group attached to the alpha carbon. A chiral carbon atom must have four different groups.

57.   **D.** The structures of cysteine, methionine, valine, and lysine are shown below, respectively.

The presence of -thio- in a name is an indication of the presence of a sulfur atoms. You must memorize the amino acids and their structures.

58. **C.** To be an amide there must be a reaction between an organic acid (1,4- butanedicarboxylic acid or adipic acid) and an amine, eliminating choices B and C, which are alcohols and esters, respectively. The passage specifies very long polymers, so there needs to be an amine on each end of the molecule to allow the polymerization to continue.

59. **C.** The pK_as of phosphoric acid are 2.15, 7.20, and 12.35.

60. **B.** In the Gabriel synthesis an alkyl halide is converted into a primary amine, which could not possibly be chiral. The Strecker synthesis prepares amino acids from aldehydes or ketones by reaction with ammonium chloride and potassium cyanide, and occurs without stereospecificity.

61. **D.** Infrared spectroscopy (IR) is associated with molecular vibrations, which are very similar for C-H bonds, but easily identified for various functional groups containing, O-H, N-H, C=O, C-O, or N-O groups. Optical rotation and deshielding (choices B and C) apply to the rotation of plane polarized light and nuclear magnetic resonance (NMR), respectively.

62. **D.** Molecular vibrations that cause a change in a dipole moment are observed in the IR spectrum.

63. **C.** In order to observe a nuclear magnetic resonance signal, a nucleus must have a nonzero nuclear spin. The nuclear spin of a proton (^1H) is 1/2 and this isotope of hydrogen is probably the most commonly used nucleus for magnetic resonance. Deuterium, with one proton and one neutron has a nuclear spin of 1 and is NMR active. A helium (^4He) nucleus, with two protons and two neutrons does not have a net nuclear spin and is not NMR active. The most abundant isotope of carbon (^{12}C) does not have a net nuclear spin, but the minor isotope (^{13}C, 1.1%) does have a nuclear spin of 1/2 and is NMR active. ^4Be is not a stable isotope of beryllium.

64. **A.** Spin-spin coupling affects the number of possible spin states (splitting patterns) for a nucleus with a particular chemical environment.

65. **C.** Absorption of electromagnetic energy occurs when an electron is excited from an occupied orbital to higher energy an unoccupied orbital.

66. **D.** In most cases, enantiomers have identical chemical and physical properties, except for their ability to rotate plane-polarized light.

67. **A.** Since electrons have a spin, they can affect the magnetic field experienced by a nucleus with spin. Removing electron density from a nucleus is known as deshielding and causes the ^1H NMR signal to shift to higher magnetic field, which is to higher ppm or to the left in a conventional plot of an ^1H NMR spectrum. Acidic protons are significantly deshielded.

68. **A.** Fractional distillation employs the use of a special distillation column with a large number of theoretical plates to facilitate separating compounds with similar boiling points.

69. **B.** Reacting the organic acid with a strong base would produce the ionic carboxylate, which would tend to have greater solubility in an aqueous solution and less solubility in the hydrocarbon solvent.

70. **D.** Vacuum distillation reduces boiling points and is most useful for compounds with very high normal (at 1 atm of pressure) boiling points.

71. **D.** The retardation factor (R_f) is the ratio of the distance that a compound has traveled to the distance that the solvent has traveled in TLC. The higher the R_f the more quickly a particular compound will elute in column chromatography.

72. **C.** If the compound is soluble in the aqueous phase and the organic solvent, multiple extractions would be most effective at achieving the most complete extraction.

73. **C.** The ethyl iodide (organic solvent) has a greater density than the salt water, and therefore would be the bottom layer.

74. **A.** Methylamine, benzene, and phenol are all organic liquids at room temperature and could easily be separated from the solid silica (sand) by filtration. Since methyl amine is a base and it could be separated from the other two organic compounds by extraction into an acidified aqueous solution. Benzene (bp 80 °C) has a much lower boiling point than phenol (mp 40 °C, bp 182 °C), which is a solid at room temperature.

75. **B.** In thin layer chromatography (TLC), the silica gel is the stationary phase and the solvent is the mobile phase, whereas in gas chromatography (GC) the stationary phase is either a solid material or a high boiling liquid coating the surface of the solid and the mobile phase is a carrier gas like hydrogen or helium.

76. **A.** Elemental iron (atomic number 26) has an electron configuration of $[Ar]3d^64s^2$ and the ferric ion (Fe^{3+}) has a ground state electron configuration where the electrons in the 4s orbital and one of the 3d electrons has removed, $[Ar]3d^5$.

77. **D.** The principal quantum number n can have nonzero positive integer values; the azimuthal quantum number l adopts integer values starting with zero up to n-1; the magnetic quantum number m_l adopts possible integer values from $-l$ to $+l$; and the spin quantum number m_s is either +1/2 or -1/2. For choice D, the highest possible value of the azimuthal quantum number is $l = 2 - 1 = 1$, so a value of 2 (d-orbitals) is not possible in the second shell.

78.   **C.** The third shell has three subshells (s, p and d), having a maximum number of electrons of 2, 6 and 10, respectively.

79.   **D.** Sodium has a single electron in its valence shell, [Ne]$3s^1$. The noble gases helium and neon have completely filled valence shells and magnesium has two valence electrons that are spin paired in the s orbital, [Ne]$3s^2$.

80.   **B.** To go from a lower energy state (n = 2) to a higher energy state (n = 4), a quantized amount of energy must be absorbed. To become ionized the electron would have to absorb enough energy to reach the n = ∞ level.

81.   **A.** Silicon has an atomic number of 14. For the vast majority of the elements there are stable isotopes that have approximately the same number of neutrons as protons, i.e. the mass number is approximately twice the atomic number. Silicon-14 would be extremely unstable, since there are no neutrons.

82.   **B.** Momentum is mass times velocity and in order to determine a particle's velocity, it must move, but since the electron moves near the speed of light, simultaneously determining the electron's position and velocity is impossible and all we can really do is predict the probability of finding the electron at a particular position in the atom relative to the nucleus.

83.   **C.** It is not possible for the principal quantum number to be zero (see the explanation for question 77), eliminating choice D. The transition in choice A would release a photon and can be eliminated. The Balmer series occurs in the visible portion of the spectrum and corresponds to emission lines for transitions to the n = 2 state. The wavelength for the transition in choice B is 410 nm. The Lyman series is in the UV portion of the spectrum and corresponds to transitions to the n = 1 state. The wavelength for the transition in choice C is 122 nm.

84.   **A.** Hund's rules states that spin pairing will not occur until each orbital for a particular subshell has at least one electron.

85.   **C.** Oxygen and sulfur are in the same column (group or family) of the periodic table and have the same number of valence electrons and similar oxidation numbers.

86.   **C.** Sodium has 11 protons and potassium has 19 protons. Nucleons are subatomic particles in the nucleus, such as protons and neutrons.

87.   **C.** Ions with an increasing number of valence electrons get larger due to the electrostatic repulsions, so Roman numeral I would increase the size of the ion. The effective nuclear charge is essentially the number of protons for an atom minus the number of inner shell electrons. The effective nuclear charge decreases from right to left in a period, which corresponds to an increase in the atomic radii, so Roman numeral II would increase the size of the atom. Neutrons are in the nucleus of an atom which is much smaller than the volume of the atom itself, which is determined by the electron clouds, so varying numbers of neutrons has no effect on the size of an atom, eliminating Roman numeral III.

88.   **A.** Electron affinity increases from left to right in a period and bottom to top in a group.

89.   **C.** Nonmetals are in the top right hand corner of the periodic table and have properties essentially opposite of the metals that are to the left side of the periodic table. The metalloids form a downward sloping diagonal line in the p-block of the periodic table and have properties intermediate between metals and nonmetals, i.e. silicon is a semiconducting material.

90.   **D.** Atomic radii decrease from left to right in a period due to increasing effective nuclear charge. See also the explanation for question 87.

91.   **B.** All of the choices are properties of metals, but the thermal conductivity is the property that is most applicable to the question.

92.   **A.** The alkaline earth metals are group 2 elements, with two valence electrons and very stable 2+ ions with noble gas electron configurations.

93.   **B.** A complex ion is formed when a Lewis base coordinates to a transition metal ion, i.e. $Co(NH_3)_6{}^{2+}$ or $CuCl_4{}^{2-}$.

94.   **C.** The number of valence electrons systematically increases from left to right in the third period.

95.   **C.** Covalent bonds are formed between atoms with the same or nearly the same electronegativities, whereas polar covalent bonds are formed between nonmetal atoms with significant differences in electronegativities. Ionic bonds are generally formed between metal and nonmetal ions.

96.   **D.** The formal charge is the number of valence electrons minus the number of lone-pair electrons and half of the bonding-pair electrons. The ammonium ion, $NH_4{}^+$ has four N-H bonds, and nitrogen has five valence electrons, so the formal charge is 5 - 4 = +1.

97.   **C.** The oxidation number of oxygen is typically 2- in most compounds, except for peroxides and elemental oxygen.

98.   **A.** In order to satisfy the octet rule for the carbon atom, one of the oxygen atoms must form a double bond to carbon.

99.   **B.** The strongest intermolecular force in propanal would be dipole-dipole forces, whereas propanol would also have hydrogen bonding and sodium chloride is an ionic compound.

100.   **D.** Xenon can violate the octet rule and in addition to the four polar covalent Xe-F bonds there are two lone pairs.

101.   **B.** Carbon tetrachloride adopts a tetrahedral molecular geometry whose symmetry results in no net molecular dipole.

102.   **C.** Hydrogen has a modest electronegativity compared with fluorine, oxygen and nitrogen, such that H-F, H-O and H-N bonds have greater bond dipoles than other polar covalent bonds between main group elements.

103.   **C.** Bronsted bases are proton acceptors.

104.   **A.** First period elements (H and He) only need two electrons to complete their valence shell. Second period p-block elements never violate the octet rule (except for boron in BH_3, in the gas phase), whereas third period p-

block elements can make use of the low lying d-orbitals to expand their valence shells and violate the octet rule.

105.   **D.** The formula for potassium chloride is KCl. The sum of the atomic masses from the periodic table is 30.0983 + 35.453 = 65.551 amu

106.   **C.** 147 g̶ H̶₂S̶O̶₄ x 1 mol/98 g̶ x 2 H⁺/H̶₂S̶O̶₄ = 3 mol H⁺

107.   **C.** The formula mass of HCl is 1 + 35 = 36 g/mol.

108.   **B.** The formula of ethanol is C_2H_6O (MW = 46 g/mol) and the percent carbon is
$$[(2 \times 12)/46] \times 100 = (24/46) \times 100 = 52\%$$

109.   **D.** This a an acid-base neutralization reaction, which is also an example of a double replacement reaction, which is also sometimes called a metathesis reaction, in which the ions are switched between reactants and products. REDOX reactions have changes in oxidation numbers between reactants and products.

110.   **A.** See the explanation for question 109.

111.   **D.** Decomposition reactions involve a single reactant forming multiple products; synthesis reactions involve multiple reactants forming a single product; polymerization reactions involve combining multiple monomers to form a single polymer; double replacement reactions involve two ionic compounds as reactants and two ionic compounds as products in which the cations and anions have been switched.

112.   **D.** This is a single replacement reaction, which is also a REDOX reaction, in which the zinc is oxidized, rather than the iron.

113.   **C.** The formula mass of the empirical formula is 12 + 2(1) + 16 = 30 g/mol. Dividing the molar mass by the empirical formula mass gives 180/30 = 6, which means the molecular formula is six times the empirical formula, or $C_6H_{12}O_6$.

114.   **A.** From the balanced reaction the mole ratios of A_2:BC_4:D are 8:1:2. The chemist uses a ratio of 60:8:20 (7.5:1:2.5), so the reactant that will be consumed first will be A_2.

115.   **C.** The rate law must be zero order in A and second order in B.
$$\text{Rate} = k[A]^0[B]^2$$

116.   **A.** The Gibbs free energy change (ΔG) for a nonspontaneous reaction is positive.

117.   **D.** Based on the information provided, the rate law with respect to A is most likely either first or second order, and the order with respect to B then must be second of first order, respectively, to provide a third order rate law overall. It is unlikely to be zero order in A, since the rate law would then have to be third order with respect to B, i.e. the probability of three molecules colliding simultaneous is very low, unless there is a catalyst.

118.   **B.** If a reaction is zero order for a particular reactant, then the rate of reaction does not depend upon the concentration of that reactant, i.e. any number raised to the zero power equals one.

119.   **C.** Increasing the temperature will increase the number of effective collisions that overcome the activation energy. For an equilibrium reaction, based on Le Châtelier's principle, the forward reaction will speed up if there are more gaseous products than reactants and the pressure is decreased, or if more reactants are added. Removing products for an equilibrium reaction will speed up the forward reaction, but an irreversible reaction is not the same as an equilibrium reaction, since the reverse reaction does not occur at any significant rate.

120.   **B.** Pure solids and pure liquids do not appear in the equilibrium expression, the ion product (reaction quotient), or the rate law. The rate of a reaction involving a solid is significantly dependent upon surface area (and difficult to predict quantitatively), so finely divided solids (powders) have a much greater effect, but a larger Pb (*s*) electrode would have much less effect.

121.   **D.** Doubling the [O_2] concentration should quadruple the reaction rate because the rate law is second order with respect to oxygen, not third order (it is third order overall). Species not involved in the reaction do not appear in the rate law.

122.   **C.** Comparing trials 1 and 2, doubling [A] while keeping [B_2] constant causes the rate of the reaction to double, so the reaction is first order with respect to A. Comparing trials 1 and 3, we see that [A] is tripled and [B_2] is doubled. Since we already know that the reaction is first order with respect to A, if the reaction were zero order in B_2, then the rate of reaction should have tripled, from 2.4 to 7.2, but the reaction rate is actually four times faster than that (28.8/7.2 = 4), so the reaction must be second order in B_2.

123.   **D.** A catalyst lowers the activation energy of a reaction, which is the energy difference between the reactants and the activated complex (transition state), which is the highest energy species in the reaction pathway or energy diagram.

124.   **B.** Since the activation energy for product 2 (kinetically more favorable) is lower than the activation energy for product 1, initially there will be more of product 2 formed than of product 1. If the reaction were allowed to proceed for a much longer period of time, the thermodynamic product 1 will be favored.

125.   **D.** By sampling just once we do not know if the reaction has come to completion (a slow irreversible reaction or an equilibrium) in 24 hours. If the reaction is at equilibrium, then the rate of the forward and reverse reactions are the same, if the reaction is not yet at equilibrium, then the rate of the forward reaction is greater than the reverse reaction. Since there are more products than reactants, then the products must be more stable than the reactants and ΔG in the forward direction must be negative.

126.   **C.** The equilibrium expression is the concentration of products raised to their stoichiometric power, divided by the concentration of the reactants raised to their stoichiometric power. Pure solids and pure liquids are not included in the equilibrium expression. See also the explanation for question 120.

127.   **D.** When carbon dioxide is dissolved in water at high pressure it produces a carbonic acid solution (H_2CO_3) that has the typical somewhat sour taste of all acids. When the pressure is released by opening the bottle,

the equilibrium shifts and carbon dioxide bubbles out of the solution, reducing the concentration of carbonic acid and raising the pH.

128. **D.** Equilibrium constants less than unity usually indicate that at equilibrium the concentration of products will be less than the concentration of reactants. See the explanation for question 126.

129. **B.** The solubility equilibrium is

$$CaCl_2 \ (s) \longleftrightarrow Ca^{2+} \ (aq) + 2 \ Cl^- \ (aq)$$

Addition of chloride will cause the reaction to shift to the left and precipitate more calcium chloride.

130. **D.** Based on Le Châtelier's principle increasing the pressure should shift the reaction towards products since this is the side with fewer moles of gas; decreasing the temperature should also shift the reaction towards the products since heat is also a product; and adding a reactant such as C would shift the reaction towards the products. Of the answer choices, only adding a product like ABC_2 would shift the equilibrium towards the reactants.

131. **A.** See the explanation for question 130.

132. **B.** See the explanation for question 130.

133. **C.** Only carbonic acid will react with the substance, since it is a pretty weak base. All the other answer choices are bases.

134. **C.** When an equilibrium reaction is reversed the equilibrium expression is inverted.

$$1/(5 \times 10^{-3}) = 1/5 \times 10^3 = 0.2 \times 10^3 = 2 \times 10^2$$

135. **D.** Isobaric means the pressure doesn't change and the plot clearly shows that the pressure changes. Likewise, isovolumetric means the volume doesn't change and the plot clearly shows that the volume changes. The stem of the question states that the temperature decreases, so it can't be isothermal. An adiabatic system is one in which heat does not flow into or out of the system, such that changes in volume and pressure result in temperature changes.

136. **B.** If the reaction is endothermic then ΔH must be positive. According to the Gibbs free energy equation, $\Delta G = \Delta H - T\Delta S$, the free energy change will be positive under all conditions of temperature.

137. **C.** Both ΔH and ΔS are negative, so that at low temperatures the $-T\Delta S$ term will be a small positive value compared to the negative ΔH and the reaction will be spontaneous because overall the ΔG will be negative. But, at high temperatures the $-T\Delta S$ term will be a large positive value resulting in a positive ΔG and a nonspontaneous reaction.

138. **D.** Both ΔH and ΔS are positive. This is the opposite situation as seen in question 137.

139. **D.** This is essentially an irreversible reaction with a very large K_{eq} because the products are so much more stable than the reactants. There are two reactions.

$$Na \ (s) + H_2O \ (l) \rightarrow H_2 \ (g) + NaOH \ (aq)$$

The heat produced by this reaction results in the combustion of the hydrogen gas, producing even more heat.

$$H_2 \ (g) + O_2 \ (g) \rightarrow H_2O \ (g)$$

140. **A.** The products of combustion reactions are gases, whereas the reactant hydrocarbon is probably a liquid. In addition, there will be many more product molecules, carbon dioxide and water, than reactant molecules (hydrocarbon and elemental oxygen), so that entropy will increase ($\Delta S = +$). The amount of energy released would depend upon the nature of the functional groups that replace the hydrogen atoms in the hydrocarbon and it is not possible to predict the relative amount of energy without knowing the chemical makeup of the functional groups.

141. **B.** We must put energy into molecules to break bonds ($\Delta H = +$) and we get energy out when we make bonds ($\Delta H = -$). The ΔH for the reaction will be approximately the sum of the bond energies of the reactant bonds that are broken

$$1(C\text{-}Cl) + 1(O\text{-}H) = 780$$

minus the bond energies of the bonds that are formed in the products

$$1(C\text{-}O) + 1(H\text{-}Cl) = 790$$
$$\Delta H = 780 - 790 = -10 \text{ kJ/mol}$$

142. **C.** This is the reverse reaction of the reaction in question 141. Just change the sign of ΔH.

143. **C.** See the explanation for question 141.

$$2(C\text{-}O) + 4(H\text{-}Cl) = 720 + 1720 = 2440$$
$$2(C\text{-}Cl) + 2(O\text{-}H) + 1(Cl\text{-}Cl) + 1(H\text{-}H) = 660 + 900 +$$
$$330 + 430 = 2320$$
$$2440 - 2320 = +120 \text{ kJ/mol}$$

144. **D.** Gases have more entropy than liquids, which have more entropy than solids. Sublimation is when a solid goes directly to the gas phase. Evaporation would also have a positive change, but it would only involve the liquid going to the gas phase and therefore would be less positive than sublimation. Both freezing and condensation would have negative ΔS values.

145. **A.** Under conditions of high pressure and low temperature, a real gas may become a liquid or solid, therefore a real gas is most likely to remain a gas and behave like an ideal gas at high temperatures and low pressures.

146. **C.** The volume of one mole of an ideal gas at standard temperature and pressure is 22.4 L. If you have to do the calculation

$$V = (2 \ \text{mol})(0.0821 \ \text{L atm/mol K})(273 \ \text{K})/(1 \ \text{atm}) = 44.8 \text{ L}$$

147. **B.** For 1 mole of the gas at STP the volume is 22.4 L, see the explanation for question 146. The density is mass per unit volume.

$$\rho = 100 \ \text{g}/22.4 \ \text{L} = 4.46 \ \text{g/L}$$

148. **D.** At the same temperature, the gas with less mass must have a greater speed in order to have the same average kinetic energy (temperature). Therefore, the helium will leak out faster than the argon.

149. **A.** Choices B, C and D are part of the definition of an ideal gas. Real gases behave most like an ideal gas at high temperatures and low pressures.

150. **C.** The reaction will produce a total of 10 moles of gas. Using the ideal gas law to calculate the pressure gives

$$P = (10 \ \text{mol})(0.0821 \ \text{L atm/mol K})(298 \ \text{K})/(2 \ \text{L})$$

$= 122$ atm

151. **D.** The average kinetic energy of the gases is the same, but there is a distribution of energies. Collisions are taken to be completely elastic in kinetic molecular theory. The sun is primarily comprised of a hydrogen plasma and undergoes nuclear fusion, not fission.

152. **A.** If the three gases are at the same temperature, their average kinetic energies are the same. Neon is the lightest gas and therefore would have the greatest average velocity.

153. **B.** The mole fraction of N_2 is

$$2/(1 + 2 + 5) = 2/8 = 0.25$$

Multiplying the mole fraction by the total pressure gives

$$0.25 \times 5 \text{ atm} = 1.25 \text{ atm}$$

154. **C.** See the explanation for question 153.

$$5/8 \times 5 \text{ atm} = 3.125 \text{ atm}$$

155. **A.** The combined gas law is

$$P_1V_1/T_1 = P_2V_2/T_2$$

Volume is directly related to the temperature, but inversely related to pressure. For choice A, if the pressure increases, the volume would decrease, but an increase in temperature has the opposite effect and should cause the volume to increase. For choice B, if pressure is held constant and temperature increases, then the volume must increase. For choice C, a decrease in pressure and an increase in temperature will both cause the volume to increase. For choice D, increasing the pressure and decreasing the temperature should both cause the volume to decrease.

156. **C.** The boiling point elevation equation is

$$DT = K_b \, m \, n$$

where m is the molality (moles of solute per kilogram of solvent) and n is the number of moles of ions produced when the solute dissolves in solution.

$$7.68 \text{ K} = (0.512 \text{ K} \cdot \text{kg/mol})(0.5 \text{ mol}/0.10 \text{ kg}) \, n$$
$$n = (7.68)(0.10)/(0.512)(0.5) = 3$$

157. **D.** The major gas present in the earth's atmosphere is elemental nitrogen, N_2 (78%), which could be considered the solvent in a solution, with the minor components of water vapor, oxygen, carbon dioxide, etc. being solutes.

158. **A.** Raoult's law states that the partial vapor pressure of each component of an ideal mixture of liquids is equal to the vapor pressure of the pure component multiplied by its mole fraction in the mixture.

159. **B.** Boiling points increase and melting points decrease when solutes are dissolved in solution, due to colligative effects.

160. **C.** Energy must be put into the system to break bonds and energy is released when bonds are made.

161. **C.** Based on the solubility rules, metal hydroxides are generally insoluble, but the negatively charged zinc hydroxate complex ion will be significantly more soluble due to electrostatic and increased hydrogen bonding interactions with the solvent water molecules.

162. **C.** The mass of sucrose is

$$2 \text{ cup} \times 240 \text{ mL/cup} \times 1.6 \text{ g/mL} = 768 \text{ g}$$

and the mass of water is

$$1 \text{ cup} \times 240 \text{ mL/cup} \times 0.98 \text{ g/mL} = 235 \text{ g}$$

and the percent mass is

$$[768/(768 + 235)] \times 100 = 77 \text{ \%}$$

In fact, you should not have wasted time doing a calculation for this question since the percentage of sugar had to be over 50 % (eliminating choices A and B) and it clearly was not 100 % sugar (eliminating choice D).

163. **D.** See the explanation for question 158. An ideal solution results when the intermolecular forces and chemical properties of the components are nearly identical (choice B). Deviations from ideal behavior can increase or decrease the vapor pressure of the components as compared to the theoretical ideal, depending upon the intermolecular forces of the components. For choice A, benzene and water are not miscible and benzene is less dense, floating on top of the water and evaporating easily. For choice C, ammonia is a gas at room temperature, not a liquid, and would not have significant solubility in a hydrocarbon. For choice D, the strong acid, will dissociate into ions and strongly interact with the water, lowering the vapor pressure of both components.

164. **D.** The Gibb's free energy equation has a negative sign in front of the entropy term, $\Delta G = \Delta H - T\Delta S$ and negative free energies are spontaneous. If both ΔH and ΔS are positive, the reaction will be spontaneous at high temperatures and nonspontaneous at low temperatures.

165. **D.** The vapor pressure is affected by the colligative properties of the solute, with the more particles (ions) produced the greater the effect. Both glucose and glycine will essentially produce a single molecule per formula unit, sodium chloride will produce two ions per formula unit and sodium sulfate will produce three ions per formula unit.

166. **B.** If the molar solubility is the variable x, then substituting into the equilibrium expression.

$$K_{sp} = [A^{2+}][B^{2-}]^2$$
$$8 \times 10^{-9} = [x][0.01 + 2x]^2$$

Since the solubility product constant is very small, the value of x will be small compared with the $[B^-]$ and we can simplify the expression and solve for x.

$$8 \times 10^{-9} = [x][0.01]^2$$
$$x = 8 \times 10^{-5} \text{ M}$$

167. **B.** Bronsted bases can accept hydrogen ions and ammonia can form ammonium ion.

$$NH_3 + H^+ \longrightarrow NH_4^+$$

HNO_2 and HF are acids and propane is neither an acid nor a base.

168. **B.** Since HCl is a strong acid the $[H^+] = 2.5 \times 10^{-3}$ M. Since $pH = -\log[H^+]$, the pH must be between 2 and 3 ($-\log 10^{-3} = 3$ and $-\log 10^{-2} = 2$).

169. **A.** The anion in chlorous acid is chlorite, ClO_2^-, which when a hydrogen ion is added to the formula gives choice A.

170. **C.** The anion in perchloric acid is perchlorate, ClO_4^-, which when a hydrogen ion is added to the formula gives choice C.

171. **C.** Bisulfate is the conjugate of a strong acid, so it is a neutral ion. Alkyl groups are electron donating, which pushes electron density towards the nitrogen atom.

172. **B.** All of the hydrohalic acids are strong acids, except for hydrofluoric acid, which is a weak acid (pK_a = 3.17).

173. **D.** For a buffer, when the pH = pK_a, the concentration of the weak acid and its conjugate base are equal.

174. **B.** When carbon dioxide is dissolved in aqueous solution it reacts with water to form carbonic acid which has an effective pK_a of 6.3, and establishes a buffer system with its conjugate base, bicarbonate.

$$H_2CO_3 \text{ (aq)} <==> HCO_3^- \text{ (aq)} + H^+ \text{ (aq)}$$

175. **D.** This is a titration curve for a diprotic acid. The horizontal plateaus, where the pH doesn't change much, are the buffer regions. The steep changes in pH are at the equivalence points.

176. **C.** See the explanation for question 175. The pH = pK_{a1} at point A and pH = pK_{a2} at point C.

177. **B.** Since sulfuric acid is a diprotic acid, the molarity of the solution is half of the normality of the solution. Note that we are making two liters of solution, 4.5 moles/2 L = 2.25 M.

178. **A.** In this reaction the oxidation number of hydrogen is +1 in the reactant HCl and 0 in product H_2. The oxidation number of chlorine in the reactant HCl is -1 and 0 in the product Cl_2. The oxidation number of oxygen in the reactant CH_3CH_2OH is -2 and -1 in the product H_2O_2. One of the carbons in the CH_3CH_2- groups is being reduced. The oxidation number of the carbon attached to the oxygen in the reactants changes from -1 to -2 in the product.

179. **B.** See the explanation for question 178.

180. **C.** Reducing agents get oxidized (oxidation numbers increase) and oxidizing agents get reduced (oxidation numbers decrease). See also the explanation for question 178.

181. **D.** See the explanations for questions 178-180. The HCl is not acting as an acid or a base in this reaction.

182. **C.** The formula for sodium borohydride is $NaBH_4$. The total charge must equal the oxidation numbers of each atom in the formula. The oxidation number for sodium and hydrogen are +1 and -1 (hydride), respectively, and the total charge is zero.

$$0 = (+1) + x + 4(-1)$$
$$x = +3$$

183. **A.** Reducing agents give up electrons (see the explanation for question 180). Roman numeral I is the electron configuration for potassium, which is an excellent reducing agent. Roman numerals II and III are the electron configurations for the nonmetals chlorine and argon, respectively. The former is most likely to be reduced to chloride.

184. **B.** See the explanation to question 183.

185. **D.** In compounds the oxidation numbers of fluorine and sodium are always -1 and +1, respectively. Unless the compound contains peroxide (-1), the oxidation number of oxygen in compounds is -2. Iron has at least two common oxidation numbers, +2 and +3.

186. **A.** The formula of formaldehyde (methanal) and the oxidation number of the carbon can be calculated [0

= 2(+1) + 1(-2) + x] is x = 0. The formula of formic acid is $HCHO_2$ and the oxidation number of the carbon atom [0 = 2(+1) + 2(-2) + x] is x = +2. The formula of methanol is CH_3OH and the oxidation number of the carbon atom [0 = 4(+1) + 1(-2) + x] is x = -2.

187. **D.** The element X has the highest oxidation number (+5) in choice D. The oxidation numbers of X in choices A, B and C are +1, +2, and +4, respectively.

188. **C.** Disproportionation reactions are REDOX reactions in which the products have oxidation numbers that are both higher and lower than the reactant oxidation number. This reaction involves changing the oxidation number of chlorine from 0 to -1 (Cl⁻) and +1 (HClO). See also the explanation of question 111. Oxidation reactions increase the oxidation numbers, only. Metathesis reactions (double replacement reactions) are not REDOX reactions.

189. **D.** Positive REDOX potentials correspond to spontaneous REDOX reactions. Zinc is oxidized to Zn^{2+}, giving up its electrons to oxygen.

$$Zn \text{ (}s\text{)} + 1/2 \text{ } O_2 \text{ (}g\text{)} --> ZnO \text{ (}s\text{)}$$

190. **C.** The reduction half reaction is
$Ag^+ + e^- \rightarrow Ag$ $\qquad$ $E° = +0.80$ V
While the stoichiometric coefficients are doubled in the overall reaction, this has no effect on the potential. The oxidation half reaction is
$Mg \rightarrow Mg^{2+} + 2e^-$ $\qquad$ $E° = +2.37$ V
Adding the oxidation and reduction potentials gives the potential for the overall reaction.
$$0.80 + 2.37 = +3.17 \text{ V}$$
This will be a spontaneous REDOX reaction.

191. **A.** See the explanation for question 190.
$$-0.34 - 0.76 = -1.1 \text{ V}$$
This is a nonspontaneous REDOX reaction.

192. **C.** See the explanation for question 190.
$$+0.80 - 0.34 = +0.46 \text{ V}$$
This is a spontaneous REDOX reaction.

193. **B.** The most positive oxidation potential (anode) would be for magnesium and the most positive reduction potential (cathode) would be for silver.
$$2.37 + 0.80 = +3.17 \text{ V}$$

194. **A.** When combined with the zinc reduction potential, the oxidation potential must provide a positive overall cell potential.
$$+2.37 - 0.76 = +1.61.$$

195. **C.** Reduction always occurs at the cathode and oxidation always occurs at the anode, regardless of the type of cell, "the red cat is a fat cat" and Roman numeral I is true. The anode is the negative terminal in a Galvanic cell, but the negative terminal is the cathode in an electrolytic cell, making Roman numeral II false. Electrons flow from anode to cathode, but current is the movement of positive charge.

196. **D.** Increasing the surface area will increase the amount of current, but does not change the voltage, which is a measure of the electric potential energy between the reactants and products.

197. **B.** Cations always move towards the cathode. Prior to applying an external voltage, the REDOX potential of

an electrolytic cell is negative and the reaction is nonspontaneous (positive free energy change). See also the explanation for question 195.

198.   **A.** See the explanation for question 195.

199.   **B.** The relationship between Gibbs free energy and potential under standard conditions is $DG° = -nFE°$, where n is the number of electrons transferred.

$$3 \times 10^5 \, J/mol = -(2)(10^5 \, C/mol)E°$$
$$E° = (3/2) = -1.5 \, J/C = -1.5 \, V$$

Since the Gibb's free energy change is positive, the reaction is nonspontaneous and the voltage is negative.

200.   **B.** Matter is considered any object (particle) with mass and there are several subatomic particles with mass, i.e. protons, neutrons and electrons. An electron is not a nucleon. The number of protons in the nucleus of an atom defines the chemical properties of that atom.

Periodic Table of the Elements

1	2	3	4	5	6	7	8	9	10	11	12	13	14	15	16	17	18
hydrogen 1 **H** 1.0079																	helium 2 **He** 4.0026
lithium 3 **Li** 6.941	beryllium 4 **Be** 9.0122											boron 5 **B** 10.811	carbon 6 **C** 12.011	nitrogen 7 **N** 14.007	oxygen 8 **O** 15.999	fluorine 9 **F** 18.998	neon 10 **Ne** 20.180
sodium 11 **Na** 22.990	magnesium 12 **Mg** 24.305											aluminium 13 **Al** 26.982	silicon 14 **Si** 28.086	phosphorus 15 **P** 30.974	sulfur 16 **S** 32.065	chlorine 17 **Cl** 35.453	argon 18 **Ar** 39.948
potassium 19 **K** 39.098	calcium 20 **Ca** 40.078	scandium 21 **Sc** 44.956	titanium 22 **Ti** 47.867	vanadium 23 **V** 50.942	chromium 24 **Cr** 51.996	manganese 25 **Mn** 54.938	iron 26 **Fe** 55.845	cobalt 27 **Co** 58.933	nickel 28 **Ni** 58.693	copper 29 **Cu** 63.546	zinc 30 **Zn** 65.39	gallium 31 **Ga** 69.723	germanium 32 **Ge** 72.61	arsenic 33 **As** 74.922	selenium 34 **Se** 78.96	bromine 35 **Br** 79.904	krypton 36 **Kr** 83.80
rubidium 37 **Rb** 85.468	strontium 38 **Sr** 87.62	yttrium 39 **Y** 88.906	zirconium 40 **Zr** 91.224	niobium 41 **Nb** 92.906	molybdenum 42 **Mo** 95.94	technetium 43 **Tc** [98]	ruthenium 44 **Ru** 101.07	rhodium 45 **Rh** 102.91	palladium 46 **Pd** 106.42	silver 47 **Ag** 107.87	cadmium 48 **Cd** 112.41	indium 49 **In** 114.82	tin 50 **Sn** 118.71	antimony 51 **Sb** 121.76	tellurium 52 **Te** 127.60	iodine 53 **I** 126.90	xenon 54 **Xe** 131.29
caesium 55 **Cs** 132.91	barium 56 **Ba** 137.33	57-70 *	lutetium 71 **Lu** 174.97	hafnium 72 **Hf** 178.49	tantalum 73 **Ta** 180.95	tungsten 74 **W** 183.84	rhenium 75 **Re** 186.21	osmium 76 **Os** 190.23	iridium 77 **Ir** 192.22	platinum 78 **Pt** 195.08	gold 79 **Au** 196.97	mercury 80 **Hg** 200.59	thallium 81 **Tl** 204.38	lead 82 **Pb** 207.2	bismuth 83 **Bi** 208.98	polonium 84 **Po** [209]	astatine 85 **At** [210]	radon 86 **Rn** [222]
francium 87 **Fr** [223]	radium 88 **Ra** [226]	89-102 **	lawrencium 103 **Lr** [262]	rutherfordium 104 **Rf** [261]	dubnium 105 **Db** [262]	seaborgium 106 **Sg** [266]	bohrium 107 **Bh** [264]	hassium 108 **Hs** [269]	meitnerium 109 **Mt** [268]	ununnilium 110 **Uun** [271]	unununium 111 **Uuu** [272]	ununbium 112 **Uub** [277]		ununquadium 114 **Uuq** [289]				

* Lanthanide series

lanthanum 57 **La** 138.91	cerium 58 **Ce** 140.12	praseodymium 59 **Pr** 140.91	neodymium 60 **Nd** 144.24	promethium 61 **Pm** [145]	samarium 62 **Sm** 150.36	europium 63 **Eu** 151.96	gadolinium 64 **Gd** 157.25	terbium 65 **Tb** 158.93	dysprosium 66 **Dy** 162.50	holmium 67 **Ho** 164.93	erbium 68 **Er** 167.26	thulium 69 **Tm** 168.93	ytterbium 70 **Yb** 173.04

** Actinide series

actinium 89 **Ac** [227]	thorium 90 **Th** 232.04	protactinium 91 **Pa** 231.04	uranium 92 **U** 238.03	neptunium 93 **Np** [237]	plutonium 94 **Pu** [244]	americium 95 **Am** [243]	curium 96 **Cm** [247]	berkelium 97 **Bk** [247]	californium 98 **Cf** [251]	einsteinium 99 **Es** [252]	fermium 100 **Fm** [257]	mendelevium 101 **Md** [258]	nobelium 102 **No** [259]